21st-Century Gothic

Great Gothic Novels since 2000

EDITED BY DANEL OLSON

THE SCARECROW PRESS, INC.
Lanham • Toronto • Plymouth, UK
2011

Published by Scarecrow Press, Inc.
A wholly owned subsidary of The Rowman & Littlefield Publishing Group, Inc.
4501 Forbes Boulevard, Suite 200, Lanham, Maryland 20706
http://www.scarecrowpress.com

Estover Road, Plymouth PL6 7PY, United Kingdom

British Library Cataloguing in Publication Information Available

Library of Congress Cataloging-in-Publication Data
21st-century Gothic : great Gothic novels since 2000 / edited by Danel Olson.
    p. cm.
  Includes bibliographical references and index.
  ISBN 978-0-8108-7728-3 (cloth : alk. paper) — ISBN 978-0-8108-7729-0 (ebook)
  1. Gothic fiction (Literary genre)—21st century—History and criticism. 2. Horror tales—
History and criticism. I. Olson, Danel. II. Title: Twenty-first century Gothic.
  PN3435.A16 2011
  809.3'8729   2010032757

♾™ The paper used in this publication meets the minimum requirements of American
National Standard for Information Sciences—Permanence of Paper for Printed Library
Materials, ANSI/NISO Z39.48-1992.

Printed in the United States of America

To my Belgrade friend
MILORAD PAVIĆ *(1929–2009)*

Contents

Foreword

S. T. Joshi

The recent efflorescence of neo-Gothic fiction—the literature of fear, terror, wonder, awe, and the supernatural admirably analyzed by over fifty independent scholars, academics, and creative writers in these two volumes—is the product of centuries, perhaps millennia, of work by a wide array of artists both celebrated and obscure. It is, after all, in the *Epic of Gilgamesh* (c. 1700 BCE) that we find such motifs as the superhero, the quest for eternal life, battles with monsters, and the like. About a millennium later, the *Odyssey* is rife with creatures of eccentric cast, from the sorceress Circe, to Polyphemus the Cyclops, to the twin horrors of Scylla and Charybdis. Greek literature and myth regales us with the Gorgon Medusa, the Furies, and the harpies. Ghosts stalk through the most elevated of Greek tragedies. Dante and Milton drew only partly upon scripture, but more upon their own imaginations, in depicting the terrors of hell and its demons. The ghost in *Hamlet* and the witches in *Macbeth* are familiar to all.

We must, however, be careful not to let our zeal for tracing anticipations of contemporary Gothic elements get the best of us. The literature of terror can only be said to have achieved independent existence when it has substantially segregated itself from religion, myth, and folklore, however much it may draw upon these rich storehouses of belief and ritual. In particular, the literature of the *supernatural* can only be said to have become viable when, in a given culture, there becomes a relatively clear sense of the *natural*. If ghosts, goblins, and vampires are commonly considered to be components of the everyday scene, the depiction of them in literature cannot be considered *supernatural* because it would not constitute a defiance of the natural laws that render such entities beyond the bounds of the possible. It is for this reason that, without perhaps being entirely aware of it, literary scholars have rightly declared that Gothicism commenced as an independent literary mode with the publication of Horace Walpole's *The Castle of Otranto* (1764). For it was only by the middle of the

eighteenth century that human knowledge had advanced to the point where it could, with some confidence, be asserted that creatures such as the ghost or the werewolf were definitively outside the limits of nature.

It is often forgotten that this original Gothic movement—running roughly from 1764 to the 1820s—did not get under way at once upon the publication of Walpole's curious little novel. It required the added impetus of German Romanticism to bring to the fore such literary figures as Ann Radcliffe, Matthew Gregory Lewis, Mary Shelley, and Charles Robert Maturin, not to mention a host of lesser talents. This movement shares many similarities with the "horror boom" of the 1970s and 1980s, in that it was energized by a quite small number of toweringly original writers and a motley crew of crude imitators who sought to capitalize on the sudden popularity of this literary genre; and there is a further similarity in that the Gothic movement could not in any sense be said to be uniform or monolithic, but quickly fragmented into numerous subgenres and offshoots. The element of supernatural terror was by no means dominant, and Ann Radcliffe (perhaps unwisely) rejected the supernatural altogether in her work, opting instead for what has been called the "explained supernatural," where supernatural phenomena are suggested but are accounted for naturalistically (oftentimes in a highly unconvincing manner) at the end. Lewis and Maturin shrewdly avoided this deflation of the reader's expectations, while Shelley's *Frankenstein* (1818), by transferring the locus of fear to radical new discoveries in science, contributed significantly to the later creation of science fiction.

In a sense, the Gothic novelists were trying to have their cake and eat it too. While depicting the most outlandish incidents in their tales, they placed many of their narratives in the Middle Ages, at a time when—in their estimation—ignorance and superstition so dominated the populace that the representation of wondrous events in fiction could be thought to constitute a backhanded kind of psychological realism. More relevantly, the supernatural, in those works that featured it, was acknowledged as beyond the bounds of the real, but because it drew upon deep, vestigial instincts centered on the fear of death and the terrors of hell, it commanded a kind of quasi-belief that was the real secret to its success.

In the 1830s, Edgar Allan Poe revolutionized the field both by confining the literature of terror exclusively to the short story and by bringing to that literature an entirely new and intense understanding of the psychology of fear. Poe's greatest innovation, quite frankly, was his immense literary talent: any one of his best tales packs more of a punch than entire novels by the Gothicists. That initial wave of Gothic literature fell by the wayside very quickly, as Poe, both by precept and by example, championed the short story as the chosen vehicle for conveying terror. His great contemporary, Nathaniel Hawthorne, was not quite so rigid in confining Gothicism to the short story; indeed, his *House of the Seven Gables* (1851) might be said to constitute one of the first instances in

American literature in which the entire premise of the work is supernatural—the curse of the dying Matthew Maule on the entire Pyncheon family—although his execution of that premise leads more to wistful melancholy than to fear or horror. Fitz-James O'Brien and Ambrose Bierce followed Poe more closely, but in England, Poe's example of concision and intensity took much longer to find favor. If anyone today is capable of wading through Edward Bulwer-Lytton's Gothic novels, especially the immense *A Strange Story* (1862), they will find that his work is more in the nature of a philosophical tract than an excursion into the supernatural. J. Sheridan Le Fanu restricted the supernatural almost entirely to the short story or novella, while a legion of Victorian ghost-story writers— Margaret Oliphant, Mrs. J. H. Riddell, Rhoda Broughton, Amelia B. Edwards, and many others—resurrected the ghost story with seemingly endless variations.

It was, however, at this juncture—the late nineteenth century—that we come upon some towering works of Gothicism that still color the popular imagination. Less than two decades separate the publication of such novels as Robert Louis Stevenson's *The Strange Case of Dr. Jekyll and Mr. Hyde* (1886), Oscar Wilde's *The Picture of Dorian Gray* (1890–1891), Bram Stoker's *Dracula* (1897), and Henry James's *The Turn of the Screw* (1898)—the first two constituting imperishable examples of the *doppelgänger* motif, while the other two remain the canonical treatments of the vampire and the ghost, respectively. It is of some significance that three of these works are short novels at best, adhering to Poe's notion of the "unity of effect" (which he believed possible only in the short story), but expansive enough to incorporate the interplay and development of character that is one of the distinguishing features of the novel. Indeed, one of the several literary failings of *Dracula* is probably its excessive length, to say nothing of the fact that its putative lead character, Count Dracula, remains offstage for large segments of the work.

What is most notable about this turn-of-the-century period is the degree to which mainstream literary figures chose to engage in Gothicism, either supernatural or nonsupernatural, for the length of a tale or novel. A substantial number of the short stories and novellas of Henry James involve ghosts or the suspicion of ghosts, as do the tales of his friend and disciple Edith Wharton. Such Americans as F. Marion Crawford (*The Witch of Prague*, 1891; *Wandering Ghosts*, 1911), Robert W. Chambers (*The King in Yellow*, 1895), the architect Ralph Adams Cram (*Black Spirits and White*, 1895), Sarah Orne Jewett, Gertrude Atherton, and Mary E. Wilkins-Freeman made vital contributions to the literature of terror. Such of their British counterparts as Rudyard Kipling, Sir Arthur Conan Doyle, Wilkie Collins, Richard Marsh (*The Beetle*, 1897), H. Rider Haggard (*She*, 1887), and H. G. Wells did the same. And what do we make of Joseph Conrad's "Heart of Darkness" (1899)? Its concluding utterance by Kurtz, "The horror! The horror!" has become almost self-parodic, but this

novella as a whole fuses the terrors of the external world—symbolized by the darkness of deepest Africa—and the terrors of the human mind as ably as any work in literature.

It was during this period that some of the most significant figures in super- natural horror—the Welshman Arthur Machen, the Irishman Lord Dunsany, the Englishmen Algernon Blackwood and M. R. James, and the American H. P. Lovecraft—emerged. Their work, very diverse in subject matter, is united by a philosophical vision that found in the supernatural a means of conveying each author's deepest metaphysical and moral vision. Machen, the implacable foe of science, which he believed was tearing the veils from the mystery of the universe, utilized the supernatural as a means of restoring the sense of wonder to the cosmos; Blackwood, not quite so hostile to the progress of human knowl- edge, nevertheless used his horror and fantasy fiction to envision a pantheistic unity of all nature; Dunsany was repelled by the onslaught of technology and commercialism and sought to depict otherworldly realms of beauty; and James, a relatively orthodox Christian, found in the ghost story a vehicle for moral ac- counts of the just punishment that descends upon sin and error.

Lovecraft, drawing upon the work of all his predecessors dating back to Poe, infused the weird tale with a cosmic vision that remains his signature achieve- ment. Recognizing that many of the standard motifs in supernatural fiction— the ghost, the witch, the vampire, the werewolf, the haunted house—had lost much of their potency because the advance of knowledge had rendered them virtually unusable in serious literature, Lovecraft refocused the locus of terror to the unbounded depths of the cosmos, thereby effecting a felicitous union with the burgeoning genre of science fiction.

Lovecraft was, of course, present at the birth of the pulp magazine *Weird Tales*, the first periodical devoted solely to weird fiction. Such of his colleagues as Clark Ashton Smith, Robert E. Howard, August Derleth, and Donald Wandrei filled the pages of that magazine, and dozens of other pulps, with a wide array of writing that spanned the spectrum from psychological suspense to pure science fiction. And yet, it must be acknowledged frankly that the great bulk of material published in *Weird Tales* and other pulp magazines was subliterary rubbish that deserved the scorn it garnered from mainstream critics. Whether the refusal of mainstream magazines to publish weird material led to the birth of the pulps, or whether the pulps' emergence led to the banishing of the weird from mainstream magazines, is a chicken-and-egg question that may be impossible to answer; but because the pulps were "popular" literature designed for a largely ill-educated public, the majority of their contents was hackneyed in conception and slipshod in execution. Only the very best of the pulp writers surmounted the hackwork of their fellow scribblers, but, because they had few other outlets to publish their work, they became tarred with the same brush that depicted *all* the material in

the pulps as beneath critical notice. The entire field of Gothic fiction thereby came to be considered a poor relation to mainstream literature.

This aesthetic cleavage was never quite so pronounced in England, perhaps because of the unusual longevity of such writers as Blackwood and Dunsany, whose work continued to be received with respect. The continuing credibility of the ghost story helped to foster a vibrant and literarily viable tradition of supernatural writing that included such distinguished figures as Walter de la Mare, E. Nesbit, L. P. Hartley, John Buchan, Robert Hichens, Elizabeth Bowen, and May Sinclair. Dunsany's work had the effect of segregating *fantasy*—a mode whereby the author creates his own realm of pure imagination—from supernatural horror. From the foundations he established came the later work of E. R. Eddison, Mervyn Peake, and J. R. R. Tolkien.

Curiously enough, the supernatural novel flourished after a fashion in the early twentieth century, whether at the hands of such an eccentric writer as William Hope Hodgson or in individual efforts by generally mainstream writers such as Barry Pain (*An Exchange of Souls*, 1911), Francis Brett Young (*Cold Harbour*, 1924), Herbert Gorman (*The Place Called Dagon*, 1927), and Leonard Cline (*The Dark Chamber*, 1927). M. R. James's work inspired a small cadre of disciples who sought to build upon his tradition of the antiquarian ghost story, although few of these writers came close to matching James's achievement. But the neo-Gothic novel all but faded out of existence by the 1930s, overwhelmed by the literary dominance of mimetic realism (Hemingway, Sinclair Lewis, F. Scott Fitzgerald, and William Faulkner) or the Modernist movement that, while drawing upon fantasy and terror to some degree, generally scorned pure supernaturalism. D. H. Lawrence wrote a handful of weird tales, but these were cast in shade when compared with his immensely influential novels of love and death.

August Derleth and Donald Wandrei's founding of Arkham House in 1939—initially to publish the work of Lovecraft in hardcover—was a mixed blessing; although the founders quickly proceeded to publish other meritorious work from the pulp magazines, their press in some senses augmented the ghettoization of weird literature by restricting it to a small and insignificant audience. The demise of the pulps in the 1940s resulted from the emergence of the paperback book, and in this market, some supernatural writers flourished—but only by writing work that could be marketed under other rubrics. Fritz Leiber and Ray Bradbury spanned the spectrum from science fiction to supernatural horror to pure fantasy, while Robert Bloch did the same but settled upon psychological suspense as his chosen mode of literary utterance. By the 1950s and 1960s, they were joined by other writers such as Richard Matheson, Russell Kirk, Theodore Sturgeon, Charles Beaumont, and Rod Serling. Then, of course, there was the odd case of Shirley Jackson, whose work sat uneasily between the domains of mainstream fiction and psychological terror, lapsing finally into the supernatural

with the stunning haunted house novel *The Haunting of Hill House* (1959). Critics rarely knew what to make of her unclassifiable work, with the result that she was largely ignored both by the mainstream community and by the cadre of Gothic devotees.

In England, the picture was in some sense not quite so bleak—the flamboyant supernatural novels of Dennis Wheatley earned him a wide following if little critical recognition, while Gerald Kersh contributed his eccentric fusions of supernatural, psychological, and science-fictional terror—but in other ways was dire indeed, as Robert Aickman was virtually the sole practitioner of pure supernaturalism in the 1950s and 1960s. It was just at this time that the media were making their impress upon the literary development of the field. Although horror movies had been prevalent since the earliest days of the film industry—it was, indeed, the popularity of *Dracula* (1931) and other vampire films that raised Stoker's novel to canonical status—the impact of film and television upon literary work only began to be substantially felt in the 1960s. Rod Serling's *The Twilight Zone* (1959–1964) enlisted the services of some of the best writers in the field, including Beaumont and Matheson, and it is arguable that it was this leavening of the popular audience for treatments of the supernatural that led to the spectacular and seemingly sudden emergence of horror as a best-selling phenomenon.

Ira Levin's *Rosemary's Baby* (1967), William Peter Blatty's *The Exorcist* (1971), and Thomas Tryon's *The Other* (1971) were all adapted into film, the first two being particularly noteworthy and popular. The synergy between film and literature gained particular force in the work of Stephen King, who for a time was the most remarkable phenomenon in the history of publishing. Virtually every one of his novels, beginning with *Carrie* (1974), achieved best-seller status and was adapted into a film or a television miniseries; he quickly became a brand name, a known quantity like a McDonald's hamburger or Tide detergent. Other bestselling writers such as Peter Straub (*Ghost Story*, 1979) and Clive Barker (*The Books of Blood*, 1984–1985) followed in his wake; a bit later, Dean R. Koontz and Anne Rice joined the ranks of the blockbusters. But this "horror boom"—which was, in reality, much more a marketing than an aesthetic phenomenon—had at least one unfortunate tendency: it impelled authors of all sorts to aim for *popular* rather than *literary* success, their goal being to reach the best-seller lists, not to produce work of genuine merit. The result was inevitable. A surfeit of the hackneyed, the uninspired, and the plainly trashy caused the entire field to implode, at least from a marketing perspective; publishers radically cut back on their horror offerings or abandoned them altogether.

The fact is that, during this entire period, any number of sincere, talented writers were working out of the limelight, and it is their work that will in the end survive and come to be seen as representative of the best that Gothicism has

to offer. Ramsey Campbell, emerging from his early devotion to Lovecraft, has produced such a distinguished array of novels and tales from the 1970s to the present that he must be given serious consideration as the greatest horror writer of our time, and perhaps of all time. Not far behind are such writers as T. E. D. Klein, Thomas Ligotti, Dennis Etchison, and Thomas Tessier. And now that Gothicism has, to some degree, returned to its roots in the small press, such writers as Caitlín R. Kiernan, Norman Partridge, China Miéville, and Laird Barron are only the most prominent of a vibrant new crop of neo-Gothicists.

What the present volume demonstrates beyond all doubt is that Gothicism is a mode of writing that writers of many different stripes—whether it be predominantly mainstream writers like Toni Morrison, Peter Ackroyd, Joyce Carol Oates, and Margaret Atwood, or genre veterans such as Campbell, King, Straub, Elizabeth Hand, Dan Simmons, Neil Gaiman, and Phil Rickman—can utilize to express themes, conceptions, and imagery beyond the purview of mimetic realism. Many of these writers draw upon the long heritage of Gothicism stretching back at least two centuries, while at the same time remaining distinctively original in their manipulation of character and incident. The blurring or melding of genres is the order of the day, and if this sometimes results in critical difficulties in classification, it is nonetheless a benefit to those privileged readers who can find in neo-Gothicism some of the best that contemporary literature has to offer.

with the stunning haunted house novel *The Haunting of Hill House* (1959). Critics rarely knew what to make of her unclassifiable work, with the result that she was largely ignored both by the mainstream community and by the cadre of Gothic devotees.

In England, the picture was in some sense not quite so bleak—the flamboyant supernatural novels of Dennis Wheatley earned him a wide following if little critical recognition, while Gerald Kersh contributed his eccentric fusions of supernatural, psychological, and science-fictional terror—but in other ways was dire indeed, as Robert Aickman was virtually the sole practitioner of pure supernaturalism in the 1950s and 1960s. It was just at this time that the media were making their impress upon the literary development of the field. Although horror movies had been prevalent since the earliest days of the film industry—it was, indeed, the popularity of *Dracula* (1931) and other vampire films that raised Stoker's novel to canonical status—the impact of film and television upon literary work only began to be substantially felt in the 1960s. Rod Serling's *The Twilight Zone* (1959–1964) enlisted the services of some of the best writers in the field, including Beaumont and Matheson, and it is arguable that it was this leavening of the popular audience for treatments of the supernatural that led to the spectacular and seemingly sudden emergence of horror as a best-selling phenomenon.

Ira Levin's *Rosemary's Baby* (1967), William Peter Blatty's *The Exorcist* (1971), and Thomas Tryon's *The Other* (1971) were all adapted into film, the first two being particularly noteworthy and popular. The synergy between film and literature gained particular force in the work of Stephen King, who for a time was the most remarkable phenomenon in the history of publishing. Virtually every one of his novels, beginning with *Carrie* (1974), achieved best-seller status and was adapted into a film or a television miniseries; he quickly became a brand name, a known quantity like a McDonald's hamburger or Tide detergent. Other bestselling writers such as Peter Straub (*Ghost Story*, 1979) and Clive Barker (*The Books of Blood*, 1984–1985) followed in his wake; a bit later, Dean R. Koontz and Anne Rice joined the ranks of the blockbusters. But this "horror boom"—which was, in reality, much more a marketing than an aesthetic phenomenon—had at least one unfortunate tendency: it impelled authors of all sorts to aim for *popular* rather than *literary* success, their goal being to reach the best-seller lists, not to produce work of genuine merit. The result was inevitable. A surfeit of the hackneyed, the uninspired, and the plainly trashy caused the entire field to implode, at least from a marketing perspective; publishers radically cut back on their horror offerings or abandoned them altogether.

The fact is that, during this entire period, any number of sincere, talented writers were working out of the limelight, and it is their work that will in the end survive and come to be seen as representative of the best that Gothicism has

the pulps as beneath critical notice. The entire field of Gothic fiction thereby came to be considered a poor relation to mainstream literature.

This aesthetic cleavage was never quite so pronounced in England, perhaps because of the unusual longevity of such writers as Blackwood and Dunsany, whose work continued to be received with respect. The continuing credibility of the ghost story helped to foster a vibrant and literarily viable tradition of supernatural writing that included such distinguished figures as Walter de la Mare, E. Nesbit, L. P. Hartley, John Buchan, Robert Hichens, Elizabeth Bowen, and May Sinclair. Dunsany's work had the effect of segregating *fantasy*—a mode whereby the author creates his own realm of pure imagination—from supernatural horror. From the foundations he established came the later work of E. R. Eddison, Mervyn Peake, and J. R. R. Tolkien.

Curiously enough, the supernatural novel flourished after a fashion in the early twentieth century, whether at the hands of such an eccentric writer as William Hope Hodgson or in individual efforts by generally mainstream writers such as Barry Pain (*An Exchange of Souls*, 1911), Francis Brett Young (*Cold Harbour*, 1924), Herbert Gorman (*The Place Called Dagon*, 1927), and Leonard Cline (*The Dark Chamber*, 1927). M. R. James's work inspired a small cadre of disciples who sought to build upon his tradition of the antiquarian ghost story, although few of these writers came close to matching James's achievement. But the neo-Gothic novel all but faded out of existence by the 1930s, overwhelmed by the literary dominance of mimetic realism (Hemingway, Sinclair Lewis, F. Scott Fitzgerald, and William Faulkner) or the Modernist movement that, while drawing upon fantasy and terror to some degree, generally scorned pure supernaturalism. D. H. Lawrence wrote a handful of weird tales, but these were cast in shade when compared with his immensely influential novels of love and death.

August Derleth and Donald Wandrei's founding of Arkham House in 1939—initially to publish the work of Lovecraft in hardcover—was a mixed blessing; although the founders quickly proceeded to publish other meritorious work from the pulp magazines, their press in some senses augmented the ghettoization of weird literature by restricting it to a small and insignificant audience. The demise of the pulps in the 1940s resulted from the emergence of the paperback book, and in this market, some supernatural writers flourished—but only by writing work that could be marketed under other rubrics. Fritz Leiber and Ray Bradbury spanned the spectrum from science fiction to supernatural horror to pure fantasy, while Robert Bloch did the same but settled upon psychological suspense as his chosen mode of literary utterance. By the 1950s and 1960s, they were joined by other writers such as Richard Matheson, Russell Kirk, Theodore Sturgeon, Charles Beaumont, and Rod Serling. Then, of course, there was the odd case of Shirley Jackson, whose work sat uneasily between the domains of mainstream fiction and psychological terror, lapsing finally into the supernatural

Acknowledgments

Texas-sized thanks to the impressive writers for putting themselves into this project and for every creative hour they gave. Few of the works you have written on have any substantial criticism yet, so you are all pioneers. What a pleasure to work with you.

My gratitude to S. T. Joshi for his inspiring works and splendid foreword.

How much I appreciate Scarecrow Press's senior editor, Stephen Ryan, whose intelligence, assistance, patience, and great questions were a boon to the project. Hats off as well to Scarecrow production editor Jayme Bartles Reed for her deep dedication to the book. Any mistakes are my own.

Special thanks to my wife Catherine and my daughters Emily Sophia and Juliana Celeste Olson, and to my parents Morris and Olga Olson.

I am much obliged for these superb works below from 1999 on, all of great help to me as a Gothic professor, and without which the present book would not exist:

Ash Tree Press's *All Hallows: The Journal of the Ghost Story Society*, and their on-line All-Hallows Group; contributing editor Ruth Bienstock Anolik's *Horrifying Sex: Essays on Sexual Difference in the Gothic Imagination* (Jefferson, NC: McFarland, 2007); contributing editor Richard Bleiler's *Supernatural Fiction Writers: Contemporary Fantasy and Horror* (New York: Scribner, 2002; 2 vols., 2nd ed.); contributing editors Glennis Byron and David Punter's *Spectral Readings: Towards a Gothic Geography* (London: Macmillan, 1999) and *The Gothic* (Oxford: Blackwell, 2003); Jason Colavito's *Knowing Fear: Science, Knowledge and the*

Development of the Horror Genre (Jefferson, NC: McFarland, 2008); *Cemetery Dance* magazine; *The Complete Review*; Ellen Datlow's yearly "Summation" from *The Year's Best Fantasy and Horror* (New York: St. Martin's, through the twenty-first annual for 2008) and now in *The Best Horror of the Year* (San Francisco: Night Shade Books, 2009 and following); Heather L. Duda's *The Monster Hunter in Modern Popular Culture* (Jefferson, NC: McFarland, 2008); the Gothic panels of the World Fantasy Convention in Saratoga Springs, Calgary, and San Jose (2007–2009); contributing editors Diane Long Hoeveler and Tamar Heller's *Approaches to Teaching Gothic Fiction* (New York: MLA, 2003); contributing editor Jerrold E. Hogle's *The Cambridge Companion to Gothic Fiction* (Cambridge: Cambridge University Press, 2002); editors Stephen Jones and Kim Newman's *Horror: Another 100 Best Books* (New York: Carroll & Graf, 2005); S. T. Joshi's *The Modern Weird Tale* (Jefferson, NC: McFarland, 2001); contributing editors S. T. Joshi and Stefan Dziemianowicz's *Supernatural Literature of the World: An Encyclopedia* (Westport, CT: Greenwood, 2005; 3 vols.); David Kalat's *J-Horror* (New York: Vertical, 2007); *Locus* magazine; Marie Mulvey-Robert's *The Handbook to the Gothic* (New York: NYU Press, 2009; 2nd ed.); Bernice M. Murphy and Elizabeth McCarthy's online *Irish Journal of Gothic and Horror Studies*; June Pulliam and Anthony J. Fonseca's online *Necropsy: The Review of Horror Fiction*, as well as their *Hooked on Horror III: A Guide to Reading Interests in the Genre* (Libraries Unlimited, 2009) and *Read On . . . Horror Fiction* (Libraries Unlimited, 2006); contributing editor David Punter's *A Companion to the Gothic* (Oxford: Blackwell, 2000); Laurence A. Rickels's *The Vampire Lectures* (Minneapolis: University of Minnesota Press, 1999); Mary Ellen Snodgrass's *Encyclopedia of Gothic Literature* (New York: Facts on File, 2005); Tartarus Press's journal *Wormwood*; Charles Tan's interviews with contemporary Gothic writers at Bibliophile Stalker (http://charles-tan.blogspot .com/); contributing editors Douglass H. Thomson, Jack G. Voller, and Frederick S. Frank's *Gothic Writers: A Critical and Bibliographic Guide* (Westport, CT: Greenwood, 2002); and Peter Turchi's *Maps of the Imagination: The Writer as Cartographer* (San Antonio: Trinity University Press, 2004).

Three cheers for my inquisitive "Horror, Ghost, and Gothic" students.

And for always answering my many e-mails about all things Gothic, a humble bow to T. C. Boyle, Terry Dowling, Guillermo del Toro, Jennifer Egan, Graham Joyce, Joyce Carol Oates, Steve Rasnic Tem, Stephen Volk, and Chelsea Quinn Yarbro.

Last, a blessing for beloved Virginia Cowen (1919–2010), a giving mother to eleven inspiring sons and daughters, and the most devoted reader and teacher of fiction I knew. May Heaven hold for her more grand novels than stars in the skies of Texas.

Introduction

Danel Olson

The New Dusk

> Are you like me, ready for the new dusk?
>
> —Ingrid Pitt, legendary Hammer Films vamp[1]

> Welcome to hell. You get the full tour.
>
> —Mark Z. Danielewski in interview[2]

> We should never have come in.
>
> —Jennifer Egan, *The Keep*[3]

As you are already holding this volume, you must be ready for the new dusk. Let this brief introduction to this reference book's mission and method serve as a torch to guide your way through these new literary catacombs. I envy you, as you are about to wind your way through fifty-three startlingly different ways to recount—and react to—a Gothic novel. More than that you will discover a new dark library for your bookshelves, and will from this moment unbury all their hidden pasts and relations.

Why Study the Gothic Novel?
Why Not Just Read It?

For my part, I understand a reader's or student's desire to simply experience the terror, untameable superstition, occasional sadism, and constant suspense of

these books. Dry academic dissection implies that these works are mostly intellectual puzzles, or some chaos to put to order. I sense they are more. They intend to chill and astonish, and they mean to be felt. They come upon us in their madness and hunger as would a wolf pack, and awe should be our first response. But I promise that the unfolding of these pages will only increase the reader's astonishment, dark pleasure, and discovery. In fact, this whole book owes its existence to a student in my "Horror, Ghost, and Gothic Fiction" course who thoughtfully asked, "But what about any good Gothic novels after Y2K?" It is a grand question, and although she has had a rather long wait for an answer, here it is. For underneath the Gothic's corseted bodices, spikes, frilly Victorian dresses, black eye makeup, gray lipstick, piercings, spandex, wigs, and laced-up boots or patterned knee-highs, what exactly is there? Behind its monsters, ghouls, ghosts, serial killers, zombies, and vampires, what thing of any meaning lurks? Within this reference guide, each of the novel's authors and critics may have a different answer as to why the Gothic is worth an academic view. My belief is that Gothdom and Gothic literature, though separate entities, have so closely crept up to the mainstream that a basic interest in the world around us demands that they be examined. Certainly when the Spanish prime minister shows up at the White House with his Goth daughters in tow, with even their mother clad in all black, and then the U.S. State Department proudly uploads the pictures to Flickr,[4] we have a phenomenon on our hands. In literary terms, this trend is just as substantial. Tracking each week of the last two months, I am staggered that Gothic-themed novels have consistently appeared in four to seven of the fifteen to sixteen slots on the *New York Times* best-sellers list (with those most favored Gothic situations appearing in the *Times*'s capsule descriptions: "a letter from his dead wife," "a family secret," "girl goes missing," "a ruthless foe," "fallen prey to an ancestral curse," "woman's body found in London cemetery," and "slave flees with her master to New Orleans"). Untold millions are reading them. It seems, however, that library shelves have a hole in them with regard to interpretations of the latest Gothic fictions. I expect the users of this book to be not only patrons of public, college, and university libraries, but also classes on contemporary novels and pop culture, postmodern seminars, Gothic Studies programs, reading-group leaders, genre publishers (some genre presses from Canada and Britain have asked for a copy already), and both university and independent scholars. Many junior high school and high school library collections will find this guidebook essential for their hooked-on-Gothic students, who stand as a major market (and I'm afraid to admit that my daughters—who have fallen deeply for both Edward Cullen *and* Jacob Black—would probably be the first to crack it open).

When an author wins the 1993 Nobel Prize for Literature in part for her powerful and popular Pulitzer Prize–winning novel of a visitant daughter

come back to the mother who killed her to save her—Toni Morrison's *Beloved* (1987)—we again must give the Gothic narrative its due. A thorough investigation, but also a salute and celebration, is what this study intends. If, like salt, the Gothic has been much abused for its deleterious effects on our health, still the Gothic is so much a part of our fashion, culture, and entertainment that it is as unimaginable to go without it as it is to forsake salt. There is some strange affinity between our lives and these works; surely to ask what allures and what terrifies us is to penetrate our minds with the most primal questions. What better kind of character self-analysis do we know than pondering our own unseemly attractions and ungodly fears? What compels one of our essay contributors, the highly regarded novelist Lisa Tuttle, is "that ambiguous, murky, and dangerous region where the very things we fear most are also those we secretly desire."[5] Is then our terror of the uncanny actually our shock over witnessing the distorted image of our own desire in these unnatural storyworlds, these zones of dark potentiality, these bizarre and opaque minds?

It's undebatable that there has been a boom in Gothic studies since 1980 to satisfy our hunger for context and meaning in these novels that challenge or enlarge our knowledge of the world and the mind, offering us narrators unreliable, psychotic, or even dead.[6] What's more, as University Distinguished Professor and former International Gothic Association President Jerrold E. Hogle muses,

> Now people realize that there's a lot of symbolic dimension to Gothic fictions. They have deep symbolic significance that extends to the use of the Gothic in film, in video games, in graphic novels. All of those, including Gothic novels, are now the subject of a lot of intense academic analysis to figure out these questions: Why do we need this kind of phenomenon in our culture and why does it keep reproducing itself?[7]

Considering how prevalent the Gothic is in our culture, the timing for this guide is right. We need an understanding of how and why the alien will within the neo-Gothic has cast such a spell on us and to show how the Gothic is evolving. Perhaps the ways we read it should evolve as well. This luminous study of macabre fiction and the death myths underneath it aims to provide these answers. Another justification for serious study is that Gothic postmodernism is revising our notions of the sublime and its inherent terror; in the elegant words of David B. Morris, "The gothic takes us deep within rather than far beyond the human sphere."[8] Isaac Bashevis Singer put it in another, droller, matter-of-fact way to his editor on a spring day in 1978, when Kirby McCauley asked him why he spent so much time writing away on demons, dybbuks, resurrected Nazis, and supernatural happenings. Singer's arresting answer: "It brings me into contact with reality."[9] Thus from this Nobel prize winner's view, the weirdest, most

estranging fiction about these others—that fiction where there is no textual evidence that the others were some narrator's unfortunate nightmare, fantasy, illusion, or hallucination—is still about human concerns, or our unreal reality. Perhaps the greatest reason why we can't quit the Gothic and why we must press deeper to disclose its secrets is because we are ensorcelled by death, haunted by the day or night of our own death, wondering if death is the definite end of our existence. More than that, will we see the dead somehow again? "The Gothic genre," as our critic contributor Judith Wilt captured it elsewhere, "always blurs the boundary between life and death."[10] This grey blur is the most stilling and captivating one of all. No doubt the Gothic saturates our culture because we crave the most intense mystery. So much is explained to us in the information overload heaped upon our heads every day from all corners that we want enigma, we want questions forever without answer, we want the riddles of Thanatos and Eros that the Gothic summons. We may believe that we would be better off not knowing our weakness for the torturous in the Gothic, what has been called its "dark other," the stuff of "slasher videos, snuff films, and violent pornography,"[11] but the novels featured in this volume (especially those from Chuck Palahniuk and Andrew Davidson) will not let us off so easily. What do we really know about our furtive longings, then, the Gothic asks, and what do we know about people? Do we actually believe that they are either simply good or simply bad, when as a dark film of the 1950s wisely put it, "good and evil can change places like light and shadow. How can we be sure where one ends and the other begins, of which side we are on at a given moment?"[12] It is our interest, our complicity, our shadow side that the Gothic lets us peer into, possibly giving us a warning, a release, but perhaps an encouragement toward viciousness. As one former American vice president eerily intoned to the world listening, "We also have to work, through, sort of the dark side, if you will. We've got to spend time in the shadows. . ."[13] (To think I once invited this spooky politician to a book launch of mine.) The point is that the ever-watchful Gothic keeps asking us, who or what is out there? And do I recognize myself in it?

Scope, Focus, Methodology, and Inclusion Criteria

The crossover appeal is that this volume offers guideposts for high school and college students, general readers, and seasoned scholars to fifty-three of the most intriguingly foreboding novels and novellas, as well as nonsupernatural Gothic narratives, appearing in their original languages between the years 2000 and 2010. Over 180 consultants and contributors were sought for cross-disciplinary conversations (see appendix A) and polled (by e-mail, phone, or in-person con-

versation at conventions) to nominate the post-2000 novels they considered the most stylistically artistic, experimentally successful, apt at genre bending and blending, influential on other writers and the market, original and emotive, metaphysically/culturally/historically significant, or authentically scary/disturbing/transgressive/shocking, all with that strange alchemy of literary elements that make them come back to us in dreams. If "myth is truth" and literature simply "words that provoke response," as the Cheshire novelist Alan Garner claims,[14] then which is truest, most provocative? Which is the one with more mystery and secrets, melodrama and murder, than you could reasonably hope for? Which innovative storytellers went beyond the conventional and best redefined the Gothic? You may be surprised by the choices, as I was by a few.

The goal was then for the fifty works with the most nominations to be meticulously described, analyzed, and evaluated in essays that average over five thousand words each (a few novels tied, so we ended up at fifty-three works). I asked the greatest lovers of the Gothic to observe how the Gothic slithers, coils, and strikes throughout these novels. These authorities are a varied lot, including mainstream and genre novelists, members of Gothic Studies departments and associations, World Fantasy Convention panelists, academics of Gothic note, esteemed independent scholars, online horror/ghost/Gothic newsgroup and literary archive founders, long-active horror and fantasy editors, publishers, humanities librarians, speculative-fiction-award board members, horror film experts and directors, true crime writers, literary biographers, editors and authors of dark erotica/noirotica, a couple of Goth girls turned academics, reference guide compilers, and a forensic psychologist whose specialty is serial killers.

To widen the range of Gothic authors discussed, I suggested that we only write on a particular author once, so some prolific fictionists with fresh and arresting premises in *several* of their novels during this fertile decade, despite getting a large number of nods, are represented only once. My apologies to them and their readers (though their nominated works are listed in appendix B, which lists all the works that received votes). From American-born authors came twenty-six of the novels featured in *21st Century Gothic*, from England thirteen, from Australia five, from Canada, Spain, and Japan came two each, and from Scotland, Wales, Belgium, and the Netherlands came one each. It is hoped that when such a study is launched again—possibly on the Gothic novels from years 2010 through 2020—we will see more novelists out of South America and Africa getting an essay.

Naturally each land, through its art, culture, technology, and history, either disinters or births a Gothic creature substantially its own. Compounding that, ambiguity, hybridization, and shape-shifting seem to be the Gothic's foggy, killing strength and nature. Thus, consensus for what the Gothic means now is not universal. Nevertheless, in a post-2000 survey that went out to a hundred Gothic

scholars from Europe and North America (for the MLA volume *Approaches to Teaching Gothic Novels* for which some of our contributors wrote), editors Diane Long Hoeveler and Tamar Heller found that scholars tended to agree on many of the Gothic's traits and tones, all of which were shared with our contributors. Their survey respondents mentioned that often the Gothic explores fantasies, hidden and forbidden desires (murder, incest, and worse), damnation, physical and emotional disease and aberration, revenge, curses, family lineage, estate battles, horror, terror, falls, the sublime, superstition, reanimation, entrapment and confinement (especially of women), the supernatural, the past, and haunted and decayed structures (castles, mansions, abbeys, or modern houses of spirits).[15] Moreover, the Gothic supplies us with unreliable or compulsive narrators, the anxiety of the displaced, bad parenting or none at all, inverted domesticity, nightmares, embedded tests and frame narratives, and a fascination with thresholds and the transgression of boundaries.[16] The Gothic involves confrontations between us and the uncanny, between us and the other.[17] Other damaging encounters include those of the politically or financially weak in conflict with the elites, reason with irrationality, science with religion, and the individual with the social order (e.g., the subaltern versus the dominant, the child versus the parent, woman versus patriarchy). All literature may ultimately be about defeat, but few genres stress it as the Gothic does, so often dwelling on our grand strivings and hopes all wickedly moving in reverse.

As the managing editor, reading or rereading a Gothic novel (or a series of them) each week for the last year has not made me completely insane, but I cannot truthfully say it has helped my mental health. It was spiky Gothic pages before breakfast, lunch, and supper, and after my midnight snack. Everything I touched seemed cut from shadows. So, the effects of this Gothic immersion have not been altogether salubrious. The books are draining; they entertain evil. They tend to make one wary, questioning the everyday simple answers people give, and absurdly looking for the dark and shaggy roots of conspiracy behind them. And if sometimes the novels' philosophizing seemed low-grade and their melancholy relentless, the recompense came in plots grandly salacious, complicated, and irresistibly manic, as I read sometimes until breaking dawn, surrounded by a cast of shambling characters spreading terror, and sometimes receiving it. I expect I will miss this year as a feral child, once acclimatized to "civilization," misses the wolf pack. The books, like the wolves, ran wild and hungry and free, and they made me *feel* more. They exist in a marvellous antiparadise.

There are so many other graceful and illuminating guides to the Gothic that I barely know where to begin naming them, and one could wonder, why one more? An answer is that Gothic Studies often seems fondly retrospective, as if the best were behind us, as if groping among "the dry bones of the past," as Emerson put it, were somehow preferable to fingering the fresh kills. A large

number of Gothic anthologies and reference books represent, describe, or deconstruct the eighteenth-century Gothic, and a huge number are under the thrall of the nineteenth-century Gothic, all understandably so. And many studies are besotted by the aberrant charms of the twentieth-century Gothic. But what about our Gothic of the new millennium? This book is a kickoff to the Gothic of our time, with radiant critical minds from Europe, North America, Asia, and Australia lighting the shadowy corners of each novel or novella. At these new literary frontiers, the contributors chart the ever-vacillating moods and actions of the neo-Gothic. In this work, we see how the new Gothic ranges from gallows humor (especially in Lauren Groff's *The Monsters of Templeton* and Neil Gaiman's book for all ages, *The Graveyard Book*, both from 2008) to outright horror (of the stalk-drop-and-chop Grand Guignol kind, all given free range in Chuck Palahniuk's *Lullaby*), from young adult angst, mixed feelings, and tender holdings (see all of Stephenie Meyer's *Twilight* and part of Elizabeth Kostova's *The Historian*) to highly metatextual experimentation that miraculously still manages to be affecting (in Jennifer Egan's *The Keep* and Mark Z. Danielewski's *House of Leaves*).

The neo-Gothic's macabre emotional territory has expanded as never before, and this collection maps the range. Until now, no one else has made a systematic investigation of the genius of expression within this new millennium's Gothic. For as far as we can see, very few of the novels investigated here have much criticism of a developed kind anywhere (only reviews of slight size and sometimes idiosyncratic or capricious judgment). No one has pondered at length how these novels fit and fight the Gothic tradition that spans the last 250 years. It is hoped that this dark treasure-box of lucid and penetrating criticism may launch a Gothic discourse that enlarges the Gothic canon, just as Morrison's *Beloved* expanded the American literary canon over twenty years ago. The Gothic has been reconceived, and these essays help readers appreciate the movements, motifs, and motives within the harrowing new fictions, informing the largest possible audience, while still stimulating and challenging even the most devoted Gothic fan/writer/editor/critic.

Questions Raised

One question curiously underasked in Gothic Studies is how and why much of the neo-Gothic in the twenty-first century differs from its ancestors, and what that difference puts at risk: what does the new Gothic mock, flaunt, or falsify? The old Gothic frame was well drawn by Jennifer Egan (*The Keep*, 2007) after an appearance in my city. On that evening, she shared her love of the "fantastic (and totally insane) Gothic novels I had a ball reading: Horace Walpole's *The*

Castle of Otranto, Charles Maturin's *Melmoth the Wanderer*, Ann Radcliffe's *The Mysteries of Udolpho*, Matthew Lewis's *The Monk*—those are all 18th century books—and then from the 19th century, Wilkie Collins's *The Woman in White*, which is an absolutely drop-dead great thriller."[18] Then came her memorable brief of the fundamental movements in the traditional Gothic plot: vulnerable strangers come to a new place, stay around long enough to seem participants in their own victimization, compromise themselves, face the uncanny, and then "leave us wondering whether it was really the paranormal or just their brains on broil."[19] Now, beyond these salient features that she limned, we also remember that the traditional Gothic manifestations of the eighteenth and nineteenth centuries broke all taboos while revealing simultaneous love-hate for the object of desire, whether that object was *a man* (Catherine Earnshaw's Heathcliff), *a process* (Dr. Victor Frankenstein wanting the worship of future generations, but still rejecting the reanimated creature from his filthy workshop of creation, which he thought would bring the fame), *a parent* (the creature's driving Dr. Frankenstein to his Arctic death, and yet regarding him as the only father he had, all confirming the Gothic's obsession of the terrified child and the tyrannical, unstable parental order), or *a power* (the Capuchin monk Ambrosio adoring eminence and honor, but despising how self-controlled you have to stay to keep such approval). And we should always keep in our hearts what was the old Gothic's predominant feeling—hopelessness. As evidence of this dismal emotion, or what Coleridge called "the grief without a pang," I recall my rereading of four Gothic classics that were separated by over fifty years (*The Castle of Otranto*, *Vathek*, *The Monk*, and *Frankenstein*), undertaken before I was to moderate a World Fantasy Convention panel on the Gothic. I was struck by seeing the same word repeated over and over again in the last five pages of each of these novels: *despair*. But the Gothic world is not what it was. We have all grown a little Gothic now and joined the movement. More of who we are now seems to reside inside the neo-Gothic "villain." As Fred Botting persuasively contends, vampires are now "mirrors of contemporary identity and sympathetic identifications." With their lives of luxurious consumption and wasted desires, they are the "normative image of the latter-day consumer."[20] More worrisome than that, he finds that in our real life, as in our neo-Gothic fictional lives, there are equal amounts of possibility and unease: "anxiety floats freely, reflecting and thus ghosting the high-speed circulation of information and commodities . . . [the c]omputer and genetic codes [that] allow everything from identity to bodies to be rewritten."[21] My own concern is that if the überfigure of the Gothic—the vampire—has changed from the articulate and merciless count of Bram Stoker's *Dracula*, one obsessed with hierarchy and battle and little prone to love in the way we understand devotion and protection, to a softhearted and mumbling boy, less a fiend than a friend, and quite capable of love, maybe even a purer love than our mortal one (enter

Edward Cullen), then we have no great monster story but a little romance. What is to dread in that? If we suck dry the mad blood from the revenant account, where has the wildness gone and the terror vanished to? And if what was fearsome and loathly is now embraced, how can we be reminded of its unpredictable animal power, its essential and awful strangeness and apartness? Has the vampire novel moved from being a great shaggy gray Carpathian wolf of violent instability in Bram Stoker's time to a trimmed and absurd black French lap poodle in ours? Doesn't the Gothic need to stay a bête noir that pounces, tears, devours, and dashes away, rather than a tame little thing that sits and broods?

All of this change from the old ways of Gothika to this softer thing of caring vampires who resemble sparkly therapists causes understandable outrage for traditionalists, and some nostalgia, even among the very characters of its novels. Our longing for the darker protagonists is best mirrored by this exchange from the most popular vampire novel of the past decade, during Bella Swan's first visit to her beau vampire's house in *Twilight* (2005), where she may have secretly hoped for something a little more dangerous and forbidden, a bit more sexually frenzied, and a lot more shadowy:

> He [Edward Cullen] followed my gaze. "Not what you expected, is it?" he asked, his voice smug.
> "No," I admitted.
> "No coffins, no piled skulls in the corners; I don't even think we have cobwebs . . . what a disappointment this must be for you," he continued slyly.
> I ignored his teasing. "It's so light . . . so open."[22]

In the 2008 film version, again this surprise and possible disappointment of hers is too vital to pass up, though it was shortened:

> EDWARD CULLEN: What did you expect? Coffins and dungeons and moats?
> ISABELLA SWANN: No, not the moats.[23]

What unearthly good is a vampire who sits at the edge of your bed at night and just looks at you? Where's the bite? Despite what my daughters tell me, it seems the great vampire story is under threat, and a dramatic corrective is needed. However, this is a question best left for our contributors to answer.

If the most popular vampire novel in this period seems underfearful and anemic, what is the health of the undead others? Perhaps the fate of all these dark fictions hinges on their ability to adapt. *21st Century Gothic* evidences that the Gothic was not so much a literary movement long past as an impulse in art that won't stay buried. The Gothic invites us deep within its cave, which may be a

reflection of our own grave. In this maw of possibilities before death, we become, through the strong and vicarious power of reader identification, part of the scariest nightmare we've never dreamed. What sexual possibilities and transgressions, violent destruction and new creation can happen in each of the novels lives for as long as we speak the book's name. To have that dreadful shivery pleasure all for yourself may well be the reason we put up with what Stephen King recently called neo-Gothic's endless queue of "monsters, murders, bastards, and ne'er-do-wells."[24] Perhaps the reason the Gothic can't stay dead for good is that it suddenly wriggles, disguises, and disappears just before its execution, avoiding extinction by constantly changing (just as literally happens in Richard Flanagan's novel of penal Tasmania featured here, *Gould's Book of Fish*). Slipping from the gibbet is the Gothic way, and its detractors will always find killing its ghost a maddening process. This guide's critics inquire where and how the neo-Gothic is twisting away from our grasp and old definitions, and remaking itself. The contributors will signal how successful the slipstream bending and merging has been. We will watch how cunningly the Gothic descends the winding staircase into the gloom, only to insert itself into memoir, comics, crime and detection novels, travel narratives, erotica, history, science fiction, and fantasy.

Specifically, the contributors to this volume were asked to meditate on eight clusters of questions in forming the dark heart of their all-original essays:

- Why is this one of the most creative or influential modern Gothic novels of the last decade? How does it have a remarkable fullness of characterization, intricacy of plot, cumulatively unbearable power of suspense, a vital symbolic or allegorical system, and the bloodred wine of astonishment—the bizarre, the sublime, the horrific, or the paranormal?
- How does this novel embody the traditional impulse of the Gothic and yet expand, explode, or revolutionize the definition of Gothicism? Does it add humor, a likable villain, some new Gothic mise-en-scène (instead of the usual castle, keep, dungeon, moat, ladies in white, and ominous men in hooded inquisition garb)? How is this novel successfully evolving the Gothic, showing it to be a genre in progress, gifting new life to an old form, dreaming freshly startling visions to the genre's moonless night?
- To where is the dark path of the new Gothic winding? How is the latest Gothic merging with the young adult novel, the metafictional experiment, fantastica, the magical realist narrative, and others?
- How does the novel stir and satisfy readers? How does the neo-Gothic project our current anxieties, dangerous fantasies, and contradictions? Where does it present cultural metaphors? How does the novel's telepathy for our own states, wishes, and dreads explain this particular book's immediately popular reception?

- What are this novel's subtexts and major themes, its perceptions of the natural and the supernatural world?
- Where are the narrative's conflicts?
- What fictional elements beyond symbol and theme have a peculiar power in the narrative, undraping a new generation's awareness of transgression and taboo, of power and its limits, of awe toward love and death? Or, how is the writer ably experimenting with Gothic characters, settings and atmosphere, dialogue, point of view, structure and suspense, style and spontaneous associations, and tone and mood (e.g., is it bitter, ironic, campy, parodic, romantic, satiric, sardonic, or something else)? What intriguing critical concerns does the novel raise independent from the above questions?
- Has Gothicism recently been defanged? Does its survivor instinct make the Gothic return to some of its old trends? What recent studies illuminate best where the Gothic is going and what the novel is doing?

Answers to these queries illustrate how the Gothic has come in from the cold, no longer languishing in the critical margins, but now demanding the most serious questioning and exploration, and even storming the castle of the established literary canon. Together these essays direct us to novels half in love with death and madness, ones that release the shades in the most unforgettable ways. There is, of course, one dark truth to all Gothic texts, despite all their transformations from the time of Horace Walpole's generative novel *The Castle of Otranto* until now, namely that not all who venture inside do get out alive. But now that you are in, and the exits seem missing or blacked out, you might as well relish the Gothic ambience. Run through these new mansions panting and adrenaline addled with our critics, take that offered hand that guides you down the silvered twirling staircase, into the maze of earth-cool torchlit passages, and finally to their terrible secrets below. Everyone may discover something different down there; from your findings, may this book raise a thousand questions. As Mark Z. Danielewski, author of one of my favorite neo-Gothic novels, *House of Leaves*, insightfully said in an interview,

> Smart horror . . . goes after the deeper origins of fear. It usually relies on specters, religion, unanticipated violence, and all of it handled with enough uncertainty it doesn't just provoke an adrenaline rush but thought. . . . What are [you] afraid of? And why? And how should [you] respond? After all, maybe what we're so frightened of will turn out to be nothing more than a dark, empty room. Then again, maybe it won't.[25]

The secrets I found were that the new Gothic, despite its fresh masquerade, still takes us back to the haunting themes of the old Gothic: the bondage of the

body, the bondage of the soul. The Gothic genre has many incarnations—this is merely the latest, but not the last. Enjoy it before it changes into something else.

Notes

1. Ingrid Pitt, "Introduction: My Life Among the Undead," in *The Mammoth Book of Vampire Stories by Women*, ed. Stephen Jones (New York: Carroll & Graf, 2001), 1–6. Sadly, Hammer Films's leading glamour-puss (and toothsome star of *The Vampire Lovers*, *Countess Dracula*, and *Beyond the Rave*) was not a stranger to real-life horrors. Ingrid was born Kasha Kotuzova on November 21, 1937, on a train carrying her mother to a Nazi concentration camp. "They did horrific things to us," she remembers. "My mother told me, 'Never be a victim' and I've never again been a victim in my life." See "Ingrid Pitt," in *Hammer Glamour: Classic Images from the Archive of Hammer Films*, ed. Marcus Hearn (London: Titan, 2009), 120.

2. Mark Z. Danielewski, interview by Sophie Cottrell, "Bold Type: A Conversation with Mark Danielewski," Random House, www.randomhouse.com/boldtype/0400/danielewski/interview.html (accessed April 1, 2010).

3. Jennifer Egan, *The Keep* (Knopf, 2006), 201.

4. "Spain's Goth First Daughters Embarrass, Embarrassed by Dad," *Gawker*, September 25, 2009, http://gawker.com/5368039/spains-goth-first-daughters-embarrass-embarrassed-by-dad (accessed June 9, 2010).

5. Lisa Tuttle, commentary on her portrait, in *The Faces of Fantasy: Photographs by Patti Perret* (New York: Tor, 1996), 142.

6. One of our own contributors lit the Gothic fuse. According to Jerrold E. Hogle, "Gothic studies as an enterprise has become a big international phenomenon. I would say it was 1980 when we had our first major scholarly study of Gothic that a lot of people responded to. It was a book called *The Literature of Terror*, by David Punter in England, and a lot of people wrote books and articles in response to it and that sort of set off a three-decades-long proliferation of studies in the Gothic. And so now there's a whole international community of scholars who go to Gothic conferences. We have an International Gothic Association of international scholars, . . . [a]nd we organize conferences every other year and we have a journal." See Jerrold E. Hogle, interview, "Employee Q & A: Gothic Expert Jerry Hogle," *University of Arizona News*, October 28, 2009, http://uanews.org/node/28183 (accessed March 28, 2010).

7. Hogle, interview.

8. David B. Morris, "The Sublime and the Beautiful: Reconsiderations," *New Literary History* 16, no. 2 (Winter 1985): 306.

9. Isaac Singer to Kirby McCauley, introduction to *Dark Forces: New Stories of Suspense and Supernatural Horror* (New York: Viking, 1980), xiv.

10. Judith Wilt, "And Still He Sees the Ghosts," in *Approaches to Teaching Gothic Fiction: The British and American Traditions*, ed. Diane Long Hoeveler and Tamar Heller (New York: MLA, 2003), 41.

11. Diane Long Hoeveler and Tamar Heller, introduction to *Approaches to Teaching Gothic Fiction: The British and American Traditions*, ed. Diane Long Hoeveler and Tamar Heller (New York: MLA, 2003), 36.

12. *The 13th Letter* (a remake of Georges Clouzot's *Le Courbeau*), director Otto Preminger, screenwriter Howard Koch, performers Linda Darnell, Charles Boyer, and Michael Rennie (Los Angeles: 20th Century Fox, 1951).

13. Dick Cheney, transcript for *Meet the Press*, September 14, 2003, Tim Russert moderator, NBC News, www.msnbc.msn.com/id/3080244/ (accessed April 2, 2010).

14. Alan Garner, commentary on his portrait, in *The Faces of Fantasy: Photographs by Patti Perret* (New York: Tor, 1996), 38.

15. Diane Long Hoeveler and Tamar Heller, "Some Results of the Survey," in *Approaches to Teaching Gothic Fiction: The British and American Traditions*, ed. Diane Long Hoeveler and Tamar Heller (New York: MLA, 2003), 4.

16. Hoeveler and Heller, "Some Results of the Survey," 4.

17. Hoeveler and Heller, "Some Results of the Survey," 4.

18. Jennifer Egan, a reading of *The Keep* with questions and answers, Inprint Margaret Root Brown Reading Series, October 15, 2007, Alley Theatre, Houston, Texas.

19. Egan, a reading of *The Keep*.

20. Fred Botting, "Aftergothic: Consumption, Machines, and Black Holes," in *The Cambridge Companion to Gothic Fiction*, ed. Jerrold E. Hogle (Cambridge, UK: Cambridge University Press, 2002), 287.

21. Botting, "Aftergothic," 287–288.

22. Stephenie Meyer, *Twilight* (Little, Brown, 2005), 329.

23. *Twilight*, director Catherine Hardwicke, screenwriter Melissa Rosenberg, performers Kristen Stewart, Robert Pattinson, and Billy Burke (Universal City, CA: Summit, 2008).

24. Stephen King, "Critical Praise for *The Monsters of Templeton*," HarperCollins Canada, www.harpercollins.ca/book/index.aspx?isbn=9781401322250 (accessed April 1, 2010).

25. Mark Z. Danielewski, interview by Sophie Cottrell.

11. Diane Long Hoeveler and Tamar Heller, introduction to *Approaches to Teaching Gothic Fiction: The British and American Traditions*, ed. Diane Long Hoeveler and Tamar Heller (New York: MLA, 2003), 36.

12. *The 13th Letter* (a remake of Georges Clouzot's *Le Courbeau*), director Otto Preminger, screenwriter Howard Koch, performers Linda Darnell, Charles Boyer, and Michael Rennie (Los Angeles: 20th Century Fox, 1951).

13. Dick Cheney, transcript for *Meet the Press*, September 14, 2003, Tim Russert moderator, NBC News, www.msnbc.msn.com/id/3080244/ (accessed April 2, 2010).

14. Alan Garner, commentary on his portrait, in *The Faces of Fantasy: Photographs by Patti Perret* (New York: Tor, 1996), 38.

15. Diane Long Hoeveler and Tamar Heller, "Some Results of the Survey," in *Approaches to Teaching Gothic Fiction: The British and American Traditions*, ed. Diane Long Hoeveler and Tamar Heller (New York: MLA, 2003), 4.

16. Hoeveler and Heller, "Some Results of the Survey," 4.

17. Hoeveler and Heller, "Some Results of the Survey," 4.

18. Jennifer Egan, a reading of *The Keep* with questions and answers, Inprint Margaret Root Brown Reading Series, October 15, 2007, Alley Theatre, Houston, Texas.

19. Egan, a reading of *The Keep*.

20. Fred Botting, "Aftergothic: Consumption, Machines, and Black Holes," in *The Cambridge Companion to Gothic Fiction*, ed. Jerrold E. Hogle (Cambridge, UK: Cambridge University Press, 2002), 287.

21. Botting, "Aftergothic," 287–288.

22. Stephenie Meyer, *Twilight* (Little, Brown, 2005), 329.

23. *Twilight*, director Catherine Hardwicke, screenwriter Melissa Rosenberg, performers Kristen Stewart, Robert Pattinson, and Billy Burke (Universal City, CA: Summit, 2008).

24. Stephen King, "Critical Praise for *The Monsters of Templeton*," HarperCollins Canada, www.harpercollins.ca/book/index.aspx?isbn=9781401322250 (accessed April 1, 2010).

25. Mark Z. Danielewski, interview by Sophie Cottrell.

From Asperger's Syndrome to Monosexual Reproduction

STEFAN BRIJS' *THE ANGEL MAKER* AND ITS TRANSFORMATIONS OF *FRANKENSTEIN*

Jerrold E. Hogle

The Angel Maker by Stefan Brijs (born 1969), first published as *De engelenmaker* in Dutch in 2005 and now available in a highly readable English translation by Hester Velmans (2008), is a vivid, arresting, and at least semi-Gothic novel in its own right. But it is also an inventive variation on the most distinctive elements in Mary Shelley's *Frankenstein* (1818), more on the contents of the original novel, in fact, than on its adaptations.[1] In the later 1980s, when Brijs begins his novel, Dr. Victor Hoppe (yes, Victor) returns to the Belgian hamlet of Wolfheim where he was born—a town importantly close to the three-borders meeting point of Belgium, Germany, and the Netherlands—and brings with him, in the backseat of a taxi, three infant boys whom a local lad views dimly through the window as having "heads . . . split apart" to the point of revealing their brains, each "like a [big] walnut."[2] This hint of visceral horror and vague misbreeding seems absent a few weeks later when Victor allows his three sons briefly out in public for the first time, at which point their heads seem healed over, if still quite "bulging."[3] These boys, however, named after the most famous Christian archangels (Michael, Gabriel, and Raphael), appear to be not only triplets but "uncannily alike," all exhibiting "ginger hair" and the same "stitched upper lip, leaving a diagonal scar," that appears on Hoppe's own red-headed face as an attempt to correct a harelip that he shares with all three boys in *exactly* the same place.[4] Triplets have never been as identical as these, nor as strictly like their father, his whole appearance in small, and those degrees of total sameness soon begin to unsettle the retired schoolteacher, Charlotte Maenhout, whom Victor hires to care for them. She notices complete correspondences between father and sons everywhere, "hair, skin, eyes and, alas, cleft palate, on the

same side, too—the right," and even a resemblance in how they, like their father, "avoid any and all eye contact" and exhibit "a rhythm to their movements, which [gives] them a robot-like air."[5] Throughout the first third of this novel, Brijs gradually exposes such telling details more and more as Charlotte observes these rapidly developing boys in the vaguely mysterious (though not especially Gothic) home of the bachelor Dr. Hoppe that used to be *his* father's house *and* doctor's office as far back as the 1940s. By the time we turn to the flashbacks in the second third of *The Angel Maker*, we are thus not too surprised to learn that the triplets are *clones*, "conceived" and produced out of a very particular scientific process invented by Hoppe, whereby his "angels" have emerged from cells whose nuclei have been infused with his sperm alone. The resemblances to *Frankenstein* are quite a few, then: an isolated doctor-scientist pursuing his self-centered, obsessive, even onanistic vision; the largely artificial production of male offspring, albeit with many "natural" ingredients; the monosexual avoidance of woman, or at least her genetic material (though a woman's body must be used in Brijs' version to incubate fetuses inseminated with only their father's DNA); children who seem almost "robot-like," with partly stitched and repellant features; and offspring who are as antisocial as their progenitor and are thus alter egos of him, as Victor Frankenstein's creature famously is for him.

What makes *The Angel Maker* most intriguing for longtime Gothicists, though, are less the fairly obvious similarities and more the very sharp differences *within* the correspondences to *Frankenstein*. Indeed, the Brijs novel says a great deal about its own times and settings—the Western world, especially Western Europe, of today—precisely by taking several motifs openly from Mary Shelley and then altering the very core of them in quite specific ways. It is as if Brijs has "conceived" his novel in a manner very like his Victor's procedure with animal and human embryos: while keeping some of the material and features from harvested cells (in this case, aspects of the original *Frankenstein*), he has scooped out the conceptual and historical nuclei of each one and replaced them with his own insights and suggestions, all of them bound up (as happens in all good Gothic novels) with deep cultural and psychological fears of his own time and place. Such a process, as a matter of fact, is visible in Brijs' fiction well before the publication of *The Angel Maker*. In his novel *Arend* (or *Eagle*, 2000), for example, Brijs offers a title character highly reminiscent of the Gregor Samsa who suddenly finds himself a huge and repugnant beetle in Franz Kafka's *The Metamorphosis* (1916). After being a "bullying foetus" in the womb, Arend is born as a "gigantic, deformed child" prone to beatings by his disturbed mother and "bullying" at school.[6] Because of all this, he meticulously withdraws into his collection of insect wings and decides to construct wings for his own flight—as though he were indeed a bug—that seem to enable his final leap, again modeled after a previous character: Icarus from ancient Greek myth. But Arend is also,

unlike Gregor or Icarus, made the product of artificial insemination (a precursor of the ones in *The Angel Maker*) and the damage inflicted by his pregnant mother on herself because of abuse in her own childhood.

Brijs' *Arend* has taken Kafka's highly symbolic suggestion of the petit-bourgeois state of urban alienation in the early twentieth century and turned it into a synecdoche of quite recent concerns over the mechanical injection of sperm, violence against children, bullying in the public schools, and (as in *The Angel Maker*, too) the causes of autistic withdrawal and obsession. In *The Angel Maker* itself, Brijs adds more semi-Gothic suggestions about dark secrets and ancestral sins, more psychological pressures wrought on key characters by a persistent Catholicism and small-town superstition (as in Matthew Lewis's *The Monk* of 1796), and more "returns of the repressed" in late reappearances of half-forgotten characters and recollections of an old-style Catholic education abruptly placed in discordant contact with modern science. All of this greater Gothicism, of course, though based in the particulars of the three-borders area, links itself readily to the many echoes of *Frankenstein* that *The Angel Maker* invokes. Yet it also allows Brijs, as he did with *The Metamorphosis* in *Arend*, to fill somewhat hollowed-out figurations from older writing with much more recent content and Western fears. After all, since Horace Walpole used medieval Catholic icons in which he did not believe to convey quite Protestant aspirations and anxieties in *The Castle of Otranto* (1764–1765), the Gothic has often been about the use of emptied constructs from the past as repositories of very present apprehensions and even anxieties about the future.[7] *The Angel Maker* is thus most Gothic when it enacts that peculiar shifting of symbols and plot points of *Frankenstein* into a quite new reflection on several "monstrosities" of the 1980s, the 1990s, and the early 2000s.

Perhaps the most obvious change that this novel makes in *Frankenstein* is its pointed shift to the technology of *genetics*. There is no transfer of sperm or anything like genes in Victor Frankenstein's artificial creation, and the key to Victor Hoppe's similar experiment is that very transfer, if only in a petri dish prior to implantation. In Shelley's novel, the primal infusion that makes the creature live is vaguely expressed as the "light" of an electrical motion in a very universal sense—the "neuro-anatomical soul flowing through the fluid of the nerves and the brain" in and among all living things, according to the science of the eighteen-teens[8]—and Frankenstein is conflicted, as were the scientific debates in Shelley's time, as to how to interpret that "power": as an infusion from a very external and transcendent source outside all bodies, as a "torrent of light" in our otherwise "dark world," or as the dynamism that results from the interplay of all the parts in any organic body, the more local "minutiae of causation."[9] The result of this conflict in *Frankenstein* is, not surprisingly, a creature at odds with itself within itself, as well as with its creator and all human society.

This controversial *philosophical* "infusion," the primal physical cause in Shelley's tale, is replaced in *The Angel Maker* by the minutiae of literal genetic manipulation, science fiction really tilting toward actual science. The experiments that Dr. Hoppe conducts in the late 1970s and into the 1980s, we discover in part 2 of the novel, were at least conceivable at that time in the history of Western genetics. They are also being recalled by Brijs and his readers from the perspective of 2005, a time of bourgeoning gene mapping and gene therapy that holds out the promise and terrors of just such human engineering, even to the point of debates and fears about cloning itself, to which Brijs' Gothic science fiction speaks with an immediate and scary resonance. At this point, as different as all this is from *Frankenstein*, Brijs still recalls Shelley's appeal to genuine fears in her audience of 1818 about where early industrial science might go, as in her suggestion that it might permit mechanical reproduction to displace human reproduction to the point where men might "do it" without women.[10] *The Angel Maker* sounds such warning notes about genetic engineering on several fronts as the novel proceeds, especially in its concluding part 3. There, while women (such as the boys' incubator) are not completely excluded from the birth process, they are downgraded to nuisances (indeed, she is called only "the woman" in part 3) if they want too much maternal participation, even if they once agreed to no involvement after birth, as some surrogate mothers have recently found in wanting to nurture the infants they had promised to give up. Moreover, Dr. Hoppe faces unexpected flaws in the actual children of his engineering and sheer self-reproduction. The "angels" retain the swollen heads, which hint that they were incompletely formed at birth, and the harelips and cleft palates that Victor hopes to remove from them, since their genetic code has to duplicate him more exactly than he had planned. Worse still, they age unusually quickly, even though they also learn rapidly once they start to outgrow infancy; hence they begin to die prematurely as soon as they are most fully alive. The genetic manipulation of *The Angel Maker* cannot forecast the effects of the variables in the process of injecting cells, so the speed of the life process once begun in the boys duplicates the excessive and anxious haste of the experiments that led to their creation. The more Brijs changes the particular ironies and fears in *Frankenstein*, the more he opens up new ones by deliberately replacing the source-of-life debates of Shelley's time with today's many quandaries over genetic medical science.

The big questions raised by parts 1 and 2 of *The Angel Maker*, though, are why Victor Hoppe has so self-obsessively made his sons the way that he has *and* why he protects them and himself from public scrutiny by hiding their unnatural development for as long as he can in the mysterious, though not especially Gothic, Wolfheim house of his dead mother and father (the equally harelipped Dr. *Karl* Hoppe). As the novel gradually answers these questions, Brijs' patterns of characterization do slightly resemble Mary Shelley's, but they ultimately

deviate quite sharply—and, again, scientifically—in exposing the most crucial motivations of the central father-creator. On one level, the Victor of the original *Frankenstein* is clearly driven by the Faustian longing, a repetition of Original Sin, to play God and be worshipped like God: "A new species would bless me as its creator and source," he hopes as he "attempt[s] the creation of a being like [him]self" (not to say in his own image), and hence he fancies that "no father could claim the gratitude of his child so completely as I should deserve theirs."[11] On another level, there are the revelations about his unconscious in Frankenstein's quite pre-Freudian dream right after he flees the first sight of his finished creature—the nightmare in which he imagines embracing his fiancée Elizabeth only to have her turn into the corpse of his dead mother.[12] The "thing" he has made turns out to be a libidinal enactor of the preconscious drives that *this* Victor cannot admit to himself, such as the desire to join himself to the nurturer he has lost (disguised in the repression of the maternal in his onanistic "child"-making), in part by fashioning the being who will vengefully destroy the very Elizabeth whose earlier scarlet fever really caused his beloved mother's death.[13] Brijs' Victor Hoppe, by contrast, though determined to "astonish the scientific community"[14] and enact his own reconception of Christianity, begins with a personal orientation much more specifically diagnosed in late twentieth-century terms: he is born with Asperger's syndrome, a "mild form of autism" recognized officially in 1981 and associated with "severe deficiencies in socialization, imagination, and, above all, communications skills" alongside preternatural capacities for left-brain intelligence, rote memory, and intense narrowness of vision.[15] Once Brijs' narrator makes this diagnosis clear in part 2, about a third of the way into *The Angel Maker, this* Dr. Victor's endemic nature makes his onanistic pursuits almost too predictable. If such a man cannot make intimate contact with others and virtually *has* to be obsessed with his own mental and bodily universe more than any other object, why should he *not* seek a self-oriented reproduction quite apart from intercourse with a woman, all according to scientific theories and minute genetic procedures for which he has the intellect? After all, he is inherently (if not entirely) oblivious to any external consequences because of an internal condition with which he has been born.

In addition, we should note, Victor Hoppe is virtually the opposite of Victor Frankenstein in his initial relationship with his parents. Brijs' part 2, right before announcing the Asperger's syndrome, flashes back to the tortuous delivery of his Victor at the hands of his father, who more or less has to breathe his own life into a half-dead fetus.[16] Soon the novel reveals the immediate rejection of the Hoppe son both by his repulsed mother, who never recovers from her postpartum depression (the antithesis of the overcaring Caroline Frankenstein), and by his father, who later even strikes his son, in part because he feels unredeemable guilt for passing on a harelipped ugliness that he had hoped to eliminate in his

offspring as much as his son later strives to eradicate it in Michael, Gabriel, and Raphael. It turns out, then, that Victor Hoppe has returned with these "angels" secretively after 1985 to his parents' empty house (Gothic only in the secrets it holds about Victor's birth and rejection) to nurture and cure them himself in the very place where his mother and father denied him nurturance from 1945 on. Consequently, he breathes—now more scientifically and less intimately—his own life into his children only to find himself constantly repairing the incompletions and the early onset of death wrought by their artificial insemination from his sperm alone. If the sins of fathers are visited upon sons from the very first Gothic novel, as *The Castle of Otranto* quite openly announces,[17] the relationship of Victor to Karl Hoppe is very Gothic indeed, much more so than the relationship of Victor Frankenstein to his father or mother. That difference, in retrospect, makes Shelley's Victor more *personally* responsible than Brijs' for the sins he visits on his offspring, certainly in ways that come back to haunt him when his creature carries out his most libidinal and selfish impulses on those closest to him. Some readers of *The Angel Maker* may therefore see the motives of its doctor-scientist as more oversimplified than Victor Frankenstein's, based more than his on one congenital psychophysical condition, or as more predetermined in Victor Hoppe because of how so many people, beginning with his parents, have unreasonably browbeaten him in ways that compound his Asperger's syndrome. Because of this contrast between novels, it can be argued with equal force that Brijs' causality, not completely unlike Mary Shelley's, comes from the discoveries of his own time and the many cultural anxieties about these discoveries that are still with us. Troubling us now, we have to admit, are the once-hidden problems emerging from the post–World War II "nuclear family" that was supposed to become the model for modern suburban life. There is the guilt of not diagnosing autistic children soon enough and not understanding them sufficiently once they are diagnosed. There is the knot of anxieties in genetic engineering itself, which at once offers cures for inherited traits but may instead lead to their proliferation, posing the question of how much or how little *truly personal* responsibility there is or should be in acts of human reproduction. If motives are more coherently diagnosable in the Victor of *The Angel Maker* than in the Victor of *Frankenstein*, the cause may be, appropriately for a Gothic novel of the early 2000s, the postmodern quandaries and fears that are cathected onto Brijs' main characters by both their author and his twenty-first-century audience.

Complicating these post-1945 concerns, after all, are the ways Brijs links them to causes more related to West European "nurture" than to genetically predetermined "nature." For example, Victor Hoppe's avoidance of heterosexual coupling in *The Angel Maker* is not rooted solely in his autistic inwardness. In the case of Victor Frankenstein, this same avoidance, because of which his creature kills his new spouse before she and Victor can consummate their marriage,

stems from his obsession with his dead mother. His nightmare of hugging her reveals paradoxically his fear of being absorbed back into her, even as he longs to return to her womb, *and* his horror at realizing that his love for his intended is really a longing for the Great Mother for whom Elizabeth is but a substitute (his mother's "replacement" after unintentionally killing her with scarlet fever). Victor Hoppe's antisexuality is built up layer by layer by how multiple human relationships intensify the basic inclinations of his Asperger's syndrome. Beginning with his own mother's total rejection of further sexuality at the same time as she rejects him as the ugly product of it, Brijs' Victor keeps seeking places of nurture that themselves turn out to denature the naturalness of sex. As an extension of their rejection, and also as self-protection from prying eyes, Victor Hoppe's parents enroll their entirely nonverbal child as a "patient" diagnosed as "feebleminded" in the La Chapelle Institute run by the traditionally Catholic Sisters of St. Claire, who find that he begins to talk only by repeating prayers and liturgy by rote. Young Hoppe utters his first independent speech only when he witnesses another boy suffocating the truly retarded lad Egon, who had until then been Victor's only object of interest outside his innate self-involvement.[18] The sole nun figure who can then get Victor to connect repeated sounds with meanings is the postulant-turned-novice Lotte Guelen, called "Sister Marthe," the closest thing to a nurturing mother Victor ever knows. Her consistent sympathetic attention and her belief in his actual intelligence finally lead him to read with understanding—until a pregnancy from secret (and rebellious) sex outside the convent leads the Sisters to forcibly abort Marthe's baby and Victor's father to wrench him back out of La Chapelle, thus breaking the bonds of trust in the child's eyes at least three times over. At such moments, young Hoppe is positioned less like Victor Frankenstein and more like the sad figure of Frankenstein's initially speechless creature, who is left neglected in Shelley's novel and in need of the kindness of strangers. In that connection, Brijs' Lotte is also somewhat like Justine Moritz in *Frankenstein*, who is unfairly seen as guilty in the eyes of those who rush to judgment when too few know the good she has done for Shelley's Victor and his family.

It is no wonder that this whole series of previous events in Brijs' part 2 is interwoven in flashbacks with the progress the grown *Dr.* Hoppe makes in the 1970s and 1980s, from inseminating rodent embryos, to depositing his own sperm in laboratory human eggs from unknown women, to finally attempting the fertilization of known eggs by promising to combine the DNA of two lesbians (though he illicitly uses his own sperm here, too, and so implants his "angels" in one of these women without her knowledge). This entire succession of events moves further and further away from heterosexual sex, and so further distances Victor from such interactions the more it proceeds. The interlaced recollections show that the psychic causes of Victor's revulsion toward sex include the

continual breakings of trust, the authoritarian cruelty, the severing of all bonds between the nurturing and the nurtured, and the external condemnation-rejections (the experiences suffered particularly by the creature in *Frankenstein*) that are all Victor Hoppe, already semiautistic, can ever associate with lovemaking. On this level, *The Angel Maker* ranges back through the Gothic tradition, even before *Frankenstein*, to recall the shifting borders between sanctioned and unsanctioned sex in *The Castle of Otranto* and *The Monk*. The result in Brijs' novel is a bringing forward of this Janus-faced group of cultural tendencies to expose how postwar Western Europe, especially at the nexus of Belgium, Germany, and the Netherlands, is still contesting the limits and sanctions of sexuality. *The Angel Maker* hints both at Western society's many retrograde pulls toward sexual repression throughout the twentieth century (from religion to education to village gossip) and at the simultaneous openings of possibility (or are they temptations?) emerging from the same century's sexual revolution that has supposedly laid sex bare only to subject it to the representations of public discourse and the asexual techniques of science with its artificial inseminations.

The vivacity in *The Angel Maker*'s dealings with sex, however, finally pales in comparison to its ultimately shocking take on Christianity, and here, too, there emerges a stark contrast with the original *Frankenstein* novel (though not as much with *The Monk*, as we will see). Mary Shelley's Victor may recall Original Sin, as rendered in Milton's *Paradise Lost* (1667), by overreaching as a "creator" toward a godlike status and level of knowledge, but he also appears admirable at least for questioning the stultifying views of reactionary scientists and theologians, partly by fashioning a monster who exposes how all ancien régimes, as well as emerging capitalism and industry, have mistreated the poor and the working classes that they themselves have created.[19] The original *Frankenstein*, after all, reflects the ideological tug-of-war in its author and her circle between important tenets of responsibility articulated in older Christian schemes (as in Milton who was considered radical in the 1660s) and skeptical resistance to the established alliance of Church and state that has too often restricted the progress of empirical science and the need for changes in labor conditions. Victor Hoppe's resistance to old-style Christianity, however, based mostly on what he hears and sees in the La Chapelle Institute, is less a skepticism struggling between positions and more an absolutism suited to an autistic inclination that has "trouble with nuances."[20] Having heard and repeated priestly articulations of God as "one who excoriates and punishes" very like his own father, and having witnessed God's "holy order" enabling the murder of Egon and the forced abortion of Lotte's child (all linked to the words "God giveth and God taketh away"), Brijs' Victor concludes that the "Father did bad things": He "destroyed cities" or "sent down plagues," whether in the Bible or in the Holocaust of World War II in Western Europe. Jesus, the son who "fed the hungry" and "calmed the storms," by contrast, "did

good things," for which God nevertheless "abandoned him," as Victor Hoppe has been abandoned (why else, he concludes, would Jesus have died crying, "My God, my God, why hast Thou forsaken me?").[21] This Victor therefore decides to become a doctor and a pioneer of new reproductive technologies precisely because he sees Jesus, *not* God, as his model, as the archetypal preserver and *re-creator* of life in the face of all the destructiveness caused by all forms of God. In a twentieth century that allowed old punitive theologies to hang on in churches and schools, and hence in everyday public prejudice, while it also "rained down" horrors as great as the Holocaust or "plagues" as vast as the spread of HIV/ AIDS from the 1980s on, Victor's view is all too immediately understandable. In this world, the *new* Christ, as Victor Hoppe sees himself, should do so much good that merely healing the sick is not enough; hence a new Christ wills that the source of life that gives rise to improved humans has to be the sperm of the re-creator himself. This *fluid* source would thus improve on the *breath* of God the Father, which has become the ultimate cause of the many destructions and betrayals in the world He has made. Again, some readers of *The Angel Maker* may see this countertheology as narrowing the wide range of quandaries found in the beliefs that motivate both Mary Shelley's Victor and his social order in the original *Frankenstein*. But given that the twentieth-century West has been able to name more diseases than it can cure (among them Asperger's syndrome) and has seen human destruction on an unprecedented scale as one result of its technological progress, should we be too critical of Brijs' worldview in *The Angel Maker*? In its most Gothic vein, this novel asks how we might rearrange the oldest forms of belief still operative in the West to transform a violent world (or whether we might already have rearranged them), just as the old Gothic raised and made us question the once-ruling powers, superstitions, and prejudices of the so-called Dark Ages.

In any case, it is this alternative theology of Brijs' Victor that most fully explains why the stunning and bloody climax of *The Angel Maker*—a scene as horrific as the dismemberment of the Mother Abbess and the genesis in reverse of the title character in the final chapters of *The Monk*—is utterly different from the closing scenes of *Frankenstein*. There, Shelley's Victor and creature face off in the frozen wastes of the Arctic as the doubles of each other they have always been; they consequently appear as exemplars to Robert Walton, the explorer who encounters them, of the potential follies in even his own "ideas of glory and honour."[22] The culmination of *Frankenstein*, indeed its whole frame story recounted by Walton, is removed from centers of civilization and human religion in order to expose, as the central and barren Sea of Ice finally exposes the most venal sins in Dante's *Inferno* (cited by Mary Shelley in her novel[23]), the naked feelings of aspiration and guilt in both Victor Frankenstein and his creature. The climax of *The Angel Maker* is staged instead at the novel's most important public center

of urban and religious display, the Vaalserberg hill, with its Boudewijn Tower now under reconstruction, which is right at the juncture of the Belgian-German-Netherlands border, squarely between the La Chapelle convent and Wolfheim. Annually, as it happens, this is the location of the widely attended "pilgrimage to La Chapelle" through the stations of Jesus at Calvary, which occurs in the novel on May 21, 1989, and ends at a large cross bearing a full-size effigy of Christ crucified near the ruins of the tower preceding its rebuilding.[24] After being unable to prevent the deaths of his "angels" and even refusing to recognize the efforts of the gestator-"mother" to reclaim the dead children that are his alone, Victor Hoppe, hitherto averse to public appearances, inserts himself, to everyone's surprise, into this pilgrimage as it reaches its (and the novel's) climax. He realizes his reembodiment of Christ to its fullest, in the only way still left to him, by taking the effigy's place on the cross, knowing he will die of both bleeding and suffocation as he nails himself to the sanctified beams before the procession arrives to confront this *extremely* religious sacrilege.[25] For Victor Hoppe, this apotheosis allows him to imagine an external recognition of his absolute goodness denied both by his earlier life and his failed effort to make life anew through the "angels" he created in his own image. For the reader of *The Angel Maker*, somewhat as with readers of *The Monk*, Dr. Hoppe's incapacity to entirely confront what he has done and why (even as he dies in such a vividly horrific way) forces a recognition of how religious *and* technological understandings clash, violently if not always so visibly, at the end of the twentieth century, often at the very heart of the most public ceremonies and discourses by which we attempt to reconcile or conceal them. As in many Gothic novels with endings that partially mute the climactic horror, Brijs offers readers a choice during the denouement, in which the characters who view the pilgrimage provide explanations far more conventional and hopeful than the ones revealed by the final flashbacks that explain, but only to the reader, what has actually happened.[26] In this way, we are given the option ourselves of resting on such explanations, or cover-ups like them, while simply "feeling sorry" for Victor Hoppe, or of fighting against them, as Brijs does, by a reexamination of the current collision of values (scientific, religious, sexual, and historical) regarding the creation of life—and tragedies such as Victor's.

It would be wrong of me to leave the impression, though, that *The Angel Maker* fictionalizes these tortuous clashes only by locating them in the institutions of laboratory science, medical practice, the Christian religion, and religious education. One of the greatest differences between Shelley's *Frankenstein* and Brijs' rejoinder to it is the distancing of academia in the former and the foregrounding of it in the latter. Victor Frankenstein may heighten his sense of the quarrels between medieval alchemy and Enlightenment science, despite his attractions to both, by formally attending the University of Ingolstadt in the original novel, but once he attempts to reconcile these irreconcilables in making

his creature, he totally withdraws from the university and all formal institutions in order to carry out a lonely sacrilege unsanctioned by any social order. In his much more recent case, Victor Hoppe, beginning with his advanced studies in the 1970s, initially becomes the darling of organized academia when his discoveries seem to promise scientific advances beyond mere *animal* cloning that could bring prestige, grants, students, and money to prominent European research universities, here to the University of Aachen just across the three-borders junction in northwest Germany. To be sure, when Hoppe's experiments become increasingly unverifiable and controversial, to the point even of involving a lesbian gestator unknown to the university, his professorial standing is challenged, and he becomes subject to academic investigation; hence his secretive flight with his "angels" back to the family house and his father's private practice in Wolfheim. Such a rendering of the university world—the location of many of us who are now offering these essays on new Gothic fiction—may seem just as exaggerated as Victor Hoppe's most Frankensteinian excesses of belief and experimentation. Yet Brijs' representation here reflects the much-publicized reality in recent years of formal investigations into possible violations of academic integrity in laboratories at American and European universities, all of which have led at least to increased regulations on research involving human subjects. What *The Angel Maker* can thus point to in academia is a genuine difficulty that has arisen in our time of determining where the line is to be drawn between experiments promising scientific breakthroughs with wide human benefit and the pushing of experimental data toward unreproducible and even morally questionable conclusions.

We cannot retreat from this problem as readers of *The Angel Maker* by claiming that it arises in this novel only in the efforts of a "mad scientist." For one thing, the Asperger's diagnosis and the manifest unfairness of the "feebleminded" label applied to Victor Hoppe release him from such a pat analysis in our eyes, as do our more recent attitudes toward the *non*insanity in many forms of mental illness. For another thing, and more importantly, the embrace of Hoppe's cloning procedures by the University of Aachen in the most usual of academic ways keeps us from judging him or his supervisors too simplistically. Indeed, we become most intimately involved with the difficulty of drawing clear lines between good and bad research when later episodes of *The Angel Maker*, particularly in the final part 3, adopt the point of view of Dr. Rex Cremer, dean of the faculty of biomedical studies at Aachen, who invites Victor Hoppe to come to the university and expend all his research support there, initially to great acclaim that raises the university's profile. As we watch Dr. Cremer begin with ambition and credulity and then gradually become skeptical and even alarmed enough to drive to Wolfheim and confront the results of the Hoppe "breakthroughs," so much as to discover in Victor's house the dead body of the woman he had used as an incubator (a Gothic secret indeed), we come to

see our own possible attraction to, and even complicity in, what Dr. Hoppe is and offers, as well as our reluctance until very late to confront what all of his extremes might mean. *Frankenstein* involves us in identifications with figures who finally defy, as well as fear, institutions for a range of reasons that have long been debated, among them the way such organizations attempt to repress and control what counterinstitutional "monstrosity" exposes. *The Angel Maker* gives us institutions that are far more consciously complicit in the miseducation of Victor Hoppe and then in the advancement of what come to be his excesses, so that the institutionalized shock at his self-crucifixion becomes clearly disingenuous—but also completely understandable. This Gothic novel thereby confronts the current reader with our very mixed views on such matters, with our unease in the face of the scientific genius at a university who can in fact change the world as we know it, mingled with our suspicion of the laboratory egghead who may only be advancing his own field or institution and may be taking public or corporate money without benefitting the general population, much of which could be true of the university itself. The Gothic novel has always exposed us to the conflicts and underlying fears in our own attitudes about many subjects, unsettling them even as it appeals to them, and *The Angel Maker* is a strong extension of that tradition precisely in its intentional parallels to, and its just as intentional departures from, *Frankenstein* again and again. Even the universities in which many of us work cannot, and should not, escape Stefan Brijs' Gothic probing of their multiple levels and motives. If *Frankenstein* the novel gains its lasting power from the great number of social and psychological issues of its day that are so vividly cathected into one fictional narrative, *The Angel Maker* can rightly claim to take on just as many contentious issues and features of civilization, along with the fears about them, that agitate the times in which *we* live. It remains to be seen how long these current issues will last, what forms they will assume in the future, and how they will be viewed, even in fiction, decades from now. It is those eventualities, depending on how they progress, that will determine if *The Angel Maker* will end up becoming as much a profoundly resonant classic as *Frankenstein* has turned out to be in what is by now the 250-year history of Gothic fiction in the Western world.

Notes

1. Reviewers have already noticed the *Frankenstein* echoes, although in terms so general that the precise parallels and contrasts between Shelley's novel and *The Angel Maker* have yet to be explored. See, for example, the review of Brijs' book by Drennan Spitzer on the *Bookslut* website, www.bookslut.com/fiction/2009-02-04149.php.

2. Stefan Brijs, *The Angel Maker*, trans. Hester Velmans (London: Weidenfeld and Nicholson, 2008), 5.

3. *Angel Maker*, 16.

4. *Angel Maker*, 15–17.

5. *Angel Maker*, 29–30.

6. See Brijs, *Arend* (Amsterdam: Atlas, 2000), and the NLVPF review of it at www
.nlpvf.nl/book/book2.php?Book=188.

7. For more discussion of this key dimension of Gothic fiction, see Jerrold E. Hogle, "The Gothic Ghost of the Counterfeit and the Process of Abjection," in *A Companion to the Gothic*, ed. David Punter (Oxford: Blackwell, 2000), 293–304. Note also the 1765 preface to *The Castle of Otranto: A Gothic Story* in Horace Walpole, *The Castle of Otranto and The Mysterious Mother*, ed. Frederick S. Frank (New York: Broadview, 2003), 65–70.

8. Denise Gigante, *On Life: Organic Form and Romanticism* (New Haven, CT: Yale University Press, 2009), 156.

9. Here I quote the book itself from Mary Wollstonecraft Shelley, *Frankenstein, or The Modern Prometheus: The 1818 Text*, ed. James Rieger, Phoenix edition (Chicago: University of Chicago Press, 1982), 47.

10. See Anne K. Mellor, "A Feminist Critique of Science," in *Frankenstein: Contemporary Critical Essays*, ed. Fred Botting (London: Macmillan, 1995), 107–139.

11. Shelley, *Frankenstein*, 48–49.

12. Shelley, *Frankenstein*, 53. For the most comprehensive look at this nightmare in Mary Shelley's novel and its progeny—including a review of the Freudian elements in it—see *Frankenstein's Dream: A Romantic Praxis Volume*, ed. Jerrold E. Hogle (College Park: University of Maryland, 2003), www.rc.umd.edu/praxis/frankenstein.

13. Shelley, *Frankenstein*, 37–38.

14. *Angel Maker*, 117.

15. *Angel Maker*, 130–131.

16. *Angel Maker*, 121–122.

17. Walpole, *The Castle of Otranto*, 61.

18. *Angel Maker*, 131–134.

19. See Paul O'Flinn, "Production and Reproduction: The Case of *Frankenstein*," in Botting, *Frankenstein*, 21–47.

20. *Angel Maker*, 196.

21. *Angel Maker*, 198–199.

22. Shelley, *Frankenstein*, 213.

23. Shelley, *Frankenstein*, 53.

24. *Angel Maker*, 328–341.

25. *Angel Maker*, 342–344.

26. *Angel Maker*, 341–346.

CHAPTER 2

The Sleep of Reason

GOTHIC THEMES IN *BANQUET FOR THE DAMNED* BY ADAM L. G. NEVILL

James Marriott

Perhaps no visual representation of night terrors has been as influential as Fuseli's *The Nightmare*. The scene is indelibly familiar: a woman lies on a bed with her eyes closed and her arms thrown back, a demonic homunculus propped on her chest, while a pale, wild-eyed horse looks on. This most enduring image of the Gothic tradition looks back to old wives' tales and folk legends of witches, incubi, and succubi, and forward to popular prestige (Freud hung a copy of this painting on a wall of his Vienna waiting room) and pastiche (the scene is recreated in Ken Russell's *Gothic*). Yet while it has long proved a touchstone for poets and novelists seeking to recreate the authentic whiff of nightmare in their fictions, rarely do these attempts approach *Banquet for the Damned*'s uncanny grasp of the claustrophobic intensity of true night terrors.

Dante Shaw, a failed rock musician seeking a second chance, leaps at the opportunity to help his idol, writer and academic Eliot Coldwell, work on a second book. Coldwell's first, *Banquet for the Damned*, had defined everything the young Dante wanted to be; now a second book offers a way out of dead-end jobs in Birmingham and a fresh start in Scotland's St. Andrews—and perhaps even renewed inspiration for Dante's band. But Eliot's tastes have moved on since *Banquet*; his occult investigations have borne fruit beyond his expectations, but what is conjured is not as easily dismissed. The students who have attended Eliot's occult group are suffering nightmares that lead them to the jaws of something impossibly long and ragged; but its appetite is growing, and easy food is running out.

The novel's power derives in part from Nevill's extrapolation from states familiar to every reader into situations of barely imaginable panic and horror. We have all had nightmares; we have all been glad to wake up. Memory is mercifully unreliable; the sense of acute claustrophobia and impotence characterizing such states usually fades into a faint echo in waking life. Fortunately we do not often bring material back.

Nevill's students suffer a trajectory of night terrors—sleep paralysis, a Fuseli-like sense of being sat on, a fear of sleep and insistence on staying awake—familiar if not from our own experience then at least from the dream demon cycle of horror films (*A Nightmare on Elm Street* onward). The reader is put into these students' minds as they wake up terrified on the outskirts of town, having sleepwalked to places remote enough to invite discreet dismemberment. Alternatively they are given the opportunity to relate their experiences to Hart Miller, an American professor of anthropology who has studied night terrors and their ghoulish aftermath around the world: in Nigeria, Guatemala, the Amazon basin—and St. Andrews.

But the most distressing terrors are reserved for the novel's protagonist, Dante—distressing not only because Dante, "a hard-luck champion who eats chips with a tarnished fork,"[1] elicits our empathy as a profoundly sympathetic and vulnerable protagonist, but also because the nightmares attributed to him are so grotesquely convincing that the reader suspects them to be direct, unwanted souvenirs from Nevill's own experiences. Indeed Nevill has in interview admitted, "I suffered dreadful night terrors while writing the book. I'd never had them before."[2] The intensity of their expression here hints at a ritual purging in the aid of some magical defense or exorcism against the danger of reexperiencing them.

Chapter 13 (which follows directly on the gory death of a student in a St. Andrews tunnel) features a dream with Dante as a boy running full tilt through a field. He is aware that he is dreaming but is unable to wake up or to prevent himself from losing his balance and tripping, "straight as a stone dropped into a well,"[3] into the mouth of a pipe in the middle of the field. His speed and the force of his fall jam his shoulders fast into the pipe. He is unable to do any more than flex his hands and kick his feet against its sides, his screams vanishing into the inky depths.

This succinct and disturbing vision of live burial is almost topped by another of Dante's nightmares in which he is mocked by Eliot and his charge Beth while his numb, impotent body is kicked into a hole in the cellar. Just before the makeshift grave is sealed with a slab, "something slips from the cement floor of the cellar, and drops into the tomb with him."[4]

The nightmares do not bring only terror. Dante and the students become convinced that something visits them while they sleep—a tall, thin thing with

too many teeth. The nightmares prepare them for victimization, tenderizing them through fear until their flesh becomes palatable to the night being. The rational, post-Enlightenment view of the dream state is rejected here: these are not just dreams but have a powerful, measurable effect on waking life. Hallucinations also play a part in the texture of the novel. The proctor's speech to a new undergraduate class is interrupted by sights and smells of which only he is aware, yet in a sense these presage an actual future, establishing an ontological insecurity that leads to profound unease in the reader.

The theme of different levels of reality is developed through slippages between modes of representation throughout the novel. *Banquet for the Damned* is not only the title of the novel but of Coldwell's first book (faintly redolent of Colin Wilson's *The Outsider*), which drew both Beth and Dante to his side. Reading, here, determines action, drawing on the Gothic fascination with forbidden knowledge and scholarship. Even Dante's name is inescapably evocative of medieval thought (as well as its infernal overtones). Eliot's response to Dante's arrival is to give him a pile of musty tomes that leave the musician feeling woefully inadequate. Hart, as an academic, fares better with his research, pointed in the right direction by a librarian (nothing like expert help) and mapping his own previous learning onto the specific history of witchcraft at St. Andrews.

There is a sense, as with Fuseli's painting, of ideas bleeding from one medium to another. Dante and Tom, his Lothario musician friend, plan a concept album based on Coldwell's second book, and the sights that most terrify Dante on a visit to Coldwell's house are the paintings lining its walls, using the thin, ragged, hungry creature referred to elsewhere as the "Brown Man" as a model.

These paintings, created by one of a growing coven of witches, all women associated with the university, represent a physical distillation of the psychic unease hanging in a pall over St. Andrews, not least in their use of blood and body parts in the service of representational accuracy. But the town itself also distils this unease, increasingly mirroring the characters' attitudes and shifting from appearing attractively Gothic to bristling with a glowering spikiness made up of "haggard, desolate"[5] buildings.

The descriptions of St. Andrews are meticulous and superbly visualized, the sense of authenticity supported by references to its celebrated golf courses and nearby airbase. Nevill has in interview described the town as "pretty much a character in the novel. . . . The wealth of history, the architecture, the tributes to martyrs, the shadowy courts, the very age of the place, just conjured macabre fantasies."[6]

The medieval parts of the town boast archetypal Gothic architecture, often referred to as such in the text, but St. Andrews also features Victorian modifications and a veneer of modern touches, suggesting a triad of Gothic, Victorian,

and modern that can then be mapped onto the novel's literary influences. The Gothic influence is clear in the novel's insistence on the dead weight of the past, its heady atmosphere of decay, sexual deviance, madness and transgression, and its backdrop of crumbling ruins. We might also align the Victorian touches with the influence of the ghost story on the novel, most visibly in the weighty scholarship of key characters and the persistence of the irrational in a rational world.

Yet, just as St. Andrews is a working, living, contemporary town, this is inescapably a modern novel, far from period pastiche; the widescreen pans and jump-cut edits of the present-tense narrative give it a pop cinematic feel that is reinforced by the scope of its cultural references—from Sir Richard Burton to Brad Pitt—while the cast of convincingly obnoxious students, casually stoned musicians, and moody Goth girls leaps off the page in one clearly defined visual tableau after another.

For all the novel's entertaining grasp of the vicissitudes of modern life, though, the dead weight of the past is inescapable. Coldwell has, perhaps unwittingly, unleashed an ancient curse on St. Andrews, in perhaps the novel's most concise expression of the malign influence of the past on the present. This theme underpins the entire novel, as explored in Dante's inability to escape a teenage obsession or to wrest a new life from the ashes of his thwarted ambitions as a musician, in an unwanted pregnancy which plays a key role in the backstory, and in Beth's possession by an ancient witch. St. Andrews may exist as a palimpsest, with each new architectural design obscuring its forebears, to be written on much as Coldwell scrawls occult symbols on his cellar floor with Hart Miller aping the act in drunkenly optimistic self-defense, but the past will out.

The Gothic obsession with "backward-looking thoughts,"[7] to use Rupert Davenport-Hines's phrase, shades inevitably into "a promise of ruin,"[8] and Nevill marries the novel's ethereal occult concerns to an earthly physicality expressed paradoxically through images of bodily disintegration. Eliot and Hart are doubled, academics who have traveled far and wide in search of occult lore and returned with bodies ravaged by tropical disease and alcoholic dyspepsia. The Brown Man and his coven eat their victims, a vision of abjection reminding us forcefully of the fallibility of the flesh. Dante suffers from a virus presented to us in feverish detail, the proctor of the university hallucinates the vicar vomiting over a row of students, there are repeated images of long hairs being pulled from mouths, and victory over evil is sought at the cost of blisters, chafing clothes, and horrific burns, to say nothing of Dante's and Hart's problems with clinging underwear.

And yet, for all the retrograde horror, whether psychic or physical, *Banquet* betrays a profoundly Gothic ambivalence toward modernity. Coldwell may be a ruin, but he is the prime mover throughout; his occult experiments *work*, and

his actions prove decisive at the climax of the novel as well. By contrast, Dante and Tom are ineffectual, locked in a cycle of guitar practice, stoned banter, and squabbling over women; Hart is a hands-off academic drunk, always arriving after the fact; and Eliot's university peers, who only hired him as a reminder of their more adventurous youth, are conservative and resolutely middle class, more concerned with appearance than substance and sexually selfish enough for their wives to consider joining an anthropophagic cult as a breath of fresh air.

But even these doyens of respectability cannot help revealing an admiration for Eliot's actions: Arthur, the hebdomidar (the university official responsible for student discipline and welfare), tells Dante the tale of witnessing the ritual that brought the curse on the town and is unable, for all his condemnation, to suppress his gleeful amazement that Eliot has actually succeeded. Their fear of the occult derives less from rational rejection than from an archaic respect for its power.

One of the novel's central questions—what if the witch confessions were actually genuine rather than the result of baseless accusation and prejudice?—might leave it open to accusations of misogyny were it not that the energy of the women is contrasted favorably with the listlessness of the men. Beth, an "insane hybrid of a harlot and a clown,"[9] proves irresistible to both Dante and Tom. Dante allows her to drink his blood; indeed he encourages it after she bites his lip during one of their meetings. He is passive, numb; she is active, sexually dominant, the archetypal witch as femme fatale, *la belle dame sans merci*.

Eliot is the only man present who is able to navigate these powerful women and their deviant tastes, having affairs with both Beth and her benign double, Janice, and even he eventually falters beneath Beth's appetites. As the coven spreads, the downtrodden university wives find renewed energy in making offerings to their dark lord; while Hart can't even suck on a bottle of Scotch without breeding a peptic ulcer, the witches can feast on human flesh without even a whisper of indigestion. Tom, the Birmingham rock scene's premier lady-killer, finds his love 'em and leave 'em approach failing to pass muster here; all he is good for now is a bloodied scalp.

The sexual politics of the classic Gothic novel are in a sense turned on their head; the theme of confinement, a key image in *Banquet*, has been traditionally associated with restricted opportunities for women, expressed in the only language and imagery available. Now it represents, by contrast, fallible masculinity, trapped in cycles of addiction (Hart) or hopeless dreams of rock stardom (Dante), and the sequence of dead-end jobs and quashed hopes that such dreams inevitably incur.

The problem remains of why the supernatural should prove such an energizing force in the novel, both for many of the characters and for Nevill's writing

itself. The theme of confinement has another meaning that may offer at least a partial solution. As they approach Coldwell's house toward the end of the novel, Dante tells Hart that he thinks they will find the coven in the basement: "That's where everything starts out here."[10] What starts in basements follows through in tunnels, and the energy unleashed by the supernatural in the novel reminds us that the dark, confined, buried spaces to which *Banquet* obsessively returns are as much caves or grottoes, sites of transformation, as they are burial chambers.

Such transformation might be overt, as in the case of Beth, whose trajectory from shy, withdrawn student to exultant, irresistible witch begins in Coldwell's basement, or it might be occult, hidden. Victoria Nelson suggests in *The Secret Life of Puppets*, her provocative history of the Western supernatural, that

> the ancient notion of the afterworld after the Renaissance . . . became attached to the form of fantastic art called "grotesque" (from *grotto*, or cave), and . . . the entire discredited worldview of Platonism eventually came to be linked with the underworld and the demonic grotesque, a connection that persisted after the Reformation in literature (and, in this century, film) of the fantastic. . . . [T]he grotto remains the physical point of connection to the transcendent in the Western imagination.[11]

But why should the transcendent translate as terror? Why should what was once *awe filling* have become *awful*? Nelson goes on to provide a secular, Freudian explanation of the horrors associated with the supernatural grotesque:

> Our culture's post-Reformation, post-Enlightenment prohibition on the supernatural and exclusion of a transcendent, non-materialist level of reality from the allowable universe has created the ontological equivalent of a perversion caused by repression. Lacking an allowable connection with the transcendent, we have substituted an obsessive, unconscious focus on the negative dimension of the denied experience. In popular Western entertainments through the end of the twentieth century, the supernatural translated mostly as terror and monsters enjoyably consumed. But as Paul Tillich profoundly remarked, "Wherever the demonic appears, there the question of its correlate, the divine, will also be raised."[12]

Divine or diabolic as the novel may be, a warning to the curious, *caveat lector*, is required. Nevill suffered night terrors while writing *Banquet for the Damned*; in interview he has revealed that several readers have contacted him after having similar experiences upon reading the book. What is summoned is not as easily dismissed. Proceed with caution.

Notes

1. Adam L. G. Nevill, *Banquet for the Damned* (London: Virgin Books, 2008), 127.

2. Adam L. G. Nevill, interview by *Horror Reanimated*, www.horrorreanimated .com/2009/08/17/micro-review-of-banquet-for-the-damned-macro-interview-with-adam-lg-nevill-by-jdl (accessed November 24, 2009).

3. Nevill, *Banquet*, 121.

4. Nevill, *Banquet*, 171.

5. Nevill, *Banquet*, 203.

6. Nevill, interview by *Horror Reanimated*.

7. Rupert Davenport-Hines, *Gothic* (London: Fourth Estate Limited, 1998), 385.

8. Nevill, *Banquet*, 255.

9. Nevill, *Banquet*, 232.

10. Nevill, *Banquet*, 382.

11. Victoria Nelson, *The Secret Life of Puppets* (Cambridge, MA: Harvard University Press, 2001), viii.

12. Nelson, *The Secret Life of Puppets*, 19.

CHAPTER 3

Beasts

JOYCE CAROL OATES AND
THE ART OF THE GROTESQUE

Peter Bell

> The surreal, raised to the level of poetry, is the very essence
> of "gothic"; that which displays the range, depth, audacity
> and fantastical extravagance of the human imagination . . .
>
> —Joyce Carol Oates[1]

The word *Gothic* as applied to fiction, especially in contemporary writing, refined as *New Gothic*, defies precise definition. Yet it is a genre with a set of recognizable motifs: an eerie, numinous setting, often associated with decay; a sombre, melancholy, menacing past overlying a deceptively secure modernity; a fascination with irrationalism, with madness and mystical states, with dreams and visions, with the strange and supernatural, with dark romance and sex, with decadence, disease, and death; narratives in which tormented souls toil under the weight of a bleak fate or else stalk the pages as Mephistophelian harbingers of doom and dread; and the epic and tragic, hubris and nemesis, the eternal battle within the human spirit between the demonic and the angelic. There can be found, in the best examples of the genre, what Joyce Carol Oates, describing H. P. Lovecraft, terms "a melancholy, operatic grandeur."[2]

Conventionally, literary Gothic dates back to the eighteenth-century Gothic romance, pioneered by Horace Walpole and Ann Radcliffe. Their brooding, gloom-laden sense of tragedy found refinement in nineteenth-century German Romanticism, typified by Heinrich von Kleist and E. T. A. Hoffmann, whose tortured visions of an ordered world in horrifying disequilibrium bring us close to the paradigm of contemporary Gothic. The great Victorian purveyors of the eerie—the Brontës, Sheridan Le Fanu, Mary Elizabeth Braddon, Elizabeth

Gaskell, Charlotte Riddell, Vernon Lee, and Bram Stoker—framed their strange visions on such foundations, as did practitioners of the Edwardian ghost story, notably M. R. James. The psychological dimension, so crucial to this vision, was reinforced in the twentieth century by Jungian and Freudian theory, fixing literary Gothic centrally within the uncharted wildernesses of the psyche, as in Robert Aickman's grimly disordered fables of a seemingly normal world where the hapless wander, beset by forces larger than oneself. Latter years—with fears of mass destruction; ever more grisly news of violence, insanity, and murder; the prospect of environmental ruin; and a general crisis of uncertainty in the Western World—have enhanced still further the fascination with such themes, finding their way into that broad spectrum of pessimism termed New Gothic. Nothing could be more wrong than to designate Gothic fiction as mere dark fantasy, crucial as that may be; it is, and always has been, a way of looking at the world, a dark surrealism, a reordering of the strange reality all around us. Joyce Carol Oates is a supreme artiste of that doom-shrouded consciousness we label Gothic, well exemplified in her novella *Beasts*.

Oates is best known as a prolific chronicler of the American Nightmare, the dark side of the American Dream. She can be regarded thus as a realist, charting the tribulations of current America. Yet, for Oates, the world is a strange, chaotic place, where reality and unreality march hand in hand, where truth may well be stranger than fiction. Even her most realistic works—*Black Water*, a fantasia on the Chappaquiddick affair; *Blonde*, a thinly disguised reflection on Marilyn Monroe; *Man Crazy*, with its resonances of the Manson slaughters—exude a Gothic sensibility. What could be more tragically macabre than a young woman breathing her last breath in an air bubble in a sinking car while reflecting on betrayal by her lover, a denizen of the privileged, powerful realm of wealth, celebrity, and politics? Or a naive girl forced to inhabit, literally, a double life, driven crazy by exploitation, such that she could not separate her own reality from that of legend? With a little adjustment, these tormented fables could form plots for a Brontë novel, a psychological horror tale by Le Fanu, or a grisly extravaganza by Edgar Allan Poe.

Indeed, Oates designates Poe as an early muse, dating back to her childhood. Poe's significance, she believes, lies in his "bold use of surrealistic dream images, the drama of his various deranged voices, the fluidity of his plots";[3] from him she absorbed the technique of "grounding the surreal in the seeming 'reality' of an earnest, impassioned voice." Her own ability to assume a variety of demented voices is exemplified in the Bram Stoker Award–winning novel *Zombie*, a first-person narrative articulating with disturbing authenticity the mind of a serial sex killer and cannibal, loosely based on Jeffrey Dahmer.[4] Poe's obsession with degeneration is echoed in *We Were the Mulvaneys*, a realist novel charting the disintegration of respectable folk traumatized by the unspeakable violation

of their teenage daughter, and equally in the supernatural novella *The Ruins of Contracoeur*, which presents a family's obscurely occasioned collapse through scandal from the children's innocent perspective. In her psychic detective trilogy *Mysteries of Winterthurn*, the very language of Poe is echoed, with its arcane musical rhythms and elegantly macabre prose-poetry, as well as in the surreal epic *Bellefleur*, concerning the decline and fall of a wealthy, accursed family and their legend-haunted mansion on the shores of Lake Noir. Significantly, Oates cites as her earliest influence of all Lewis Carroll's *Alice* books, with their potent blend of wonder and horror, where reality and fantasy bewilderingly interchange, sanity blurs into madness, and the narrative unfolds with a crazy, inexorable logic.[5]

Much of Oates's writing, especially her short stories, which number in many hundreds, apply multiple facets of the Gothic, with supernatural, occult, strange, psychological, and horrific themes. These she defines as "tales of the grotesque," taking her cue from Southern Gothic writer Flannery O'Connor, who used the same epithet for her own stories, and Poe's *Tales of the Grotesque and Arabesque*. Oates's own definition of the term *Gothic* is eclectic, and though she eschews this oft-misused and overused word, we can recognize components of the Gothic in her words:

> The "grotesque" is a sensibility that accommodates the genius of
> Goya and the kitsch-surrealism of Dali; the crude visceral power of
> H. P. Lovecraft and the baroque elegance of Isak Dinesen; the fatal-
> istic simplicity of Grimm's fairy tales and the complexity of vision
> of which, for instance, William Faulkner's "A Rose for Emily" is a
> supreme example—the grotesque image as historical commentary.[6]

Beasts, set on a Massachusetts university campus during the 1970s, exemplifies Oates's skillful command of the Gothic, displaying various facets of what is understood by that term in a modern setting. The seventies provide a sufficient distance to invest the macabre experiences of the female narrator, Gillian Brauer, with that patina of unreality and disbelief that often marks the recollection of traumas instinctively denied with time's passage, yet which we know to have happened, however improbable. Like Jane Eyre, the naive Brauer undergoes a grim rite of passage in a world of dark passions, scarcely comprehended until they overwhelm her. It is a Gothic romance, the story of a young woman's obsessive affair with "two people I'd loved, a long time ago."[7] It is also a compelling tale of Gothic horror by an author who, perhaps more than any living writer, has absorbed its rich heritage and dexterously applied it to the familiar, reassuring world of New England.

Within the genteel groves of academe, Brauer, a literature student at Catamount College, falls under the spell of her charismatic tutor, Andre Harrow, and his French wife, Dorcas. First as a talented pupil in Harrow's poetry

workshops, beguiled by his charm, awed by his erudition, insidiously she becomes an intimate of their Bohemian household. Dorcas, a sculptress, has acquired a scandalous reputation on the staid campus for her grotesque humanoid carvings, totems of man's bestial side, far removed from the noble qualities of the arts which the college represents and which have drawn Brauer into its scholarly portals. Brauer's love of poetry is exploited by her unscrupulous mentor and subverted to perverse ends. Harrow is an expert on D. H. Lawrence, yet it is the dark side of this passionate writer which excites him, paralleling his wife's brutal artistic vision. Despite unsavory rumours, Brauer becomes their acolyte, seduced by her naive emotions and love of learning. The Harrows prove to be sexual voyeurs, luring young women into pornographic rituals. "*We are beasts and this is our consolation*" (119): Dorcas's slogan for her exhibitions has more than arty relevance; it is the expression of their amoral, nihilistic philosophy. They are psychological vampires preying on the vulnerable and innocent. Throughout the story, in an unresolved subplot, the campus is scourged by mysterious fires suspected as arson, and the story ends, in true Gothic fashion, in purging flames, which consume the sleeping Harrows, gorged on gluttony, alcohol, and sex, in an apocalyptic act of retribution by their once complicit victim.

Beasts, though, is no mere exposition of social abuse, much less a feminist tract; it is a surreally macabre story, with the texture of a constantly unfolding nightmare, resonating with the voice of Oates's Gothic heritage. The surreal, as in much of her fiction, is a potent device, as with Poe, for expressing disturbing truths through hyperbole and metaphor. It is a parable about half-willing sexploitation. Brauer's fate at the hands of her mentor, Andre Harrow, the archetypal devil in disguise with whom she is infatuated, is a recognizable one, especially, perhaps, in the libertarian 1970s when the advocacy of sexual liberation all too often became a cover for abusive license. "You would wonder," reflects Brauer, "that I could be so emotionally inexperienced, or undernourished, as well as sexually immature, at the age of twenty, in 1975" (11). She, like her classmates Marisa, Sybil, and Dominique, her predecessors, is fair game for the corrupt Harrow, with his "low, gravelly voice, like a rough caress," a "lean, lanky man with a quicksilver manner, energetic, restless," who in contrast to other tutors appears sincere: He "made us squirm sometimes with his candor" (28, 30). Harrow breaches the defenses of his innocent protégés behind a mask of literary brilliance, as Brauer experiences during a class on Lawrence's poem "Peach":

> In rapt astonishment, I listened. I was seated in the front row in Mr. Harrow's large lecture class of about one hundred fifty students and I was staring intently at Mr. Harrow and I realized that, though I'd read "Peach" previously, as I'd read numerous other poems by D. H. Lawrence, I had not understood it until now. Until hearing it in Mr. Harrow's voice. In Mr. Harrow's voice, which was itself

velvety-voluptuous-heavy. It seemed to me that as he read, Mr. Harrow glanced up to look at me. It seemed to me that Mr. Harrow was himself the poet and the words of the poem were his words, intimate and shocking. And consoling. For I understood now that the true subject of the poem wasn't a peach devoured by the poet, a peach he finds delicious, juice running down his fingers, the true subject of the poem was the female body. (28–29)

In her naivety, she feels exultant, pleased to be told that her body "harbors unexpected beauty," that "we must not be ashamed of our bodies, but proud of them" (29). Throughout the lecture, she is mesmerized, believing that Harrow, "stroking his short spade-shaped beard that resembled D. H. Lawrence's," has eyes for her (30). She listens avidly to his evocation: "Lawrence is the supreme poet of Eros. No recriminations, no reproaches, no guilt, no 'morality.'" Morality is a "leash around the neck," a "noose." His message is "that love—sensual, sexual, physical love—is the reason we exist" (30).

Through her infatuation, Bauer becomes a complicit victim of Harrow and his kinky, manipulative wife, Dorcas, a partner in sexual debauchery masquerading as self-liberation, the shedding of the straitjacket of "morality." Oates's fascination, in much of her work, with victim-centered exploitation may seem at odds with narratives of women's empowerment, yet through her relentless, merciless depiction of degradation, she conveys a devastating critique of sexploitation, not least in *Beasts*. Lawrence has a specific relevance here. The "core of our human tragedy," she notes regarding his literary vision, has less to do with society than with the individual, "with the curious, self-destructive condition of the human spirit."[8] This could be the leitmotif of *Beasts*. The victim as tragic accomplice in his or her own damnation is central to Gothic sensibility, the Faustian bargain.

A parallel can also be drawn in this context between *Beasts* and Henry James's *The Turn of the Screw*, a work Oates greatly admires for its Gothic sensibility (and to which she has written two tributes, "Accursed Inhabitants of the House of Bly" and "The Turn of the Screw"). Regarding James's novella, she has remarked that "this is the forbidden truth, the unspeakable taboo—that evil is not always repellent but frequently attractive; that it has the power to make of us not simply victims, as nature and accident do, but active accomplices."[9] Harrow can be seen as a Quint-like figure, a demonic seducer, an emotional vampire. "Of all monstrous creatures," Oates has observed, "it has been the vampire that by tradition both attracts and repels, for vampires have nearly always been portrayed as aesthetically (that is, erotically) appealing."[10] The gauche Brauer is in love with evil posing as enlightenment, personifying in contemporary mode a classic Gothic paradigm.

A feature of Oates's artistic skill is her ability to transform stereotypes into believable characters. Andre and Dorcas Harrow are recognizable types,

especially to anyone familiar with the Bohemian undercurrent of campus life, albeit drawn in hyperbolic form. But despite the hyperbole—essential to the Gothic mode—they are chillingly real, especially as seen through the eyes of the enchanted Brauer. One of the things that makes Brauer's fate appear that much more chilling is that her infatuation is not portrayed simply in line with the clichéd plot of a naive girl seduced by her mentor, by an older, charming man; nor is it merely a tale of the exhilaration of adultery. Crucial to the story is her parallel infatuation with Dorcas (though not in lesbian terms). Dorcas becomes a fascination for Brauer as a figure through whom she relates by proxy to the object of her desire: the (to her) unapproachable Andre Harrow. Brauer, and other students fixated upon Andre, are drawn to Dorcas because of who she is, a mixture of admiration and envy: "If you love a married man you exist in a special, secret, undeclared relationship with his wife" (10). Brauer takes to following her, "drawn into the woman's wake like a fluttering scrap of paper in the wake of a rushing vehicle" (11). This is how she is first introduced into the narrative, even before her husband, in the form of a secret journal entry by Brauer:

> "Dor-cas"
> I whispered the name to myself.
> I was following the woman through a hilly wooded area, along a path strewn with pine needles into the village of Catamount, Massachusetts. My third year at Catamount College. The woman called herself, with arrogant simplicity, "Dorcas." She had no idea that anyone was following her. She had no idea of my existence. She was the wife of a man I believed I loved. *Loved more than myself,* I might have said.
> The conviction, or maybe it was the sensation, to which I gave the name *love,* coursed through my veins like liquid flame. (9)

Dorcas also possesses for the inexperienced, conventional Brauer a mesmeric aura, deriving from her striking dress and looks, her eccentric personality, and her scandalous artwork. None of the girls refer to her as "Mrs. Harrow," such an appellation being "ludicrous in reference to Dorcas"; it was impossible to imagine her "belonging to any man" (13). She was said to scorn both academic life and "conventional bourgeois life" and to possess a shadowy past: "There was some mystery or secret—or there was a rumor of a mystery or secret—regarding Dorcas's children, or child. It seemed to be known, but vaguely, that Dorcas was a 'mother'—that Dorcas had children, or a child. Not with Andre Harrow? In a time predating her arrival in Catamount?" (13). Oates here skillfully creates through her choice of language a vista of unfathomable depths of mystery, the kind of abysses impinging on the present that one finds in, say, Sheridan Le Fanu, Wilkie Collins, or Emily Brontë.

Brauer learns that the Harrows sometimes take into their studio an intern or model, a "special" girl from the college. Like a moth to a flame, she is drawn into the fire of their perverted passions. It is Brauer, significantly, who takes the first step, the complicit victim, insinuating herself into Dorcas's presence. Awed by her proximity, she reflects upon her outré appearance:

> Close up I saw that Dorcas was wearing handwrought aluminium earrings that swung like scimitars from her pinkened ears. Chunky silver rings gleamed on her fingers. Her nails were short as a man's, ridged with dirt or black paint. She'd made up her face in her usual lavish style, with an artist's skill and what may have been an artist's wit, for perhaps Dorcas, living in a small New England college town in 1975, was meant to suggest a sloe-eyed, savage-voluptuous female portrait of Picasso. . . . Her face was a mask of pale, grainy powder, like a geisha's. She wore her usual denim smock with paint-stained cuffs, a long denim skirt stencilled in rainbow colors, and leather sandals that displayed her startlingly small, attractive bare feet. (With blue-polished toenails.) Around her fleshy shoulders, to complete this costume, she'd tied a coarse-knit, parrot-green shawl with fringes, halfway down her back. Dorcas was sexy, seductive. She was big-breasted, big-hipped. When she walked, her buttocks swayed. It was impossible not to stare at her, as customers in the post office were doing. (19–20)

Dorcas is a classic Bohemian. She is a sculptress of the bizarre, a passionate artist, "her hands lacerated by splinters, her fingernails broken." "You admired her work or hated it. You admired her or hated her. It was that simple, and yet it wasn't simple at all." Dorcas's sculptures are celebrations of the primitive, the beast in man, totems of nihilism; the story is significantly framed by Brauer's encounter twenty-five years later with a crude aboriginal carving, a "maternal figure" triggering horrific recollections. Dorcas's exhibition, Totem and Taboo, is sexually explicit and, from a conventional perspective, a scandalous, obscene mockery of the respectable and noble.

> Her sculptures! They were made of wood, larger than life-sized, primitive and dramatic. They were raw, crude, ugly. Most were of women, and were defiantly sexual, with protuberant breasts and bellies, exaggerated pudenda. Rounded buttocks, with a crevicelike crack between. Heads tended to be small, and faces minimal. Like others I was disturbed by these figures, and excited. I remember when I saw them for the first time, I was literally openmouthed. (14)

Inspiring as much outrage as the sculptures is Dorcas's justification for them. Catamount alumni, the older generation, protest, "We are not beasts who

have been proudly created in God's likeness and possess immortal souls" (15). Current students condemn it as "gross," "putrid," "sexist," and "a betrayal of feminism" (15); for, even as it confounds old-fashioned conservatism, it fails to endorse the new liberalism. It is a credo of nihilism. It is, however, forbidden fruit for Brauer, and thus perilously delicious. Dorcas's dark art, burning with its sexual brutalism, directly parallels Harrow's vision of Lawrence, and thus Brauer is doubly entrapped.

Permeating the novella is the motif of fire. Oates introduces it in the first lines of the second chapter, which is in fact the first chapter of the narrative, as chapter one is a flash-forward, a framing device for Brauer's recollections. "*In the night, sirens erupting. In the night, the terrible beauty of fire*" (5, 133). The second chapter, titled "The Alarm," describes the evacuation of a student hostel in the early morning hours in subzero temperatures, the confusion, the fascination, the curiosity: "*Whose house is it, burning?*" (7). Yet this chapter, too, is framing the narrative; the same-titled chapter reappears as the penultimate one, much of it repeating Brauer's identical words, her impressions. Significantly, though, this forms the conclusion of her experiences in the Harrow household. Reading the original paragraph, it appears that, in her confusion then and with a twenty-five-year lapse, Brauer is distorting reality: "My hair, too, was burning. My braided hair, so beautiful." Yet this cannot be so, for it is a false alarm; the fire is elsewhere. "Never," she remarks, "would it seem other than a confused dream." What this opening psychic conflagration relates to, however, is the novella's apocalyptic climax. Brauer has invoked, in exquisite Gothic mode, "the terrible beauty of fire." "*Whose house is it, burning?*" It is, in fact, the Harrows' residence, whose burning Brauer has deliberately caused by taking from an ashtray a smouldering cigarillo stub and placing it upon a sofa amidst combustible materials, including several of Dorcas's canvases.

> Her luridly bright Aztec-inspired primitive abstracts. I carried these
> to lean against the side of the sofa. It was not that I was thinking,
> *These, too, are flammable.* I was not thinking at all. I moved by in-
> stinct. (131)

By incinerating not simply her wicked lover-oppressors, but also their bestial images, Brauer is no mere avenger; she is acting as the agent of a purging destruction, a symbolic liberation from the beast in man, from naked evil. Her own act of arson constitutes both revenge and redemption.

The mystery surrounding the fires also serves to enhance the novella's power as a Gothic narrative. They are only vaguely resolved, if at all, retaining their aura as an arbitrary, enigmatic force of evil: "We never knew (we told each other, with grim humor) whether we might be 'burned alive' in our beds." Reflecting a quarter of a century later, Brauer recalls that two teenage boys made confessions,

retracted them, and then admitted partial responsibility, and also that, following a police inquiry into the deaths by arson of a woman and two children, the suspect, her estranged husband, was released due to lack of evidence. Were all the various fires related? Was there a single arsonist, many, or none? The uncertainty causes the girls, Brauer's fellow students, to speculate that it could be "one of us." It is concluded that whoever it is, is "crazy in love." They giggle nervously, and Brauer feels "a humiliating blush" lifting to her cheeks: "Each of us was thinking *Andre Harrow. But we must not utter the name.*" Brauer records,

> You heard rumors . . . I had no idea who the arsonist was but her random acts seemed to me logical, like a message in code. In my journal I wrote, *She's in love, too. They scorn her. They look through her, invisible.* (22)

Brauer's grim voyage of self-discovery is linked to the fiery motif. She may not be literally responsible for the fires, but they resonate in her mind and indeed serve as an omen, perhaps even an inspiration, of her climactic act of self-deliverance from evil. An omen is implicit also in a trash-can blaze ignited beside the Humanities Department, "in fact, just below the second-floor office of Professor Andre Harrow."

Beasts is a macabre cogitation on innocence and evil. Significantly, Brauer first confronts her "hopeless infatuation" with Andre Harrow in a place of holy purity, the campus chapel, "a place of stark, chaste, white walls, a minimal altar draped in white like a tablecloth, and no religious iconography to hint that Catamount College had once been, before the revolutionary sixties, a Presbyterian-founded women's college." In demonic contrast is the Harrows' home, where Brauer goes to live and work as an "intern." Dorcas's vile totemic carvings—a pregnant woman whose belly "swelled like a malignant growth"; another in childbirth with "an ugly infant's head peeping from her wounded vagina"; others gaunt and elderly, "their sexual organs withered, with death's-head grins"; a "muscled man with enormous erect genitals"; and a "plump, preening adolescent girl cupping her breasts in both hands"—overshadow the darkly erotic proceedings. A demonic pet parrot, named Xipe Totec, provides a macabre touch, a "fierce, bedraggled creature," shrieking angrily at Brauer. One of his beady eyes "looked loose in its socket," his "sharp curved beak had a hairline crack," and his breast feathers were "thin and speckled with blood," for he pecked himself, Dorcas tells her, "out of deviltry" (94).

Brauer is plied with alcohol and Quaaludes, violated by husband and wife. Their first violation is described with vampire resonance, the couple taking turns kissing her upon her "bruised, sticky mouth," conversing in sexy French: "*Voilà, une petite surprise. Un morceau délicieux. Une belle* little animal, eh!" (94). Confused and drugged, the many violations blur into unreality in Brauer's mind,

their very vagueness imbuing them, in the reader's mind, with unspeakable filth and revolting abuse. They occur like "a film in which scenes are dreamily spliced together." The fire motif is brought in, for "our love-making was confused and fantastical as a film run faster and faster until it burst into flame" (95). Brauer discovers repulsive evidence of the extent of her patrons' abuse in a pornographic archive hidden at the bottom of a filing cabinet, in an office ranged with the works of Lawrence, underneath documents and a book of poetry by Harrow. They are all the more shocking for featuring Brauer's classmates, and rivals in love, with dazed expressions, in degrading sexual activities, in lewd association with Dorcas's monstrous sculptures.

> "Gillian, do you believe in evil?" asks her friend, Penelope, whom Brauer believes she has seen in one of the photos.
> "Evil? No." I spoke quickly, embarrassed.
> "Just—'No'?"
> "Not in the old way. I don't think so."
> "What's the 'old way'?"
> I wasn't sure. But I needed to speak. Andre Harrow would have been furious with me if I'd kept silent.
> I said, "God and Satan. 'Good' and 'evil.' A supernatural principle."
> "There's no evil, without the supernatural?" Penelope crinkled her forehead. Her fair, moon-shaped face was comically incongruous with her theological concerns. (107)

Herein lies the perennial debate, one of the central dilemmas of the human condition, at the heart of all the world's philosophies. It is equally at the heart of Gothic fiction, from Faust to Frankenstein. Is evil something out there, conditioning human behavior? Or does it emanate from within, from free will, from man as architect of his own fall? The Gothic does indeed address these questions, dealing in fundamental truths, mediating reality through the prism of the darkly surreal. *Beasts*—with its all too recognizable horrors—is a chronicle of realism, yet simultaneously of surrealism. The reader, like Brauer reminiscing, is challenged by incidents all too true, all too iniquitous, which we would much prefer to believe merely part of dark fantasy. As Oates has stated, *à propos* another fable of sexual abuse, her short story "The Bingo Master," there are truths, sometimes, to impart, which can only be faced through the surreal.

Notes

1. Joyce Carol Oates, introduction to *American Gothic Tales*, ed. Joyce Carol Oates (New York: Penguin, 1996), 9.

2. Oates, introduction, 7.

3. Joyce Carol Oates, "Edgar Allan Poe," in *The Oxford Book of American Short Stories*, ed. Joyce Carol Oates (Oxford: Oxford University Press, 1992), 91.

4. Joyce Carol Oates, interview by Oates biographer Greg Johnson, *Atlanta Journal-Constitution*, March 12, 2000, republished at Celestial Timepiece: A Joyce Carol Oates Home Page, http://jco.usfca.edu/works/novels/blonde.html (accessed April 26, 2010).

5. Joyce Carol Oates, *The Faith of a Writer: Life, Craft, Art* (New York: HarperCollins, 2003), 10.

6. Joyce Carol Oates, "Reflections on the Grotesque," Celestial Timepiece, usf.usfca.edu/fac-staff/~southerr/grotesque.html (accessed April 6, 2010).

7. Joyce Carol Oates, *Beasts* (New York: Carroll & Graf, 2002), 2. Page numbers appear hereafter in parentheses in the text.

8. Joyce Carol Oates, "Lawrence's *Götterdämmerung*: The Apocalyptic Vision of *Women in Love*," Celestial Timepiece, http://jco.usfca.edu/womeninlove.html (accessed April 6, 2010).

9. Joyce Carol Oates, afterword to *Haunted: Tales of the Grotesque* (New York: Penguin, 1994), 305.

10. Joyce Carol Oates, afterword, 305.

CHAPTER 4

The Blind Assassin by Margaret Atwood as a Modern "Bluebeard"

Karen F. Stein

1

The Bluebeard story of a newly married woman isolated in a private space (a castle keep, convent, mansion, or suburban house) at the mercy of a tyrannical and brutal husband, confronted with terrible secrets and possessing few resources, may be the fundamental female Gothic story. It reappears dramatically in the works of many early Gothic writers, including Horace Walpole, Ann Radcliffe, and the Brontë sisters, as well as in contemporary authors such as Angela Carter, Gloria Naylor, and Margaret Atwood.

Full of secrets and complications, Atwood's tenth novel, *The Blind Assassin*, features the memoir of an eighty-three-year-old Ontario woman named Iris Chase, who will die in 1999. She retells her sufferings at the hands of a Bluebeard figure in one of contemporary Gothic's more revelatory and satisfying retellings. The ominous but well-to-do lady-killer from Charles Perrault's "Bluebeard" and the brothers Grimm's two stories "The Robber Bridegroom" and "Fitcher's Bird" walks again in the guise of Iris's husband, Richard E. Griffen.

In Atwood's version, both this twentieth-century Bluebeard and his wife have secrets: he has seduced her sister, and Iris engages in an adulterous affair. Atwood's career as a writer has been one of accretion: themes are piled upon themes, images upon images. Although written in the realist tradition, her novels are deeply grounded in fairy tale and myth and are rich in irony and paradox. Her successive texts have grown in scope and complexity as they paint key recurring themes on broader canvases. *The Blind Assassin* is especially rich in Gothic

plots, stories, and narrative techniques. Many familiar Atwoodian motifs—the storyteller's complex configuration of power and powerlessness, the paradoxes of women's speech and silence, myth, the compelling power of the unknown, the difficulties of understanding another person, descent, death by drowning, entrapment, and the power struggles between men and women—resonate in this novel.

Richard Griffen (whose name immediately evokes the lion-bodied griffin/gryphon of myth, which built its nest out of gold) likes to rule. While the Greeks believed the griffin was a protector of treasures, Richard Griffen does not protect Norval Chase's treasured factory or daughters, Iris and Laura. He is the rich suitor that Iris has doubts about but agrees to marry, just as wealth (and a week of parties at Bluebeard's country house) convinces the younger sister in Perrault's tale that the widower gentleman's beard is not *so* very blue. More than that, Norval Chase offers his innocent and unworldly daughter Iris to the wealthy clothing manufacturer Griffen in return for his promises to support Iris and to save Chase's failing button factory during the Great Depression. Norval tries to reassure Iris about Richard (as it turns out, he is wrong): "I believe he's sound, underneath it all."[1] Iris later concludes that Richard is not leonine at all, but instead, "He was ruthless, but not like a lion; more like a sort of large rodent. He tunneled underground; he killed things by chewing off their roots" (479–480).

Iris has been badly educated and lacks skills that would make her employable; during that time there were few jobs open to middle-class women, and therefore marriage to a man who can support her seems the safest option in Norval's estimation. Iris agrees, for she repeatedly refutes her younger sister Laura's suggestion that they could support themselves. Once married, Iris displays less curiosity than Bluebeard's wife. Iris is the dutiful wife and does not go searching for Richard's secrets. Because she fails to probe her husband's secrets until it is too late, she is unable to protect her sister.

Laura is the more curious one, the one who questions and challenges conventional beliefs with her earnest questions about sacrifice, God, and the books she reads. Laura "frightens people" because she does not hide "some odd, skewed element" that most people hide (89). Nevertheless, she has a terrible secret which she reveals by leaving clues that Iris is slow to read. Laura colors the photos in a family album and paints Richard's head with red flames, and his hands as red and bloody as the hands of the dismembered brides in the Grimms' stories. Yet Iris does not interpret these clues in time to save Laura from Richard's devious machinations.

However, after Laura has been abused and has committed suicide, Iris manages to save herself through trickery, incorporating both storytelling and disguise. Like the young woman in "Fitcher's Bird," Iris disguises herself by using Laura's name. Like the young woman in "The Robber Bridegroom," she tells her

story in the guise of fiction that saves her from her Bluebeard when she publishes the novel attributed to Laura. Her novel about an affair with an unnamed man is Iris's story, but Richard assumes it is Laura's. Atwood has commented on the power of such fictions before, in a review of a book on fairy tales and their tellers: "The more women as a group were misprized by society, the greater the level of disguise required by any who dared to break silence. In times of oppression, wisdom of certain kinds can safely be spoken only through the mouths of those playing the fool."[2] Nevertheless, Iris is unable to save her sister or her daughter Aimee; unlike the fairy tale characters, these dead women do not return to life. The sad truth is that Iris is partly responsible for Laura's death. She tells Laura that the disreputable socialist activist Alex Thomas is dead and that she had an affair with him. Laura had believed that she had protected Alex by yielding to Richard's sexual advances and that Alex would contact her when he returned from serving in World War II. Iris's tactless revelation of her affair, and of Alex's death, drives Laura to suicide.

2

In Gothic narratives, things are seldom what they seem. The wizard in "Fitcher's Bird" appears to be an old beggar; the wizard, the robber bridegroom, and Bluebeard all hide murdered and dismembered bodies in their homes. In *The Blind Assassin*, Richard Griffen appears to be an upstanding citizen, active in politics, and en route to elected office. Yet he reneges on his promise to keep the button factory running. He preys on Laura's innocence to gain her consent to what is in effect rape and then labels her as delusional when she asserts that she is pregnant. His sister Winifred poses as an affectionate sister-in-law and mentor to Iris, yet she colludes with her brother in his nefarious schemes. Winifred and Richard whisk Laura off to an abortion facility under the pretext that she has had a nervous breakdown. They destroy her letters to Iris, thus keeping their plot secret and preventing Iris from acting to help Laura.

Imagery of keys and codes recurs through the novel, reiterating the theme of secrets and mysteries. Griffen is sexually abusive, brutally bruising Iris in places such as her thigh, where the marks will not be seen in public. Iris thinks of these bruises as "a kind of code" and wonders, "if they were a code, who held the key to it?" (371). Madeleine Davies notes, "Iris represents herself as a blank space or page encoded by others: with no autonomy over her own body she has no rights over the words written onto it and no access to them anyway since they are inscribed in a code to which she does not hold the key."[3]

The disconnection between appearance and reality occurs in the form of the narrative itself. Atwood points out there are five layers of narrative (Iris's mem-

oir, the science fiction stories, the Laura Chase novel, newspaper articles, and bathroom graffiti), and some of them contradict others.[4] The newspaper stories are superficial and are based on the falsified statements issued by Richard and Winifred to hide their family problems. Iris writes a novel within a novel and passes the novel off as the posthumous work of her sister Laura. When she explains that the Laura Chase novel was her own work, she qualifies her statement:

> I didn't think of what I was doing as writing—just writing down. What I remembered, and also what I imagined, which is also the truth. I thought of myself as recording. A bodiless hand, scrawling across a wall. . . . I can't say Laura didn't write a word. Technically that's accurate, but in another sense—what Laura would have called the spiritual sense—you could say she was my collaborator. The real author was neither one of us: a fist is more than the sum of its fingers. (512–513)

By contrasting different layers of discourse, this novel functions like a prism, separating the seemingly unified and clear light of fiction into its constituent colored bands of discourse. Put another way, the novel's polyphonic, multivoiced text points to the impossibility of unified discourse and thus exposes the contradictory and duplicitous nature of storytelling and of narrative itself. Iris even hints that perhaps she and Laura are not separate people. Throughout Atwood's fiction, many characters act as doubles. Starting with her early self-published poetry collection, *Double Persephone*, many of her protagonists are paired with characters who double them and act as foils, as for example in *Edible Woman*, Marian McAlpin is contrasted with her roommate Ainsley Tewce as both of them experiment with different approaches to the problems of courtship and marriage. Similarly, Mary Whitney in *Alias Grace* is a double (perhaps even an imagined one or a separate personality) for Grace Marks. The role of Laura in *The Blind Assassin* is similar. In any event, in this novel, Laura represents a part of Iris's self with feelings and ideas she tries to silence and deny.

Outspoken and forthright, Laura acts out fears and asks questions that the more docile Iris is unable to voice. As a child, Iris finds that she receives better treatment when she is quiet, and she maintains this stance throughout most of her life. Often Laura functions as Iris's alter ego, raising the issues that Iris would rather not acknowledge. For example, on the night before Iris's wedding, Laura tries to talk her sister out of the marriage, for she knows that Iris does not love Richard. Laura suggests that they get jobs. She tells Iris to "run away tonight and leave a note." Iris insists that she will be all right: "I've got my eyes open." But Laura sees through this bluff. "Like a sleepwalker," she comments tellingly, finishing the conversation with the rather snide observation, "well, you'll have nice clothes, anyway" (237). When she is married to Richard, Iris thinks she can

be safe by hiding. "I thought I could live like a mouse in the castle of tigers, by creeping around out of sight inside the walls; by staying quiet. . . . I didn't see the danger. I didn't even know they were tigers. Worse: I didn't know I might become a Tiger myself" (328).

In some ways, Laura's role is similar to that of Bertha Rochester's in *Jane Eyre*.[5] Bertha is the madwoman locked in an attic; Laura is falsely labeled mad and sent to a sanitarium/abortion facility. Both Bertha Rochester and Laura Chase to some degree act out—in ways that are impossible for the more pragmatic protagonists (Iris Chase Griffen and Jane Eyre)—the rage of a woman victimized by a patriarchal society. Both Edward Rochester and Richard Griffen lie to the women they are courting and attempt to possess them by underhanded means. Rochester hides the fact that he is already married and cannot get a divorce, while Richard reneges on his promises to Norval Chase, rapes Laura, and weaves a tissue of lies to maintain his bullying control of Iris and Laura. Dramatizing a rage and terror that Jane Eyre cannot acknowledge, Bertha sets fire to Jane's bridal veil, and eventually to the house in which they both have been imprisoned, Bertha literally and Jane figuratively. Bertha's death in the fire makes possible Jane's marriage to Rochester. But while Bertha's death frees Rochester to marry Jane, perhaps just as importantly it also leaves him blind. His disability reduces his power and gives Jane the possibility of a more equal relationship. By this means, Jane achieves her happy ending.

Jane Eyre marries a tamed Bluebeard, but the story of Bluebeard opens another option for women: escape from the marriage and the Gothic trap. Atwood finds women's power to resist inscribed within the Bluebeard story, especially in its "Fitcher's Bird" version. The female protagonist of this story rescues her sisters and saves herself by disguise and trickery. Following this tradition, *The Blind Assassin*, a contemporary iteration of the female Gothic subgenre, empowers Iris to escape from her Bluebeard.

3

Starting with Ellen Moers, critics have been investigating the subgenre of the female Gothic. Scholars have approached these fictions from the perspectives of psychology, mythology, psychoanalysis, and literary and cultural history. Diane Long Hoeveler's reading accommodates a range of approaches that open up a discussion of this genre. She argues that female Gothic novelists construct "a series of ideologies—a set of literary masquerades and poses—that would allow their female characters and by extension their female readers a fictitious mastery over . . . an oppressive social and political system."[6] The Gothic novel is "a coded and veiled critique of all those public institutions that have been

erected to displace, contain, or commodify women."[7] Because these systems have relegated women to the private sphere of home rather than the public sphere, and to positions of relative powerlessness in the family, the patriarchal family is the site where the female Gothic novel and its traumas are enacted. Michelle A. Massé explains, "Horror returns in the new home of the couple, conjured up by renewed denial of the heroine's identity and autonomy. The marriage that she thought would give her voice (because she would be listened to), movement (because her status would be that of an adult), and not just a room of her own but a house, proves to have none of these attributes. . . . The heroine again finds herself mute, paralyzed, enclosed."[8] Complementing Massé's view, Margery Fee observes that "the terror of male rejection or violence" is at the heart of the female Gothic tradition, and "another part of the terror is that of the loss of identity."[9] Ann McMillan writes that "enclosure and the chastity it represents have long remained the ideal for women. . . . [However,] by giving women chastity as their protection, patriarchal society gives women a weapon effective only against those whom social constraints can bind."[10] According to McMillan, there are two Gothic traditions, the Gothic romantic fantasy in which the villain becomes a rescuing hero and Gothic naturalism which ends with the heroine mad or dead. While Gothic fantasy "maintains . . . a conservative relationship to social norms. . . . Gothic naturalism shows that the bargain—remain powerless and you'll be taken care of—has long failed to protect women. Its heroines . . . live in danger . . . from forces in society and in themselves."[11] Atwood, however, refuses "the simpler resolutions of both Gothic traditions."[12]

Atwood's imaginative response to the Gothic, and especially to the Bluebeard stories, was shaped in her early childhood. When she was six years old, she first read the unexpurgated, original, gory Grimm brothers' fairy tales, replete with "barrels of nails, red-hot shoes, removable tongues and eyes."[13] At that time, her family spent "over half the year in the forest lands of Northern Quebec," where her father ran a forest insect research station.[14] While she was living in a rural environment—before TV and beyond the range of shopping malls, movie theaters, zoos, and museums—reading the Grimm's stories made a deep impression on her. Reading and making up stories were her chief entertainments during much of her early childhood, and "*Grimm's Fairy Tales* was the most influential book I ever read," she told Linda Sandler.[15] To Donald Haase, she asks, "Where else could I have gotten the idea, so early in life, that words can change you?"[16] Another idea that she took from these stories is the concept that "anyone might turn out to be someone other than you thought they were."[17] She explains,

> Stories like these . . . were important to me, as a writer because they convey an idea of what a story is. They give a sense of pattern, of design. They also do not color within the lines of "realism"; they spill over into the areas of dream and the paranormal, which are also an

important part of human experience. . . . Writers use references to known stories to give resonance and pattern to their work, and I have found some Grimm's tales . . . useful for that purpose. I think the Grimm's stories are often more available to women writers—when featuring women characters—than the Bible or the Greek myths, because they contain a larger number of active female protagonists— possibly because many of these stories were retold by women.[18]

Atwood observes that, contrary to the modern expurgated, popularized versions of Cinderella, Snow White, and The Sleeping Beauty, "women in these stories are not passive zombies; they do as much rescuing as the princes do, though they use magic, perseverance and cleverness rather than cold steel to do it."[19] They "show considerable wit and resourcefulness and usually win, not just by being pretty virtuous, but by using their brains."[20]

Atwood reiterates that her favorites remain "The Juniper Tree" and "Fitcher's Bird."[21] Rosemary Sullivan observes that "Fitcher's Bird" is "a story that would haunt Atwood, to the extent that its motifs can be found throughout her mature writing."[22] One such recurring figure is, of course, the Bluebeard figure. He appears frequently in Atwood's poetry (as in "The Robber Bridegroom" in *Interlunar*) and fiction, for example as Arthur, the Polish count, and Chuck Brewer (also known as the Royal Porcupine) in *Lady Oracle*, the commander in *The Handmaid's Tale*, and Ed in the title story of the collection *Bluebeard's Egg*. The novel *The Robber Bride* reverses the gender of the Grimm's story.

Maria Tatar describes the Bluebeard story as one that "begins with marriage (rather than ending with it), but also engages with the nexus of knowledge, sexuality, evil, and mortality."[23] Furthermore, this story "begins on the outside—in the realm of the familiar, common, and quotidian—and moves to the inside—the exotic, dangerous, passionate, and barbaric."[24] Tatar explains that there are two parts to the Bluebeard story: the violent, demonic Bluebeard and the curious, questioning woman.

4

Bluebeard appears in several variants; the three best known to English speakers are Charles Perrault's "Bluebeard" and the Grimms' two stories, "The Robber Bridegroom" and "Fitcher's Bird." In each version, the woman is reluctant to marry the Bluebeard figure. In the Perrault story, she is swayed by his courtship and lavish display of wealth. Her disobedience is emphasized, and the rescuers are her brothers who fortuitously arrive in time to save her. When her husband leaves her with a key, she rushes down to unlock the room where she discovers the murdered brides. She cannot clean the bloodstain off the key, which she

drops in horror. Bluebeard sees that she has disobeyed his orders and prepares to behead her. She stalls for time by asking to pray. When Bluebeard grabs his wife by her hair and is about to kill her, the brothers arrive and put him to death. The wife remarries and uses the money she has now inherited to reward her brothers with promotions in military rank, and her sister with marriage.

The twenty-first-century novel is more skeptical of marriage, and contemporary novels often end with women leaving rather than entering marriage. Whereas Charlotte Brontë's Bertha Rochester sets a house on fire, Atwood's Laura Chase puts on Iris's white gloves and drives off a bridge. Her death and the notebooks she leaves behind provide a key (and certainly this is a roman à clef in more ways than one) that finally enables Iris to understand her coded messages about Richard's sexual predation. Through this means, Iris's eyes are opened. Thus Laura's death makes it possible for Iris to obtain a divorce from Richard and thereby gain her independence. By taking action, Iris rejects the role of innocent victim and assumes the role of independent agent. She now works to support herself, as Laura had previously urged.

One of the themes of Gothic literature is the male desire to keep his bloodline pure, to guarantee heirs for transmission of his property. Bluebeard denies himself this possibility; he doesn't have children because he kills his wives too soon to produce progeny. And in *The Blind Assassin*, we learn that Richard Griffen has no children either. For Iris has another potent secret: Alex Thomas is the father of her daughter, Aimée, and therefore Richard Griffen has produced no living heirs. Ironically, in arranging for Laura's abortion, Richard prevented the birth of his only child.

As she writes her memoir, Iris wonders for whom she is telling the story. She thinks, "For myself? I think not. . . . For some stranger, in the future, after I'm dead? . . . Perhaps I write for no one" (43). As she grows more infirm, her writing assumes a greater urgency; she is eager to finish her tale, and she now directs it to a specific reader. She is writing her story for her granddaughter, Sabrina. Iris's intent in leaving her manuscript for Sabrina is liberatory. She intends her revelation of her granddaughter's ancestry to free Sabrina from misconceptions about her heritage, and to invite her to "reinvent" herself as she wishes (513).

What meanings does this new iteration of the traditional Bluebeard story hold for contemporary readers? Perhaps we readers may consider this novel as an invitation to reinvent ourselves as well. Sharon Wilson demonstrates that in much of Atwood's poetry and fiction the Bluebeard story functions as a subtext or intertext, representing the protagonist's metaphorical, or even literal, marriage to death. According to Wilson, the danger the Bluebeard figure poses is great; he "is not simply a male or even patriarchy *per se* but [a] kind of death or death-worshipping culture."[25] Another critic, Margaret Homans, argues persuasively that the Gothic literalizes—gives fictional form to—subjective states.[26]

If Homans is correct, then as long as women experience anxieties about the emotional vicissitudes of marriage, or feel threatened by their husbands—or, as Wilson teaches us, as long as people are enmeshed in patriarchal and death-worshipping cultures—Bluebeards will continue to haunt our literature. But Gothic narratives such as *The Blind Assassin* can lead their protagonists to "talk back to Bluebeard [and thus to] give voice to the formerly silent, allowing them to express their encoded wisdom, their dangerous knowledge," and can thereby lead to liberating strategies of resistance and survival.[27]

Notes

Special thanks to Danel Olson for the many helpful comments on this essay.

1. Margaret Atwood, *The Blind Assassin* (New York: Random House, 2000), 227. Page numbers appear hereafter in parentheses in the text.

2. Margaret Atwood, "Not So Grimm: The Staying Power of Fairy Tales," review of *From the Beast to the Blonde: On Fairy Tales and Their Tellers*, by Marina Warner, in *Moving Targets: Writing with Intent 1982–2004* (Toronto: House of Anansi, 2004), 182.

3. Madeleine Davies "Margaret Atwood's Female Bodies," in *The Cambridge Companion to Margaret Atwood*, ed. Coral Ann Howells (Cambridge, UK: Cambridge University Press, 2006), 61.

4. Margaret Atwood, "Fifty-two Ways of Making Butter," interview by Ann Heilmann and Debbie Taylor, in *Waltzing Again: New and Selected Conversations with Margaret Atwood*, ed. Earl G. Ingersoll (Princeton, NJ: Ontario Review Press, 2006), 236–237.

5. Charlotte Brontë, *Jane Eyre* (Mineola, NY: Dover, 2002).

6. Diane Long Hoeveler, *Gothic Feminism: The Professionalization of Gender from Charlotte Smith to the Brontës* (University Park: Pennsylvania State University Press, 1995), xii.

7. Hoeveler, *Gothic Feminism*, xiii.

8. Michelle A. Massé, *In the Name of Love: Women, Masochism, and the Gothic* (Ithaca, NY: Cornell University Press, 1992), 20.

9. Margery Fee, *The Fat Lady Dances: Margaret Atwood's* Lady Oracle (Toronto: ECW Press, 1993), 62–63.

10. Ann McMillan, "The Transforming Eye: *Lady Oracle* and Gothic Traditions," in *Margaret Atwood: Vision and Forms*, ed. Kathryn VanSpanckeren and Jan Garden Castro (Carbondale: Southern Illinois University Press, 1988), 51.

11. McMillan, "The Transforming Eye," 52.

12. McMillan, "The Transforming Eye," 50.

13. Margaret Atwood, "The Pleasures of Rereading," *New York Times*, June 12, 1983, book review desk, sec. 7, p. 14.

14. Margaret Atwood, "Grimms Remembered," in *The Reception of Grimms' Fairy Tales*, ed. Donald Haase (Detroit: Wayne State University Press, 1993), 290.

15. Margaret Atwood, "A Question of Metamorphosis," interview by Linda Sandler, in *Waltzing Again*, 24.

16. Margaret Atwood, "Grimms Remembered," 292.

17. Margaret Atwood, "The Pleasures of Rereading," 14.

18. Margaret Atwood, "To Write Is to Wrestle with an Angel in the Mud," interview by Rudolf Bader, in *Waltzing Again*, 191–192.

19. Margaret Atwood, "The Pleasures of Rereading," 14.

20. Margaret Atwood, "My Mother Would Rather Skate Than Scrub Floors," interview by Joyce Carol Oates, in *Waltzing Again*, 39.

21. Atwood, "My Mother Would Rather Skate," 39.

22. Rosemary Sullivan, *The Red Shoes: Margaret Atwood Starting Out* (New York: HarperCollins, 1998), 35–36.

23. Maria Tatar, *Secrets Beyond the Door: The Story of Bluebeard and His Wives* (Princeton, NJ: Princeton University Press, 2004), 3.

24. Maria Tatar, *Secrets Beyond the Door*, 2.

25. Sharon Rose Wilson, *Margaret Atwood's Fairy-Tale Sexual Politics* (Jackson: University Press of Mississippi, 1993), 199.

26. Margaret Homans, "Dreaming of Children: Literalisation in *Jane Eyre*," in *New Casebooks: Jane Eyre*, ed. Heather Glen (New York: St. Martin's Press, 1997), 147–167.

27. Karen Stein, "Talking Back to Bluebeard," in *Margaret Atwood's Textual Assassinations*, ed. Sharon Rose Wilson (Columbus: Ohio State University Press, 2003), 170.

CHAPTER 5

Death and *The Book Thief* by Markus Zusak

Steve Rasnic Tem

A great deal has been written endeavoring to define the Gothic sensibility. My own inclination is to define that particular impulse to both read and write about dark materials as broadly and as fluidly as possible. However, there is one characteristic which I seldom see acknowledged directly, but which I believe cuts through all the usually identified Gothic elements like the haunted settings, the hidden and suppressed histories, the forbidden fantasies, the sublime and the spiritual. That characteristic is a heightened awareness of death.

In its simplest, most workmanlike manifestation, this heightening may simply consist of putting the characters in mortal danger. In the contemporary mainstream novel, this threat is usually (but not always) compromised. The thrill comes in seeing how cleverly our protagonists escape certain death, but as readers we take comfort in knowing that our most favored protagonist will cheat death yet again. One or two important characters whom we have been coaxed into caring about may be sacrificed along the way in order to make the threat appear real, but we trust the author not to take us too far out of our comfort zone. Spouses may be sacrificed, but children rarely. The assumption that publishers and authors appear to be making in such novels is that readers want to be thrilled, but they do not want to be made too uncomfortable—they do not like to feel personally threatened, because where's the fun in that?

In the Gothic novel, such reassuring protections are removed, or are at least held in abeyance. We must be prepared for the demise of any character, including the protagonist (although even in Gothic fiction many editors still shy away from the death of a child). It is this expectation, I think, which finally separates the Gothic from the mainstream popular novel, and why some readers find the

Gothic intolerable. For such readers, entertainment needs to be reassuring, and they may even exhibit disbelief that the dark events of the Gothic could possibly be considered entertaining.

I believe the gulf that separates these two continents of readers—those who find the Gothic enthralling, even enlightening, and those who find such fiction suspect—may be broader than most of us appreciate. At times the division seems to go as deep as politics or religion. It would appear that everyone knows that he or she is going to die, but how far and in what way that awareness should infiltrate our common consciousness is broadly debated.

Few books in recent memory provide this heightened awareness of death more directly than Markus Zusak's *The Book Thief.* Zusak pushes the character of Death out of the shadows at the rear of the stage to narrate this novel as a somewhat shy and reluctant actor instead of as some grand "effect." But like many reluctant actors, he quickly warms to the role out of a need, perhaps, to explain himself. Everything we know is filtered either through his senses or through the notebook the young girl Liesel Meminger has written recording the most traumatic events in her life. At the time of the narration, this notebook has come into Death's possession, retrieved from a garbage truck. Liesel's book has the singular distinction of being a book that Death carries around with him and studies, much the way a religious person might carry and consult a Bible (or a Nazi of that period might have consulted *Mein Kampf*).

Zusak's version of Death is a character whose modesty appeals to us. Even as he is brought forth to narrate, we get a sense—in part through a technique of asides, interjections, and billboardlike proclamations—that this is a character eager to ingratiate himself, to counter that grim clichéd image we have of him, to get his *own* story told, but at the same time he appears to have lingering doubts as to whether it is his place to have his story told. He is eager to make friends, to be understood, and yet clearly a human being's ability to understand such a creature and his role in our lives must be limited. He presents himself as a functionary, simply fulfilling his role in the grand scheme of things, forced to abide by unparsable destinies and inevitabilities, doing a job that has been assigned to him by some higher cosmic power. But even as we recognize that he fulfills this role with at times an astounding gentleness, we cannot escape that obvious echo of all the Nazis who defended themselves by saying they were only doing their jobs, following orders.

Death, as Zusak portrays him, is not the scythe-wielding grim reaper familiar to most of us from art and animation. In fact, he makes a bit of fun of this sinister psychopomp of himself. ("I only wear a hooded black robe when it's cold."[1]) Instead, Zusak presents him as an overworked entity who performs his duties reluctantly, at the behest of an unreasonably demanding boss. He has the soul of a painter, composing his portraits of this war-torn landscape with a

German Expressionist's stark brushstrokes of black, white, and red, an emotional palette of death, peace, and passion (which are also the colors of the Nazi flag). At times he is a kindly dark angel who gently separates the soul from the body and carries it away as if it were a babe in arms.

In these things, Death is highly sympathetic. Indeed Death is uncannily like us, or at least like generations of Gothic readers who devour shudder novels. They need a diversion of pathos and danger, and so does Death, as he notes by the second page. Death both opens and closes this long novel with a link to us, with the need for a pleasurably unpleasant story. He admits at the end of the book, "There's a multitude of stories . . . that I allow to distract me as I work."[2] The account of a girl whose birth parents can no longer save her and who keeps a secret (a Jew that's hidden in her foster family's basement) from the Nazi authorities is a modern, grim variation of the orphaned maiden threatened in countless Gothic novels (a girl whose desire the lord of the manor must control). This girl's story will be Death's distraction all along. And yet, for all that, he cannot be our friend. He tells us on the very first page that he can be "amiable. Agreeable,"[3] but "nice has nothing to do with me."[4]

He certainly cannot be nine-year-old Liesel's friend. He knows what is going to happen to her. He knows he cannot change it. And, as he admits himself, he sees the colors before he sees the people. He is as different from us in his sympathies as the weather.

Having Death as the narrator provides Zusak with some rather unique opportunities for foreshadowing. Because he is Death, we assume he is timeless and completely reliable in his predictions of what is to come. This is no unreliable narrator. So when he tells us that Liesel's world is ending, we are chilled because we cannot doubt him. There is something matter-of-fact about the way he drops in these observations that also seems a bit cruel, but not purposefully so. They simply remind us that Death is not human, and our human dilemmas necessarily have a different meaning and context for him. And in this attitude he folds us back comfortably into the Gothic, with its clear message that we will all die (the characters we love, our own loved ones, and ourselves).

Although this message is implicit in most forms of literature, I believe the Gothic in its obsessive dissection of perception and its emotional directness makes it abundantly clear to its readers that *they* are included. If anything makes the Gothic a "risky" literature, it is this insistence that its readers will share the same fate as its characters, perhaps sooner than anyone guesses. Sometimes fiction gives us an escape from this final truth into an eternal world of the imagination where beauty is celebrated and deathless. But the Gothic approaches this truth head on and does not waver: Beauty dies, and to ashes goes all our passion for it.

And who better to deliver such a message than Death? Can we expect anything else from a creature who hands "souls to the conveyor belt of eternity?"[5] In the grand scheme of things, after all, we are patterns of light and shade, colors. Death has had to deal with so many of us. Our spirits may be beautiful, but the sheer numbers overwhelm. At times the best he can offer us is a thread of poetry. "Five hundred souls. I carried them in my fingers like suitcases. Or I'd throw them over my shoulder."[6]

He lets us know early on that it is the survivors who trouble him most—"the leftover humans,"[7] as he calls them—and he tries to limit his exposure to them as much as possible. But Liesel trips him up; he lingers longer with her than he knows he should. Death can be *very* detached. As Allied bombings of Germany increase, Death observes it obliquely: "There was the smell of a freshly cut coffin. Black flowers. Enormous suitcases under the eyes. . . . It was a very busy day all around, really."[8] Liesel, then, offers Death the mystique of *feeling* more over "the chaos of goodbye . . . a goodbye that was wet with the girl's head buried into the wooly, worn shallows of her mother's coat."[9] Death cannot die; he can never sense separation and mortality in the overwhelming way that we do. Death thus is as entranced with the idea of finitude (with "leaving") as we are with infinity. In a sense, Liesel humanizes him.

At least one critic[10] has complained that this is a Harry Potterish portrayal of Death, and I must admit that from time to time I found myself wishing this Death had a bit more edge. Certainly the author might have made more of the intrinsic cynicism of a supernatural being who is only doing his job. There are hints of it in the text—sometimes the asides are a bit too sharp, too caustic, too fatalistic for us to ever like this character entirely ("It kills me sometimes, how people die"[11]). But Zusak's choices have delivered to us a Death who can be gazed at for a length of time even by more squeamish readers, who does reassure us even while talking about extremely disturbing things. For example, when Death talks about catching souls as they plummet over the cliffs at the Mauthausen concentration camp, "'Saved you,' I'd think," he says about catching their souls midair.[12] This poetic quality removes some of the barriers this subject matter might have had to popular appeal.

Indeed, this kindlier, more subtle personification of Death manages to cut us to the very bone with such painterly observations as "the sky was the color of Jews,"[13] a metaphor which is both fanciful and yet appallingly realistic. The sustaining strength of this book is that supporting this supernatural narrator are Gothic elements based on harsh, but very real events and characters (unless one insists on being part of some disbelieving fringe group of revisionists). Instead of asking us to suspend our disbelief with elaborately devised monsters and vampires and haunted castles and imaginatively supercharged slaughters, Zusak

appeals to those Gothic perceptions of the spiritual and the sublime in his readers with some very real, and more powerful, elements of history.

There are historical events of such social power and psychological influence that they have become in a sense mythic, part of the collective unconscious in a way similar to how the myths and fairy tales of deities and holy places and vampires and werewolves and demons have become part of the dream life of most human beings. The dropping of the atomic bomb is one such event. The mass extermination of the Jews, with all its accompanying paraphernalia (trains, ledgers, camps, and piles of eyeglasses), is another.

Here, in order to focus the book on the daily lives of ordinary Germans during wartime, Zusak has kept this extermination event just offstage, over the next hill, beyond the next town, intruding on the ordinary lives of these people by means of the Nazi troops who march through their community, or with the ongoing effect of the cruel death of Liesel's brother in the opening scene, or with the character of Max who hides out of sight in the cellar, or with the spreading tide of destruction which each day creeps closer to their street.

But the Holocaust haunts the entire enterprise, and the novel's mostly offstage elements—the concentration camp, the soldiers, the cartoonish figure of Hitler—are its Gothic haunted castle, its werewolf, its vampire. These are people struggling to live out their ordinary lives, and yet at all times they are aware that over the next hill, or sometimes as close as next door, there lies nightmare.

This balance between ordinary life and nightmare is a crucial formula for making *The Book Thief* work as well as it does. It is also a formula which may prevent some readers from seeing this novel as truly Gothic. One of the aesthetic pleasures of the traditional Gothic novel is that it seems all of a piece. The characters and the setting and the story are all grim mirrors of one another. In terms of the color metaphors of *The Book Thief*, the Gothic is a palette of grays, with the occasional stark white or depthless black, and a splash of red. And death personally likes a chocolate-colored sky, "dark, dark chocolate."[14] But this symmetry, this aesthetic purity, tends to come with a cost. Nonfans of the genre may legitimately complain that there tends to be a scarcity of "real life" in these works. Often the stories have been conceptualized in such a way that the normal lives of their characters have been excluded. Because the characters' lives are subsumed by a Gothic obsession, we rarely see what appears to be normal interaction.

Much of *The Book Thief* is devoted to dramatizations of the normal play of children, such as the ongoing soccer game in the street, the races at school, and even the thieving forays outside the town. And although there is certainly a shadow cast by the immediate historical circumstances, for the most part these scenes tend to illuminate how children continue to play even under the worst conditions. These small humans are survivors in the purest form.

Such a lengthy focus on the ordinary might seem to be a risk on Zusak's part, but I believe the novel gains strength from such scenes, and that they add

a depth that many Gothics do not achieve. Sometimes it is important to remind the reader of the significance and value of what a character has to lose before it is taken away. The novelist's higher goals of balance and resonance, I believe, necessitate that a heightened sense of death be accompanied by a heightened sense of life.

So, does this heightened sense of life add a certain optimism to the proceedings? Given the number of readers who have expressed how much they have been moved by the book, I would suspect so. But it is not the optimism of "everything will get better" at work here (which would be a very un-Gothic idea), but rather the more practical optimism that "terrible things can be survived, at least until the moment of death" (a much more Gothic idea).

Liesel survives through words, both the ones she has stolen and the ones she has learned to create on her own. Through the course of the book, her words grow in strength and meaning, becoming a kind of compensation for all she has lost. Liesel steals her first book, *The Gravedigger's Handbook*, as a way of dealing with the death of her brother. She uses this first book as an instrument for learning how to read. She eventually learns to use words to protect herself and—in a dramatic form of self-therapy—to tell her own story.

As she tells us again and again, she both loves the words and hates the words. The words have helped her survive (and for Max, carrying *Mein Kampf* has saved his life), but at the same time, Hitler has used words to hypnotize the German populace and to grotesquely distort the image of the Jews. And finally, of course, Liesel is spared the fate of everyone else in her neighborhood simply because she is in the basement reading when the bombs are dropped. In itself, the very idea that words could be so important seems a highly optimistic theme.

The Second Book Thief

Holocaust literature as a whole concerns the burden of one terrible period in history, a set of near-unimaginable, unchangeable events. Implicit in such fiction is a nod toward the hope that, by telling the stories, these atrocities might not someday be repeated. There is a thread of optimism as well in the idea that human beings have a spirit which allows them to survive such events. But also implicit is a doubt, I think, a pessimism, that human beings could ever be prevented from doing their worst. "Say something enough times and you never forget it,"[15] Death tells us at the end, and that would seem to suggest that the vow of "Never again" will be upheld. To not remember the Holocaust is to kill the victims a second time. On the other hand, we remember too well Nazi propagandist Joseph Goebbels' words to feel safe: "If you tell a lie big enough and keep repeating it, people will eventually come to believe it."[16]

In his *The Death of Tragedy*, the philosopher George Steiner claims that the Holocaust was an event so awful that it killed the possibility for expression. Numerous other authors have posited that the experience of the Holocaust defies the imagination. I was on a panel at the World Fantasy Convention some twenty years ago at which several authors opined that the Holocaust couldn't be used in horror fiction because the actual horrors were so unimaginably great. And yet writers continue to challenge the unimaginable by imagining even further, and I wonder if perhaps that is the only way we *can* deal with such events.

When Death actually goes to the garbage truck and retrieves Liesel's notebook, it is a startling scene, in part because this interest by a supernatural, eternal entity in a transitory human being's personal ephemera would appear to be so unlikely, an elaborate pathetic fallacy. Death's behavior feels transgressive here, a forced congress between the spiritual and the actual, a violation of the natural order. Our imaginations naturally speculate on the practical complications of such a scenario. Can Death's spiritual garment contain such a physical object? How does he carry it? Death himself apparently feels awkward with what he has done, and although he has simply retrieved something thrown away, he has misgivings about having such an object in his possession and is eventually compelled to return it. It is here, I think, that Zusak wants us to see that there are two book thieves in his novel.

Clearly Death has taken an unusual step in his career. Since he mentions no other "souvenirs," this would appear to be a one-time acquisition. And of course it is not so much the book he has borrowed, or stolen, that is an important object of study; it is Liesel's story contained within. In making such an exception, he raises Liesel's story to a very high level of importance.

It is a common human trait that we would each like to believe our personal stories are of such importance. And yet we have created vast libraries of religion, philosophy, and psychology, which, combined with our own personal misgivings, teach us that our individual lives are at best simply one small thread in the human fabric, virtually lost in the grander sweep of the world's drama.

And yet here is a personification of one of the elemental forces of nature—a player in the even grander drama of the rise and fall of the universe—raising the importance of one human individual's story and confessing in the book's final words that he is "haunted by humans."[17] Perhaps this confession is pure hubris and manipulation, an author's overstatement in an attempt to appeal to his all-too-human readership. But as an act of the imagination, it takes the breath away.

Notes

1. Markus Zusak, *The Book Thief* (New York: Knopf, 2006), 307.
2. Zusak, *The Book Thief*, 549.

3. Zusak, *The Book Thief,* 3.

4. Zusak, *The Book Thief,* 3.

5. Zusak, *The Book Thief,* 23.

6. Zusak, *The Book Thief,* 336.

7. Zusak, *The Book Thief,* 5.

8. Zusak, *The Book Thief,* 506.

9. Zusak, *The Book Thief,* 25–26.

10. Janet Maslin, "Stealing to Settle a Score with Life," *New York Times,* March 27, 2006, www.nytimes.com/2006/03/27/books/27masl.html (accessed December 18, 2009).

11. Zusak, *The Book Thief,* 464.

12. Zusak, *The Book Thief,* 349.

13. Zusak, *The Book Thief,* 349.

14. Zusak, *The Book Thief,* 4.

15. Zusak, *The Book Thief,* 529.

16. "Joseph Goebbels," *The Holocaust Education & Archive Research Team/University of Northampton,* www.holocaustresearchproject.org/holoprelude/goebbels.html (accessed December 18, 2009).

17. Zusak, *The Book Thief,* 550.

CHAPTER 6

Cinematic Femme Fatales and Weimar Germany in Elizabeth Hand's *The Bride of Frankenstein: Pandora's Bride*

Marie Mulvey-Roberts

There is a cartoon by "Bestie" (English humorist Steve Best) of Boris Karloff standing behind Elsa Lanchester, the bandaged bride of Frankenstein, with her characteristic bouffant hairdo. While she stares in frozen horror at a pile of unwashed dishes, the caption below reads, "She suddenly realized why Dr. Frankenstein had created her."[1]

Elizabeth Hand's novel, too, is a feminist re-creation of *The Bride of Frankenstein* (1935), directed by James Whale, which was the first sequel to the influential *Frankenstein* (1931), also directed by him. Set in Weimar, Germany, during a time of disease and starvation, the novel looks toward the reconstruction of society through scientific experimentation and a new world order within which Gothic and science fiction coalesce. By way of Whale's film, Hand connects with Mary Shelley's novel *Frankenstein* (1818), on which the film is based.

Pandora, Hand's bride of Frankenstein, is the product of male desire, the brainchild of two scientists, Henry Frankenstein and his mentor Septimus Pretorius. Frankenstein had created her to marry another manmade monster of his creation. Pandora joins the ranks of runaway brides, fleeing Dr. Frankenstein, whose speciality is to create "ambulatory corpses"[2] from the dead bodies of murdered women. By contrast, Dr. Pretorius, like Shelley's Victor Frankenstein, refrains from murder for body parts and is more inclined toward grave robbing. Yet, unlike Shelley's scientist, Pretorius nurtures his female creature, whom Henry Frankenstein attempts to victimize. In this sequel of a sequel, Hand's

skillful ensemble of "gods and monsters"[3] takes full circle the transformation of text into film and back.

Whale's film is framed by a scene in which Mary Shelley explains to Percy Bysshe Shelley and Lord Byron that her intention in writing *Frankenstein* was to impart a moral lesson. She is played by Elsa Lanchester, who doubles as the monster in a mirroring of author as creator and creation. In her preface to the 1831 edition of the novel, Shelley describes the birth pangs of her own authorial creativity as having been formed not out of the void but from the chaos of preexisting materials. In *Frankenstein*, Mary Shelley's stitching together of creation myths and literary texts parallels Victor's suturing together parts of dead bodies for his grisly experiments. Both partake in acts of recomposition from decomposition. Similarly, Hand splices together cinematic extracts for the body of her text. In addition to *The Bride of Frankenstein*, she incorporates references to German Expressionist films including *The Cabinet of Dr. Caligari* (1920), *Metropolis* (1927), *Pandora's Box* (1929), *The Blue Angel* (1930), and *M* (1931) by marching characters off the screen into the pages of her novel. These films appeared between the two world wars during the Weimar Republic, a period of liberal democracy, yet it is the war between the sexes and the inequalities for women within marriage that are the main focus of Hand's attention. These were also a particular concern for Mary Shelley's mother Mary Wollstonecraft, the author of *A Vindication of the Rights of Woman* (1792), who fictionalized them in her Gothic novel *Maria; or, The Wrongs of Woman* (1798), which tells of how a woman was wrongly incarcerated in a lunatic asylum by her husband.

From the start of Hand's novel, her heroine, after having been the property and product of two male scientists in Germany, takes ownership of herself by resisting the nuptial destiny mapped out for her. She declares, "I was to be no male's bride. . . . I am no man's creature and no man's possession" (9), since she realizes, in relation to her raison d'être, "I had no other purpose, than to be the playmate and companion, yes, wife and *friend*, to that *thing*" (11). This harkens back, not only to Shelley's novel, but also to her Miltonic source in *Paradise Lost* (1667) and Genesis, when God created Eve, the first woman, as a companion for Adam. In Shelley's novel, Victor agrees to create a mate for his male monster, but when he reneges on his promise by destroying her, the creature takes revenge by killing his fiancée, Elizabeth. While tearing her to pieces, Victor even desexes his female creature by referring to her as "the thing on which I was engaged."[4] It is this discourse of thingification which Pandora uses against her male counterpart. After Victor has returned his female creation to the fragmented state from which she had been assembled, Hand virtually pieces her back together in a montage of textual and cinematic fragments. This Gothic reintegration and resurrection of the bride of Frankenstein threatens to bring into being Victor Frankenstein's fears of her propagating a race of devils.

This patriarchal nightmare is particularly prescient toward the end of the novel, when the Amazonian Pandora is invited to join a triumvirate of deadly females, which includes the fembot, a metallic woman, and Elizabeth, the cross-dressing, estranged Medusa-like (49) wife of Henry Frankenstein, in a new world order dominated by women. The threat of this power shift is symbolized by "a rayed sun surmounted by a crescent moon" (129).

The novel orbits the tensions between free will and predeterminism in an exploration of destiny and fate. Pandora appears to have inherited an Eve-like thirst for knowledge. In this bildungsroman, she educates herself by using Pretorius's library, where she reads Goethe's *Faust* (1808), to which references are made in Shelley's novel. Pandora is grateful for the gift of reading, saying, "I might never know the identity of the woman whose mind and memories ticked inside my skull, but every day I thanked her for knowing how to read" (37). Here Hand may be paying homage to Mary Shelley, who was allowed to read books from the library of her father, the writer and philosopher William Godwin, who did not restrict the education of his daughters on the grounds of gender. Pandora exults in having a woman's brain, even though she realizes that it has been taken from someone else. This opens up an ontological dilemma in regard to self and identity. Can she have ownership of herself when her skin, limbs, and organs have been harvested from dead girls? Is she subject to a Cartesian mind-body split? How do the parts relate to the whole? In a parody of self-exploration, Pandora looks within, literally, by cutting into her own body. By penetrating her own flesh, she discovers that she is a woman who does not bleed. Instead of blood, horror courses through her veins. Her bloodlessness makes her a "deathly pale woman" (132), a pallor shared by the vampire and the femme fatale, who converge in Bram Stoker's *Dracula* (1897). Stoker characterizes the latter as having the light of hell in her eyes.[5] For another of Hand's femme fatales, Lulu, eyes hold an "almost inhuman detachment" (137). Detachment is key to Henry Frankenstein's vision of the world as a vast slaughterhouse within which women have become detached from themselves by being reduced to mere body parts.

The pursuit of creation by creator in Shelley's novel is played out in Henry's hunt for Pandora. He plans to vivisect her and replicate the work done on her by Pretorius and Cesare. Vivisection and cross-species grafting are the secret horrors in H. G. Wells's *The Island of Dr. Moreau* (1896), which is another recreation of Shelley's *Frankenstein*. Dr. Moreau's horrific experiments qualify him to take his place in the pantheon of mad scientists ushered in by Victor Frankenstein. Wells's evil genius metamorphoses animals into humans to produce some horrific and dangerous mutant forms of life. The female puma he vivisects in agonising experiments manages to escape from his laboratory and kill her creator. Prior to that, her terrible cries emanating from the "House of Pain"[6] rip through the novel. In a harrowing echo, Pandora hears "the most ter-

rible, most solitary cry I have ever heard" (62). Like Wells's hero Prendergast, she realizes that the howl is not that of a brute but of a human. Hand may have responded to Wells's chapter nine entitled "The Thing in the Forest" with her tale of Wendigo, a monster who lives in the great North Woods. She aptly describes this as "a ripping yarn" (102) since, after calling you by your name, it then tears you limb from limb. Dismemberment is evocative of Pandora in that it helped, ironically, to bring about her own somatic integrity, the beginnings of which are remembered by her when she tries to recall the point at which she came into existence. When she enters Frankenstein's laboratory, it is as if she reenters the "void" (191), her cradle of creation, his operating theater. Once she had come into being, Pandora's sense of selfhood is consolidated further when she chooses her own name.

Naming is pertinent in *Frankenstein* as well as throughout its literary and cinematic progeny. The film industry named Mary Shelley's unnamed creature after his creator, thus identifying him with a slave or wife, since both are named after their "master." Dr. Pretorius, however, is determined that his female creation be given a name of her own. He suggests naming her after Lilith, the strong predecessor of Eve who possessed the ineffable name of the almighty and was created independently of Adam. Nevertheless, he insists that it must be her choice, saying, "*Everything* is your own choice" (26). So she exercises this freedom by rejecting the name of Lilith in favor of that of Pandora, the first woman in Greek mythology. As Pretorius points out, unlike Eve, his creation was not molded from Adam's flesh, nor, as in Milton's *Paradise Lost*, was she relegated to that of helpmate. In earlier versions of the myth, Pandora was created by Hephaestus, the blacksmith to the gods, who forged Zeus's thunderbolts as a punishment for Prometheus's theft of fire. Pretorius assigns an abbreviated form of this name, "Smith" (160), to his male monster, who had appropriately been singed by the fire he started in Henry Frankenstein's laboratory at the start of the novel. As far as Pandora is concerned, one can never fully escape the patriarchal myth that woman was born of man.[7] Yet Hand offers the reader some of the hope released from Pandora's Box when she writes, "Someday, a woman will write of the New Eve" (26). Since the novel is set in the 1920s, the author might be looking forward to Angela Carter's *The Passion of New Eve* (1977), or even to herself in the present work. Pandora may be seen as a female re-creation of Shelley's new Adam, while both Victor and his dark twin Henry Frankenstein are versions of a new Prometheus, the transgressor who stole fire from the gods. Another version of this Greek myth tells of how Prometheus breathed life into clay figures to create mankind. Nevertheless, Smith insists that Henry Frankenstein "did not create me! He served merely as a conduit between a lump of dead flesh and the fire of heaven" (150). This, in turn, serves as a reminder of how the light of creation can be refracted from its source.

The subtitle of Hand's novel, *Pandora's Bride*, is a reply to that of Mary Shelley's novel, *The Modern Prometheus*, whereby the Promethean creation myth has been superseded by a revision of the Pandoran. The en*gender*ing of these myths is broken down by Pandora's dressing as a man after her bridal gown is consigned to the flames and by the cross-dressed Elizabeth usurping her husband's Promethean role by attempting to create a super race of dominant women. Pandora not only crosses the boundary of gender but also that which lies between the human and the monstrous, into the domain of the femme fatale.

Hand draws on silver-screen femme fatales to people the pages of her novel. Her Lulu is based on the vaudeville dancer played by Louise Brooks who starred in the silent melodrama *Pandora's Box*, directed by Georg Wilhelm Pabst. Like Brookses, Hand's Lulu has a "black lacquered bob" (200) and "lovely dark eyes," along with an "unsettling combination of female beauty and feckless abandon" that "invited attention even while displacing it" (137). In the film, Lulu persuades her wealthy lover, Dr. Schön, to marry her. He realizes his mistake even before his wedding night, when he tries to force her to shoot herself but ends up getting shot himself. Even though it is he who is the monster and not Lulu, it is she who is put on trial for murder and then demonized by the prosecutor, who links the cultural myth of the annihilating female with the misogyny of the legend of Pandora, a woman who opens her box to unleash evil upon men. After arriving in foggy London, Lulu falls into destitution and is finally murdered by a Jack the Ripper kind of serial killer. As Angela Carter points out in her essay on screen sirens, Lulu's "only hope, now, [is] to accede to death as if it were some kind of grace."[8] This penitential erasure is the price she pays for unrestrained sexual behavior in a society which distorts sexuality, for as Carter explains, "This is the true source of the fatality of the *femme fatale*: that she lives her life in such a way her freedom reveals to others their lack of liberty."[9] The runner-up for the part of Lulu was Marlene Dietrich, who attained stardom the following year in *The Blue Angel*, directed by Josef von Sternberg, who had inherited the project from Pabst. Here she plays the role of another showgirl, Lola-Lola, whose name echoes that of Lulu. Like her predecessor, she too makes an unfortunate marriage by marrying Immanuel Rath, a schoolmaster at the local gymnasium (a college preparatory high school) who falls under her "spell." As a result of his association with her, he loses his job and is eventually forced to find employment as a clown in Lulu's troupe of cabaret artists. Returning to his home town, he is jeered and ridiculed by the former patrons of the Blue Angel club where he met his wife. Feeling humiliated and emasculated, he tries to strangle Lulu after seeing her with a rival and is restrained by a straitjacket. Later, he is found dead in the classroom where he used to teach. His death represents a fatal collision of bourgeois male with bohemian female.

In Hand's novel, Rath is paralleled by Professor Unrat, who also gives up teaching to marry a cabaret performer called Lola. But in contrast to Rath, he

relishes the opportunity to work as a clown and aspires toward "the great comic roles" (133) of Falstaff and the ham contemporary actor Viktor Hempel. Unrat denies rumors circulated by his former colleagues and students that he has descended into dissolution and madness by insisting, "In fact, I enjoy my work and have gotten very good at it" (133). Through this admission, Sternberg's Lola is exonerated for causing Rath's spiral into self-destruction. In common with Carter, Hand exposes the femme fatale as a cultural myth that is fraught with contradiction. As the desired object, the femme fatale is subject to libidinal projections which grossly misrepresent her. As Pandora, "deadliest of beauties" (57), points out, "Beauty is a temporary disfigurement. . . . Death will cure you of it, in no time. But I have survived death" (105). She is not unlike Angela Carter's vampire in her short story "The Lady of the House of Love" (1970):

> She is so beautiful she is unnatural; her beauty is an abnormality, a deformity, for none of her features exhibit any of those touching imperfections that reconcile us to the imperfection of the human condition. Her beauty is a symptom of her disorder, of her soullessness.[10]

Since Pandora, the undead devouring seductress, is without hamartia (a painful or destructive flaw that leads to catastrophe), which according to Aristotle was brought about through human procreation, her very existence becomes an affront to the jealous prerogative of deities.

Conflict in the novel revolves around competing scripts of gods, myths, and writers. One such author is Christopher Isherwood, whose *The Berlin Stories* (1945) inspired the film *Cabaret* (1972). The ghost of his heroine, Sally Bowles,[11] haunts Hand's trilogy of femme fatales, whose final member is the showgirl Thea, who boasts of having multiple fiancés. She befriends Pandora, who later rescues her from Dr. Frankenstein's second laboratory. In a collision of creative myths, Pandora prepares to be introduced to the show by Thea in the role of Eve, with serpents inscribed on her skin (70). It is a reminder that the femme fatale is another version of Freud's phallic, castrated, and castrating woman.[12] Thea is sister to Cesare, whose narcolepsy is being treated by Dr. Pretorius with cocaine, a drug favored by Freud, not only for recreational purposes but also as a cure. Cesare confides to Pandora that Pretorius, almost like a Freudian psychoanalyst, is teaching him to "live my life as a dream from which I might never awaken" (29). His mission is to free the inner world imprisoned in the outer.

The kohl-rimmed eyes of Cesare evoke the student somnambulist in the silent film *The Cabinet of Dr. Caligari*, directed by Robert Wiene. Dr. Caligari exhibits his loyal sleepwalking companion Cesare in a carnival, boasting that he can answer any question pitched by the audience. Similarly, in Hand's novel, Cesare performs in Dr. Pretorius's traveling freak show, as a mind reader. The main plot of Wiene's film concerns a series of murders in a German town.

Similarly, the film *M*, directed by Fritz Lang, to which Hand obliquely refers, is about a child murderer, Hans Beckert, played by Peter Lorre. This stalker and serial killer lures children on the streets of a city suggested as Berlin.[13] In an indirect allusion to the film, Hand describes a man offering a doll to a child before receding into shadow. Her child murderer is known as the Pfeifer (German for "piper" or "whistler"), who, like Lang's villain Beckert, whistles a tune from Edvard Grieg's "In the Hall of the Mountain King."[14] Eventually Beckert is captured by beggars and subjected to a kangaroo court run by the criminal underworld.[15] His plea of insanity and his defense by a "lawyer" are echoed by the words of Hand's Smith, who reasons with Professor Rotwang that though the Pfeifer is "a bad man; a sick man. . . . He is a man and not an animal. And you must deal with him as such, with justice but also with pity" (183–184). Here Smith demonstrates how a manmade monster can have more humanity than the scientific rationalism of Professor Rotwang allows.

The even more inhuman scientist, Henry Frankenstein, had manipulated the Pfeifer by promising to help him, on condition that he supply him with women for their body parts. The mendacious rumor circulated by Frankenstein was that they were being murdered by Pretorius, with Pandora as his accomplice, thereby causing people to believe that "he's creating an entire army of uber-women to take over the countryside, kill off the men, and set up a new republic of free-thinking *blau-stockings* in their place" (43). Fears of powerful women are expressed in Edward Bulwer-Lytton's dystopia *The Coming Race* (1871), where seven-foot women called *gys* were not only capable of defending themselves "against all aggressions from the males, but could, at any moment when he least suspected his danger, terminate the existence of an offending spouse."[16] Fear of women prompted Henry Frankenstein to conspire in the subjugation of his own wife Elizabeth. For this reason, she later forms an alliance against him with his assistant the fembot, known as Elfi, who is a technological version of the femme fatale. Straight out of Fritz Lang's *Metropolis*, with her "glowing crystal limbs and torso, [and] glowing crystal eyes in a face that seemed made of molten steel" (135), Hand informs us that she will never cry out during childbirth (197). Her maker is Professor Rotwang, who had designed her to lead the underclasses in revolution, maybe as part of the communist contingent in the battle waged on Berlin's streets against the fascists with their Frankenstein-like aspirations. But because Rotwang failed to give his tabula rasa a moral consciousness, she is hijacked by Henry Frankenstein for his own sinister political purposes.

Pretorius is a creator in stark contrast to Frankenstein. He is compassionate toward Pandora and his other creations, called the children of Cain, whose prototypes appear as homunculi in Whale's *Bride of Frankenstein*. In Hand's novel, they are exhibited in the cabinet of curiosities of "Professor Faust's Fantastical Panopticon" (56). Through them, Pretorius observes simultaneous drives to de-

stroy, love, and procreate. Pandora sees herself and her grotesque mutant siblings as "throwaway experiments" (98), yet their creator refuses to dispose of them. As Cesare points out to Pandora, Pretorius does not punish his creations, judge them, or insist that they worship him. Her response is to marvel, "A strange sort of God" (30). The three scientists in the novel set out to recreate the world anew in their different ways, for as Wendigo, the leader of an alternative society in the form of a community of wild boys living in the woods (the equivalent of Whale's gypsies), declares, "Our country is broken. . . . Our world is broken. Someone has to fix it" (105). For him, that someone is Professor Rotwang, who intends to build a new city and then a new world, but only after destroying the old one first and all its inhabitants. The novel is about the clashes and convergences between creation myths and the new world orders lined up by Dr. Frankenstein, Dr. Pretorius, and Dr. Rotwang, which include the creation of a new kind of woman. The rebellion of these neowomen is a replay of the revolt of Adam and Eve against God.

The Faustian pact, which represents in some ways a means of reversing the effects of the Fall, is offered to Pandora when she is invited to join forces with Elizabeth Frankenstein and the fembot in order to seize the power to create life from the male scientists on the grounds that "the giving and taking of Life is too important a matter to be left to the likes of men" (197). She has the chance of deification, for as Elizabeth predicts, "we will be like the Three Fates, watching over the world" (197). Pandora draws on another Greek myth for her answer by recalling how her prototype had originally opened a jar, a bridal gift from Zeus, and released *keres*, or sprites of nightmare. These female death spirits of Greek legend, red in tooth and claw, thirsted after human blood. But after closing the container, Pandora opened it again to release a *ker* of hope, which would be capable of sustaining humanity through all the miseries of existence. Even though Hand's Pandora initially dismissed the tale as "a stupid story" (31), she fulfils her chosen destiny by playing one legend against another in renouncing the Mephistophelian path of Faust for that of Pandora, as redeemer of mankind. By doing so, she renounces the misogynous myth that holds woman responsible for the destruction of the world, and absolves from blame not only the Greek Pandora but also the Judeo-Christian Eve.

Pandora has also resisted subjugation through marriage, which Henry Frankenstein believed would cure her of rebellion. Her response to this suggestion is to hit him and eventually, with the help of Smith, to destroy him as a prophylactic against further destruction. As well as proving herself not to be Pygmalion's pliable subject, at the start of the novel she saves her other creator, Dr. Pretorius, from fire as well as from being destroyed by a race of dominant females. Her choice is for a world in which men and women coexist on equal terms. Her refusal to be the bride of Frankenstein, in favor of the bride of Pandora, is recognition that marriage has been used as an opiate to restrain and

numb women from political realities. Dr. Frankenstein wants to exchange her brain with that of a monkey or a cat and to turn her into the perfect servant, who is interchangeable with "the ideal wife" (76). He is even prepared to enslave his own wife, which proves to be his undoing, for when she discovers this dastardly plan, she retaliates by turning the fembot against him. Frankenstein had also intended to control men through his subjugated women. The false propaganda he disseminated about Dr. Pretorius "creating an entire army of uber-women to take over the countryside" (43) chimes with Nazi rhetoric of the 1930s concerning an Aryan super race and their attendant slave societies, anticipated in Lang's *Metropolis*, probably covertly condemned in *M*,[17] and more explicitly attacked in his *The Testament of Dr. Mabuse* (1933). Under the Third Reich, even Aryan women would lose the freedoms they had enjoyed under the Weimar Republic. Hitler's 1933 Law for the Encouragement of Marriage, which was part of a process to force women back into the home to become reproductive machines, bears similarities with Henry Frankenstein's mission to enslave women as docile wives and to father a race of superbeings.

Hand's novel is an allegory warning of the dangers of totalitarianism and contains veiled allusions to the rise of fascism in Weimar Germany and its culmination in the horrors of the Third Reich: the ideology of a super race, medical experimentation, enslavement, mass death, and more than one Promethean overreacher. In the films, a lightning rod brings fire down from heaven to animate the monsters with electricity. Fire begins and ends Hand's novel. These conflagrations are purgative as they destroy Henry Frankenstein's two laboratories. In Whale's film, the bride and Pretorius burn alongside the monster. The opening words of the novel, "How could you imagine that fire would kill me? Fire gave me life" (9), embody Pandora's message of hope to the reader. It also picks up on the beginning of Whale's *The Bride of Frankenstein*, which in turn is a continuation of the end of his previous film *Frankenstein*, in which German villagers gather around the burning windmill, cheering the apparent death of the monster. Fires would one day consume far more of Germany. As Hand's recreation of Christopher Isherwood counsels, it is wise to visit Berlin "before it burns completely to the ground" (22). This may be a premonition of the fire-bombing of Berlin by the Allies during World War II, as well as that of around 150 other German cities as documented in Jörg Friedrich's book entitled *The Fire: The Bombing of Germany 1940–1945* (2006). Berliners took shelter from the bombings and the meltdown of their city in sewers and other underground shelters in a reliving of Dante's inferno. This is a modern version of the epic journey to the underworld, the realm of death, which is reenacted in Hand's novel through the descent of the main characters into the Undercity, the *Unterstadt*, an immense network stretching beneath Berlin. Here the forces of evil are ultimately destroyed and, as in Nazi Germany, the real monsters are laid bare as totalitarianism, war, and genocide.

The insistence that woman is the cause of humanity's downfall is also refuted in Hand's novel as "cruel and egregious" (198). She casts away the specter of the femme fatale and implicitly repudiates the Aristotelian equation of monstrosity and the feminine. Through her dissection of these mythologies, she exposes and unmans the misogynies which gave them life. In an evocation of the perennial forces of creation, destruction, resurrection, and redemption, Hand has given us a new creation myth though her witty, powerful, and complex rendition of the legend of Pandora and Mary Shelley's *Frankenstein*.

Notes

1. Steve Best, *All the Bestie* (London: Index Books, 2002), 55.
2. Elizabeth Hand, *The Bride of Frankenstein: Pandora's Bride* (Milwaukee: Dark Horse Books, 2007), 186. Page numbers appear hereafter in parentheses in the text.
3. In *Bride of Frankenstein* (1935), directed by James Whale, Dr. Pretorius toasts Dr. Frankenstein, "To a new world of gods and monsters." *Gods and Monsters* (1998), directed by Bill Condon, concerns the last days of Whale's life.
4. Mary Shelley, *Frankenstein, or The Modern Prometheus*, ed. Joanna M. Smith (New York: St. Martin's Press, 1992), 141.
5. See Bram Stoker, *Dracula*, ed. Maurice Hindle (London: Penguin Books, 1993), 225.
6. H. G. Wells, *The Island of Dr. Moreau* (Rockville, MD: Phoenix Pick, 2008), 152.
7. Other versions see Pandora as part of a splintering of the Great Goddess or as representing aspects of Gaia and Demeter.
8. Angela Carter, "Femme Fatales," in *Nothing Sacred: Selected Writings* (London: Virago Press, 1982), 123.
9. Carter, "Femme Fatales," 123.
10. Angela Carter, *The Bloody Chamber* (Harmondsworth, UK: King Penguin, 1981), 94.
11. Sally Bowles appears in Christopher Isherwood, *Sally Bowles* (1937) and *Goodbye to Berlin* (1939). The latter was published with *Mr. Norris Changes Trains* (1935) as *The Berlin Stories* (1945).
12. Hand's character, Dora, might be a reference to Freud's well-known case history.
13. Peter Kürten, the German serial killer dubbed the Vampire of Düsseldorf, is thought to have inspired the film, made in the year of execution, though this was denied by Lang.
14. This is taken from the *Peer Gynt Suite* no. 1, opus 46. The premiere was February 24, 1876, in Christiania (now Oslo), Norway.
15. Karl Pfeifer defended himself in numerous court cases after criticizing an anti-Semitic article written by a right-wing politician in 1993.
16. Edward Bulwer-Lytton, *The Coming Race* (Stroud, UK: Alan Sutton, 1995), 31.
17. The Nazis were opposed to this film and used Lorre's acclaimed monologue in their anti-Semitic propaganda film *The Eternal Jew* (1940), directed by Fritz Hippler.

CHAPTER 7

Ghosts in a Mirror

TABITHA KING AND MICHAEL MCDOWELL'S *CANDLES BURNING*

Nancy A. Collins

Although best known as the screenwriter for the Tim Burton films *Beetlejuice* and *The Nightmare Before Christmas*, Michael McEachern McDowell (1950–1999) was first and foremost a novelist. In fact, he wrote what is arguably some of the best Southern Gothic literature of the late twentieth century. However, since McDowell's novels were marketed as straight horror and focused on the supernatural aspect inherent in the term *Gothic*, his contribution to the field has been largely overlooked or dismissed as "horror."

As McDowell stated more than twenty years before the publication of *Candles Burning*, "I am a commercial writer and I'm proud of that. I am writing things to be put in the bookstore next month. I think it is a mistake to try to write for the ages."[1] Such humility is rarely rewarded within an artist's lifetime.

Upon his untimely death at age forty-nine, Michael McDowell was already a couple hundred pages into the novel that would become *Candles Burning*. According to his posthumous collaborator, Tabitha King, there were no real notes or outline for her to work with. In her preface, Mrs. King explains that the finished product isn't the story that McDowell set out to tell, but rather the story she "drew from his manuscript."[2] Although an author in her own right, Tabitha King is best known for being married to Stephen King, the most successful writer of American horror fiction in the twentieth century. McDowell and the Kings were friends and colleagues during his lifetime, with Mr. King having once praised the Alabama-born writer as "the finest writer of paperback originals in America today."[3] A few years before his death in 1999, McDowell had adapted King's pseudonymous *Thinner* for the big screen.

Despite the stylistic blurring that comes from such posthumous collaborations, *Candles Burning* allows a final glimpse of the man doing what he did best—crafting believable, three-dimensional characters and recreating the manners and mores of a time and place long gone within a contemporary narrative, all while trailing an icy finger down the reader's back.

It is important to remember that McDowell intended *Candles Burning* as a coda for his career, if not his life. There is a scene in the book where a ghost appears in a parlor mirror and comments on the similarity of the house to that of another, grander house, which was destroyed long ago. I view it is an analogy for the book itself. For *Candles Burning* is littered with ghostly mirror images—some exact, others reversed—of characters, plots, and situations from McDowell's previous horror novels.

For the most part, *Candles Burning* has all the tell-tale ingredients found in Danel Olson's theory on the Southern Gothic. Most of the story is set in the (then) small resort community of Pensacola Beach, Florida, in an isolated boarding house. Outmoded customs on display include hoodoo and sympathetic magic, as well as the practice of making one's own soap, shampoo, and home medicinal cures. The underclass grotesques are represented by a dim-witted chambermaid and an even dimmer cook, who conspire to kidnap, and then murder, the father of the protagonist. The story itself is set during the transitionary period between the Old South and the New, where old social traditions came into violent conflict with modern civil rights. The humiliation associated with downward social mobility is a major motivator throughout the novels, and although there is very little violence in the book, explosive, gruesome death does comes into play, in one case quite literally. There is an obvious reversal in parenting, as the protagonist is, at times, more of a parent to her wastrel mother. As for the narcissism necessary to make a Southern Gothic worth its salt, *Candles Burning* has two of the best examples of hell on wheels this side of Cruella DeVille.

Where his previous Southern Gothic novels were clearly influenced by William Faulkner, Flannery O'Connor, and Tennessee Williams, the overall tone of *Candles Burning* owes more to McDowell's fellow Alabamans, Harper Lee and Truman Capote. Unlike McDowell's previous works, *Candles Burning* is written as a memoir-style first-person narrative, in the vein of *To Kill a Mockingbird*. Indeed, the narrator, Calliope "Calley" Dakin, is an even bigger daddy's girl than Scout Finch. Then again, Scout never had the ability to communicate with the dead or the power to mimic any voice she hears. There is also a later holiday scene with a kindly (if not exactly living) female relative that reads like a twisted version of Capote's "A Christmas Memory."

As the story opens, Calley is the seven-year-old daughter of Joe Cane Dakin, a self-made millionaire from Montgomery, Alabama, and Roberta Ann Carroll,

last in the line of a prestigious southern family. The blue-blooded Roberta Ann dotes on her bratty son, Ford, but is shockingly casual in her cruelty toward her daughter, apparently because the child has oversized ears that make her look "feeble-minded."[4]

In 1958, Joe Cane Dakin takes his family with him on an important business trip to New Orleans. While shopping with her mother, Calley meets a mysterious woman who takes an unusual interest in the child after all the clocks in the store mysteriously fall silent. Later Calley's father becomes the victim of a bizarre kidnapping plot. Joe Cane Dakin is tortured, chopped up, and shoved inside a footlocker. His head is never found. Roberta Ann arranges for a million dollars to be placed inside an identical footlocker in hopes of buying back her husband, but it is too late.

At her father's wake, Calley and her mother are approached by a woman named Fennie Verlow, who claims to be a distant relation. Fennie suggests they escape the media circus created by the trial of the murderers by spending the summer at her sister's home in Pensacola Beach. The next day, Roberta Ann learns that her husband had leveraged virtually every aspect of his business, leaving his family destitute. Forced from their home in Montgomery, they end up moving to the backwater town of Tallassee to live with Roberta Ann's mother, the venomous Deidre "Mamadee" Carroll.

Where Roberta Ann is narcissistic and prone to spite and fits of rage, Mamadee is absolutely loathsome. Jealous of her daughter's youth and beauty, she is verbally abusive to Roberta Ann and exceptionally vicious toward Calley. However, she displays a near-incestuous obsession with her grandson, who she views as the rebirth of the vaunted Carroll legacy.

Ignored and uncomforted by her family, Calley investigates her new surroundings and finds an old Audubon Society field guide that belonged to her uncle. She also discovers that her mother once had two sisters named Faith and Hope, whom Mamadee "gave away as if they were old clothes" to their grandmother years ago (125). Neither woman is willing to talk about what happened to the sisters, nor are they willing to talk about Roberta Ann's brother, Bobby, who died mysteriously.

Living under her mother's roof proves impossible for Roberta Ann. When it becomes clear that Mamadee and the family lawyer are in cahoots to gain guardianship of Ford, as well as to implicate her in her husband's murder, Roberta Ann decides to take the ransom money and run. She wakes Calley in the middle of the night to help her load the footlocker full of money, as well as a few choice family heirlooms, into her Edsel. Surprised by her mother before she can fetch Ford, Roberta Ann drives off with Calley, leaving her son in Mamadee's dubious care.

Once she is safely away from her mother, Roberta Ann opens the footlocker to find not only the money gone, but the locker apparently switched with the

one that contained her husband's mutilated body. Unsure what to do next, Calley reminds her mother of Fennie Verlow's sister in Pensacola Beach.

Upon arriving at the beach house, called Merrymeeting, Roberta Ann is shocked to discover that it is identical, inside and out, to the house belonging to her beloved grandmother, Cosima. But that house was located in Banks, Alabama, and had burned down years ago.

The owner of the house, Merry Verlow, welcomes the runaways and seems to have known they were coming. Although Roberta Ann resents being reduced to a penurious widow living in a distant cousin's boardinghouse, Calley has no problems adjusting. However, Calley senses that there is a dark motive behind "Miz Verlow's" willingness to accept them as permanent guests. Not long after taking up residence in Merrymeeting, Calley experiences a strange interlude on the beach that results in the loss of her hair, which later grows back the same color as Miz Verlow's.

One night, while playing cards by candlelight, the voice of Mamadee is heard, claiming to be dead. While everyone in the room can hear the disembodied voice, only Calley can see her grandmother's face in the mirror over the mantelpiece. Mamadee's ghost recognizes the interior of Merrymeeting as being identical to her mother's home. The ghost also reveals that Roberta Ann was responsible for burning down the house in Banks, killing her grandmother and sisters. Believing her daughter and granddaughter to be already dead, Mamadee laughs unpleasantly, telling Calley, "I will not have to warn you about what's going to happen to you" (190).

Subsequent investigation reveals that Mamadee is in fact dead, having passed away under extremely mysterious circumstances the same day Roberta Ann ran away. Calley's brother—and the Carroll fortune—is now under the guardianship of the family doctor, as Mamadee had disowned Roberta Ann.

Calley is introduced to the enigmatic Mrs. Mank, a sophisticated older woman from Boston who is a regular visitor to Merrymeeting. Mrs. Mank takes an uncommon interest in the Dakins, at first arranging for a lawyer to help Roberta Ann regain custody of her son and her share of her mother's estate. Later, though, she threatens to have Roberta Ann killed if Calley tries to run away and reunite with her relatives on her father's side of the family.

That Christmas, several guests, whom Miz Verlow refers to as her "regulars," begin to arrive, and on Christmas Eve the voice of Great Grandmother Cosima speaks from the artificial Christmas tree, instructing Roberta Ann to allow Calley to stay up late in order "to watch that the candle in the window does not go out" (268).

Once everyone is finally asleep, Cosima's ghost—speaking from the flame in the candle—tells her descendant that she is the "eye of a storm . . . not of your doing" (271), and sends her a visitor in the form of an emaciated ghost named

Tallulah Jordan, who urges Calley to "listen to the book" before disappearing (276). As for the ghostly admonition to "listen to the book," Calley somehow manages to forget it for several years.

Some time later, Calley and a couple of friends are playing in the attic when they stumble across a mysterious old poster advertising the Dexter Brothers' Circus. Calley sees that the various acrobats, fortune-tellers, and lion tamers bear a strong resemblance to the "regulars" who come to Merrymeeting every Christmas, despite the poster being nearly a hundred years old. After that, Calley begins to view Miz Verlow and the "regulars" with far greater suspicion.

For the next hundred pages, the narrative abandons its plot of ghostly intervention and supernatural manipulation and turns into a coming-of-age novel set in the mid-to-late 1960s. Calley grows from awkward child to strong-willed young woman while Pensacola Beach becomes racially integrated, Kennedy is shot, and the Vietnam War goes on amid domestic protest.

Several more years go by before Calley finally gets around to remembering the ghostly Tallulah's instructions to "listen to the book." She decides that the ghost meant the Audubon Society field guide that once belonged to her uncle. She goes out to an isolated spot on the beach to try and learn the secrets of the book and discovers that it was actually owned by her Aunt Hope, and that she was named after (or might possibly be a reincarnation of) her great grandmother Cosima's treasured pet parrot, Calliope.

Meanwhile, Roberta Ann announces that she has decided to remarry and informs Calley that once she graduates from high school she will be sent to Boston to live with Mrs. Mank in order to attend college. Before she leaves the South for good, Calley arranges to have a friend drive her to Tallahassee to try to find her brother. Once she arrives, she discovers the ancestral estate burned to the ground, the family lawyer crippled by a stroke, her brother gone to live in New Orleans, and her grandmother buried in an untended and misspelled grave with a marker that reads "deirdre dexter caroll 1899–1958," without even "a Bible verse or an R-I-P" (365).

Upon returning home, Calley finds Mrs. Mank and Miz Verlow waiting for her. Mrs. Mank reveals that she once knew Calley's grandmother and states that Mamadee "ruined your mama and she would have ruined you" (368). Calley resents the old woman's intrusion into her life but feels powerless to stop it.

While in the attic looking for a suitcase, Calley hears the voice of her old mammy, Ida Mae Oakes, who leads her to the footlocker that once contained the million-dollar ransom. When she opens it, she finds that the missing money has returned. She also finds a grotesque rag doll that seems to be a crude effigy of herself, which she burns. She smuggles the ransom out of the attic in an old duffle bag and gives it to a trustworthy friend for safekeeping.

As Calley debates whether to go to Boston or take the money and try to find her brother, Roberta Ann receives a letter from Ford, asking her to meet him in Mobile. Disappointed that her brother makes no mention of her, Calley decides to leave for Boston. A week later, Hurricane Camille hits the Gulf Coast the day Roberta Ann is supposed to meet her son in Mobile. Her body is later found "floating tits up" in a hotel pool in Pass Christian, Mississippi (398).

Calley receives an invitation from her brother to attend their mother's funeral back in Alabama. The night before they leave, a tipsy Mrs. Mank reveals that she is actually Mamadee's sister, Calley's great-aunt. According to Mrs. Mank, their mother, Cosima Dexter, was a woman of considerable power who married the owner of a circus as a means of attracting and providing camouflage for "people with special talents . . . who stand out of a crowd" and "draw the sometimes murderous hatred of all those sadly untalented people who make up the mob" (402).

Mrs. Mank's sister, Mamadee, did not inherit any of these abilities and sought to escape her humble origins by marrying into the wealthy Carroll family. However, to her chagrin, her daughters Hope and Faith were born "special." Mamadee tried to kill them, but they were saved by Cosima, who took them in. Mrs. Mank reveals that Roberta Ann was jealous of the attention her grandmother Cosima gave her special sisters, and in a fit of rage she burned the house to the ground, killing everyone inside. Mrs. Mank views herself as continuing the Dexter family tradition of recognizing and using "the talents the rest of the populace would gladly smother in infancy" (403), and sees Calley as a particularly important investment, one that had to be safeguarded from the corrupting influence of her own family.

Upon arriving in Alabama, Calley is finally reunited with her brother. He reveals that the reason he never contacted her before is because, following Mamadee's death, Mrs. Mank became his legal guardian and sent him to a military academy run by some of the "regulars" at Merrymeeting. He only recently gained control of the Carroll fortune, in part because he was able to blackmail Mrs. Mank. It turns out he saw Fennie Verlow give Mamadee's cook something to put in her food the day she died.

When confronted, Mrs. Mank confesses that she wanted access to Calley's powers after seeing her silence the clocks in the New Orleans antique store. She then used Mamadee's hatred of her redneck son-in-law so that she would help arrange Joe Cane Dakin's kidnapping and murder, as well as the theft of his estate. Once Calley's father was out of the way, Mrs. Mank turned the tables on her sister by having her poisoned. Mrs. Mank insists that everything that was done was to protect Calley's powers from being destroyed, and now she claims that Calley "owes" her. Calley decides that she will beat her great-aunt at her own game by pretending to go along with her, so she agrees to return to Boston.

The next thirty-five years pass in a couple of pages, and the story ends with Calley returning with her brother to the long-abandoned Merrymeeting after the deaths of Mrs. Mank and Miz Verlow. Hurricane Ivan has destroyed the derelict beach house, and it is there that they find the missing skull of their murdered father. Calley and her loving daddy are finally reunited after forty-six years.

Candles Burning is the fifth book in McDowell's series of Southern Gothic novels. The others are *The Amulet* (1979), *Cold Moon Over Babylon* (1980), *The Elementals* (1981), and the six-volume *Blackwater* (1983). All five are set in rural communities close to the Alabama-Florida border, near the Gulf of Mexico. And, like the others, *Candles Burning* is essentially a tale of tangled family secrets and supernatural revenge. For the dedicated fan of Michael McDowell's work, the true pleasure to be found in his final novel comes from identifying the shadows cast by his earlier books. While there are a couple of blatant shout-outs, mostly in the form of place names (as well as thinly veiled references to several Stephen King novels, including *The Green Mile* and *The Shining*), you sometimes have to squint your eyes and tilt your head to see the shapes hiding inside the plot and characters of *Candles Burning*.

The numerous similarities between *Candles Burning* and McDowell's earlier works range from the plot to swindle a family out of money via murder (*Cold Moon Over Babylon*) to an isolated, haunted beach house (*The Elementals*) and the appearance of a scarlet macaw as a family pet (*The Elementals*). But the strongest link between *Candles Burning* and its predecessors is its cast of strong-willed women.

McDowell's vision of rural southern society (especially that of the Old South) is decidedly matriarchal. Like fellow Alabaman Truman Capote, McDowell had an uncanny understanding of the female soul, whether kind or evil.

Any reader born and raised in the South before 1980 is sure to recognize a particular grandmother, aunt, or other outspoken female relation in Mary Love Caskey (*Blackwater*), Big Barbara McCray (*The Elementals*), and Becca Blair (*The Amulet*). However, this sympathy for the female condition was counterbalanced by a deep ambivalence, as evidenced in this passage from *Blackwater I: The Flood*:

> That was the great misconception about men: because they dealt with money because they could hire someone on and later fire him, because they alone filled state assemblies and were elected congressional representatives, everyone thought they had power. . . . [Yet] these were only bluster. They were blinds to disguise the fact of men's real powerlessness in life. Men controlled the legislatures, but when it came down to it, they didn't control *themselves*. Men had failed to study their own minds sufficiently, and because of this failure they

were at the mercy of fleeting passions; men, much more than women, were moved by petty jealousies and the desire for petty revenges. . . . Women, in their adversity and superficial subservience, had been forced to learn about the workings of their brains and emotions.[5]

For the most part, the men in McDowell's Southern Gothics fall into one of two camps: incompetent and ineffectual, or crass and villainous. None of them come close to being protagonists. For example, *Blackwater*'s Oscar Caskey, the supposed patriarch of the most powerful family in town, is little more than a pawn to be picked up and moved around by first his mother, then his wife, and finally his daughter; the head of the McCray family in *The Elementals* is a duplicitous redneck who cheats on his wife and is well versed in the art of insurance fraud; Jim Larkin of *Cold Moon Over Babylon* is not only unable to avenge his sister's murder, but he proves helpless to prevent his own; and *The Amulet*'s Dean Howell is no more than a lobotomized zombie swaddled in bandages like a giant burned baby.

Candles Burning is almost entirely bereft of men, with the only male characters of any significance being Calley's father and brother—the former murdered within the first forty pages, while the latter disappears around page 125 and does not reappear until page 407, à la deus ex machina (the book is 423 pages long).

In the twenty-seven years I have spent reading and rereading McDowell's work, in particular his Southern Gothics, I have come to recognize four types of female characters that he liked to use. I call them the Ogress, the Matriarch, the Strange Child, and the Ditherer.

The Ogress is always an older woman who is cruel, manipulative, verbally abusive, selfish, vain, snobbish, arrogant, vindictive, and occasionally homicidal, even toward her own flesh and blood. Often the Ogress starts off as a genuinely affectionate mother, but somewhere along the line inherent narcissism turns her love into tyranny; imagine Livia from *I, Claudius* sipping a mint julep while fanning herself with a paper fan from the Methodist Church.

The Ogress in *Candles Burning* is Mamadee Carroll, an amalgamation of the venal, piggish Jo Howell (*The Amulet*) and the overly possessive Mary-Love (*Blackwater*). The resemblance between Mary-Love and Mamadee is especially pronounced, as both women are the widowed heads of prestigious families who steal custody of their firstborn grandchildren. They also share a cruelty toward their own family relations born out of a distrust and dislike of a younger woman's otherness. In Mary-Love's case, she is deeply suspicious of the enigmatic Elinor Dammert's designs on her son, while Mamadee views Calley as a freak of nature and an embarrassing reminder of her own modest origins. Mamadee's obsession with her grandson and shabby treatment of Calley reflects Mary-Love's lionization of her firstborn granddaughter and her dismissive behavior toward her second grandchild. The demises of the two women are also similar, in that

both are poisoned: Mary-Love by drinking tainted blackberry nectar, while Mamadee smears contaminated butter on her morning brioche.

In terms of sheer viciousness and unpleasantness, Mamadee is one of McDowell's finest villains, and is disposed of entirely too early. She is the kind of character you love to hate and can't wait to see get her comeuppance, but not offstage.

The second archetype is the Matriarch, usually a woman of childbearing years, or slightly older, who is levelheaded, highly manipulative, and extremely pragmatic. Not only is the Matriarch unafraid to give orders, but she expects them to be carried out to the letter, and she is willing to do whatever it takes—including murder—to protect those under her aegis. She is portrayed as ruthless, but not maliciously so, and as having her good points. More like a force of nature than a flesh-and-blood woman, she is definitely "deadlier than the male."

Candles Burning offers up a trio of Matriarchs: Merry Verlow, Mrs. Mank, and Cosima. Of these, Mrs. Mank bears the closest resemblance to McDowell's über-Matriarch, the otherworldly Elinor Dammert (*Blackwater*). Like Elinor, Mrs. Mank possesses supernatural abilities and is willing to manipulate and murder to achieve her ends. However, while Elinor killed her niece Grace's mother and her friend Queenie's husband in order to protect them both from continued abuse, Mrs. Mank's motivation for arranging the kidnapping and murder of Calley's adored father is completely self-serving.

The same can also be said for Merry Verlow, who secretly manipulates the Dakins by drugging Roberta Ann's foot cream and feeding Calley birth control in the guise of vitamins, as well as changing the color of the young girl's hair. Therefore Mrs. Mank's and Miz Verlow's secret agendas and dark intent also place them in the Ogress category. While Mrs. Mank is clearly supposed to replace Mamadee as the central villain, she is seldom center stage and doesn't make nearly the impression her social-climbing sister does.

Cosima Dexter, Calley's great-grandmother, is perhaps the true, hidden Matriarch of *Candles Burning*, much like Odessa Red, the Savage family maid, is the hidden Matriarch of *The Elementals*. Both Cosima and Odessa have supernatural psychic powers of some sort. While Cosima's are never revealed, Odessa has the ability to see what she refers to as "spirits." Both women also serve as tutors to a Strange Child. Odessa shows India McCray how to photograph the mysterious elementals that haunt the third house and later bequeaths the girl her vision, while Cosima speaks from beyond the grave in an attempt to instruct Calley on the proper use of her gifts.

The third stock female character in McDowell's world is the Strange Child. They are always young girls with some tie to the supernatural, and they are usually Matriarchs-in-training. It is clear that McDowell closely identified with

these Strange Children, as they no doubt represented his own sense of "otherness" growing up gay in the Deep South.

Calley, the Strange Child of *Burning Candles*, is easily recognizable as a mixture of India McCray (*The Elementals*), the precocious young girl who can photograph spirits (and who is also the template for Winona Ryder's character in *Beetlejuice*), and Frances Caskey (*Blackwater*), the shy young heiress who can shapeshift into something resembling Lovecraft's amphibian Deep Ones.

Of the two, Calley has the most in common with India, as she shares this character's extreme precocity. Whether this is because Calley was born listening to the voices of the dead or simply because the narrative is told from the viewpoint of a woman in her mid-fifties recalling what happened to her as a child is open to debate. Calley can hear the dead and mimic the voices of people she has never met, while India can see the dead and draw exact pictures of those who died long ago. But, most importantly, the biggest similarity between India and Calley is that both children are dyed-in-the-wool daddy's girls who are forced to deal with abusive, emotionally stunted mothers.

It should be noted that Calley bears a physical resemblance to another Strange Child found in *The Elementals*: the hideous monster baby that haunts the third beach house, easily the most disturbing image in the book. The horrifying apparition is described as not having "eyes to see with and no nostrils to smell, but its ears were very large,"[6] while Calley has ears so big that the adults who meet her automatically assume she is mentally defective.

The final female archetype is that of the Ditherer, which McDowell tended to use as a comedic foil. The Ditherer is usually shallow, ineffectual, and clumsy in her attempts at manipulating others. She is indecisive and prone to weakness (drinking, spending money, laziness, talking nonstop, and so on). She is portrayed as a pathetically silly woman with a tendency for being codependent and a deep fear of rocking the boat. Despite these very human flaws (or perhaps because of them), the Ditherer is often the most likable character in the book.

The Elementals' boozy Big Barbara; *Blackwater's* wheedling Queenie Strickland, spinsterly Sister, and vapid Lucille; and *Cold Moon Over Babylon's* timid Evelyn Larkin are all excellent examples of this character.

However, Ditherers rarely remain as such in McDowell's world but instead undergo a personal trauma that transforms them into either a Matriarch or an Ogress. In *The Amulet*, browbeaten Sarah Howell is finally shocked into taking action against her evil mother-in-law after witnessing the death of her best friend. In *Cold Moon Over Babylon*, poor, ineffectual Evelyn Larkin is murdered and comes back as a vengeful, waterborne zombie. Big Barbara's narrow escape from the title creatures in *The Elementals* enables her to kick the bottle and be a real mother to her widowed daughter during her pregnancy.

The multivolume, multigenerational saga *Blackwater* is chock-full of Ditherers, all of whom suffer some type of transformative trauma: Queenie Strickland's rape by her brutal husband turns her from crass and flighty chatterbox into a humble, levelheaded woman and valued helpmate; Lucille Strickland's violent assault at the hands of an escaped convict turns the shallow, self-obsessed flirt into a hardworking lesbian farmwife; and Sister's fall down the stairs and subsequent invalidism transforms her into a pale copy of her Ogress mother, Mary-Love.

In *Candles Burning*, there is a mirror-reverse transformation, as Ogress-in-training Roberta Ann Dakin deteriorates into a Ditherer after the disappearance of the ransom money and her subsequent arrival at Merrymeeting. Unfortunately, Roberta Ann's metamorphosis from a Maggie the Cat–style spitfire to a Blanche DuBois clone robbed the novel of one of its more compelling characters. Sometimes a book just needs a really good bitch to hold your interest.

At the time of his death, Michael McDowell had not published a book in over a decade. Before that, he had turned out more than twenty novels within eight years time, both under his own name and under several pseudonyms. The reason for this curtailment was simple enough. Like Faulkner before him, McDowell had been lured to Hollywood and the far more lucrative (if no less stressful) life of a professional screenwriter. He had left the Alabama of his youth long ago, relocating to Boston in the 1960s in order to attend college, as Calley did in *Candles Burning*.

Surely McDowell knew he was dying when he set out to write *Candles Burning*. He was diagnosed with HIV in 1987, and he watched his good friend and writing partner, Dennis Schuetz (with whom he had collaborated on a series of gay-themed murder mysteries under the pseudonym Nathan Aldyne), die of AIDS in 1989. He knew what the disease could do and what it inevitably held in store for him. That he set out to write a novel—and a lengthy one, at that—in what proved to be the final days of his life says a great deal about the man's passions, as does the fact that he chose to revisit, one last time, at least in fiction, the hot, lazy summer days unique to the Gulf Coast.[7]

In the end, it seems apropos, in a novel about how the dead speak from beyond the grave to those who have ears to hear, that the most memorable ghost on display belongs to the author.

Notes

1. "About Michael McDowell," *Fantastic Fiction*, www.fantasticfiction.co.uk/m/michael-mcdowell (accessed January 9, 2010).

2. Tabitha King, acknowledgments in *Candles Burning* (New York: Berkley Books, 2006).

3. "About Michael McDowell," *Fantastic Fiction*.

4. Tabitha King and Michael McDowell, *Candles Burning* (New York: Berkley Books, 2006), 169. Page numbers appear hereafter in parentheses in the text.

5. Michael McDowell, *Blackwater I: The Flood* (New York: Avon, 1983), 86.

6. Michael McDowell, *The Elementals* (New York: Avon, 1981), 225.

7. I can testify to the accuracy of McDowell's descriptions of the Gulf Coast during full summer. My father's side of the family came from Alabama, and every summer until Camille hit, we would spend a week in either Gulf Shores, Alabama, or Biloxi, Mississippi. After Camille, we summered in the Ozarks.

CHAPTER 8

Repositioning the Bodies

PETER ACKROYD'S *THE CASEBOOK OF VICTOR FRANKENSTEIN* AND OTHER MONSTROUS RETELLINGS

Judith Wilt

Looking at the best-seller list in the two decades around the turn of the third millennium, it would seem we are mainly in a vampire age: Dean Koontz's third *Frankenstein* series paperback, for instance, debuted atop the *New York Times* best-seller top twenty in August 2009, but there were seven vampire novels already there. We might attribute this to the highlighting of sensation and sexuality in the search for "knowing" conducted by *Dracula* and its children, but also to the fact that the most popular narratives in this genre are relatively simple first- or third-person narratives, and that the sexually alive vampire appeals to the continuing elements of Victorian Puritanism in the twenty-first century.[1]

The children of *Frankenstein* are very much with us, though. They are branded in those genetically modified "Frankenfoods" we uneasily rely upon and attenuated in the clones and cyborgs of popular novels, films, and TV programs, where supremely rational machines probe their own programming for those evidences of affect, impulse, invention, and autonomy that make, we want to believe, the human difference.[2]

Over the years the novel has had its share of casual rewrites and monstrous adaptations, offering homage to the novel's timeless themes. But Mary Shelley's *Frankenstein* also attracts writers who aspire to reproduce that novel's very particular blend of destabilized narrative, anguished experiencing, and dark prophecy. They dwell at that tipping point of biopolitical change, as the Enlightenment suffers the nightmares of reason and Romantic idealism tries to seize a new future from the ruins of empire. These writers aspire to take us to the novel and get us lost, to make us think our way out of the problems of epistemology and

ontology that took us and them to *Frankenstein* in the first place. These novels would have us explore with all the new knowledges that we can the old enigma for which *Frankenstein* is the key text, the enigma of the body and that peculiarly human aspect of the body's electricity we call consciousness.

I want to recommend three Frankenworks published within fifteen years of each other which succeed wonderfully in this attempt. Each of them implies questions for the others, and two will significantly help us understand the themes of Peter Ackroyd's *The Casebook of Victor Frankenstein* (2008). Theodore Roszak's *The Memoirs of Elizabeth Frankenstein* (1995) offers the perspective of Victor's sister-spouse on their lives as an expression of the intellectual battles of their times, recovering the lost voices not just of the feminine but of the maternal.[3] The author of the popular pedagogical sensation of the 1970s called *The Making of a Counter Culture*, Roszak saves the monster until almost the end of the novel, making the Great Mother the pivot of the tale in a crazy but fascinating revision of the figure of Caroline Beaufort. Another compelling revision comes from the poet and teacher Laurie Sheck, who turns to fiction in *A Monster's Notes* (2009); this epic doorstopper, fragmented and wide-ranging almost to the point of disintegration, centers on a brilliantly humanized monster with two centuries of self-educated knowledge, lonely for the writing "hands" of the Shelley circle which brought him to being out of their own traumas and then disappeared into haunting memory.[4] And in perhaps the most accessible and yet mysterious of these contemporary treatments, the biographer and novelist Peter Ackroyd offers *The Casebook of Victor Frankenstein* (2006), like *Memoirs* raising the issue of gender, like *Notes* promiscuously mixing the fictional and fiction-making characters of Mary Shelley's life and tale, and like all of his other seriously playful works presenting the real magic of humanity and its history.[5] Urgent and sly, outrageous and inventive, *The Casebook* makes its brilliantly dislocated way through a territory which includes real and invented characters, but the Victor who narrates the novel owes no debt to the past for his rage at the human condition of mortality.

The Memoirs of Elizabeth Frankenstein presents the mythic Mother, in all her antique and second-wave feminist glory, as the source of that embodied imaginative natural magic which stands over against the mathematical-mechanical model of the new science and the new post-Enlightenment vision of humanity.[6] Theodore Roszak's heroine is a noble child stolen by gypsies and educated in the women's magic there; adopted by the Frankenstein family, she observes the love but also the cultural chasm between the Voltairean Baron and the Rousseauvian Caroline Beaufort, who has looked beyond the forward-driving science and capitalist energy that is the obvious source of power of the line of Frankensteins to explore the hidden corners of their mansion in which more ancient magics have been practiced and preserved.

Mary Shelley's Victor noted that his parents believed in giving the children freedom to educate themselves from the resources of their libraries; Roszak's

Walton finds Elizabeth's diaries and letters, which emphasize her early immersion, and Victor's, guided by Caroline Beaufort, in an alchemical-hermetic tradition envisioned as profoundly matriarchal and sexual in its way of imagining power. Shrewd and humane, but as ambitious and aggressive in its way as Enlightenment reason is in its way, this philosophical tradition unites Western and Eastern lore, deeply body centered, in a fantastic knowledge project aimed at the opposite of analysis—fusion. In a hundred or so leave-little-to-the-imagination pages, *The Memoirs* fleshes out the original novel's semi-incestuous compulsion about Victor and Elizabeth's necessary marriage in scenes of Greek and Egyptian and Tantric practices of preejaculatory sexuality designed to enable the couple to move beyond sexuality into nirvana, and with them, the universe itself.

The Memoirs, then, like *The Making of a Counter Culture*, is both defending and mourning dualities. Caroline Beaufort's hope is to unify the "questing current" with "the river of remembrance"; the battle is between the Mother as "defender of ancient springs" from which humanity is born as "a dream of the slumbering earth," and the Father, setting out from his "Island of Enlightenment" to bring civilization to wild places.[7] The Mother cultivates a patient braiding of the two currents; the Father is full of "thrusting aspirations."[8] The image of rape represents for Roszak, and for the radical feminist and Gaia traditions he works in, the hyperpatriarchal twist in the natural order of the person, and the planet.

And so, in this novel, Victor's "fall" happens well before he departs for Ingolstadt and its laboratories; it is choreographed as rape. Young Victor's failure to achieve the discipline that stops short of consummation prefigures his "drive on" haste in all things; impatient and engorged, he short-circuits "the training" in a violent rape that alienates Elizabeth and sends him to the opposite extreme represented by his skeptic though gentle father, by the knowledge-hungry teachers of his college, and by the project that results in the masculine birth project. In elegant counterpoint, Roszak's Elizabeth moves through natural processes both tender and violent, including a "feral" period in the wilderness, and then returns home to interpret Victor's letters, and his silences, as evidence of his human self-alienation. She records curious visits from a new arrival in the neighborhood, a creature who calls himself "Adam," strong and articulate, disheveled and misshapen, resistant, needy and mysteriously obsessed, who admires her and warns her, but she is ready to meet her fate: "The air is full of electricity. . . . They are taking the world to pieces."[9]

Roszak's aggressively feminist reinvention is enclosed, like the original, in a narrative by the patriarchally conventional explorer Robert Walton. Roszak has fun with him, and so does the reader; he is even more shocked by the erotic illuminations of Elizabeth's fragmented memoir than by the driving ambition of Victor, which of course he shares.

Yet in transcribing Elizabeth's earth- and birth-centered reflections, her willing self-sacrifices, and her vision of a damaging modern separation between man and (feminine) nature, Walton absorbs and transmits Elizabeth's own uneasiness about the direction of history. In this way the protagonist, Elizabeth, remains in charge of her own story—Roszak's salute, across the decades, to Mary Shelley herself.

Laurie Sheck finds a more direct way to put Mary Shelley back into her story. *A Monster's Notes*, gathered, transcribed, and written by the immortal creature now camping out in a ruined building from post-9/11 Manhattan, is an epic rumination haunted by its own ontological status—"made," as creator, creature, and creation alike were made, of some ineffable combination of flesh, action, and words. Ferociously didactic and autodidactic from the beginning—whenever that was—the originator of the *Notes* leaves both a written manuscript and an "old" computer, the fruit of two centuries of reading, thinking, imagining, writing, and finally that virtual talking to oneself and the world made possible, mandatory, by the computer and the Internet. Computer and manuscript texts are addressed to the male hand who rocked his cradle, the laboratory table, but at the center of the text is Mary Shelley, whom Victor Frankenstein's creature discovered sitting by her mother's grave, yearning for the maternal voice, authenticating and socializing and teaching, which he then became to her in her girlhood, while afterward she became, inscrutably to him, the hand who wrote him into the world's culture as the wounded and wounding, tender and violent, interrogating and evading, mystery that he remains.

We never quite go back to the laboratory table; the narrative touches Victor only obliquely, if poignantly, in the sections of *Notes* which chronicle the Monster's continual self-housing in blank spaces/cold places, researching and remembering his own and others' Arctic explorations, the alternately elating and numbing journeys of twentieth-century astronauts, and the frozen rooms in Manhattan in which he lives. His creator never "comes" to him, in responsible parenthood or empathetic humanity; his condition after creation is one he recognized later in a book accidentally picked up, Melville's "Bartleby the Scrivener"—memory, identity, and desire all a blank page he prefers not to inscribe or enact. It is as if the tellable part of his tale doesn't begin until his re-awakening, and revisioning, by the woman, and women, of the Godwin-Shelley circle, where Romantic radicalism enabled, and enforced, the extremities of understanding about the human condition.[10]

A section is devoted to imaginary letters (based on scholarship enabled by the wide publication of journals and diaries from and about Mary Shelley's parents, Mary Wollstonecraft and William Godwin, and about Mary, Percy, and all their complex legitimate and illegitimate siblings and offspring) between Claire

Claremont, her stepsister by her father's second wife, and Fanny Imlay, her half sister by her mother's lover. Hidden or half-claimed children litter the lives of the Shelley circle in those years, as well as maternal death or despair; *Notes* puts these at the heart of the crises about identity and abandonment that are the engines of *Frankenstein*. As "mind" cries out its tale of extremity, the hand seeks an expressive task, and the memory of the creature fixes on the writing hand of Claire Claremont, seeking to order experience to the dead Fanny, to the distant and guarded Mary.

As the novel develops, the Monster reenters "his own" story, again through a writing hand that leads/encompasses his own, through a long imaginary correspondence between Victor Frankenstein's literary friend Henry Clerval, translating and reflecting on the eighteenth-century Chinese classic novel *The Dream of the Red Chamber*, and the "friend" living in the Italian Alps who could, or perhaps should, be the Victor Frankenstein who simply pursued medicine, married, and lived happily with his children and his work.

The invented Monster's invented relationships fade; "Then Claire came to me, and Clerval. . . . Or was it I who went to them?" he muses, knowing that at some level he needed to invent the writing relationships that make up the first two-thirds of the novel, because they made meaning for the unbearably blank page of his identity, which he confronts more directly in the last third.[11] "Here in a city of neon and digital billboards, news zippers, vibrating pixels . . . vast terrain of glass and steel and blasted towers," he finally works his way out of his "Bartleby" trance, to engage and reproduce the mind of the young and then slowly aging Mary Shelley.[12] Remembering/inventing her as she invented him, he creates a poignant pas de deux that uncovers Mary's hidden motive for the fictional murders and traumas of her novel.

Frankenstein encoded the fundamental trauma of awareness itself: whether awakened in a flash of lightning on a laboratory table or in the educative fires of childhood reading and experience, "thought was a violent thing to me, in me," the Monster's Mary writes; "I still feel this, that thinking is a violent act."[13] And again, "I felt . . . the need to hurt him, make him pay. . . . But what had he murdered?—The deluded place in me that thought there could be answers, clear meanings in the world? Or the place that believed abandonment, fear, and shame could be eluded? Or the place that hoped I might one day hear my mother's voice?"[14] In the Monster's imagination and on the page of *A Monster's Notes*, the hand of Mary Shelley, probing her own history, revealing his, writes its way toward its end, scoring through sentences, abandoning words, and then thought. Muteness engulfs the writing Monster, too, but his final recorded bodily sensation, before abandoning communication, if not thought itself, returns us to ourselves: "I hear pages turning."[15] Somebody is still reading. Last

page. Somebody, perforce, has stopped reading. But the violence of thinking, of course, continues.

The violence of thinking, and the desperation that attends it, is the continuing subject of the novelist, critic, and biographer Peter Ackroyd, who has been working a Gothic seam in both material and prose style during a writing career of more than thirty years. His biography of Dickens (1990) is also a novel and a work of criticism; his esteemed novel *Hawksmoor* (1985) narrates itself in multiple voices and the English of the twentieth and the seventeenth centuries; and the bulk of his work in fiction seems to have been a preparation or condition for two massive English meditations—*London: A Biography* (2000) and *Thames: Sacred River* (2007)—two entities, or presences, whose history lies both above and below ground, reason, and awareness. As the first of *Hawksmoor*'s two Hawksmoors says, "The Mind in Infancy, like the Body in embryo, receives impressions that cannot be removed and it was as a meer Boy that I was placed in the extremity of the Human State."[16] Continuing the mindfulness on beginnings, the twentieth-century owner of *The House of Doctor Dee* reasons, "This was some monstrous fantasy . . . to create an artificial life within a tube of glass."[17] Ironically, this character—Ackroyd's Matthew Palmer—has in fact been inhabiting the house in which the famed mathematician and alchemist had experimented with creating new life, "the homunculus," and, more, he is at some level the dwelling of the spirit of John Dee, and his London contains both material and spirit passages to the pre-Christian London which whispers all around Ackroyd's twenty-first-century biographies of the living city and its sacred river.

No wonder then that Ackroyd's first twenty-first-century novel is *The Casebook of Victor Frankenstein*, and that he moves the laboratory of mystic and material creation and destruction from Mary Shelley's Switzerland to the London that Ackroyd has made his own, where music and mathematics, according to the ancient masters in *Doctor Dee*, are the hermetic "signatures" of the spirit everywhere at work, and the city and the body are the same; "this city is formed within the spiritual body of man."[18]

Two questions are paramount for the reader taking up a new treatment of *Frankenstein*: what desires and concepts are taking body in the Monster? And what will be the upshot of the mutual pursuit of creator and creature, the human and his idea/l? The questions proceed from Mary Shelley's original, with its interlocking parables of creation and education, of thinking isolation and the blessing/curse of community, or the dark side of community which Ackroyd will call "aggregation." To the echoes of the original parables in *Frankenstein*, Ackroyd adds two more, interlocking parables of the city, and of art.

Like Sheck, Ackroyd sets his novel in a realm which includes the lives of the Shelley circle as well as their inventions, and goes one step further, exploring

embodiment itself. Shelley's Victor was emphatically a product of continental culture, and his creature self-educated by reading Goethe; Ackroyd's Victor has bullied his Swiss father into allowing him to train in England, "a place of practical learning,"[19] where he meets Percy Shelley at Oxford and then joins the Shelley circle in the much more dynamic and dangerous education enforced by the city of London itself, a place of no body, and of every body. "We have repealed habeas corpus," Ackroyd's radical "Bysshe" Shelley tells his new friend early in the novel; he is correcting the Switzer's naive assumption that England is a land of political freedoms, but the metafictional possibilities inherent in the legal phrase and its question are multiple, and Ackroyd means to exploit all of them.[20]

Have we a body? Somebody? Manybody? A repressive English government cracking down in fear of the spread of French revolutionary ideas now claims it doesn't need a body—material evidence of a crime—to throw a body in jail. A scientist needs bodies to explore for the invisible but surely material "fluid" which animates life and manifests as lightning, but it is knowledge, not the material or even the (re)animated body, that "matters." A natural philosopher-poet, a dreamer, a madman, "casts off the vesture of the body, and in their pursuits becomes pure spirit," says the idealist Bysshe, but "pursuits" work both ways: elated after hearing the scientist Humphrey Davy lecture on the galvanic properties of electricity, Victor rushes from the room "as if fleeing from someone, or something, but the nature of my pursuer was not known to me. . . . Someone else was running beside me"; "someone was lying beside me."[21] Two chapters later, the cautious demonstrations at university and his own experiments on dog and cat corpses being unsatisfying, Victor is making plans to overcome the vexatious "scarcity of corpses" by illegal transactions with the grave-robbing Resurrection men who can help him turn his someone or something into . . . some body.[22]

Percy Shelley is the equivocal exemplar for two "ordinary" ways of making a body. Shelley is a lover and eventually a father, and also a perfectabilitarian. He is creating a "new woman" by essentially buying and then tutoring to his specifications a female body which will bear his child and become his wife, the teenaged sister of a radical shoemaker named Harriet Westlake. It is a project exactly comparable, he says himself, to Victor's work on animating bodies through "voltaic plates" that capture and target electrical "fluid."[23] Shelley's theory of the improved human species relies on the Greek recognition that suffering is essential not just to the production of the new, but to the human condition itself; his romantic engagement with the path to joy through pain invokes Keats's "Ode on Melancholy" and in Ackroyd's hands is a gesture toward the original novel's curious competition between Victor and his creature as to who can suffer the most. And which of them can consider the root cause of suffering—the violence of thinking?

Both Shelley's and Ackroyd's Victor were originally emotionally formed by the confluence of Alpine heights and storms and take from these early impressions that license to mental gigantism and spiritual inebriation and longing for self-dissolution that form the Monster. But Ackroyd's Victor and his creature acquire an extra dimension of savage potency from the "aggregated" maelstrom and lodestone of their mutual (re)birth in the great city. "No Alpine storm . . . can give the least idea of the roar of the city," Victor rhapsodizes, suggestively; "what power human lives have in the aggregate! To me the city resembled some vast electric machine . . . sending its current down every alley and lane. . . . London seemed ungovernable, obeying laws mysterious to itself, like some dim phantasm, stalking through the world."[24] Prowling dazed and engrossed through the worst slums, "I had not known that such monstrousness, such abstract horror, could exist in any Christian country. How had this fetid body grown?"[25] Caught up in the crowd overflowing the seats of a theater, he feels terror, and inspiration; in its "animation," the crowd "resembled some restless creature in search of prey. Could many lives make up one life?"[26]

This is the mob, the species, the swelling of mass man in occult purposefulness, assessed as political revolution, calculated in the new political economy of Malthus and Ricardo, soon to be theorized by Darwin and Marx. Is manybody organic? Mechanical? Human? The image of electricity combines these two, satisfying with its beauty and sublimity both benign desires for a human unity, saturating matter with mind moving toward progress, and the darker desires associated with dissolution and fatality—devolution.

But the power of the aggregate is also the artistic experience. Texts multiplying in receiving minds, drawing bodies across borders of materiality, of time and space, of idea and action. Theater scenes in *The Casebook* reinforce the permeability of bodies and minds: one actor becomes two; the audience becomes one. The imagination, another form of electricity, passes through matter and shapes it. Ackroyd's Victor plays cards in London with a teenaged surgeon's apprentice named Jack Keat, who in a parallel universe as John Keats wrote that the imagination, like Milton's Adam, need only dream an Eve to have it embodied. Who killed John Keats? asked Percy Shelley's "Adonais" in that same universe. The answer is an unresponsive aggregate of readers. In a sly melding of universes, Ackroyd's Jack Keat, stricken by poverty and consumption, sells his dying body for coin to support his sister and is resurrected, forcibly, on Victor Frankenstein's laboratory table. Rebuffed by its startled creator, the body displays its preternatural strength and its own horror and then rushes to the sacred Thames and flings itself in: this is the origin of "body." Staggered by his own presumption, Victor reels from his Limehouse laboratory into the streets, a different kind of sacred river, "joining without choice or thought the steady stream of people."[27] This was the origin of thought, and choice.

As the novel moves to its second half, it engages the second question readers want to ask of any version of *Frankenstein*; what is the consciousness of the new creature like—fixed or flexible, natural or made, capable of sublimity, depravity, humanity? And what will these two minds be to each other—objects of inquiry, of passion, of recognition? Complementary as fusion, or fission? Some fragments of answers Ackroyd inherits from the original and uses. Awareness is indeed natural; the body's own creation as the city is the river's. Consciousness is innately expressive, exploratory, inventive.

But above all, consciousness is desperation; it is terrified equally and alternately of nonbeing and of being. Seeking an equilibrium of these terrors, consciousness is an outlaw and an actor. When Victor saw an actor playing the great Gothic antihero Melmoth the Wanderer, he marveled that a man could be two—his civilized, controlling, actor's self, and "the desperate man."[28] And as with Mary Shelley's creator and creature, Ackroyd's Victor and the new Jack Keat, in their passionate encounters and debates, each play both of these parts.

But what is the root of the anxiety of mindfulness? the reader always asks. Is it bad parenting by divine or human maker, an initial mysterious neglect or rejection that might, in a perfectible world, be healed by a substitute spouse/companion/institution? Shelley's plot, and those of all three novels treated here, considers this, but the matter seems deeper. Is it masculine birth envy, the social ills of hierarchy, ownership, property? Is it curiosity, ambition? These are unsatisfactory approximations of the answer, it seems.

In *The Casebook of Victor Frankenstein*, as in the original, the wrestling of creature and creator with the desperation of human consciousness begets a gravity or maelstrom which pulls other people in, to their wonderment, to their deaths. Onlookers marvel, but those closest die, especially women. *The Casebook* offers a final death that figures Ackroyd's special contribution to the story. Fred, a cockney street kid with an aggregate family, a deep knowledge of London's hidden places and persons, and the sidekick sweetness of Dickens's Sam Weller, has been Victor's servant and in some ways guide, and is mysteriously missing, possibly murdered, by Jack Keat or even by Victor himself. In many ways Fred is London itself, the coin obverse of its monstrousness, the counterpart and contrary of Jack Keat. The sweetness perhaps can die or disappear; the monstrousness, never.

Monstrous London is an occult fatality both unified and divided in the novel's symbolic structure as river and city. The reanimated creature travels by river and makes his home on the estuary. He challenges Victor to take his urban/maker's responsibility—"This [laboratory table] was my cradle . . . or will you pretend that the river gave me birth?"[29] If his creator revives the dead on land, the creature will kill them in the water, drowning his substitute victims and sending Victor the prophetic dream of his own drowning. "Man had created London. Man had not created the estuary. I was seized with a great fear that the

land had just emerged from the sea, and that the incoming water was about to overwhelm me. . . . Then I found myself walking down a street in London . . . of black stone. . . . The stone began to shriek . . . in agony, in fear, in consternation."[30]

If the creature's first expressed fear was that he will be "returned to that state of non-being from which [he] had come," it can only be assuaged by the "recognition" of another consciousness.[31] Indeed, as in the original, the creature's desire goes in this direction. The possibility of a solacing recognition, of a "mate" for the new consciousness, is the lynchpin of the original. And when in Shelley's novel Victor promises to make a mate but later tears it to pieces before his creature's spying eyes, the more wretched one withdraws "with a howl of devilish despair and revenge."[32] But Ackroyd's novel will not make such promises. In *The Casebook*, Victor's immediate refusal of the creature's request and the creature's immediate acceptance put the spotlight on the darker desperation. Being is more insufferable than nonbeing and has no assuagement at all. The ultimate wish is for "Death. Forgetting. Oblivion, and darkness."[33] Victor's assent to this, his perfection of a "reversal" process to the electric animation, offers the last turn of the screw of agony. The process worked on an ape but not on the reanimated consciousness of Jack Keat: maker and creature are both condemned to sentience. Both of them remain "the desperate man."

At this stalemate point in the original, Victor goes to the police and finds himself thrown into a madhouse for his story, later to be released and submitted to the mutual pursuit which culminates in his Arctic death and the creature's enigmatic disappearance on a quest to destroy his body, in the uncertain hope that it will destroy his consciousness. At the same point in Ackroyd's novel, with only one more page to go, Ackroyd plays his last trick. Shelley's friend Dr. Polidori enters the laboratory, confronting the two desperate creatures, and tells Victor he sees only one body, one consciousness.

Habeas corpus? Was there all along in fact no creature at all, only a desperate scientist who like all men in the grip of an idea had murdered his unity to create two, had self-split a phantasm of his own consciousness in order to explore the despair of life?

Or, reading between the lines, might *The Casebook* signify a conspiracy between the occult rationalist Polidori and the physician at the Hoxton Mental Asylum for Incurables, who we find on the last page has transcribed the story of his patient, two doctors trying to reduce the unthinkable possibility and danger of Victor's actual history to the ravings of a madman? Or, given that the asylum doctor signs himself Frederick Newman, might the reporter of this story be the London cockney servant Fred, returned a new man, obscuring the matter still further?

Or maybe *The Casebook* is itself pure text, a monster aggregated from parts of both Shelleys, and Byron and Keats and Dostoevsky and Conrad, and

Ackroyd's own pre-texts about mystical London? Early in the novel, before he found a body, Victor's own hand, experimentally self-electrified, suddenly started writing in an unknown handwriting John Keats's private letter from 1817 authorizing negative capability to the man of imagination, prescribing the only possible solution to painful awareness, which is to live life "suspended among uncertainties, mysteries, doubts, without any recourse to fact or reason."[34] Hauntingly, *The Casebook*'s Mary Shelley catches a glimpse of the monster's face "crumpled, creased rather, like a sheet of paper hastily thrown away."[35] Jack Keat's body travels to its laboratory/cradle with its hand trailing in the water; John Keats wanted his epitaph to read, "Here lies one whose name was writ in water."[36]

Is Ackroyd the author in any better control of his cascading ideas and ghost characters than his Victor Frankenstein, whose contradictory testimony we have here? No, not much better. But his Keatsian license to maneuver his darker materials around the edge of fact and reason, clarity and probability, still beckons and holds, repositioning the reader inside this inherited and invented workshop of filthy creation, rewriting the journey of desperate consciousness with the one fact we at bottom want to be assured of, that "we wandered out, the creature and I, into the world, where we were taken up by the watchmen."[37]

Notes

1. I worked a little with the similarities between *Frankenstein* and *Dracula* in my *Ghosts of the Gothic: Austen, Eliot and Lawrence* (Princeton, NJ: Princeton University Press, 1980), and so have many others. But the indispensable treatment of this is Franco Moretti's historical-cultural argument that Mary Shelley's monster represented the industrialized worker just coming into critical consciousness at the beginning of the nineteenth century, while Bram Stoker's Count Dracula played to the equivocal end-of-century English craving for an aristocracy which the nation was unseating in politics and resituating in culture, in *Signs Taken for Wonders: Essays in the Sociology of Literary Form* (New York: Verso, 1988).

2. Mary Shelley's novel has always garnered attention from students of Gothic romance and science fiction; it became a staple of the mainstream literary (and teaching) canon at least as early as George Levine's influential *The Realistic Imagination: English Fiction from Frankenstein to Lady Chatterley* (Chicago: University of Chicago Press, 1981).

3. Theodore Roszak, *The Memoirs of Elizabeth Frankenstein* (New York: Random House, 1995); I am using the Bantam paperback published a year later.

4. Laurie Sheck, *A Monster's Notes* (New York: Knopf, 2009).

5. Peter Ackroyd, *The Casebook of Victor Frankenstein* (London: Chatto & Windus, 2008).

6. Mary Shelley's work and life, especially as figured in *Frankenstein* and amplified in her journals, became central to feminist literary analysis in the 1970s, starting with Ellen Moers's *Literary Women* (New York: Doubleday, 1976) and Sandra Gilbert and Susan

Gubar's *The Madwomen in the Attic* (New Haven, CT: Yale University Press, 1979), and a little later, Kate Ellis's *The Contested Castle* (Chicago: University of Illinois Press, 1989).

7. Roszak, *Memoirs*, 122.

8. Roszak, *Memoirs*, 121.

9. Roszak, *Memoirs*, 416.

10. The starting place for a study of the network of relationships and ideas which produced Mary Shelley and her novel is probably Anne K. Mellor's *Mary Shelley: Her Life, Her Fiction, Her Monsters* (New York: Methuen, 1988). Interest continues unabated in such recent texts as Janet Todd's *Death and the Maidens: Fanny Wollstonecraft and the Shelley Circle* (Berkeley, CA: Counterpoint, 2007) and Julie Ann Carlson's *England's First Family of Writers: Mary Wollstonecraft, William Godwin, Mary Shelley* (Baltimore, MD: Johns Hopkins University Press, 2007).

11. Sheck, *A Monster's Notes*, 316.

12. Sheck, *A Monster's Notes*, 353.

13. Sheck, *A Monster's Notes*, 358.

14. Sheck, *A Monster's Notes*, 451.

15. Sheck, *A Monster's Notes*, 519.

16. Peter Ackroyd, *Hawksmoor* (New York: Harper & Row, 1985), 14.

17. Peter Ackroyd, *The House of Doctor Dee* (London: Hamish Hamilton, 1993), 124.

18. Ackroyd, *The House of Doctor Dee*, 273.

19. Ackroyd, *Casebook*, 2.

20. Ackroyd, *Casebook*, 4.

21. Ackroyd, *Casebook*, 6, 23, 30.

22. Ackroyd, *Casebook*, 57.

23. Ackroyd, *Casebook*, 27.

24. Ackroyd, *Casebook*, 12.

25. Ackroyd, *Casebook*, 15.

26. Ackroyd, *Casebook*, 32. Films to the contrary notwithstanding, there are no crowd scenes in *Frankenstein*. Studies of "the crowd" in literature abound, though, and a good companion to Ackroyd's theorizing about "the aggregate" would be John Plotz's treatment of early nineteenth-century literature in *The Crowd: British Literature and Public Politics* (Berkeley: University of California Press, 2000).

27. Ackroyd, *Casebook*, 155.

28. Ackroyd, *Casebook*, 33.

29. Ackroyd, *Casebook*, 164.

30. Ackroyd, *Casebook*, 233.

31. Ackroyd, *Casebook*, 167.

32. Judith Wilt, ed., *Making Humans:* Frankenstein *and* The Island of Dr. Moreau (New York: Houghton Mifflin/New Riverside, 2003), 131.

33. Ackroyd, *Casebook*, 293.

34. Ackroyd, *Casebook*, 126.

35. Ackroyd, *Casebook*, 198.

36. See Stephen Coote, *John Keats: A Life* (London: Hodder & Stoughton, 1995), 325.

37. Ackroyd, *Casebook*, 296.

CHAPTER 9

Marvels and Horrors

TERRY DOWLING'S *CLOWNS AT MIDNIGHT*

Leigh Blackmore

Long before the existence of Australia was ever confirmed by explorers and cartographers, it had already been imagined as a grotesque space, a land peopled by monsters. The idea of its existence was disputed, was even heretical for a time, and with the advent of the transportation of convicts its darkness seemed confirmed. The Antipodes was a world of reversals, the dark subconscious of Britain. It was, for all intents and purposes, Gothic *par excellence*, the dungeon of the world. It is perhaps for this reason that the Gothic as a mode has been a consistent presence in Australia since European settlement.

—Gerry Turcotte, "Australian Gothic"[1]

Gothic themes encompass such diverse elements as werewolfery and vampirism, ghosts and doppelgängers, transgenerational curses, spontaneous combustion, the evil eye, and even science fiction. Characteristics of Gothic literature include an appreciation of the joys of extreme emotion, the thrills of fearfulness and awe inherent in the sublime, and a quest for atmosphere, which may often include mysterious, fantastic, and superstitious rituals. Early examples of the mode evince a fascination with persecuted heroines and with architecture, often remote, crumbling, and medievally gloomy.

Conger identifies Gothic's "cluster of now-familiar macabre themes: crime and punishment, death and dying, terror, and the supernatural."[2] He also points out that Gothic romance continues to serve

"this invaluable compensatory function, somewhat different from age to age, but persistent in its attention to anything assumed to be noncivilized or taboo, for example, necrophilia, incest, domestic violence, or murder."[3] Gothic texts are useful for negotiating a sense of expectation or disappointment about what one might find in terra incognita, and this is particularly relevant to what I will term "Australian Gothic."

There is a long history in Australian writing of material that draws on Gothic tropes, though naturally this writing reflects conditions that are transplanted from those of the UK and Continental Europe where the classic Gothics emerged in the late eighteenth century. The idea of Australia as a colonial outpost of the UK naturally figures largely in Australian fiction of the nineteenth century, and during this period the demonization of the Australian bush and desert, which are largely seen as hostile, unforgiving environments, informs much of the fiction that might be cited as examples of "Australian Gothic."

Turcotte highlights Gothic aspects in the work of such writers as Marcus Clarke, Barbara Baynton, and Henry Lawson in the nineteenth century, and in the twentieth century in the work of writers including Christina Stead, Hal Porter, Kenneth Cook, Joan Lindsay, Thomas Keneally, Frank Moorhouse, Peter Carey, Louis Nowra, Barbara Hanrahan, Kate Grenville, Janette Turner Hospital, Gabrielle Lord, and Elizabeth Jolley. Anthologists James Doig, Ken Gelder, and Rachel Weaver have now assembled valuable compilations of early writings that can well be termed "Australian Gothic."

Other modern novelists such as Rodney Hall and Andrew McGahan have certainly contributed to what is now a well-established tradition of Australian Gothic writing. A course at Sydney University examines the Gothic mode in Australian literature and film from the nineteenth century to the present, taking in such issues as "weird melancholy," ghosts, bunyips, badlands, and postcolonial (dis)enchantment.

Perhaps the modern horror genre may be regarded as a mere branch of Gothic fiction as a whole, or at least as the most recent development of it. It is in this light that I will consider Terry Dowling's *Clowns at Midnight*, an existential horror novel that draws extensively (though not exclusively) on Gothic tropes for its effects. Terry Dowling is an acclaimed Australian writer whose work in the late years of the twentieth century initially appeared to be primarily science fiction and speculative literature. But interspersed among his short stories were always tales of dark fantasy and horror, and as he has turned more and more to this form, the balance of his work has become clearer, with horror and ghost stories forming at least half of his output to date. He has won as many awards for his horror fiction as for his science fiction, the most relevant collections here being *An Intimate Knowledge of the Night* (Aphelion, 1995), *Blackwater Days* (Eidolon, 2000), and *Basic Black: Tales of Appropriate Fear* (Cemetery Dance,

2006), which won the International Horror Guild Award in 2006 for best single author collection. *Amberjack: Tales of Fear and Wonder* (Subterranean Press, 2010) will also contain horror tales by Dowling.

Dowling's disquieting novel *Clowns at Midnight*, written for his 2006 Ph.D. and first excerpted in *Exotic Gothic 2: New Tales of Taboo* (Ash-Tree Press, 2008), concerns family secrets and ancient rituals in present-day Australia; it features a very special kind of clown. *Clowns at Midnight* takes its place as one of the most imaginative examples of modern Australian Gothic, expanding the boundaries of what Gothic means in the twenty-first century. There is no doubt that Dowling's novel partakes in a discourse "predicated on the darkness and anxiety specific to Australian experience."[4]

The protagonist of this four-part novel is David Leeton, who, like Dowling, is from Sydney. David is a coulrophobe; that is, he suffers from a paralyzing fear of clowns and their images, not only in film, art, and literature, but in everyday life. He also suffers from another condition, as we will learn.

In part 1, we find David staying at Starbreak Fell, a property near Casino in rural New South Wales that he is minding for his friends Beth and John Rankin. Dowling signposts the Australianness of the setting by frequent mentions of southerly winds, cicadas, and local plants and trees. Separated from his former girlfriend Julia for three months now, David is at work on a novel titled *The Riddling Tree* and is also writing lyrics for a band, Shock Salamander. He is attempting to cope with his condition, which tests him to the limit, via tolerance tests (abbreviated *TTs*), which have been provided by Jack, his psychiatrist. These take the form of images of clowns faces, masks, and statues, all of which terrify him, but to which he is drawn in order to understand and overcome his condition.

Clowns are a recurrent motif in Gothic and horror literature. In the *Cambridge Companion to Gothic Fiction*, it is pointed out that Honoré de Balzac, in a preface later omitted from *Le Peau de Chagrin* (1831), describes Gothic as a literature *sanguinolent* and *bouffon* ("bloody" and "clownlike").[5] *The Castle Spectre* is a 1797 Gothic dramatic romance in five acts by Matthew "Monk" Lewis that introduced the clown, Motley, as a privileged commentator figure,[6] though this use of the clown was more akin to the wise fool or jester, such as Feste in Shakespeare's *Twelfth Night*. It seems that evil clowns as a horror trope are primarily a modern phenomenon, with examples such as the monstrous Pennywise in Stephen King's *It* or the menacing ritualistic clowns disturbing Thomas Ligotti's *The Nightmare Factory* (along with mannequins, puppets, and harlequins) springing readily to mind.

As David explores the forested hilltop behind the house, he comes upon a mysterious granite tower in the bush on the neighbors' property, with a wooden cross close by, something he calls "Scarecrow Cross." That Dowling is con-

sciously utilizing Gothic tropes is hinted by David's declaring that the tower has "a keyhole. A lovely Gothic touch and so tantalising."[7] Hearing a fluting wail, he explores further and discovers three odd structures—"bottle trees"—on the slope beyond the forest. His clown fear is triggered. Wondering about his new neighbors, he reflects, "I knew only too well how far we ended up from where we started, how different our lives became from what we intended" (10), a statement that will be applicable to him by the novel's end.

David then receives an unexpected dinner invitation from these neighbors, the Risis, initiating a sequence of events that will echo throughout the narrative. When he next performs a clown image self-test on the computer—one of the TTs prescribed by his psychiatrist—we learn more about his condition: that he is also afraid of masks, dolls, painted figures, and statues, and is a full-blown counterphobe as well, someone drawn to the very thing feared. Hauntingly, an extra image that should not be there appears amid the TT images, a completely black page, which triggers another episode of clown fear. This intrusive rogue image is never entirely explained, but it is an apt symbol for the haunting blackness that threatens to overwhelm him, and it ties naturally to all the dark fears that come up for him (and the reader) during the novel.

David naturally suspects that his psychiatrist planted the TT surprise, but during their next phone call, neither of them mentions it. David then decides to build his own bottle tree—his response to "unwanted mystery" (23). When he has done this, he sets off for the Risi home, where his hosts Carlo and Raina Risi have brought together for a dinner party twenty or so guests, one of whom, Gemma Ewins, David finds himself attracted to. At the insistence of his hosts, he learns he must perform a memorization of his fellow guests' names—a clue to their focus on ritualized activity. Carlo then shows David a hedge maze on his property. Just as in Gothic romances where a heroine finds herself returning to a maze or labyrinth (from traditional American romantics like Nathaniel Hawthorne, in "Rappaccini's Daughter," to contemporary Australian romantics like Kate Morton, in *The Forgotten Garden*), Dowling uses them repeatedly, from the story "The Maze Man" (now optioned for filming) to "Nights at Totem Rule" (from his *Tom Rynosseros* cycle of stories). I have written elsewhere about the Jungian significance of this topos.[8]

Though David assumes Carlo and his family are Italian, it happens they are in fact Sardinian. The locale of Sardinia as a background to the novel's events is significant. Though none of the events take place there, the myths and customs the Risis have brought with them from their Mediterranean home have an unfamiliar quality that intrigues David and lures him deeply into their lives. Sardinia, according to D. H. Lawrence (as quoted by Carlo Risi to our protagonist) is "outside the circuit of civilisation" (32), a hint that introduces a note of anxiety to the narrative.

When David asks about the tower, Carlo tells him it's an old silo that he remembers going into as a boy. Then, to David's embarrassment and anger, Carlo tells the other guests about David's clown fear.

David feels exposed, embarrassed, and angry. After the other guests have gone, Gemma with them, Carlo explains that a grinning terracotta face mask usually sits above their fireplace. The Rankins have told the Risis about his condition, and the mask was removed for the evening out of consideration. David now wants to see it, as a tolerance test. It is difficult for him, and we begin to see how clown fear affects him:

> Then he hefted the grinning mask and carefully restored it to its place. It immediately commanded the room with its mad grin and unbridled delight. . . . The mask presided over everything: the dark chambers of its eyes surveying all that had happened in this golden heart of the Risi household. There was no escaping it. I stood no chance. . . . The grin was everything. The manic gaze; the eyes filled with night. The power was incredible. (39)

We see here how easily our narrator might slip into panic or actual madness.

Returning home, David finds his bottle tree smashed, and the original ones nearer to the forest destroyed as well. He suspects some sort of conspiracy may be afoot, though he is reassured when Carlo phones to ask if he reached home safely. We then learn that, at David's own request, Beth Rankin left out one thing to test him (Mary Renault's novel *The Mask of Apollo*, with an image of a mask on its cover), but everything else that might trigger his fears has been stowed away in an unused spare bedroom. Confronting his fears, David rechecks the disks and images.

Events accumulate with increasingly sinister overtones. When David goes to clean up the bottle tree glass the next day, he finds that all traces of them on the Risi property have gone.

The uncertainty created by Dowling as to his protagonist's state of mind is broadly hinted at when David works on his writing and does the TT's again. During this exercise, David himself is manically grinning, foreshadowing doubts later in the novel as to whether he may himself be mad. He then discovers that at image 30 on disk 5 another intruder image has surfaced, a hieroglyph shape he does not recognize.

Throughout these happenings, Dowling provides much fascinating cultural material regarding the role of masks in society, with David particularly intrigued by the role of the "maschera" in the Commedia dell'Arte. Despite his condition, he even wants to celebrate their role by writing about them in an article that Carlo expresses interest in reading.

Hoping to meet Gemma again, David leaves a draft of the article in the Risi mailbox on his way into the township of Kyogle. When he encounters Gemma by chance in a local pub, he is hurt when she doesn't talk to him. He is lonely and needs redemption. He then discovers a sprig of gumnuts in both the Risi mailbox and his own—another token of something (but what?) that adds to his feelings of persecution and paranoia. Investigating the storeroom at Starbreak Fell, he is simultaneously repelled and attracted by the many shrouded shapes it contains and learns that a mannequin is included among them. In his eyes, this is a "domesticised Iron Maiden," a "quadruple amputee mockery" (65)—images evoking classical Gothic tropes.

He finally uncovers this demon mannequin (which he has long called "Madame Sew") and closes the door on it, but he later wakes up terrified of it being so close at hand. The next morning, even as he makes arrangements for his neighbor Len Catley to take care of the mannequin, he seems on the verge of a breakdown: "I was crazy, crazy, grinning . . ." (72). Returning to Starbreak Fell after dropping the mannequin off, he decides to revisit the tower. This time the "cross" has a flower garland draped across it, and more gumnuts. Are these more signs calculated to tip him into his own private madness? He then encounters a group of neighborhood women from the dinner party pushing each other on a swing. Gemma is among them. In sections like this, the novel recalls Thomas Tryon's classic rural Gothic *Harvest Home*, with its closely guarded local traditions and luring in of an outsider. David joins the women in a picnic, drinks mead, and falls asleep.

Afterward, waking alone, he tries the tower door again, finding it still locked. Relentless curiosity drives him to do a Net search on Sardinia, from which he learns that these watchtowers are called "nuraghi." As he immerses himself in Sardinian history, he hears weird night cries echoing outside—cries that sound like "Yakkos"—accompanied by the sound of bells. Again his clown mania is activated.

Part 2 opens as David goes shopping in the nearby township of Casino, wondering if the night sounds were merely auditory hallucinations. Encountering Connie Lambert, the librarian from the Risi dinner party, he requests contact details for Gemma, but Connie cannot recall them. Driving to the Risis' through a storm, David encounters Gemma sitting in an old swing and gives her a lift into Kyogle. This time she shows interest in him, so he uses the opportunity to divulge some of his life story before returning home.

David then arranges to visit Carlo Risi to photograph the terracotta mask, and while being shown the maze again he learns that the dinner with the neighbors had been on January 6—Twelfth Night—the original date of Christmas. They discuss the Etruscans and the predominance in those times of Goddess

worship and the importance of the Earth Mother. This, Carlo asserts, is anamnesis—lost knowledge.

While later writing at the kitchen table, David sees a misshapen dark form standing at the edge of the forest and becomes terrified. Could it be another hallucination? But then the figure moves: "The grotesque form simply swung about in a quick flurry of black, tan and brassy glints, showed its deformed, hunched shoulders and strangely crusted back, and vanished into the scrub" (118). It is a shivery moment. David scrabbles for explanations. Is it a costume? Is someone simply out to scare him? He reinvestigates the tower, only to find that the cross is decorated again, this time with a strange black mask and a fleece:

> Draped over the short transverse bar was the black covering the figure had worn: black fur, a fleece it looked like, most of it falling down the back of the cross, with a huge swelling of coppery pots? gourds? something, attached to the shoulders and spilling down behind. The head of the creature—a glossy black mask—was fitted over the top of the cross and hooded with a dark kerchief, completing the effect. (121)

Approaching this object despite his terror, David discovers that the fleece is covered with bells, the sort that might make a troika sound if someone ran with them through the forest at night. He also notices that on the carapace of the fleece is "the brilliant red stickiness of blood. Lit by late summer sunlight through the trees, it seemed to glow there, so dramatic, so melodramatic, almost comic, the sort of Grand Guignol flourish you expected to find in over-the-top Hollywood and Hammer films" (124). He manages to get home despite his terror at what might be happening.

In the morning, David checks the cross but finds it unadorned again. After breakfast, he conducts net searches on Mamoiada, Carlo's village in Sardinia, and learns that the black-fleeced figure is a *mamuthone*, a pagan god/man/animal combination and a Shepherd's Carnival figure, one of the demonic forms connected historically with the expulsion of the Moors from Sardinia. He phones Carlo and asks about these mamuthones and then says he has seen one on the hill. To David's relief, Carlo says he has seen it too. David tells Carlo about the bottle trees as well and plans to come over.

Before doing so, he goes to Gemma's place, only to find that the house where she had been on the swing is not her home. At the Risis' place, David tells them of the Yakkos' calls and of the bush figure he saw, "how it had stood weighed down by its panoply of bells like some fantastic insect, like a bush demon, yes, like a banksia-man with gaping seedcases on its back" (140). They agree that someone is playing a prank. Carlo tells David the significance of the mamuthone within the old Dionysian rites and how the cross near the tower suggests the *stulos*, or mask pole, for these rites. He also mentions that "wisdom

has to be protected by enigma" (140). The maze, the enigmatic woman of desire, the visions, and Carlo's own unveiling of ancient mysteries to David all recall the flavor and strangeness of John Fowles's classic novel *The Magus*.

Further revelations are forthcoming—about the *charontes* (Etruscan demons of death) and the fact that *Yakkos* probably means "Iackhos," the equivalent of the god Dionysus. But when David asks about the significance of the gumnut sprigs, Raina becomes afraid, though she won't say why. Despite this, they agree to visit the tower the following day. It turns out that Raina has had the key to the tower all along but dreaded going there.

Before leaving, David gets Gemma's address in Kyogle and drives there to leave a note in the mailbox, not only asking her to call, but, at Raina's urging, asking to meet someone named Zoe. The next day, Carlo, Raina, and David visit the tower but find it empty. There are references here to "appropriate fear," a continual motif of Dowling's (his horror collection *Basic Black* is subtitled "Tales of Appropriate Fear"). David then discovers the mysterious hieroglyph from his TT disk carved on one of the granite blocks. Raina becomes suddenly unwell, and they part company.

When Gemma phones, David questions her about having a twin, Zoe, but she denies knowing anyone of that name. After telling her more about his condition, she in turn reveals that Carlo is more than he appears; he is an archaeologist. The symbolism of the swing is part of an ancient Greek tradition. David is troubled, suspecting that, if the twins don't exist, perhaps Gemma herself is Zoe. Dowling plays magnificently here with the old Gothic trope of the doppelgänger, and the uncertainty of whether Gemma has a twin sister or not further plays on David's mind, adding to his anxieties.

Disturbingly, Len Catley phones to say that the clothes dummy left at his place has disappeared. Then, on checking the TT disks, David finds yet another new image that adds to his paranoia: an image of Nascone from the Commedia. Unable to stand this tampering any longer, David destroys the disks and considers replacing the locks.

Carlo later phones to say he has discovered that the petroglyph represents the Night Sun motif, or "aporesis" (176), meaning those answers that lead to further questions. They have an extensive discussion on the symbolism of Dionysus and Apollo, and David learns that the tower was built by Carlo's father and his uncle, Tomaso, but Tomaso denies putting a carving there. Curiously, all this information comes not from a comparative religion scholar, archaeologist, or professional historian, but from "Carlo the 'peasant' pig farmer" (175).

That night, David goes into Kyogle to wait for Gemma. Knocking at her door, he finds another sprig of gumnuts. When there is no answer, he leaves, only to find another gumnut sprig at Starbreak Fell. These tokens, if meant to frighten him, are working. Waking in the dark, David becomes convinced that the mannequin has returned. When he checks, he finds the storeroom

completely empty—*everything* has gone!—and the lights go out. A trap! He is then confronted by the mannequin, draped. When he touches her, she shatters, covered in blood.

Part 3 sees a fast escalation of the action. Unfortunately, to recount here the various thrills and ratcheting-up of the events would spoil the twists and surprises on which so much of the enjoyment of *Clowns at Midnight* depends, so the temptation to reveal how the novel ends must be resisted. Suffice to say that in part 3 there are more clowns, more mysteries (it is not saying too much to reveal that they are women's mysteries), and a venerable Gothic trope in the use of an attic as the site of disturbing events. There is also a culminating ritual in which we learn the true significance of maenads, about the continuation of a tradition of the ancients, a revelation that "Dionysos [*sic*] stood for indestructible life, not *bios*, the individual life that dies, but the archetypal, continuous life that inhabits it for a time" (246).

Part 4 finds our protagonist meditating on where the tests, ordeals, and masks near Starbreak Fell have taken him, how they have opened him to a state of becoming, to the constant sublimity around us, to the greater life promised by the Night Sun. In this, part 4 follows Carlo's promise of a final test and of "someone uninitiated, wild and natural, completing it" (258).

Gothic Landscape in *Clowns at Midnight*

One imagines that Terry Dowling had no Strawberry Hill on the banks of the Thames at Twickenham, as did Walpole, in which to pace the lonely galleries and (as Varma speculates) "yield to strange imaginings."[9] But the setting of Dowling's novel was inspired by real locations, as revealed by photos accessible under the heading *Process* at his official website: www.terrydowling.com.

The landscape's power to amplify unease, so central to the Gothic, is well evidenced in *Clowns at Midnight*. Consider David's view outside:

> My bedroom faced south, so what wasn't the shifting intense black-
> ness of treetops through the shuddering insect screen was that other
> deeper blackness, again filled with more stars than I could ever
> remember seeing. With it came the smells of dry grass, resins and
> night blossoms, gathered up, carried along, vivid cargoes in the night.
> Whatever moon there was came and went in that darkness, now out
> of sight behind the great galleons of cloud, dimly seen, now with its
> rich, fragile light shivering in hints and quick enamellings. (85–86)

Dowling is able to deftly introduce uniquely Australian elements of the land-scape to this Antipodean Gothic, all potent in their sense of ancient lurking evil. Again, we read,

> Perhaps it was just the landscape itself. The Australian bush in sum-
> mer is rarely threatening. There are some venomous snakes and
> spiders, certainly, but no natural predators for humankind. But it
> can be unsettling. Without that constant wall of cicada song, with-
> out the twittering and burble of birds because of the heat, there is
> an uncanny quality. . . . On a hilltop like this, pulled back from that
> wide bright expanse into close-filled corridors of tree shadow, there
> is a compression. The silence fills something with itself, is no longer
> the containing vessel but the thing contained. (115–116)

In such a passage, Dowling enables the reader, via the acutely aware protagonist caught up in his phobia (almost as crippled by perception as Poe's Roderick Usher's oversensitive ears), to cross the zone between the known and the
unknown menacing world. We sense how richly Dowling's language is loaded
with Gothic associations—words such as "shuddering" and "shivering" subtly
suggest the required reader response, while "darkness" and "blackness" imbue
the otherwise straightforward description of the bush with the unknowable
(85, 86, 181). Other British Gothic images such as old-fashioned sailing ships
are vividly evoked by "cargoes in the night" and "galleons of cloud," while
"dim shapes, shadows in shadows" manage to conjure haunted castles (85,
188), despite all the novel's action taking place ten thousand miles from British shores.

Imparting a menace all the more convincing for its solid grounding, Dowling's writing is akin to Gothic Australian writers such as Barbara Baynton
(1857–1929) who in works like *Bush Studies* (1902) presented an intensely realistic picture of the Australian bush. *Clowns at Midnight* situates its narrative firmly
within the Australian landscape, yet it draws on old European myth and legend
for much of its suspense and terror, exploiting the eeriness of both traditions.

Dreams, Mythology, and
Surrealism in *Clowns at Midnight*

As Varma points out, "dreadful nightmares and gloomy dreams occupy an
important place" in the Gothic.[10] This is certainly the case in *Clowns at Midnight*.

The close relationship of dreams to the supernatural has long been explored
in Gothic literature. Such famous examples as Walpole's *The Castle of Otranto*
(the outcome of a dream in which Walpole dreamed about medieval structures)
or Mary Shelley's *Frankenstein* (the product of a romantic dream in Villa Diodati) illustrate the centrality of dream for apprehending supernatural manifestations. Dowling's interest in the unconscious, which he shares with the Surrealist

painters and writers, all of whom explored the dividing line between reality and unreality, between logic and fantasy, surfaces anew in *Clowns at Midnight*. As it was of Mary Shelley in writing *Frankenstein*, Dowling's aim appears to be to write a story that would "speak to the mysterious fears of our nature, and awaken thrilling horror—one to make the reader dread to look around, to curdle the blood, and quicken the beatings of the heart."[11]

However, to simply scare is a slim purpose; Dowling has deeper ambitions in this latest work. As well as horror, he wants to evoke a sense of the marvellous. By rooting the material in the rich mythology of the ancient Greeks and of the Etruscans of Sardinia, he imparts to the work multiple levels of shivery emotional and intellectual discovery. Just as the protagonist David Leeton is gradually awakened to the meaning of the strange hieroglyph that he finds in his TT disks, and the way in which it represents the Night Sun and all it evokes, a reader may gradually awaken to the life-giving potential of an ever-living mythology.

In a sense, the narrative knowingly uses mytho-Gothic tropes both to thrill and to horrify, and to undrape the exotic Other, creating suspense that keeps us turning the pages. There is also (as commonly with Dowling) a powerful epiphany at the end, when much is revealed in a manner that reroutes some of our horrific expectations. Whether this makes the novel a successful Gothic novel or a departure from the form is a matter for debate, but Dowling certainly turns his narrative to different purposes than are found in most contemporary offerings.

Dowling's novel is also informed by his deep understanding of the surrealist realization that (in Varma's words) "there exists a world more real than the normal world, and this is the world of the unconscious mind. The Surrealists' aim is to achieve access to the repressed contents of the unconscious and then to mingle these elements freely with the more conscious images. . . . They . . . find a key to the perplexities of life in the material of dreams."[12]

The question of the numinous or inexplicable supernatural versus the rational mind which is able to explain away any vestige of the actual marvellous is central in *Clowns at Midnight*. As in many tales of psychological darkness (from James's *Turn of the Screw* onward) Dowling employs an unstable narrator, who may occupy a place anywhere on the spectrum from simply unreliable to actually deranged, filtering the story through his or her own eyes, thus leading to ambiguity about the actual nature of events.

Ehrfurcht in *Clowns at Midnight*

Clowns at Midnight is a sophisticated tale of the weird which provides unpredictable rhythms of terror and release. Dowling avails himself here of literary motifs that derive from the European Gothic tradition, in particular the mysterious castle or tower and mysterious noises in the night, among others.

Dowling has seldom stressed the physically gruesome or gory in his metaphysical horror fiction. Rather, his work usually invokes a sense of *Ehrfurcht*—reverence or awe for the mysterious and the inexplicable. He often prefers the psychologically uncanny to the supernatural. This is largely the case with *Clowns at Midnight*, though there are certainly scenes that may disturb, depending on one's own sensibilities and whether one is susceptible to a degree of clown fear.

Nevertheless, there are at least two scenes in *Clowns at Midnight* that verge on the luridly grotesque, involving sex and violence. Like Ramsey Campbell, another *imagier* who has extensively utilized the terrors of inanimate but anthropomorphic beings and objects such as dolls, puppets, mannequins, and masks, Dowling realizes there is a deep well of fright to be found in this arena of totemic representation.

Some of *Clowns at Midnight*'s most memorable scenes involve the utilization of Gothic tropes such as the suggestive mystery of the tower and the masks, but we also have unique conceptions, such as the bottle trees, which impart a different flavor to this Gothic. And while the mamuthones with their strange costumes and carnival-like rites are spookily convincing, it is perhaps not these elements from European myth and history that grip us in suspense as much as the careful buildup of atmosphere and tension which Dowling expertly manipulates. More concerned than many grim scribes with deciphering the irrational archetypes and artifacts of the Gothic world in a modern context, Dowling has characters sift through the symbols' underlying meanings and potential for life-changing realization.

It could be said that Dowling is fundamentally concerned with transcendence, with what he calls the "indominatibility of the human spirit" (57), not in a mystical sense unconnected with the quotidian, but in a sense that reawakens us (as readers and human beings) to the immanent wonder of being alive. This can be seen in the ultimate outcome of *Clowns at Midnight*, and in the crucial significance of the character of Zoe, of her nature and what it means for David Leeton.

Secret Societies, Conspiracy, and Paradoxical Pleasure in *Clowns at Midnight*

One aspect of *Clowns of Midnight* involves what might be described as a secret society, a trope which has featured in Gothic novels as early as Carl von Grosse's *Horrid Mysteries* of 1796, and in the old fictions of the Brotherhood of the Rosy Cross.[13]

Dowling is also in good company among contemporary writers who have tapped the theme of ritualistic Dionysian rites. Donna Tartt's *The Secret His-*

tory explores similar territory, though Tartt's novel is far more concerned with murder and its effects on her characters. Dowling's book, however, plumbs both the mysterious and (to the modern mind) at times the shadowy and frightening nature of these ancient rites, while ultimately seeking a restoration to their rightful place in the world, a way of seeing that makes such rites a deep, positively life-changing experience. This elevates *Clowns at Midnight* from a mere spine tingler to an example of the literary and philosophic Gothic, redolent with profound messages about the human condition and the possibilities for change and redemption.

David Leeton, as a counterphobe, partakes of a paradoxically deep pleasure in his own fear that might be seen as parallel to the experience of the reader who is drawn to the macabre or Gothic as reading matter. The need to confront our fears, to be attracted to the spine tingling and the monstrous, is a psychological phenomenon that underlies the ongoing popularity of the horror genre. Whether it be seen as a process of calling our fears out in the open in order to name and banish them, or as a process of deepening our ability to be unafraid in the face of what would in real life be overwhelming terrors, the nightmares of the Gothic can provide a cathartic and safe release for repressed neuroses as a rehearsal for actual engagement or confrontation with the unknown and uncanny.

As Turcotte has pointed out, "Perhaps what is most exhilarating about the Gothic mode, and what has made it so enduring, is that unlike many other literary forms, it has been at its most exciting when least obeyed—which is ironic given that the mode is frequently dismissed for being formulaic."[14] For Dowling, the *overcoming* of estrangement and entrapment appears to be as important as the depiction of that psychological estrangement. Not content, then, to leave his protagonist a hapless victim of the forces that plague him, the novel concludes on a note of optimism in which sinister Gothic tropes are ultimately turned to a life-affirming conclusion.

Terry Dowling's *Clowns at Midnight* aptly demonstrates a range of affects and topoi that, while rooted in the traditional Gothic, continue the modification of the Gothic into transformative directions today, not least of which is the continuing development of that subgenre known as "Australian Gothic."

Notes

The author would like to acknowledge the useful suggestions made by Margi Curtis during the preparation of the final draft of this essay.

1. Gerry Turcotte, "Australian Gothic," in *The Handbook to Gothic Literature*, ed. Marie Mulvey-Roberts (Houndmills and London: Macmillan, 1998), 10, http://ro.uow.edu.au/cgi/viewcontent.cgi?article=1060&context=artspapers.

2. Syndy McMillen Conger, "Gothic Romance," in *The Penguin Encyclopedia of Horror and the Supernatural*, ed. Jack Sullivan (New York: Viking, 1986), 179.

3. Conger, "Gothic Romance," 179.

4. Turcotte, "Australian Gothic," 14.

5. Jerrold E. Hogle, ed., *The Cambridge Companion to Gothic Fiction* (Cambridge, UK: Cambridge University Press, 2002), 79.

6. James Watts, *Contesting the Gothic: Fiction, Genre and Cultural Conflict, 1764–1832* (Cambridge, UK: Cambridge University Press, 2006), 94.

7. Terry Dowling, *Clowns at Midnight: A Tale of Appropriate Fear* (Hornsea, East Yorkshire, UK: PS Publishing, 2010), 6. Page numbers appear hereafter in parentheses in the text.

8. Leigh Blackmore, "Deep in the Reality Crisis: Individuation, 'Mytho-realism' and Surrealistic Traces in Terry Dowling's *Tom Rynosseros* Cycle," honors thesis, Faculty of Creative Arts, University of Wollongong, 2009; forthcoming in *Science Fiction: A Review of Speculative Literature*.

9. Devendra P. Varma, *Gothic Flame: Being a History of the Gothic Novel* (Metuchen, NJ: Scarecrow Press, 1987), 68.

10. Varma, *Gothic Flame*, 80.

11. Mary Wollstonecraft Shelley, "Introduction to the Standard Novels Edition (1831)," in *Frankenstein, or The Modern Prometheus*, ed. D. L. MacDonald and Kathleen Scherf (Petersborough, ON: Broadview Press, 1999), 356.

12. Varma, *Gothic Flame*, 222.

13. For an in-depth discussion of secret societies with the traditional Gothics of Shelley, Godwin, Bulwer-Lytton, and others, see Marie Roberts, *Gothic Immortals: The Fiction of the Brotherhood of the Rosy Cross* (London: Routledge, 1990).

14. Turcotte, "Australian Gothic," 19.

CHAPTER 10

What We Hide Within Us

THOUGHTS ON ALBERT SÁNCHEZ PIÑOL'S *COLD SKIN*

Brian J. Showers

> The sky was tinged a gloomy shade of tarnished silver, with the even darker tones of a rusty suit of armour. The sun was no more than an orange suspended halfway up, small and continuously covered by clouds that grudgingly filtered the light. A sun that, because of its latitude, would never reach its zenith. My description isn't trustworthy. It is only what I saw. But the landscape we see beyond our eyes tends to be a reflection of what we hide, within us.
>
> —Unnamed narrator in Albert Sánchez Piñol's *Cold Skin*[1]

The notion of the Gothic is nebulous and somewhat difficult to define. The characteristics of the genre—exotic locales, uncovering the hidden both within and without, the gradual blossoming of terror, and the externalization of metaphor—are so universal that they are frequently, and often effortlessly, incorporated into other genres. One could argue that Gothic sensibilities have been around since the shaman's fire first caused shadows to flicker and dance upon the cavern wall, long before the genre's key components crystallized in the late-eighteenth-century works of Horace Walpole, Ann Radcliffe, and M. G. Lewis. Albert Sánchez Piñol's 2002 debut novel *Cold Skin* firmly pays homage to the established Gothic traditions of strange landscapes, invasions from the "outside," the intermingling of love and hate, and the raging beast within. While these conflicts also exist in genres decidedly non-Gothic, what sets the Gothic apart from its more realistic counterparts is that the internal often becomes the external: the darker elements of human nature and the soul are given tangible

form, manifesting as a physical and often exaggerated topography through which the story and characters move. This is true of *Cold Skin*, and throughout the course of the novel the protagonist's inner turmoils are projected and become terrifyingly real. This is the world of the Gothic.

Piñol sets *Cold Skin* against the backdrop of the First World War, an era not generally associated with the Gothic. The stark horrors of modern warfare were startlingly vicious and more immediate to everyday experience than the shadowy world of oblique terror as typified by the Gothic. International diplomacy had failed on an unheard-of level, and science had developed new and increasingly impersonal ways of killing people, which were utilized during the subsequent death throes of nineteenth-century imperialism: fragmenting artillery, automatic weaponry, and chemical warfare. Not even the most fervent prayers to God could provide adequate protection against strategic aerial bombing. A cynic might see *La Guerre Pour la Civilization* as an oxymoron—like Frankenstein's monster, the simultaneous epitome and failing of human progress, in short, the complete breakdown of a supposedly enlightened world, a world in which logic can no longer be trusted. And though not necessarily Gothic in itself, the commonalities are there, and Piñol uses this chaotic milieu, this backward step into darkness, as a reason to propel the story into Gothic territories. Dark corners can once again be shadowy and unknowable.

The novel begins with Piñol's protagonist, an unnamed narrator en route to the center of one of these dark and unknowable shadows: a remote island near the Antarctic Circle. Direct information about the narrator is parceled out sparingly in the opening chapters of the English-language edition. And like a classic Byronic hero, whose erratic or extreme actions and thoughts are not immediately understood, we piece together a fragmented understanding of the protagonist's background from his reactions to his current situation. Each player in this drama, even those who enter on the periphery, has a past at which is only hinted. John Donne's philosophy that "no man is an island" has no place in the Gothic world of *Cold Skin*—indeed, the inverse of Donne is the dominant reality. Some men are islands. As the narration unfolds, the reader gets the impression that the protagonist is not necessarily *sharing* his story with us, the act of sharing being a communion between two people, but rather that we are eavesdropping on the narrator's private thoughts. In fact, the whole of chapter 7 is presented as diary extracts, reinforcing the notion of the reader as a detached observer—and perhaps also an invocation of the epistolary conceit famously utilized by Wilkie Collins in *The Moonstone*, later by Bram Stoker in *Dracula*, and in the final chapter of Poe's *The Narrative of Arthur Gordon Pym* (a forerunner to *Cold Skin* in other ways, as well, as Poe's is a novel of Antarctica, of being overrun by freakish natives, and of moral and physical disintegration). This degree of disconnection only serves to increase the Gothic sense of isolation, both

literal and metaphorical, surrounding each character. But there is still enough interpersonal identification to give the proceedings context and meaning from page one; it is this sense of mystery (another component of Gothic literature), the incomplete puzzle of personality, and this urge to forge a connection with and an understanding of the narrator that compels readers onward.

With the above in mind, readers should also be aware that, as a review in the *Independent* notes, "some fifteen early pages explaining the narrator's background as an IRA volunteer in the 1920s have been left out [from the English language edition]."[2] While the author's original opening with extra information might be construed as "less Gothic" in effect, the loss of these pages does not adversely change the novel. But this opinion is sure to vary from reader to reader. In any case, the publisher of the English-language edition should have noted this expurgation.

Throughout the early chapters, there are notes of cynicism in the narrator's observations, which emphasize his Byronic traits—barbed yet vague commentary not only about his shrouded past, but also about the world he has left behind. From his viewpoint, it is not so much he who is forsaking civilization, but rather civilization that has failed him—and humanity. This loss of faith in his fellow man drives the narrator to accept (after having *actively* lobbied for) the position of weather official at a station on a desolate island, far removed from the ruins of postwar Europe. He sheds some light on this drastic decision for seclusion—"No one accepts such a fate for money" (3)—and in saying this he verifies in his oblique way that the job is not just a duty, but also that this self-exile was a conscious and deliberate choice. He is creating the possibilities for his own hell. For the narrator, both place and state of mind are synonymous; indeed, in the Gothic, place is often an extension of a state of mind, which is nearly always turbulent. As such, the island is an inevitable destination.

The narrator goes on to describe his somewhat peculiar post as "a job as monotonous as it [is] insignificant: to log the intensity, direction and frequency of the winds" (3). Far from the populated shipping lanes, this distant corner of the Atlantic Ocean is hardly a concern to the rest of the world. But it is its geographical remoteness that leaves the island open to fantastic possibilities. On a map the island might be labeled with a banner that reads "*Hic sunt dracones.*" And because this is the Gothic, we know there will be. Even the island's lighthouse, civilization's lonely beacon, which the narrator eventually comes to inhabit, is essentially an abandoned outpost. It stands alone on the opposite end of the island from the weather station. We even learn later in the story that it no longer serves the intended function of a lighthouse, having become the domicile of a madman. In fact, no one can now say which country was responsible for its erection. It stands as a monument to gratuitous progress, like a lone flag of some Earthling nation planted on distant, inhospitable Pluto. The island is one

of civilization's dead ends, a place never fully explored or understood, a literal terra incognita.

The insignificant job in the above quotation refers to the absolute futility of the narrator's assigned chore. The very existence of this job begs the question: Why? To what end? This is record keeping for the sake of recording keeping, an action seemingly stripped of function, perhaps more about the baroque bureaucracy than it is about discovery. It is science existing purely for its own sake rather than for the betterment of mankind. Ironically, the narrator's excuse for adjourning to the island, a meaningless task, is the embodiment of what he is trying to escape: a world where politics, religion, and science no longer serve mankind but seemingly conspire to destroy it. Even on a remote island, the moribund excesses of civilization dog him. By chapter 2, the narrator's cynical attitude toward the world reaches a fever pitch.

Unloaded from the ship, along with his personal effects and provisions for the forthcoming year of isolation, is a box labeled "22-E." The narrator's description of the box's contents not only underscores his cynicism but also reveals a complementary sardonic humor. The box contains requests from various world institutions, each seemingly more absurd than the last: a request from Kiev University to populate the island with rabbits to serve as a food source for passing ships (there are few if any passing ships), an application from the Geographical Society of Berlin to collect *Hydrometridae halobates* and *Chironomidae pontomyia* (efficient directions translated into eight languages that omit any explanation of what specifically these creatures are), and an appeal from a Catholic missionary who wants the narrator to quiz the island's Bantu chiefs on their knowledge of Christianity (there are no indigenous people within thousands of miles of the island, at least not human). Depending on your mindset, the absurdity in Piñol's writing borders on outright comedy, making chapter 2 an entertaining section for readers who share a similar worldview.

Absurd humor pops up again in Piñol's follow-up novel, *Pandora in the Congo* (2008), which shares not only many of the Gothic sensibilities of *Cold Skin*, in particular an isolated and unsympathetic wilderness, but it is, according to the author, the second installment of a loose thematic trilogy. *Pandora in the Congo*'s protagonist is employed in a similar functionally deficient position as a ghostwriter for a ghostwriter (for a ghostwriter), and at a point later in the book he is unknowingly assigned to write a review for his own novel. In one scene, set during one of the book's darker moments, is a brief rumination on laughter, which in Piñol's literary cosmos might be a defining quality that makes us human. Both humor and horror are extreme perceptions of reality, one antithetical to the other, and there may just be salvation from horror in understanding that life is comedy, even during its darker moments. Given the narrator's situation,

the futility of human activity in *Cold Skin* comes off as bizarre and even ridiculous (though perhaps no more so, albeit in a less fantastical manner, than the image of the giant helmet crushing young Prince Conrad at the beginning of *The Castle of Otranto*). Box 22-E as metaphor for institutionalized folly is abundantly clear, and its near implausibility, a signpost just before we enter the world of the Gothic, prepares us for fantastic events yet to come.

"My description isn't trustworthy. It is only what I saw" (16), muses the narrator in the opening chapter of *Cold Skin*. What he describes is pure Gothic. In keeping with the Gothic tradition, the island is seemingly sympathetic to his turbulent mood. Vague coordinates for the island are given, and a quick look at a map will confirm that it lies somewhere near the Antarctic Circle, surrounded by nothing but the cold, blue Atlantic for thousands of miles. "The nearest land mass is Bouvet Island, claimed by the Norwegians" (13). This is as far from Europe as one can get without crossing over into the absolute unknown regions of the Antarctic. Let us not forget that Cocytus, Dante's ninth circle of hell, is a frozen wasteland. Fortunately, the narrator stands on the "threshold of a border [he] would never cross" (2), a literal edge of the unknown. This also implies the possibility of redemption.

The narrator describes the borderland island in a manner that verges on the hostile, without considering that its ecology, which he deems unusual, is simply one he does not, or possibly cannot, understand. Nevertheless, the ominous landscape seems to him harsh and unearthly: "A sliver of land crushed between the greys of the ocean and the sky" with an "eerie sense of desolation" that saturates everything, yet "its nature [is] hard to grasp" (2). The "treacherous moss" that hides "pockets of mud and black ooze" (7) calls to mind Arthur Conan Doyle's Grimpen Mire in *The Hound of the Baskervilles* and suggests, perhaps, something even more primeval. And, as if to echo the toxified terrain surrounding Poe's mansion of gloom in "The Fall of the House of Usher," with its "rank sedges [and] a few white trunks of decayed trees,"[3] Piñol employs similar descriptions: The island's wind-twisted trees grow like "a herd of huddled animals seeking their own kind" and are stained with an unusually dense moss of blue, violet, and black, "like a three-coloured blight" (2). The bold and unsettling coloration also evokes Pym's description of an island stream from the far southern latitudes: "It flowed every possible shade of purple; like the hues of a changeable silk, . . . made up of a number of distinct veins [that] . . . did not commingle."[4] A peculiar sense of noiselessness also pervades the island, a complete absence of "melodies associated with forest wildlife" (7). At least by European standards, the island can be taxonomized as decidedly not normal. Even the inveterate sailors who deliver the narrator to the island react subconsciously to the landscape: they are restless and impatient to leave without quite knowing why (15). Seafarers are a breed traditionally known for their heightened perception of the natural world

and practice a reverential deference to superstition when navigating unpredictable leagues of sea—another terrain that at times does not obey expected laws or conventional behavior. The sailors' nonverbal commentary, like a barometer or, even more ominously, like a canary in a cage, echoes what the narrator is just beginning to learn. This hints at the supernormal nature of the island.

Perhaps the most Gothic feature of the island's landscape is "a solid rock elevation crowned by a lighthouse" (2) with "a rounded and compact surface to withstand the ocean's violence" (8) and the "solidity of a megalith" (2). As with Dracula's Transylvanian stronghold, Manfred's castle Otranto, the house of Roderick Usher, and a myriad of other such brooding structures that regularly appear in Gothic novels, such "castles" typically snare protagonists in either physical or psychological capacities, though quite frequently both. The lighthouse on the island becomes just such a prison for the narrator when at first he willingly seeks shelter there. Like the castles of Gothic literature, the narrator is drawn to it; he is compelled to go there for survival, at first to escape the deadly terrain that surrounds it, only to find out that the "castle" is the epicenter and possibly the source of the unnaturalness. The lighthouse is the home of the madman Gruner, a former Austrian artilleryman, and his bellicose way of life—a way of life that seems to cast a pall of ruination across the entire island. And it is the lighthouse, this island on the island, which becomes the stage where the crux of the drama plays out.

The island is like a glass that distorts everyday expectations, everything from human habit to the reliable progression of time. The blurring of place and mood allows stories written in the Gothic manner to border on the unreal, to exist in the betwixt and between lands of twilight. Indeed, in the southerly latitudes of *Cold Skin*, the sun never quite reaches its zenith. The procession of time begins to have no meaning for the narrator, as if the island exists in a place wholly removed from the Greenwich chronometer. The irregular diary entries that attempt to mark the progression of time in chapter 7 give way to a later scene in chapter 11 in which the narrator struggles to reconstruct a calendar. Descriptions of the passage of time are disproportionate to each other: details of a single day can be expanded over the course of many pages, while events of a week are sometimes compressed to less than a sentence or two. The narrator's urge to keep track of time, like a prisoner scratching days onto a gloomy cell wall, is a desperate link to the civilized world. "I neglected to cross off days simply because I had little hope of seeing the morrow," the narrator writes (158). In a savage world, where the monotony of survival is the daily goal, timekeeping becomes a futile effort as one day merges into the next.

The island seems neither an independent reality nor a projection of temperament but an alchemical fusion of both. In either case, the island, far removed from civilization, serves to create the same necessary sense of remote and exotic

otherworldliness that one finds in Stoker's Transylvania, H. G. Wells's island of Dr. Moreau, or even in Joseph Conrad's dark heart of the Belgian Congo (also the setting for Piñol's similarly Gothic *Pandora in the Congo*). "I was at the end of the world, the middle of nowhere," says the narrator about his new home (2). The general impression one gets is that the island is responding to the benighted narrator's brooding qualities. Perhaps it could even be said that the island has risen up out of the sea for the sole purpose of accommodating the narrator, that it has been patiently awaiting his arrival. This journey is a fate which cannot be avoided. The island is a place where the narrator would have eventually ended up, and if not the island, then some other dark corner of the globe. "'Look, on the horizon. *Your* island,' the captain said to me" (1, italics added). An ominous portent, indeed, as if the captain knows that this island belongs solely to the narrator, an albatross that he alone must bear.

The celebrated ghost-story writer M. R. James, ruminating on his craft, wrote, "Let us, then, be introduced to the actors in a placid way; let us see them going about their ordinary business, undisturbed by forebodings, pleased with their surroundings; and into this calm environment let the ominous thing put out its head."[5] This is sound advice for storytellers working in any genre, but when it comes to horror and the Gothic, where the inversion of "ordinary business" is the general aim, conveying this contrast is absolutely essential for atmosphere and a unified effect. In *Cold Skin*, Piñol gives James's advice its due airing, and in keeping with the Gothic tradition, the concept of "normal," at least as defined within the context of the novel, is manifested in the captain of the ship that delivers the narrator to the island. Though the novel does not necessarily start in a placid way—the Great War made sure that the world would never be "normal" again—the confused mindset of the narrator, already en route to his self-imposed exile, is juxtaposed against the collected attitude of the captain. The captain is the embodiment of composure; an august man who, unlike the still young, idealistic narrator, has found a way to disentangle himself from the complexities of terra firma and has come to terms with the necessary evils of the world. The captain and his vessel are a link between Europe and the island, a temporary oasis between the madness that the narrator is leaving behind and the trials that await him. From bow to stern, the captain is the absolute master of his ship—his own sovereign nation. While a harsh man, he is not unfair. As the narrator notes, "He scrutinised others with the shrewdness of an entomologist. . . . Some would have mistaken this for severity. I believe that it was his way of expressing the benevolence he hid in the recesses of his soul. He would never confess this love for his fellow man, but it was evident in all his actions" (3). The captain's depth, his accumulation of understanding and world experience, are hinted at, but the details are kept hidden.

Though the stoic demeanors of both men would prevent either of them from admitting so, the captain may also be seen as a sort of role model or father figure to the narrator. During the voyage, the narrator identifies an understanding "that sometimes arise[s] between men of different generations" (3). It is plausible to anticipate that, after his trials on the island, the narrator might someday grow into a man like the captain, perhaps never quite reassimilating into civilization, but creating his own world, not unlike the captain's ship domain, in which to feel content. Clearly the narrator's opinion of the captain is high. Even after a fundamental disagreement over the necessities of the military—the narrator is an avowed pacifist—he still exclaims, "With fifty men like the captain I could found a new country, a free nation, and call it Hope" (36).

Even more importantly, the captain appears to have an unspoken and seerlike understanding of the narrator's reasons for turning his back on civilization: "'Some disillusionment has brought you here,' [the captain] stated with conviction. . . . 'You've come here out of spite.' . . . His gesture said: 'There's nothing more I can do for you'" (14–15). The impression is that the captain has had a similar cathartic experience in his past and intimately understands the importance of the narrator's decision for absolute isolation: he *must* go through this ordeal, a removal that is simultaneously a choice and a predetermined fate beyond anyone's control—yet another invoking of the Gothic. And while the captain understands the narrator's need for isolation and self-discovery, he also understands the dangers of disconnecting from civilization.

Before the ship weighs anchor, the captain offers the narrator one last chance to leave the island. When the narrator refuses, as the captain likely anticipates, he gives him a final piece of advice, perhaps a warning meant to foreshadow the fate that has befallen Maritime Signalman Gruner, the mad occupant of the lighthouse: "'Eat well, work hard, and keep looking in the mirror to remember what you look like. Talk to yourself so you don't lose the habit of speech'" (15). It is as if the captain is aware of the inherent dangers of distancing oneself from the constraints of the civilized world. Just as the captain represents equilibrium attained, a projection of whom the narrator *could* become, Gruner represents the complete antithesis of the captain: the embodiment of uncivilized discord and a wild beastlike nature—another possible projection of the narrator's future. If the captain is Dr. Jekyll, then Gruner is most certainly Mr. Hyde.

The most terrifying monsters are generally those that retain human traits, whether physical or otherwise. The possibility of transition from human into something less than human presents a terrifying prospect, one that is often explored in Gothic literature. After all, as we are reminded by Curt Siodmak's famous couplet from *The Wolf Man*, "Even a man who is pure in heart and says his prayers by night, may become a wolf when the wolfbane blooms and the

autumn moon is bright." In the Gothic, when we see a monster, often we are seeing a reflection of ourselves, an image of man's darker possibilities. In *Cold Skin*, the reptilian humanoids that maraud the island nightly are, on the surface, most easily identified as monsters, but the character of Gruner, the island's human resident, is the real metaphor for man's bestial and destructive capabilities.

Gruner, as the narrator will come to learn, is his nightmare incarnate. He is the embodiment of all that the narrator is fleeing: war, territorialism, abuse of power, blind reactions to a demonized "other" (in this case the amphibious Sitauca creatures), and mankind's self-destructive tendencies. Gruner lacks empathy and a conscious morality—this is what makes him so frightening and unpredictable. He is a monster that wears human skin. Most importantly, the narrator must face the fact that, even on a tiny island in the South Atlantic, the corrupt and monstrous facets of man cannot be avoided.

Piñol, who has a career as an anthropologist in addition to that of a novelist, describes Gruner in terms of an animal, as something perhaps less than human—and the lighthouse is his cage. The imposing structure is highlighted throughout the opening chapters and serves as an extended introduction to Gruner's own dominant personality, which infuses the island with an air of inhospitality. From our first introduction to him, we know that Gruner will be the world's worst roommate. And like Gruner's inner workings, the abode he has created for himself is virtually inaccessible.

The exterior of the lighthouse is like a defensive castle, composed of "sticks and crossed posts, often with their points sharpened" (8). This echoes Gruner's rather brusque personality. Even when the narrator gains access to the lighthouse for physical protection, it still prevents the island from becoming the spiritual refuge that he seeks at the beginning of the novel. Gruner's interests lay primarily in eradicating "toads," and conversations between the two men, when they do happen, are usually to this end. Irritable and unruly, it seems only a matter of time before Gruner turns on his human companion. Instead of refuge on any level, the narrator becomes trapped between the unpredictable Gruner and the throngs of amphibious sea creatures.

Albeit in an oblique way, Gruner's fortifications also serve to introduce the narrator to the Sitauca. Initially thought to be the manifestation of a fractured and lost mind, the lighthouse's defenses, which make the building look like a "makeshift hedgehog" (24), are in fact a testament of Gruner's general demeanor: he has barricaded himself physically, spiritually, and mentally. Gruner reacts to the bizarre, humanoid sea creatures with hatred and violence as if incapable of any other rational consideration. He sits at the lighthouse balcony each night, shooting them with his rifle like a sniper; they are aggressors that must be fended off. Gruner must protect his domain; it is his only purpose in life. Even

his Sitauca concubine, Aneris, is treated with disgust. She is his servant, his beast of burden—and also the passive recipient of his brutish lust.

Knowing nothing of the island or its Sitauca inhabitants, the narrator does not at first question Gruner's violence, although he initially finds the lighthouse's barricade bewildering, a "ridiculous fortification" (25). This reaction to the barricade being "ridiculous" foreshadows the eventual questioning of Gruner's aggressive tactics and destructive methods, indeed what would appear to be Gruner's entire philosophy of life. But after his first night in the ramshackle weather station, with hordes of Sitauca groping for entry, the narrator quickly comes to accept Gruner's hostile reaction to the monsters. It is in this way that the narrator comes to question his own personal values: Is the bestial nature of mankind sometimes necessary? Questions such as these are often at the heart of Gothic literature.

At the start of the book, the narrator is an avowed pacifist, yet when survival is at stake, he falls into Gruner's way of life without question. The island seems to justify violence, and thereby justifies Gruner: "No good man, no philosopher, poet or philanthropist could survive in this place, only Gruner" (50–51). As if to underscore this point, the narrator builds a defensive bonfire with the books he brought with him for study and meditation. The great thinkers, philosophers, and writers of humankind are listed before being tossed into the flames: Goethe, Aristotle, Rilke, Marx, Milton, Voltaire, Rousseau, and Cervantes—the island's brutal environment renders all their philosophies useless. A heavy-handed metaphor for sure, but in doing this, Piñol also emphasizes the precivilized and bestial state of mankind. It is true that men fight over philosophies, but one of the questions raised in *Cold Skin* is, if we could somehow cast off the philosophies and higher thinking that set us apart from beasts, would we be better off? And yet Gruner continues to epitomize the bestial at its worst.

Gruner's clothes, which fill an old oil drum, are filthy. Under the bed lies a chamber pot filled to the rim with urine, and no attempt has been made to hide the stench that permeates the lighthouse. When the narrator and the ship's crew first meet Gruner, as he rises from his bed they are shocked to see that his "organ [is] covered with hair up to his foreskin. . . . His beard was as wild as a patriarch's . . . [his] hairline begins barely an inch and a half above his eyebrows . . . his lids opened and closed like a bat's" (12). To emphasize this animalistic description, Gruner is also apparently unashamed of his naked, disheveled physical state and filthy living conditions. It is as if Gruner wears his animalism with a sense of pride.

Near the fountain that supplies the island with its only source of fresh water is a sign that is a profound assertion of brute territorialism: "Gruner is Gruner and Gruner is Gruner. . . . *Dix it et fecit* [*sic*]" (He said and he did) (23). Gruner's

belief in his own authority is self-evident; he is interested only in perpetuating his lordship over the island at all costs. This includes defense against the Sitauca as much as it does any threat posed by the narrator's presence. Like the literary touchstone of autonomous, godlike authority Mr. Kurtz in *Heart of Darkness*, Gruner answers to no man: "Gruner [is] an authentic demon, a desperate Viking, the marauding pirate Red Beard; all this and more" (105). And yet despite this power, Gruner is still a prisoner of the lighthouse, damned to the island for the rest of his existence. After all, how could a man like Gruner possibly return to civilization? And so he paces back and forth like an animal in its cage.

The Gothic is ultimately a metaphor for ourselves and our world. Dracula was, presumably, once a man; Frankenstein's monster was many men (with a few animal parts from the slaughterhouse); and Mr. Hyde was a single, amplified facet of man, cruelty in extremis. Like all noteworthy Gothic monsters—supernatural, scientific, or psychological—the Sitauca are recognizably part human. Just as Gruner, a man, exhibits traits that are recognizably animal, the Sitauca are monsters that are humanoid in appearance and exhibit what might be a developed culture, or at least a harmony with their world.

Aneris, a female of her race, is described by Piñol in delicate, almost sensuous terms, despite her monstrous (at least to the narrator) form: "The eyebrow lines appeared to have been drawn by some Sumerian calligrapher. . . . Its eyes were the very blue of the African sky. . . . The subtle nose was thin and pointed with high-set nostrils. . . . It had smooth cheeks and a long, thin neck" (53–54). Even to the reader, descriptions of this exotic woman are strangely alluring. To the narrator, though, the creature remains an "it" until he notices her sexual organs: "bare, untrammeled by pubic hair" (54). He continues to refer to her as a beast throughout the novel, but after the revelation that Aneris is female, possibly in an act of humanization, he starts using feminine pronouns.

Still, Aneris is a monster, and the narrator is plagued by conflicting emotions over his attraction to a being so unlike himself. At times the narrator treats her as a lover and confidant, his solace from Gruner; other times he treats her as a possession, like a dog he can kick when he's possessed by a dark mood. Yet when they make love it is she who gains control of him: "Her body was a living sponge spilling forth opium. My humanity was annulled. . . . Her sexuality was free from any encumbrance. . . . That act reduced our bodies to their most elemental, basic state. . . . I had reached the zenith of human experience" (118–120). Aneris is pure sexuality, the forbidden woman of Gothic literature, and through her the narrator is able to catch a glimpse of experiences beyond what was previously known to anyone. "Europe had no idea that it was living in a state of perpetual castration" (119). The narrator's guilt and inability to come to terms with his passion for Aneris instills him with a fear. Worse yet, it makes him in some ways an equal to Gruner, who also enjoys Aneris's sexuality: "How

could he lie with one of the very same monsters that plagued us every night? How did he manage to justify the act, in defiance of all obstacles set down by civilisation and nature? It was worse than cannibalism" (85). It is this mixture of shame and self-disgust that drives the narrator back to Gruner. And so they set about contriving a way to retrieve explosives from a sunken ship that they might use to obliterate six or seven hundred Sitauca at once.

Perhaps the most distressing metaphor in *Cold Skin* comes during its finale. Just as with most of the novel's characters, true identities and personal histories are obfuscated; Gruner is no exception. At the beginning of the novel, when we are introduced to Gruner, it is the captain who makes the assumption that Gruner is the maritime signalman assigned to the lighthouse. Gruner, who is clearly of unsound mind and never affirms this attribution one way or another, could just as easily have arrived on the island as the weather station official (who is missing at the start of the novel). The narrator, who has arrived on the island with noble intentions for self-improvement, witnesses Gruner's bestial lust for violence and unbridled sexuality: "Was he in himself cruel, or did he carry cruelty like a disease, spreading it to others?" (50). It would seem the latter is the case.

Over the course of the novel, the narrator contracts Gruner's "disease" to the extent that he replaces Gruner in his role as the mad, embattled hermit. At the novel's end, after the passing of a year and Gruner's death, a new weather official arrives at the island. The new weather official addresses the narrator as "Mr. Gruner" (229). The narrator, seemingly resigned to his fate, does nothing to correct him and even hints that he can now never leave the island.

One of the book's final scenes closely echoes the first encounter with Gruner—only this time the roles are reversed in a sort of twist on the doppelgänger motif:

> "With whom am I speaking? What is your rank?" the captain de-
> manded. "Are you deaf, dumb or ill? Do you not understand me?
> What languages do you speak? What is your name? Answer! Or have
> you gone mad? Of course; he is insane." He paused, sniffing the air.
> "Where does this stench come from? If fish could sweat, this is what
> it would smell like! The whole building reeks." (223)

Much is made of Gruner's pungent odor, a smell that still lingers in the above scene. It would be valid to question the source of the stench; perhaps it does not belong to the man but rather to whichever man fills the role of maritime signalman. Perhaps it is the lighthouse, a diseased entity in itself. The narrator passes a warning to the new weather official: "That lighthouse is a mirage. There is no refuge to be found within its walls. Don't go inside. Leave; go home" (231). The safety of the lighthouse is illusory; much worse things can happen

within. But the role of the lighthouse keeper must always be filled. There must always be a Gruner, and so the stench persists. The lighthouse is not unlike Hell: the Sitauca are its devils and the signalmen and weather officials are its eternal parade of tormented souls who come willingly to the island.

We are left with a set of dichotomies that two centuries of Gothic fiction have been unable to reconcile: real versus unreal, man versus beast, passion versus apathy, civilization versus destruction, and—most importantly—how easy it is to pass from one extreme to the other. Ultimately, Gothic literature questions human nature: what lies within each of us? It is a fiction of possibilities outside of expected reality. The genre's appeal in the twenty-first century, while varied in its theme and manner of conveyance, is ultimately no different from what fascinated the readers of Walpole, Radcliffe, and their scions (Piñol included among their number). Gothic storytellers drag from the depths these dreams of dark possibility, of which we are all guilty, and sprawl them out across the pages like entrails so that we might infer meaning. The possibilities that Gothic storytellers explore are mostly subjective—we each divine the relevant wisdom. It is in this way that we can all be like the primitive shaman, who no longer lays exclusive claim to these otherworldly visions. Metaphors, their essences always shifting and elusive, must be decoded by each reader. They are cyclical and labyrinthine, often turning in on themselves to reveal new corridors to explore, and this makes the prospect of finding the truth a difficult one. But this is the lasting pleasure of the Gothic: through careful detection, we can all glimpse our raging beasts within.

Notes

1. Albert Sánchez Piñol, *Cold Skin*, trans. Cheryl Leah Morgan (Edinburgh, UK: Canongate, 2006), 16. Page numbers appear hereafter in parentheses in the text.

2. Michael Eaude, "*Cold Skin* by Albert Sánchez Piñol: Today's Forecast—Angst, Fantasy, Action, and Unidentified Monsters," *Independent*, March 13, 2006, www.independent.co.uk/arts-entertainment/books/reviews/cold-skin-by-albert-saacutenchez-pintildeol-trans-by-cheryl-leah-morgan-469666.html.

3. Edgar Allan Poe, "The Fall of the House of Usher," in *Complete Stories and Poems of Edgar Allan Poe* (New York: Doubleday, 1984), 177.

4. Edgar Allan Poe, *The Narrative of Arthur Gordon Pym of Nantucket*, ed. Richard Kopley (New York: Penguin, 1999), 168.

5. M. R. James, introduction to *Ghosts and Marvels: A Selection of Uncanny Tales from Daniel Defoe to Algernon Blackwood*, ed. Vere H. Collins (Oxford, UK: Oxford University Press, 1924), vi.

CHAPTER 11

Michel Faber, Feminism, and the Neo-Gothic Novel

THE CRIMSON PETAL AND THE WHITE

Mary Ellen Snodgrass

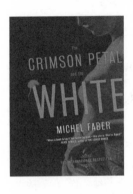

A domestic fiction master, Michel Faber hybridizes the Gothic terror novel by blending sensationalism with the epistolary novel, the novel of manners, stories of everyday duplicity, accounts of coercive medical treatments, and improbable melodrama.[1] He exudes literary savoir faire by delineating male perceptions of female passion. Gothic chiaroscuro enhances his diction, sensory detail, homegrown brutality, and aberrant behavior. His masterwork, *The Crimson Petal and the White* (2002), flavors the Victorian revenge novel with post-Freudian psychology, an anti-Catholic burlesque of mysticism, naturalism bordering on soft porn, and a nineteenth-century female panorama from madwife in the attic[2] and child in the nursery to ambitious hooker gracing the business world. A globe-trotting allegorist from The Hague reared in Melbourne, Australia, and now residing forty miles north of Inverness, Scotland, the author brings to Gothic fiction an unusual combination of Dutch, Anglo-Saxon, and Middle English rhetoric as well as training in nursing and two decades of literary research into Victorian erotica. He is adept at turning droll episodes of London squalor into the incongruous, with its "overbearing stench of perfume and horse dung, freshly-baked cakes and old meat, burnt mutton-fat and chocolate, roast chestnuts and dog piss."[3]

Faber's novel draws from the remarkable woman-powered Gothic of the nineteenth century the conventions prefigured by publishing phenomena Ann Radcliffe, Joanna Baillie, Elizabeth Braddon, Marie Corelli, and Gertrude Atherton.[4] Set against a cast of the usual suspects more Bunyanesque than Dickensian—the idler and tormentor, William "Bill" Rackham, Esquire; the nineteen-year-old doxy, Miss Sugar, nicknamed "Shush"; the bawdy house toll collector,

Colonel Leek; the cocoa-crazed do-gooder, Emmeline Fox; and a potential bride, Lady Constance Bridgelow—the subtext flaunts enough eccentric character names to stage the picaresque goings-on of London's mid-1870s subculture.[5] A telling East End progression transforms Sugar's strumpet mother, Mrs. Jettison, into the conniving procuress renamed Mrs. Castaway, who sells her thirteen-year-old daughter into whoredom. With sarcastic precision, the sporting-house mistress delivers the watchword of the stews: "Men love to wallow in sin; we are the sin they wallow in."[6] At her death, she leaves in charge Amelia Crozier, bearer of the fallen woman's cross.

Faber chooses the pre–Jack the Ripper gaslight paradigm as a footing on which to hoist his lever and shift the world's perspective on the gentleman's carnal fun. An overlay of secrecy serves Gothic innovation by shadowing the lurkings of the demon lover, William Rackham, an antihero amid urban unease with "vertiginous stacks of decaying housing,"[7] a lapse of upkeep parallel to the default in public morals. To heighten the air of corruption and menace, Faber coordinates a tableau of peril from a wrecked vehicle picked clean of recyclables by scavenging ghetto urchins, the next generation of Soho bottom feeders. He skewers the male focus through his observations of leisure-class values: to William, "a high-class umbrella is worth more than a low-class woman."[8] The action further discredits William through scatology by describing his delight in the Great Flatelli, a performer at the Oxford Music Hall who turns flatulence into a "One-Man Wind Ensemble" playing "Greensleeves."[9] With frat-boy guides, Edward Ashwell and Philip Bodley, son of Bishop Bodley, William surveys the nooks and hideaways of Soho in a show of rakish bluster and daring. The text compares the red-light district to a rookery, one of Charles Dickens's pet terms for a blighted district or breeding ground for crows and rooks, an avian metaphor for footpads, cutpurses, beggars, and bawds.

Implying a metafictional I-thou relationship with the postmodern reader, Faber opens with a genial warning, "Watch your step."[10] The after-hours sum-up of slum life requires diction at full-organ precision, like an introit to *The Phantom of the Opera*. Even the architecture bears an underworld visage of imposing verticality, looming infirmity and pestilence, and putrefaction from the dribbling of night wastes out of skeletal window sashes. At Church Lane, St. Giles, at 2:50 a.m., "where no Gods are being thanked,"[11] Faber develops a Dantean atmosphere of "Abandon hope, all ye who enter here," with cinders in the air on an ashy night, an intimidating introduction to London's hellmouth and the "[persons] worth next-to-nothing" who inhabit it.[12] A glum exposé of church disinterest in the underclass, the opening chapter pictures malnutrition and unemployment of such magnitude that do-gooders depart "with despair in their hearts and shit on their shoes."[13] The narrator, in a soothing tone, promises to guide the reader over unstable steps and declares, "I know the way," a subtextual

nod toward the novelist's skill at researching London's underbelly and recreating its skanky abyss in November 1874.[14]

An experienced pilot, Faber treads a narrow footpath between Gothic detail and city-bred invective. In describing the no-win life of twenty-nine-year-old Caroline, he declares her better off than "fellow factory slaves" because her sale of sex is "not as dirty as the factory, nor as dangerous, nor as dull."[15] Caroline's "lay and lodgings"[16] abuts a commercial center, a "benign monster called manufacture,"[17] a foreshadowing of the story to come and its melding of degeneracy with capitalism. Staring from the window at female drudges and a man who sells paper windmills, she rationalizes the practicality of earning her keep as a fallen woman: "What did God make cunts for, if not to save women from donkeywork,"[18] a coarse approximation of Zora Neale Hurston's declaration in *Their Eyes Were Watching God* (1937) that women are the "mules of the world." In flight from joblessness, Caroline, a single parent of an unhealthy son, leaves temporary housing at Chitty Street and moves deeper into the heart of darkness of "the capital of the civilised world,"[19] Faber's sarcastic gesture toward the British Empire's paganism and smuggery.

Faber excels at reflecting female survivalism in a man's world. He subverts the nineteenth-century tradition that women require chivalric shielding from startling sights, physical toil, and emotional shock. Unlike William, an undisciplined layabout, his paramour is well read in Shakespearean tragedy and pre-Romantic funereal verse. To his surprise, she discusses intelligently the prefeminist philosophies of her day. Before William's first coupling with his red-haired temptress, he naps and wets his pants, an infantilism that Sugar pities. In sponging him clean of too much ale and murmuring "Poor baby," she prefigures her reclamation through pseudomotherhood.[20] For contrast, Faber pictures the era's sanctimonious prig in the forays and dalliances of the "frightfully sincere"[21] Henry Rackham, William's older brother and alter ego, a hairy masturbator, voyeur, and obvious newcomer to the dissolute life. Tantalized by paintings of nude saints at the Royal Academy, Henry takes on the comic qualities of the "werewolf . . . ravaging virgins, then scourging his flesh in remorse."[22] In retort to Henry's aspiration to be a parson, Bodley quips, "We had prayers twice a day in our house. I owe my atheism to it,"[23] an unbeliever's explanation of the failure of mid-1800s piety. Unlike his mimsy brother, William, a roguish narcissist, negotiates outright for control of Sugar's sexuality and loyalty. The contractual agreement boils down to "marvels for a guinea," a cents-for-sex subjugation and twenty-first-century recap of white slavery.[24]

Male and female perspectives jostle Faber's novel like duelers. Ashwell reduces Sugar to a mathematical commodity: "Three men; three holes—the arithmetic of it is perfect!"[25] an even-steven summation of the Victorian orgy. Out of sympathy for the child derelicts of St. Giles whom Henry attempts to uplift

from perdition, Emmeline comments that there is no need for hell for fallen women, who have "already endured the worst" on earth.[26] Together, the Rackham brothers combine foibles into a rank plunder of the nuclear family cloaked by the respectability of two of the era's surface purifiers—Christian proselytizing and the perfume business, a miniaturization of Industrial Age consumerism. In private, Sugar sees through the pretext. She abases William's ejaculation on her pantalettes as "the snot of male ecstasy . . . the making of another pompous little man,"[27] her diminution of the British swell. Grown surly toward the era's optimism, for the third time since the opening chapter, she speaks the apostasy of John Milton's Satan: "God damn God and all his horrible filthy creation,"[28] a curse that resonates through the text. The imprecation supplies Faber's explanation for the late nineteenth century's abandonment of Christianity.

Ironically, the gamesmanship that accompanies whoring on Silver Street devalues females at the same time that it valorizes them. Intent on "[snatching] victory from the orifice of defeat,"[29] William, under the alias of writer and critic George W. Hunt, prepares for an evening of prime wenching. In his den, he studies the animalesque descriptions of More Sprees in London, which divides female choices into trotters, hocks, prime rump, and mid loin.[30] In a coin game with his initial conquests, Claire and Alice, William enjoys watching the pair squat and capture in their labia the coins he tosses. Delving deeper into perversity, he rotates the girls' bodies in search of undiscovered orifices to titillate his fancy. At Sugar's hangout at the Fireside, he hears group songs about "military defeats," "shipwrecks," "broken hearts," and "Death itself,"[31] in which God takes the blame for human destitution. On William's first assignation with Sugar, he awards himself victory in her shape-shifting from polite lady to winsome siren. In contrast to his fascination with an obedient girl toy, she rejects the handsome-prince syndrome by gaining for herself the perks of the kept woman.

In an updating of the Beauty and the Beast motif, Sugar maneuvers William's obsession to her advantage. Bestiality endears her for her willingness to turn her genitals into innovative sex toys, an indecency performed at her Priory Close quarters at a price that separates her from Soho's low-life debauchery. At one of the novel's misogynistic epiphanies, she pours water into her vagina and lowers herself on all fours to crawl like a crab and squirt a stream at William for his amusement. The outré genital trick degrades her sex organs while dehumanizing her to the level of a crustacean, reminiscent of J. Alfred Prufrock's "pair of ragged claws scuttling across the floors of silent seas." In justification for his deviant tastes, William makes the sybarite's demand: "I must not be denied,"[32] a peculiar blend of arrogance with the petulance of a three-year-old.

A reverse Jane Eyre, Sugar understands the power of playacting and the profit motive. Early on, she poses as delectably defenseless but privately declares, "It's not possible to save anyone in this world, except oneself."[33] Nefarious thoughts

clog her mind in an unending plot cycle, leaving her confused about "her lover . . . her employer . . . whatever he is to her now."[34] In a slap at antiwoman myth, she derides her era's fiction for its polarized images of pink-cheeked governesses and crazy women locked into straw-floored cells. She shocks William into a blush by asking about business, a taboo subject that he condemns as "a great deal more transgressive than talk of cocks and cunts."[35] Faber creates low comedy from Sugar's questions about Rackham's product line while William disappears under her skirts to sniff her female musk and plunder her pudenda. Through reverse psychology, like Scheherazade, she inculcates him in packaging and advertising and convinces him of "the inevitability of Rackham's one day being the foremost manufacturer of toiletries in England."[36] While plotting a getaway, the kept-woman-turned-governess does more than teach the young. She defeats her dominator with a stash of bank notes to finance the abduction of seven-year-old Sophie, a naïf appropriately named for the Greek "wisdom." To William, Sophie is "a daughter, unfortunately,"[37] who can do nothing to retrieve the Rackham house, "a grand pretentious gravestone for an illustrious family that reached the end of its line."[38] The child's artlessness suggests a suitable tabula rasa for Sugar's cynical truisms, for example, "A man requires constant, tireless flattery to keep him from turning nasty."[39] In proof of her philosophy, she condones his sexual vice and flatters his "pego,"[40] a bordello term for "penis." With a saucy fillip directed at erectile function, she adds, "One careless remark can make his fragile forbearance shrivel."[41]

Significantly titled with a line from a cloying seduction ditty in Alfred, Lord Tennyson's *The Princess* (1847), *The Crimson Petal and the White* peruses a range of women's roles—wives, daughters, servants, and reformers at one end of the continuum and procurers and harlots at the other. Ironically, the female gender shares sisterhood bound by a curse, control by men who rule women's existence simply by being male. With artful profusion, Faber spikes his prose with rummagings in bedcraft, body effluvia, drugs, spying, and Hogarthian detail, including a lying beggar woman guffawing at her mate's public urination and pleading for a coin to buy "Mother's Blessing," a tincture of laudanum meant to quiet whimpering babes. In a strumpet's quarters, a tureen of spermicide and a sponge-on-a-stick method of neutralizing sperm in the vagina reassure the trollop alongside her fail-safe, a collection of abortifacients blending borax with sulphate of zinc or tansy with wormwood, a bitter herb. Faber extends the Gothic edge with a satire of Rackham venturing into the demimonde with the aid of the rake's Baedeker, *More Sprees in London: Hints for Men About Town, with Advice for Greenhorns,*[42] a real handbook to gaming and sensuality published around 1844. Black humor dominates Faber's plot and subplot—the snide religious mockery in William's choice of Priory Close, Marylebone (Mary the Good),[43] in April 1875 as Sugar's haven and love nest; Emmeline's overt seduction of Henry

as a last-ditch seizure of happiness from her impending death from tuberculosis; and Henry's demise in a cottage conflagration, as though unhallowed passion set him literally aflame. For Agnes Unwin Rackham, the neurasthenic maiden, in so sullied a world, morbidity prevails. She bewails, "Black, black, all is Black . . . I am shrouded in darkness,"[44] an admission of the failure of her truant fantasies and Catholic raptures.

Faber's impact derives, not from imitation of the Gothic classic, but from subversion of a longstanding Gothic framework and its moral assumptions of light/dark, yin/yang, revered/downtrodden, and worthy/transgressive. The classic faceoff between the monstrous Bertha Mason Rochester and the angelic governess from Charlotte Brontë's *Jane Eyre* (1847) takes a salvific direction after Rackham installs Sugar in the tony Notting Hill section at the governess's room in his "doll's house," a prefiguring of Henrik Ibsen's feminist drama, published in 1879.[45] Precise details insert Faber's take on the anomaly of a residential seraglio, particularly Sugar's cracking lips and scaly ichthyosis, a trope of the sere spirit that echoes the desiccation of Offred's carnal servitude in Margaret Atwood's dystopic fable *The Handmaid's Tale* (1985). Faber's emblematic punning implies that an impressionable virgin, Agnes "Always-Sick" Unwin Rackham,[46] chooses a mate unworthy of her affection and innocence. By marrying a bounder like William, she secures for herself an oppressive gender role, a metaphoric torment on the rack, the medieval version of adult life devoid of affection, friendship, curiosity, adventure, and artistic expression. In a symbolic dismembering of the matriarch's role in polite society, she, like Atropos, one of the three Greek *Moirae* (Fates), applies dressmaking shears to "a chaos of cannibalised ballgowns and bodices" by hacking and sewing them into bird shapes as a wifely comeuppance to "everything disagreeable,"[47] a euphemism for marital misery. No longer the failing invalid and domestic pawn, Agnes pedals furiously at her sewing machine, a boon to the female realm from the mechanized age since 1850. Significantly, Sugar boosts Agnes's morale in female fashion by purchasing a cloak from a strawberry vendor's back to enfold the fallen wife in tender reassurance.

With the yearning of the isle-bound Daedalus and Icarus in Greek myth, Faber's homebound victim reaches toward the sky. He lightens Agnes's travail by picturing her formation of images in flight—"dozens of humming-birds,"[48] a fluttery puff of whimsy and mobility. An imaginary guardian angel "with a mysterious pale glow shimmering in front of its torso"[49] promises Agnes release from her immurement by William and from weekly male-controlled medical gropings by the odious Dr. James Curlew. In league with William, Curlew diagnoses Agnes's ill health as the fault of a troublemaking womb, thus blaming her gender for persistent malfunction. Instead of Brontë's deranged cast-off wife stalking the heroine in a dark hallway, Faber presents wife Agnes with a greater solace to terror in the form of a radiant seraph—Sugar—as a heaven-sent comforter

endowed with agape, the benevolence that doesn't have to be deserved. Rather than sacrifice one woman for another as Brontë does with Bertha and Jane, Faber empowers Sugar to rescue herself and Agnes, as well as Agnes's daughter Sophie, who flees the unwholesomeness of idealized ladyhood proposed by Lady Bridgelow and the new governess. The triple play elevates females to greater efficacy through strength in sisterhood, an antidote to Agnes's stymied faculties and to impending disaster for Sugar.

Through the tending of Sophie, the next female generation, Sugar discovers the joys of mothering, a post abandoned by Agnes, the raving lady of the house, an Anglo-Catholic version of La Llorona, the Central American phantom who mourns and despoils her own offspring. A Gothic epiphany, Agnes's horror at her crimson menses leaps from the page with its graphic perception of women's biological downfall—the cyclic flow of bloody uterine discharge that becomes a visual link between womanhood and death. For literal substantiation of the image, Faber names the wife "Agnes," a derivative of the Latin for "lamb," the tremulous antibride on the altar whom her husband subdues with house arrest and enough morphine to keep her "doped halfway to fairyland."[50] Extending the horror of martyrdom is William's plan to dispatch Agnes three days after Christmas 1875 to Labaube Sanatorium in Wiltshire northwest of London. A further censure of William's character is his planned business trip to Frome, Somerset, a retreat of the cowardly husband while five men from the asylum terrorize and abduct his wife. In a waggish insertion of bathos, William pictures himself as Ozymandias, the despairing Egyptian ruler Ramses the Great reduced to wreckage in the desert in Shelley's 1818 sonnet. Faber snickers at his wimpy antihero's decision to withdraw from Agnes's permanent departure: "William could have wept."[51] His consolation is typical, a retreat to the Jolly Shepherdess tavern where the bar clock long ago "stopped at midnight."[52]

The text evens out Gothic extremes through the hyperomniscient narrator,[53] a genial insurgent who metes out pity to the madwoman for having a brain tumor undiscoverable and untreatable in the mid-1870s. The speaker also accords blessing on Sugar, an escapee from William's private netherworld at Chepstow Villas. In the ensuing domestic chaos, Sophie contrasts her father's demeanor by remaining calm while William "sulks and stammers and bawls, and falls asleep in mid-task, like a querulous infant."[54] Sugar's prize is extrication from captivity, self-actualization through surrogate motherhood, and the writing of a prophecy, *The Fall and Rise of Sugar*,[55] an autobiographical novel through which she acts out the female murder of males. Faber draws comedy out of her harangue by describing bloodletting as a flow, spill, spurt, pour, or leak. At length, she chooses "spew"[56] before a quick urination and the tossing of the evidence out the window before it can offend William. In a bondage scenario suggestive of the apocryphal decapitation story of Judith and Holofernes, the fictional Sugar "[busies] myself

with my whet-stone and my dagger" and offers a choice to the male tied to
the bedpost: "Where is it your pleasure to have the blade enter you?"[57] Sugar's
S-and-M fiction, composed in purple ink and renamed at her whim from its
initial title, *Women Against Men*, inventories a line of brutes, "a jostling queue
of human refuse, filthy, gin-stinking, whisky-stinking, ale-stinking, scabrous,
oily-nailed, slime-toothed, squint-eyed, senile, cadaverous, obese, stump-legged,
hairy-arsed, monster-cocked."[58] The text, like the neo-Gothic genre itself,
morphs into an eyewitness account of Rackham's atrocities and vilifies Dr. Curlew as "Satan's lackey, the Demon Inquisitor and the Leech Master" for calmly
leading Agnes away to an asylum,[59] an aboveground version of premature burial.
At such villainy, Sugar struggles to conceal revulsion and rage at males in general,
even the happily-ever-after novels concluding with rescue through marriage. At
Adam, the human progenitor in Eden, she frames an indictment; at androcen-
trism, she hurls "unprettified truth" followed by an antimale screed: "There's a
new century coming soon, and you and your kind will be dead!"[60]

With more feminist zeal than nostalgia for old-style Gothic, Faber wraps
up his lengthy vendetta tale with a surge of energy. For the setting of chapter
27, he chooses the female command post of the house: "the kitchen, in whose
mausoleum frigidity a glum, sleepy-headed company has gathered" to search
for Agnes, the runaway wife.[61] A mystic voice in Sugar's head directs her away
from the search party in the snow, a subtextual parallel of the freezing of Molly
Farren, the fallen woman, laudanum addict, and failed mother congealed in
pure white in George Eliot's *Silas Marner* (1861). Sugar's voice leads her to the
carriage, a symbol of engineless mobility that stands in "a puddle of chains and
leather straps," the symbolic constraints of the sadomasochistic world of women
like Agnes and Sugar and of constraints on the insane rigged up by heinous
mad scientists like James Curlew. Faber extends ties to standard Gothicism by
picturing the delusional Agnes in thick magenta silk "in an oriental style,"[62] a
subtle gesture toward the Victorian flair for Asian exoticism that barely covers
her innocent white cotton nightgown. Paranoia causes Agnes, a hapless Alice
in Wonderland, to suspect her husband of slowly poisoning her, a metaphoric
description of patriarchy's incremental negation of female autonomy. Before her
complete erasure, she rejects fairy-tale promises of connubial bliss and seizes on
a realistic hope that Sugar has indeed retrieved her diaries, a female outlet and
self-vindication for a throttled life. In one of Faber's prevalent olfactory touches,
Agnes disdains the odor of the Rackham house, which reminds her of "people
trying terribly hard to be happy, without the slightest success."[63] At a peak of delight, Sugar, the replacement mother who escapes Rackham's sanctum, swoops
Sophie up in play, experiencing "more physical joy than she's felt in a lifetime
of embraces."[64] Sugar's chance at selfhood and maternity far from the Rackham
domain contrasts the despair of Sophie's grandfather, Henry Calder Rackham,

the family patriarch who grieves for his dead son Henry and longs for grandchildren, preferably boys.

For Sugar, self-rescue, the sine qua non of postmodern feminist Gothicism, follows an operatic dustup. Betrayed by William, a shallow hedonist, she bears blame for an unforeseen pregnancy, a unilateral fault thrust on her by her fellow copulator. Caroming about her conscious mind is an amorphous foreboding, the danger of coitus she learned in prepubescence from her mother's sacrilegious jingle: "One squirt of slime from the man, one fishy egg in the woman, and behold: they shall call his name Emmanuel,"[65] a tweak at the Old Testament prophet Isaiah. William, meanwhile, stutters his way through an epiphany: Victorian males foist on themselves distasteful roles as "an ogre, a f-fraud, a f-fool, a gaoler, a w-well-dressed prop to be s-seen w-with in the S-S-Season."[66] He opts for the ogrish persona after Sugar's self-dosing with brewer's yeast and pennyroyal, a potentially lethal folk emmenagogue producing uterine contractions, vomiting, and menstrual flow. Faber enlarges on the infanticidal implications of abortion as Sugar's mental image progresses from a clump of cells in her womb to an innocent victim "scalded with sulphate of zinc and borax, its mouth gasping for clean nourishment amidst the poisons that swirl in Sugar's innards."[67] At an inopportune moment on a tour of William's soap factory in Lambeth, she must locate the washroom and relieve the spasms in the birth canal. Too late, she realizes that the "blood and other hot, slick material"[68] erupting from her vagina and slithering down her thighs is the miscarriage she has courted with lavage, drugs, and a deliberate but ineffectual tumble down the stairs. Faber wrings grim humor as the entourage turns homeward over Waterloo Bridge. After Sugar's four months of concubinage in the Rackham household, like Napoleon's downfall, the crossing prefaces her ouster for immorality.

Fine-tuned with Gothic sensibilities, *The Crimson Petal and the White* flaunts extremes of coarse sexuality and phobia to heighten escapism, Faber's controlling theme. From a Machiavellian view of profit, blasphemous scenarios depict Ashley and Bodwell exploiting their parodic pamphlet *The Efficacy of Prayer* as well as corrupting pubescent girls equipped with riding crops as sources of sexual exhilaration for their adult johns.[69] Out of terror of solitude, Agnes longs for female stories by the authors of her day, including Eliza Lynn Linton, Charlotte Riddell, and Scots novelist Margaret Oliphant, producers of "a steady supply of noble and attractive human beings" to relieve isolation.[70] William congratulates himself on ensnaring "the girl of a life" but manages to swathe himself in self-pity.[71] Picturing himself "as a restless beast" confined in a cage twisted from "silvery '£' symbols," he regrets a fiscal deficit that prevents him from "[raping] the world into submission," an impasse that captures the author's concept of commercial impotence.[72] The goad to his manhood, a yearning to restrict Sugar from public trafficking in the sex trade, becomes the jolt that

saves William from bankruptcy and from his father's carping about "[opening] his mind to the mathematics of manure," an agrarian image of the materials of perfumerie.[73]

The height of Faber's feminist diatribe reveals Sugar as femme fatale to William's inept Bluebeard. With the resolve of a Medea, Medusa, or Lilith, she commandeers poses and guises from taunting slut to kittenish man pleaser, each intended to further her aims to dominate the male and to free Agnes from death in life as a walled-up invalid. Sugar's stimulus is an undercurrent of rage and sorrow at the unspeakable—the memory of her mother devaluing her in childhood to a saleable commodity. In the resolution, William's hero story backfires into a fool tale through the female trickster's victimization of an easily gulled male. For the sake of public approval, he frees himself from an unsuitable wife by identifying a drowned wretch on a morgue slab as Agnes. As a form of exorcism, Sugar's memoir calls down the Almighty's wrath on philanderers like William who aggrandize themselves by degrading and dehumanizing women, like Lucy Fitzroy, Madam Georgina's prize strumpet, whom a client beats and disfigures with her own riding crop. In a deplorable spoonerism on persecution, Bodley chortles, "How the fighty are maulen."[74] Bodley further discredits himself by referring to Sophie's injury as "drama, bloodshed—and feminine charm . . . a proboscidiferous haemorrhage [nosebleed]."[75] With stereotypical male illogic, Rackham interprets Sugar's laudable self-rejuvenation as evidence of transgendered depravity, ironically a trait that could belong only to a man. Unlike male Gothic, which banishes the rebellious or threatening female from her rightful domestic place, female Gothic reclaims the woman's place as householder, mother, and fount of goodness. A self-acknowledged robber bride and outlaw from Victorian proprieties, Sugar adopts a new identity free of coercion and depersonalization. Thus she recedes from view, presumably into a shadowed lair in which to groom Sophie into the unfettered New Woman.

Notes

1. *The Crimson Petal and the White* blossoms just after those works at the end of the twentieth century that pushed genre parameters into darker, more intense, more profuse realms by combining horror with postcolonialism, feminism, bondage, and satires on materialism and social and economic orders. See Mary Ellen Snodgrass, *Encyclopedia of Gothic Literature* (New York: Facts on File, 2004). These neo-Gothic treasures of the late 1900s include the following titles:

- Isabel Allende's Chilean colonial Gothic *The House of the Spirits* (1981)
- T. Coraghessan Boyle's phantasmagoric historical novel *Water Music* (1982)
- Patrick Suskind's Bavarian blockbuster *Parfum* (1985)

- Laura Esquivel's best-selling Tex-Mex melodrama *Like Water for Chocolate* (1989)
- August Wilson's ghost-busting postslavery play *The Piano Lesson* (1990)
- Peter Carey's reclamation of Dickens's Abel Magwitch in *Jack Maggs* (1997)
- Margaret Edson's "mad scientist" play *Wit* (1999)

2. See Sandra Gilbert and Susan Gubar, *The Madwoman in the Attic*, 2nd ed. (New Haven, CT: Yale University Press, 1984).

3. Michel Faber, *The Crimson Petal and the White* (New York: Harcourt, 2002), 717.

4. Similarly, other innovative works of the early 21st century, like

- Carlos Ruiz Zafón's Barcelona-based quest novel *The Shadow of the Wind* (2001),
- Sarah Waters's lesbian Victoriana in *Fingersmith* (2002),
- Virginia Renfro Ellis's gentle post–Civil War revenant tale *The Wedding Dress* (2002),
- Dan Brown's convoluted crusader's mystery *The Da Vinci Code* (2003), and
- Ariana Franklin's twelfth-century historical thriller *The Serpent's Tale* (2008) hone

character dilemmas and choices that have the immediacy of *Lady Audley's Secret*, the peril of *The Hound of the Baskervilles*, the claustrophobia of "The Yellow Wallpaper," and the menace and prurience of the Marquis de Sade. The best of the genre take the pragmatic approach by putting sensational elements to better use than generating shivers or eliciting sexual depravity.

5. Masters of female Gothic, Angela Carter, Toni Morrison, Joyce Carol Oates, and Anne Rice, also apply updated visions of seduction, stalking, and Newgate novel violence to a reevaluation of fairy tale and myth as sources of insight into male-female egalitarianism and gender empowerment.

6. Faber, *The Crimson Petal*, 655.

7. Faber, *The Crimson Petal*, 238.

8. Faber, *The Crimson Petal*, 226.

9. Faber, *The Crimson Petal*, 217.

10. Faber, *The Crimson Petal*, 3.

11. Faber, *The Crimson Petal*, 831.

12. Faber, *The Crimson Petal*, 4.

13. Faber, *The Crimson Petal*, 4.

14. Faber, *The Crimson Petal*, 5.

15. Faber, *The Crimson Petal*, 12.

16. Faber, *The Crimson Petal*, 19.

17. Faber, *The Crimson Petal*, 21.

18. Faber, *The Crimson Petal*, 12.

19. Faber, *The Crimson Petal*, 13.

20. Faber, *The Crimson Petal*, 115.

21. Faber, *The Crimson Petal*, 658.

22. Faber, *The Crimson Petal*, 240.

23. Faber, *The Crimson Petal*, 143.

24. Faber, *The Crimson Petal*, 84.

25. Faber, *The Crimson Petal*, 225.

26. Faber, *The Crimson Petal*, 183. See also Barbara Braid, "Monster/Angel Dichotomy in the Representation of Women in Michel Faber's *The Crimson Petal and the White*," www.inter-disciplinary.net/wp-content/uploads/2009/04/ewf1braid.pdf (accessed June 19, 2009).

27. Faber, *The Crimson Petal*, 123, 124.

28. Faber, *The Crimson Petal*, 124.

29. Faber, *The Crimson Petal*, 89.

30. Faber, *The Crimson Petal*, 83.

31. Faber, *The Crimson Petal*, 92.

32. Faber, *The Crimson Petal*, 74.

33. Faber, *The Crimson Petal*, 41.

34. Faber, *The Crimson Petal*, 749.

35. Faber, *The Crimson Petal*, 233.

36. Faber, *The Crimson Petal*, 649.

37. Faber, *The Crimson Petal*, 296.

38. Faber, *The Crimson Petal*, 299.

39. Faber, *The Crimson Petal*, 650.

40. Faber, *The Crimson Petal*, 238.

41. Faber, *The Crimson Petal*, 650.

42. Faber, *The Crimson Petal*, 68.

43. Faber, *The Crimson Petal*, 261.

44. Faber, *The Crimson Petal*, 477, 478.

45. Faber, *The Crimson Petal*, 200.

46. Faber, *The Crimson Petal*, 239.

47. Faber, *The Crimson Petal*, 222.

48. Faber, *The Crimson Petal*, 222.

49. Faber, *The Crimson Petal*, 427.

50. Faber, *The Crimson Petal*, 300.

51. Faber, *The Crimson Petal*, 660.

52. Faber, *The Crimson Petal*, 300.

53. See Paul Dawson, "The Return of Omniscience in Contemporary Fiction," *Narrative* 17, no. 2 (May 2009): 143–161.

54. Faber, *The Crimson Petal*, 681.

55. Faber, *The Crimson Petal*, 411.

56. Faber, *The Crimson Petal*, 197.

57. Faber, *The Crimson Petal*, 227.

58. Faber, *The Crimson Petal*, 335, 228.

59. Faber, *The Crimson Petal*, 752.

60. Faber, *The Crimson Petal*, 229, 172.

61. Faber, *The Crimson Petal*, 638.

62. Faber, *The Crimson Petal*, 641.

63. Faber, *The Crimson Petal*, 643.

64. Faber, *The Crimson Petal*, 705.

65. Faber, *The Crimson Petal*, 686.
66. Faber, *The Crimson Petal*, 783.
67. Faber, *The Crimson Petal*, 739.
68. Faber, *The Crimson Petal*, 739.
69. Faber, *The Crimson Petal*, 61.
70. Faber, *The Crimson Petal*, 221.
71. Faber, *The Crimson Petal*, 127.
72. Faber, *The Crimson Petal*, 67.
73. Faber, *The Crimson Petal*, 138.
74. Faber, *The Crimson Petal*, 144.
75. Faber, *The Crimson Petal*, 145, 146.

CHAPTER 12

Shedding Light on the Gothic

PETER STRAUB'S *A DARK MATTER*

Brian Evenson

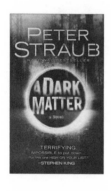

In his afterword to the "New Gothic" portfolio that he edited for *Conjunctions* magazine in 1990,[1] Patrick McGrath suggests that, as early as Poe, the Gothic began "shifting away from an emphasis on props and sets—dark forests and lugubrious caverns, skeletons and thunderstorms—and toward a particular sensibility characterized by transgressive tendencies and extreme distortions of perception and affect."[2] In the place of an externalized sublime, we find instead an increasing focus on the way in which an event or an experience is transformed by the consciousness of an individual, most often a narrator. For instance, the way someone can be driven mad by the imagined beating of a heart beneath the floorboards, the beating itself a distortion of perception that is a result of a transgression that the perceiving mind has committed (in this case murder). In Poe, we see this distortion expressed prominently in syntax, in the starts and hesitations and recoils of Poe's narrators (for instance, "TRUE!—nervous—very, very dreadfully nervous I had been and am; but why *will* you say that I am mad?" from "The Tell-tale Heart").[3] In Lovecraft, the narrator's awareness that his perception and the world's opinions do not coincide manifests itself in a kind of baroque thickening of vocabulary and structure, an attempt to make something seemingly unbelievable believable through a language become palpable. In both cases, we find narrators who are often unable to believe the evidence of their own eyes but also helpless not to recount what they saw.

Straub is very aware of this; indeed, his *Mr. X* (1999) consciously, and seemingly effortlessly, pastiches Lovecraft. A careful reader of other texts and a conscious stylist in his own right, Straub can write like Lovecraft when he wants to, and no doubt could also write like Poe. But whereas these earlier authors,

and many ostensibly Gothic authors since, have focused on "extreme distortions of perception," Straub's *A Dark Matter* focuses less on overdetermined distortions of perception than on perception, full stop, and in this he has as much in common with Henry James as he does with the Gothic or Late Gothic writers as McGrath defines them. Indeed, *A Dark Matter* provides a link between the way in which the Gothic in its various forms ostensibly deals with perception and consciousness and the way that literary works do. It does so in a way that makes the pretended distinction between literature and genre that critics are fond of making seem misguided.

In his anthology *Poe's Children: The New Horror*, Straub makes the point that with contemporary genre-influenced work, "You have to be open-eyed and flexible as to category to get what is going on, but some vital individual breakthroughs are in the wind."[4] I think this point applies equally to Straub's own work in *A Dark Matter*. Perhaps Straub's most complex work to date, it utterly erases the line between the literary and horror in a way that makes us feel that that distinction was "designed mostly to keep everyone in their proper place,"[5] and makes us wonder if that line has all along been a mechanism either of protection or of control. As early as the 1990s, Straub was suggesting that "horror was a house that horror had moved out of,"[6] a category that the best work had outgrown.

More recently, on March 9, 2010, Straub suggested of horror that

> Crime writers and academics of genre fiction like to denigrate horror by pointing out that unlike "mystery," "western" or "romance," "horror" specifies no content beyond the emotion it is intended to arouse. I think this absence of specificity is not at all a limitation but the reverse, a great enhancement. That no situational templates are built into horror grants it an inherent boundarilessness, a boundlessness, an inexhaustible unlimitedness. If the "horror" part is not stressed all that overtly and the author spares us zombies, vampires, ghosts, haunted houses, hideous things in bandages, etc., what results is fiction indistinguishable, except in one element alone, from literary fiction.[7]

If this is in fact the case, then one would expect Straub's work not to fit snugly into a particular genre category, be it horror or literature or Gothic.

It is interesting that McGrath defines the Gothic not dissimilarly, suggesting that "the gothic is precisely this, an air, a tone, an atmosphere, a tendency. It is not a monolith, and there is no objective gauge by means of which one can detect its presence or absence. It's a matter of subjective arousal, indistinct and unreliable, which is as it should be, the gothic wouldn't have it any other way."[8] Indeed, one of the difficulties with a book like *A Dark Matter* (not unlike much

of Robert Aickman's work) is that, while it contains elements that can be clearly identified as coming from literature, horror, and the Gothic, the way it combines and manipulates them makes any of these categories feel, ultimately, inadequate to defining the book as a whole.

In other words, there are many other books that fit much more snugly into their category and that would be much easier to discuss in a scholarly book on the Gothic. At the same time, books like *A Dark Matter* are the ones that project toward a future of the genre. For this reason, they are precisely the works that we need most to discuss; they are the works that show limitations in our thinking and in our neat categories, the works that suggest where a genre is capable of going. *A Dark Matter* illustrates what both horror/Gothic and the literary can be as they evolve and progressively outgrow their categories.

With that disclaimer, there are numerous elements of both horror and the Gothic in the novel: transgressions, pacts attempted with the supernatural world, losses of identity, disappearances, the notion of a past haunting a present, deliberate slips from one time to another, the revelation of the world as potentially not what it seems, the illumination of the world at one point as a pretense or as a kind of cheap toy, a proliferation of narrators each with a slightly (and sometimes dramatically) different perception of events, and so on. Though the novel takes place roughly around the year it was published, at the heart of *A Dark Matter* lies an event that occurred more than forty years earlier on October 16, 1966, in Madison, Wisconsin. On that evening, a group of high school and college students led by Spencer Mallon, an older charismatic hippie type, gathered in the University of Wisconsin's agronomy meadow (hardly the Gothic's typical setting) to perform a forbidden ritual. They are not exactly clear on the ritual, and even Spencer Mallon, despite being confident in his own abilities and despite his dabbling in various mysticisms and Dionysian ideals, really has very little idea what he's opening up. He promises them "a great transformation and rebirth," which he admits, hedging his bets, might last "only a second or two" and "might take place only in their minds, as the opening of a fresh vision, a truer, more essential way of seeing things."[9]

What they seemingly get, however, is something quite different. Of the eight people who follow Mallon into the meadow, only six come out. One, Keith Hayward, a college boy whom several of the others find creepy or damaged, is killed, his body "hideously mutilated, ripped to shreds" (16). Another, Brett Milstrap, simply vanishes, seemingly having stepped out of the world. The remaining six scatter. Mallon flees, with a high school kid named Dill Olson, now a Mallon acolyte, following in his wake.

These are the facts we have. What actually happened in that meadow is something that has, for forty years, remained unclear. Meredith Bright, Mallon's

girlfriend (one of several), took "off at a dead run, packed up her clothes, and camped out at the airport until she could get a flight back home to Arkansas, where the police questioned her for hours, day after day . . ." (39). Of the remaining three, one, Howard "Hootie" Bly, has become a permanent resident of a psychiatric ward as a result of his experience in the meadow. There he speaks only in quotations from Hawthorne and from a dictionary by a certain "Captain Leland Fountain." Another, Jason "Boats" Boatman, leaves school to become a full-time professional thief. Another, Lee "the Eel" Truax, "the most beautiful woman in any room she happened to enter, blessed with intelligence, courage, excellent health" (40), who is married to the book's primary narrator, seems initially to have come out of the experience whole, but as time goes on, what she has seen in the meadow begins to darken her vision and finally takes it away entirely, leaving her blind.

In a case of doubling (and inversion, since "Eel" is "Lee" backward), the Eel's husband is also named Lee. He is Lee Harwell, a writer stuck on his latest book when he stumbles across a homicide detective's poorly written memoirs that suggest links between the "Ladykiller Homicides" and the events of the meadow. Lee is closer to Fitzgerald's Nick Carroway than to Poe's or Lovecraft's implicated narrators; though he was to some degree part of the group, he did not go to the meadow with the others and thus stands perpetually as a stranger to their experience: "I had missed the boat, definitively, and so had been spared the mysterious experience that came to define their lives. There was a magic circle and I stood beyond its periphery" (39).

Over the years, Lee hasn't learned much about the events at the meadow. The Eel has refused to speak about it in any kind of detail with him, and they both fled to New York not long after, leaving the events submerged. Though there have been hints over the years, and though he knows Eel is periodically in touch with the others, he thinks of it as her own business, considers the past to be, well, past. But the detective's memoir, combined with an encounter with a homeless man whose way of speaking reminds him of Hootie, imbues him with a need to learn the answer to a question that has remained unasked for so long: "Why had they, each in his or her own way, not only jumped off the rails but jumped into such distorted lives?" (41).

In a traditional Gothic novel, asking such a question might be the beginning of the end. It might open the door to something likely to destroy them all. But, as Lee admits, "my need was stronger than the fear of whatever might crawl out of the knowledge I might turn up" (41). And as he also realizes, things have already been off the rails for forty years. The problem is not asking the question, but in having failed to ask it for so long—not the destruction by an unleashed secret but the slow, gnawing destruction by something never quite faced up to. Add to that Lee's knowledge that, "all this time, I admitted to myself, I had

been jealous of them for whatever they had *seen* out there, no matter that it had screwed them up, each in a different way" (41). By asking the question, Lee is trying to find a way to enter back into the magic circle of his friends, a circle that he has flitted around for years now. He asks Eel to put him in touch with Dilly, the person who had gone off with Mallon, to see if he can find some answers. In the Gothic of the past, Lee most likely would receive more than he bargained for, more than he could take in, but as we will see, Straub will take the ending of the novel in a different direction, one of acceptance and acknowledgment rather than destruction.

What follows are Lee's attempts to see the old friends, to gather them close again. There are multiple narratives from all the different characters, different perceptions, none of which are the whole truth about what happens, but all of which, gathered by Lee and brought together, add up to a kind of complex and discordant truth. These are allowed to jostle one another and to conflict. As in Orson Welles's *Citizen Kane*, we get the impression that we're getting something real with each new story, but that no single story, no single gesture, reveals the truth.

After the introductory section, we have a section entitled "Hootie's Blues," which Lee's introduction to it tells us was originally a story called "Tootie's Blues" but is based on stories that, as the narrative anticipates, Hootie tells him after being released from the hospital. In other words, after changing the names and showing the story to Hootie (and receiving Hootie's approval—"It's like you were there, right there with me" [48])—Lee returned the names to their original form and presents the story as Hootie's truth. The effect of this is to give a slight instability to the story being told, to emphasize not only its subjective quality, but the way in which it consists of a complex interaction between a writer and the person upon whose experience the narrative is based.

Hootie has long had an ability to remember almost everything he read and often expresses himself in long quotations from Hawthorne or by peppering ordinary conversation with odd words from *Captain Leland Fountain's Dictionary of Unknown, Strange and Preposterous Words*. For him, Fountain's book demonstrated "the existence of a secret code that if fully understood would surely reveal the unknown and hidden structure of the world, or at least of what was called reality" (49). The events in 1966 he saw as "so terrible that [he] had encircled himself with the sacred stones of his words" (52), and it has taken him nearly forty years to get the courage to step outside of that protective circle.

In his story, in which at moments the events of the distant past seem to exist cotemporally with Hootie's life in the present, we see Hootie's view of the days just before the event in the meadow, get his sense of the interactions of and tensions between the other characters, including a dream about Hayward as a murderer and a strange and menacing interaction with Hayward's uncle. Together they troop out to the agronomy meadow for a rehearsal and paint a white circle

in the grass for their ceremony, and during that experience Hootie realizes that they are surrounded by strangers, by "humane, upright dogs: dogs in handsome but outdated human clothes" (84). He is the only one who can see them, along with, very briefly, a "tormented white scrap" that flies over the grass and seems to have "*escaped* into this world" (85), and both sights unnerve him. Later that night, at a fraternity party, he catches a glimpse of a man in a gray suit whom he associates with his dream of Hayward's uncle and who seems to be paying unnatural attention to Eel. The scene is wonderfully full of threat, giving the sense that things are about to come seriously unwound, and then the scene itself ends.

This is followed by a short italicized section from Mallon of things he said to Hootie, a glimpse into his thoughts and patterns, that gives a sense of his charisma and appeal as well as how manipulative he is. The juxtaposition of this section to "Hootie's Blues," the introduction of the reader to it on the fading edge of the panic of the party scene, ends up catching the reader off guard and making it all the more powerful.

The following section returns initially to Lee's narration, beginning with a description of Dilly, just out of prison, getting back in touch with him, and Lee, reluctantly at first, helping him out and allowing him to stay with him as he gets on his feet. Slowly they begin to talk, and both realize they have had the same experience with Boats: when asked by each of them separately, years after the event, to describe what he saw in the meadow, he describes a "tower of dead children . . . . With little arms and legs sticking out" (123) and then breaks into tears. Dilly admits his experience has been different: he describes light streaming in "like through some crack in the world," and a terrible odor, which he thinks the others smelled as well (124). What he saw wasn't a tower of dead children but a "dog, standing up inside a little room with a rolltop desk," wearing human clothes. But the dog, he came to realize just as Mallon grabbed his elbow and pulled him away, was trying to hide something from him, "things I was not supposed to see." These hidden things were like humans, "but bright, almost shiny, as if they were made of mercury or something." Among them was a sort of queen carrying a distaff. "It terrified me," Dilly admits. "No, it *horrified* me, it filled me with *horror*" (125).

Together, Dilly and Lee decide to visit Hootie, the first time for Lee, and drive to Madison together. There Hootie's doctor indicates to them their friend's panicked response to dogs and asks if they have any explanation. The section ends with Lee discovering (through Dilly, not Hootie, who is still speaking just in quotations) that Mallon called the Eel his skylark, and with Lee being "pierced by the bright, sudden memory" of a skylark that he and his wife had seen soaring in London (142).

The following section begins with Lee and Dilly at their hotel reflecting on the end of their visit to Hootie, where Hootie, at first seemingly scared out of

his mind, has a breakdown and then a kind of breakthrough. Their talk moves from there to thoughts about Hayward's uncle and whether he was the killer that the detective thought he was. Not only is Lee convinced he was, but he's also convinced that Hayward himself probably helped him.

The narration becomes fairly complex after this. In one italicized thread, there is a story that Eel has told Lee about how she got a thief to confess to working with the American Confederacy of the Blind and how she had felt a shadowy, evil figure become present in the room with her, listening in ecstasy. In the other, we are getting Don's reaction to this story as told earlier in the evening. The story of the theft exists simultaneously on three levels: as it was originally told to Lee by Eel, as it is retold to Don by Lee, with his and Lee's comments added in, and in the way Lee rethinks and reconsiders it later that evening. But the way the narrative is arranged gives the impression of all three of these tellings existing simultaneously, the interaction among the three being exceptionally complex. The fact that it is difficult to summarize *A Dark Matter* without talking extensively about the narration should indicate that Straub is doing something very intentional with how the story is told, and one of the greatest joys of the novel—and one of the things most difficult to get across without simply reading the book itself—is the deftness with which Straub manipulates the book's many thematic and narrative strands.

Dilly and Lee take a trip to see Meredith Bright, now Meredith Walsh, in search of further answers. When trying to buy a plane ticket to Milwaukee, Lee finds himself dragged out of line by a strange man, perhaps Spencer Mallon, who knows his name and tells him not to fly. The event unsettles them enough that they drive, only later learning that the flight has crashed. Meredith, Lee discovers (Dilly has known all along), is the wife of a senator, her past life carefully hidden. She's got as an assistant a suitably black-clad cadaverous Hungarian named Vardis Fleck who might be an extra in Edgar G. Ulmer's *The Black Cat*. Meredith herself seems ageless and still stunning, though also weirdly calculating, and as time goes on, her smooth surface, both physically and emotionally, begins to crack.

Meredith's version of the story is as much about her sense of hurt because Mallon was insufficiently attentive to her. She also focuses on how the police had attempted to shut down an off-campus demonstration against the war on the day of the event in the meadow, leaving in their wake "a stunning chaos" (219), everything in motion, enraged policemen and fallen protesters. This is something nobody else has spoken about: for Dilly, it only slowed them down a little and wasn't worth mentioning, but for Meredith it gets them off schedule and puts them behind the star chart she had worked up to find the perfect time for the ceremony. As a result, things had changed, and they should have gone home.

There are jabs at the Eel, too, of whom Meredith is jealous and who, Lee discovers, might have had more of a relationship with Mallon than she had admitted.

For Meredith, the ceremony in the meadow didn't center on dogs or dead babies or monsters but on something else entirely. According to her, "A queen gave me a gift, and that changed everything" (223). But as she begins to speak, it is clear that she saw her monsters too. She saw things that are "more like scenes than mere beings or creatures" (233). There were several of these dioramas, all soundless: an old man and an old woman with second faces on the backs of their heads standing with an enormous pig and a small, scaly dragon; a man in bloody rags waving a sword, with an animal rearing behind him; a naked woman greenish white in color; a king riding a bear and a "Roaring Queen" (234) with a staff, both made of shiny liquid silver. The mad queen pointed the staff at Meredith, a light came out that struck Meredith's forehead, and, according to Meredith, "The great blessing had been bestowed and received" (235). She also watched as Brett Milstrap found a seam in space, tugged it open, and then was sucked into the chaotic world of the king and queen and was instantly gone.

But all of that was obscured by a terrible creature with a smell so awful that it was almost beautiful, a smell that made her dizzy. The creature "gave her a beatific smile only slightly undercut by the fact of the smiling lips being red with the blood of Keith Hayward, and the parallel fact that Keith Hayward's limp and utterly dead body, minus its head and right arm, dropped from the great creature's hands" (237).

Meredith's story is destabilized by her inability to fully describe what she saw, by the incommensurable and sublime aspect of what she saw. There were, she admits, upright dogs, but the dogs were there because "*they were what kept us from seeing that which we are not equipped to see*" (239). And as they moved away, she knew what they really looked like, "but she could not, not ever, describe them. It wasn't possible. Our words don't go that far, sorry" (239).

Her story is further destabilized by an odd sensation Lee had that she is at once lying and telling the truth at the same time. Lee believes that Meredith is empty, that there's "nothing there but hunger and the desire to manipulate" (243).

What follows is a return to Hootie, with his own telling of what happened during the ceremony in the meadow, told in the third person but in a highly allusive literary style that could only belong to Hootie's consciousness. Hootie saw beings "*laying in wait*" and smelled their sharp rank smell (269). He saw a creature that "did not *want* to be seen. . . . It did its work unseen, Hootie understood" (269). And seeing this creature leveled everything, turned it to dust. It is the "demon of midday, the Noonday Demon" (270), and now that it has seen Hootie, he is sure it intends to kill him. At that precise moment, Brett Milstrap

is worming his way out of the world. Simultaneously, the psychotic Keith Hayward is running toward Eel, his hands outstretched like claws as if to attack her, and he collides with the creature to become a "sudden fountain of blood" (271).

Hootie's realization is a startling one. He realizes that what is coming toward him, intending to kill him, is made of many, many words and sentences, "thrashing and boiling like monstrous, endless, interconnected snakes. And he knew all those sentences; they were within him" (271). This realization is enough to save him; he slips out of his body and threads into language, though as we already know, it takes him many years to thread his way out again.

After Hootie comes Jason "Boats" Boatman's version of the story, but the story he tells doesn't take place in the meadow at all; according to him, it "came from the meadow, I'm sure of that. It took a lot longer to get here, that's all" (283). Boats has a name for it, for the thing he felt, and this is the title of the book itself: "the dark matter" (282).

Boats tells about going out on Lake Michigan in a stolen boat and hearing voices coming over the water, as if there was an ocean liner anchored just out of sight, among them a voice that says, "I need what you need" (289). The noises come and go, and he realizes that the voice is Spencer Mallon's. He leaves his boat and goes onto a beach where he thinks the voice is coming from, and he hears it again. But this time he knows the words; he knows he is hearing a conversation from years ago, from the past. There is a brief moment when the past and the present seem to sink, where the Spencer Mallon of the past and the Boats of the future are together and speaking, with Mallon explaining that time isn't linear, and then, just as suddenly, he is alone again.

But this isn't the end. Something seems to be going wrong, and Boats is made to start the experience several times over again, the world resetting. In its last manifestation, the scene itself is reduced to Boats dragging a triangle of polished wood across a concrete floor, with words representing the scene he has just experienced written on notebook paper. His tower of babies in the meadow has become a pile of dolls, but when he gets too close, it becomes babies again, and then nearly instantly transforms back, leaving him in his make-believe "dead world of the wire hanger" (308). The implication is not only that nothing is what it seems, but that it is all make-believe, a representation, and as such a kind of life-in-death. This suggestion, that what is actually behind everything may be paltry, may be nothing, may be only the "dark matter," is at least as terrifying—if not more so—as the myriad creatures the friends have seen at the ceremony in the meadow. But this sensation, too, may be a function of "the noonday demon," the depression that works slowly and carefully to take someone apart, that reduces the world to a husk. As a disclosure, I should say that in his acknowledgments, Straub cites a chapter from my novel *The Open Curtain* as an inspiration for some of the techniques of this chapter, though he manages

to push it further and make it entirely his own. Ironically, the confusion and doubling of place in *The Open Curtain* was most likely inspired by a story of Straub's, "The Buffalo Hunter."

The final version, the one that gathers all the others into it and integrates them, not so much into a single "real" version of what happened, but into a complex fabric of multiple perceptions, is Eel's. She tells her story not only to Lee but also to her other close friends, Boats, Dilly, and Hootie, only insisting that they allow her to tell it her way and don't interrupt. What she adds, among other things better left for the reader of the novel to discover, is the skylark, a figure that she has herself become and occupied in a way that has allowed her to flit across time and space in a fraction of a second.

The skylark might be read, as Cameron suggests in his commentary on Percy Bysshe Shelley's poem "To a Skylark," as "a symbol of liberty and happiness, a force from nature that . . . might inspire others to produce a better world."[10] The actual poem asks, "Teach us, sprite or bird, / What sweet thoughts are thine" (lines 61–62).[11] As humans, however, we remain dissatisfied with our lot: "We look before and after / And pine for what is not" (lines 86–87). As both a symbolic and a literal skylark, the Eel is positioned to move the other characters from their own limited perspectives and troubles to a grander perspective that acknowledges them.

In Eel's case, by becoming a skylark, "she understood that Mallon, all unknowing, had given her access to the heart of time, which lay like a huge map on all sides, neither two-dimensional nor three, but both simultaneously. With the addition of breathing, static time, the fourth dimension had been set in place. Across its great map she was free to travel as she wished" (357–358). For this privilege she has traded her sight, and she considers this a fair trade, one that has given her a sense of herself and the world that she would not have had otherwise. Near the end, she finds herself inside Hayward, experiencing Keith's memory of having "given" a friend of his to his uncle for killing (an event alluded to several times in *A Dark Matter* but recounted in full only in Straub's separate novella *A Special Place*, 2009). And then she watches the demon that occupies Hayward pack up and move on. "In this line of work," he admits to her, "you're never really out of a J-O-B" (371).

All the groundwork for what Eel sees and perceives has been prepared for in the sections that come before, and indeed, as in each of the previous accounts, we see an addition of one or two new elements, but also a reevaluation of what has been already discussed before, a shift in perspective that ends up not neutralizing the earlier visions of other characters but contextualizing them, giving us a different way to see them. With Eel, the result is to bring in a ray of hope and light, though it is not unmixed with darkness as well. Indeed, she finds herself "Assailed by both love and terror, an unbearable combination" (386), and we are even left with at least a glimmer of hope that Hayward himself wasn't all bad.

"How certain are you, anyhow, that what you call 'unpleasantness' is not a necessary, even crucial, part of our experience?"[12] asks Straub. I read *A Dark Matter* as an answer to that question. *A Dark Matter* is a book about what it is like to bring a shared trauma, experienced differently by several people, to the surface and talk it through as a group, thinking it out and breaking its grip. It is a book not only about being damned by what one has seen and has attempted to bury, but about survival. Though shot through with Gothic elements, *A Dark Matter* is ultimately a novel about stepping out of the nonluminous world of the Gothic and into a world that has more than one ray of light. It is a captivating 397-page meditation about individual perception and shared perception that ends with a moment of joyous laughter. Suspensefully and gracefully, it discloses how the behavior of a larger shared story cannot be predicted by the behavior of the individual narratives that compose it, by its separate witnesses' agonies and memories. What makes *A Dark Matter* extraordinary is this: it is one of the first successful twenty-first-century experiments to take the traditional elements of the Gothic and of horror and design with them a residence all its own, one that in the end turns the lights on. Straub's *A Dark Matter* shows what may happen to the Gothic as it floats through the house that Walpole, Lewis, Radcliffe, and Shelley built, and then builds anew.

Notes

1. Peter Straub contributed an excerpt, "Mrs. God," to this same groundbreaking issue of *Conjunctions* 14.

2. Patrick McGrath, afterword in *Conjunctions* 14 (Spring 1990), par. 1, www.conjunctions.com/archives/c14-pm.htm (accessed March 9, 2010).

3. Edgar Allan Poe, "The Tell-tale Heart," in *Complete Stories and Poems of Edgar Allan Poe* (New York: Doubleday, 1984), 121.

4. Peter Straub, introduction to *Poe's Children: The New Horror*, ed. Peter Straub (New York: Doubleday, 2008), x.

5. Straub, introduction to *Poe's Children*, x.

6. Straub, introduction to *Poe's Children*, viii.

7. Peter Straub, "What about Genre, What about Horror?" *The Millions*, March 9, 2010, par. 10, www.themillions.com/2010/03/what-about-genre-what-about-horror.html (accessed March 9, 2010).

8. McGrath, afterword in *Conjunctions* 14, par. 10.

9. Peter Straub, *A Dark Matter* (New York: Doubleday), 27. Page numbers appear hereafter in parentheses in text.

10. Kenneth Neill Cameron, *Shelley: The Golden Years* (Cambridge, MA: Harvard University Press, 1974), 295.

11. Percy Bysshe Shelley, "To a Skylark," in *The Complete Poems of Percy Bysshe Shelley* (New York: Modern Library, 1994), 640–641.

12. Straub, "What about Genre," par. 1.

CHAPTER 13

Gothic Western Epic Fantasy

ENCOMPASSING STEPHEN KING'S DARK TOWER SERIES

Tony Magistrale

Near the end of *Book VI: Song of Susannah*, Stephen King, the author of the 3,872-page The Dark Tower opus, the longest published novel ever written in English, invents a literary character named Stephen King. Anyone who is a fan of the Hollywood films adapted from King's fiction will recognize here an extension of his homage to Alfred Hitchcock, as the writer often makes a personal appearance in movies adapted from his books. Moreover, a King-like writer—alive, or dead, or in between—surfaces as a protagonist in many of his works, short and long. From *Misery* to *Lisey's Story* to "The Road Virus Heads North," a curious, compulsive, and fan-hounded East Coast author of bestsellers may be seen, or remembered. But *Song of Susannah* is the first time that Stephen King has ever featured himself as a self-named functioning character in one of his own books. In doing so, he has literally tried to answer the metafictive question E. M. Forster initially raised in the 1920s when considering the role of novelist to his own novel: "Instead of standing above his work and controlling it, cannot the novelist throw himself into it and be carried along to some goal he did not foresee?"[1]

Writing this tome in the first decade of the twenty-first century, the fictionalized King who appears in it is a throwback to a portrait of the artist as a young man: Roland and Eddie, two of the principal characters in The Dark Tower, go back in time to meet their creator, the young father and fledgling novelist in 1977. The Stephen King that Roland and Eddie encounter in the kitchen of a summer home somewhere in central Maine has not yet become America's Storyteller; he is an unassuming guy who is not just a little afraid of the gunslinger protagonist he has invented and who, at this moment, absurdly, confronts him

in the flesh, seeking answers to questions King hasn't thought of yet. Ironically, King's literary character Roland, because he possesses the benefit of future time, knows more than the writer who created him. King began to write about Roland as early as 1970, but in this time-warped conversation set in 1977, he is forced to acknowledge that the gunslinger "started to scare me, so I stopped writing about you. Boxed you up and put you in a drawer."[2]

The Dark Tower can be appreciated as an umbrella text encompassing the whole of King's fictional oeuvre; by that, I mean that it encapsulates and interfaces with many of the core plots, characters, and themes that constitute King's canon. It contains multitudes, including an epic western plot and a Gothic plot. The Dark Tower is therefore a kind of unified field theory for King—that is, he has constructed a grand narrative which not only provides the keystone to all his other works, but also unifies the realms of fiction with those of nonfiction (e.g., the autobiographical element). This, too, is in keeping with the science-fiction elements of time travel, wormholes (portals to other worlds), and multiverses, all of which many physicists seriously posit are real possibilities as scientists themselves similarly struggle to create a united field theory designed to reconcile the theory of relativity and quantum mechanics. King the wordslinger and Roland the gunslinger share something in common, despite their occupational differences; it is as if they are alter egos or twinners. Both would appear to maintain deeply held convictions and ethics that often leave them socially alienated and misunderstood. It is the storyteller's job to make sense out of chaos, to find forgotten truths hidden under heaps of broken images. Roland would seem an integral part of this enterprise in his effort to find and sustain the beams that hold up the Dark Tower. Both King and Roland believe there are codes of heroism that transcend and interconnect with the codes of prior eras; it is their respective jobs to rediscover these codes and put them into play.

The Evolution of a Gunslinger: Roland's Western Mold

Let us return again to Stephen King's nervous admission in *Song of Susannah* that he abandoned work on The Dark Tower early in his career because Roland started to scare him. How could a mere literary invention, Roland Deschain of Gilead, provoke such an overreaction? Perhaps it wasn't just Roland's aggressive personality that was responsible for King's professed reluctance; the envisioned length and scope of Roland's story might also have constituted part of the author's fear. When we consider the size and amount of time involved in producing this opus, especially when viewed from the perspective of a young, nascent writer uncertain about the details of the story beginning to unfold, the

intimidation potential grows exponentially. So, if this is an honest admission by the metafictive author, why then did King feel compelled to continue revisiting this figure over the next thirty years in six long subsequent volumes, making Roland Deschain the single most important character to emerge from his fictional canon? The explanation King supplies in the last volume of The Dark Tower is that Roland and Jake, the latter sacrificing his own life in order to rescue King from his real-life car accident back in 1999, were ultimately responsible for bringing him back to writing about the beams and the tower. Without their miraculous metafictive intercession, the novel would have us believe, Stephen King would have never finished his magnum opus: "'I lost the Beam,' King said. . . . 'You didn't lose it, you turned your coward's eye away [Roland counters]. My friend had to save you for you to see it again.'"[3] While this speculation becomes an integral part of Roland's quest as well as fueling his amusing antipathy toward his author-creator, there may also be other, less specious reasons that King felt compelled to return to his long saga of the gunslinger.

His link to Childe Roland and the heroic epic tradition notwithstanding, King's gunslinger is also representative of a primal American archetype. For while the saga conjoins primarily the worlds of medieval fantasy and postmodern America, it is also very much shaped by the classic American western, informed as it is by the masculine code of ethics that informs the genre. We have seen some version of this western before, rooted as it is in the work of John Wayne and Clint Eastwood, but The Dark Tower doesn't quite fit comfortably in the twentieth century, as King finished it in the twenty first, remaking the image of the western hero for one more and perhaps the last time. The Dark Tower thus poses yet another window on King's career-long exploration of the American character, as the gunslinger embodies the spirit of the American wanderer. Like the *Huck Finn* prototype that has influenced so many of King's texts, from the Danny-Hallorann relationship (evoking Huck and Jim) in *The Shining* to Jack Sawyer's character in *The Talisman*, The Dark Tower features again a young social outsider–outlaw whose restive quest for adventure and forgetting takes him to places that are often as dangerous as they are lonely. Americans remain inordinately fond of personalities that drift in and out of settled society, testing its mores and levels of tolerance before lighting out again for the territory ahead of the rest. Even today, two in ten American households move every fifteen months to two years, to say nothing of the frequency of movement among individual Americans who are devoid of familial ties. Although a majority of Americans are not loners, there is something about the myth of the archetypical loner figure that Americans seem to identify with. And the most forbidding of these personalities are those drifters that emerge from western dust: Billy the Kid, the Dalton Brothers, Ted Bundy, Charles Manson, Bonnie and Clyde, and so on. An anomalous combination of western myth and alienated American reality, all these

Americans, those from fiction as well as those real enough to gain mythological status, must be seen as kin to Roland Deschain: nihilistic and unanchored, when they venture into society, they often end up killing, or dead, or both. Roland is, finally, a figure who blends both the medieval romance of Mid-World with traditional definitions of American masculinity. Perhaps this explains his choice of a *ka-tet* (a group that shares a destiny) composed exclusively of Americans and his fascination (he remains in awe of aspirin's miraculous ability to heal) to learn as much as he can about the culture from which they came. For Roland is unconsciously linked with those American males, both real and imaginary, who are associated with a fiercely independent spirit and will and an *otherness* distinct to American culture; in other words, you would be far less likely to find a Roland Deschain emerge from Europe or Japan.

While always aligned with those fighting against the forces that serve the Crimson King, Roland is not much of a negotiator; words ultimately matter less to him than action. In fact, he is most comfortable in active opposition to authority—providing orders to his allies about how to conduct themselves in combat or planning an effectively gruesome battle strategy. As King informs us early in the journey, the gunslinger "had never been a man who understood himself deeply or cared to; the concept of self-consciousness (let alone self-analysis) was alien to him. His way was to act—to quickly consult his own interior, utterly mysterious workings, and then act."[4] Roland reveals his humanity sparingly, and most notably as a young man, when he falls in love with Susan Delgado in *Wizard and Glass*. But this adolescent version of the gunslinger—dreamily preoccupied with sexual liaisons and romance—is so foreign to his temperament elsewhere in The Dark Tower that Cuthbert and Alain, his warrior sidekicks, are baffled and disturbed by his atypical behavior.

In Roland, we see the essence of the American cowboy-mercenary-politician—an ambivalent figure who is as fearful as he is fascinating, as likely to destroy a village as he is to save it. Alongside his restlessness exists a reliance on violence; indeed, violence is his instinctual response to all conflicts. Roland conducts himself by modeling nearly an identical ideology to the one that has framed American foreign policy since World War II: anytime verbal negotiations threaten to break down, he pulls out his gun and initiates a bloodbath. Moreover, as we journey further along into the epic, Roland's tendency is to abandon negotiating altogether, although it should be noted that the closer the *ka-tet* gets to the tower, the less human are its enemies. The Wolves of the Calla, for example, are actually cyborgs wearing wolf masks, and the guards at Algul Siento are a bizarre mix of spiritless low men, humanoid bird-rodent hybrids called *taheens*, and rejects from the American penal system, such as Pimli Prentiss. Nevertheless, Ted Brautigan, who has spent enough time in Connecticut to understand the gunslinger in distinctly American terms, recognizes Roland's propensity for

aggression within a very short time after meeting him, noting, as the two plan their attack on the prison at Algul Siento, "You mean to spill an almighty lot of blood." And Roland's reply is just as emphatic: "Indeed I do. As much as I can."[5]

King understands well enough that his readers will recognize in Roland a version of Dirty Harry, Shane, the Man with No Name, Walt Kowalski, and all the other convoluted versions of outlaws and avenging American iconoclastic antiheroes that have roamed across our collective cultural consciousness for the past half a century. All of these are embodied in Roland's ideology and physical gestures, from his clear attraction to mortal combat even when he is massively outnumbered, to his moral righteousness in his dogmatic belief that he is fighting the good fight, to his silent grimaces of pain each time he must overexert his arthritic hips and hands. These spectral cultural figures, totems of masculinity and avatars from a distinctly American sense of a heroic tradition, are what give substance to Roland's personality; his regal ancestry rooted in Mid-World as the son of the last Lord of Gilead, descendent of Arthur Eld, pales in importance to his mythic inheritance as a son of Sergio Leone, Sam Peckinpah, and Clint Eastwood.

David Davis, in writing about the codes of western behavior, includes violence as an elemental rite of passage: "Of course, most cowboy books and movies bristle with violence. . . . These bloody escapades are necessary and are simply explained. They provide the stage for the hero to show his heroism, and since the cowboy is the hero of the preadolescent, he must prove himself by [preadolescent] standards."[6] In Tull, when the townspeople attack the gunslinger at the urging of the dark man, it is clear that Roland has no compunction about his use of force. It is probably true that violent force remains Roland's hallmark throughout the saga, but in the early books he lacks any sensitivity to the moral complexity and responsibility that attend its usage. King tells us, for example, that after completely eliminating the town of its human inhabitants, Roland "ate hamburgers and drank three beers. . . . That night he slept in the bed where he and Alice had lain. He had no dreams."[7] The Slow Mutants lose whatever humanity they may still retain when the gunslinger shoots indiscriminately into their midst "without allowing himself to think."[8] The gunslinger may hunt the man in black for a reason that is semi-comprehensible to himself alone, but it is apparent from the first four stories of The Gunslinger volume that Roland has much in common with the amoral dark man he pursues. One becomes what one sets out to destroy, as the dweller Brown memorably suggests, with Roland offering no direct protest.[9]

In the afterword to The Gunslinger volume, King alludes to Robert Browning's poem "Childe Roland to the Dark Tower Came" as the primary influence in the construction of his own epic saga: "I played with the idea of trying a long romantic novel embodying the feel, if not the exact sense of the Browning

poem."[10] Browning's Childe Roland has spent a life training for the sight, and his journey to the Dark Tower is heroic if for no other reason than the knight's perseverance. In many ways, King's narrative is characteristic of the same epic tendencies found in Browning's poem, given the difference in genre, as an epic is traditionally a poem rather than a novel. Roland is the central heroic figure, and while he is not literally superhuman, he does possess skills and talents that seem to stretch the limits of human potential (e.g., his ability to shoot unerringly despite missing fingers on his right hand, his telekinesis). Like the Browning poem, The Dark Tower is filled with perilous journeys and adventures full of physical and mental dangers that fail to deter the progress of the main character. As is also the case with King's last gunslinger, Childe Roland seeks a vision he neither understands nor precisely knows where or how to pursue.

King's Roland Deschain comes to parallel Browning's protagonist in each of the aforementioned aspects, but his spiritual evolution is as slow and tentative as the quest to find the Dark Tower. In the first two volumes at least, it is clear why the Stephen King character in *Song of Susannah* acknowledged some anxiousness in writing about Roland: the early gunslinger is a man without attachments; he is loved by no one, and there is no one for him to love. He lacks a sense of community or purpose beyond the incessant hunt for the man in black and, by extension, the tower itself. Indeed, in his rootlessness, his belief in violence as a solution to most problems, and his studied amorality, he most resembles the man in black himself. Throughout most of the epic's first volume, Roland is at the nadir of his spiritual development; he must learn why "the man in black travels with [Roland's] soul in his pocket"[11] and how best to extricate it so that it may belong to Roland once more and serve the greater good affiliated with the tower's beam. Roland's early spiritual malaise is perhaps best illustrated in his failure to save the young boy, Jake. Forced to choose between capturing the man in black and letting Jake fall to his death, Roland lets the young boy die. This choice parallels Roland's obsession with the tower: he is willing, at least early on, to sacrifice everything and everyone in his life in pursuit of this amorphous goal. The Roland who enters the second book, *The Drawing of the Three*, is best summed up by Eddie Dean, who pronounces an accurate condemnation of the gunslinger: "There are people who need people to need them. The reason you don't understand is because you are not one of those people. You'd use me and then toss me away like a paper bag if that's what it came down to."[12]

There is, however, a discernable difference between this Roland and the man who evolves in subsequent volumes of The Dark Tower. Just as Father Callahan undergoes a metamorphosis during his years in exile, Roland likewise modifies as a result of his commitment to the members of his *ka-tet* and the gradual understanding of his role as the last gunslinger, a force of rough justice in the world bound by the code of his kind to help those in distress. One might

argue that Roland's metamorphosis begins as early as the second volume in the series, *The Drawing of the Three*. Here, Roland's propensity toward violence is definitely tempered—more appropriate to the situation and to the behavior of a heroic personage. Moreover, by serving as the distraction that saves Jake from being murdered by Jack Mort, Roland displays the fullest extent of his development as a moral agent. Unwilling to allow the boy to die a second time as a result of his own selfishness and negligence, Roland relinquishes his hold on Mort long enough to permit Jake's escape. It is the first time in The Dark Tower that the gunslinger demonstrates a determined willingness to sacrifice the successful completion of his quest because of its cost in human life. The gunslinger's choice of self-sacrifice, risking the quest for the tower itself, is repeated elsewhere in the series, such as in his willingness to comb the booby-trapped city of Lud in his search to rescue Jake when he is kidnapped by Gasher and the Tick-Tock Man in volume 3, *The Waste Lands*.

Epic versus Gothic: The Price of Answering the Tower's Call

The Dark Tower is built on a series of backstories—every member of the *ka-tet* has a history—and it is through the interweaving of these stories that the group shares in one another's past and achieves community. As they persevere toward the tower, each member of the *ka-tet* grapples with his or her own destiny as well as working to uphold the unity and power of the group dynamic. Thus each member develops his or her sense of selfhood as both independent beings and as a part of a larger gestalt. The individual coexists within the group's identity, but the two never completely merge.

Roland's ambiguous love for Eddie and Susannah grows in depth and intensity as the story progresses. From Roland, Eddie and Susannah learn the combat skills and mental discipline tied to the gunslinger lineage. Eddie, in particular, evolves from a pathetic junkie desperate for a fix to a "man who behaves with all the dignity of a born gunslinger despite his addiction."[13] From Eddie and Susannah, Roland is properly educated in virtues that in him are sorely underdeveloped: friendship and love, certainly, but also the knowledge that the *quest* to find the tower is just as important as the tower itself. The people he has loved in the course of his long journey—the *ka-tet* most of all, but also Susan Delgado, Ted Brautigan, Sheemie, Cuthbert and Alain, and even Oy the billy-bumbler—teach Roland that his life's goal is less physical than it is spiritual, and in this way the gunslinger comes most to emulate the heroic tenets of Browning's Childe Roland. As Joseph Campbell argues throughout his monumental study

The Hero with a Thousand Faces, the epic journey is always an instrument for the hero's moral education.

In *The Theory of the Novel*, however, Georg Lukacs limits Campbell's faith in the epic as a tool for education by placing chronological restrictions on its effectiveness. Lukacs posits that the epic form loses its significance once it tries to cross over into modern literary narratives, and that the explanation for this is that society has moved beyond the "age of the epic," never to return again, because "we have invented the productivity of the spirit. . . . We have invented the creation of forms: and that is why everything that falls from our weary and despairing hands must always be incomplete."[14] The epic can no longer accurately represent our fractured world because the belief system of the epic—synonymous with the equipoise inherent in a medieval cosmology—is no longer possible to sustain in a fragmented, unsettled world. Instead of maintaining its faith in tradition and a viable past worth fighting to preserve, the epic tendencies available in The Dark Tower are undercut by the presence of more modern, Gothic sensibilities, and this holds true in explaining both the general erosion of the form's potency as well as its specific employment in King's seven-volume text. The romance tradition that embodied the epic structure is undermined by the intrusion of modernity's chaos, its violence and corresponding loss of meaning, and its palpable sense of alienation and corruption. Even Mid-World, King's own projection of a medieval universe, cannot remain insulated from the intrusions of modernity and its overriding sentiment of doubt.

So, while we might acknowledge The Dark Tower as a unique blend of Gothic horror and epic fantasy, as is the case in *The Stand* and *The Talisman* as well, this admixture is a restive one. The Dark Tower's Gothic sensibilities, after all, clash most blatantly with the noble intentions that define its epic quest. The endangered quaintness of Mid-World and the justifications for why the beams supporting it need to be restored and fortified are continually challenged by the Gothic wastelands that permeate places such as Calla Bryn Sturgis and Lud in Mid-World, and Kansas and New York City in King's parallel universe. Outside of the immediate members of the *ka-tet*, there are also precious few human beings worth saving in The Dark Tower, and many of those who are, such as Susan Delgado or Father Callahan, are destroyed by the very forces that Roland seeks to thwart. In fact, as Roland slouches toward his tower, he comes more and more to resemble the Gothic antihero than the traditional epic hero; by the end of his long saga, there is not much more left for Roland to learn, and as he looks back on his education he cannot help but see it soaked in blood and grief. There is something of the Byronic figure in his melancholic sense of loss, especially following the deaths of Susan and Jake. Like many Gothic monsters and villains, Roland's suffering—physical, emotional, and psychological—defines his character; he is the emotive center of this journey, and his behavior sets the tone

for everyone else, including the reader. Critic Frederick S. Frank believed that the Gothic tradition embodied an ancestry of anguish, manifesting itself in the actions of the Gothic antihero, which symbolize defiance and outrage as well as suffering.[15] This cry of anguish can be heard from Manfred in Walpole's first Gothic, *The Castle of Otranto*, and from such characters as Lewis's Ambrosio, Shelley's Victor Frankenstein, Stevenson's Henry Jekyll, and many of the central protagonists in the fictions of Poe, Hawthorne, and Melville. In King's Roland, we see the brooding darkness of the handsome and psychologically distressed Gothic male. In spite of his long association with the *ka-tet* and the occasional female lover, such as Rosalita Munoz in *Wolves of the Calla*, Roland remains essentially a solitary figure, impossible to know, who only reluctantly shares the intimate details of his life. Like many Gothic protagonists throughout literature and film, Roland generally tends to maintain a lonely and sinister independence from social ties. His quest comes to resemble closely the prototypical Gothic obsession, as he willingly sacrifices a large piece of his own humanity in his relentless pursuit of the tower.

The early Gothics from the last decade of the eighteenth century sought a return to the ambiance of the Middle Ages, with a renewed fascination for the mystical and the inexplicable as well as an intensified interest in the battle between good and evil. Politically it embodied the awareness of social upheaval that characterized an age of revolution. Psychologically, the Gothic signaled a turn from the portrayal of manners in an integrated society to the analysis of lonely, guilt-ridden outsiders. Roland and his *ka-tet* grow increasingly estranged from the inhabitants of both Mid-World and New York, the two primary locales for the saga. In fact, the single bond that unites all the members of the *ka-tet*, including the late addition of Father Callahan, is that they are all alienated figures estranged from their native worlds. Jake is a single child of parents who do not understand him, Eddie is a heroin abuser lost in the shadow of his mean-spirited older brother, Susannah is a black woman struggling with multiple personalities, and Roland never does completely recover from the loss of Susan Delgado in *Wizard and Glass*. It could be argued that Roland's obsession with the Dark Tower is transformed into a surrogate replacement for the loss of Susan; he displaces his guilt and anger over losing her onto the quest to save the universe by righting the tower. As a young man, he may have failed to rescue his besieged maiden, but he will make up for it as an old man in rescuing the besieged tower.

The Gothic environment of crumbling castles, supernatural animation, and mysterious forests is revisited in The Dark Tower as King's *ka-tet* wanders along a blasted landscape where the divine order is under siege and the vacuum created by social upheaval typically leads to lawlessness and power oligarchies in the hands of the most ruthless. Despite the vastness of their journey, the *ka-tet* encounters very little beauty along the way—no descriptions of inspiring

landscapes, few examples of kindness unselfishly bestowed among humans, or even much gratitude from the supernal beams that are rescued at such a tremendous human cost. The dark road they travel, whether along the interstates of contemporary America or the dusty dirt paths of Mid-World, is more reminiscent of Cormac McCarthy's *The Road* than it is of Walt Whitman's sunny journey of hopefulness. The sickness caused by radiation poisoning and the long-term consequences of unattended petrochemicals permeates the landscape. The threatened status of the tower requires a multidimensional explanation, but surely its endangerment is both reflected in and caused by the collapse of an ecosystem to which the tower is intricately connected. In Mid-World in particular, genetic deformities and abnormalities abound. North Central Positronics, the computer corporation that produced Shardik the Bear, Blaine the Mono, Andy the Robot, and the Wolves of the Calla, remains a faceless entity that symbolizes the disastrous consequences of unregulated corporate "progress" and an amoral reliance on computers and robotic life forms. This is also another way that The Dark Tower intersects with Gothic science; the abuse and misuse of cyborg robotics is an issue that ties King's saga to other dystopic texts confronting the same issue, such as *Frankenstein, Blade Runner, Total Recall, Minority Report*, and *The Matrix*. Although King does not develop it sufficiently, there even appears to be an unholy collusion between the polluted physical environments of Lud, the Mejis, and Calla Bryn Sturgis on the one hand and the computer technology that is discarded or left barely functioning on the outskirts of these cities and towns on the other. Indeed, the cities and villages that the *ka-tet* visits in both worlds are fallen and corrupted. Thus the Gothic's characteristic fascination with evil, its fixation on rebellion against optimistic virtues and the righteousness of social convention, and its emphasis on disorder, chaos, and fear for the future resonated with some darkly sympathetic cord in King's construction of his narrative.

One of the most Gothic elements in The Dark Tower is the increasing sense of doom that grows ever more palpable as Roland nears his destination. Despite his deepening association with the other members of his *ka-tet* as the series evolves, there is an essential part of Roland that none of the others is capable of penetrating: the brooding Gothic man of violence that defines himself via his isolation from human society and his alacrity for aggressive action. Each of the last four books shares an identical narrative design structure that builds to a climactic crescendo of brutality in the final chapters. And although Roland never does relinquish his reliance on violence as a solution to all conflict, the grief he experiences as a result of this commitment ever darkens him. Indeed, the Roland who exits this epic has, in the course of many years, lost most of the people he cared about to the violence he has dedicated himself to perpetuating: "*I only kill my family*, Roland thought."[16] The recurring Gothic fascination with

family destruction—a fallen heir to a great lineage, a son who suffers the curse of distant, secretive, or depraved parents—is well satisfied. He has dragged others into his quest and made them both kill and die in pursuit of a life's mission that Roland imposes on his associates. As such, Roland must accept some measure of responsibility for what he has set in motion and forced others to participate in. The gunslinger acknowledges at least this much late in the last volume as he prepares to say good-bye to Susannah: "And he did owe this woman a debt, he reckoned, for had he not pretty much seized her by the scruff of the neck and hauled her into this world, where she'd learned the art of murder and fallen in love and been left bereaved? Had he not kidnapped her into this present sorrow?"[17] Although Roland's life's work has been of his own choosing, this is also an apt description of himself as well.

By the time he actually reaches the end of his voyage, the young stud warrior that readers followed in *The Gunslinger* and *Wizard and Glass* with some of the same fear and awe that the Stephen King character confessed to back in 1977 has transformed into a world-weary old man, arguably defined more by what he has lost on the road to the tower than by the values that the tower purportedly represents: "He felt quite sure that this was his last march. He didn't believe he would ever leave Can'-Ka No Rey, and that was all right. He was tired. And, despite the power of the rose, sad."[18] At the end of this long saga, the amorous suitor of Susan Delgado has transformed into Mordred's "Old White Daddy," a hobbled adult, full of adult aches and pains, adult darkness, corruption, remorse, and regret. In short, the idealistic epic adventurer slips into the brooding Gothic antihero, an elaborate illustration of the shadow side of a decent man, the corrosive product of violence. The gunslinger in volume 7 is still desirous, but also confused, alone, and bereft. His tragic trajectory thus follows those life histories perhaps most readily identifiable with Gothic scientists from the nineteenth century, such as Victor Frankenstein and Henry Jekyll: what begins as a quest to enhance the world ends in a somber and sobering cautionary tale about the dangers of hubris and the indulgence of personal obsession. We make choices to bring out the good or evil in ourselves, spawning monsters in spite of our pursuit of righteous causes. Gothic literature abounds with characters who begin their tales with good intentions and confidence, only to be seduced by their own ambitions, tumbled by their tragic innocence, or thwarted by nature itself—in any case, leaving dispossessed men in the valley of sorrow. Self-knowledge may be one of the major identifiable traits of the epic narrative design, but in the Gothic, introspection tends to occur too late or not at all.

Roland relinquishes the crystalline focus, the defiant virtue that characterizes his early vision and motivation. Wracked by pain and exhaustion (both spiritual and physical), bereft of his *ka-tet*, and carrying the burden of his own history that casts a shadow as long as that of the tower itself, the gunslinger that

exits this narrative resembles closely the depleted Gothic antiheroes, Manfred, Don Juan, Henry Jekyll, Victor Frankenstein, the Ancient Mariner, and even Roderick Usher, as well as the epic heroes, Odysseus, Achilles, Don Quixote, and Childe Roland, but most of all Frodo at the end of *The Lord of the Rings*, men whose journeys have exacted a severe toll. Campbell tells us that the epic hero must lose himself to find himself, and at the end, when his duty is completed, he "brings back from his adventure the means for the regeneration of his society as a whole."[19] However, of all the aforementioned epic heroes, only Tolkien's Frodo seems to be as singularly empty as Roland at the end of The Dark Tower; that is, they both resemble more the Gothic antihero than the triumphant epic hero who returns to be welcomed back and claim his rightful place in the community. Critics, readers, and King himself may be most comfortable viewing The Dark Tower saga as an epic, but in truth it ends with probably more in common with the Gothic tale of the psychically lost, guilt-ridden outsider. In their quests to uphold a semblance of goodness in a fallen world, Frodo and Roland, like their fellow Gothic brethren, have wandered a long way from home and from any unequivocal definition of goodness, so far afield that home becomes just a vague, barely recognizable memory no longer accessible, and goodness merely a relative concept.

I have always believed that the most emotive part of Tolkien's wonderful trilogy centers on the displaced Frodo that we leave at the story's conclusion. He occupies a psychic space that is very close to where we leave Roland at the end of The Dark Tower. Although both are triumphant in their adventures, they end their respective tales diminished. The Shire that Frodo and his friends return to find—with its corrupt bureaucratic officials and weak-willed hobbits, the vile odors and polluted streams that have displaced the domain's sweetness, and the general air of civic and environmental degradation and indifference—resembles the Mid-World wasteland that Roland and his *ka-tet* endeavor to fix. In the end, the battle to save Mid-World and Middle Earth is as much about saving the physical environment from the multifarious corruptive forces that would poison it as it is about defeating the more obvious avatars of evil, the Crimson King and Sauron. Thus both sagas embody the theme of the destructive consequences inherent in change and the need to protect the earth from those who would debase it in their bid for dominance. This general theme of debasement enlarges to include Roland's *ka-tet* and Frodo's fellowship of hobbits as well. Roland and Frodo pulled these individuals out of their former lives, as mundane or self-destructive as many of them were, and took them on an amazing adventure. Each of the characters that embarked on these adventures was changed by it; in the process, they all became something better than their former selves. Perhaps Roland's and Frodo's personal journeys were self-paved paths to hell, yet these paths were nonetheless worthy of a grand story. Education through experience

and suffering enlarges the spirit, gives it confidence and stature, especially for a naive little hobbit and a monomaniacal gunslinger who were both transformed into world-wise (and world-weary) wordslingers. Frodo and Roland were capable of revivifying their respective worlds and their respective *ka-tets*, but their own psyches were woefully depleted as a direct consequence of their redemptive quests. While they may be the transcendent heroes of their individual books, they also exit them exhausted, in the absence of friends and devoid of purpose.

Books in the Series

American hardbacks from The Dark Tower series were all initially published by Donald M. Grant publishers (note that Penguin Putnam would rerelease the first four of them in 2003 as hardbacks).

1. *The Dark Tower: The Gunslinger* (Donald M. Grant, 1982)
2. *The Dark Tower II: The Drawing of the Three* (1987)
3. *The Dark Tower III: The Waste Lands* (1991)
4. *The Dark Tower IV: Wizard and Glass* (1997)
5. *The Dark Tower V: Wolves of the Calla* (2003)
6. *The Dark Tower VI: Song of Susannah* (2004)
7. *The Dark Tower VII: The Dark Tower* (2004)

The Dark Tower series in American trade paperbacks appears below, then after the semicolon the American mass-market release.

1. *The Dark Tower: The Gunslinger* (Plume, 2003; Signet, 2003)
2. *The Dark Tower II: The Drawing of the Three* (mass market, Signet, 1990)
3. *The Dark Tower III: The Waste Lands* (Plume, 2003; Signet, 1993)
4. *The Dark Tower IV: Wizard and Glass* (Plume, 2003; Signet, 2003)
5. *The Dark Tower V: Wolves of the Calla* (Scribner, 2005; Plume, 2006)
6. *The Dark Tower VI: Song of Susannah* (Scribner, 2005; Pocket, 2006)
7. *The Dark Tower VII: The Dark Tower* (Scribner, 2005; Pocket, 2006)

Notes

1. E. M. Forster, *Aspects of the Novel* (Orlando, FL: Harcourt, 1927, 1955), 145.
2. Stephen King, *The Dark Tower VI: Song of Susannah* (New York: Scribner, 2004), 286.

3. Stephen King, *The Dark Tower VII: The Dark Tower* (New York: Simon and Schuster, 2004), 564–565.

4. Stephen King, *The Dark Tower III: The Waste Lands* (New York: New American Library, 1993), 29.

5. King, *The Dark Tower VII: The Dark Tower*, 421.

6. David Davis, "Ten-Gallon Hero," in *The Western: A Collection of Critical Essays*, ed. James K. Folsom (Englewood Cliffs, NJ: Prentice Hall, 1979), 28–29.

7. Stephen King, *The Dark Tower: The Gunslinger* (West Kingston, RI: Donald M. Grant, 1982), 64.

8. King, *Gunslinger*, 179.

9. Brown hauntingly tells Roland, "I think you're very close to your man in black," in King, *Gunslinger*, 65.

10. King, *Gunslinger*, 221.

11. King, *Gunslinger*, 90.

12. Stephen King, *The Dark Tower II: The Drawing of the Three* (New York: New American Library, 1987), 170.

13. King, *Drawing of the Three*, 156.

14. Georg Lukacs, *The Theory of the Novel*, trans. Anna Bostock (Boston: MIT Press, 1971), 33–34.

15. Frederick S. Frank, "Proto-Gothicism: The Infernal Iconography of Walpole's *Castle of Otranto*," *Orbis Litterarum* 41 (1986): 199–212.

16. King, *The Dark Tower VII: The Dark Tower*, 960.

17. King, *The Dark Tower VII: The Dark Tower*, 921.

18. King, *The Dark Tower VII: The Dark Tower*, 944.

19. Joseph Campbell, *The Hero with a Thousand Faces* (Cleveland and New York: World, 1956), 38.

CHAPTER 14

Wonder and Awe

MYSTICISM, POETRY, AND PERCEPTION IN RAMSEY CAMPBELL'S *THE DARKEST PART OF THE WOODS*

Adam L. G. Nevill

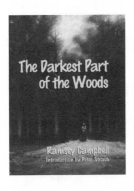

A Gothic novel would struggle to affect us if its setting were a sun-bathed beach or a brightly-lit shopping mall. Within the perceptions of the cast, and in the reader whom the cast guides, in order to create the right receptivity to the mystical, to embrace the presence of supernatural evil and the cursed legacy embedded in the past from which the evil presence arises, we must have the right setting for Gothic horror. We must have age. We must have shadows and the unlit places from which the shadows flow outward and seep backward.

Campbell's great Gothic creation in *The Darkest Part of the Woods* is . . . the wood. A forest that affects like a towering mountain range, a cathedral, a castle, or a sprawling seventeenth-century estate; those universes of stone that have facilitated the Gothic field so well. From the opening scene to the final page, what is consistently extraordinary about *The Darkest Part of the Woods* is its setting: Goodmanswood.

With their highest digits, the trees of the wood forever claw at the sky. At any moment faces will appear in the growths and fungi on trunks. Great woody limbs beckon and wave to those on the boundary of the trees. Shadows swell outward on the surrounding common, or retract suddenly, taking on new forms as they move, while only barely staying within the rules of how shadows work. A giant but indistinct form paces your every step through the glades and trails, a form constantly constructing and reconstructing itself from the patterns and motions in the wind-stirred foliage. The air currents, birdsong, and insect activity are always uncanny, guided by the will of this much larger presence that inhabits a region beneath the damp earth, as well as the bewitching air of the

forest, and even the region above the highest reaches of the treetops, as is its want. The wood is its own inhabitant—an entity. And eventually we learn it serves a much higher purpose: a passage from this world to another place that human comprehension struggles to even make sense of.

A reader would struggle to find a single page within the text in which the wood is not *active* upon their imagination, and active in a way that barely complies with natural law:

> The far edge of the common was crowded with shadows bent on clawing the ground into the woods. Of course it was the wind and not the shadows that kept urging the grass towards them in waves, but he couldn't shake off the notion that there were more elongated spindly shadows than trees bordering the forest to cast them.[1]

We are literally spoiled by the wealth and diversity of description. It is intentionally oppressive, omniscient, claustrophobic. It is entrapping, timeless, wondrous, dreadful, and loaded with malevolence. The very spirit of Goodmanswood is imbued with the essence of the Gothic. Sustaining so complex a variety of lyrical descriptions to create a specific effect on the reader over such a long novel reflects a writer at the very height of both his own game and that of what the horror genre has ever produced (possibly only matched by the same author's previous work, *Midnight Sun*, and the very best of Algernon Blackwood's and Arthur Machen's mystical stories). And in such a lowering, restless, ancient setting, we more readily accept the forgotten books malodorous with age and what they prophesy; and we are more inclined to acknowledge, though also dread, the subterranean power that exists beneath Goodmanswood's mound. Our primal fear of deciduous woods is a great facilitator of the suspension of our disbelief in this story. Forget the piney vastness of conifer forests, or the alien lushness of the jungle that is exhilarating to the explorer, but think of the prehistoric and unmanaged boreal spirit of the cluttered and spindly limbed deciduous woods of old Europe—impenetrable, shadowy, skeletal in winter, and feared for generations for the old things that linger from ancient times, like sprites, fairies, and trolls (not the cutesy late-Victorian versions). Arguably, it is in the tangled virgin woodland, as much as the period house, that a supernatural presence can still seem to exist most plausibly to the Western mind. And so sustained is the range of nightmarish effects that Campbell produces in depicting this old English forest of Goodmanswood that no reader will be able to simply rush through this novel to see the mystery unraveled. We are forced to walk slowly and look up, to behold

> the highest branches contorting themselves into shapes he wouldn't have dreamed they could take, leaves fluttering or gliding through the air in patterns too elaborate for his mind to grasp, then fitting them-

selves into a mosaic of decay that was the forest floor. Some stirred as if
they weren't entirely dead. . . . The leaves were most hectic between the
trees at the limit of his vision, where they swarmed like insects caught
up in some nervous ritual.[2]

Indeed, the history of the very forest that is Goodmanswood is not only
steeped in witchcraft from pre-Roman times, but it also once produced a crop of
hallucinogenic moss. And the language—the sheer range of metaphor and simile
employed by Campbell to create his setting—produces the same sensations of disorientation, of bewilderment, of paranoia often described as a bad trip. When we
are immersed in any character's point of view within the wood, we are immediately
cast into a region that confines and swells around us like nightmare, one we cannot
awaken from. There is no release from it. Even when some uneasy resolution has
been found to the problem of the mage Selcouth's lingering presence and activity
among the trees—indeed, his determination to return from the past—there is no
stilling of the leaves or release from the shadows. No, at the book's end, the next
vigil merely begins, to be on watch for Selcouth's next appearance.

And into this place that taints our perception so darkly, that confounds and
bewilders, is placed a cast, a family with secrets. Every family has secrets, but a
family in the Gothic horror tradition hides more than most. And those mysteries
they *have* will not let them rest. In fact, whatever happened in the past of this
family—whatever anyone saw, or did, or didn't do when they should have done
something—is in the process of returning to a point in the future too close for
the reader's comfort.

Typical of the characters in latter-day Campbell novels, the cast here be-
guiles itself. Confusion, defensiveness, the potential for mishearing things, or
seeing things that are not there, or could have been there, the terror of social
humiliation, the acute sufferings at the hands of such, and the inability to
overcome reticence are all Campbell trademarks that are amplified here to a suffocating pitch by the shadows and the ever-present waving limbs of that place:
Goodmanswood. It whips anxiety to a point of hysteria; it perpetually distorts
any attempt at reason or clear thought. Goodmanswood hampers, agitates, and
thwarts, as a spiky thicket of undergrowth will delay a visitor's passage through
a forest. The wood haunts the characters' waking and their sleeping. Not for a
moment are any of them free of the trees:

He felt as though the depths of the forest or something they were
concealing were effortlessly pacing the car. He couldn't think for the
Beethoven which kept repeating itself louder like someone shouting
at a deaf person or a foreigner while the treetops seemed to describe
shapes more sinuous and patterns more complex than any music. He
couldn't grasp how long it took the car to pass the woods. He saw
them shrinking in the mirror as the motorway glittered with traffic

ahead, but he felt as if they were dwindling only to reveal more of themselves, to increase themselves somehow. They remained a hovering restless, many-limbed presence in his mind.[3]

And the realm of psychology that Campbell excels at exploring in his fiction is that of the disturbed in the process of being disturbed. His characters inhabit a region of consciousness that is often both difficult and painful to empathize with. By immersing oneself in a dialogue with the thoughts and emotions of Ramsey Campbell characters, one enters a world of the acutely vulnerable, the anxious, the manic, all tormented by everyday slights and words, because their defensive reactions to the mundane represent a volatile core of a much greater unresolved angst that lies deeper, buried. In his pages, the hypersensitive and the delusional endlessly challenge and withdraw from each other in exchanges either taut with tension or fraught with misunderstanding. The labyrinthine psychological complexity of a Ramsey Campbell cast most often confounds readers of horror seduced to his books through a lurid cover and the sensations it promises. But there are few literary critics who would not be surprised by the sophistication of his characterization within what is called "genre" or "category" fiction. And Campbell's is a thoroughly posthistorical characterization. It is rare that his characters pit themselves against grave physical horrors like war, violence, hunger, poverty, or exile, those traditional tests of a character's endurance. But it is the gradual and the insidious, the ever-subtle influences of the macabre, that drive his characters mad. In the same way that the stresses and pressures of modern life—the whole gamut of performance and professional and physical anxieties—are literally driving us crazy in the modern Western world, it is through incremental psychological pressures that the minds of his characters are unraveled. And as madness and despair have always formed the DNA of Gothic character profiles, there are few more thoroughly modern Gothic novels than *The Darkest Part of the Woods*.

The entire family that lives on the border of Goodmanswood is no exception to this range of damage. The parents, Margo and Lennox, are too far gone in their addiction to Goodmanswood to be proactive. Lennox swallowed too much trippy moss to ever do much but watch the trees from the asylum that teeters on the brink of the forest. And it was his addiction to the trees and their mystery that dragged the rest of his family into its influence. He introduced them to his dealer: Goodmanswood, that procurer of strange dreams and weird thoughts, showing you how to exist half in this world and half in another, in the hidden life of the trees. Like Blackwood's narrator in the short story of the same name, he is "the man whom the trees loved."

His wife Margo is an artist. Despite her clear affection and regard for her family, her compulsion is to recreate the wood from the wood, as a sculptor and then as a video artist. Her purpose is to observe the trees and process their effects,

to make others see what she can see within those cursed but bewitching groves. But, like Lennox, she is of the wood and cannot see beyond or break free of its spellbinding presence. She is trapped and in thrall to the godforsaken.

Sam, the grandson, is as bewildered, confused, and seemingly aimless as the latter-day incarnation of his grandfather, Lennox, that old figure at the asylum window, committed to the care of the hospital, from which he periodically escapes to race like a child into the trees. The forest took most of Lennox's mind. It took Sam's leg too, literally. As an environmental activist, he tried to protect Goodmanswood from a bypass and fell (or was he pushed?) from his perch, and now he walks with a limp that he will carry for the rest of his days. Buried under layers of resentment, self-absorption, and depression, like so much heavy wet earth, tormented Sam wants to articulate his own vision. It will probably take the form of creative language, and the subject will almost certainly be something about Goodmanswood. Sam is the tortured soul, the tormented and baffled Gothic antihero through whom the cursed wood's powerful reach is most acutely received. And he is conflicted, deeply so. His instincts for self-preservation tell him he should leave, in fact flee.

This escalation of disorientation, confusion, dysphasia, paranoia, and hypersensitivity to manic episodes—so profound at times that it is impossible for the characters to articulate to each other what it is they feel—is most astutely voiced by Campbell in the character of Sam as he tries to flee Goodmanswood by car; it is probably one of the most disturbing scenes in the entire novel. Sam is both half awake and glued-down in a nightmare driven by persecution:

> He felt he wasn't driving so much as being driven, but to where? . . . And the children did their utmost to transform the faces they were presenting to him into objects he wouldn't have cared to meet in the dark. . . . They and the relentless lowness of the sun, the traffic swelling in the mirror, the utterance that felt embedded in his skull. "The calling of the void." It could have been his aunt's voice imitating a child or the reverse. . . . The heat and noise seemed to mass within him as his panic did. He felt like a child, very lost and very small. . . . He felt as if his skull was being goaded onward by the lowering sun, aided by the protracted shadow that was dragging the car.[4]

But though Sam can hardly bare to admit it to himself, the forest has bequeathed him a role. He is a sleeper cell and will be activated soon. Until then, he cannot leave and must flounder, baffled and haunted, in his hometown, his own prison. Just like Lennox, Sam's past won't let him go. All of his roads just lead back to the mound, in the darkest part of the woods, to the Gothic dungeon where things are buried. And that is because he is one half of one of those family secrets mentioned earlier.

Sylvia, the youngest daughter of Margo and Lennox, does not so much return home as she is drawn home, by Goodmanswood. Sylvia—enigmatic, painfully thin, evasive, and pregnant—an author and academic like her father, she wants to continue his legacy by studying the folklore and the origins of this patch of woodland. You could say she has been seduced by the woods, if not summoned to them, just like her father. But who is the father of her child, and why has she been banged up inside an American asylum? Family secrets again, the worst kind that you need to keep from each other. And she is the other half of the secret that is driving Sam deeper into himself, into despair.

Which leaves us with Heather, Sylvia's elder sister and Sam's mother, the firstborn of Lennox and Margo. She is the bedrock, the center, the unimaginative one, the daughter who stayed home to watch over her parents and do the best she could as a parent in her own right. She is kind and unfailingly supportive to the array of *gifted* family members who orbit her. She is diligent and hardworking, a homemaker and librarian. But let's not underestimate Heather, most importantly her continued resistance to that place she can see from every window of her house and smell like freshly turned earth on every draft: Goodmanswood. She gives it the proper respect it deserves: she fears it, because it is dangerous. The way it moves, the things it whispers, what seeps from it to terrify the schoolchildren—it is all wrong and it is taking the best part of her family from her piecemeal. Perhaps Heather is the only sane one, the reason before unreason, an unlikely heroine, but perhaps all the family has to save them from whatever is stirring out there, thrashing impatiently around its dark heart, from where it will rise again, from the mound.

And in this mound, for which the restless trees have made us ready, we enter into a dialogue with the most acute fear and despair of all, and down here we are ready to meet the truly godforsaken, the one who lurks in the shadows of such a place. Count Dracula and Frankenstein's monster were godforsaken and furtive, and so is Goodmanswood and its adept Selcouth—Selcouth of the mound, whose incantatory voice Heather hears in the night:

> *Goodman's Wood, which is a Site of great Powers forgotten by the Herd and a fit Setting for the Completion of my Experiments . . . where once an ancient Ring of stone was raised to Summon and containe the Daemon of this Place.*[5]

The Gothic tradition needs the godforsaken. It romanticizes and sensationalizes the derided messiahs, the misunderstood, the cast down, the banished, the fallen angels. And within the role of the rejected or self-exiled, the godforsaken can transgress at will. Unlike the forgiving martyred Christ, the godforsaken can murder and lust and finally dominate; they can be unrestrained and wallow in damnation. The seeking of arcane, unstable, and dangerous knowledge is a

good route to facilitating vengeance and immortality, because it allows one to consort with demons and devils and call upon great dark powers for personal enlightenment and enrichment. The godforsaken is the focus of our own hidden contempt for our fellow man and his vapid endeavors. It is an imaginative exploration into regions of thought and deed that we forbid ourselves; in fact, we are forbidden to engage with anything but this imaginative level. We are men, not gods. The banished one in this novel, Selcouth, is willingly damned. Unfettered by morals, he will pursue his own purpose: to harness the power of the gods, to look through the eyes of the gods and to throw off all earthly manacles and obstructions like justice, compassion, obedience, cooperation, and any other ethical behavior. His will is to become a god. Selcouth's story is one of the empowerment of an outcast through dark forces, and at the expense of everyone else's well-being.

To be a god is to preside over the mysteries of burial and resurrection, a perception deeply rooted in the Gothic tradition whose tendrils of madness and dysfunction are fed from what refuses to be forgotten, as we observe in the action of this novel. And, literally, in the darkest part of Campbell's Goodmanswood, there is a barrow under which something is buried. But the forest itself, and what lies beneath its roots, forbids access to the mound. Only the chosen can enter the very dark womb of the mystery, with a spade and the requisite amount of curiosity or compulsion. Obsessive amounts of each of these impulses drive Aunt Sylvia and her young nephew out there to it in a collaboration sugared with the electricity of inappropriate arousal. And down there, where forbidden rites were once performed, and upon the mound where incestuous yearnings were consummated, once we begin the excavation, we merge the Gothic with another great twentieth-century tradition of dark fiction: the Lovecraftian.

It was awe and wonder that Lovecraft claimed were necessary for the weird tale to work, something he observed in those mystical writers Arthur Machen and Algernon Blackwood. And it is "The White People" and "The Man Whom the Trees Loved" by Machen and Blackwood, respectively, that are most closely conjured in the effects of Campbell's novel. The wonder and awe here arise not from a reaction to beauty, though there is a dreadful beauty in these woods. It is not joy but euphoria, a kind of mad euphoria produced in a mind reaching its furthest limits while attempting to comprehend something cosmic like eternity, timelessness, and what waits there, the very same things Lovecraft's own protagonists were forced to behold. And feelings of awe and wonderment are produced by one's utter insignificance before these phenomena, the kind of revelation that makes you irreparably unhinged, like poor old Lennox.

Maybe Lennox even chooses to die so that he will be swept up in the wonder of the impossible that inhabits these woods. We never really know. But Sylvia embraces the sense that she and her child belong down there in the dark, under

the mound. For her, this curious martyring of mother with child, this willing entrapment, is transcendent like her father's demise. Her own father even buried her in Selcouth's mound shortly before his death. It is believed that the madman was attempting to bury her alive, though later revelations suggest that he was trying to give his daughter and her unborn child, begot incestuously, to something down there, or more specifically, to a *place* designated a very long time ago for the miracle of this kind of birth.

The mound is a kind of blasphemous manger, a nativity scene that no one sane would readily choose. But a woman in the grip of awe and wonder at what Selcouth achieved here, what he pulled into these woods from another place among, or even beyond, the visible stars, might well choose this place for the destiny of herself and her child, because the past will not be denied; the will of the trees cannot be defied.

We are in the presence of mighty cosmic forces down there in the mound. Selcouth's own diary, found hidden in an alcove, attests to as much. Remnants of Lovecraft's own mythical texts are alluded to in the novel, and burned fragments of such are also discovered inside the mound, as are the degenerate remains of the mating of men and things from the stars. Even poor Heather reads what Sam and Sylvia bring back from their first excavation of the mound, and it forces her to immerse herself in the impossible: that which was once dead is coming back, coming home. And from a distant time and place, it seems the dead Selcouth will be accompanied by other uninvited visitors. Earthy compassionate Heather must also take that leap of imagination and unwillingly acknowledge the extraordinary with awe and wonder, along with the jolt of its bedfellow, terror.

Heather's own flesh and blood—Lennox, Sam, and Sylvia—have facilitated this renewal of activity. This is the most terrible revelation she must endure. The impossible truth of it, and the terrible oceanic raging of the bewitched wood in the climax, becomes the very essence of sustained awe through Heather's point of view. A woman with more imagination might not have returned from what she goes into the forest, and then the mound, to finish:

> At first it seemed that her surroundings had been reversed—that the woods were rooted less in the earth than in the darkness the familiar sky would have masked. This left her utterly disoriented, in the grip of a vertigo that let more of the truth come for her. Her mouth opened as did her mind, but she no longer knew if she was desperate to cry out or breathe. The entity whose thirst she'd sensed was using the forest to reach for her and the world. The forest was a memory with as many claws or digits or tendrils as there were trees. It was the end of a gigantic limb that stretched into a blackness she was terrified to contemplate. . . . The prospect of looking up appalled her, and yet her head was tilting helplessly skyward as if her neck was being

manipulated like a puppet's. Any moment she might see more than blackness overhead. She might see what its inhabitant had for a face.[6]

Can we finally say with any certainty that the fate of our heroine Heather—the new watcher of the woods from an asylum window, like her father before her—is the end of this matter? All that is certain is that the cast, like so many of Lovecraft's characters, are either destroyed, broken, or forever changed. But the catalyst that facilitated this change in our characters' perspectives, or that crafted their destruction, remains unchanged, remains as timeless and uncanny and seductive as it did before—the entity of Goodmanswood. The wondrous journeys in dream, and the sheer terrors it inflicts upon the waking, continue as its legacy. We can but watch and wait.

The very components of the novel—the motivations and actions of the principal contemporary English characters (which are rarely entirely their own); the history of the wood as a Neolithic place of worship, later adopted by the mage Selcouth for his dabblings with the blackest arts; the unearthing of the subterranean past and its relics; the collision between the living and what was once buried—are all the dark will and the ever-animate presence of the neo-Gothic.

There is even something Stoker-like, or Carpathian, about Goodmanswood. One could even believe it to be Campbell's Transylvania. It certainly is as memorable and as evil, though even older than Dracula's home. And, after reading this novel, the reader cannot be blamed for deciding that the setting and milieu of the classic Gothic novel has now been vitally reinterpreted and bought howling into the twenty-first century by Ramsey Campbell.

Notes

1. Ramsey Campbell, *The Darkest Part of the Woods* (New York: Tor, 2003), 79–80.
2. Campbell, *The Darkest Part of the Woods*, 39.
3. Campbell, *The Darkest Part of the Woods*, 83.
4. Campbell, *The Darkest Part of the Woods*, 237–242.
5. Campbell, *The Darkest Part of the Woods*, 317.
6. Campbell, *The Darkest Part of the Woods*, 355.

CHAPTER 15

Drac the Ripper

JAMES REESE'S *THE DRACULA DOSSIER*, CONSCIOUSNESS DISORDERS, AND NINETEENTH-CENTURY TERROR

Katherine Ramsland

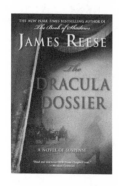

A striking fact about the case of Jack the Ripper is that it is so elastic. Still unidentified, the killer of between four and nine women from 1887 to as late as 1891 has been tagged variously as a lunatic, physician, magician, prince, minister, painter, and suicidal med student, to name a few. Advocates strenuously promote their favorite candidate, and while feeling right is not the same as *being* right, some spend millions on their campaign. A common tactic for angling readers toward a specific suspect is to inject a character like Sherlock Holmes into a fictionalized Ripper investigation, or to fictionalize the lives of real people who were alive at the time. That's the great thing about gaping holes in police records, especially when so many notables were Red Jack's contemporaries.

In *The Dracula Dossier*, James Reese exploits not just incomplete police reports but also Bram Stoker's spare biography to offer a titillating *what if?* Adopting the Gothic frame of cryptic correspondences, journal entries, and discovered treasures that have quietly collected dust under everyone's noses, he offers an obscure collection of Stoker's notes that depicts a supposed close encounter with the Ripper. Along the way, we hear gossip about William Butler Yeats and Oscar Wilde. Reese choreographs disparate elements to suggest that Stoker's most famous novel, *Dracula*, may be a disguise for actual events to which Stoker was witness. So, the story is fiction coating fact to present a theory which can itself only be fiction. However, authors who hope to successfully mimic nineteenth-century Gothic style must achieve more than good form; they must also grasp the anxieties of the era that fueled such tales and make their own version credible for a new age. Mashing *Dracula* with Red Jack is clever, but to achieve a compelling convergence, Reese must assimilate the dialectic of possession and violation

on two levels: how it worked for Stoker's readers and how it works for us. Reese's moody panache may fit Stoker's era, but, sadly, the psychological dynamic is flat.

The metaphor of monstrousness surrounding the Ripper, even if similar to a nineteenth-century vampire tale, should still bristle with emotional tones appropriate for its readers. I suggest that today's possession narratives must be more conversant with the science of neuropsychology, that is, they should absorb and convey the embodied terror of consciousness disorders. What made Stoker's characters tremble in the 1890s we now face in much more sophisticated form. In this chapter, I explore several forms of possession and propose the idea of possessed figures as liminal beings. This image accommodates the larger-than-life serial killer, possessed people, and archetypal vampires that populate both novels. All are part human and part "other," and within this otherness, their situation can be either terrifying or marvelous. The liminal being of our time will similarly attract and repel because it addresses *our* desires and fears.

The Ripper

First, let's review the facts that frame the novel.

The official story of Jack the Ripper focuses on the murders of five prostitutes in London's East End slums in the fall of 1888. Some criminologists (and Ripperologists) believe there were more than five victims, and a few say there were less, but to sidestep these arguments I'll concentrate on the "official" five murders on which most experts agree.

The first was forty-five-year-old Mary Ann "Polly" Nichols. On the night of August 31, an hour after a friend saw her, she was killed and left on the street. Her skirt was pulled up to her waist, her legs were parted, and there were severe cuts across her abdomen and throat. About a week later, Annie Chapman ended up on the wrong side of a similar knife. Her throat was cut, her stomach ripped open, and her intestines pulled out. Her bladder and uterus were missing.

A note arrived on September 29 that appeared to be a lead. Signed, "Yours Truly, Jack the Ripper," the author claimed to be "down on whores," and he intended to keep killing them. The next night, September 30, saw the murders of two women, Elizabeth Stride and Catherine Eddowes. Stride's throat was cut, but Eddowes's intestines were removed and placed over her right shoulder. In addition, her face was oddly mutilated, and her uterus and kidney were missing.

Then came a letter "from Hell" to the head of the Whitechapel vigilante organization, enclosed with half of a pickled kidney that seemed to be afflicted with Bright's disease—a disorder from which Eddowes had suffered. The note's author indicated that he'd fried and eaten the other half. He offered to send "the bloody knife" in due time, and taunted, "Catch me when you can." The police

could not track down who had sent the gruesome package, but the handwriting was different from that in the Jack the Ripper letter.

It was the last victim, Mary Kelly, twenty-four, who took the brunt of the offender's frenzy. On November 8, she apparently invited a man into a rented room, and after he killed her, he spent about two hours skinning and disemboweling her.[1]

Among the diverse array of suspects, Reese selects a real personage, the self-educated American herbalist, and possible quack, Francis J. Tumblety, who was also suspected of complicity in the assassination of Abraham Lincoln. Tumblety disliked women and was associated with the deaths of several patients, but to avoid arrest he kept moving, landing in London at an opportune moment to possibly be the Ripper. He befriended British writer Thomas Henry Hall Caine and was arrested on November 7, 1888, on a charge of "gross indecency," which meant that he'd allegedly engaged in a homosexual liaison. To escape a humiliating trial, he fled to France just after Mary Kelly's murder and then returned to the United States. One researcher insists that Tumblety's handwriting is consistent with the letter "from Hell."[2]

Enter Bram Stoker, also a friend of Caine's (dedicating *Dracula* to him). It does not require much suspension of belief to accept Reese's premise that Stoker might actually have met Tumblety on some social occasion. Reese exploits their mutual acquaintance to support his suggestion that *Dracula* is a metaphorical map to actual events. Thus, we must review Bram Stoker's life story.

Stoker

Born November 8, 1847, in Dublin, Ireland, the third of seven children, Stoker was an avid reader. As he grew up, he developed a love for the theater, and in 1871 he began reviewing theatrical productions. At one point, he gave actor Henry Irving a favorable review in a production of *Hamlet*. The two men became friends, and when Irving purchased the Lyceum Theater in London, he invited Stoker to manage it. In addition to this acquaintance, Stoker trumped Oscar Wilde for the attentions of Florence Balcombe, whom he then married. As the theater prospered, the Stokers moved among London's elite, giving dinner parties and salons. In his spare time, Stoker also wrote stories, and after he met a scholar in 1890 who told him tales from Eastern Europe, he envisioned a fictional vampire. On his travels (never to Eastern Europe), he visited many places that became settings for his tale. When the Lyceum fell on hard times, Stoker supplemented his income with novels, publishing *Dracula* in 1897. His publications earned little money, so he died nearly destitute in 1912 at the age of sixty-four.

Stoker had an interest in the occult, especially the use of hypnosis, and he was rumored to be a member of the mystical Hermetic Order of the Golden Dawn. The order would attract many influential writers—including Algernon Blackwood, Aleister Crowley, Maud Gonne, Arthur Machen, E. Nesbit, and W. B. Yeats. Indeed, some of Stoker's close friends and associates were known members, as were several people who thought that one among them was Jack the Ripper. Stoker was also conversant with anthropological theories that offenders were primitive throwbacks whose criminality was evident in their thuggish features. Stoker used this notion to create Count Dracula as a criminal degenerate.

While not wildly popular when Stoker was alive, *Dracula* has never been out of print. On the contrary, it has inspired countless plays, fictional spin-offs, critical interpretations, scholarly treatises, dance productions, and films. Told as an epistolary novel via a series of letters, clippings, telegrams, and diary entries from several different characters, the plot involves an English solicitor's clerk, Jonathan Harker, who travels to northeastern Transylvania in 1893 to assist the aristocratic Count Dracula with purchasing a home in England. The count welcomes him, but Harker finds the man disturbing, especially when Dracula scales the castle walls like a spider. Harker discovers that Dracula thrives on human blood, and the rest of the tale involves him trying to alert others back in England. A vampire hunter named Abraham Van Helsing steps in and explains that the *nosferatu* is a dangerous blood drinker with the strength of twenty men. This monster uses necromancy, which involves gaining special knowledge from corpses. The count is both animal and devil; he can command rats, wolves, and the elements, and he can change his form. Among his secret powers is the ability to vanish into a mist and see in the dark. For repressed Victorians, a ravenous, seductive vampire was a titillating figure.[3]

An additional detail of interest is that among the people whom Stoker met in London was Sir Arthur Conan Doyle, famous for creating Sherlock Holmes (with the first story featuring Holmes being published the year before the Ripper's attacks). It is not a stretch to deduce that Reese tapped their acquaintance for his detective-like rendition of Stoker. In fact, we can take this connection further; in 1892, Stoker encouraged Henry Irving to buy the stage rights to Conan Doyle's story, "A Straggler of '15." That same year, Stoker and Conan Doyle were two of twenty-four collaborators in a literary experiment, wherein each added a chapter to an ongoing tale, and in 1907, Stoker interviewed Conan Doyle for publication. During their period of acquaintance, Conan Doyle also published "The Parasite," in 1894, a story about possession via hypnotic trance induction. It shares with *Dracula* certain thematic preoccupations, notably the presence of the occult in a scientific age, sexual possession, and psychological invasion.[4]

This story conveys the male distrust of hypnosis and the notion that vulnerability to a trance was a sign of weakness bordering on the feminine. The plot

features a petite Trinidadian crone with "powers" who seduces the protagonist and erodes an Englishman's autonomy. He learns with horror that his ego boundaries are permeable, that he can be directed by another's mind to commit crimes, and that his subconscious can be forcefully colonized. That is, he can be raped. Was there anything more disturbing to a straitlaced Victorian male?

Stoker was clearly enthralled with this notion as well, but Count Dracula is intent on more than mere sexual possession. He aspires to penetrate and colonize a great empire. In tales from those times, the tool is the unseen influence of mind control, which makes penetration and possession possible. We watch helplessly while an outside being moves us like pawns and determines our fates. Although Victorians knew nothing about consciousness disorders, they had experimented with hypnosis. From what little they knew, they feared that this technique could annihilate their free will, entrap them, and make them vulnerable to possession. Part of *Dracula*'s power to frighten derives from this sense of nebulous threat.

The Fortress is Weak

It was Franz Anton Mesmer who first brought hypnosis into popular consciousness, making theatrical displays and unwarranted claims, and while conservative medical professionals regarded "mesmerism" as quackery, some found trance induction to be a powerful tool. John Braid coined the term *hypnosis* in 1843, in reference to Hypnos, the Greek god of sleep, and Jean-Martin Charcot, head of the Salpetriere Hospital in Paris, heralded its medical benefits. Charcot was a leading neurologist during the 1870s who believed that alterations in the brain caused the majority of psychopathologies. He used hypnosis to treat disorders such as hysteria. Charcot's student Pierre Janet hypothesized that hypnosis was a dissociated state in which part of one's consciousness split off from the rest.

These ideas clearly influenced Stoker, and he gave them a fictional twist. As Dracula selects and connects with his victims, seducing them with trance induction, he creates a telepathic bond that forces them under his control. Dracula proclaims to Mina Harker, "When my brain says 'Come!' to you, you shall cross land or sea to do my bidding."[5] However, he also plants the seed for his destruction: The vampire hunters learn that when Mina is in a trance they can track his movements. Thus they locate him via his own powers and destroy him.

Back to Reese's idea that *Dracula* is a disguise for reality. Stoker witnesses secret ceremonies in which Tumblety becomes possessed by the Egyptian god Set. When Stoker learns about the Ripper murders, he thinks of Tumblety. It turns out that Set is using Tumblety's human form to murder prostitutes and remove their organs for a nefarious purpose. Thus we are back to the mechanisms of a possession narrative. An evil force possesses the count to make a former

human thrive on blood and transform others into monsters, while an equally bloodthirsty entity controls Tumblety, with equally evil intent. Now we enter an inner landscape of violators and victims.

The Irresistible Impulse

Stoker's notes, as Reese depicts them, provide glimpses of Stoker's London experiences while directing readers beyond the descriptive text into a psychologically charged subterranean realm. As with *Dracula*, an indistinct presence haunts these busy details, as if the narrator is finding distractions that deflect his reluctance to face whatever is in the darkness. "In fiction," writes Charles Baxter in *The Art of Subtext*, "the half-visible and the unspoken—all those subtextual matters—are evoked when the action and dialogue of the scene angle downward, when by their multiplicity they imply as much as they show."[6] In other words, we are directed to pressing secret panels, going down stairs, exploring basement rooms, digging into the ground, and submerging into deep water. The same can be said for subtle hints about other disturbing things. Yet, despite suggestions in *The Dracula Dossier* of outsider sexuality—represented by Oscar Wilde's entourage—the novel lacks *Dracula*'s charged eroticism, perhaps because demonic possession is less sexy than a ravenous vampire. However, the possibility that a demon might be driving Jack the Ripper explains why he always got away, despite close calls, and why he was so brutal. Thus we should examine the narrative of spirit possession as a manifestation of human psychology similar to how the vampire narrative has been interpreted. If it is not about the dread of surrender to sexual possession, perhaps there is another way to appreciate it. Like *Dracula*, Reese's depiction is about unspeakably extraordinary events that threaten ordinary lives.

In *Horror and the Holy*, existential psychologist Kirk J. Schneider describes reasons why the extraordinary captivates us: in our monster tales, we find elements of the sacred. "Creation, destruction, the monstrous—each of these touches on the extraordinary as well as on the pathological."[7] He notes that the human soul is endlessly caught between attraction to freedom ("the expansive") and the safety of limits ("the restrictive"): we want something that offers deliverance from limits, but losing our moorings also scares us. Constriction threatens to stultify and obliterate, while freedom might drown us in chaos. Schneider says that, within this frame, *Dracula* is a study in hyperconstriction. Despite the vampire's promise of immortality and suprahuman powers, the novel undermines this with images of entrapment, deterioration, and trespass, as well as beating back the fantastical (occult expansion) with a return to the ordinary, and thus to safety. The vampire's form of expansion, enticing to consider, comes at too dear a cost—the soul.

In Reese's vision, *Dracula* is not really about a vampire. Instead, this image is merely a prop to suggest how Jack the Ripper was "born." At the Hermetic Order's temple, "Isis-Urania No. 3," possibly near the British Museum, Reese lets a shaken Stoker wonder if Set, a demonic entity, has just filled the kneeling and intoning man at his side, Tumblety. Can an ancient spirit make a modern man into a bloodthirsty monster? Toward this question rushes the book's secrets that could ruin one, in the form of esoteric wisdom, ambiguities, and Gothic melodrama:

> As for the Hierophant himself [Tumblety], I saw, or rather thought I saw, his eyes back-roll to their whites and the scar upon his cheek redden and twist . . . till it appeared like lips. . . . All present hung upon his every word as he continued extempore in a voice seeming not his own. . . . "I am He who casteth Lightning and Thunder. I am He whom the showers of righteousness shall not douse. I am He whose mouth ever flameth. I am He who hath come back from Condemnation. I am He who refuseth Exile. I am He who riseth from the sands Vengeful. I am he whose heart was wrongly Weighed. . . . I am Set, . . . risen to Right the Scales of Maat.'[8]

In ancient Egypt, the *ka* is a double that lived inside a tomb with a person's corpse, holding the life energy. If not fed, it would emerge and devour whatever it could find. The Ripper and the count are both former humans possessed by something darkly fantastic. Set (or Seth) is the Egyptian god of the desert, associated with powerful sandstorms. During certain periods, Set was Egypt's chief deity, and a hero. He then killed and hacked up his brother Osiris, and the myths made him the embodiment of evil, like the Christian Satan. Thus he enters Tumblety as a demonic entity, representing a threshold between good and evil, human and divine. Set makes Tumblety a liminal being. Set will make Tumblety go "ripping hores at will," ultimately to reenact a damning ritual for Set. This is the weighing of a dead person's heart on "the Scales of Maat" against an ostrich feather (symbolically the "feather of truth") and the interrogation of the heart for its sins against any god or goddess.[9] In some versions, the jackal-headed god Anubis actually brings the heart to Set's slain brother Osiris—the King of the Dead—to weigh.[10] Without a balance on these scales of justice/order/morality, the soul cannot progress into the afterlife. If the heart scale tips downward, the heart is devoured by the female demon Ammit, condemning the deceased to eternal restlessness.[11] More menacingly, and making this all an Egypto-Gothic work, Tumblety insists in letters that Stoker assist him in the weighing-of-the-heart ritual—just as fourteen gods and goddesses, the falcon-headed sky god Horus, and the ibis-headed god of wisdom Thoth would assist heart judgment in many ancient *Books of the Dead* papyri recovered from tombs along the Nile.[12]

If Stoker refuses, Tumblety promises to use Stoker's kukri knife to cut out and place Stoker's own heart on the scales.

The word *demon* derives from *daimon* in ancient Greek and refers to liminal beings that were more than human but less than divine. Liminality joins two distinctly different states of existence within a single physical body. Thus, such creatures can be both good and evil, dead and alive, mortal and immortal, attractive and dangerous. Examples in myth or fiction of liminal people are Merlin in the Arthurian tales, the Green Man, the horse-man Chiron, and the vampire.

The vampire is animated by something that can bring a corpse back to life with its cognitive faculties intact. The creature, archetypally, is immortal and thrives on human blood (or whatever else a given culture considers to be the essence of life). The vampire has no life spring within itself, so it must seek this from others. It represents an insatiable void, seducing us via our own compliance in order to drain us of our best resources. The ironic spring in such Gothic novels is that the victim participates in, and even welcomes, the victimization. In the process, we might experience the ecstasy of surrender and perhaps gain immortality, but once we cross this threshold, we are no longer human. We, too, are now liminal creatures.

In real life (which *The Dracula Dossier* imagines), cases of alleged possession provide a glimpse into what happens to people who willingly or unwillingly acquire an entity. It also shows us the psychological dimensions of this metaphor of vulnerability and trespass. Some cultures fear and resist it, while others embrace its power. This in itself makes possession a liminal experience.

Possessed

In September 2009, scientists reported a bizarre case: a thirty-seven-year-old woman with no history of mental illness, other than signs of depression in late adulthood, experienced a seizure in 2006 that sent her to a German epilepsy center. She offered a list of her symptoms and experiences: frequent déjà vu, nausea, sudden fear, . . . and oh, there was this other thing: Sometimes she came out of a seizure perceiving herself as a man. Her arms were transformed into hairy male arms, and her voice sounded lower in pitch. In fact, not only did she see herself as a man, but other women in the room appeared to be men as well. A benign tumor in her brain near the right amygdala, affecting the right temporal lobe, was diagnosed as the cause.[13] Although anticonvulsive drugs relieved her symptoms, her condition raised many questions for neuroscientists about perception.

Scientists have already associated human identity with the amygdala, and the right temporal lobe with sexual identity, but this case suggests that there are brain circuits specifically for the perception of gender. When they are disturbed,

a person might lose the sense of gender identity and feel possessed by someone of the opposite gender. That is, they lose their psychological boundaries.

In fact, many people who commit crimes claim to have been possessed while in the act, and perhaps there is more to their claim, neurologically, than a case of malingering. Since the hypothesis before us involves a demon that fuels the Ripper's rage-filled, bloody spree, let's examine a case of five similar murders in which the killer, "Gainesville Ripper" Danny Rolling, described the entity that supposedly controlled him.

During the summer of 1990, there were five gruesome rape-murders in Gainesville, Florida, in quick succession. The first crime scene involved two freshmen at the University of Florida who had been repeatedly stabbed, mutilated, and posed for shocking effect. That same night, investigators found a missing eighteen-year-old in her bedroom; her head was propped on a bookshelf, and her nude mutilated body was bent over on the edge of the bed. Two days later, a mile away, a male and female student were killed in their home. As with the others, entry to the apartment had been forced with a pry tool.

In the nearby woods, police found a black bag with a screwdriver, money taken during a bank robbery, duct tape, a cassette recorder, and clothes. But when the screwdriver failed to match the pry marks from the crime scenes, these items were forgotten, until Danny Rolling was arrested for robbing a store. The police retrieved and listened to the cassette in the recorder, which began, "This is Danny Rolling." He sang a song about being insane and signed off with, "Somethin' I gotta do."[14] Confronted, Rolling confessed to all the murders but blamed an alter ego, Gemini—inspired by the movie *The Exorcist III*.

In this 1990 film, derived from the novel *The Exorcist*, a demon-possessed lunatic begins killing people in the asylum where he is locked up. He calls himself the Gemini Killer, and his modus operandi is to paralyze his victims with succinylcholine, which leaves them alert and aware of their torture. Gemini is the "thing" inside the killer, using the man's body to perform his gory deeds. Although Rolling did not get a pass on this attempt at a multiple personality defense (he was convicted), the scenario leads us to an actual disorder that suggests why our possession tales can be so frightening.

Throughout history, the less we have known about the brain, the more we have relied on metaphors to convey ideas about it, for example, a blank slate, a wax block, a recorder, or a computer. With the establishment of psychology and neuropsychology, we more fully understand how possession narratives might arise from somatic anxiety over the potential for consciousness disorders. The healthy waking mind formulates consciousness and self-awareness, but certain pathological states interfere with functional awareness, such as stupors, comas, dementia, and delirium. A comatose patient lacks both wakefulness and awareness, while someone in a vegetative state has periods of wakefulness but no

awareness.[15] Yet sometimes these are misdiagnosed in patients who actually suffer from a much more frightening condition: "locked-in syndrome."

In 2006, a car crash victim in the Netherlands, Rom Houben, managed to communicate with doctors after twenty-three years of what they had believed was a vegetative state. In fact, Houben seems to have been fully aware during all this time but had been unable to make anyone understand. Recent brain scan technology allowed doctors to see that his brain was more active than it should be, and they set him up with a computer. Through a guide, he stated that he had felt "utterly powerless."[16] Apparently, this man is not alone in being misdiagnosed, but only recently have we understood how to distinguish such disorders.

Our worst nightmare is the possibility of being buried alive, that is, to have wakefulness but be unable to move. Locked-in syndrome is a similar experience. This neurological condition is in an important way parallel to what we find in possession narratives that inspire terror today: Something has paralyzed our will and forced us along for the ride.

Yet we must not rush to a culture-bound judgment. As noted earlier, possessed people are liminal beings, which can be either positive or negative—or both. The fact is, many cultures have embraced possession as a spiritual experience. The Dionysian cults of ancient Greece induced voluntary possession by the gods to gain a form of wild madness that brought unusual insight. The ritual spread throughout Greece until the Romans suppressed it in 186 BCE. In addition, priestesses such as those at Delphi went into trances to channel the pronouncements of Apollo. Israel, too, had prophets who entered an ecstatic state, as did the Sufis, who danced to draw down the gods.

Spiritualists and mediums through the ages have claimed to be possessed by entities who deliver messages from beyond the grave. In some cases, they do even more. In Brazil, João de Deus (John of God) operates in the remote village of Abadiânia as an unlicensed medical consultant and healer. He claims, however, that it is not him doing the surgeries but the spirits who possess him. "I am unconscious," he insists. According to him, when he was sixteen, the spirit of King Solomon entered his body and began to heal people. Now he says that more than thirty different entities can enter his body, most of whom were once living people and some of whom were themselves medical men. The "incorporation" occurs quickly. As João prepares to perform a surgery, his body jerks. This means an entity has come into him and he now sees through its eyes and has its skills. He might heal without breaking the patient's skin, or he might penetrate the organs with surgical knives. Observers have reported that his eye color may change to match the person inhabiting him. Whether he is effective is anyone's guess, thanks to the placebo effect and the self-healing powers of human beings. Often mere expectation can stall a tumor's growth or make a rash disappear. However, believers flock to him. He charges no fee, yet he is wealthy from the gifts of grateful patients.[17]

Some psychologists think such entities are real. During the 1980s, Dr. Edith Fiore published *The Unquiet Dead* to explain psychological disorders as resulting from "spirit attachment," which inspired the methods of spirit release-ment therapy and remote depossession. While not officially recognized among establishment practitioners, these treatments have had their promoters. More conservative practitioners reframed spirit attachments as "negative thought forms," which echoed what Swiss psychoanalyst Carl Jung had said. He viewed the phenomenon of spirit possession as a psychological manifestation. The possessed person had become overly fascinated with an archetypal figure that represented an unconscious issue. Jung warned that there was a danger that "the archetypal figures, which are endowed with a certain autonomy on account of their numinosity, will escape from conscious control altogether and become completely independent, thus producing the phenomenon of possession."[18] In other words, we project our intolerable issues away from ourselves. We see demons "out there," but they are actually from within us.

This idea evolved into the possibility of personality fragmentation. In some corners of the psychological community, mental disorders such as schizophrenia, demonomania, and multiple personality disorder (dissociative identity disorder) are today associated with spirit possession.[19] From about 1982 until 1995, many psychotherapists used hypnosis, guided imagery, dream analysis, and other techniques to persuade patients to "remember" childhood abuse. People turned up with dozens, hundreds, or even a thousand alter personalities, some of which were not even human. (Often, these "alters" identified themselves as demons.) Although the diagnosis is controversial, it proposes that, due to overwhelming trauma, a person fractures into several alter personalities and that two or more subpersonalities share a single body. Each takes turns inhabiting the personality and controlling the person's behavior.[20] For some alters, it is a nightmare of Gothic entrapment and violation, while others like the opportunity to take charge. Someone who truly has such a condition would be a liminal being in its most concrete form.

Liminal people, whether possessed by an entity, undermined by unconscious complexes, or locked in by physical disabilities, may be terrified at the loss of their autonomy. Or they may recognize the opportunity to expand their powers. In either case, the interplay of attraction and revulsion could empower narratives of possession with a suffocating cultural dread.

Summary

Altered states of consciousness can cause perceptual changes, some of which can seem like pressure from an external entity. However, anxiety about possession is

not so much about an entity subsuming us as it is about our complicity in the process. Our darkest fear is not of the "other" but of the self-destruction and self-paralysis of which we are capable. No one wants to be "locked in," but even worse would be to know that one did this to oneself. Reese has nicely mimicked Stoker's style, but the disturbance produced by liminal beings is potent only when the creature absorbs current collective issues. We know too much about hypnosis to be as nervous about it as the Victorians were, but we are only just discovering things inside our brains that can violate and possess us as surely as demonic spirits. Despite the possibilities that lure us, drawing out gods or devils from within could exact too great a cost.

Notes

1. Katherine Ramsland, *The Human Predator: A Historical Chronicle of Serial Murder and Forensic Investigation* (New York: Berkley, 2005), 79–83.

2. Stewart P. Evans and Paul Gainey, *Jack the Ripper: The First American Serial Killer* (Lanham, MD: Kodansha America, 1998).

3. Katherine Ramsland, *The Science of Vampires* (New York: Berkley, 2000), 1–7.

4. Catherine Wynne, ed., *The Parasite*, by Arthur Conan Doyle (Kansas City, KS: Valancourt Books, 2009), x–xxiv.

5. Bram Stoker, *Dracula*, ed. Glennis Byron (Peterborough, ON: Broadview, 1997), 328.

6. Charles Baxter, *The Art of Subtext: Beyond Plot* (St. Paul, MN: Graywolf, 2007), 4.

7. Kirk J. Schneider, *Horror and the Holy: Wisdom Teachings of the Monster Tale* (Chicago: Open Court, 1993), xi.

8. James Reese, *The Dracula Dossier* (New York: HarperCollins, 2008), 128.

9. Denise Dersin, ed., "And None Have Returned," in *What Life Was Like on the Banks of the Nile: Egypt 3050–30 BC* (New York: Time-Life, 1997), 137–181.

10. Dersin, "And None Have Returned."

11. Susie Hodge, "The Judgment of Hunefer from *The Book of the Dead*," in *Egyptian Art* (New York: Metro Books, 2008), 86–91.

12. Hodge, "The Judgment of Hunefer from *The Book of the Dead*."

13. Charles Q. Choi, "Seizure Makes Woman Mistake Herself for a Man," *LiveScience*, www.livescience.com/culture/090903-seizure-switch.html (accessed December 8, 2009).

14. Fiona Steel, "Savage Weekend: Danny Rolling," *TruTV Crime Library*, www.trutv.com/library/crime/serial_killers/predators/rolling/11.html (accessed December 5, 2009).

15. James L. Bernat, "Chronic Consciousness Disorders," *Annual Review of Medicine* 60 (2009): 381–392.

16. "Man Says Emergence from 'Coma' like a Rebirth," MSNBC, www.msnbc.msn.com/id/34109227/ns/health-more-health_news (accessed November 23, 2009).

17. Heather Cummings and Karen Leffler, *John of God: The Brazilian Healer Who's Touched the Lives of Millions* (Hillsboro, OR: Beyond Words Publishing, 2007).

18. C. G. Jung. *The Basic Writings of C. G. Jung*, ed. Violet S. de Laszlo (New York: Modern Library, 1959), 323–324.

19. Mark Bancroft, "The History and Psychology of Spirit Possession," Enspire Press, www.enspirepress.com/writings_on_consciousness/spirit_possession_exorcism/spirit_possession_exorcism.html (accessed August 27, 2009).

20 Joan Acocella, "The Politics of Hysteria," *New Yorker*, April 6, 1998, www.newyorker.com/archive/1998/04/06/1998_04_06_064_TNY_LIBRY_000015295 (accessed November 23, 2009).

CHAPTER 16

The New Southern Gothic

CHERIE PRIEST'S *FOUR AND TWENTY BLACKBIRDS*, *WINGS TO THE KINGDOM*, AND *NOT FLESH NOR FEATHERS*

Don D'Ammassa

The Southern Gothic is commonly thought of as a regional adaptation of the literary tradition that began with novels like *The Castle of Otranto* by Hugh Walpole. Although Southern Gothics are not necessarily horror novels and do not require supernatural content—as is the case with writers like Flannery O'Connor and William Faulkner—they are invariably strongly atmospheric, they frequently involve elements of terror or dread, and the often make use of other traditional elements like the persecuted female, family secrets, and slightly to very grotesque characters. Typically they at least allude to a lingering racial and social stratification. This can be more pronounced when the author chooses to incorporate more overtly horrifying elements, including ghosts, family curses, insanity, and images of darkness and decay. Writers including Robert R. McCammon, Michael McDowell, and Joe Lansdale are among others who have worked in this tradition in recent years. Cherie Priest, a relative newcomer, draws on most of the facets of the Southern Gothic in her work, perhaps most notably in the Eden Moore trilogy, and with a surprising degree of maturity for a new writer.

Priest places her stories of the supernatural in Chattanooga, Tennessee, and imbues each with elements that evoke a strongly regional atmosphere. Some of these are obvious and overt, while others are subtle and often not crucial to the story line although they provide a richer backdrop for her characters by describing an identifiable but distinct subset of American culture. This is often accomplished through reference to seemingly inconsequential details, perhaps as slight as the mention of a Confederate flag sticker on a bumper. More effective, however, is her depiction of a culture which maintains its distinctive flavor

despite the increasing homogeneity of American life. There are suggestions that the author finds this cultural enclave archaic, particularly in the third novel, wherein her protagonist characterizes people in Chattanooga as shortsighted and inward looking, smothering the younger generation who frequently flee the city in order to better themselves. This is somewhat contradicted by the unwillingness of the protagonist to cut her own ties to the region and move on, but as is the case in real life, Eden is frequently torn between conflicting impulses.

The subsequent volumes embellish the southern flavor. Memories of personal favors or affronts cross the barrier of generations, with hints of old feuds and obligations both within and between families. The simmering, ever-present conflict that lurks within most personal relationships is as much a product of class barriers as racial background. Ghosts of Confederate soldiers appear on a historic battlefield, their presence almost taken for granted. We are told that there is no such thing as a private matter in the South, that scandals and secrets necessarily become fodder for the public at large. Those individuals who are subject to this public examination hardly even seem to resent the intrusion. There are scenes which remind the reader that many individuals remain incapable of putting the Civil War behind them, and which hint at a code of honor that governs everything from funeral attendance to the appropriateness of graffiti. Even gossip has a regional tone, elaborating upon itself and conferring an aura of celebrity even when the subject of that notoriety is not necessarily admirable. The role of the family is strongly emphasized and suggests obligations that transcend other considerations, and these matters are perceived as being outside the realm of external agencies, including the police. Superstition plays an active role in everyday life; the existence of ghosts and monsters and black magic comes as no surprise to the characters, with the notable exception of Eden's journalist friend, who is a displaced northerner.

Priest avoids some genre devices that readers might expect to find in her work, which bears some similarities to the currently popular paranormal romance novels. Eden is a feisty young woman with more than human powers who lives in an urban environment, has predominantly male friends, encounters various supernatural entities, and triumphs over them by demonstrating both intelligence and physical courage. There is, however, virtually no romantic content other than a mild flirtation between Eden and a journalist late in the third book; the challenges she faces usually apply to the world at large rather than to her specifically. Eden's internal conflicts are almost always related directly to her predicament, not to regrets about past actions or missed opportunities. She is rarely introspective and prefers to move on from her mistakes rather than agonize over them. Although all three of the novels are set primarily in Chattanooga or the surrounding area, the stories themselves have a much more rural than urban feel, with the exception of the prolonged flood sequence in *Not Flesh*

Nor Feathers, and even in this case her wanderings in the drowned city suggest flooded ravines, mysterious caverns, and abandoned wastelands.

Although Priest's novels are intensely character driven, she spends little time developing their personalities outside of the fantastic context, introducing a variety of the devices of supernatural horror in the first few chapters of *Four and Twenty Blackbirds* (2003, revised 2005) even as she describes the rather turbulent life of her protagonist. Eden Moore is an orphan whose unwed mother died during childbirth under peculiar circumstances. Even as a child she could see ghosts, she believed herself to have lived previous lives, she experienced visions, and she was pursued by a mentally unstable, religiously obsessed killer. Eden's mother, Leslie, died while institutionalized, for reasons revealed late in the novel, and Eden is raised by her formidable Aunt Lulu—her mother's sister—and Uncle Dave. Although not an overtly unhappy child, she tends to be introverted and feels separated from her classmates, in part because of her mixed racial heritage. She also begins to lapse into dream states in which she sees images from a former life, events sometimes quite disturbing, including the presence of a book that contains a dried human hand. During one of these episodes, she inadvertently stabs a counselor at school, which raises suspicions about her mental stability. It is likely that Priest either did not expect to write a sequel or had given it little thought, because much of Eden's preternatural talent is absent from the other two novels.

Eden also sees and hears ghosts, specifically those of three women, sisters who were killed by a man they trusted, their bodies dismembered and thrown into a swamp. Although she is initially frightened by her visions, Eden adjusts to their presence after her aunt tells her that the ghosts are there to watch over her, and they do in fact help her to escape when Malachi Dufresne first tries to kill her during a nightmarish chase through a stretch of forestland. He insists that she is not who she appears to be but rather a demon in human form, the reincarnation of someone named Avery. She outwits him, and he is committed to a mental facility, but she is stunned to discover later that he is her cousin, that his mother is her great-aunt Eliza. Eventually she will learn that the relationship is even closer, that Malachi is her half brother. Eliza, a particularly fearsome matriarch, hints that there is some dark secret connected to Eden's heritage which marks her as extraordinary, though not in a good way. Most of the first novel consists of Eden's quest to discover the truth about her own heritage, much of which is known to her aunt. Lulu insists that Eden is not old enough to hear the truth, a misjudgment that helps fuel the story. Eden also has vague memories of the name Pine Breeze, a mysterious place that she instinctively fears, eventually identified as the facility where her mother was confined at the time of her death. Lulu also knows the significance of this name but refuses to explain. Although this leads to Eden's eventual quest to discover her heritage, Lulu's desire to withhold the information is not always credible given the circumstances.

The number of Eden's persecutors grows steadily as the novel progresses. Her teachers pretend to be neutral, but she is aware that they are secretly making fun of her and have underestimated her perspicacity. A new girl in school, April, makes racist comments and provokes a fight for which Eden is ultimately blamed, and the counselors at a summer camp immediately classify her as an oddball and consign her to the company of the other campers who don't fit in with the majority. Eden is not, however, a shrinking violet who wilts under the pressure of other people's displeasure or even animosity. She physically attacks April, outwits Malachi under extreme circumstances even though she has been injured, confronts her teachers despite their thinly disguised contempt, and refuses to accept even Lulu's presumably benign attempts to keep her from learning the truth.

Eden briefly makes a friend at camp. Cora is also troubled by ghostly apparitions, and one evening they share an experience in which a cloudy shape manifests itself in a mirror. Unlike Eden's ghosts, this entity feels malevolent, is able to manipulate objects in the physical world, and evinces an interest in Eden rather than its original prey. Cora helps her escape this first encounter by using a doggerel version of the rhyme "Four and Twenty Blackbirds" as a kind of prayer or mantra to hold it at bay. Eden learns a potentially valuable lesson, but she never sees Cora again after she goes home from the camp, and the malevolent spirit vanishes as well. Although this sequence helps establish the fact that Eden is resourceful and courageous, it feels oddly out of place and incomplete. There is also an inconsistency in Priest's depiction of ghosts, who are not supposed to be able to manipulate physical objects, although the ghostly Caroline Read in the third book proves to be both a ghost and a poltergeist, a distinction which Priest never resolves.

When Eden reaches the age of sixteen she finally discovers—following some clandestine assistance from her uncle Dave—that her mother was sent to Pine Breeze, at that time a home for troubled teenagers, where she died during a botched childbirth, a tragedy that was instrumental in the subsequent decision to close the facility. She also learns that Pine Breeze was at one time a tuberculosis clinic that experienced such a high death rate that one of the buildings was turned into a crematorium in which the corpses were disposed of. This is another side issue that helps to establish atmosphere but which is not germane to the actual story. Pine Breeze is currently closed and abandoned and is scheduled for demolition. The aura surrounding Pine Breeze contributes to the atmosphere of suspense, but the explicit ramifications of its existence and history are never fully explored. Where most contemporary horror writers feel compelled to tie up loose ends, Priest prefers to leave them unresolved, part of an indistinct tapestry of the supernatural that serves as context rather than to advance the plot.

Priest is also well aware of the convention of the woman-in-jeopardy suspense device and directly alludes to it when Eden discusses her days as a performing poet. "Everyone loves a lost little girl in a black corset top and leather pants."[1] They are caught up in the "illusion that she is innocence and pain in search of defilement and rescue," an illusion which she characterizes as "a lascivious parody of worship."[2] Eden not only performs in the role of the persecuted Gothic heroine but also repudiates the validity of the stereotype by acting to effect her own salvation—by taking the initiative to hunt down her antagonist rather than simply defend herself. This near worship is inverted by the religiously obsessed Malachi, however, who follows his escape from state custody by fatally shooting another female poet under the mistaken assumption that it is Eden. To Malachi, Eden is an instrument of Satan to be destroyed, not venerated. In the aftermath, Eden directly confronts Malachi rather than recoiling in horror; she is angry rather than frightened.

Eventually Eden begins to unravel the convoluted web of her past. Avery was the son produced by a love affair between a Union soldier and a slave woman during the Civil War. The soldier later married and fathered Eliza, which suggests part of the reason why she and Malachi might not look favorably on Avery's return in another body—although this proves to be a red herring, since Avery has magically prolonged his life. Avery's wife and her two sisters are the three ghosts who watch over Eden, and Avery is Lulu's grandfather as well. These convoluted family relationships are reflected in the extended—if sometimes informal—family structure typical of the Gothic novel. Although Lulu finally tells Eden as much as she knows, or at least admits to knowing, she also warns against investigating further, suggesting that curiosity was what caused the crisis in Leslie's life which led to her incarceration and ultimately her death.

The first-person narration allows the author to structure *Four and Twenty Blackbirds* much like a traditional detective story. The reader only knows what the protagonist learns during the course of her investigation, which is spread out over several years. There is no omniscient viewpoint to fill in the gaps or drop additional hints. As a teenager, Eden does finally locate Pine Breeze, where she recovers several papers relating to her mother from files which unaccountably were neither destroyed nor safeguarded. Although these provide some explanations—Eliza was paying for the treatment—they include more new questions than answers. Among the papers is a threatening letter that refers to Leslie's unborn child, unsigned but obviously not from Malachi, who would not have been old enough by then. There is also a letter from Leslie's lover, Eden's father, signed only "A" and suggesting that Leslie's pregnancy was known before she went to Pine Breeze, which contradicts everything else Eden has heard on the subject. The fate of Malachi's mother, Rachel, is yet another unresolved question.

Frustrated by her inability to convince Lulu to divulge the whole truth, if she even knows it, Eden travels to Georgia to confront Eliza, only to learn that her murderous cousin has escaped for a second time and is believed to be in the area. It is only then that Eden finally begins to uncover the true story in enough detail to explain most of the unusual events that have marked her life. Avery was the follower of John Gray, a quasi-voodoo sorcerer who died 165 years earlier and whose followers must restore him to life within ten days to prevent his soul from being lost forever. This is also the point at which we learn that Eliza is Avery's sister, and that both of them have extended their lives unnaturally by means of potions that Gray developed before his death.

Priest provides another revelation at this point, never foreshadowed. A priest has posed as Eliza's servant for years while attempting to find the mysterious book of power that Gray left behind, the same book about which Eden has had unsettling dreams, although the book actually plays little part in the resolution of the conflict. Priest provides a sketchy but interesting system of magic in which the power of an individual is dissipated through his children, which explains Avery's attempts to kill all of his descendants and reclaim their life force. Other than providing a motive and an incentive for Eden to act quickly, this disclosure contributes little to the resolution, which is actually a rather violent physical confrontation between Eden and Avery. The three watchful ghosts observe but do not intercede even in the limited way available to them. Although Avery is killed and his plans of resurrection are disrupted, the absence of overt fantastical elements during the violent climax is mildly discordant, but it is not fatal to the novel's effect. The mix of conventional and unconventional supernatural elements is an overall success, immersing the reader in a setting that is both realistic and fantastic.

The second book in the series, *Wings to the Kingdom* (2006), opens a few months after the events in the first. Eden has developed an unwanted reputation as someone who can speak to the dead and is sought after by bereaved people who are convinced that she can put them in touch with their loved ones, even though this is not the case. In the opening chapter, we learn that she is still living with her aunt and uncle but has not told them the whole truth about her encounter with Avery. Uncle Dave, in particular, seems determined to discover the truth, even if his curiosity has dissipated by the end of the novel. Although Eden avoids lying to them as much as possible, she conceals much of the truth, including the fact that she is now resistant to disease and that even moderately serious wounds heal with surprising rapidity. Nor does she contradict their belief that Malachi died in the fire when Avery's cabin burned. Malachi is in fact now living with Harry, the undercover priest, and has more or less reformed, although his mental stability is still questionable.

Fresh tension emerges slowly this time, starting with manifestations of Civil War ghosts attempting to issue enigmatic warnings although they cannot speak. Priest invokes the omniscient author to describe the initial appearance of the apparitions but soon returns to first-person narration, although there are occasional diversions. There is also a rumored monster on the Chickamauga battlefield, Old Green Eyes, about whose existence Eden remains skeptical. Old Green Eyes is an actual legend connected to the battlefield, and Priest has chosen from among various contradictory stories about his origin and appearance. Her preference is a version that likens the apparition to a yeti or some other inhuman creature rather than a ghost, although at times he is apparently immaterial. Once again, Priest chooses not to provide a comprehensive explanation, and we never receive more than vague hints about the apparition's origin and nature.

A husband-and-wife team of psychic investigators are supposedly investigating the manifestations, but Eden resists the temptation to become involved, in large part because she wants to avoid any further publicity, but also because she suspects the motives of the married couple leading the inquiry. Malachi is no longer trying to kill her under the misconception that she is the reincarnation of an evil sorcerer, but he still manages to place her life in jeopardy by returning unannounced to Chattanooga and having his car break down within the grounds of an insane asylum—not Pine Breeze—where someone, or something, has reportedly been haunting the area at night, disturbing some of the patients.

Malachi is searching for information about his mother, Rachel, who was reported dead in the first novel and who might well be the malevolent female ghost that Eden encountered during her investigation of Pine Breeze. They meet near the mental institution, and Priest deliberately invokes one of the hoariest plot elements of horror movies—the asylum was built on top of an ancient Native American burial ground—although apparently it is based on an actual institution on an actual burial ground. The author somewhat ameliorates the cliché by drawing our attention to its overuse. Following this encounter, we learn that Old Green Eyes is a kind of supernatural overseer of the ghosts at the battlefield, who for some reason has abandoned his post to wander the grounds of the asylum instead, to the consternation of the ghosts. We also learn of a lost ledger probably buried somewhere at Chickamauga which lists the location of a hidden cache of Confederate gold, information that leads to Peter Buford's attempts to retrieve it. His first encounter there is certainly the most effectively atmospheric sequence in the novel, but the brief jumps to third-person narration of Buford's activities are jarring.

Eden and two friends sneak onto the battlefield one night and encounter several ghosts, but they are able to record only bits and pieces of their speech, which suggest that some sort of bargain has expired and that this is connected

to the Dyer House, an area in the park which Buford believes contains the missing ledger. The professional ghost chasers are there also, as is a sniper who kills the male half of the pair, leaving his wife Dana a widow. This latter encounter is a fairly suspenseful sequence, but none of the six adults present appears to have brought a cell phone, despite the fact that one of their crew was shot and wounded at the same location only a day earlier. Although we know that Eden carries one, she fails to use it even when stalked by the mysterious killer. Eden and Dana escape with the aid of some benevolent ghosts, who can only speak audibly when one of them occupies Dana's body briefly, contradicting what we are told about ghosts in both the first and third novels in the series. He indicates that Old Green Eyes made a pact to protect the dead until the last descendent of a fallen general has died. A casual reference to the disappearance and assumed death of a college student suggests that this was the crucial event that gave the "digging man,"[3] who is also the sniper, freedom to desecrate the graves.

Not surprisingly, the sniper turns out to be Peter Buford, who was chased away by Old Green Eyes during his first attempt to retrieve the ledger. Buford learned about the creature's agreement with the Boynton family to watch over the battlefield in a very contrived sequence in which he consults another ex-con who just happens to have heard the truth and knows how to end the pact, even though no one else seems to be aware of it. Buford killed the last of the Boyntons in order to eliminate Old Green Eyes as an obstacle, and now he is chasing off human interlopers as well, although his methods are illogical in that they draw unnecessary attention to his presence.

Priest introduces but never really confronts a troubling moral question. Eden is able to open communication with Old Green Eyes, whose simple nature leaves him confused and unable to act now that he has been released from a century-long obligation. No longer compelled to protect the dead, the creature finds itself without purpose, unaware of the fact that it can choose a course of action rather than simply respond to some exterior imperative. Eden makes a convincing argument that it is now free to make use of its own initiative and strongly suggests that it is no longer bound not to physically injure those who defile the battlefield. Although her immediate objective might be admirable—Buford is holding one of her friends hostage and is threatening to kill him—the consequences of her actions cannot be predicted and could very well turn a frightening but harmless legend into a relentless killer. Dana, the surviving ghost buster, attempts to convince her of this, but Eden shrugs off the objection, and after Buford is disposed of, Eden (and the author) ignores the potential harm she might have done. Eden is similarly unwilling to face the consequences of harboring Malachi after the climax of *Four and Twenty Blackbirds*, and he reappears intermittently in the two sequels. Although he is presumably no longer homicidally inclined, the fact is that he is mentally unstable and has committed

at least one murder renders her decision to allow him to remain free, though in hiding, questionable at the very least. This decision to shield him from the authorities is justified in her own mind because he is family, her half brother, but her unwillingness to confront the possibility that he could present a danger to others is never addressed.

The changes in viewpoint are particularly striking because part of the novel is told in third person focusing on Buford, part in omniscience, and the bulk in first person. There are several jumps back and forth during the course of the novel, and they often disrupt the story flow. The second-person viewpoint is employed primarily to provide the background concerning the missing Confederate gold, which might have been more smoothly accomplished by having Eden stumble upon the legend herself, and to establish the character of Buford and the circumstances which drove him to commit murder. Although these contrivances are occasionally distracting, the novel as a whole is extremely suspenseful and maintains balance between realism and the supernatural.

The third and to date final novel in the Eden Moore series is *Not Flesh Nor Feathers* (2007). Once again, the author's choice of first-person narration presents some minor problems, this time during the opening sequences, because we need to witness events that took place before Eden was born. This is accomplished more effectively than in *Wings to the Kingdom* by casting these scenes as her speculation about the past, a mildly awkward contrivance which fortunately does not last long. The viewpoint shifts almost immediately to Eden in the present, and once again the format is very much that of the detective story until the actual disaster is under way. The diversion is designed to establish that something dangerous is stirring, but since her aunt was present during those events, it might more seamlessly have been accomplished by having her tell Eden the story.

The lead-in describes the experiences of Leslie and Lulu, who were briefly trapped in a warehouse during a flood and who heard what might have been creatures rising from the riverbed. Although there is nothing to confirm their story, it is reflected in the present when Eden learns that a number of homeless and poor people have been disappearing in the vicinity of the riverfront. She initially ignores these reports, although she has uncharacteristically agreed to help a reporter look into stories of the Lady in White, a ghost resident in a historic hotel whose recent appearances have frightened off staff and customers alike. What she finds is a confused but powerful poltergeist who attacks her after a cryptic warning that "they are coming"[4] to get everyone and refers to some mistake made in a church. Eden suspects that these manifestations were inspired by the appearance of construction people who are remodeling the hotel, but readers will conclude immediately that there is a connection with the disturbances in the river.

The next clue that something is wrong comes in the form of an anonymous letter to a newspaper from a construction worker at an apartment complex who claims that management is covering up the discovery of something "weird" at the site. Since this is the same apartment building where Eden has placed a deposit, despite Lulu's objection that the area isn't safe, Eden begins to have second thoughts, which are intensified by her suspicion that recent vandalism there was committed by the same friend who told her that people have been disappearing. She is also experiencing some disquieting physical changes. Her incredibly fast healing and immunity to disease have begun to leave her exhausted and feeling ill. She is finally driven to consult her Aunt Eliza, despite the near certainty that the older woman will not tell her the truth. Since she learns nothing, this sequence seems to have no real purpose other than to explain what has happened to Eliza since Avery's death.

The various plot threads begin to come together just as a supernaturally inspired flood turns Chattanooga into a disaster area, where charred corpses wrapped in chains rise from the river to kill the living. The petulant ghost at the old hotel is Caroline Read, who was judged insane during the early part of the twentieth century and who feels guilty about the burning of a church. The reader will undoubtedly pick out the connections more quickly than Eden does. The church in question had one of the few mixed-race congregations at the time it was burned, along with its occupants, by Klan members acting upon a lie told by Caroline when she was a child. Another ghost leads Eden to a ruined building decorated in part with Klan artwork, and Caroline refers to charred corpses, suggesting some kind of massacre. Caroline also refers to the tragedy as a "mistake," but just as with oracles in fantasy stories, the various ghosts who speak to Eden are either cryptic or just refuse to answer questions. At one point, Eden tries to explain this: "I think maybe they like the attention, because being dead makes them feel left out."[5]

When the flood occurs, Eden finds herself among the refugees deep within the city. She agrees to confront the ghost of Caroline Read again in a desperate effort to find out what the revenants want and possibly how to send them back to wherever they came from. She and her journalist friend undertake a risky plan to destroy or at least trap some of the creatures by setting off an explosion, but their effort only succeeds when Malachi makes an unlikely appearance and restores some balance to his recurring role by sacrificing himself on their behalf. Malachi's final act is consistent with what we have learned of his behavior in the past, and he and the rest of the major characters take on new depth during the course of the story.

Despite some structural problems, all three of the novels are suspenseful, inventive stories that draw on a strong and varied cast of characters and a distinctive setting that brings fresh life to stories of ghosts, black magic, and the

revenant dead. While Priest recognizes those elements that make the southern United States a distinct culture, she is not nostalgic for them, and in fact Eden characterizes the city and its traditions as having a negative impact on her generation. Her rejection of gentility and her frequently active physical response to problems is a sharp contrast to the traditional role of the southern lady as pampered and delicate. Almost all of the strong characters in the series—Eden herself, Lulu, Dana, and Eliza—are women. Priest's stories illustrate that we cannot escape history, either as individuals or as a society, but that we need to move on from those experiences and shape a future that incorporates but does not venerate the past. The three novels have left many questions about Eden Moore's life unanswered, but it remains to be seen whether or not Priest will tell us any more than she has already revealed.

Books in the Trilogy

1. *Four and Twenty Blackbirds* (Tor, 2005)
2. *Wings to the Kingdom* (Tor, 2006)
3. *Not Flesh Nor Feathers* (Tor, 2007)

Notes

1. Cherie Priest, *Four and Twenty Blackbirds* (New York: Tor, 2005), 78.
2. Priest, *Four and Twenty Blackbirds*, 78.
3. Cherie Priest, *Wings to the Kingdom* (New York: Tor, 2006), 242.
4. Cherie Priest, *Not Flesh Nor Feathers* (New York: Tor, 2007), 48.
5. Priest, *Not Flesh Nor Feathers*, 241.

CHAPTER 17

Margot Livesey's *Eva Moves the Furniture*

SHIFTING THE HOUSE OF GOTHIC

Tunku Halim

One similarity between Margot Livesey's *Eva Moves the Furniture* (2001) and the founding Gothic novel, Horace Walpole's *The Castle of Otranto* (1764), is that both works are set in the past. Walpole's work was allegedly printed in Naples in 1529 and written between 1095 and 1243. This is the fictitious claim in the Preface to the First Edition, meaning that the events are supposed to have occurred more than five centuries before Walpole wrote it.

In comparison, the main proceedings in *Eva* are more recent. Eva is born around 1920, eighty-one years before the novel was published, and her story spans the period before, after, and during the Second World War. Nevertheless, in what may be seen as a recognition of the novel's Gothic antecedents, the opening of the novel provides a snippet of an event that occurs in 1551, when "the Italian surgeon Fiorovanti was travelling in Africa when he came upon two men fighting a duel."[1] This is significant, for it is not long after the fictitious printing date of *The Castle of Otranto* and, one speculates, provides a link back to the genre's origins. The Italian connection in both works should also not be overlooked.

A significant motif in Gothic literature is the inclusion of a mystery that relies on elements of the supernatural. Maggie Kilgour has pointed out that the emergence of the genre in the eighteenth century has "been read as a sign of the resurrection of the need for the sacred and transcendent in a modern enlightened secular world."[2]

In the twenty-first century, the inhabitants of a multitasking, Internet-dominant, and gadget-driven existence may have an even greater desire for the mysteries of the supernatural than their eighteenth-century predecessors. After all, as individuals become further alienated from each other, notwithstanding

their numerous "friends" listed on social-networking sites such as Facebook, there arises a greater need to find connection. The supernatural is attractive because it may offer that.

These supernatural mysteries surface early on in *Eva*. In chapter 1, Eva, who is five years old, is playing house when she encounters a white-haired woman and a girl of twelve or thirteen. Eva serves them tea in acorn cups, which they pretend to sip. This is her first introduction to her companions who will remain with her for the rest of her life.

We know early on that these visitors are not of the usual human variety, for they come and go as they choose, appearing and disappearing at will. Yet they are undoubtedly more than mere apparitions, for, other than being able to speak to Eva, they readily interact with the physical world:

> [The woman] held the bowl for me while I went from nest to nest, and I noticed she had to stoop to avoid hitting the cobwebby roof, whereas Lily could stand upright with ease. "See?" she said, at the last nest. "You don't need to be scared of the hens." She placed the bowl in my hands. (16)

Even at the tender age of five, Eva is aware that her visitors are neither human nor mere ghosts.

> In my mind there was already much confusion between two categories commonly held to be opposites: the living and the dead. As for the third category, the ghosts in my storybook were filmy, insubstantial beings who did not graze their knees or chase hens. The companions did not seem to fit into that group either; they existed in their own peculiar dimension. (18)

The woman and the girl are supernatural beings, but their ability to speak and to interact with the physical world, let alone pretend to sip tea, make them almost human. Soon it becomes obvious that Eva can readily touch and feel them like she would any friend. It is this physicality, no different from a human's, that provides Eva's visitors with a greater vitality and presence in the narrative. Moreover, the intentions of the companions are not clear: are they there to hinder or assist? This will be explored later, but for the moment we should recognize that not knowing the companions' motivations compounds the mystery.

The idea of a hidden secret, often found in old Gothic, is also apparent in *Eva*. Stephen King has observed that "all of these books . . . have certain things in common, and all of them deal with the very basis of the horror story: secrets best left untold and things best left unsaid. And yet [their authors] all promise to tell us the secret."[3] In the current work, the secrets are neither dark nor threatening.

The companions are presented in a straightforward manner, like normal people, and they simply exist, viewed by Eva as a "deformity" in her life. It is their very existence, though, that has to be kept secret from everyone, including her own family, and even writing about her encounters in a diary is viewed as treachery.

The intentions of the companions, their very presence, and how their actions will impact Eva's life is a secret that has to be uncovered. Eva wonders if she has a purpose similar to Saint Joan and studies the life of saints for answers. Her future seems to be a secret kept from her, for she has less control of it. When she starts a new job at a legal firm, her companions, who had ironically helped her find it, sabotage her work, and she is asked to leave:

> "How could you?" I demanded. . . . But the air remained empty.
> They would not appear to answer my charges. This was their prerogative, to come and go in my life as they pleased, meddling or helping, while I was left to cope with the consequences. (62)

Answers to some secrets can be found in the distant past, and there are two references in the novel to myths and folklore far from the book's Scottish setting. The relevant ones are Jewish and Nigerian. The dybbuk is a spirit from Jewish legend that takes possession of a person. It can only be exorcised by a rabbi, and when the spirit is gone, the person dies. Similarly, in Nigerian folktales, an *abiku* is a baby that has been taken over by a spirit, and the child dies when the spirit leaves the body. These references, and the similarities to Eva's situation, can be viewed as adding to the secrets inherent in the novel, but they may also hint at some of the answers.

Beyond a kinship with the supernatural elements, mysteries, and secrets of old Gothic literature, *Eva Moves the Furniture* also shares the telling element of fear. Wolf explains that fear and violence have always been present in literature, including classical Greek plays and the Bible. Centuries later, it was Gothic literature that embraced this primal element. As Wolf states,

> What distinguishes Gothic fiction from mainstream literature is that its goal is to delight the reader by creating fear. . . . Because of its narrower scope, the Gothic novel became the fictive rug under which every unspeakable human act or fantasy could be swept. Atrocities of every kind—incest, murder, torture, rape—found their way into Gothic fiction.[4]

The question we are faced with is this: does *Eva Moves the Furniture* contain the element of fear we have come to expect from traditional Gothic? Although we as readers know what fear is and what it is not, it is our individual response

to a particular work that causes difficulty. If we are to discuss fear, whether in the Gothic novel or anywhere else, we will need to grasp and examine it in detail.

Fear is subjective. Every person is different, and each response may vary. Reader A may find my first novel, *Dark Demon Rising*, frightening and yet may find that element sorely lacking in my subsequent novel, *Vermillion Eye*. Reader B may find the opposite to be the case. Both novels were written with the intent to terrify, yet both observers reacted differently. It may be that reader A finds vampires frightening, but not reader B. Reader B may instead have problems with reincarnated serial killers.

We may therefore hypothesize as follows: an observer's emotional response to a specific work, whether it is literature, art, music, manga, or film, will depend on that observer's emotional makeup. A person's emotional makeup is directly affected by his or her life experience. This experience will certainly also depend on the time period in which that person was or is living. A twenty-first-century observer, who may well be fed on a diet of *The Blair Witch Project* and the *Saw* franchise, will respond to a particular work far differently from an eighteenth-century observer. Our reactions would be alien to them, and theirs to us.

It is therefore no great surprise that our modern reader will not find *The Castle of Otranto* particularly terrifying. Wolf has suggested that the novel is "not likely to find many admirers today" and is "a cumbersome, stiff and occasionally quaint story with almost no relevance to human experience."[5] In some ways tied to one's time, fear is subjective, and an eighteenth-century reader must have responded much differently to make that novel so popular then.

This, on the face of it, means that we cannot be objective about fear. We cannot objectively determine which books contain the element of terror and which do not. Other than conducting a costly and time-consuming polling of readers, or perhaps convening a council of literary critics, it would be impossible to make such a determination. This places us in a seemingly ludicrous position of not being able to state that Jane Austen's *Pride and Prejudice* does not contain the element of fear, whereas William Peter Blatty's *The Exorcist* does.

Fortunately, the problem is not insurmountable. The question that should be asked is not whether a novel causes a reader to be afraid but whether that novel contains the *ingredients* that may cause such fear, those elements that expose characters to danger or make them expect pain, loss, corruption, or damnation. For example, if a person desperately clings to the edge of a cliff with a long drop below, this satisfies the fear-element requirement. But if she then climbs back onto the top of the cliff, then the danger and consequently the fear is removed. This scenario can be found in many action novels and movies, and these are rightly not classified as Gothic. This is because in the action genre the ingredients of fear are intermittent. In a Gothic novel, however, these ingredients

are usually prolonged and will of course, as part of the narrative, include other pleasurably unpleasant Gothic motifs.

The usual scenario in the genre is that a person is physically threatened by someone or something. Because of the continuing nature of the threat, we can conclude that the narrative contains the ingredients of fear usually associated with the genre. The subject matter of the narrative is less significant, so it is not vital whether it deals with vampires, serial killers, zombies, werewolves, murderers, evil spirits, or a host of other malevolent entities. Such creatures may be no threat at all in the tale and may even be parodied in a comedy; the movies *The Addams Family* (1991) and *Scary Movie* (2000) are but two examples.

We may now ask the first question, and it is a subjective one: Does *Eva Moves the Furniture* cause the reader to be afraid? It can, as previously stated, only be answered based on personal observation. In *Eva*, I found that the presence of terror was lacking. I venture that most other readers would also find this to be the case.

We can then pose the second question, and it is an objective one: Does the novel contain the *ingredients* of fear? The answer is in the affirmative. In fact, the physical threat to Eva occurs early on in the novel:

> In the hallway she stopped aghast. Sixteen steep wooden stairs led up to the bedrooms and there, within inches of the topmost stair I lay. . . . When her terror receded, she carried me back to my room; what she saw made her startle all over again. My crib was in the corner, with the bars . . . still in place. (9–10)

The protagonist, a mere baby, is under physical threat. But as the novel progresses, as Eva grows up and becomes acquainted with her companions, the threat recedes. It should be noted that it is the *threat* that is the key ingredient and not death itself. The reason can be illustrated in an early example in the novel, which is immediately after Barbara has given birth to Eva:

> "What is it?" asked Barbara drowsily.
> "Some Magpie squabbling in the apple tree." The midwife leaned towards the glass, counting. "One, two . . . six," she declared.
> "Six magpies? Are you certain?"
> But already we had turned away. "Take a nap," the midwife repeated from the door. "I'll be back in a trice." (5)

Barbara dies soon after. The ingredients of dread are served up to readers who are aware of the superstition that six magpies signify death. They are aware of the threat and will be anxious for Barbara. For those who are not apprised of this superstition, it is only several pages *later* that all is revealed when Lily and the midwife repeat the rhyme:

> One for sorrow, two for mirth,
> Three for a wedding, four for a birth.
> Five's a christening, six a dearth,
> Seven's heaven, eight is hell.
> And nine's the devil his ane sel'. (8)

If this information were provided before Eva's birth, then the threat to Barbara and the ingredient of fear would exist for all readers. A death may invoke sadness in the reader. But the threat of death will likely cause fear.

The threat of physical harm is also likely to invoke fear. Such a threat arises later in the novel when Eva is accosted by a man and a boy:

> I raced along the river's edge, dodging bracken and fallen branches. Just when I thought I had got clean away, my foot caught in a rabbit hole.
> Even now, I have only a confused sense of what happened. The boy was upon me. Behind me the man loomed. And somehow, miraculously, they were gone. In their place were the companions. (38)

Although the components of apprehension and menace are present, they are short lived and exist for no more than half a page. Instead of describing the imminent attack, the reader is pulled out of the scene with the time-shifting words, "Even now . . ." These words push readers forward in time, detaching them from the assault, and the threat is dissipated.

The fear factors are mild, intermittent, and used sparingly in the novel. It is not necessary or desirable to explore the author's motives, although from her past meditations on lost things, including a story about an abandoned baby (*Criminals*), amnesia (*The Missing World*), a missing pregnant woman (*Banishing Verona*), and faithfulness and friendship (*The House on Fortune Street*), it is clear that Margot Livesey does not set supernatural horror high on her agenda. *Eva* appears to be an exception, and Livesey's motivation behind the novel was because of a ghostly event witnessed by her adopted father.[6] It may have been because of this unusual subject matter that it took the author thirteen years to write the book.

We should also note that, unlike its Gothic predecessors, no atrocities occur in *Eva*; there is a lack of Wolf's "incest, murder, torture, rape." Other than the patients in the infirmary who succumb to their war wounds, no one in the novel dies an unnatural death. No one is blood-sucked, murdered, slaughtered, or decapitated. Barbara dies from childbirth, and Eva's father, David, passes away due to illness.

This may be contrasted with the "cumbersome" *The Castle of Otranto*, where unnatural death, this one seemingly a bizarre accident, occurs from its

inception: Manfred's son is crushed to death by an enormous helmet. Toward the end of the novel, Manfred tries to kill the woman who refuses to marry him and, due to mistaken identity, murders his daughter instead. In Matthew G. Lewis's *The Monk* (1796), the monk Ambrosio kills the mother of the fifteen-year-old girl he intends to seduce. These unnatural deaths have been the fatal inheritance of later Gothic works.

Perhaps *Eva*'s sparing use of fear and scenes of unnatural death will be the path that the twenty-first-century Gothic novel will continue to follow, leading it further away from its less charming progeny, the horror novel. We may now ask the question, where does the Gothic novel end and where does the horror novel begin? Bloom has observed that horror and Gothic are often interchangeable, though there are Gothic tales which are not horror fiction and horror fiction that contains no Gothic elements.[7] The scenes of gore and ghastliness in the horror genre, particular the movies which have become more popular, possibly motivated by the desire to outdo the immediately preceding movie, may have caused the rift to widen between the two genres. Revulsion and fear are different creatures.

Closely associated with fear is that other motif of old Gothic, the tyrannical villain. These rogues include Manfred in *The Castle of Otranto*, Montoni in *The Mysteries of Udolpho* (1794), and others, including the science-fiction-based ones as in Mary Shelley's *Frankenstein* (1831) and the supernatural ones as in *Dracula* (1897). On the face of it, the villains in *Eva* are the two companions: the white-haired woman and the girl of twelve or thirteen.

From the outset, we realize the intentions of these visitors are ambiguous. The crib incident, which was mentioned earlier, was an act that put Eva in physical danger, for the baby lay precipitously inches from the topmost stair. When Eva was older, the girl companion, like many girls her age, also misbehaved:

> Now that I was closer to her age, she seemed to enjoy my company, but I had mixed feelings about her. . . . Besides, I never knew what she would do next. One minute she would be wonderfully sweet . . . and the next, for no reason, bad-tempered. Once, when I said I didn't like porridge, she shoved me into the ditch. (20)

Yet when Eva is at the athletics club, her companions lift her up so that she is able to clear the bar at high jump. They not only assist her, but they may even have saved her from being raped. The incident at the riverbank in which a man and a boy attack Eva has already been mentioned. It is her visitors' ambivalence that provides continuing tension in the novel. Are they a force for good or evil? Will they interfere with Eva and her plans? This is a question that continually arises in the reader's mind as Eva grows up and makes her way in life.

Although they may have once put Eva in physical danger, the companions, through their ambiguity, are not the typical villainous villains of old Gothic. Although initially physically threatening, the dangers they pose as the novel progresses become no more than potential interferences in Eva's personal life. These visitors are not real villains, and they do not fit the traditional Gothic mold. Later on in the novel, we doubt they are villains at all when they rescue Eva after an air raid in Glasgow. When the companions, with the assistance of ghost soldiers, pull Eva's collapsed father out of the river, we realize they are not villains but saviors.

One of the foundations of Gothic literature is architecture. As Mulvey-Roberts states, "Associated with the Gothic Novel is an ivy-covered haunted ruin, a swooning heroine replete with sensibility, and a tyrannical villain, bequeathed with a lock, a key and a castle."[8] Other associations include an old mansion, a monastery, and a ruin. These are the traditional Gothic settings, which may also include the landscapes of "precipitous mountains and windswept moors."[9]

We should note that Gothic literature and architecture were intrinsically bound at its inception as Walpole also came to significantly influence the Gothic Revival architectural style. This architectural form has been described as a movement that began in England to revive medieval Gothic forms, and "Horace Walpole's Strawberry Hill, Twickenham (c. 1760–1776) made the style fashionable."[10] In the preface to the first edition of his novel, Walpole fictitiously speculates, "I cannot but believe that the groundwork of the story is founded on truth. The scene is undoubtedly laid in some real castle. The author seems frequently, without design, to describe particular parts."[11] Clearly, it is *with design* that Walpole described the innards of the castle in order to ground his narrative in a particular setting and to provide authenticity.

In *Eva Moves the Furniture*, Eva is not brought up in a medieval castle but in a stone house called "Ballintyre," with the steep wooden stairway linking the two levels being "scarcely wider than a tea tray." While the initial setting for the novel may be a stone cottage, it is the town of Troon itself that provides the milieu in the first few chapters.

Troon is not a decaying atmospheric place that we may expect from an old Gothic novel but has a rather more cheerful disposition.

> I was born in 1920 in the lowlands of Scotland, outside the town of Troon. . . . It is a mild mannered part of the country. The fields are fertile and predictable, with foaming hawthorn hedges and woods of beech, chestnut, and birch. (4)

The reader will come across Larch House, Station Hotel, the riverbank, and the churchyard of Saint Cuthbert's. The town has its own co-op, labor exchange, munitions factory, forge, chemist's, library, and dramatic society. It is a safe,

"predictable" place. "Even as a little girl I judged the landscape inferior to the one I knew from stories, the fierce, dour Highlands where my mother had spent her childhood" (4). The thought of spending the rest of her life in this "predictable" and "inferior" place troubles the teenage Eva. Troon is not a fictitious place, but rather a town situated in South Ayrshire on the west coast of Scotland.

The author certainly had the option of creating a make-believe town, perhaps even a decaying Gothic-type village filled with an oppressive atmosphere, for her narrative, but she has instead chosen to ground her setting in reality. It is this very ordinariness of the setting that emphasizes Eva's alienation. The presence of the companions in her life has singled her out as different. When she tries to tell a friend about them, the girl companion throws a rock into the bird bath, and the friend is soaked. This effectively ends the friendship, and the feeling of alienation is made more acute.

> All my daydreams were gone and I was terrified to think that she had nearly seen the girl. At home it was easy to overlook the strangeness of my situation. But in Catherine's garden I had understood that the presence of the companions in my life was like a hidden deformity: ugly, mysterious, and incomprehensible. (28)

In the second part of the novel, Eva moves to Glasgow and lives in a nurse's hostel. Not a great deal of description of the hostel is provided other than that it "bore a strong resemblance to the grammar school at Troon," and the infirmary where she works is not described in much detail either.

In the third part of the novel, Eva finds herself in Glenaird, the birthplace of her mother, where she has accepted the position as a school matron at a boarding school. This is located in the country, in "the fierce, dour Highlands where my mother had spent her childhood" (4), and it is here that we obtain a real sense of her environment: "The afternoon was so clear and still that, as we descended the stairs to the river, I could hear each separate leaf falling in the woods around us. We crossed the bridge and followed the track up the hill, between fields of sheep" (147). The big city has been left far behind, and the country setting is now described in an intimate manner:

> [W]e decided to walk across the river to the village. . . . Matthew pointed out the pheasants rooting in the frozen stubble, the bull-finches pecking at last summer's shrivelled rose hips. . . . The sun had broken through and the weathercock was glinting on the church steeple. (159)

This is not a place of mystery, filled with ruins and decay. It is a beautiful setting, filled with hope and renewal: "The field below us was occupied by a flock

of sheep, many of them ewes newly brought to lamb, and as we leaned on the gate, the back and forth of their bleating filled the air. I felt as if the world had been made afresh" (162).

Eva has come full circle. Her mother was born in Glenaird, and now she has returned to this idyllic place. There is a sense of belonging. She visits the Grange where her mother had spent her childhood. She discovers her mother's initials carved on a desk in the schoolhouse she attended, and in the churchyard Eva finds the graves of her grandparents.

Perhaps, one could argue, *Eva* does remain faithful to the traditions of old Gothic, for its idyllic rural setting and uplifting highland landscape in Glenaird are reminiscent of the soft and glowing descriptions of the countryside in *The Mysteries of Udolpho*. These similarities, though, are not substantial, for in *Eva* the renderings of the landscape are more pastoral and less romantic. Furthermore, Radcliffe later confines the protagonist to a gloomy stony castle, whereas no such castle or decaying mansion looms forth in *Eva*. As an aside, both novels, we may also note, are coming-of-age stories, or *bildungsromans*, a feature that may find its way into many genres.

Jerrold Hogle has observed that the architectural integrity of old Gothic is maintained as long as the setting is in an antiquated or seemingly antiquated place.[12] How do we define an antiquated place? Perhaps as long as the reader is under the impression that such a setting, because of its age, may be haunted, then that would suffice as a Gothic setting. This ghostly possibility creates the mood in which the genre thrives. As such, the settings in *Eva* would appear to satisfy the definition.

However, are Ballintyre and the infirmary in Glasgow antiquated places? Although from the narrative one would infer that they are sufficiently old, the author does not emphasize the age of these buildings. Moreover, she does not use any of these antiquated places to create an atmosphere of decay. So, although the settings may be sufficiently aged, the mood or atmosphere of the Gothic architecture do not sufficiently surface in *Eva*.

The firm link between the Gothic novel and the Gothic setting appears to have weakened in *Eva*. Harvey has stated that "Gothic architecture symbolizes the fiction's themes: dungeons and labyrinths suggest confinement, the secret and forbidden; castles embody the past's oppressive weight."[13] Such atmospheric settings, the decaying castle, the ruins associated with traditional Gothic literature, are absent from *Eva*. Ballintyre, Troon, Glasgow, the infirmary, and Glenaird are normal places which any reader may encounter in daily life.

Eva is not a heavy novel. It is not dominated by dark moods, furtiveness, curses, and enigma brought about by some external force, usually the villain springing from the pages of old Gothic. The companions are the cause of an *internal* oppression, and as such the narrative does not require the symbolism

evident in the architecture of old Gothic. *Eva* is an example of how the twenty-first-century Gothic novel, once liberated from the traditional milieu of the genre, can offer more varied settings in its narrative. A consequence of this is that it will be able to deliver a different Gothic experience to readers.

Lastly, we should consider romance. Gothic literature was an early manifestation of the Romantic movement, creating stories where readers became emotionally bound to the protagonists. In our case, however, the term is more narrowly defined to mean "love story." *The Mysteries of Udolpho* includes a romantic relationship between Emily and Valancourt and, as such, is said to have been responsible for creating a subgenre called the "Radcliffian Gothic" or "Gothic romance." The novel also brings to mind later works by the Brontë sisters and Jane Austen. Although Tracy has observed that "romance in the popular sense, the pursuit of love, is less of a presence [in the Gothic novel] than one would suppose, in part because the plots stress separation and isolation,"[14] we should note, however, that romance, in many Gothic novels, forms at least part of the unfolding plot.

Eva's love for Dr. Samuel Rosenbaum, a Jewish surgeon at the Glasgow Infirmary, resonates throughout the novel. Even though the couple do not meet until Eva is working as a nurse in Glasgow, we are made aware of him early on through a series of flash-forwards. We should note that the 1551 incident involving Fiorovanti was in the opening chapter and was a story related to Eva by Samuel, and this further underlines the surgeon's importance in the novel. Even when Eva moves to Glenaird and agrees to marry someone else, she still longs for the "fluttering of the heart, the eagerness to touch and hold" (163):

> Marriage, it turned out, did not entirely banish memories of Samuel. I meant to forget him, I had the best of intentions, but . . . he sometimes slipped into my mind, and before I knew it I was picturing him as he bent over a patient or leaned towards the cinema screen. (175)

Eva is a coming-of-age tale, a story of development, and as sometimes, or often, happens in life, the girl does not get her man. Her relationship with Samuel is thwarted by the existence of her companions. She tries to share her secret with Samuel, but he believes they are only a figment of her imagination and that she needs psychiatric help. He asks her to give them up, but she says she is not able to, and this ultimately ruins the relationship. This breakup, we discover, is by far the most significant damage that the companions inflict on Eva. Nevertheless, Eva's love for Samuel remains strong, and it is felt from the beginning to the end of the novel.

It may be that in the twenty-first century, the Gothic genre will find itself more often holding the delicate hand of romance when it treads its dark, winding path. If the ingredients of fear become less prominent, it may be that the

love story will find a greater presence in today's Gothic. While the horror genre becomes more obsessed with gruesomeness and revulsion, its Gothic parent may rely less on fear and may instead choose romance. The incredible popularity of the *Twilight* series for young adults, often labeled "paranormal romance," may shift the genre in this direction. There is no doubt that a plethora of such novels will be written for the adult market.

The Gothic genre, beginning with *The Castle of Otranto* and all that followed, has come to be recognized by certain motifs. Not all of these characteristics, of course, need be present for a novel to be recognized as Gothic, but it is self-evident that at least some of them need to subsist. The genre itself, we should note, is a "notoriously shifting and complex object of study"[15] because, we assume, its embrace is wide, and it drapes around itself many motifs. New motifs may edge into the genre, while others, which may in the past have had a minor presence, may blossom. Romance could well be one of the latter.

In *Eva Moves the Furniture*, the features of old Gothic, including the supernatural, mysteries, and hidden secrets, continue to be woven into its pages. Other motifs, including the tyrannical villain, feelings of fear, and antiquated architecture are less distinct. *Eva* underscores certain motifs and diminishes others. A novel is often said to be the child of its author, and naturally the author's own psychological makeup and contemporary experiences will be imprinted like DNA in and behind the lines of text. As such, each new narrative will be different. Each novelist will draw upon certain Gothic characteristics, fortifying some while diminishing and even ignoring others, and this will create a rich, but no doubt still dark, diversity in the twenty-first century. Nevertheless, they will all share the same Gothic antecedents and the same desire to darkly delight the reader.

Notes

1. Margot Livesey, *Eva Moves the Furniture* (New York: Henry Holt, 2001), 3. Page numbers appear hereafter in parentheses in the text.

2. Maggie Kilgour, *The Rise of the Gothic Novel* (London: Routledge, 1995), 3.

3. Stephen King, *Danse Macabre* (New York: Berkley, 1987), 50–51.

4. Leonard Wolf, *Dracula: The Connoisseur's Guide* (New York: Broadway Books, 1997), 76.

5. Wolf, *Dracula: The Connoisseur's Guide*, 77.

6. Margot Livesey, "In the Author's Words," www.margotlivesey.com/eva-moves-the-furniture.html (accessed November 25, 2009).

7. Clive Bloom, "Horror Fiction: In Search of a Definition," in *A Companion to the Gothic*, ed. David Punter (Oxford: Blackwell, 2000), 155.

8. Marie Mulvey-Roberts, ed., *The Handbook to Gothic Literature* (London: Macmillan, 1998), xv–xviii, xvi.

9. Catherine Spooner and Emma McEvoy, "Gothic Locations," in *The Routledge Companion to Gothic*, ed. Catherine Spooner and Emma McEvoy (Oxon, UK: Routledge, 2007), 51.

10. James Stevens Curl, *The Oxford Dictionary of Architecture and Landscape Architecture* (Oxford, UK: Oxford University Press, 2006), 833.

11. Horace Walpole, preface to the first edition of *The Castle of Otranto: A Gothic Story*, ed. W. S. Lewis (Oxford, UK: Oxford University Press, 2009), 8.

12. Jerrold E. Hogle, "Introduction: The Gothic in Western Culture," in *The Cambridge Companion to Gothic Fiction*, ed. Jerrold E. Hogle (Cambridge, UK: Cambridge University Press, 2002), 2.

13. Benjamin Harvey, "Contemporary Horror Cinema," in *The Routledge Companion to Gothic*, ed. Catherine Spooner and Emma McEvoy (Oxon, UK: Routledge, 2007), 234.

14. Ann B. Tracy, "Gothic Romance," in *The Handbook of Gothic Literature*, ed. Marie Mulvey-Roberts (London: Macmillan, 1998), 104.

15. Michael Gamer, "Gothic Fictions and Romantic Writing in Britain," in *The Cambridge Companion to Gothic Fiction*, ed. Jerrold E. Hogle (Cambridge, UK: Cambridge University Press, 2002), 86.

CHAPTER 18

Fatal Women and Their Stratagems

TANITH LEE WRITING AS ESTHER GARBER

Mavis Haut

Before we can even turn to the first page of *Fatal Women*, we have already been confronted by a miniature enigma. The preliminary information about the author(s) suggests that Tanith Lee is no longer quite the Tanith Lee we know. Who then is she? It quickly becomes clear that the name under which this collection has been written is something beyond the usual authorial pseudonym. Esther Garber is a person with a distinct and separate identity, deserving of her own biographical notes, although these secondary notes express considerable uncertainty about her. Described as only "apparently" the person she purports to be, she has shifting, discontinuous origins as "a European Jewess" and is further deracinated by unexplained early years in Egypt. No attempt is made to account for her special focus on Paris. And, with a career in writing that has only emerged in later life, Garber's own precise age is almost as debatable as the degree to which her work may or may not be autobiographical. One thing, however, is patently certain: whatever she is or is not, Garber is a creature with a life of her own. And so, our narrator arrives shrouded in mysteries, herself a fiction enveloping her own fiction, and, well before any story has begun, the makings of the Gothic have already been assembled. Meanwhile, this quintessentially unreliable narrator has *apparently* recast Lee as amanuensis to a phantom author, as ghost-writer for a ghost.

But the Gothic needs more than merely external trappings to raise it above recycled cliché and the same old fancy dress. The Gothic has powers particular to itself and offers its own special possibilities. The Gothic is able to penetrate into those human imaginings, desires, and strivings that contravene the primary tenets and conventions of a rationally ordered, governable society. When that

new Prometheus, Dr. Frankenstein, creates his monster, he is guilty of more than the hubris so often associated with the scientist. By usurping the right to create life that, in the eyes of his contemporaries, belonged exclusively to God, he is undermining the fundamental stability of his society. The Gothic also descends into the well of myth, ancient or modern, where reason is not supreme, and monsters, demons, and uncontrollable, possibly unappeasable, forces from the dreamworld haunt the daily lives of men. Myth has always haunted the work of Tanith Lee.

The consistent social transgression that accompanies Lee's altered authorial personality in *Fatal Women* is the rejection of heterosexual conformity. The model heterosexual woman is manifested differently in each of the periods delineated in the three novellas of this collection, and the female protagonists emerge from their historical backgrounds tempered by the preoccupations of their eras. All three have been extracted from a rich seam of psychological experience which, one way or another, culminates in women who refuse to be confined to the mundane or to accept sexual servitude to male custodians. Their homosexuality is understood in depth and detail as it modifies three intelligent and complex characters whose self-determination creates personal and social problems in and around them. The problems are all of a fatal or potentially fatal nature, but these women are not perceived as deviants, merely as humanly flawed and inevitably fallible characters who must learn the lessons their desires and deliriums produce. Though the sexual writing is intensely erotic at times, it is never voyeuristic.

Using realistic period settings, the novellas examine the experiences and strategies of women searching for ways to conduct their lives beyond the control and intervention of a male-dominated society. Lee/Garber's women refuse unconditionally to give up any of their innate capacities, and it is in the pursuit of their own desires and destinies that their sexuality adapts to their needs. They are mostly portrayed as alienated by the brutalities and betrayals of the men with whom they are, have been, or refuse to become involved. They are risk takers, people prepared to move in little-tried directions, either for their own private advancement or as women stretching out toward a love that includes personal independence. Of course, they do not necessarily reach real emotion or self-knowledge. And when they do, the price tends to be very high.

Women of this kind, with their own passionate needs and desires, are already familiar to us from Lee's earlier work. In Lee's first published work of adult fantasy, *The Birthgrave*, the protagonist chooses self-understanding over love. Esther Garber, now a being in her mature years, discreetly demonstrates that a capacity for love is a sine qua non of self-understanding and self-realization. This applies here to love in any form, whether it be domestic and homely or dramatic and tragic, and irrespective of whether it ends well or disastrously or

whether the process is even fully apprehended by the character involved. These women are as damaged and vulnerable, as corruptible and redeemable, as any others. However, they differ from women who are regarded as normal by the moral standards and conventions of a given time. These women are willing to go to the furthest extremes and to suffer any consequences in order to preserve the integrity of their own perceptions and actions. They lack neither courage nor conviction. The passive woman-awaiting-rescue of much earlier Gothic literature has no place here.

Rherlotte, the longest of the three novellas, is set in the late nineteenth century. It introduces a classic fatal woman—in fact, two fatal women, although one is a harbinger only of death, the other of both love and death. Phèdre is virtually predestined to become a murderer of abusive and unfaithful men. Her mother, a woman habitually in thrall to faithless men, commits suicide. Phèdre, still a child, is raised by her coldhearted grandmother, a wealthy former prostitute. When the grandmother sends her off into the world equipped with an allowance and a sinister little bottle of poison that she has found among her dead mother's effects, Phèdre does her best to emulate her grandmother's ruthless antisentimentality. She shuns men and indulges her rapacious bodily appetites with venal or naive young women. She makes use of the income with which she has been provided, and quite soon also the bottle of poison, with which she dispatches the violent lover of a young actress with whom she is having an affair. This leads seamlessly to a second murder, in this instance, of the philandering husband of a woman who approaches her for help. She returns the money when this woman tries to pay her.

Phèdre's crimes have no real material motive. She believes herself to be perfectly cool and rational in matters of both death and love. At her first meeting with the uncomely woman who commissions her second murder, she describes her own calm demeanor: "I looked at her cooly, and thought, *She sounds like a lover*. But I could never have been tempted."[1] Rherlotte describes Phèdre as, "made of this cold, cold snow."[2] "How could you know anything about love?" she asks.[3] It is true that Phèdre's early experiences allowed her to see vice in the man who was Rherlotte's beloved, but the reality remains that her crimes are pointless and devoid of reason.

A reader may be reminded of *Crime and Punishment* or the equally perverse and purely psychological motives of the protagonist in Poe's "The Tell-tale Heart." However, *Rherlotte* is most perfectly offset by a novella that comes from Colette, an author Lee values greatly. In *The Rainy Moon*, a woman writer is mesmerized by a younger woman's efforts to kill her unfaithful lover by means of magic rituals. Colette's protagonist is familiar with ungovernable passion. She neither commits nor conceives of murder, but when the woman's lover dies suddenly, she feels a vicarious revenge for her own youthful hurts and recognizes

a dark satisfaction in herself. The common core of both Lee's and Colette's narratives is the untamed female response to the cruelties of men.

Phèdre's reaction to her mother's repeated betrayals in love and eventual suicide is emotionally logical: she determines to go to any lengths to avoid a similar fate. Men are "filthy brutes," her grandmother says.[4] She is selfish, but also a survivor. Phèdre informs us, "At fourteen Constance took the mysterious bottle away from me, but about five years later, she gave it back."[5] Phèdre resolves to have nothing to do with men, love, or any emotion that might render her vulnerable. Even with women, her sexual liaisons are predatory and have nothing of herself invested in them. Her need for absolute control leads smoothly into executing murders to order. And it is only through the agency of another woman that Lee's protagonist comes to perceive the shadow cast across her by what she has always until that time regarded as cool reason. It takes Rherlotte, the bereaved mistress of her second victim, to force her to an experience of passion. When Rherlotte seduces Phèdre into falling truly in love with her and then kills herself, her suicide causes Phèdre to suffer exactly what Rherlotte herself has suffered: "She taught me her own lesson," Phèdre muses.[6] The death also repeats the trauma of her mother's earlier suicide, the loss that had originally frozen Phèdre's capacity for love. From this act of revenge she learns the meaning of passion, and the hidden cruelty at the core of reason is revealed for what it is.

Careful attention is paid to details that enhance the Gothic character of this novella. There is the little bottle of poison, the classic woman's weapon, and the red, theatrical wig which both disguises Phèdre when she performs her murders and parodies the pale marigold hair that her mother and Rherlotte share. There is the room festooned with ice in which Phèdre discovers Rherlotte's pale, blood-drained corpse, and the grandmother's two eerie, feral daughters, whose normal, childish responses to the warmth of Phèdre's cleaning woman underline the icy emotional childhoods that they, like Phèdre and her mother before them, have had to endure. Many such delicate touches give depth to the psyche and psychopathy of a protagonist who is pivotal in Lee's particular re-creation of the Gothic in this novella. Phèdre's intense fear of Rherlotte has overtly mythological qualities. Rherlotte has the "face of the moon goddess Diane. . . . She is the huntress, not I. She rides them down, the fleet deer in the forest, even the tigress she rides down."[7] This initial sense of terror intensifies, and at a second interview, she asks herself, "What is this feeling of falling, of panic, of heat, of ice? . . . trembling, shivering, a sickness lying under my breastbone."[8] Phèdre is already infected by the sickness she dreads, already contaminated by passion. Later, dreaming of her mother, Phèdre is lost in a flood of intense emotion. She has traveled a long way since she dismissed her mother as a "whore courtesan who had died of a broken heart when an Italian pastry cook, fifteen years her

junior, had told her they were done."[9] In her dream, she gives way to Rherlotte "in terror" and screams "in agony, torture and delight."[10]

The novella concludes with an extended description of the icy, shattered beauty of Rherlotte's room. The dead woman, seated in a chair, has eyes "now an unearthly blue. Her face also bluish. She's old."[11] Phèdre, too, is suddenly much older as the shocking scene is frozen forever into her memory. At the same time, she is moving with quiet restraint through a previously unknown range of feelings that belong to the love she only just discovered: "Although I've learnt your lesson, Rherlotte, I learnt it as a child learns speech. Before ever I could understand."[12] This moment of realization also becomes frozen and immobile. She continues, "After some hours, I wanted to put my arms around her, put my head on her bosom. But she would be hard and stiff as a dead tree. . . . Besides, she'd never wanted me to touch her. She'd fought me away. How could I do it now?"[13] And finally, "All days, all nights like this one, always."[14] But the reader is fully aware that nothing could persuade her to renounce these feelings and that Rherlotte's act of revenge has, perhaps involuntarily, been tempered by love. By the end of the novella, Phèdre's story has moved close to that of Raskolnikov. Phèdre embarks on adult life as a deeply damaged person who only recognizes the reality of her crimes after she has caused the suicide of Rherlotte. Like Dostoevsky's distraught hero, even though forced to endure terrible suffering, she is redeemed through a love that awakens the passionate self she has refused to acknowledge. Love does not come easily to Lee's fiercely intelligent, willful young woman. As she is falling in love with Rherlotte, she muses, "When I first look at her, each time, this sensation of falling, falling down, but into an abyss which has no floor. . . . Will it kill me, this fall? Or is it only flight, the sole form of flight of which I am capable?"[15]

The second novella is set very early in the twentieth century. Like *Rherlotte*, it makes reference to the moon goddess and huntress Diana and takes place in the little town of Bois-de-Diane.[16] *Virgile, the Widow* records a girl's personal and quasi-mythological journey toward an understanding of the meaning that love has for her as she outgrows her romantic craving for a tragic passion. Lee describes this phase in a sensitive girl's adolescence without a trace of cynicism. In a lighter vein, it works toward a reconciliation of the conflict between Eros and Thanatos, between the comedic muse of love and the tragic muse of death. The narrative also provides an affectionate analysis of the extravagances that, in everyday life, can cause the Gothic to degenerate into melodrama or even parody. The young protagonist's perception of reality is bred mainly out of a desire to experience a fatal passion. She is naive in the way of a very young girl whose imagination is her foremost refuge. After the crimes and grand passions of *Rherlotte*, Laure's story comes with the innocence that belongs to inexperience.

Laure's lesbian preference is established early. She is initiated by her best friend from her schooldays and provided with the space to explore her sexuality by the old lady of the village chateau. This chatelaine offers hospitality and a retreat to young women seeking respite from the demands of husbands, families, or just the bourgeois respectability of provincial life. Laure is twenty—the age of the unhappy Phèdre when she encountered Rherlotte—when she first sees the beautiful stranger, Virgile. Like Phèdre, Laure has also been orphaned young and taken on by an older relative. Her elderly aunt, however, is devoted to her young charge and shows her every kindness and indulgence, even freely permitting her niece to remain unmarried if she so pleases. Laure, who has a romantic spirit, yearns for "earlier eras," is "offended" by the present, and considers it the "single advantage of modernity that no one had forcibly married her off."[17]

The aunt is well aware of what happens at the chateau. She makes no attempt to pretend it is otherwise, as the parents of certain other girls do in the hope that this connection may lead to social advancement or monetary profit. She remarks, "Well, it will pass. . . . One day you'll meet someone. It will be for him to deal with."[18] And, for her part, the aged chatelaine tells Laure, "I give you liberty, my little birds."[19] She likes, she says, to hear "those footsteps, the laughs and little cries. . . . At least you will have tasted happiness, to recognise it, or passion."[20] It may be meant especially for Laure, maybe even with a touch of prescience, when she adds, "Perhaps great passion, if you are very fortunate and very unlucky."[21] Certainly the old lady's stories of innocent maidens; depraved, cannibalistic aristocrats; and magical jackdaws enhance the decaying beauty of the ancient chateau.

The woman Laure sees walking along the canal bank makes an indelible impression on her. To Laure, Virgile seems to have "a timeless look."[22] Black haired, she is dressed in unrelieved black and has "long black eyebrows, cruel-arched like scimitars," and black eyes with a "glassy obsidian surface."[23] The stranger is at once exotic, beautiful, and menacing and immediately becomes an object of fascination for Laure. In fact, Virgile in her black mourning garments is many times a widow, a woman who marries old men who are approaching death, bringing them pleasure and easing their passage out of life in exchange for money. Laure is not yet aware that she has come to the village to perform the same service for the chatelaine. When her friend, Sophrine, familiar with Laure's flights of fancy, suggests that the mysterious widow may be a figment of her imagination, Laure concedes that this is possible and then elaborates—Virgile may be the "ghost of a young woman who drowned herself in the canal. In mourning for her own death."[24] But privately she tells herself that the woman is "as real as the street."[25] Laure's thoughts are frequently ambivalent, as if her imaginings are equally "as real as the street."

It is precisely this recurrent ambiguity that gives strength and shape to a narrative which, until it reaches its resolution, takes place almost as convincingly in Laure's imagination as in the material world around her. At moments, the authorial voice (Lee's? Garber's?) fuses with Laure's to a degree that makes it difficult to know just what or whose consciousness is finding its way onto the page. Laure's blurring of realities is described explicitly. Following her first evening at the chateau, after hearing a story, "just antique enough to interest her at once,"[26] of a death averted by an emblematic jackdaw, Laure dreams herself so deeply into the part of the sacrificial maiden that, on waking to the noises of domesticity, "it was more than surfacing from dream or sleep . . . her nightlong experience had gone elsewhere."[27] The experience is so real that she thinks, "This place has nothing at all to do with me."[28] A lesser degree of the same fusion also happens through the internal mechanisms of language, often making it impossible for the reader to know whether or not Laure is passing judgement on her own behavior—"*And all those curtsies*, thought spiteful Laure, *on account.*"[29] We are left to decide for ourselves whether or not Laure is consciously remarking her own spitefulness. Small and large fusions of reality and personal interpretation—notably in matters concerning death—are woven right through the narrative. They are there in Laure's reading of the chatelaine's appearance as "a beneficiary of the embalmer's art, made ready for the casket,"[30] at which, immediately, "the room spun. Or in fact not the room, but Laure herself, spun round, inside her body. . . . Everything when she came back, was removed far off. And so she drifted to the table, miles away from all of them."[31] We can read this as fear of death, the same impetus that fills her with disgust at her aunt's old age. Yet, at the same time, she is helplessly drawn toward the thing she fears, and to Virgile, whom she perceives as "a symbol of death."[32] Sophrine tells her that she is waiting for the "kind of love that smashes you to pieces—kills you—that's what you want."[33] And it is also Sophrine who tries to rouse her: "I won't let you throw yourself down into a—a pit of vipers. . . . It isn't fate. You—*you*—have made it happen, and you can make it stop."[34] Laure's guilty idea that her romantic longings for death have been the cause of her aunt's close brush with it reveals the same magical thinking that pervades superstition, the child's imagination, fairy tales, and all forms of Gothic literature. "*Have I really made this happen? Made her die so I can die, so I can have Virgile and languish in the arms of Virgile?*"[35] This is the turning point at which she resolves, "I sacrifice my death for you. My magnificent death in the arms of ebony and agate."[36]

Laure has long been aware of her own "self-harming habit of sometimes seeing magic in persons and things where it didn't exist."[37] When she finally begins to emerge from the erotic torments of her dreams of death and love and her obsession with the beautiful, mysterious, and apparently deadly stranger, Virgile,

it is in a curious reversal of the myth of Diana and Acteon, the hunter torn apart by his own hounds after beholding her naked. It is only when the bewitching Virgile removes her clothes, when the goddess reveals herself naked, that Laure is released from her spell and is content to find an ordinary happiness waiting for her in the adult world. Love is not, after all, a deadly abyss into which she must fall; love is all around her in the provincial village that had previously appeared so worthless and commonplace to her. She recognizes and is reconciled to love as "banal. It was affectionate, it shared memory, bickered and had arguments, and in the case of the sexual lover, desire, the games of delight which ended in spasms not remotely deathlike. Love . . . was more like the mad dance of *life*."[38]

Green Iris is short. Set just after the Great War, it tells the story of a woman less concerned with self-understanding than with how others perceive her. Sabia does not wish to have anyone know she is homosexual. She is described as "both cunning and naive, as she herself had always known."[39] Even so, the opening may be telling us more about the protagonist than perhaps she herself wishes to know. "She thought: After a certain age, most women are with a man."[40] She is determined to appear to conform with the model, to seem like most women, especially women possessed of money and some degree of social standing. The reader immediately understands that Sabia's difficulties are compounded by lack of money. At a party, she sees Helen, the suave epitome of what she would like to be—and therefore like to have. She inveigles herself into the employ of Helen's husband, a thing easily done, as she is a typist by trade and he a successful writer. She flirts with him so as to embed herself more firmly in Helen's household, then finds herself embroiled in an unintended affair with him and shortly reaches the point of no return. Agreeing to a holiday in Italy, where they will certainly become lovers, she precedes him there by a few days. He does not arrive. She is told that Helen, the original object of her desire, has jealously shot her husband and herself. Sabia is advised to keep out of the way during the police inquiry, and we last see her, now known as Sacha, sharing a squalid flat and life with an office coworker in a dull provincial town.

Sabia's struggles to produce an image of herself that has no basis in reality are precisely what make her cunning, naive, and fatal to any others who are sucked into the complexities of the illusions she creates. She gives no thought to the effect of her elaborate deceptions except when her own interests are threatened, and she has only the sketchiest idea of what she is doing—"What now, what now? If I had any sense I'd run . . . . But Helen . . . . This itch now, not only of lust . . . not every possibility had yet been tried."[41] At the same time, she recognizes her own shallow motives: "*I'm not in love with her. In fact, I don't even like her much. It's only her. That turn of her head, for example.*"[42] It is not Helen that Sabia wants to possess but what Helen represents to her, what Helen seems to be. And, although Edmund Driver's advances initially frighten her, she

continues to prevaricate, to fend him off, yet simultaneously to encourage him. When he invites her for dinner, "while she played with this fantasy of avoidance, Sabia was taking a bath, dressing herself in an evening frock, powdering her face."[43] Once she reaches the Italian villa where she is to wait for Edmund, she barely gives him a thought. This is an ideal setting. "She had so often (always?) acted out a role, and now framed by such magnificent and almost convincing scenery, here was simply another role for her. That of a pampered woman cut adrift and quite alone, a rich woman in a romantic villa."[44] Even when she is told of the double shooting, she thinks primarily of herself "flirting, not with a lover but with Normalcy—more dangerous than any man."[45] As the man who has brought the news describes the shooting, she thinks him "really rather a bad actor. . . . But then the dialogue was awful."[46] Thus, he too becomes as inauthentic as the whole affair, the "almost convincing" location, and in fact all of the actors in the melodrama—the people she has perhaps simply "imagined into existence."[47]

The vignette that concludes the story is an indication of where such unrealities are bound to end. The undiscriminating flatmate in the town where Sabia/ Sacha has gone for anonymity is thinking of buying some waxed-paper irises she has seen in a florist's window. But the "unreal irises" were turning "a curious acidulous lime green" in an ugly discoloration of artifice.[48] "That can't be meant to be like that," Phyllis comments. "It gives the game away, doesn't it?"[49]

Initially, none of the women in the three novellas understand themselves in relation to others. Two are redeemed by love—loves existing at far extremes of sorrow and happiness. The third, giving nothing of herself, learns nothing, except perhaps that she must go back to her beginning, as in a game of snakes and ladders, and try again with some modicum of honesty. Lee's sequential use of a repeated theme in three specific periods[50] provides an active cultural critique of the gradual arrival of modernism, which in literary terms gets placed a little before the First World War, a point in time when cultural significances and the behavior that emerged out of changing meanings were shifting rapidly. In fact, Esther Garber comes out of exactly such an unstable and fragmented world, and, under her name, Lee measures the underground shifts and instabilities on which the Gothic stands. By the late nineteenth century, the essentially Romantic configurations of the original Gothic were just beginning to disintegrate. Lee is wary. She eschews both the outright supernatural and the sentimental that belong with fully fledged Romanticism. What she retains in its place is the need for intensity of feeling, especially in the distilled form of love, that allows the individual to reach her mature emotional potential, regardless of the shape it may take.

However, the releases of Phèdre's frozen emotions and the youthful Laure's less deep-seated malaise require strategies that belong to different eras. Phèdre's

need to avoid the role of the abused and submissive woman that constituted the male ideal of her period is expressed in crimes against the male sex, murders that serve as a means of impersonal retribution for the sufferings and death of her mother. Laure yearns for the past and what she imagines to be vanished passion, culminating in the absolute immolation of death. She is finally able to leave these dreams of the romantic past behind and enter a more realistic, everyday modern context. Sabia/Sacha's fluctuating name, her substitution of identity with role, her uncertain class affiliations, and the ambiguity of her sexual signals result in a drama she never intended. These unmistakably modern problems are set in a cracked social order, where, though the old center no longer holds, the fatal woman is still present in its midst. She has wandered a long way from the tragic, deliberate Phèdre and is no longer even aware of the part she will accidentally play in the ensuing bloodshed. The sure moral and emotional focus of the earlier realities has gone forever. Without a renewed center, only empty imitations of passion and authenticity remain, leading to deaths that have no meaning left. And all the while, keeping discreetly in the shadows behind these three novellas, Lee is illustrating a history of the progression of the Gothic as it moves on from its origins and enters the modern era.

Notes

1. Tanith Lee (as Esther Garber), *Rherlotte*, in *Fatal Women* (Bexhill on Sea, East Sussex, UK: Egerton House, 2004), 26.

2. Lee, *Rherlotte*, 124.

3. Lee, *Rherlotte*, 124.

4. Lee, *Rherlotte*, 29.

5. Lee, *Rherlotte*, 40.

6. Lee, *Rherlotte*, 142.

7. Lee, *Rherlotte*, 63.

8. Lee, *Rherlotte*, 78.

9. Lee, *Rherlotte*, 27.

10. Lee, *Rherlotte*, 105.

11. Lee, *Rherlotte*, 141.

12. Lee, *Rherlotte*, 141.

13. Lee, *Rherlotte*, 142.

14. Lee, *Rherlotte*, 143.

15. Lee, *Rherlotte*, 98.

16. Carlo Ginsburg's study of rural Italian superstitions (*Ecstasies: Deciphering the Witches' Sabbath* [Chicago: University of Chicago Press, 2004]) concludes that practices that in the Christian era came to be seen as witchcraft were originally female nocturnal cults celebrating the moon goddess Diana. Diana/Artemis was associated with trees and forest temples, where she was worshipped as a huntress and moon queen who made women fruitful and assisted them in childbirth.

17. Tanith Lee (as Esther Garber), *Virgile, the Widow*, in *Fatal Women* (Bexhill on Sea, East Sussex, UK: Egerton House, 2004), 151.

18. Lee, *Virgile, the Widow*, 179.
19. Lee, *Virgile, the Widow*, 161.
20. Lee, *Virgile, the Widow*, 161.
21. Lee, *Virgile, the Widow*, 161.
22. Lee, *Virgile, the Widow*, 149.
23. Lee, *Virgile, the Widow*, 149.
24. Lee, *Virgile, the Widow*, 151.
25. Lee, *Virgile, the Widow*, 151.
26. Lee, *Virgile, the Widow*, 163.
27. Lee, *Virgile, the Widow*, 188.
28. Lee, *Virgile, the Widow*, 188.
29. Lee, *Virgile, the Widow*, 194.
30. Lee, *Virgile, the Widow*, 196.
31. Lee, *Virgile, the Widow*, 196.
32. Lee, *Virgile, the Widow*, 201.
33. Lee, *Virgile, the Widow*, 231.
34. Lee, *Virgile, the Widow*, 232.
35. Lee, *Virgile, the Widow*, 248.
36. Lee, *Virgile, the Widow*, 249.
37. Lee, *Virgile, the Widow*, 162.
38. Lee, *Virgile, the Widow*, 250.
39. Tanith Lee (as Esther Garber), *Green Iris*, in *Fatal Women* (Bexhill on Sea, East Sussex, UK: Egerton House, 2004), 302.
40. Lee, *Green Iris*, 277.
41. Lee, *Green Iris*, 303.
42. Lee, *Green Iris*, 307.
43. Lee, *Green Iris*, 324.
44. Lee, *Green Iris*, 336.
45. Lee, *Green Iris*, 341.
46. Lee, *Green Iris*, 341–342.
47. Lee, *Green Iris*, 343.
48. Lee, *Green Iris*, 348.
49. Lee, *Green Iris*, 349.
50. Lee has always shown an exceptional ability to root her fiction not only in the external trappings of the historical eras she sometimes uses but also in their mind-sets. I gave considerable space to this in my book, *The Hidden Library of Tanith Lee: Themes and Subtexts* (Jefferson, NC: McFarland, 2001). Note particularly an analysis of her novella *Malice in Saffron*, which is set in the Middle Ages. Lee has also written an explicitly historical novel, *The Gods are Thirsty*.

CHAPTER 19

A Monster Sensation
VICTORIAN TRADITIONS CELEBRATED AND SUBVERTED IN SARAH WATERS'S *FINGERSMITH*

Lisa Tuttle

The "sensation novel," usually considered a subgenre of the Gothic, emerged in the 1860s. Among the most successful of that once-booming genre are such books as *East Lynne* by Mrs. Henry Wood, *Lady Audley's Secret* by Mary Elizabeth Braddon, and, most popular and earliest of all, *The Woman in White* by Wilkie Collins.[1] These books not only caused a sensation, but they were about sensational events, and they were very much of their day, drawing on high-profile court cases that were well-known to the Victorian reader, featuring murder, domestic violence, bigamy, forced marriage, and false imprisonment. Yet, despite how society has changed and how far it seems we have come since a time when women could be denied access to their children or locked away from the world simply on the word of their husbands, these books with their emphasis on suspense, reversals, and complicated plots, remain highly enjoyable today. I don't think *The Woman in White* has ever gone out of print, and it not only continues to be widely read, but it is still an active influence on the work of modern authors.

Before she became the popular and successful novelist she is now, Sarah Waters received her Ph.D. in English literature from Queen Mary, University of London, with a dissertation entitled, "Wolfskins and Togas: Lesbian and Gay Historical Fictions, 1870 to the Present."[2] Having immersed herself in Victorian literature as a student, it is not surprising that her first novel was set in that period. After *Tipping the Velvet*, a self-proclaimed "lesbian romp" set against the background of late Victorian music halls, she wrote *Affinity*, another "neo-Victorian" novel, but this time in the Gothic mode, featuring a darker side of London life, particularly prisons and spirit mediums. Her third novel, *Fingersmith*, achieved even greater heights of fame, was widely and respectfully

reviewed, and was nominated for the Booker and the Orange prize, as well as being a popular best seller and TV production.

In interviews, Waters has said that she was "drawn to the gothic since I was a child, when I was fascinated by the macabre and supernatural, and watched all the Hammer House of Horror films."[3] She also specifically cited the works of Wilkie Collins and Elizabeth Braddon, and she explained, "I wanted to take all the classic scenarios and tropes of sensation fiction and to take a different path through them, pursuing lesbian attraction and making them mean different things."[4]

The connection between *Fingersmith* and *The Woman in White* is impossible to miss. Although I had read Wilkie Collins's novel at least thirty years before and had only vague recollections of it, one of my first, delighted impressions of *Fingersmith* was that Waters had taken *The Woman in White*, turned it inside out and upside down, and given it a vigorous shake. I do not mean to imply that her novel is a pastiche—it is much too powerful and sophisticated for that.

What Sarah Waters has managed to do is write something that feels authentically Victorian and yet is clearly a book that no Victorian could have written. She has picked up and followed certain traditions of the sensation novel absolutely faithfully: her plot is as satisfyingly complex and full of twists as anything Wilkie Collins could have devised, and her narrative is just as tense, with the richness of texture and detail that we expect from that period. There are no obvious anachronisms and no distanced or ironic perspectives to provide escape. At the same time, she subverts a number of Victorian traditions and expectations. Her narrators may not be aware of it, but their author knows very well how differently modern readers will respond to certain revelations.

After *The Woman in White*, the other book I was reminded of was John Fowles's *The French Lieutenant's Woman*. Although I don't think Fowles's novel is likely to have been a direct influence on Waters, and she obviously has a very different aim from his metafictional interrogation of the novelist's art, she has written in a convincingly Victorian style while taking an approach toward women, and sexual relations, that would have been impossible for any true Victorian. Like Fowles, Waters re-creates the expansive Victorian mode of storytelling and offers a rich, immersive reading experience. But where he deliberately broke up that escapist experience with his authorial presence, forcing his readers to confront the limits of fiction by sharing his struggles to write it, Sarah Waters allows us to read on. She gives us the same sort of reading pleasure an intelligent Victorian reader might have taken from *The Woman in White*, not stopping where the Victorian author—whether through "delicacy" or cultural blindness—would have been forced to turn his or her gaze away.

Yes, this is about forbidden sex. Despite their self-publicized image as guardians of morality and instigators of sexual repression, the Victorians *did* write

explicitly and obscenely about sexual activities—but not in the novels published for public consumption. *Women* read novels, and their delicate sensibilities were never to be offended. Pornography was written and privately published for men only. Of course women must have read it occasionally, and some of the anonymous authors may have been women—who knows? It was written, always, with the aim of exciting and pleasing a male reader, so that even lesbian scenes were really about the man who watched, or controlled, or inserted himself between the women who performed for his pleasure rather than their own.

In *The French Lieutenant's Woman*, John Fowles added sex to the Victorian novel, not in the style of Victorian pornography, but with realism and sensitive artistry. However, his point of view—male, heterosexual, self-consciously modern—was probably not so far from the Victorian norm as he may have liked to think.

Lesbianism doesn't play as large a role in *Fingersmith* as it did in Waters's two previous novels, but the sexual connection between women remains at the heart of her story, its most hopeful vision, like a single gleam of light in the pervading Gothic darkness, and the only escape from the labyrinthine snares of plot.

Fingersmith is the story of two young women, Sue and Maud.

Susan Trinder has been raised in London, in a den of petty thieves (or "fingersmiths") presided over by Mrs. Sucksby, a baby farmer who doesn't usually keep the children left in her care for so long, or so well. She has told Sue that her real mother was hanged for murder committed during a robbery, and she has more than hinted that someday Sue will make her fortune, for reasons she is not ready to disclose.

Maud Lilly is another orphan, although of gentler birth. But after her mother's death in a madhouse, she is sent to live in her uncle's remote country house. Her guardian, Christopher Lilly, is a cruel, peevish eccentric who cares only about his collection of books and rare prints. But his isn't an ordinary library; late in the novel, as one more blow of Gothic melodrama, we find out he is a self-confessed "curator of poisons"[5] and has assembled an ambitious bibliography of pornography.

Sue becomes Maud's maid when she is enlisted in a scheme by Mrs. Sucksby and a con man known as "Gentleman." He has been hired as Maud's drawing teacher (the same role played by the upright Walter Hartright to Laura and Marion in *The Woman in White*) and says he needs Sue's help in convincing Maud to elope with him. Once they are legally married, he will have her confined in a private insane asylum and will control her fortune. A story as old as the first Gothic novels commences: who will have the heir's fortune, and what will be done—what taboos violated—to get it?

Gradually, an unexpected intimacy grows between Maud and Sue. Despite the class differences between them, they are the same age (seventeen) and are

isolated from the rest of the world. Every day, Sue must dress and undress Maud, a prisoner of Victorian corsetry, as women of that class tended to be, and help her wash. Because of the oddness of her uncle, Maud has no friends, so there is no one but her maid to turn to when she wants advice on how to dress, a game of cards to pass the time, or another perspective on whether what she feels for her handsome drawing master is truly love, or if she is frightened by a bad dream and wants company in bed.

Sue has been raised to be a good little criminal and to gull the rich, but she can't help feeling sorry for Maud and growing fond of her. Her heart feels the sympathy of one orphan to another, when one night:

> I made my way to the crack of [Maud's] door and peeped through. She had leaned out of the curtained bed, and had the portrait of the handsome lady—her mother—in her hand. As I watched, she raised the portrait to her mouth, kissed it, and spoke soft, sad words to it.[6]

She begins to have her doubts about Gentleman's scheme. Can she really go through with it? Gothic romances traditionally have tests and trials of character—which nearly everyone lamentably fails—and this is a severe one for Sue. The first part of *Fingersmith*, through page 175, is narrated by Sue, and her experience, especially the development of her relationship with Maud, is wonderfully rich, gripping, and suspenseful, culminating in a shocking trap that reveals how Sue has completely misunderstood her own situation (and, with her, the reader has also been kept in the dark). The real plot, it so transpires, was devised between Gentleman and Maud, with Sue their unsuspecting victim.

Now Maud tells her side of the story, revealing quite a different character from the nervous, naive innocent that young Miss Sue thought her to be. Telling the same story twice is a risky strategy for any author, but there are so many distinctly different details in Maud's recounting of the events we have heard about from Sue that the reader is never tempted to skip ahead and is actually more likely to go back and reread the first part again in search of missed clues, while admiring the consummate skill with which the false trail was laid. And there is much more to come after we reach the point where Sue, expecting to betray Maud, is herself betrayed—more mysteries from the past to be revealed, and more struggles for both women to seize control of their own lives. Because it is in the characters of Sue and Maud, and the author's decision to present the entire complicated edifice of her plot as *their* story, that *Fingersmith* departs so dramatically from the traditional Victorian tale it resembles, and reveals itself as an entirely modern Gothic.

The relationship between the two women transgresses so many Victorian values and beliefs that it would have been unimaginable in a novel written in the

1860s. Wilkie Collins might have found a minor part for Sue, or even Maud, but only one of them, and only as an undoubted villain.

Close, loving relationships between women were certainly permitted in morally unimpeachable Victorian fiction, often written about in a way that can sound suspiciously erotic to a modern reader, as the women clutch at each other, kissing, petting, and stroking, and sighingly proclaiming their undying affection for one another. The love between "ugly," mannish-looking Marian Halcombe and her "irresistibly beautiful" half sister Laura Fairlie in *The Woman in White* is so strong that they refuse to be parted even after Laura is married, but these are both unambiguously *good* women, and they also belong to the same (respectably elevated) social class.

Take away their only sexual encounter (and there is only one, although it is described twice), and Sue and Maud's relationship would still be unacceptable, because it is between a lady and her maid, and, perhaps more importantly, because neither of them is either innocent or good. They are neither of them the self-sacrificing angel a Victorian heroine was required to be. To write about the ordinary, inevitable physical closeness between a servant and the woman she serves in eroticized language would be scandalous enough, but to allow the women involved to be aware of their feelings, and to welcome them, would have led a book to be considered coarse, at the least, or outright dangerous in its wickedness. Nor would the relationship between Sue and Maud have been suitable as pornography, because there was no room to insert the colonizing male gaze. These sisters are doing it for themselves. Besides, Victorian pornography is known for its fantastical ease—easy in, easy out, and nothing as obstacle, save for many layers of clothing. Titillation and trysts, without consequence, unless the consequences should give rise to more teasing temptations, were to be repeated ad infinitum. Such salacious and popular Victorian novels, all reissued by the Wordsworth Classic Erotic series, are these: *My Secret Life, My Lustful Adventures: A Nocturnal Meeting, Venus in India, Man with a Maid, A Night in a Moorish Harem,* and even *Randiana: The Adventures of Grace & Anna.* Canings, soundproof rooms replete with iron rings and rope pulleys, "firm bubbies," "glorious sheaths," and orgiastic splendor are promised, all highly charged and very funny to the postmodern eye, but distinctly lacking in anything more than the most basic narrative arc aimed at inspiring a quick release of sexual tension. Foreplay, too, is as rudimentary as the plot. Passions are always ready to rise, so long as the right equipment is present, as if sex were mere mechanics, a far cry from the highly psychological, very female, woman-centered, dark Gothic romance of *Fingersmith.*

The Gothic, according to Lorna Sage, "has had from the beginning a suggestive relationship with rebellion, and particularly with the laying bare and transgression of gender roles," which has long made it especially appealing to women as both readers and writers.[7]

Reflecting on her long interest in the Gothic, Sarah Waters points out, "Women have often been victimized within the genre, they have never been powerful—but there has often been this frisson around female sexuality and female transgressions."[8]

Both of her main characters are victims, or at least potential victims, throughout much of the book—victims of a male-dominated society, victims of schemes put into motion while they were infants, victims of greed, and victims of each other. Yet, at the same time, they are, as narrators, practically the authors of their own fates, and, through a combination of cunning and determination, both women manage to triumph, breaking free of the snares set by others. By the end of the book, the possibility of "happily ever after" is within their grasp, a conclusion I feel certain no writer of the Victorian era, whether male or female, would have dared provide.

In an interview, Sarah Waters was asked why she thought so many contemporary writers, not just herself, were drawn to write "neo-Victorian" novels. Her reply follows:

> I've sometimes thought that it's a way of addressing issues that are still very, very current in British culture, like class and gender, and submerged sexuality or sexual underworlds. Things that we think we're pretty cool with, and actually we're not at all, and we keep on wanting to go back to the nineteenth century to play these out on a bigger scale, precisely because they're still very current for us.[9]

I agree. The Victorian era may at first seem long ago and far away, an easy target for both idealization (of their "family values" and many achievements) or mockery (how little they knew! how quaint and repressed they were, despite the output of their erotic fiction and the glut of prostitutes and brothels in Queen Victoria's London!), but a closer acquaintance forces the recognition that, for all the scientific and technological advances of the last century, we are still struggling with the same social and personal issues now as they were then, even if we use different terminology and feel less certain that we know what's right. Take the subject of class. Class tension, or the fear and anger of lower and middle classes toward the lawless, rich aristocracy (in both the UK and France), inspired many of the earliest Gothic novels. Although British society today is no longer rigidly stratified, an awareness of class distinctions has never gone away, and the socioeconomic class into which one is born remains the strongest predictor of future success, higher education, career, and even health and average age of death.

We are probably even more obsessed with the issue of heredity than were the more class-conscious Victorians. Those staple elements of the Gothic romance—disguise, inheritance, confusion surrounding parentage, babies switched at birth—remain powerfully resonant today. In the 1860s, proof of identity was

more easily forged and often relied on the trustworthiness of people who claimed to know the truth. Nowadays, when laboratory tests on skin or blood samples, or even a few hairs filched from a comb, can establish genetic relationships beyond a doubt, we are practically hysterical about the burgeoning crime of "identity theft."

Women can no longer be imprisoned, legally, at the whim of their husbands or fathers, yet the fear of this sort of domination still haunts us, as evidenced by the popularity of the "misery memoir" and headlines blaring the fortunately rare criminal cases. Sexual discrimination is outlawed, but people still argue and worry over whether this is *right*: Are children damaged by mothers who go out to work? Are little boys being deprived because they are taught only by female teachers, while girls do better in class?

For a brief period in the late 1960s through mid-1970s, there was a popular fictional genre known as the "Gothic romance" or "modern Gothic." These books were aimed at women readers, as they were category romances with a sinister edge. The plot always focused on a young woman in some remote location—often in a big house—where she found herself in a threatening situation that could only be resolved by figuring out whether the man she thought she loved was in reality a villain or a suitable romantic partner. The title of Joanna Russ's critical essay pretty much says it all: "Somebody's Trying to Kill Me and I Think It's My Husband: The Modern Gothic."[10] The covers of these books were as formulaic as the plots, with a nervous young woman in the foreground and a castle or house (with a single lighted window) looming darkly behind her. In fact, when I first read *The Woman in White*, it was a paperback edition packaged to appeal to the same audience.

The urtext of the modern Gothic was Daphne du Maurier's *Rebecca* (1938), and it is significant that the genre was at the height of its popularity not then or in the revisionist postwar years, but later in the 1960s, at the very moment when the modern feminist movement was taking off in America and women were breaking down all kinds of outdated barriers, refusing to accept that the choice of who they married was the only significant action they would ever take.

The classic Gothic novel of the nineteenth century generally included a love story in the mixture, but this was largely a matter of convention and the feeling that a happy ending should involve a marriage. The marriage plotted as a way to gain control of a woman's fortune (as featured in both *The Woman in White* and *Fingersmith*) is a fairly straightforward act of villainy, rather than a means of psychologically tormenting the heroine, and the story is about much more than a series of obstacles set in the path of true love.

Readers of Gothic romances in the 1960s might well have enjoyed *The Woman in White*, but it is impossible to imagine *Fingersmith* repackaged in the

same way. It could not have been published as popular fiction by a mainstream or literary publisher in the 1960s, and while it is possible to imagine it being written in the 1970s, it could only have been published then, if at all, by a small feminist press.

The obstacle to a wider readership in earlier times is not the lesbian sex (only one scene, after all, and written in a way that is subtle and emotional rather than explicitly, graphically physical) but the two main characters and the roles they play.

The male antihero has a well-established history. A villain may tell his own story and charm his readers into accepting him as good company, even if they wouldn't want to encounter him in real life. Bad girls also appeal to readers of both sexes—especially when they are bad in the eyes of society because they flout convention, but prove they are really good beneath the tough exterior through some self-sacrificing act. But a female antihero, a true counterpart to the masculine figure, someone who acts entirely out of brazen self-interest, who refuses to be victimized, and who doesn't conform to accepted moral standards, is still impossible for many readers to accept.

I was surprised when, during a discussion of *Fingersmith* in my local book group, one of the women commented that although she'd found the story quite gripping and had kept on reading, driven by the need to know what happened next, she hadn't liked any of the characters and felt that everyone in the book was basically horrible. Two other women chimed in their agreement. I think it is fair to say that (apart from me) none of the group is a big fan of supernatural or Gothic fiction, and they certainly would not have read *Fingersmith* if not for my suggestion. So it says something for the pleasures of the book's well-constructed plot and suspenseful atmosphere that they all stuck with it, and even enjoyed it, despite not liking the company of either narrator.

Personally, I had no problem with this. Of course, both main characters are (like practically everyone else who features in the story) villains who behave badly, pursuing their own interests regardless of what it will mean for anyone else. I like Sue, who fits very much in the tough, spunky character who wins against the odds. It is true that Maud is rather horrible, cruel, spiteful, and worse, but it is also so clear how her background has made her what she is that I was inclined to sympathize. But the comments of these other readers made me consider that women are still expected to be *much better* than men; they can take revenge but should not strike the first blow, and if they are to commit crimes, it should be for a good reason, or because they have to, either because they are forced (they are victims) or because they are driven by love or altruism to save someone else. Although we have come a long way since the Victorian era, we are still inclined to judge men and women by different standards.

And it may just be that chipping away at those standards and subverting our expectations is something that the modern Gothic tale is especially good at. At least it is in Sarah Waters's hands.

Notes

1. Wilkie Collins, *The Woman in White*, ed. and prefaced by John Sutherland (Oxford, UK: Oxford University Press, 1996).

2. Sarah Waters, "The Politics of Lesbian Fiction: Sonja Tiernan Interviews Novelist Sarah Waters," *Irish Feminist Review*, September 1, 2006, www.highbeam.com/doc/1P3-1178240241.html (accessed November 24, 2009).

3. Sarah Waters, "Her Thieving Hands," *Virago Press*, www.virago.co.uk/author_results.asp?SF1=data&ST1=feature&REF=e2006111617063697&SORT=author_id&TAG=&CID=&PGE=&LANG=en (accessed October 10, 2009).

4. Sarah Waters, "Interview with Abigail Dennis," *Neo-Victorian Studies* 1, no. 1 (Autumn 2008): 41–52, www.neovictorianstudies.com/past_issues/Autumn2008/NVS%201-1%20A-Dennis.pdf (accessed October 10, 2009).

5. Sarah Waters, *Fingersmith* (London: Virago Press, 2002), 198.

6. Sarah Waters, *Fingersmith*, 85.

7. Lorna Sage, "Gothic," in *The Cambridge Guide to Women's Writing in English* (Cambridge, UK: Cambridge University Press, 1999), 284–285.

8. Sarah Waters, "Interview with Abigail Dennis."

9. Sarah Waters, "Interview with Abigail Dennis."

10. Joanna Russ, "Somebody's Trying to Kill Me and I Think It's My Husband: The Modern Gothic," in *To Write Like a Woman: Essays in Feminism and Science Fiction* (Bloomington: Indiana University Press, 1995), 94–119.

CHAPTER 20

Fairy Goth-Mothers

MATERNAL WISH FULFILLMENT IN KATE MORTON'S *THE FORGOTTEN GARDEN*

Walter Rankin

The Gothic Fairy Tale Defined and Revisited

Gothic literature, at its most basic, focuses on our confrontation with the unknown and the unknowable. The most celebrated Gothic works have, ironically, been defined by that which ultimately cannot be defined, quantified, or proven: monsters, ghosts, vampires, witches, doppelgängers, and any other psychological terrors that go bump in the night, sending shivers down our literary spines. As H. P. Lovecraft explained in his *Supernatural Horror in Literature* (1927), in true Gothic works (and in his specialty, "weird tales"), "There must be a hint, expressed with a seriousness and portentousness becoming its subject, of that most terrible conception of the human brain—a malign and particular suspension or defeat of those fixed laws of Nature which are our only safeguard against the assaults of chaos and the daemons of unplumbed space."[1] Drs. Frankenstein and Jekyll famously enter this world through science, each discovering uncontrollable, murderous monsters that reflect the most sinister and taboo part of our human natures. Count Dracula psychically preys upon poor Jonathan Harker who is nearly driven mad during his stay at the isolated castle. Preparing for her wedding day, Jane Eyre learns that her betrothed has secretly confined his first wife as the original madwoman in the attic.[2] And while much of the Gothic often hinges upon abstract supernatural beings and hallucinations, the classic Gothic settings are remarkably concrete locations: laboratories with bubbling chemicals and lightning rods, castles with hidden passageways and oubliettes, and locked rooms and attics in rambling old houses. In *The Gothic*

Text (2005), Marshall Brown posits, "What would be left of a person, these novels ask, if all human society were stripped away, all customary perception, all the expected regularity of cause and effect? They ask, in other words, what are people in themselves, when deprived of all the external supports that condition ordinary experience? What resources, if any, does the mind retain in isolation?"[3]

We can readily apply Brown's critique to such subgenres as Gothic romance and Gothic horror novels. In the context of this discussion, we could also substitute the term *novels* with the term *fairy tales* in Brown's supposition, particularly when we look at the Gothic themes and imagery that infuse the tales collected and revised by Jacob and Wilhelm Grimm in nineteenth-century Germany. For the most part, these tales isolate our heroes and heroines, stranding them in the dark forest of fetishes where they encounter cannibalism ("Hansel and Gretel" and "Snow White"); necrophilia ("Brier Rose" and "Snow White"); vengeance ("Cinderella," "Hansel and Gretel," and "Snow White"); and sexual obsession ("Cinderella," "Rapunzel," "Brier Rose," and, yes, again "Snow White"). Wolves, witches, and sorceresses abound, but the tales repeatedly teach us that the greatest dangers dwell within our own homes, frequently at the hands of our (step)parents. At best, the children are ignored, while at worst they are abandoned, bartered, abused, or nearly murdered by their caregivers. The tales also share the Gothic attraction to location and architecture, invariably sending our young heroes and heroines out into that foreboding forest, but also revealing the dangers lurking within those candied cottages and stolid castle walls. Snow White's jealous stepmother conjures her poisons in a secret room of her castle, while Brier Rose finds her way to an abandoned tower with a narrow, winding staircase up to the kingdom's last spinning wheel. The beautiful Rapunzel is held captive in a tower room with no stairs or door, while Cinderella is forced to sleep in the ashes of her own home. In *Why Fairy Tales Stick* (2006), Jack Zipes posits essential questions that arise in these tales and that mirror those asked of Gothic literature by Marshall Brown: "What must an individual do to adapt to a new and unexpected situation? Does a person become heroic through a special kind of adaptation? How will the heroine or hero survive?"[4] It is important to keep in mind that, while the journeys of Gothic and fairy-tale heroes and heroines into the unknown share a number of similarities, the effect of those trips on the characters' psyches tends to be radically different. We know our fairy-tale namesakes will, in spite of all supernatural dangers, survive, adapt, and return to the natural world (stronger and, arguably, changed for the better), while their Gothic cousins more often than not remain lost in that dark forest of madness.

In *The Forgotten Garden* (2008), Kate Morton recognizes Gretel, Snow White, Brier Rose, Cinderella, and Rapunzel as the prototypal "Goth chicks" that they are, incorporating iconic aspects of their stories into her own Gothic work, directly and symbolically.[5] And while these tales exist in similar versions

across the world and through other storytellers (such as Charles Perrault and Joseph Jacobs), Morton references only the Brothers Grimm specifically as the inspiration for the authoress. As a young girl, Morton's Eliza proclaims, "I'm going to collect stories. Ancient stories that no one here has heard before. I'll be just like the Brothers Grimm I was telling you about."[6] Morton weaves together her series of tales using the common thread of motherhood—birth mother, step-mother, surrogate mother, grandmother—as she spans five generations of lost girls to solve a mystery that begins in London, 1913, with an unnamed girl on a boat, wondering, "in the vague, unconcerned manner of much-loved children, where Mamma [is]."[7] As the story unfolds, we discover that the key to her identity is found within her favorite book of fairy tales "about eyeless crones, and or-phaned maidens, and long journeys across the sea" by the mysterious authoress.[8]

Summary of *The Forgotten Garden*

In *Gothic* (1996), Fred Botting explains, "Gothic atmospheres—gloomy and mysterious—have repeatedly signaled *the disturbing return of pasts upon pres-ents* [emphasis added] and evoked emotions of terror and laughter."[9] Charles Dickens may have provided literature's most famous temporal, otherworldly creations with the time-traveling ghosts of Christmas past, present, and future in *A Christmas Carol* (1843), while William Faulkner scrambled the concept of chronology altogether in his Southern Gothic works like *As I Lay Dying* (1930) and *The Sound and the Fury* (1929). One of the joys of Morton's work lies in unraveling her complex and multiple asynchronous story lines that jump across decades from chapter to chapter, connecting each of her heroines—Georgiana, Eliza, Nell, and Cassandra—and her one arguable villainess, Adeline, through her respective mother/daughter role. Morton recognizes that, culturally, almost nothing links the past and the present more than family, as stated simply by one of Cassandra's great-aunts, "You know, family, blood, the past . . . they're the things that make us who we are."[10] One of the challenges in summarizing Mor-ton's work is that it requires revealing major plot developments while ascribing a linear continuity to each heroine's tale. Such a summary is essential, however, to allow for further exegesis.

Although the novel begins with a nameless child, we learn on her twenty-first birthday that she was found and adopted in classic fairy-tale style by a young couple who longed for children. Upon the death of her adoptive mother, the adoptive father decides that the young woman, called Nell, has a right to know about the past which she has long forgotten. Learning this secret sets Nell apart from her younger sisters and compels her to find the mother who (she believes) abandoned her. She employs a detective who eventually finds her birthplace,

Cliff Cottage in England, hidden behind a maze on the rambling Blackhurst Estate. Nell buys the cottage and prepares to continue her search when her own daughter, Lesley, with whom she has never been close, drops off her daughter, Cassandra, for Nell to raise. Nell willingly abandons her dream to raise the girl, bequeathing her the cottage and the unsolved maternal mystery on her deathbed.

Cassandra is stunned to learn that her grandmother was a foundling, and she continues the search (believing "the puzzle was her inheritance"[11]), using her grandmother's illustrated book of fairy tales, *Magical Tales for Girls and Boys*, by Eliza Makepeace, as her guide. Along her journey, she discovers that Eliza was the daughter of Georgiana Mountrachet, a well-bred lady shunned by her family and society when she fell in love with a lowly sailor. The sailor dies under mysterious circumstances, likely at the hands of Mr. Mansell, her brother's hired henchman, and a pregnant Georgiana flees into hiding, later warning her twins, Eliza and Sammy, to beware of "the Bad Man." Eliza is completely orphaned following the death of her mother, due to illness, and then her brother, who is trampled in the London fog by a black horse. Shortly after Sammy's death, the Bad Man—a shadowy figure known as Mr. Mansell—finds her and takes her back to the Blackhurst Estate, where "[d]ark grey clouds drooped towards the earth, heavy with intention, and the air beneath was thick with fog."[12]

At the Blackhurst Estate, Eliza meets her uncle, Linus, who obsessively protects a single photograph he took of Georgiana before she fled; Adeline, his wife, who has managed to overcome her own low upbringing to become the lady of the house; and Rose, her sickly cousin who stays hidden from the world. Eliza and Rose become like sisters, with Eliza entertaining her with grand tales of adventure and her own versions of fairy tales. As they grow into young women, Adeline comes to view Eliza as a threat to both herself and her daughter. The matured Eliza now so resembles her mother that she has awakened latent incestuous feelings within Linus. Additionally, her beauty and intelligence make her a true rival for her own beloved Rose. Adeline takes Rose abroad where she finds a handsome suitor, Nathaniel Walker, to marry. Returning to Blackhurst, Adeline convinces Eliza to give the couple privacy by moving into the isolated cottage at the edge of the estate. Here, Eliza plants a glorious garden to symbolize her undying love of Rose.

Despite Eliza's efforts, Rose and Eliza drift apart, especially as Rose becomes increasingly focused on having a baby. After the doctor confirms that she cannot bear children, Rose becomes deathly ill, leading Adeline to devise a new plan: Eliza must serve as the secret mother to Rose's child, even if that requires Nathaniel's infidelity. Eliza agrees, hoping once more to share a bond with Rose, but their relationship cannot overcome the emotionally fraught circumstances. After giving birth to a daughter, Ivory, Eliza and Rose seldom communicate, and Eliza leaves the estate for a few years. When she returns, she gives Ivory,

who is still a toddler, a book of fairy tales she has written, including a symbolic one called "The Golden Egg," in which a maiden gives her precious egg to save the princess and the kingdom. Nathaniel removes this one tale from the book, however, effectively excising the one story that could have one day given the child a clue to her parentage.

In spite of the century covered in the characters' backstories, the novel races to its conclusion over just a few days. Rose and Nathaniel are killed in a train crash, and Eliza decides to kidnap Ivory to start a new life. Adeline figures out Eliza's plan and employs Mr. Mansell once again to bring them back to the estate; however, Eliza has already hidden Ivory aboard the ship when Mr. Mansell locates Eliza, alone, back at the house where she and Sammy were orphaned, and where Eliza long ago had hidden an expensive family brooch that Georgiana had given her to sell in an emergency. Mansell drugs Eliza who awakens half dazed in a carriage speeding back to the estate. Echoing Botting's description of Gothic atmosphere that opens this section, a lifetime of memories and relationships washes over her ("Time folded over on itself: all moments were one, past was present was future"[13]), and, recalling her abandoned daughter, she flings herself out the door and to her death, leaving little Ivory, the foundling who begins the tale, to start her voyage on the Gothic seas, not knowing where she is going, nor where she is from.

Once Upon a Time in *The Forgotten Garden*

Once upon a time—with this four-word introduction, fairy tales invite us into a world that exists outside of standard time and place. The events, whether real (being abandoned in an enchanted forest and threatened by a conniving step-mother) or supernatural (battling the witch, awakening from a one-hundred-year spell), could have unspooled yesterday or centuries ago. By the story's conclusion, however, we are almost always assured that the good characters will live ever after within a timeless vacuum of happiness. Having experienced the sorrow that can still occur after getting, and losing, her own prince, Georgiana contrasts fairy tales to life, urging the fanciful Eliza to recognize that "[they] have a habit of ending too soon. They never show what happens afterwards, when the prince and the princess ride off the page."[14] Through the course of the novel, Morton keeps her princes and princesses firmly page bound, showing the reader what happens following "happily ever after" in the Gothic setting. Brown asserts, "Natural time does not exist in the gothic except in the form of a simple illusion; all true experiences in the novels are filtered through the grid of four types of unnatural time: inner and outer stasis, inner and outer frenzy."[15] Maggie Kilgour (1995) sees a similarly tense psychological and temporal framework

which operates on competing levels: "The gothic is thus haunted by a reading of history as a dialectical process of alienation and restoration, dismembering and remembering."[16]

Morton creates a world that epitomizes these Gothic struggles with representing time, being, and ultimately truth. She may begin each chapter with a helpful time-and-place header (London, 1913; Brisbane, 2005; Maryborough, 1914; Cliff Cottage, 2005; and so on), but the resulting feel remains one of a realm that fluidly dissolves such concrete markers in service to the heroines' individual stories. And while Morton allows Cassandra to solve the central mystery of her grandmother's bloodline, bringing fairy-tale closure to the novel, each of the other mothers represented dies while entwined in that Gothic void of unnatural time, having actively rewritten the past and further altering her child's ability to perceive the present and future. The novel's maternal mystery is thus formed by rambling umbilical cords tied in purposeful knots that span generations: Georgiana warns of "the Bad Man" without preparing her children for the dangers awaiting should they be found and carried home to Blackhurst; Eliza and Rose, equally complicit in hiding Ivory's birthright, both die in midtransport aboard an old-fashioned carriage and a modern train, symbolizing the collapse of time and movement toward truth; Adeline buries "Ivory," creating a fiction that the girl passed away from scarlet fever, and then enters into a state of madness herself; and, while alive, Nell never lets her granddaughter know about the secret that altered her forever. As she works to uncover these ladies' pasts and relationships, Cassandra can only lament, "It's like the closer we get, the more tangled the web becomes."[17]

The elements of time and maternal ties are neatly symbolized by Georgiana's mourning brooch, which contains strands of hair "taken from the women in my family. My grandmother's, her mother's before, and so on. It's a tradition."[18] Eliza is captured by Mr. Mansell when she attempts to retrieve the brooch, and it remains with her after she dies while attempting to escape the carriage. When Eliza's remains are found—buried under the apple tree in her hidden garden—the brooch is recovered as well, and Cassandra examines it: "She turned it over and ran her fingertip over the engraving on the back. *For Georgiana Mountrachet*, read the tiny print, *on the occasion of her sixteenth birthday. Past. Future. Family.*"[19]

Transforming Fairy-tale Archetypes into Gothic Mistresses

In "The Horrors of Misogyny: Feminist Psychoanalysis in the Gothic Classroom," Anne Williams suggests,

> Gothic plots are family plots. The patriarchal family is the cultural
> structure always already in place that generates Gothic plots. These
> plots tend to focus on certain pressure points that are situated at the
> intersections of nature and culture within patriarchy. . . . This is also
> the reason why in early Gothic at least (1764–1830), incest is so
> frequently the horror of horrors, for as the foundation of patriarchal
> culture incest is the Gothic mansion's heart of darkness.[20]

The Grimm Brothers did not shy away from these horrific patriarchal themes, addressing incest symbolically in "The Girl without Hands," in which a fair maiden's only defense against the hands of the devil (and her father) are her virtuous tears and prayer, and directly in "Allerleirauh," in which a king demands—and ultimately gets—his daughter as his bride, with no negative consequences. In "The Robber Bridegroom," a poor maiden barely escapes her husband, a murderous cannibal who has planned to kill and eat her. These kinds of tales are the anomaly, however, and they remain little-known stories, likely shunned from bedside readings.

In contrast to these few examples of patriarchal dominance and danger, most fairy tales tend to create a world in which birth fathers are almost uniformly impotent in comparison to female characters: Hansel and Gretel's father twice leaves his children to starve in the woods at the behest of their stepmother; Rapunzel's father allows the neighboring sorceress to take his daughter away in exchange for feeding his wife rampion lettuce; and the fathers of Snow White and Cinderella ignore their daughters' suffering at the hands of their stepmothers. The fabled saving princes are, for the most part, a boring lot as well. They tend to be nameless, generically good-looking young men who stumble into love, marrying the first beautiful maiden they happen to rescue. They each have their fetishes, of course—Cinderella's prince covets the perfect foot; Snow White and Brier Rose have princes who share a taste for necrophilia; and Rapunzel's prince is awed by her voice and bountiful hair—but these Grimm princes are no threat to Heathcliff or Mr. Hyde or Count Dracula. In each of these tales, female characters drive the story; it is the heroine we remember and the powerful woman stalking her whom we learn to fear.

One of the most striking features of *The Forgotten Garden* lies in Morton's adherence to this fairy-tale tradition. The male characters are mostly weak or absent. Eliza's father (Georgiana's love), Nell's husband, and Cassandra's husband and son have all died when we are introduced to them. While Mr. Mansell is classically terrifying (dressed in dark fabrics with his pince-nez, dark cane, pale hands, and bushy mustache), he remains a purely one-dimensional character who serves primarily at the behest of Adeline. Linus, the most connected of the male characters (Georgiana's brother; Adeline's husband; Eliza's uncle; Rose's father; Nell's grandfather; Cassandra's great-great-grandfather), is physically

disabled and haunted by his incestuous love for his lost sister. While he carries with him a true element of danger—having impulsively cut Georgiana's throat when she told him of her new love—he is ultimately controlled by Adeline as much as Cinderella and Snow White's birth fathers are by their new wives. When we learn that he loses his fortune traveling to "voodoo places" (as one character informs Cassandra at the end), we can only savor the irony of his having lived as a zombie ever since losing Georgiana. Likewise, Nathaniel, Rose's ersatz prince, settles into a loveless marriage while allowing his mother-in-law full control over his career, his wife, and his daughter.[21] The one true prince emerges in the form of Christian, a handyman and doctor, who helps Cassandra repair Cliff Cottage while assisting her in solving the mystery. He even possesses his own complete copy of Eliza's fairy tales, including the missing tale of "The Golden Egg" that reveals Eliza's sorrow and loss.

Morton's female characters serve as the embodiment and amalgam of the Grimms' iconic female figures, at times fighting against their roles, and at other times accepting and embracing them. While Georgiana had warned Eliza against the apparent ease of fairy-tale lives, her own great-great-granddaughter sighs over a century later, "Life'd be a lot easier if it were like a fairy tale, if people belonged to stock character types." Her friend, Julia, then offers, "Oh, but people do, they only think they don't. Even the person who insists such things don't exist is a cliché: the drear pedant who insists on his own uniqueness."[22] Georgiana and Cassandra bookend the generations while respectively filling the roles of Cinderella's mother (who dies while her daughter is young, inadvertently leaving her in the hands of a cunning surrogate) and Cinderella herself (landing her prince charming after suffering great personal loss and finding a loving mother figure in Nell). Nell's character is primarily a tribute to Brier Rose, a character whose life is changed forever on her eighteenth birthday because of a secret curse brought about by her parents' not issuing an invitation to a powerful woman. When Nell turns twenty-one, her adoptive father decides to tell her the truth about her past, and "the bottom fell out of her world and the person she had been vanished in an instant."[23] Her mystery envelopes generations and spans over one hundred years, casting a filial shadow as long as Brier Rose's slumber. In addition to being featured symbolically throughout Eliza's own tales, the cousins Eliza and Rose are each informed by Grimm fairy-tale tradition. Eliza, like Cinderella, loses her mother and comes under the rule of Adeline, a "stepmother" of unsurpassed malice. Like Rapunzel's mother, Eliza gives away her own daughter to be raised by a powerful woman in a stone manor she cannot access. And like poor Brier Rose, she is walled off from society, hidden within a nearly inaccessible garden for over a hundred years while awaiting rescue. Rose, herself, begins her journey like Brier Rose, shielded from society in a dark room of the Blackhurst Estate. Much like Cinderella's stepsisters, she is too easily manipulated by a domineer-

ing mother to marry the prince at all costs. And like Snow White's birth mother, she longs to have a child, even though doing so could mean her death. Each of these women also contributes invaluable clues to their shared family history through their varied means of telling stories: Georgiana's family brooch and tales of "the Bad Man" feed Eliza's imagination and fuel her need to tell stories. Eliza's published tales serve as an autobiography of her trials and loss, while Rose creates detailed scrapbooks, and Nell records her thoughts in private journals. Only by taking pieces from each, acting as the family editor, can Cassandra bring their stories to genuine closure.

In *The Gothic Tradition in Fiction* (1979), Elizabeth MacAndrew posits, "The Gothic villains have an interesting potential for ambiguous, suggested meanings. When provided with the necessary sublime setting, these villains of the early Gothic are paradoxically more nearly recognizable as depictions of human beings than the good sentimental characters who are the victims."[24] This statement could easily be applied to the fairy-tale stepmothers of Snow White and Cinderella, as well as to Adeline, a complex figure who combines elements of both characters while standing alone as the Gothic queen determined to obscure painful truths with fanciful fictions. Her Grimm counterparts are too easily vilified in my opinion, given their Disney-ready caricatures in comparison to their seemingly wholesome heroines. However, these figures are indeed more recognizably human, desperate, and creative than those they torment. Snow White's stepmother sees her beauty fading fast before the honest mirror, a beauty that has gotten her a husband and castle with a secret room to conduct her dark magic. Envy and jealousy consume her as she witnesses her stepdaughter mature into a genuine rival. Likewise, Cinderella's stepmother—single and with two daughters of her own to support before marrying the widower—puts her own children first in trying to hide Cinderella's beauty (and perfect feet) from the daft prince. Adeline, with "skin as white as snow, lips as red as blood,"[25] has also worked hard to get her prince and castle, and she is determined to keep them and to provide for her daughter. We learn that Lady Adeline Mountrachet began her life as a simple country girl brought to the Blackhurst Estate to serve the beautiful Georgiana. After discovering Linus's taboo desire for his sister, she is able to secure her place as his "protective" bride, recreating her history by "banish[ing] all mention of the truth" so that "most who knew it had been terrified into wiping it from their memories, and those who hadn't were too mindful of their position to dare breathe a word about Lady Mountrachet's origins."[26] She perfects her storytelling using actual people, defining and refining them to her advantage. She transforms Nathaniel from simple artist to famed portraitist; she determines that Eliza should provide the child her daughter so desperately wants after Rose confides to her, "Without a child I cannot go on. I would do anything for a baby, even at my own cost. I would rather die than wait"[27]; she

creates the fiction that missing Ivory has died of scarlet fever; and she decides that Eliza "must be buried where no one would ever find her. Where no one would ever think to look."[28] *The Forgotten Garden* is, ultimately, her creation, and it takes five generations of women working together across time to undo her near-seamless work. That is power.

Happily Ever After in *The Forgotten Garden*

The Grimm Brothers typically let their readers know where their sympathies lay by providing gruesome conclusions to the wicked and happy endings to the virtuous. Snow White's stepmother is invited to the new queen's wedding, only to be strapped into red-hot iron boots and forced to dance to her death on that fateful day. Cinderella's stepsisters have their eyes pecked out by birds during her ceremony. Morton, too, concludes her novel with endings befitting her characters' actions. We learn that Adeline dies from blood poisoning (what could be more all consuming?) within months of Rose, "Face all contorted so that she looked to be grinning like a ghoul, escaping from her sickbed to lurch along hallways with a great ring of keys in hand, locking all the doors and raving about some secret that no one must know."[29] In stark contrast, Cassandra finds true love with Christian, while an epilogue brings closure that ties together the Gothic and fairy-tale realms that have infused the entire novel. On her deathbed, Nell sees the authoress, the mother she searched for her entire life, emerge from the shadows, telling her that she is home. Morton juxtaposes this ethereal scene with the concluding paragraph to one of Eliza's tales, now the concluding paragraph to her own novel, as "the wicked Queen's spell was broken, and the young woman, whom circumstance and cruelty had trapped in the body of a bird, was released from her cage" to fly home.[30]

Notes

1. H. P. Lovecraft, *Supernatural Horror in Literature* (New York: Dover Publications, 1973), 15.

2. In *Gothic (Re)Visions* (New York: State University of New York Press, 1993), 64, Susan Wolstenholme asserts that Charlotte Brontë's *Jane Eyre* (1847) should be viewed as "post-Gothic Gothic," with a narrative that links "storytelling and nightmare." In *The Classic Fairy Tales* (New York: W. W. Norton, 1999), xvii, Maria Tatar makes a compelling argument that the novel "can be read as a one-woman crusade and act of resistance to the roles modeled for girls and women in fairy tales," interpreting the "plain-Jane" heroine as the anti-Cinderella.

3. Marshall Brown, *The Gothic Text* (Stanford, CA: Stanford University Press, 2005), 12.

4. Jack Zipes, *Why Fairy Tales Stick: The Evolution and Relevance of a Genre* (New York: Routledge, 2006), 27.

5. Morton's direct references include the following: Adeline is described as having "[s]kin as white as snow, lips as red as blood," 195; Cassandra falls asleep after eating a golden apple, 306; a gate at Cliff Cottage is discovered under "ropelike tendrils" while the garden behind it is referred to as "Sleeping Beauty, fast asleep until the enchantment is broken," 344; at her first ball, Rose is described as "the fairest of them all" with "[b]eauty equaled by her purity of heart," 333; and Cassandra warns her friend, Ruby, not to prick her finger on an antique spinning wheel, with Ruby responding, "I don't want to be responsible for putting us both to sleep for a hundred years," 424.

6. Kate Morton, *The Forgotten Garden* (New York: Atria, 2009), 283.

7. Morton, *The Forgotten Garden*, 3.

8. Morton, *The Forgotten Garden*, 4.

9. Fred Botting, *Gothic* (London: Routledge, 1996), 1.

10. Morton, *The Forgotten Garden*, 26.

11. Morton, *The Forgotten Garden*, 152.

12. Morton, *The Forgotten Garden*, 190.

13. Morton, *The Forgotten Garden*, 531.

14. Morton, *The Forgotten Garden*, 122.

15. Brown, *The Gothic Text*, 73.

16. Maggie Kilgour, *The Rise of the Gothic Novel* (London: Routledge, 1995), 15.

17. Morton, *The Forgotten Garden*, 503.

18. Morton, *The Forgotten Garden*, 124.

19. Morton, *The Forgotten Garden*, 543.

20. Anne Williams, "The Horrors of Misogyny: Feminist Psychoanalysis in the Gothic Classroom," in *Approaches to Teaching Gothic Fiction: The British and American Traditions*, ed. Diane Long Hoeveler and Tamar Heller (New York: MLA, 2003), 80.

21. Both Linus and Nathaniel are artists, the former a photographer and the latter an illustrator and portraitist. Linus, however, clings to a single picture of his sister that he keeps hidden from Adeline, while Nathaniel gives up illustrating after working on Eliza's book to focus on portraits. In both cases, the men devote their art to capturing the female who excites and ultimately eludes them. They are as obsessed as Snow White's prince, who is content to take away the presumed dead beauty in the glass coffin as his prize.

22. Morton, *The Forgotten Garden*, 349.

23. Morton, *The Forgotten Garden*, 11.

24. Elizabeth MacAndrew, *The Gothic Tradition in Fiction* (New York: Columbia University Press, 1979), 49.

25. Morton, *The Forgotten Garden*, 195.

26. Morton, *The Forgotten Garden*, 245.

27. Morton, *The Forgotten Garden*, 413.

28. Morton, *The Forgotten Garden*, 538.

29. Morton, *The Forgotten Garden*, 498.

30. Morton, *The Forgotten Garden*, 549.

CHAPTER 21

In Praise of She Wolves
THE NATIVE AMERICAN ECO-GOTHIC OF
LOUISE ERDRICH'S *FOUR SOULS*

Danel Olson

Let me be powerful like the *shunk-tokecha* (wolf).

—Native American War Song[1]

"She Wolf" came to me very mysteriously. I was in the studio in a bad mood that day, then I got inspired and went to a corner and I wrote the lyrics and the melody in 10 minutes. The image of the she wolf just came to my head, and when I least expected it I was howling and panting.

—Shakira in interview[2]

In the white distance one mansion shimmered, light glancing bold off its bland windowpanes and turrets and painted rails. Fleur blinked and passed her hand across her eyes. But then, behind the warm shadow of her fingers, she recovered her inner sight and slowly across her face there passed a haunted, white, wolf grin.

—Louise Erdrich, *Four Souls*[3]

Sometimes the buried secrets of a Gothic past and novel are by chance tied to one's own home. When I was a boy in Minnesota, I traveled on a school bus with other fifth-graders to a nearby reservation to see Indians. The Chippewa, or Ojibwe, Natives had been placed on this originally 61,000-acre plot of land by the shores of Mille Lacs Lake by the U.S. government in 1855,[4] but that fact wasn't stressed to us on the ride over. Once we arrived at the somewhat small museum in the sun, our teacher

directed us to a glowing white birch-bark canoe. We discovered the Chippewa art of crafting and patching canoes, but we didn't learn that in 1862 the ancestors of this reservation had defended the lives of my own white ancestors from aggression by neighboring Native tribes during the Dakota War.[5] Next, some beautiful beaded cradleboards and necklaces of bear claws were shown to us, but we didn't really hear that in 1879, the U.S. Interior Department had allowed large areas of timber to be stripped off this very land by non-Indians.[6] Instead of such boring, ugly, implicating history, we were trotted out to a less-than-lifelike diorama of Natives harvesting wild rice. In the 1880s, the U.S. government adopted a policy of assimilation for American Indians that prohibited the Native culture we were seeing now,[7] breaking their traditions that stretch back nine thousand years.[8] By the 1930s, their children would be sent to government boarding schools where they were "forbidden from speaking the Ojibwe language in an attempt to assimilate them into mainstream society."[9] We weren't told about this, nor about how in 1889 the U.S. government passed the Nelson Act, carving reservation land into allotments for each eligible Indian, partitions that could be sold, but that also would be annually taxed, and upon failure to pay the taxes, forfeited and sold to whites.[10] This didn't come up in the tour, but some earthenware jugs were found for us. In 1915, many of Mille Lacs band members from this reservation joined the U.S. Armed Forces to serve in WWI, and more than twenty-five of them would serve in WWII, with their families moving to large cities to work in defense industries.[11] We saw no statues of them, though, and none of the missing, injured, or dead were named on any of the plaques at my city hall. In the United States, Native Americans would not be allowed to become citizens until 1924.[12] But nobody told us kids: We all left thinking a reservation was not such a bad place to live. So much struggle and ruin and betrayal had taken place on that soil we walked, but it was all kept sealed underground by my own people. That such culture death could be fully hidden from all of us is an enduring example of how the suffering of a people can go unnoticed at any time and place, even during an "educational tour." The next duped generation unintentionally will let the loss stay buried. In an astonishing footnote, my neighboring county sued this reservation in 2004 for more land,[13] despite that fact that the Mille Lacs Reservation band of natives currently possesses only 3,500 acres of land (tribally owned)[14] from the original 61,000 they were corralled into by the U.S. government in the first place a century and a half ago. I share this memory of my miseducation as a backstory, because the Native American novelist (Karen) Louise Erdrich, whose novel *Four Souls* dwells on such abuses, was born in 1954 in Little Falls, Minnesota, only thirty-three miles as the crow flies from this reservation.

Though Native American lands decreased by "about ninety million acres during the fifty-year period of allotment,"[15] their struggle has not passed. That

Natives should have so much taken away—land, freedom, culture, and life—and that more is still being demanded from them forms the cruellest irony of this hard land. Thus racism, government persecution, forced reeducation, language deprivation, institutional swindles, killings, and the resulting revenge-and-reclamation fantasies make up the Native-American-meets-white story in America. But this chronicle of shame has seldom poured itself so hauntingly into a Gothic narrative until now. This chapter suggests that the abiding motifs of its author, an enrolled member of the Anishinaabe Nation at Turtle Mountain Reservation in North Dakota, are essentially Gothic ones in an Anishinaabe tongue (sometimes literally so, as the novel's Anishinaabe passages, including its long epigraph, are untranslated). The chapter describes and evaluates the novel *Four Souls*, asking about its literary, historic, and cultural significance, and how it sees the Native struggle freshly. Evidence will be offered to suggest how Erdrich simultaneously exploits the conventions of the Euro-Gothic model, from its crude but influential urtext *The Castle of Otranto* on, and the Ameri-Gothic of the nineteenth and twentieth centuries. How she grafts these Gothic developments to Chippewa storytelling and longings, and complicates our expectations, is also investigated, making the Chippewa story in Minnesota and North Dakota[16] known to the wider world.

Summary of Conflict

"I've finally figured out that I'm just working on one long novel,"[17] Erdrich said to a question regarding the layers of legend and meaning that accumulate with each of her novels, starting in 1984 with *Love Medicine*, followed by *The Beet Queen* (1986), *Tracks* (1988), *The Crown of Columbus* (1991), *The Bingo Palace* (1994), *Tales of Burning Love* (1997), the World Fantasy Award–winning *The Antelope Wife* (1998), *The Last Report on the Miracles at Little No Horse* (2001), *The Master Butchers Singing Club* (2003), *The Painted Drum* (2005), *Four Souls* (2006), *The Plague of Doves* (2008), and *Shadow Tag* (2010). Erdrich muses that "I think it is useful to have read the other books. But I try very hard to make each book its own book. It is its own book. But they all connect in some way."[18] *Four Souls* is part of her Lake Matchimanito saga, a series of novels named for an imaginary Ojibwe homeland in north-central North Dakota, near where her own actual band resides. Taking place between 1924 and the mid-1930s, *Four Souls* completes a chronological gap between her *Tracks* and *The Bingo Palace*.[19] Erdrich's original plan had been to "expand and double *Tracks* at twice its original length, . . . [but] she was eventually persuaded to leave the original *Tracks* as it was and to issue the new material as [the] fresh and complete novel [*Four Souls*]."[20]

The novel's protagonist, Fleur Pillager, was born of a family of healers who lived beside the fictional Lake Matchimanito in North Dakota, and her adoptive father is Nanapush, who becomes one of the three narrators in *Four Souls* (the second is Polly Elizabeth, the sister-in-law of the man that Fleur plans to kill in slow agony; and the third is Nanapush's Native American lover, Margaret). Through her lapsed payment of the property tax on her allotment during a famine and epidemic that swept the reservation (when Natives sold off their land for a bit of flour to eat), she loses her property. Its great oaks are cut and eventually hauled off to help make the mansion for a magnate in the neighboring state of Minnesota. Fleur, a woman who has been raped, has almost drowned, has had her first child die prematurely, and has had to give up her second child to a federal government school, wants nothing less than this—all her land and all the wood back. It seems a wild dream, but such is her destiny. Historically speaking, courts would never have given her restitution during this period. In fact, in the devastating 1903 case of *Lone Wolf v. Hitchcock*, the U.S. Supreme Court ruled "that losses suffered by Indians during allotment were no losses at all."[21] When the Kiowa Indians challenged the allotment of their treaty-guaranteed lands on the grounds that it violated the Fifth Amendment's prohibition against taking property without compensation, the Supreme Court held that Congress's action was "unreviewable."[22] So Fleur must nab it back through her wolf wiles, instincts, and cunning, prompting narrators to call her a she wolf four times in *Four Souls*.

Though short by comparison to the expansive length of many neo-Gothic tomes, Louise Erdrich's *Four Souls* (at 210 pages) makes up for its size by being arguably the most incantatory of the novels included in this *21st Century Gothic*, and as lyrical as anything she has written. Readers have waited sixteen years to find out what happened to Fleur and to see her again, not dreaming that her story would take these turns. From the first chapter, we are submerged in a trance from the language. A lone Native American woman is wandering east by foot on a vengeance quest, nailing tin grooves to the wheels of her cart so that she can ride it along train tracks to the Twin Cities (Minneapolis and St. Paul, Minnesota) and kill someone. The novel's first chapter sets a suitably somber tone but also prepares Indian snares through its grim fortitude for many later surprises, including dark deceit, absurdity, wild irony, and impossible unions:

> She wore her makizinan to shreds, then stole a pair of boots off the porch of a farmhouse, strangling a fat dog to do it. She skinned the dog, boiled and ate it, leaving only the bones behind, sucked hollow. She dug cattails from the potholes and roasted the sweet root. She ate mud hens and snared muskrats, and still she travelled east. She travelled until the iron road met up with another, until the twin roads grew hot from the thunder and lightning of so many trains passing and she had to walk beside.

> The night before she reached the city the sky opened and it
> snowed. . . . She found a tree and under it she buried the bones [of
> her ancestors] and the clan markers, tied a red prayer flag to the high-
> est branches, and then slept beneath the tree. That was the night she
> took her mother's secret name to herself, named her spirit. . . . She
> would need the name where she was going. (2)

We find Fleur, who will take her mother's name "Four Souls" (a woman who
was a healer and also the daughter of a healer), animalistic, slinking to the
outskirts of the cities as a wolf would. She fulfills the Native belief that she has
multiple souls and can toss one of them out each time she is to be killed, thus
living again with the remaining souls, or lives, remaining. She will find, in her
pursuit to murder the capitalist John James Mauser who took the ancient oak
trees off her island allotment, an antagonist who is worse than she originally
thought; he has both pretended to love and then married Native women in
order to con them out of their land, and he has not paid his own workers. His
schemes finance him as one of the wealthiest men of St. Paul and the husband of
a well-heeled but frigid woman named Placide. Fleur/Four Souls should come to
hate him all the more with these revelations of greater crimes, so why, later, will
she make love to him? Becoming the lover and then wife of the man you were
supposed to kill, and then having his child, is deep Gothic irony. In the New
World or the Old, revenge scenarios just don't play out right; they are never as
successfully or cleanly cruel as envisaged.

One of the reflections that may adjust how we appreciate retribution in
Four Souls is George Orwell's observations from the end of WWII as he came
into a just-liberated concentration camp. Seeing ample evidence left behind of
how one people tried to take the property, work to death, and obliterate the
memory of another, Orwell was horrified. But he was more curious about the
reactions of the liberated. He watches a former Jewish inmate drub a shoeless SS
man stretched out on the ground, offering little resistance, and he sees officers of
the Reich drowned in a nearby pool of water. The acts appear merely pathetic,
though, drained of whatever power or peace they were supposed to bring to the
Nazi victims. Orwell reasonably concludes,

> Revenge is an act which you want to commit when you are powerless
> and because you are powerless: as soon as the sense of impotence is
> removed, the desire evaporates also. Who would not have jumped for
> joy, in 1940, at the thought of seeing S.S. officers kicked and humili-
> ated? But when the thing becomes possible, it is merely pathetic and
> disgusting. . . . Somehow the punishment of these monsters ceases
> to seem attractive when it becomes possible: indeed, once under lock
> and key, they almost cease to be monsters. Unfortunately, there is

often a need of some concrete incident before one can discover the real state of one's feelings.[23]

Orwell's discovery (first published in London's *Tribune*, November 1945) offers a haunting insight into this entire novel. Here a retaliation fantasy (both by Fleur against Mauser, and also by the narrator Nanapush against a romantic rival) helps victims cope during their distress, but the execution of the fantasy offers them nothing and only further entangles them with their victimizer.

Traces of the European Gothic

Revenge fires this novel, but the author adds to the blaze ten other classic Euro-Gothic features. These tropes I briefly parallel with Robert Harris's short but helpful illustration of the most influential Gothic memes[24] from Horace Walpole's *The Castle of Otranto*, those that would extend their influence over 250 more years of Gothic storytelling. Applied to *Four Souls*, we see the seven motifs of the Euro-Gothic creating dark spaces all over *Four Souls*. Dominating are suspense (what is this fatal mission of the she wolf on the opening page?) and mystery (what will happen to the one who took trees from Fleur's land? Where is Fleur's daughter? How will the narrator Nanapush win his Margaret? Will he kill too?). Prophecies are implied or spoken (the twentieth century promises to be a long dark night for the Chippewa, now that the buffalo are dead, the old ways are dying, and the land of their ancestors' graves is robbed). The implied prophecy must be that Fleur will have some role in returning a portion of Native land and dignity. Visions and portents intimating the empty future occur along with supernatural and highly symbolic events, especially that of souls migrating into animals whose bodies are trapped and cut open, like the white racoon into which Fleur's mother transmigrated, a furry creature found to be absolutely hollow—"No heart. No lungs. No guts" (56). Moreover, "the metonymy of horror, gloom, and doom"[25] that characters operate in (the creaking steps, the breeze, the snow, the animal calls, and the smell of blood and spoor) give the novel added stress points and sensuous depth. There are tense, high, and even overwrought dramas (the bedtime near-killing scene of Mauser; a long, drunken, high-stakes poker game played by Fleur to win her property from an Indian agent on the reservation; and Fleur's collapse at the end of the novel and her retreat to her tree-cut island). And the classic Gothic torment—women in physical and spiritual distress—is at the novel's center. Fleur has had her property yanked away, she has almost died three times and has but one soul left, and now she has come to live in the powerful man's house who ruined her and her community. Her fellow Natives insist that she gave her daughter away, but

her adoptive father still defends her, invoking her she-wolf nature again: "Fleur merely took the girl off to hide her the way a wolf hides a pup when she must do battle to protect her standing" (73). Any mention by Nanapush of a she wolf hiding her pups summons a moving truth and what seems at first a fatal fore-shadowing that readers from active wolf-pack zones (like those mid-Minnesota counties Erdrich and I were born to) know well, namely that "female wolves have been known to bury their dead pups, making wolves one of the very few animals besides humans to interact with their dead."[26] While her daughter Lulu has a grim and silencing fate at a government school where it was thought she could be hidden and protected, her mother Fleur seeks restoration, just as the Ojibwe myths tell of wolves that protect people and provide food and clothing for them.[27] Both mother and daughter are haunted or humiliated heroines at the start of the novel, like the Gothics of old, but Fleur has become the beast, furtive and fierce. The question is whether they will stay that way by the end. Sadly, in Fleur's efforts to save what she has, her daughter seems to side with those Na-tives who call her mother "Leaves Her Daughter" (206). Lulu only spits on the ground to hear her mother's name.

One obvious objection to the comparison of Erdrich's novel to its supposed Euro-Gothic progenitors is that, because *Four Souls* takes place in North Dakota and Minnesota, the usual mise-en-scène is not to be found. There are none of the usual black castles and keeps, dungeons and treacherous moats, or ladies in white holding candelabras as they descend stairs, while ominous men in brown, hooded inquisition garb lurk late to chase, defile, and murder them. But Erdrich makes up for this lost atmosphere with an eerie mansion of her own, one that continues to register horror and loss. Glittering on a hill from far away, the new Mauser Manse (situated on a hill where an Ojibwe woman gave birth "during a bright thaw in the moon of little spirit" [4]), despite its being new, still cries, groans, sweats, and breathes out the stench of pig and cow blood which were used to color its bricks, mixing with the pungent still-bleeding sap aroma from its oak boards, the ancient timber taken from Fleur's now desecrated island on sacred Lake Matchimanito. These boards are from that felled oak that once gave shade in the scorching summer and provided a windbreak in the howling winter (a needed thing, as Minnesota and North Dakota have some of the wild-est weather extremes in the world, with winter temperatures occasionally below $-100°F$, if one factors in wind force, and summers sometimes above $100°F$). That protector oak, as it fell, smashed her island cabin. In this, Erdrich's novel has eco-Gothic concerns and elements—echoing a few other recent writers, including Elizabeth Bear, Chelsea Polk, Peter Watts, and Caitlín Kiernan. The rape of Fleur (when she was attacked by three men in a smokehouse) and the rape of her land are not far apart in time, and Fleur ends up returning to that cut

land to heal herself, a sister bond with the land that makes this one of the more memorable and involving of eco-Gothic narratives.

Like the oldest Gothic novels in existence (especially from Horace Walpole, Matthew Lewis, and Ann Radcliffe), as well as the second wave of Gothics (particularly from Mary Shelley, Charles Maturin, and the Brontë sisters), this novel mesmerizes by raising many of their same problems and subjects, but it expands or explodes the Gothic canon's treatment of them. Consider how all of these extremely traditional features are present in *Four Souls*, yet how they are metamorphosed, or a new tone or mood is taken toward them. Widely apparent in *Four Souls* is the undying Gothic theme of self-torture, but now it is felt by a whole people. Nanapush philosophizes about his and Fleur's survivor guilt: "I shared with Fleur the mysterious self-contempt of the survivor. There were times we hated who we were, and who we had to become, in order not to follow those we loved into the next world. . . . We were clumsy with knives, fire, boiling water, steel traps. Pain took our minds off . . . the mistake that we still existed" (21). There are old Gothic beguilings and trickery, tests and trials, but they are often abetted by the government and then resisted by the aboriginals: to take the land away in the first place, and then to get it back; to plan an execution of a usurper, and then for that man to escape the attempted murder. Along with such deceptions is that Gothic standard of mistaken identity (as Fleur's future White, upright, and uptight employer and sister-in-law-to-be Polly Elizabeth will say in her racist way, "Nothing in the look of her and the ignorant silence told me she could possibly end up connected to me" [13], and "It is the savage woman" [19]). The racism is compounded by a burning class tension, with the fear and anger of lower and middle classes toward the influential lumber baron who makes them toil and then goes bankrupt, unable to pay them. Unfolding with tragic Greek power are the violations and curses that riddle the novel, in the classic Gothic way. One of the damning vows a Gothic novel makes (besides the possible damnations of degeneration, infanticide, fratricide, patricide, matricide, and incest) is that a helpless or partially lame heir will be born. In the earliest Gothics arose lamentable inheritors—those sickly ones, puny, addicted, lazy, cowardly, slow, or otherwise unfit to defend the family's honor, land, wealth, and castle. Erdrich will take from this but will also find some surprise victory: her unnamed son from Mauser, a mixed-race boy, "damaged, unwhole, fractured in mind," cannot recite the alphabet, but he can play poker. With his *Rain Man*–like memory and humble appearance, her autistic savant son will win back his mother's ancestral island from the unsuspecting Indian agent Tatros at the novel's end. But no victory is complete here. What may explain his other developmental difficulties are all her own doing: she simply drank too much whiskey while pregnant and probably harmed him in vitro. The boy apparently suffers

from what has hurt a disproportionally high percentage of children among my state's Native American population: fetal alcohol syndrome. It is yet another great tragedy, and it is the novel's new and sad twist on the old Gothic's despair.

Nights with Mauser, when Fleur is not careful enough in counting between the moons of her cycle, produce their damaged heir, whom she revealingly never names but simply calls in Ojibwe, "*n'gozis*," or "the boy." It is weird sex here that, as it was in the traditionally transgressive and taboo Gothic early works, is of foremost interest to the characters, and probably to us. In *Four Souls*, the partners with the most grotesque, torturous, or alarmingly dull and quite literally anticlimactic sex must be Mauser and his first wife Placide, who would have been better named "Frosty." Human sexuality always shows the strangeness, inadequacy, and dysfunction lurking beneath the glittering surface of power and mansions and money, and here it is no different. Caressing Placide seems

> like touching the frozen body of a window mannequin whose temples, only whitened and throbbing, showed the strain. . . . Her arms were stiffly cocked and raised, her legs sprawled, her face as he formed an apology in panic was lean and mournful and suddenly gopherlike . . . her long front teeth showed. She was like a meek animal mad with fear. He fell back and turned away. (7–8)

With grim humor, Erdrich shows that Placide Armstrong Gheen is a devotee of a system called "Karezza" (37), believing that both husband and wife should save their sexual fluids. "It has had the most exciting effect on my artistic output!" (37), Placide gushes. Mercifully, one who does not know the least thing about Karezza is Fleur. She, beyond her control, makes love with this man she came to kill, a devourer of Indian land and destroyer of Indian culture. This betrayal cannot be stressed enough, for the land is everything, as without it, Natives "los[t] their trees and homes, food and subsistence lifestyles, sacred lakes and ceremonies, physical and emotional health, family patterns and members."[28] The most ironic, harrowing, and damning love within this Gothic romance unfurls when Fleur clandestinely arrives in his room in darkness, hovers over his bed, gently coaxes his head to the pillow of her breast, and whispers into his ear: "I have come here to kill you . . . slice you open . . . and take out your guts and hang them on the walls" (44, 45). It is widely known that among wolves, the alpha female is usually dominant over most members of a pack, including the males,[29] and Fleur is flouting that power now. In his unexpected answer to her, he generates our first wave of sympathy for him: "What took you so long?" (44). He is now just a rich man with an awful burden. Her heart stirs because he is seeing into her now, speaking to her in Ojibwe and pledging "to serve you" (45). "To look into the eyes of a wolf is to see your own soul," Aldo Leopold surmised,[30] and it seems the case here. Mauser looks into her bottomless eyes, identifies with her quest, and offers his body to the sacrifice. Lust in a blind moment steps in and offers more satisfaction than revenge, and "gradually,

he felt the woman's curiosity gain the upper hand" (45). He has become in Ojibwe her *g'dai*, her animal. The love scene is admirable in its easy grace, a smooth glide from taking a life to discovering a lover: "He only knew at that moment the fabulous relief as her hand lifted away from his throat. And then the shift of her body told him she was considering something else" (46).

This "something else" is the sexual theme ubiquitous in werewolf fiction. But death is supposed to come as well in these wolfish accounts. In one of the earliest notable Gothic werewolf novels, *The Phantom Ship* (1839) by Captain Frederic Marryat, there is a demonic femme fatale (ironically named Christina, or "little Christ") who transforms from woman to wolf. She digs up and devours those she has slain and proves a most difficult wife. Our Fleur is more the Shakira-type of she wolf, though, the kind with the antigravity lean and hip twitch, rather than the Christina kind. Indeed, Shakira's platinum album and song "She Wolf" bristles with the most accidental yet uncanny resonance here. For, like the moonstruck woman in the song, Fleur, too, is "in disguise," seeming to be "a domesticated girl." Fleur wanders the mansion as an "undercover" laundress, sexy yet slightly absurd in her French chambermaid's collar and cuffs, and very little understood. Fleur's nightly prowling at Mansion Mauser and her attempts to land in the master bed prove that "there's a she wolf in your closet . . . coming out, coming out, coming out," as Shakira would have it. But Fleur's failure to practice the ancient Native method of birth control with Mauser suggests, as the song goes, that "nocturnal creatures are not so prudent." In that bed of Gothic fears and delights, Fleur's body insists, just as Shakira would sing and shake it, that "it is no joke, this is lycanthropy. . . . My body's craving, so feed the hungry."[31] And who are we to argue with Shakira? And what else should a man do but oblige such compelling she-wolf logic (just as Mauser has)? On the other paw, as the narrator Nanapush concludes regarding Mauser, perhaps too bitterly, "He hadn't a notion that it would have been easier for him if she'd used her knife" (46). That there are some fates worse than being eaten by a she wolf is what the old man divines, and it could be so, but this night is theirs, and none can take away its howling joy. A strained love has blackly bloomed—that great Gothic kind, from *Wuthering Heights* forward, where, at base, love and hate are surprisingly and distressingly similar emotions, and one character (a victim) can feel simultaneous attraction and repulsion for another character (a victimizer). As the proverb goes, "When a wolf befriends you, you will be moved close to tears," and so it seems with Mauser, for better or for worse.

American Gothic Influences

Onto this Euro-Gothic Erdrich grafts a New World Gothic, an identification with animals and totemic spirits, and a belief that we have several souls at one

time in our lives, an unending battle with the outsider culture, and justified fears of both genocide and ethnocide. She is disarmingly called "Fleur" (literally, "Flower," given by a French trader's wife), yet that is a ruse. She would be better called "White Wolf," that sublime creature that blends with the snow, attacks from it, and disappears into its drifts. What Erdrich will do in her *Four Souls* is not only have her characters reappropriate some of their land, but also reclaim some derogatory and violent images, moving them from pejorative to acceptable, from base to proud, and giving us the deeper causes and meanings behind them, reclaiming and altering this depiction of "Indians on the warpath." In her sly way, Erdrich will make readers identify and vicariously enjoy Fleur's passions, her planned violence, and her enacted lust. More ambitiously, Erdrich helps herself to an Anglo-American-dominated literary movement and recurring impulse—the Gothic model—to tell a First Nation story. It is a case of double appropriation.

In a recent interview, Erdrich confessed, "Most of my books are about revenge."[32] Much of America's Gothic treatment of Native Americans is overwhelmingly written by whites and pervaded by a threatened tone and fear of vengeful attack. There were exceptions. Gothicist Washington Irving wrote that there is much "in the character and habits of the North American savage, taken in connection with the scenery over which he is accustomed to range, its vast lakes, boundless forests, majestic rivers, and trackless plains, that is, to my mind, wonderfully striking and sublime."[33] More significantly, Irving found, at an unpopular time to say it, that

> It has been the lot of the unfortunate aborigines of America in the early periods of colonization to be doubly wronged by the white men. They have been dispossessed of their hereditary possessions by mercenary and frequently wanton warfare, and their characters have been traduced by bigoted and interested writers. The colonists often treated them like beasts of the forest, and the author has endeavored to justify him in his outrages. The former found it easier to exterminate than to civilize; the latter to vilify than to discriminate.[34]

However, a more common treatment by nineteenth-century American Gothic writers is to simply depict Natives as wanting to avenge the land stolen and tribes destroyed, and as willing to do anything to the settlers. This goes back as far as America's earliest Indian Gothics, including Nathaniel Hawthorne[35] and the unapologetic Philadelphia physician Robert Montgomery Bird's bloody *Nick of the Woods* from 1837. Bird's hero, Nick, is a Kentucky frontiersman who is "struck on the head, scalped, and left for dead after the Shawnee massacre his family. He develops a demonic doppelganger who bears a . . . secret identity as Nick or Nathan the Jibbenainosay."[36] His new persona and name, translated as "the Spir-

its that Walks," allows this former Quaker to commit sudden and savage serial killings of Native Americans, sometimes leaving "a knife cut, or a brace of 'em, over the ribs in the shape of a cross."[37] For his part, Bird, in his preface, makes no apologies for this portrayal but vigorously defends it as what the Indians are and what they deserve. He says his book is a realistic remedy to the romantic notions engendered by Chateaubriand and James Fenimore Cooper, who had both "thrown a poetical illusion over the Indian character . . . [seeming to be] the embodiments of a grand and tender sentiment."[38] The Indian, says Bird, is exactly in life (unless improved by European teaching) as pictured in this fiction. What's more, Bird informs us that the American Indian has "nothing to employ him or keep him alive except the pleasures of the chase and of the scalp-hunt. . . . He is a barbarian—and it is not possible he could be anything else."[39]

Emerging from this conflict between Native Americans and explorers and settlers, "American Gothic works have traditionally incorporated hatred, secrecy, and guilt as controlling elements. Set against the backdrop of the primeval forest, the indigenous American Gothic presents destructive forces that do not exist in European experience."[40] Snodgrass describes the entrance of an American "female Gothic," starting with Louisa May Alcott's sensationalistic thrillers (over thirty of which have been recovered since 1975, showing Alcott writing as "A. M. Barnard") featuring "aggressive female protagonists . . . [having] an earthy, menacing, tempestuous streak."[41] This seems to describe Fleur's lupine character well. As Snodgrass points out, "lacking the architectural ruins and medieval backdrop of European Gothic, American Gothic derived its own conventions of terror from the motifs of law and order and survival of the fittest, . . . the threat of genocide [for the Sioux in Mari Sandoz's *Crazy Horse*, 1942], . . . graphic violence, . . . the perils of living in the wild among hostile factions, . . . melancholy, . . . vigilantism, . . . and hasty Western-style execution."[42] Beyond these dark Old West themes are the nineteenth-century Gothic developments of Edgar Allan Poe that Erdrich uses, where the great Gothic haunted house is the human mind (and Fleur tiptoes about the actual mansion each night on a mission to kill, eerily evoking the narrator of "The Tell-tale Heart"). Into the twentieth century, perhaps the greatest American Gothic influence is William Faulkner, whose family secrets and falls, dysfunction, alcoholism, ruined heirs, and forsaken communities all hold sway over *Four Souls*. What we uncover in *Four Souls* is all the salient features of the European Gothic romance melded with the harsh American Gothic of the forest and prairie, new city and old village, all with a First Nation woman who has to be more aggressive and resourceful to reclaim what is hers than nearly any remembered Euro-Gothic heroine across the sea. No one can deceive the eyes of such a she wolf. She always knows.

In the fall of 2009, the American Congress finally passed the Native American Apology Resolution, admirably pushed by Senator Sam Brownback,

Republican of Kansas.[43] The president has yet to read the historic statement aloud to any Native tribes at the time of this writing, and the resolution includes no financial reparations for past wrongs. It simply speaks regret "on behalf of the people of the United States to all Native peoples for the many instances of violence, maltreatment, and neglect inflicted on Native peoples by citizens of the United States."[44] With an inerasable debt owed by whites, and the fact that treaties with Indians were always broken, there still exists (despite this formal apology), in fiction and in life, an intense suspicion, sorrow, and rage over the massive human injuries done to Natives, a despair more inconsolable than that found in any Gothic novel from thousands of miles away, an anger that has led to addiction, self-contempt, spouse abuse, and many early deaths. But, through the compressed, poetic, and nearly intolerable beauty of her language, Louise Erdrich reminds us that Native Americans have not vanished from this earth. They will not be forgotten. Their long listening to nature and deep patience has given an understanding that should humble us. And they have the stories to hurt, horrify, and heal us now.[45] She has used, in this case, Gothic models to form a moving allegory for her people and their losses, and for the dispossessed everywhere. In *Four Souls*, we find that our grandest dreams of justice cannot be predicted, and they may trap us. We may come to kill, and then to love an enemy in a way that changes everything, mingling two bloods (Anglo and Indian) into new heirs who will have to sort out the histories, or not:

> As in all of Erdrich's books, revenge is a theme—but a complicated one, as families involved . . . intermarry. Memory is a battleground. The tribal members keep the story alive through folklore; the whites try to pretend it never happened. "In the beginning, the whites had all the power," Erdrich says, "but as one reviewer put it: The Indians have the history."[46]

The woman who wears her fur on the inside, the one with the history, our would-be Indian executioner Fleur Pillager, ends up marrying Mauser, mingles the blood, and bears his son. She even has some emotion for Mauser besides hatred, letting him take her to "theatres and great halls . . . [and] places where a thousand pictures were stored on the walls. He fed her the flesh of animals she'd never tasted" (74). Nevertheless, she won't stay with him. In this, Fleur fulfills the proverb of the forests ringing the towns where Erdrich and I were born: "However well you feed the wolf, she still looks at the woods." At the end of the book, returned to her despoiled island and away from the now foreclosed St. Paul mansion she won, does she still think of John James Mauser? "Maybe she desired him," her adoptive father Nanapush concludes, "though she never would admit it to me. . . . He seemed to get a hold over her in bed" (73, 74). This is the

tart, red, ripe truth of *Four Souls*: there is no revenge, properly speaking; there is only love, loss, and a memory of a sting in the mouth.

Notes

1. Amber Rose, ed., *Wolves: A Photographic Celebration* (New York: Metro Books, 2008), 8.

2. Shakira, interview with Caryn Ganz, "Behind Shakira's Hot Electro Groove: The Making of 'She Wolf,'" *Rolling Stone*, July 15, 2009, www.rollingstone.com/rockdaily/index.php/2009/07/15/behind-shakiras-hot-electro-groove-the-making-of-she-wolf/ (accessed April 1, 2010).

3. Louise Erdrich, *Four Souls* (New York: HarperCollins, 2004), 3. Page numbers appear hereafter in parentheses in the text. HarperCollins should be encouraged to reconsider the cover for future editions. Both the hardback and paperback feature a photograph of Hudson, New York, where no Ojibwe are, and where the natural and cultural history are as far from the novel's actual Minnesota and North Dakota settings as can be. What's more, better proofreading is hoped for in forthcoming editions to remove distracting errors such as these, appearing in both the hardbound and paperback versions: "suck doctoring frightened away the disease" (51) and "So that was how I made myself essentials again" (120). A great American writer deserves better.

4. "Culture & Traditions: A Short History of the Mille Lacs Band of Ojibwe," Mille Lacs Band of Ojibwe, 2009, www.millelacsojibwe.org/Page_History.aspx (accessed April 2, 2010).

5. "Culture & Traditions."

6. "Culture & Traditions."

7. "Culture & Traditions."

8. "Mille Lacs Kathio," Minnesota DNR, 2009, www.dnr.state.mn.us/state_parks/mille_lacs_kathio/index.html (accessed June 1, 2010).

9. "Culture & Traditions."

10. "Culture & Traditions."

11. "Culture & Traditions."

12. "Culture & Traditions."

13. Mille Lacs County would have their 2004 case for yet more land thrown out by the U.S. Supreme Court (see "Culture & Traditions").

14. "Culture & Traditions."

15. Kristen A. Carpenter, "Contextualizing the Losses of Allotment through Literature," *North Dakota Law Review* 82 (2006): 611. See also Judith V. Royster, "The Legacy of Allotment," *Arizona State Law Journal* 27 (1995): 1.

16. The long-persecuted population of Natives in these two states is now extremely low. Chippewa and other Native bands currently make up the smallest minority population in Minnesota, or 1.7 percent of its total population (see "The State of Minority Business," U.S. Department of Commerce, 2008, www.mbda.gov/?bucket_id=926&portal_

document_download=true&download_cid=6238&name=Minnesota+Profilepdf&
legacy_flag=false, accessed April 3, 2010). In North Dakota, the Chippewa and other
Native bands currently compose that state's largest minority as 5.5 percent of the population, or 35,228 people (see "Statewide Data," North Dakota Indian Affairs Commission,
2008, www.nd.gov/indianaffairs/?id=37, accessed June 1, 2010).

17. Louise Erdrich, interview with Alden Mudge, "Louise Erdrich Explores Mysteries
and Miracles on the Reservation," *Indie Bound*, 2008, www.indiebound.org/author-
interviews/erdrichlouise (accessed April 4, 2010).

18. Erdrich, interview with Alden Mudge.

19. Peter G. Beidler and Gay Barton, *A Reader's Guide to the Novels of Louise Erdrich*,
revised and expanded ed. (Columbia: University of Missouri Press, 2006), 162.

20. Beidler and Barton, *A Reader's Guide*, 56.

21. Carpenter, "Contextualizing the Losses," 609.

22. Carpenter, "Contextualizing the Losses," 609.

23. George Orwell, "Revenge Is Sour," in *The Collected Essays, Journalism and Letters
of George Orwell* (New York: Harcourt, 1968), www.orwell.ru/library/articles/revenge/
english/e_revso (accessed April 5, 2010).

24. Robert Harris, "Elements of the Gothic Novel," *Virtual Salt*, October 11, 2008,
www.virtualsalt.com/gothic.htm (accessed December 13, 2009).

25. Harris, "Elements of the Gothic Novel."

26. Rose, *Wolves*, 468.

27. Rose, *Wolves*, 343.

28. Carpenter, "Contextualizing the Losses," 612.

29. Rose, *Wolves*, 35.

30. Sam Endicott, John Hill, and Shakira Isabel Mebarak, "She Wolf," *Lyrics Mode*,
2009, www.lyricsmode.com/lyrics/s/shakira/she_wolf.html (accessed June 1, 2010).

31. Endicott, Hill, and Shakira, "She Wolf."

32. Erdrich, interview with Alden Mudge.

33. Washington Irving, "Traits of Indian Character," in *The Sketchbook of Geoffrey
Crayon* (1848; Read Print Publishing, 2010), www.readprint.com/chapter-6039/The-
Sketchbook-of-Geoffrey-Crayon-Washington-Irving (accessed April 1, 2010).

34. Irving, "Traits of Indian Character."

35. See Margaret B. Moore, *The Salem World of Nathaniel Hawthorne* (Columbia:
University of Missouri Press, 1998), 256: "In truth, Hawthorne never seemed to see the
Indian as yet civilized, an opinion he shared with most of his countrymen. In some of
the early stories he refers to Indian savagery. In 'An Old Woman's Tale' one character
has the scar of a tomahawk on his head. In 'Alice Doane's Appeal' an Indian massacre
deprives young Alice and Walter of their parents. He refers to the war cry in 'The Seven
Vagabonds' and in 'Young Goodman Brown.' At times he indicates the early view of
some of the settlers that the Indian was with the Black Man or the Devil in the forest as
in 'The Haunted Quack' or 'Young Goodman Brown.' The fear of captivity plays a part
in 'Roger Malvin's Burial' and 'Etherege.'"

36. Mary Ellen Snodgrass, "*Nick of the Woods*," in *Encyclopedia of Gothic Literature*
(New York: Facts on File, 2005), 253–254.

37. Robert Montgomery Bird, *Nick of the Woods: or, The Jibbenainosay: A Tale of Kentucky* (New York: Redfield, 1856), 24.

38. Bird, preface to *Nick of the Woods*, iv.

39. Bird, preface, iv–v.

40. Snodgrass, "Frontier Gothic," in *Encyclopedia of Gothic Literature*, 132.

41. Snodgrass, "American Gothic," in *Encyclopedia of Gothic Literature*, 6–7.

42. Snodgrass, "Frontier Gothic," 132–133.

43. Rob Capriccioso, "Native Apology Said Out Loud; Obama Still Silent," *Indian Country Today*, June 1, 2010, www.indiancountrytoday.com/home/content/95111209.html?m=y (accessed June 3, 2010).

44. Capriccioso, "Native Apology Said Out Loud."

45. Many more Native stories await discovery at Louise Erdrich's warmhearted, independent Birchbark Books in Minneapolis, Minnesota, next to the beautiful lakes, at 2115 West Twenty-first Street. My visit was a treasure, for it is a rare experience to stroll a bookshop where a major author kindly leaves handwritten Post-it-note suggestions to you for good reading on the shelves! At her Birchbark Books, writers from all over the country come to read their new works, while children are busy fetching books of wonder and hauling them up to their fort upstairs, with Native American purification herbs scenting the store and soulful art glowing from the walls. And you just might learn something of her latest creation there.

46. Louise Erdrich, interview, "Louise Erdrich: Secrets in the Indian File," *Independent*, June 6, 2008, www.independent.co.uk/arts-entertainment/books/features/louise-erdrich-secrets-in-the-indian-file-841027.html (accessed April 3, 2010).

CHAPTER 22

Andrew Davidson's *The Gargoyle*

CANADIAN GOTHIC

Karen Budra

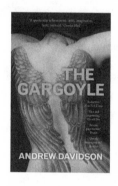

No vampires. No avenging ghosts. Not a single zombie. Instead, Andrew Davidson's lyrical first novel, *The Gargoyle*, features just that—a drug-addicted, orphaned pornographer, reduced, in a fiery car crash, to a charred ruin—a human gargoyle, as well as a possibly insane sculptress who creates stone gargoyles in penance for a sin she committed in another lifetime. We discover that these two, who meet in the burn ward of a local hospital, have been lovers in different incarnations during times of great romance: the Viking era, ancient Japan, the era of courtly love, Renaissance Italy, and Victorian England. Davidson prefaces the novel with an epigraph from Christian mystic Meister Eckhart, which sums up their relationship neatly: "Love is as strong as death, as hard as Hell."[1] Throughout the tale, Davidson grapples with themes of inspiration, love, transcendence, and art. And yet *The Gargoyle* is not a romance; it is definitely Gothic, and definitely postmodern. Most importantly, however, it is Canadian. And that, as Robert Frost says, "ma[kes] all the difference."

Canadian literature is predominantly "dark." Our most famous narrative artists, like Margaret Atwood, Barbara Gowdy, Atom Egoyan, and David Cronenberg, all write what can be called dark fiction. But Canadian Gothic, like Canadian identity, is amorphous, because Canada is a postcolonial country that was never granted independence. Reliant on England and the United States for its cultural history, Canadian Gothic art is a strange hybrid of individualism and conservatism. Canada in general, and Canadian Gothic in particular, are indeed postmodern; their reflexive nature stems from a Canadian understanding of the power and emptiness of functioning as the simulacrum or cipher of others' desires.

The Gothic has traditionally been obsessed with the past: bits of old paper, avenging ghosts, and the impossibility of escaping the ravages of time. Both British and American Gothic, in addition, focus on the monster: What does he see? Whom does he consume? And, most importantly, why is he a monster? What is his motivation? British Gothic has traditionally dealt with the dangers of class and of reaching beyond one's station in life: Manfred's desire for the title of lord of the Castle of Otranto; Victor Frankenstein's usurpation of divine creative power and his subsequent rejection of his "son," the monster he creates; Henry Jekyll's attempt to impose scientific principles on morality; and Dracula's aristocratic need for fresh territory to conquer and fresh blood to drink.

American Gothic, similarly interested in motivation, or "backstory," tends to explore the importance of family to the monster. Both Norman Bates's and Freddy Kruger's mothers have a lot to answer for, not to mention Leatherface's cannibal clan in *The Texas Chainsaw Massacre*, and even *Scream* 1 through 3 reveal that the reason Sidney, the main character, is being tortured is her mother's infidelity, and that she is being stalked by her formerly unknown half brother. Heritage is easy to trace in countries with long histories. The British and Irish can look to Lewis, Shelley, Stevenson, Stoker, LeFanu, Dickens, Hitchcock, and Clive Barker, to name just a few. Hawthorne, Melville, Poe, Lovecraft, Stephen King, and Anne Rice offer precedents to American Gothic writers.

However, Canadian Gothic has no past. Cultural critic Northrop Frye (a Canadian) confirmed this in 1982, in a series of lectures entitled "Divisions on a Ground: Essays on Canadian Culture," when he pointed out that "Canada never defined itself as a unified society. . . . [T]here is no Canadian way of life, no hundred per cent Canadian, . . . no symmetrically laid-out country. . . . [Canadians] are conditioned from infancy to think of themselves as citizens of a country of uncertain identity, a confusing past, and a hazardous future."[2]

Our history is borrowed, originally from England, and most recently, from America. Political scientist David Taras points out that "95 per cent of the movies that we watch are American. So are 84 per cent of the retail sales of sound recordings, 85 per cent of the prime time drama that we watch on English-language television, and 75 per cent on French-language TV."[3] Or at least that is what we are told we see; ironically, much of what we see when we watch America on-screen is Canada in disguise. Canadian artists have long had to "go south" to make money; traditionally, the bland, uninflected accent and nondescript Canadian "look" has made us perfect talking heads. Because of attractive exchange rates, highly trained crews, and—well—Canadian politeness, many American films are shot in Canada. In fact, according to Chris Carter, the creator of *The X-Files*, which was shot in Vancouver for its first six seasons, "Vancouver is Hollywood's biggest backlot!"[4] This Canadian city alone (in which Davidson studied English at the University of British Columbia) has doubled as Nagoya, London,

twenty-two different American states, Hong Kong, a Norwegian fishing village, the Bronx, Italy, Russia, Fantasia, and both the apocalyptic future and the Ice Age in American productions. In her 1998 story, "Death by Landscape," Margaret Atwood acknowledges Canada's cipher status, describing Canada as "nowhere definite," which can therefore "be anywhere."[5]

What Canadian Gothic writers like Andrew Davidson have done is acknowledge and embrace our cipher status by making our own, distinctive Canadian Gothic art, which explores the transgressive power of "ex-centrism" from point zero: the body. In fact, much Canadian Gothic explores the empty, or multivalent, and yet eerily familiar human body. The Canadian Gothic plot often centers on characters who suffer a change in their bodies and their relationships to the bodies of others in the exploration of their empty, lonely state. "Straight" behavior is portrayed as not only dull, but impossible for the Canadian Gothic character. Instead, the desire to cross over physical and moral boundaries is represented as a necessary part of the experience of the empty self.

Literary critic Linda Hutcheon (yet another Canadian) points out that in a postmodern world, the only place from which to criticize the status quo is from within.[6] And the bland Canadian subject exists as a kind of Trojan horse in North American culture. In short, we can get away with almost anything because no one expects us even to exist. Thus, we can say that the shock in much Canadian Gothic derives not just from the transgressions perpetrated by its characters, but by their celebration of the intense anarchic power of the unfettered imagination.

Fredric Jameson identifies an extreme attachment to intensity as a hallmark of the postmodern schizophrenic, before whom "the world comes . . . with heightened intensity, bearing the mysterious and oppressive change of affect, glowing with hallucinatory effect."[7] David Harvey elaborates on this, explaining that thus, "the image, the appearance, the spectacle can all be experienced with an intensity (joy or terror) made possible by their appreciation as pure and unrelated presents in time."[8] Shades of Burke's sublime, in which emotional intensity "lifts" the subject from ordinary existence and helps him (or her) transcend and connect in a mystical union with the spirit.[9]

This is particularly appropriate to *The Gargoyle*, in which Marianne Engel, schizophrenic, beloved, carver of gargoyles, "caress[es and] . . . coaxes the gargoyles out of their stony caverns . . . lov[es] them out of the stone" (228). She describes the experience of making her art as a "feel[ing]." She says that her "body sinks into the contours and then I feel weightless, like I'm floating . . . it's wonderful. . . . It's like being so aware . . .that I can't move because it's so overwhelming" (103). Of course, transcendence is impossible in a postmodern world, and who better than a Canadian, perhaps the perfect model of Jameson's schizophrenic, to be aware of this fact? Temporary crossing or transgression is,

however, possible for the Canadian Gothic character, and is often repeated in escalating cycles as a kind of substitute for transcendence or flight out of the monotony of ordinary life.

Before the nameless narrator of *The Gargoyle* meets Marianne Engel, his only experiences with transcendence are mediated through violence, sex, and death. Indeed, the car accident that marks the beginning of his voyage from porn star to enlightened lover, from drug addict to near ascetic, is described as "a glorious moment [in which] you achieve the empty bliss that Eastern philosophers spend their lives pursuing . . . transcendence" (2). His life until this point has been "shitty," his only coping mechanism to "imagine better [worlds]" (12). His life begins, as many Gothic characters' do, with his mother's death, and is punctuated by the subsequent deaths of his emotionally cold grandmother, who dies as "she [is] pushing [him] on a playground swing. [He goes] up into the air and stretch[es] his legs toward the sun. [He comes] back towards the earth expecting her hands to catch [him]. Instead, [he] sails past her doubled-over body" (10). And the deaths of the ironically named crack-addicted Graces, his foster parents, whose abusive treatment of him is leavened by only one day, when they take him to an air show, where he witnesses "skydivers . . . falling from sky to earth, a Hephaestian plummet . . . [that seems] like a miracle . . . the most amazing thing [he] had ever seen" (17). What Davidson does not mention is that this "exhibition" is part of the Japanese festival of O-Bon, or Day of the Death, when families float paper boats in waterways to guide the spirits of their ancestors home. In other words, it represents a kind of transcendence, a crossing of the border between death and life, past and present.

The only other times he experiences something close to transcendence are when he has sex, "so aware of the other person that I'm unsure of where she ends and I begin" (38). He says that "skin is the dividing line between people. . . . But in sex, all that changes. If skin is a fence that divides people, sex is the gate that opens your body to the other person" (148). And then he points out something central to Canadian Gothic identity: "Who you are is not permanent" (148). It is this lack of permanent identity, this cipher status, that marks this novel as quintessentially Canadian.

The gargoyles, too, are liminal, transcendent. Upon first seeing them, our narrator notices that, "in every body, disparate beasts co-existed; it was difficult to determine where one ended and the next began" (198). Which brings us to another important element of the novel: religion and myth. Because Marianne Engel (Mary Angel) is carving the gargoyles to "empty [herself] of potency to become as close as [she] can to pure art. . . . God is pure art" (206).

Just as the narrator has tried, unsuccessfully, to transcend his "shitty life," Marianne is driven to make art that frees the hundreds of hearts placed within her as penance for having sacrificed her love. In typical Gothic fashion,

however, instead of transcendence, she and the narrator are caught in what William Patrick Day calls "the Circles of Fear and Desire."[10] He argues that the Gothic exists as a mirror image or the antithesis of the romance. Like the romance hero, the Gothic hero descends into the underworld to undergo a series of "transformations." However, the Gothic hero descends against his will, often led by his unnatural desires. In *The Gargoyle*, our pornographer, high on cocaine and unfortunately gripping an open bottle of bourbon between his legs, drives off the road and over a cliff. His series of journeys through the underworld, beginning with his stay in the burn unit, force him to undergo Day's "transformations and ritual sufferings."[11] Our narrator, who describes himself as a "Kentucky Fried human," (29) whose penis has been "disposed of as medical waste" (14), is forced to undergo transformative, extremely painful medical procedures like debridement, jejunostomy, and escharotomy, or the removal of burned flesh, which is "rather like the uprising of your secret inner being, finally given license to claw to the surface" (7). Davidson, like all postmodern Gothic writers, revels in the gory details, comparing the pain of the burns to the pain of pressing one's cheek to the coils of an electric stove, which recall the circles of Dante's hell. Kelly Hurley points out, in *The Gothic Body*, that this fascination with the "plasticity of human and other bodies" is one of the central motifs of the Gothic narrative.[12]

Just as Marianne describes her obsessive gargoyle carving as "backwards art [in which you] end up with less than what you started with" (73), our narrator undergoes a recurring series of physical reductions. In fact, the motif of repetition, "of inescapable circles," continues throughout the novel. Her body, like that of the narrator, bears physical witness to her attempts to do penance for a crime of love. It is covered in mystical tattoos, including two paradoxical Latin tautologies: "*Certum es quia impossibile est*" (It is certain because it is impossible) and "*Quod me nutrit, me destruit*" (That which nourishes me also destroys me) (96). She, like other Gothic characters, is impossible for the narrator to describe: *unheimlich*. He describes her eyes as "unsolvable" (50).

She describes herself as "a vessel that water is poured into and splashes out of . . . a circle, a flowing circle between God and the gargoyles and me" (104). Indeed, the first time the narrator sees her body naked, he is struck by a sense of repetition: "my fingers felt not as if they were visiting her body for the first time but as if they were returning to a familiar location" (351). This motif of repetition arises whenever Marianne and the narrator try to connect. It also arises when, toward the end of the novel, the narrator discovers himself first buried alive, then in each of the tragic love stories Marianne has recounted to him in order to explain the fateful nature of their relationship. At one point, our narrator walks across frozen tundra with Sigurðr, a Viking who sacrificed his life for love. In an exchange that could be taken from *Waiting for Godot*, they acknowledge the fact that they are walking toward nowhere in particular:

"Where are we going?" I asked.
"I don't know."
"When will we get there?"
"I don't know." He squinted against the horizon. "I've been travel-
ing a long time. I must be getting close." (381)

In the end, they plod "ever onwards, heading to the place that he couldn't define
and I couldn't imagine" (382).

Time and space are circles in this novel. As is love. Vicky, a nineteenth-
century lover who waits twenty-two years on the cliff for her husband to return
from sea, says, "Love is an action you must repeat ceaselessly" (405). In fact,
the narrator's accident happens on Good Friday, the first day in the movement
toward Christ's resurrection, the first arc of the circle of love and redemption.
Even the serpent who lives in the narrator's spine, personifying the morphine
which keeps his pain at bay, is described in circular terms. She arrives early in
chapter 2, "slowly swimming up [his] spinal cord, swallowing it with her dis-
jointed jaw" (22). And she has a tendency to repeat herself. Most frequently,
she announces, "I am coming" (7, 22, 42, 44, 202, 234). She keeps the narrator
addicted, enslaved by his conviction that "morphine is good" (35), and that he
is, in her words, an "asshole, loser, whiner, addict, demon, monster. Devil, fiend,
beast, brute, goblin, has-been. Never-was. Never-will be. Unloved. Unlovable.
Unperson" (115).

Davidson adds an extra layer of circularity to the novel by spelling out two
messages, acrostics formed by the first letters and last letters of each chapter. Forward, it reads, "All things in a single book bound by love." And backward, "*Die
liebe ist stark wie der Tod*, Marianne" (Love is as strong as death, Marianne). This
reliance on circular structure underscores the mystical depth of the love between
Marianne and the narrator, the possibility of transcendence of the self via merging with the other. In addition, Davidson is able to dispense with the idea that
time and space are absolutes. As Day points out, once this occurs,

characters can [no longer] perceive a common reality and act in . . .
a secure relationship to the world. Rather, [time and space] become
relative functions of perception. Protagonists find that conventional
measures of time and space break down into aspects of their own
experience. . . . [Gothic] characters faint, lose consciousness, fall into
swoons or undergo blackouts [to suggest] the collapse of time and
space.

In fact, both Marianne and the narrator spend much time hallucinating,
sleeping, drugged, or entranced. We never discover how Marianne has made it
from fourteenth-century Germany to twenty-first-century America. But it does
not seem to matter because the laws of time and space are continually being

breached, not just by the characters' frequent movement between conscious and unconscious states, but because of the breaching of the main plot by Davidson's inclusion of a series of tragic love stories. They range from the story of the Italian Renaissance couple, Graziana and Francesco, forger of the arrow that shoots through time to confuse the drunken, stoned narrator as he drives along the road at the beginning of the novel; Vicki and Thomas Wennington, whose love inspires the narrator to realize, as he lies in the hospital, that "all things are inexplicably connected" (144); Old Japan's Heisaku and Sei, whose glassblowing talent brings the words "*Aishiteru*" (I love you) to the narrator; and Icelandic warriors Einarr and Sigurðr, who escorts the narrator to hell.

Most of these stories are accompanied by Marianne's provision of a lavish, beautifully described feast, both echoing the culture in which the lovers lived and the postmodern cultural mosaic that makes up most Canadian cities. They replace the narrator's experience of consuming drugs, alcohol, and empty sex, and his sense that his burned flesh is "like the steak your old man forgot on the barbecue when he got drunk" (13), with sensual bliss. Davidson describes "freshly baked round[s] of focaccia, still smelling of wood smoke, and bottles of olive oil and balsamic vinegar, . . . steaming wraps that looked like crepes but had a most bawdy smell. . . . Bastardly plump green olives. . . . Sheaves of pita and cups brimming with hummus and tzatziki" (107). "Chubby green stems of asparagus, sweating butter" appear, along with "a plump eggplant's fecund belly pregnant with stuffing" (136). When he sees Marianne naked, eating a vegetarian pizza, he notices "a cheese strand dang[ling] from her mouth to the edge of her left nipple, and . . . want[s] to rappel it like a mozzarella commando to storm her lovely breasts" (229). By the time we get to page 235, where "beady red fish eggs lolled on seaweed beds; and shrimps curled into each other, as if hugging tightly during their final moments on earth," it is clear that Davidson is both a fine poet and a gourmand, and that this neo-Gothic novel is not one to read while on a diet.

Notes

1. Andrew Davidson, *The Gargoyle* (New York: Doubleday, 2008), epigraph. In 2009, the novel won the Sunburst Award for Canadian Literature of the Fantastic, a prize for the best novel written by a Canadian using either science fiction, fantasy, magic realism, horror, surrealism, le fantastique, myth, or legend. The jury perceptively found that "an unquenchable thirst for story and a phenomenal command of his craft make Andrew Davidson's *The Gargoyle* a reader's dream. This ferociously ambitious, incendiary (at times literally) story of one man's phoenix-like transformation at the hands of a woman, possibly mad, who claims to have known him for 700 years, is prepared to fall on its own highly charged imaginative sword at any time, but never does. Davidson

manages to evoke squirm-inducing horror and abiding love with the same unblinking powers of observation and self-consciousness. As the relationship between narrator and Marianne deepens and her tale of their shared history unfolds, past and present converge in ways tragic and redemptive, and immensely satisfying." The Sunburst Award, www .sunburstaward.org/content/2009-winners (accessed April 22, 2010). Page numbers from the novel appear hereafter in parentheses in the text.

2. Northrop Frye, *Divisions on a Ground: Essays on Canadian Culture* (Toronto: House of Anansi Press, 1982), 48.

3. David Taras, "Media, Globalization, and Identity in Canada: An Introduction," in *How Canadians Communicate II: Media, Globalization and Identity*, ed. David Taras, Maria Bakardjieva, and Frits Pannekoek (Calgary, AB: University of Calgary Press, 2007), ix.

4. Chris Carter, quoted by Serra Ayse Tinic in *On Location: Canada's Television Industry in a Global Market* (Toronto: University of Toronto Press, 2005), 49.

5. Margaret Atwood, "Death by Landscape," in *Wilderness Tips* (New York: Anchor, 1998), 117.

6. Linda Hutcheon, *The Politics of Postmodernism* (New York: Routledge, 1989).

7. Frederick Jameson, "Postmodernism and Consumer Society," Athenaeum Library of Philosophy, http://evans-experientialism.freewebspace.com/jameson_postmodern ism_consumer.htm (accessed April 21, 2010).

8. David Harvey, *The Condition of Postmodernity: An Enquiry into the Origins of Cultural Change* (Oxford, UK: Blackwell, 1990), 54.

9. Edmund Burke, *A Philosophical Enquiry into the Origin of Our Ideas of the Sublime and Beautiful* (Oxford, UK: Oxford University Press, 1998).

10. William Patrick Day, *In the Circles of Fear and Desire: A Study of Gothic Fantasy* (Chicago: University of Chicago Press, 1985).

11. Day, *In the Circles of Fear and Desire*.

12. Kelly Hurley, *The Gothic Body: Sexuality, Materialism, and Degeneration at the Fin de Siècle* (Cambridge, UK: Cambridge University Press, 2004), 156.

CHAPTER 23

The Perils of Reading

THE GOTHIC ELEMENTS OF JOHN HARWOOD'S *THE GHOST WRITER*

James Doig

Some insight into the paradoxical nature of nineteenth-century *mentalité*—on the one hand a supreme confidence in the triumph of science and reason, and on the other a profound fear of the unknown—can be gained by studying the parallel development of the detective story and the ghost story. In the detective story, an event occurs that at first sight appears insoluble; the characters whisper among themselves that some supernatural agency must be at work until the brilliant detective banishes superstition by exercising the pure light of reason. By the 1890s, a subgenre of the detective story had developed in which the solution has a scientific or medical foundation that draws on the latest discoveries in, say, radiology or psychology. The other side of the coin is the ghost story, a darker and more unsettling narrative altogether in which events cannot be satisfactorily explained. In Henry James's *The Turn of the Screw* (1898), we are left wondering if the children, Miles and Flora, are the victims of the demonic attentions of Peter Quint and Miss Jessell, or if the governess is suffering from some internal affliction that she projects onto the outside world. How are we to interpret the story? James does not make it easy for us; he is the master of suggestion and ambiguity. It is this indirectness and understatement that makes *The Turn of the Screw* such a brilliantly realized ghost story.

In *The Ghost Writer* (2004), Australian poet and academic John Harwood utilizes the forms and devices of the Victorian detective story and ghost story— an epistolary narrative, family secrets, cursed legacies, crumbling mansions, discovered documents, madness, and delusion. At first glance, this seems to place *The Ghost Writer* firmly in that class of fashionable novel that attempts to imitate the Victorian mystery tale. However, this is no mere homage or pastiche,

but a reinterpretation. Harwood skillfully utilizes the techniques and tropes of nineteenth-century fiction to create a rich and complex contemporary novel that is both genuinely unsettling and enjoyable.

Much of the enjoyment is in the numerous obscure Victorian references, in the complex structure that owes something to A. S. Byatt's *Possession* (1990), and in the wonderful images and metaphors that are scattered throughout the novel. These are literary games perfectly executed by an author in complete control of his material. Harwood openly alludes to both James's *The Turn of the Screw* and his baffling *The Sacred Fount* (1901), and in Alice Jessell we have a name that combines Miss Jessell from *The Turn of the Screw* and James's sister Alice, herself a published author who suffered from delusions and died young from breast cancer.

The protagonist Gerard Freeman is a young boy growing up in the South Australian country town of Mawson. The drab, quintessentially Australian bungalow where he grows up is perfectly rendered and will be familiar to many Australians:

> Like every other house in our street, it sat squarely on a quarter-acre of dead flat ground. There was one step up to the front porch and into the hall, which was always gloomy once the door had closed. We had plaster walls, cream with an odd brownish tinge, and dark green patterned carpet that smelled faintly of dog, even though we'd never had one. To the right was my mother's bedroom, the largest of the three, then the sitting-room (never to be called "the lounge"). To the left was my father's bedroom, then mine, then the kitchen with its grey linoleum, green-painted plywood cupboards, Laminex table and chairs, and an old yellow fridge which opened with a pull handle. At night I could hear the wheeze and rattle when the motor started up. You went on through a doorway to the bathroom and laundry and a tiny alcove we called the study, on the left opposite the sunroom. The sunroom itself was a lean-to extension made of cement sheet and hardboard, the only room in the house where it was light all day.[1]

When I read this passage, I thought, "I know this house!" It was my grandparents' house that I knew so well while growing up in the 1970s, described with uncanny accuracy even down to the noisy pull-handle fridge and Laminex kitchen table, and typical of thousands of Australian suburban houses of the era.

The physical and spiritual blight of both Mawson and the house is symbolized by the constant rearguard action being played out against armies of various insects—Portuguese millipedes, bull ants, redback spiders, and the inevitable bluebottle flies. Graham, Gerard's father, devotes most of his leisure hours to the toy train set he has built in the garage; he quietly passes away at his stationmaster's chair one night watching his trains circling the track, an apt image of his own ineffectual life.

If Mawson is a sort of characterless, middle-class purgatory, a release into a richer life is provided by the vivid stories told by his mother, Phyllis née Hatherley, of her childhood in England, where she lived in a fine country house called Staplefield with her grandmother, Viola, and a cook and a maid.

Our first glimpse of just how dangerous stories can be occurs when Gerard steals into his mother's bedroom when she is asleep in the sunroom; in a drawer of the dressing table which his mother keeps locked, he finds an old paper-covered book, a typed manuscript, and a photograph of a beautiful young woman in period dress:

> I had never seen the woman in the photograph before, and yet I felt I knew her. She was young, and beautiful, and unlike most people I had seen in photographs she did not look straight at you, but gazed away to one side, her chin tilted slightly upwards, as if she did not realise anyone was looking at her. And she did not smile, at least not at first. As I went on staring at her I began to think I could see the faintest trace of a smile, just at the corner of her mouth. Her neck was amazingly long and slender, and though the picture was in black and white, I felt I could see the changing colours of her skin where the light fell across the back of her neck and touched her forehead. . . .[2]
>
> I was still kneeling in front of the drawer, lost in the photograph, when I heard a hissing sound from the doorway. My mother stood rigid, fists clenched, nostrils flared. Tufts of hair stuck out from her head; the whites of her eyes seemed to be spilling out of their sockets. For a long, petrified instant she didn't move. Then she sprang, hitting and hitting and hitting me, screaming in time to the blows that fell wherever she could reach until I broke away and fled wailing down the hall.[3]

The contrast between the ethereal photograph and the almost insane fury of Gerard's mother is unexpected and shocking. We expect a tranquil, cerebral puzzle to unfold at a leisurely pace, but the sudden intrusion of violence creates a sudden suspense and tension that makes us sit up. Harwood is a fine stylist—he can build or lower the tone of his story with a few deft strokes, and he is able to sustain our complete involvement throughout the course of the novel.

For Gerard, the greater punishment for his "sin" is that his mother never again tells him the tales of Staplefield that had been so important to him. He still clings to them, however, and his main refuge from the miseries of school are his memories of Staplefield. If Phyllis's silence is meant to extinguish Gerard's curiosity about Staplefield and her mysterious past, she fails miserably. Some time later, when Gerard is thirteen and a half, and much against his mother's wishes, he begins a pen friendship with an English girl named Alice Jessell. As a result of a car accident that killed her parents, Alice is a paraplegic living in an orphanage,

and, like Gerard, she is fond of books and reading. She describes the English countryside to him, which evokes the magic of his mother's accounts of Staplefield. This long-distance, and as it turns out long-term, relationship becomes the center of Gerard's life, and he withdraws from the company of his fellows at school and later into his work as a university librarian. The two imagine a future life in which Alice is cured of her paralysis and the two can lead a normal life together. In the meantime, they are sustained by their mutual imaginative life and by flights of telepathic autoeroticism that bind them even closer together.

A couple of years after the first exchange of letters with Alice, Gerard once again breaks into his mother's dressing table, hoping to discover information about the Hatherleys and Staplefield. He finds that the photograph and manuscript are gone, but the book is still there. It turns out to be a periodical, *The Chameleon: A Review of Arts and Letters*, volume 1, number 2, June 1898. The pages are uncut except for the last item, a ghost story by "V. H."

V. H. is Viola Hatherley, Phyllis's grandmother from Staplefield, and presumably the woman in the photograph that Gerard had seen as a child. We learn that Viola wrote several ghost stories, some of which were published in *The Chameleon* in the 1890s, others written in the 1920s that existed only in manuscript. Gerard comes across the narratives at several critical junctures in the book—filed in the British Library, found during a short trip to London to research the Hatherleys; hidden in his mother's cupboard in Mawson, found shortly after her death; and stashed in a decayed London house, the real Staplefield, found on a second trip to London during which he hoped to meet and marry Alice and finally solve the mystery of his ancestry.

These fictions are not only an integral part of the multilayered text of the novel, but they are also fabulous stand-alone tales written in perfect Edwardian style, as engaging as the Ash/LaMotte Victorian pastiche in *Possession*. In Viola's "Seraphina," Lord Edmund Napier, in pursuit of a pre-Raphaelite figure who somehow eludes him through the winding London streets, finds himself at a pawnbroker's shop at the end of a cul-de-sac:

> He paused, irresolute at the threshold, willing his eyes to penetrate the gloom within. In the light from the open door he could discern the outlines of chairs and tables and other articles of furniture crowded and heaped high, one upon the other, so as to fill both sides of the room, leaving only a narrow central passageway receding into darkness. Scents of ancient timbers and musty fabrics, of decaying paper and chill metal, of dust and rot and mould, floated about him. It was not as he had imagined a pawnbroker's shop should be; there was no counter, no sign of a proprietor; only the heaped and crowded furniture and the artificial passage, scarcely wide enough to admit him, into whose Stygian depths he continued vainly to peer. . . .[4]

How long he remained thus he could not tell, but a light began to glow dimly at the far end of the passage, or tunnel, as he perceived in the brightening gleam, for the aperture was not only framed but roofed over by the heaped furniture. Like a man under mesmeric compulsion, Lord Edmund found himself drawn into and along the passageway, which extended a surprising distance, given the mean proportions of shopfront and alley. As he emerged from the confinement of the tunnel, he was at first dazzled by the light of a single lantern held aloft by a motionless figure a few paces off to his left.[5]

The style is plain, direct, and elegant; we can effortlessly visualize the image of the shop's interior as if we are contemplating the scene in a painting. What's more, we know we are at the threshold of the supernatural, that this is the territory of the ghost story. We are compelled to follow Lord Edmund, and as we hold our breath to learn what awaits him, we realize that we are in the presence of a master of suspense. This type of "discovered text" is a common technique in ghost and detective stories—when well executed, it lends verisimilitude and a genuine sense of mystery. M. R. James used the technique frequently, brilliantly imitating medieval documents, and, in the detective story, John Dickson Carr, writing as Carter Dickson, inserts a celebrated supernatural pastiche into *The Plague Court Murders* (1935).

The Viola stories work within the novel to provide an additional layer of meaning and possibility within the different texts. Harwood alternates between Gerard's narration, his correspondence with Alice, and Viola's fictions to create an increasing sense of unease and displacement. This switching between past and present, between "fiction" and "reality," is used to great effect. The sense of disquiet becomes even more acute as Gerard comes to realize that Viola's stories seem to have the power to shape reality, to anticipate later events. To what extent can Gerard trust these texts? To what extent can we trust Gerard's interpretation of events? As in *The Turn of the Screw*, we are left wondering what is reality and what is fantasy. While *The Ghost Writer* is a compelling read that never wavers in its dramatic purpose, at another level it is a study of the nature of interpretation and the power of stories to shape our lives. In this sense, the novel has a postmodernist intent.

However, the Viola stories are more than an effective literary technique; they are fine stories in themselves, and it is not surprising to learn that Harwood wrote them first and that Gerard's narrative evolved around them. They are told in a natural, elegant period style and contain genuinely eerie moments in which an attractive yet dangerous supernatural world impinges on a lovingly described, late-nineteenth-century London landscape. Harwood is aware of the paramount importance of atmosphere and restraint in this type of story, which makes the overt descriptions of supernatural horror all the more effective when they come:

He was all in black, with what looked like a great travelling cloak draped over his shoulders, yet she could see the earth upon his clothes, for his face was lit from within by a pale blue light that shimmered and crackled in the air around him, glowing in the sockets of his eyes and in that terrible, insinuating smile. She began to back away; he did not instantly follow, but spread out what she had thought were arms before the great black cloak revealed itself as wings, unfurling hooked and leathery as he launched himself upon her with a shriek that rose in pitch and volume until it tore at her throat and went echoing out across the hillside where she found herself in the pavilion alone.[6]

Harwood is adept at fashioning the right combination of narrative tension and *frisson* that creates those hair-standing-on-end moments, but the real power of the Viola stories emerges in the context of the terrible family secret that unfolds as Gerard's quest progresses. Even Viola is spooked by their prescience: "sheer coincidence," she writes in a letter, "but there was something *unheimlich* about it." And on her deathbed, his mother chillingly tells Gerard, "*One came true.*"[7]

The true horror of the novel, the Gothic heart of it, is the awful consequences of jealousy, rivalry, and familial hatred. Harwood brings it into the light at the end of the novel, abandoning all restraint:

Lamplight gleamed upon a bald, mummified head, skin stretched like crackling over the dome of the skull, with two black holes for nostrils and a single eye burning in a leprous mass of tissue, fixing me, half a life too late, with the enormity of my delusion.[8]

On one level, *The Ghost Writer* is a homage to both Victorian Gothic romance (the sort where sibling or family rivalries and jealousies lead to feuds, exile, and worse) and the classic mystery novels of J. S. Le Fanu and Wilkie Collins (and there is certainly something of *Great Expectations* in it). Harwood draws on the tensions that exist between our rational minds, exemplified by nineteenth-century developments in science and technology, and the suggestive power of the unknown. That Anne Hatherley's demise is brought about by a "new" nineteenth-century invention is a nice touch that would not be out of place in a late-Victorian or Edwardian detective story. But it is our irrational fears that hold sway for most of the novel, and this is where the novel derives its greatest power; in this way, *The Ghost Writer* draws most of its energy from the traditions of the English ghost story.

The 1890s are wonderfully realized in the novel (perhaps not surprising for someone who has written a biography of Olivia Shakespear, the fin de siècle novelist and the woman who relieved W. B. Yeats of his long-preserved virginity), and Harwood delights in obscure references and allusions that make you reach

for reference books. Thus, a couple of Viola stories appear in *The Chameleon*, an 1890s periodical that included poetry by Victor Plarr, Olive Custance, and Theodore Wratislawe, and essays by Richard Le Gallienne and G. S. Street. In fact, *The Chameleon* is the name of a chapbook published in 1894 that lasted, evidently, for a single issue, and which published decadent fiction. Harwood displays a particular interest in Victorian art (in particular the pre-Raphaelites, John Atkinson Grimshaw, and John Martin), and paintings play a central role in several of the ghost stories, invariably as conduits to the supernatural. Again, this is a common enough trope in supernatural tales, and we see parallels with Wilde's *The Picture of Dorian Gray* and M. R. James's "The Mezzotint."

But *The Ghost Writer* is also an Australian novel. We see in it the mystery and romance of Britain as perceived by generations of Australians through books, television, and film. Gerard contrasts his dreary life in Mawson with the culturally and aesthetically superior life his mother lived at Staplefield. This is another haunting in the book—Gerard is haunted by the ghost of some imagined land of romance full of things he did not have in Mawson:

> . . . chaffinches and mayflies and foxgloves and hawthorn, coopers and farriers and old Mr. Bartholomew who delivered fresh milk and eggs to their house with his horse and cart. When she wasn't away at boarding-school, she lived with her grandmother Viola, and a cook and a maid in a house called Staplefield which had staircases and attics and more rooms than you could count.[9]

Of course, when Gerard finally goes to England, the reality is very different: "Ragged beggars lined the underpasses, wrapped in sodden cardboard, lying in pools of unspeakable filth. . . . The chaffinches had all mutated into scrofulous pigeons." Gerard does find the spirit of Britain, not in some fairy-tale vision in an English romance, or in *The Lady of Shalott*, which in his childhood daydreams he imagines to be Alice, but in the real and imagined ghosts of his own family.

Even "Staplefield" is not the country mansion of Phyllis's tales, but Ferrier's Close, a secretive house in London hidden behind high walls and massive trees. Harwood again uses a tunnel image in describing Gerard's first view of it:

> I was standing at the entrance to a tunnel about eight feet high, formed by hooped metal frames over which branches of some kind had been trained. Dim twilight filtered through an arched roof of dense greenery; a few spots of sunlight glowed on the flagged stone floor. At the far end, some thirty feet away, I could just make out two steps leading up to another door. Vines and creepers and climbing roses had grown up amongst the gnarled branches; the metal hoops were heavily corroded.[10]

Again we realize we are on the verge of the supernatural, of some tangled mystery, and we enter at our peril. Despite the novel's e-mail exchanges, Internet researches, and expert realism, we yet find ourselves in pursuit of love and an elusive family secret as our protagonist investigates a haunted house of shadowy corridors, dusty rooms, and unknown corners. We are well and truly in the realm of the Gothic—in a novel that draws inspiration from the Victorian ghost story traditions without becoming trapped in them—while Gerard Freeman gropes for the truth. Through his bitter experience, we learn the power of stories to shape lives.

Notes

1. John Harwood, *The Ghost Writer* (New York: Harcourt, 2004), 8.
2. Harwood, *The Ghost Writer*, 4–5.
3. Harwood, *The Ghost Writer*, 5.
4. Harwood, *The Ghost Writer*, 40.
5. Harwood, *The Ghost Writer*, 40–41.
6. Harwood, *The Ghost Writer*, 268.
7. Harwood, *The Ghost Writer*, 121.
8. Harwood, *The Ghost Writer*, 367.
9. Harwood, *The Ghost Writer*, 7.
10. Harwood, *The Ghost Writer*, 233.

CHAPTER 24

Making Fish Out of Men

GOTHIC UNCERTAINTY IN *GOULD'S BOOK OF FISH* BY RICHARD FLANAGAN

Robert Hood

> The question that haunts me as they chase me & as I chase brine-scrimp & lurk around the fish-rich reefs off Bruny Island that I have made my home, is this: is it easier for a man to live his life as fish, than to accept the wonder of being human?

—Richard Flanagan, *Gould's Book of Fish* (400)

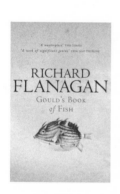

Metamorphosis and the violation of social and physical norms is a recurrent theme in Gothic literature. The living become the dead, and the dead mimic life. Werewolves prowl as humanity takes on the form of animals and animals become demonic phantoms. Arcane and sinister realities hide their true nature under a veneer of normality, while external environments reflect the guilt and passion that drive human protagonists.

The imagery of physical transformation and the intrusion of abnormal potentialities into established, consensual reality are metaphorical conceits that offer powerful entry into the dark, mortality-haunted world of the Gothic. The metamorphosis that sees words giving form to emotion and desire is what creates the ghosts and monsters that dwell in the Gothic's dark world. It is a world where words have power, and that is why books and the dark places associated with books play such an important part in the construction of the Gothic genre.

Gould's Book of Fish, though ostensibly a work of literary fiction, fits into this shadowy literary menagerie easily, representing a modern Gothic sensibility despite its particular historical setting and deliberately odd, and self-consciously archaic, language. Its Gothic credentials are many, ranging from a bizarre fram-

258

ing narrative, to the frequently macabre world it explores and the characters that inhabit it, to its constantly morphing themes of change, mental or physical imprisonment, corrupt authority, unreliability of memory, and the histories that these give birth to. Flanagan's book depicts a world that is shadowy, exuberant, sensual, grim, joyous, dangerous, stubborn, and changeable.

It is a world entered through a book.

Gothic Libraries

Bookshops are dark, exotic places in which dangerous strangers, perversions, and fantastical creatures lurk. Not the brightly lit, safe kind—not the chain stores where everything is sanitized and neatly ordered—but those cramped, labyrinthine repositories of wonder and fear and desire that are becoming rarer and rarer as the art of browsing and the lure of the past are shoved aside by catalogued best sellers and prepackaged wish lists. *Real* bookshops are Gothic in their internal architecture, creating narrow corridors, dark backwaters, and sinister hideaways, barely restraining the chaos of human imagination, stinking of ancient truths and dark lies, its rotting deep-sea detritus denying the possibility that any "official history" is an absolute depiction of reality. They are repositories of the past crammed into a narrow space. The possibilities that such places winkingly offer can be unexpected and familiar, modern and ancient, comfortable and comfortably disturbing. Above all, such living mausoleums and the books they house act as a prison colony for words—beautiful, foul, brilliant, black, sickening, enchanting, unspeakably enchanting words. Words change everything. What's past is past? No, let words loose on what's lost and see what happens to our memories. Words open a path to the ineffable.

For this reason, cluttered, secondhand bookstores, moldy libraries, and their artifactual kin, the bric-a-brac emporiums and junk shops—along with the curios and dusty tomes they contain—are a mainstay of the Gothic imagination. Necronomicons, books of blood, grimoires, coded manuscripts, ancient volumes of forgotten lore, terrifying autobiographies, and unexpected, apocalyptic diaries can be found in the pages of Gothic narratives, waiting to ensnare the unwary protagonists and drag them willingly or unwillingly into a darkness from which they cannot escape.

Controlled Chaos

Gould's Book of Fish has two central images for the eldritch power of books and the words they contain, images that explore the impact of words on reality and define the novel's structure.

The first and most encompassing is the *Book of Fish* itself. Despite its innocent title, *Gould's Book of Fish* represents controlled chaos, a fearful outpouring not just of truth but also of change. It is a book about transformation—dark, violent, glorious transformation. It is also about the intolerable suffering of victims and the ultimate mutability of history, or human memory's susceptibility to decay. As Sid Hammett, its secondary creator and initial narrator—a con man who "repurposes" junk furniture as valuable antiques—makes clear from the first paragraph, the *Book of Fish* is a mystical artifact, changing like the sea creatures it contains and causing those who read it to transmogrify:

> My wonder upon discovering the *Book of Fish* remains with me yet, luminous as the phosphorescent marbling that seized my eyes that strange morning; glittering as those weird swirls that coloured my mind and enchanted my soul—which there and then began the process of unraveling my heart and, worse still, my life into the poor, scraggy skein that is this story you are about to read. . . . We—our histories, our souls—are, I have since come to believe in consequence of his [Billy Gould's] stinking fish, in a process of constant decomposition and reinvention, and this book, I was to discover, was the story of my compost heap of a heart.[1]

The actual Tasmanian-born author of *Gould's Book of Fish*, Richard Flanagan, has his antique-forging narrator present Gould's original version of the book as a pseudosupernatural object right from the get-go, in a modern Gothic sequence that exudes all the uncanny antiquarian foreboding of Poe or M. R. James. Hammett recounts how he found the *Book of Fish* one "fateful" winter's morning in a junk shop in Hobart, Tasmania—inside an old galvanized-iron meat safe, under a heap of women's magazines. He describes his first reactions thus:

> Oddly, it smelt not of the sweet must of old books, but of the briny winds that blow in from the Tasman Sea. I lightly ran an index finger across its cover. Though filthy with a fine black grime, it felt silky to the touch. It was on wiping away that silt of centuries that the first of many remarkable things occurred. . . . For beneath that delicate black powder something highly unusual was happening: the book's marbled cover was giving off a faint, but increasingly bright purple glow.[2]

The air of supernatural oddity gets more obvious as the cover becomes "a mass of pulsing purple spots," and trying to scratch away the phosphorescence only transfers the effect to his hands, "as if I had already begun a disturbing metamorphosis."[3] What he finds when he investigates the inside of the book is a "dreadful hodgepodge" of paintings and words—beautiful images of fish surrounded by a

mass (and a mess) of heavily layered scribblings. It is the diary of a convict—a convict named William Buelow Gould—his private, and illicit, *Book of Fish*.

It is not, however, the one already known to us. There is in the Tasmanian State Library a work known as W. B. Gould's *Sketchbook of Fishes*, containing paintings by William Buelow Gould (1801–1853). History tells us that Gould was a porcelain painter from Liverpool who was transported to Van Diemen's Land for stealing "colors." His National Library of Australia biographical description reads as follows:

> In 1832, after committing several offences, [Gould] was sentenced to Macquarie Harbour, where he was assigned to work as a house servant for Dr. William de Little. De Little, a student of natural history, provided the impetus for the *Sketchbook of Fishes in Macquarie Harbour*, asking Gould to paint subjects he had collected from the beaches.[4]

What Hammett finds is not this authorized collection of beautiful zoological sketches, but a different, subversive *Book of Fish*, one, we learn, with identical pictures that Gould made in order to tell his personal story—painstakingly scrawled in whatever writable liquid he could find, on the scraps of paper he managed to secret in his cruel, damp jail cell toward the end of his life. This *Book of Fish* tells the "true" story of colonial Tasmania—dark, funny, violent, messy, horrific, and fantastical though it may be. It obsesses Hammett. He tries to get the book published, but despite authenticating date testing, no one is able to accept its deviations from standard historicity. The last word comes from an eminent colonial historian, who states that while it is clever, it is clearly a fake, and suggests that the only way to get it published might be as a *novel*—which is, of course, exactly the form in which we have received it.

The book's occult nature doesn't end with its remarkable behavior when Hammett found it, nor with the coincidental existence of two divergent books of fish.

The book seems to write itself as Hammett reads it, as though time is bending back on itself—and then, once he is finished, it disappears mysteriously. Distraught and filled with Gothic obsession, Hammett rewrites the book from memory. So we have four layers of individual input onto the *Book of Fish* as it exists for us in the present—not counting our own.

Alternate Realities

The second major collection of books to appear is toward the novel's end, when Gould finds a huge archive of journals in a room above his prison cell, to which

he gains access thanks to the sea that regularly floods his prison. Filled with curiosity, he begins to read the journals, which had been written by Danish clerk Jorgen Jorgensen, the official record keeper for the colony. In vain, Gould looks for an account of the oddities and brutalities that have characterized his experience of the place. Where is the commandant's insane nation of "Nova Venezia"? Where is the Great Mah-Jong Hall, the commandant's purchase of South American locomotives, his sale of vast tracks of wilderness, or his various audacious economic schemes, including bartering the Australian mainland for tourist merchandise?

Most significantly, where was the account of the extremes of barbarism, the insane and ongoing humiliation of the indigenous population and the convicts? None of it is there. Instead, Gould finds an intricately depicted alternate reality, an official account that turns the extreme past into a more rational history of gradual, civilized development.

But the "old Dane" goes beyond the mere bureaucratic obscuring of the negative aspects of colonization, as demanded by Governor Arthur and the Colonial Office, who had requested "full acquittals, reports, inventories & audits, all of which demanded an untruthful response, the portrayal of the penal colony as they might imagine it & not as we knew it to be."[5] In the exhilaration of his rejigging of history, a moment came for the Dane when, "dipping his quill in demons," he discovered that imagination took over. In himself, he discovered, "was all men & women: all good, all evil, all love, all hate, & all time." In his account, says Gould, "everything was different":

> Every life, every action, every motive, every consequence. Time, which the Commandant understood to be something of which we were all inexorably composed, our essential substance & lifeforce, was in these accounts something separate from us—so many equally weighted bricks that together made the wall of the present that denied us any connection with the past, & thus any knowledge of ourself.[6]

This deception denied everything and stole real connection with the world from Gould and his fellow sufferers. In short, the register usurped reality. It was a product of imagination corrupted by authoritarian power: "A book now existed with the obscene ambition of becoming the world."[7]

After Jorgensen discovers Gould in his registry and through a gargoyle fog of hysteria accuses him of being a "counterfeiter," attacks him, and in the struggle is killed by his own tomes, Gould determines to salvage the library—a determination that ends in disaster, scheduled execution, failed revolution, and personal transformation into a fish.

Gothic Mutability

The significance of all of this is what it says about the novel's themes. The book's labyrinthine structure, where everything is mutable and where the story is perpetually filtered through a multitude of consciousnesses, is itself an image of our awareness of reality—a confused mixture of experience and official history that is impossible to pin down. Experience, memory, and history are all mutable and subject to change. Even physical form changes. Gould's experiences and his obsessive concentration on drawing the fish that abound in the waters surrounding them provide the impetus for his own metamorphosis. As a metaphor for mortality, this transmogrification represents both transcendence and an escape from the horrors, and glories, of human existence.

Mutability is a theme that recurs throughout Gothic literature, whether the metamorphosis reflects the physical transformation of man to beast (as in werewolves or Robert Louis Stevenson's *Dr. Jekyll and Mr. Hyde*) or the perceived transformation of a loving husband into a cruel tyrant as familiarity brings out the reality he has kept hidden. Our understanding of the world and what it is capable of is something that we continually create and re-create—in order to survive (like Gould) or to gain power (like the commandant). Change and mortality are intricately bound together.

Gould's Book of Fish, as we have seen, is structured around processes of change, and the imagery of change and death is everywhere in it. Natives are killed and their bones and skulls repurposed. Starvation leads to changes in form. A forger becomes an artist. Mr. Lempriere—an anatomical naturalist who had turned black heads into white skulls in his pursuit of spurious scientific justifications for the principles of racial superiority—transforms into a pile of excrement thanks to Castlereagh, the pig he constantly regaled with his philosophies. The commandant metamorphoses into "a cetacean legend" as he is gutted on the quarterdeck of a black whaling ship by mutineers. Even Gould is transformed into a fish at the end—and his transformation, though equally ironic as the other acts of mortality described in the book, is more embraced and liberating. Nevertheless, it is an image of death and the "sea change" it brings.

Governing these changes is the power of the word to transform reality, because words carry the current of imagination. The change can be tyrannous or liberating—that is up to us. Mystical poet William Blake knew this. He, too, wrote of the changes that come through the power of rational tyranny on the one hand (which is intent on changing our perception of the world into a form that holds us captive), and the imagination on the other (where breaking the "mind-forged manacles," as described in his 1794 poem "London," frees us from a rigid perception that keeps us bound to a nonspiritual falsehood). The "rational"

colony and its historical renovation is what Gould leaves behind when his mind is freed and he astounds those who were set to execute him by becoming a fish, possibly a striped cowfish, and swimming away.

"Official versions" and the reality they fail to reflect, as well as the very forms of life itself, were always mutable, metamorphosing things to the Gothic imagination, and *Gould's Book of Fish* appends this vision to Tasmanian colonial history in a way that is both unique and liberating. Sometimes truth can only be revealed by overturning the official versions of history. This, too, was something Blake understood and embraced in his "Prophecies." He created a "Bible of Hell" (an apocryphal text) in order to cut through the repressive chains of official church dogma. His personal mythology is full of gods and demons of his own creation, struggling to free humanity from the monstrous forms it has been forced to adopt. Flanagan's book attempts the same liberation.

Flanagan evokes another colonial history that reflects on this liberation in the rather enigmatic line with which he opens *Gould's Book of Fish*: an epitaph from a writer who may be America's most renowned literary Gothicist, William Faulkner. Faulkner's inexplicable words (unless alcoholism is implied)—"My mother was a fish"—suggest both the inspiration for one of the book's major thematic elements and an affinity for mutable truth that draws parallels between the Tasmania that Gould's tale illuminates and America's own colonial "New World" illusions.

At the book's end, as Gould takes the metaphor of change from an intellectual conceit into the actuality of history by becoming a fish, he offers a test and an exemplar of a central observation by the father of American poetry—perhaps still its most mystical prophet of the line where love, life, and death meet—Walt Whitman. Whitman, who continually questioned what we have lived and loved for, and why, mused in 1855 that animal company was far superior to that of humans:

I think I could turn and live with the animals . . . they are so placid and self contained,
I stand and look at them long and long.
They do not sweat and whine about their condition,
They do not lie awake in the dark and weep for their sins;
They do not make me sick discussing their duty to God;
Not one is dissatisfied . . . not one is demented with the mania of owning things;
Not one kneels to another, nor his kind that lived thousands of years ago,
Not one is responsible or industrious over the whole earth.[8]

Though never mentioned in *Gould's Book of Fish*, Whitman's return to natural innocence and scorn of external authority—like Blake's—parallels that of William Gould. Fishy Billy is given an unprecedented and firsthand opportunity to test Whitman's claim, and, uncannily echoing Whitman's language, Gould-

as-fish restates the great American poet's dark speculation that the animals we eat are truly better company than humanity will ever be. Hell is other people—and the authoritarian illusions they impose—but fish are divine. Swimming in the waters of natural innocence, Gould concludes,

> I like my fellow fish. They do not whinge about small matters of no import, do not express guilt for their actions, nor do they seek to convey the diseases of kneeling to others, or of getting ahead, or of owning things. They do not make me sick with their discussions about their duties to society or science or whatever God. Their violences to one another—murder, cannibalism—are honest & without evil.[9]

That Whitman's revolutionary *Leaves of Grass* was published two years after the historic William Gould died makes this underwater verification of *Leaves of Grass* all the weirder and more time tossed.

The Creation of New Forms

While the practice is hardly new, recent times have seen an increasing tendency for literary forms to cross-breed, blurring the borders between genres in order to forge new ways of seeing the world and telling its stories.

A recent, particularly gaudy example was a surprise best seller and came about when a modern author playfully took a classic "official text" (now conveniently in the public domain) and changed it in ways that reflect a contemporary popular obsession: the zombie apocalypse subgenre. *Pride and Prejudice and Zombies*, written by Jane Austen and Seth Grahame-Smith (2009), takes the words of Austen's Regency romance and injects them with heavy doses of "Ultraviolent Zombie Mayhem," turning Elizabeth and her sisters into Buffy-esque slayers of the undead. So successful was the book that it created what amounts to its own subgenre. Ben H. Winters has subsequently cowritten *Sense and Sensibility and Sea Monsters* (2009, again with Jane) and the Tolstoyan mash-up *Android Karenina* (2010), which translates the classic work into an alternate steampunk nineteenth-century world of robots and space travel.

As well as these literary mash-ups, there are historical mélanges, such as Grahame-Smith's *Abraham Lincoln: Vampire Hunter* (2010). In fact, it seems that transposing Gothic monstrosities and the tropes that flow from them into history and less fantastical literature works remarkably effectively, going on public response. Sherlock Holmes, for example, has received the hybridization treatment many times. Sir Arthur Conan Doyle's Sherlock Holmes stories—themselves often Gothic in atmosphere, as illustrated by the best-known Holmes tale, *The Hound of the Baskervilles*—have been a target of this sort of artistic mutation

for well over a decade. The anthology *The Improbable Adventures of Sherlock Holmes*, edited by John Joseph Adams (Night Shade Books), features stories written by major authors in which the iconic consulting detective must deal with cases that are rather more fantastical than had been recorded previously by Holmes's official biographer, his good friend Dr. Watson: Holmes versus aliens, ghosts, demons, and even dinosaurian refugees from Doyle's own novel *The Lost World*. After all, as Holmes was wont to say, "When you have eliminated the impossible, whatever remains, however improbable, must be the truth."

In many ways, *Gould's Book of Fish*, published in 2001, was a precursor of the trend—though more subtle in execution and with stronger, and deeper, thematic intent. Flanagan has reenvisaged an official history, giving it a heavy injection of Gothic sensibility. The hybridization takes place at almost every level. As we have seen, the book structurally reflects the major preoccupations of Gothic literature, and the imagery of the Gothic is strong throughout. Darkness, monstrous behavior, forbidden sex (with both German pastors' wives and also striped cowfish), skulls, cannibalism, grotesque torture devices, weird and gruesome scenes of death, and a savage distancing from normality (or perhaps the classic Gothic revelation that normality is a facade that is too easily punctured)—all of these provide a rich Gothic texture. Gould uses frequent supernatural metaphors to describe the landscape and events that take place in it, for instance, "The huge fire was wild with it all, & then the surrounding bushes spontaneously combusted from its banshee-breath & the night sky began to thrum to its growing banshee-wail."[10] And when, in the midst of an increasing delirium, Gould realizes that his past life has been obliterated thanks to the old Danish clerk's register, he feels "a sickening horror" of the old Gothic kind: "Gargoylish faces seemed to cluster at the windows far above & plead for something to appease their endless suffering that went unremembered & unrecounted."[11] He even refers to the Tasmanian bush as "the wild woods of Transylvania,"[12] as, exiled from the past and human norms, he escapes into the wilderness.

The Dickensian eccentricity of the people Gould must work under, and their obsessive and bizarre schemes, all form a sensual lusciousness that is Gothic in its invitation to madness. The failed attempts to build civilization (or impose it) amid the primal forests establishes a familiar Gothic human fragility and a devouring nature. The narrator as victim (Gould was convicted of stealing "colors") evokes characters in traditional Gothic works who are often seduced by beauty, becoming victims of an uncontrollable passion. All these illustrate how profoundly Flanagan has grafted a Gothic sensibility onto the story of William Gould.

There is no doubt that Flanagan's novel is too original and eccentric to be easily classifiable. Its darkly cheeky multilayering, historical distortions, and convoluted narrative turn history on its head, but that it offers a Gothic view

of history is evident on every page. Flanagan has used these Gothic qualities to powerfully retell history, to force it to reveal the truths that "authority" has clouded and hidden from view. In the end, the novel meditates on the cost of the human desire to control, to manipulate history, that governments—and perhaps all of us—are prone to. Perhaps it is best, then, to transform oneself, casting off the oppressive human form to live as a fish, free to swim the depths and watch the endless procession of human history as it goes its fraudulent, cruel, and controlling way. At this point, Billy is finally beyond the penal horrors of "convicts [that] flogged convicts & pissed on blackfellas & spied on each other, . . . blackfellas [who] sold back women for dogs & speared escaping convicts."[13]

Still, as a fish, the desire to be human remains. The power of human speech and the possibility that his pictures, too, would speak, and the "wonder of being human,"[14] all haunt him. What's more, another dark end awaits beneath the waves:

> For out there, only just beyond our vision, the net is waiting for us all, ever ready to trap & then rise with us tangled within, fins flailing, bodies futilely thrashing, heading to who knows what chaotic destiny. Love & water.[15]

Conclusion

In its labyrinthine way, *Gould's Book of Fish* is about the mutability of narrative, indeed of reality itself. Words, as the couriers of imaginative power and desire, take the world and turn it into something else—convict to artist, fiction to history, man to fish. This transmogrification takes place at the level of Flanagan's writing and questions its relationship with history itself. Flanagan's use of Gothic imagery and themes allows him to forge a complex vision of the present's relationship with the past and to meditate on the dark passions and cruelties that are the result of the will to dominate and control.

Notes

1. Richard Flanagan, *Gould's Book of Fish: A Novel in Twelve Fish* (Sydney: Pan Macmillan, 2001), 1–2.

2. Flanagan, *Gould's Book of Fish*, 11–12.

3. Flanagan, *Gould's Book of Fish*, 13.

4. "W. B. Gould's *Sketchbook of Fishes*," National Library of Australia, http://nationaltreasures.nla.gov.au/index/Treasures/item/nla.int-ex5-s2 (accessed December 27, 2009).

5. Flanagan, *Gould's Book of Fish*, 284.

6. Flanagan, *Gould's Book of Fish*, 285–286.

7. Flanagan, *Gould's Book of Fish*, 291.

8. Walt Whitman, *Song of Myself* (facsimile edition from the Rare Book and Manuscript Library, University of Pennsylvania), *American Poetry Review*, 2009, lines 684–691.

9. Flanagan, *Gould's Book of Fish*, 398.

10. Flanagan, *Gould's Book of Fish*, 339.

11. Flanagan, *Gould's Book of Fish*, 290.

12. Flanagan, *Gould's Book of Fish*, 336.

13. Flanagan, *Gould's Book of Fish*, 401.

14. Flanagan, *Gould's Book of Fish*, 400.

15. Flanagan, *Gould's Book of Fish*, 402.

CHAPTER 25

Raised By the Dead
THE MATURATIONAL GOTHIC OF NEIL
GAIMAN'S *THE GRAVEYARD BOOK*

Richard Bleiler

Whether Neil Gaiman's *The Graveyard Book*[1] should be considered a twenty-first-century Gothic novel depends entirely on the many ways in which the word *Gothic* can now be defined. There was at one time an established body of historical literature that one could point to when discussing Gothics—works listed in such bibliographies as Montague Summer's *A Gothic Bibliography*[2] or discussed in Frederick Frank's *The First Gothics*[3] and cited in his *Guide to the Gothics I,*[4] *II,*[5] and *III*[6]—and be certain that one's audience would agree that these works were indeed Gothic, that they shared certain elements, reused certain plot devices, and had a certain commonality of theme, and that works not listed in these bibliographies might reasonably be excluded from discussion. Similarly, one could reference a handful of notable critics—in addition to the two named already, Edith Birkhead[7] and Devendra Varma[8] should be named—and find a reasonable similarity of canon and definition. Those times are no more. When authors as stylistically and thematically diverse as Raymond Chandler, Anton Chekhov, Brett Easton Ellis, William Faulkner, Thomas Hardy, Joyce Carol Oates, Walter Pater, and Ruth Rendell can be called and have been identified as Gothic writers—and they have—one may justifiably argue that the word *Gothic* has been applied in so many ways, in so many places, and to so many authors and works that it has effectively lost all of its original meaning. It has, as David Punter states, "a range of different applications" while failing to acquire a new meaning among either critics or anthologists.[9] The 1991 anthology *The New Gothic* is a case in point.[10] It is an excellent anthology, but it is successful despite its editors, Bradford Morrow and Patrick McGrath, being largely unable to define what they have assembled.

Their introduction is primarily historical and external, tending to focus on what they describe as the *furniture* of the historical Gothic: "subterranean passages, vaults, dungeons, cellars—these are all staples of the early gothicists."[11] Only in their concluding paragraphs do they attempt to define the contemporary Gothic and link the twenty-one works in their anthology to it:

> That the gothicists of the past created an artistic vision intended to reveal bleaker facets of the human soul is a given; that such an impulse is very much alive in contemporary British and American fiction is the assumption that underpins this anthology of stories and excerpts from novels. Though no longer shackled to the conventional props of the genre, the themes that fuel these pieces—horror, madness, monstrosity, death, disease, terror, evil, and weird sexuality—strongly manifest the gothic sensibility.[12]

For all that this definition is intuitively understandable, acceptable, and accessible, it is based on assertions that cannot be proven and claims that cannot be measured. What are "the bleaker facets of the human soul" and "the gothic sensibility"? Who defines them, and how? Furthermore, in casting their net, Morrow and McGrath cast it too widely, for virtually any reader should be able to locate stories that feature "horror, madness, monstrosity, death, disease, terror, evil, and weird sexuality," and to say these are all Gothic is, again, to show that the term is so widely applied that it has lost all meaning.

For all that one may fault Morrow and McGrath, their concepts and conclusions largely anticipate those of many later scholars. The critic and theorist Jean Paul Riquelme, for example, devotes a significant portion of his "Gothic History, the Gothic Tradition, and Modernism" to creating a linkage of "the Gothic with literary modernism, an influential body of writing and writers generally associated with the first half of the twentieth century whose limits and defining character remain to be convincingly described by critics of literature and culture."[13] He reasonably identifies a variety of works and genres, but a solid, convincing, and different definition does not emerge. Works by other critics possess similar problems: the word is defined partially in terms of its history, partially in terms of its "furniture," and partially in terms of the emotions it evokes or is intended to evoke. At this point, any literary work possessing, among other elements, stylistic bleakness, thematic morbidity, and outré characters, behaviors, settings, or descriptions may be called and considered Gothic by somebody, and there are few who would disagree.

If one accepts that the word *Gothic* is now not only largely undefinable but has achieved a peculiar and convenient kind of transcendence, meaning almost all things to almost all people, and then returns to *The Graveyard Book*, what is one faced with? *The Graveyard Book* is at its core a bildungsroman, describing

the maturation and education of an English boy, Nobody "Bod" Owens, who is raised by the ghosts in a graveyard after his parents are killed. Bod is loved by the ghosts and during the course of his development establishes a variety of relationships with the graveyard's denizens; he learns of the powers of friendship and the importance of life. In addition to the ghosts, Bod is instructed by, and bonds with, Silas, the graveyard's caretaker, and with Miss Lupescu, who assists Silas. He briefly attends school in the "real" world but must leave when he becomes the subject of unwelcome attention. Scarlett, a little girl he befriended near the beginning of the novel, returns near the end and is peripherally involved when Bod is menaced by the organization that killed his parents. With the assistance of his friends and through the use of his wits, he emerges victorious, but Scarlett misunderstands his actions and leaves, breaking his heart. At the novel's conclusion, the adolescent but mature Bod leaves the graveyard and death and embraces the mysteries and wonders of life: "Bod walked into it [life] with his eyes and his heart wide open."[14]

Although fantastic incidents and events have been omitted, such are the surface events of *The Graveyard Book*, and if one accepts the surface events as the story of *The Graveyard Book*, it is not and cannot be considered a Gothic work, even if one permits great liberties with the term. It is a work that, while not completely lacking in Morrow and McGrath's "horror, madness, monstrosity, death, disease, terror, evil, and weird sexuality," does not focus on these and, when presenting them, does not offer them in the context of "an artistic vision intended to reveal bleaker facets of the human soul." Nevertheless, there is significantly more to *The Graveyard Book* than its surface narrative, and it is possible to argue that Gaiman's narrative contains a variety of Gothic motifs, occasionally presented explicitly but more often than not presented allusively and adumbratively. In this vein, when its allusions are followed, *The Graveyard Book* can be seen as a work whose models tend to be those works in which humans are frail and vulnerable, adrift in a dangerous and constantly menacing world in which the certainty of death is the only guarantee of safety. Nevertheless, rather than simply presenting the motifs, Gaiman subverts them, adapting them to his story. The remainder of this chapter will identify some of the most overt Gothic elements and then ask whether these are sufficient to justify describing *The Graveyard Book* as either a Gothic or a neo-Gothic work.

The Graveyard Book begins with an evocative series of horrific images: "There was a hand in the darkness, and it held a knife."[15] The knife is held by the black-clad Jack—whose name of course evokes Jack the Ripper—who has just killed Bod's parents and older sister. That their deaths occur offstage and are described in passing makes them none the less horrific, and whether Gaiman intended it or not, the blackness surrounding their deaths offers an odd echo of the black first death in Horace Walpole's *The Castle of Otranto*, in which

Manfred's son Conrad is found crushed by "an enormous helmet, a hundred times more large than any casque ever made for a human being, and shaded with a proportionable quantity of black feathers."[16] There are few enough semblances between *The Graveyard Book* and *The Castle of Otranto* that it is worth mentioning one additional linkage: in both works, the behavior of the main characters and the subsequent development of the stories are motivated by and conceived as responses to unexpected and untimely deaths. This in itself means nothing, however, for the same can be said about such works as *Hamlet* and any number of western and suspense novels.

Not linked with *The Castle of Otranto* but more directly linkable to many Gothic novels are the graveyard, a staple of the traditional Gothic; that Bod is an orphan with a mysterious past; and, somewhat more tenuously, Gaiman's Jack, who is later revealed as a member of a secret society of magicians, all having *Jack* as their forename and a thematically related surname (e.g., Dandy, Frost, Ketch, Nimble). This secret society of purposeful criminals—their goal is power and world domination—echoes the many bandits, brigands, and ruffians that abound and propel the plot in such novels as Ann Radcliffe's *The Mysteries of Udolpho* and *The Romance of the Forest*. Graveyards, orphans, and villains do not make a novel a Gothic novel, of course, but they nevertheless should be mentioned as three more such elements in *The Graveyard Book*.

Bod escapes Jack because he takes refuge in a nearby graveyard, where the ghosts protect him and their caretaker Silas misdirects the pursuing Jack. As the ghosts argue what to do with the boy, they are visited by a woman on a white horse, "of the kind that the people who know horses would call a 'grey.'"[17] This is the Lady on the Grey, and though Gaiman never explicitly states it, she is Death's hypostasis or Death's harbinger. Death riding a pale horse is not necessarily a Gothic image—it is medieval and long predates the start of the Gothic movement—but it is nevertheless a traditionally horrific one, linking the Lady on the Grey to one of the four horsemen of the Christian apocalypse in the biblical Book of Revelation. Nevertheless, even though the Lady on the Grey may be linked to a horrific image of death and destruction, Gaiman subverts the linkage by making it gentle and almost benevolent: it is a Lady on the Grey, not the skeletal Death wielding a scythe to reap human souls.

When Bod is six years old, Silas briefly leaves the graveyard and leaves him in the custody of his friend Miss Lupescu, whom Bod finds unfriendly, unsympathetic, and demanding. The reader recognizes that she is none of these, but before Bod discovers the depths of her affection for him, he must learn the consequences of ignorance and rash decisions. Miss Lupescu deserves attention: though she uses a Russian word (*Da*), her name is probably Romanian, but whatever her ethnicity, hers is a name that is relatively uncommon in fantastic literature. The only other character bearing this name appears to be in Anthony

Boucher's "Mr. Lupescu."[18] In Boucher's tale, Mr. Lupescu, though he is mortal, appears to be a terrible vampire in order to misdirect a little boy while committing murder; in Gaiman's story, the opposite occurs: Miss Lupescu appears to be a rigid old woman, but she is in fact much more, and before the story's conclusion, the reader learns that she is a heroic werewolf, a tenacious Hound of God who "will pursue an evildoer to the very gates of Hell."[19]

Furthermore, Miss Lupescu's lessons touch upon the outside world, but hers is not the reader's world. Rather, through Bod's recitations of her lessons, one learns that the outside world is a place of different kinds of people: "There are the living and the dead, there are day-folk and night-folk, there are ghouls and mist-walkers, there are the high hunters and the Hounds of God. Also, there are solitary types."[20] Silas, it transpires, is a solitary type, and as the reader later learns, Silas is neither living nor dead; he would appear to be an undead being, for though he does not appear to need blood in order to survive, he possesses the vampiric powers of flight and hypnotism, the vampiric trait of failing to reflect in mirrors, and the vampiric dislike of the day and daylight. As with the idea of a werewolf, the image of a vampire tends toward the horrific, but in *The Graveyard Book*, it too is subverted, for Silas is wise and benevolent, if not exactly gentle, and he is the caretaker of the graveyard and friend of the ghosts before he becomes Bod's guardian and instructor.

From Miss Lupescu's lessons, Bod learns more of ghouls and their world, and of night-gaunts, which "have hairless wings" and "fly the red skies above the road to Ghûlheim."[21] Bod learns to imitate the cry of a night-gaunt, and though they play a role in the story, little more is said about either their appearance or their history. Nevertheless, evocative though the name is, night-gaunts are not original to Gaiman, though the idea and spelling of Ghûlheim appear to be. Rather, night-gaunts originated with American writer H. P. Lovecraft (1890–1937), who used them first in *The Dream-Quest of the Unknown Kadath* (written 1926–1927; first published 1948),[22] a tale in which Randolph Carter enters the world of dreams to search for the city of Kadath.[23] Carter's journey takes him across lost deserts inhabited by faceless night gaunts and ghouls, one of whom used to be a man. Ultimately, his quest completed, Carter completes his journey by awakening and leaving Dreamland, albeit with a heightened awareness of beauty and reality. Critics have disagreed about the merits of *The Dream-Quest of the Unknown Kadath*, but whether it is a success or not, Lovecraft's tale has been strongly linked to William Beckford's "Oriental tale of terror" *Vathek* (1786), a work that is frequently—though not consistently—considered one of the great Gothic novels as well as one that is largely sui generis.[24]

Gaiman's somewhat tongue-in-cheek homage to Lovecraft and *The Dream-Quest of the Unknown Kadath* becomes even more explicit when, within but a few pages after having learned of the ghouls and Ghûlheim, a disgruntled Bod

encounters ghouls and is kidnapped by them. Though the ghouls are "small, like full-size people who had shrunk in the sun,"[25] they possess extravagant titles— the Duke of Westminster, the Honorable Archibald Fitzhugh, the Bishop of Bath and Wells, the Thirty-third President of the United States, and the Emperor of China. These are ghouls of prominence operating in our world, much as Lovecraft's previously human Richard Upton Pickman is described as a "ghoul of some prominence in abysses nearer the waking world."[26]

For all that the ghouls are described as "parasites and scavengers, eaters of carrion,"[27] they do not initially convey a sense of menace: they are almost comical, their dialogue deliberately reminiscent of stage buffoons. (In combining comic and menace, however, the ghouls are reminiscent of Mr. Croup and Mr. Vandemar from Gaiman's *Neverwhere*.)[28] Ghûlheim, however, is immediately evident as a place of nightmares, and when Bod first glimpses it, he "could see that all of the angles were wrong—that the walls sloped crazily, that it was every nightmare he had ever endured made into a place, like a huge mouth of jutting teeth. It was a city that had been built just to be abandoned."[29] Can Ghûlheim be seen as a Gothic element? As with so many things, the answer depends on the definition of *Gothic*, but as a description, the city evokes a sense of *wrongness*, of *discordance*, and in this aesthetic it can be argued that Ghûlheim evokes a staple of the Gothic, the ruined place in which horrors occur as a matter of course. Ghûlheim is not a traditional Gothic castle or an abandoned abbey of the sort Ann Radcliffe describes in *The Romance of the Forest*, "sinking into ruins . . . awful in decay . . . half demolished,"[30] but at the same time, it is not far from such. Nor is the disturbing Ghûlheim terribly distant from Shirley Jackson's disquieting Hill House:

> No human eye can isolate the unhappy coincidence of line and place which suggests evil in the face of a house, and yet somehow a maniac juxtaposition, a badly turned angle, some chance meeting of roof and sky, turned Hill House into a place of despair, more frightening because the face of Hill House seemed awake, with a watchfulness from the blank windows and a touch of glee in the eyebrow of a cornice.[31]

The Haunting of Hill House is of course a classic of the modern Gothic.

After Bod is rescued from the ghouls by Miss Lupescu and the night-gaunts and returned to his graveyard, his next encounters are more benign, though fraught with menace. He meets with the young witch Eliza Hempstock, buried in unconsecrated ground near the graveyard. She was a genuine witch murdered by intolerant and superstitious villagers, her body burned until it "was nothing but blackened charcoal"[32] and buried in an unmarked grave. Witches and crones are Gothic staples, but Eliza is young, attractive, flirtatious, and tragic, a life destroyed by human intolerance: a Gothic staple immediately subverted.

It is Bod's generous attempt to procure funds to pay for a headstone for Eliza's grave that leads him first into braving the Sleer, a guardian monster inhabiting a chamber at the bottom of the hill in which the graveyard rests. Like Ghûlheim, the Sleer appears to be original to Gaiman rather than a direct homage like the night-gaunts, but although the Sleer is intriguing—a powerful smoky being whose menacing essence evokes fear and cold, yet withal bounded and limited—it is hard to justify as a Gothic element. It is, rather, overtly fantastic, not quite justifiable as either foundation or furniture.

Following Bod's misadventures in the world of the living—the person to whom he attempts to sell the Sleer's treasure attempts to steal it and imprisons him, Eliza assists him in escaping, and he returns the stolen treasure to the Sleer—he participates in what the residents of the graveyard call the Macabray, but what the reader recognizes as the Danse Macabre. The Danse Macabre is a unifying festival, a joining of all, living and dead, rich and poor, in a festivity designed to show the brevity of human existence. (Silas, being undead, is unable to participate and may not even be able to observe.) During the dance, without recognizing her identity, Bod dances with the Lady on the Grey and has a pregnant conversation with her about her horse, which she promises him he will ride, "one day. Everybody does."[33] At the same time, eerie and evocative though the whole scene is, neither the encounter with Death's hypostasis nor the Danse Macabre itself may be directly linked to the Gothic: both are medieval, predating the existence of the Gothic movement by several hundred years, and both were apparently unutilized as symbols by Gothic novelists, who preferred to concentrate on more physical horror.

The festival of the Macabray occurs approximately two-thirds of the way through *The Graveyard Book*, but rather surprisingly the remainder of the book introduces few new concepts and consists primarily of revisiting previously introduced ideas—the society of Jacks, the Hounds of Hell, Bod's increasing desire to interact with living humans, Ghûlheim, and so forth—and expanding and deepening the reader's awareness of the world outside the graveyard. (This is not in any way meant to disparage the narrative.) Only one additional element should be mentioned, one that the narrative barely touches upon: Silas, Miss Lupescu, and their compeers are engaged in a titanic struggle for the safety and future of humanity, battling the warrens of evil Jacks in an effort to thwart their plans. They succeed, though at great personal cost; and though humanity will never know the losses incurred, its future is assured. The bildungsroman concludes positively.

At this point, then, one may reasonably ask, do the scenes and references that were mentioned above, and the sometimes tenuous linkages that have been established, permit one justifiably and reasonably to describe *The Graveyard Book* as a Gothic (or neo-Gothic) work? How explicit—or, if one will, how

derivative or referential—does a work need to be in order to be considered Gothic? The answer is not easily determined, for unlike such terms as *fantasy* and *science fiction*, *Gothic* is not inherently a transformational term. One overtly fantastic or supernatural element can and often does transform a hitherto mimetic work of fiction into something else, whereas one piece of Gothic furniture does not necessarily transform an entire edifice into a Gothic castle.

In order to reach a partial conclusion, one must finally move to consider *The Graveyard Book*'s genre and tone and the narrative focus. The bildungsroman is not a genre that tends to offer negative outcomes; by its nature and definition, it depicts the maturation and education of a child over time. There are frequently philosophical discussions and discourses, for the bildungsroman tends toward the didactic, and the work itself is almost uniformly optimistic. These things cannot be said about the Gothic novel in any of its incarnations. Philosophical discussions do not occur, although there are frequently lengthy disquisitions and revelations that add to one's understanding of motivations. In addition, although children may figure in the plot, the Gothic neither depicts the maturation and education of a child nor offers these as the primary focus. Rather, the literary Gothic tends to focus on the actions of adults, and it depicts these adults at narrative crisis points. By these elements, then, a bildungsroman is not able to be a Gothic work; though congruous elements may exist, the two genres are inherently different.

It is always dangerous to make generalizations about entire genres, but in general the narrative tone of a work of Gothic fiction is overtly sensational, in the sense that the narrative is intended to generate sensations in the reader. The tone of the Gothic also frequently conveys heightened emotions, generally concentrating on depicting scenes of excitement and an urgency. More, the Gothic concentrates its narrative on its depictions of the aforementioned "horror, madness, monstrosity, death, disease, terror, evil, and weird sexuality." Parenthetically, this is not to say that the tone of the Gothic work is unrestrained; quite the opposite—the Gothic tone must be kept constant, for if it flags, suspense dwindles, and the narrative thrust is diminished when the reader becomes aware of the literature's sensationalism.

As befits a traditional bildungsroman, the narrative tone of *The Graveyard Book* is not sensational. Rather, it is quiet, almost journalistic in its depiction of events and characterizations. As implied above, there are numerous suspenseful moments, but even at the tensest of times, exclamation points—and such traditional elements of suspense as blood and thunder—are kept to a minimum. The focus on character and the concurrent lack of sustained sensation again do much to mitigate against *The Graveyard Book* being considered a Gothic work.

Finally, closely allied to narrative tone, there is the narrative focus. The writers of the traditional Gothic presented their narratives of "horror, madness, monstrosity, death, disease, terror, evil, and weird sexuality" to an audience that

thrilled to episodic descriptions of these things. Softer and gentler emotions were also depicted, of course, but these were not the narrative focus of the traditional Gothic. Rather, the softer emotions were presented in contrast to the horrific narratives and were shown as being vulnerable to destruction by them. The protagonists of the traditional Gothic struggled as much to keep hope and family and love alive as they did to prevent themselves from being murdered, their rightful causes and quests from being thwarted, and injustice and villainy from emerging triumphant.

However, the narrative focus of *The Graveyard Book* is not on the negative and precarious aspects of existence, or even on the horrors of the world. These of course exist—as stated above, its adumbrations and allusions are often to works in which humanity is constantly threatened, or to works in which death is real and terrifying—but the novel's narrative focus is on the quiet and important lessons of life and maturation. The episode involving Miss Lupescu, the ghouls, and the night-gaunts, for example, teaches Bod that those who disagree with him are not necessarily his enemies, that those who claim to be interested in him are not necessarily his friends, that dangerous situations can arise from being careless, and that learning one's lessons can have unexpected and immediate benefits. The traditional Gothic did not concern itself with presenting such lessons, which remain the province of the bildungsroman.

The conclusion, then, would seem to be inescapable. *The Graveyard Book* definitely references much that is traditionally Gothic, utilizing works, characters, themes, and settings that generations of scholars have identified and classified as Gothic. At the same time, although these Gothic elements and references are undeniable, Gaiman frequently subverts them and develops the novel by focusing on the positive aspects of maturation, concentrating on the values of learning, friendship, and sacrifice, and the importance of life and exploration. *The Graveyard Book* is, then, in the final analysis, a literary hybrid of a kind that literary critics and genre historians do not yet appear to have identified, perhaps because it is among the first of its kind: it is Gothic bildungsroman. It is a fitting hybrid to start the twenty-first century.

Notes

1. Neil Gaiman, *The Graveyard Book* (New York: HarperCollins, 2008).
2. Montague Summers, *A Gothic Bibliography* (London: Fortune Press, 1941).
3. Frederick S. Frank. *The First Gothics: A Critical Guide to the English Gothic Novel* (New York: Garland Publishing, 1987).
4. Frederick S. Frank, *Guide to the Gothic: An Annotated Bibliography of Criticism* (Metuchen, NJ: Scarecrow Press, 1984).

5. Frederick S. Frank, *Guide to the Gothic II: An Annotated Bibliography of Criticism, 1983–1993* (Metuchen, NJ: Scarecrow Press, 1994).

6. Frederick S. Frank, *Guide to the Gothic III: An Annotated Bibliography of Criticism, 1993–2003* (Lanham, MD: Scarecrow Press, 2005).

7. Edith Birkhead. *The Tale of Terror: A Study of the Gothic Romance* (London: Constable, 1921).

8. Devendra P. Varma, *The Gothic Flame, Being a History of the Gothic Novel in England: Its Origins, Efflorescence, Disintegration, and Residuary Influences* (New York: Russell and Russell, 1966).

9. David Punter, *The Literature of Terror: A History of Gothic Fictions from 1765 to the Present Day* (London: Longman, 1996), 1.

10. Bradford Morrow and Patrick McGrath, eds., *The New Gothic: A Collection of Contemporary Gothic Fiction* (New York: Random House, 1991).

11. Morrow and McGrath, *The New Gothic*, xiii.

12. Morrow and McGrath, *The New Gothic*, xiv.

13. John Paul Riquelme, "Dark Modernity from Mary Shelley to Samuel Beckett: Gothic History, the Gothic Tradition, and Modernism," in *Gothic and Modernism: Essaying Dark Literary Modernity*, ed. John Paul Riquelme (Baltimore, MD: Johns Hopkins University Press, 2008), 5.

14. Gaiman, *The Graveyard Book*, 307.

15. Gaiman, *The Graveyard Book*, 2.

16. Horace Walpole, *The Castle of Otranto: A Gothic Story*, in *Three Eighteenth Century Romances*, ed. Harrison R. Steeves (New York: Charles Scribner's Sons, 1931), 9.

17. Gaiman, *The Graveyard Book*, 29–30.

18. Anthony Boucher, "Mr. Lupescu," in *The Sleeping and the Dead*, ed. August Derleth (New York: Pelligrini and Cudahy, 1947), 344–348.

19. Gaiman, *The Graveyard Book*, 97.

20. Gaiman, *The Graveyard Book*, 71.

21. Gaiman, *The Graveyard Book*, 72.

22. S. T. Joshi and David E. Schultz, *An H. P. Lovecraft Encyclopedia* (Westport, CT: Greenwood, 2001), 70.

23. H. P. Lovecraft, *The Dream Quest of the Unknown Kadath* (New York: Del Rey, 1986).

24. Joshi and Schultz, *H. P. Lovecraft Encyclopedia*, 74.

25. Gaiman, *The Graveyard Book*, 74.

26. Lovecraft, *Dream Quest*, 45.

27. Gaiman, *The Graveyard Book*, 82.

28. Neil Gaiman, *Neverwhere* (New York: HarperTorch, 2001).

29. Gaiman, *The Graveyard Book*, 82.

30. Ann Radcliff, *The Romance of the Forest*, in *Three Eighteenth Century Romances*, ed. Harrison R. Steeves (New York: Charles Scribner's Sons, 1931), 264.

31. Shirley Jackson, *The Haunting of Hill House* (New York: Viking, 1959), 22.

32. Gaiman, *The Graveyard Book*, 111.

33. Gaiman, *The Graveyard Book*, 161.

CHAPTER 26

Death Comes in the Mail

THE RELENTLESS MALEVOLENCE OF JOE HILL'S *HEART-SHAPED BOX*

Darrell Schweitzer

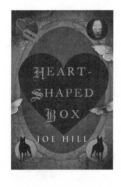

At first remove, Joe Hill's debut novel seems a very remote descendant of the earlier Gothics, even though it contains some easily recognizable Gothic motifs, notably the sins of the past manifesting themselves in the present, and a very active, vengeful ghost. It is very much a novel written from an awareness of genre, as if the writer is not only aware of the conventions of the modern horror novel but assumes that his readers are too. This, in any genre, robs the narrative of many opportunities for ambiguity. In a science fiction story, the strange light in the sky almost certainly *is* a spaceship. This is evident from the context that the story is published as science fiction. Likewise, in a horror novel published as a horror novel, there can rarely be subtle, Henry Jamesian dithering about whether or not the supernatural is actually occurring. Whereas in real life, someone confronted with the inexplicable most likely will exhaust every possible rational explanation and may even resort to outright denial before finally admitting that, yes, indeed, this is beyond nature, in a modern supernatural horror novel labeled as such, if it looks like a ghost and acts like a ghost, we assume it is a ghost. That being so, the reader expects the writer to get on with the story rather than circle endlessly around the point.

Sure enough, in Hill's 374-page novel, the ghost is unambiguously up and running by page 29. One of the very few classic novels to follow this strategy is Bram Stoker's *Dracula* (1897), where the Count's vampiric nature is clearly established in the first four chapters, and the bulk of the book follows the vigorous plot, without any pause for further questions.

Hill's protagonist is Judas Coyne (born Justin Cowzynski to a Louisiana pig-raising family), a leather-clad, heart-scorched, and unpleasantly egotistical

heavy-metal rock star in his fifties, well past his prime, having outlived most of his fellow band members, but still famous, still trying to live up to his own bad-boy image. Being a fictional character has not stopped him from making an actual page on MySpace.com, where a glance shows Keith Richards to be one of his role models. Totally unlike the same-titled Nirvana song that topped *Billboard* in 1993, this novel shows us a lead singer who is no Kurt Cobain, not devoured by the "meat-eating orchids" of women, or cut on some groupie's "angel hair" as Cobain's song described. He is hard and mean on the women and unforgiving, to say the least, noting about his last girlfriend, "She was a natural psycho, so I threw her ass out, . . . [though] when she was manic she was a hell of a lay."[1] He has a collection of macabre items, including notably a genuine snuff film and artwork by the serial killer John Wayne Gacy, to which he adds a dead man's suit which comes in the heart-shaped box of the title, complete with ghost. As he rapidly discovers, the description of this item on an online auction was no joke. Furthermore, the auction itself was fixed, to make sure that he and no one else would "win" the item, because the ghost is that of the late stepfather of one of Coyne's now deceased groupies. It seems that after Coyne tired of the increasingly neurotic young woman, he sent her back to her family, whereupon she (as he is led to believe) committed suicide out of grief. The dead groupie's sister explains on the phone that her late stepfather, one Craddock James McDermott, an occultist, hypnotist, and psyops veteran of the Vietnam War, remains attached to that suit and is out for revenge.

Once again, we leap past generic explanations. When Coyne's current lover/groupie, Georgia (not her name, but he calls his girls after their states of origin; the dead one was "Florida"), suggests the conventional strategy of trying to find out what the ghost wants so that it may perhaps be laid to rest, Coyne laconically replies, "He didn't come for talk" (66).

It's still quite early in the novel. The ghost's presence and existence have been established beyond the doubt of anybody in the cast. There is no mystery about its motives either. We know what the ghost wants. It wants Judas Coyne dead, preferably miserably, by his own hand. It will settle for nothing less. Before long, McDermott has demonstrated his terrifying power of persuasion, having caused the suicide of Danny, Coyne's personal assistant, who is otherwise innocent of any of Coyne's misdeeds. Danny had nothing to do with Florida's troubles, or her death, but *this* ghost is out for satisfaction, not justice. It wants Coyne to die alone and will kill anyone who remains too close to him.

Less than a quarter of the way into the book, Hill has already taken care of most of the "business" which would have occupied at least half (or even nearly all) of a novel written a few decades earlier. But Hill's audience has grown up reading horror novels, such as those of Ira Levin, William Peter Blatty, or Stephen King. Hill is modestly careful not to ride on his father's coattails, but he

is the son of Stephen King (and like his father's novels and tales, this one works with fearful children, now and then a kind aunt, and muscle cars). He surely must have been brought up in a household in which horror novels and ghost stories were very much taken for granted. For such readers, any sort of delay about "Is there a ghost? What does it want?" would only lead to impatience.

What follows is a vigorous chase. Judas Coyne is not a quivering, Lovecraftian protagonist who will passively research his predicament and then faint or go mad. At the novel's climax, even the ghost compliments him for his tenacity. After Georgia has burned the dead man's suit (a bad idea, because it reduces the chances of getting rid of the ghost), Coyne and Georgia drive south to confront their tormentors at the source, the house of the late Florida (whose real name was Anna) and likewise deceased but very lively stepfather. The rules seem to change a little, as it is discovered that the ghost can be held at bay by Coyne's two fierce dogs—or not so much by the animals themselves, but by their souls.

Much of the book may be described as a duel between Craddock, who is trying to engineer the deaths of his victims, and Coyne and Georgia, who are trying to stay alive. It is to Hill's credit that he manages to keep the narrative going at a lively pace. Interest never flags. Inventively scary moments and striking images occur with admirable frequency. Again, one can think of this in terms of a second-generation horror film, for audiences brought up on horror films, from *The Exorcist* and *Night of the Living Dead* onward. We know it's a horror film. There is little patience for a subtle buildup to a few barely glimpsed frights. The audience wants a lot of scares, they want them quickly, and they want them to be intense.

What is surprising is how good a novel Hill can write within such aesthetic constraints. The key to it is that he has not neglected to genuinely care about his characters. In the course of events, as he has to depend more and more on the assistance of Georgia (whose real name is Marybeth, which he begins to use as things progress), Coyne grows and becomes a better man, ultimately passing from his much belated middle-aged adolescence into a genuinely mature relationship with Georgia/Marybeth.

Inevitably, all sorts of personal and sexual secrets come out. Where previous horror stories frequently had sexual subtexts, sometimes very repressed, sometimes (as some critics have suggested of *Dracula* in particular) not entirely under the author's control, *Heart-Shaped Box* brings everything out into the open, not necessarily because the author is an unsubtle fellow who feels a need to explain everything, but because the latter-generation, almost postgenre reader *already knows all the deep, dark secrets*. Think of the hidden sexuality virtually bubbling just below the surface of Arthur Machen's work, "The White People" or "The Great God Pan" in particular. Suppose the author, due to his audience's expectations, had to bring all that out clearly into the open and *then* make the story good. This is the challenge that Joe Hill has taken up.

It is not so much a secret, but rather a steady part of the character's background, that Judas Coyne was raised by a monstrously abusive father, or that what is really going on in the lamented Florida/Anna's family, what is motivating the ghost itself, is all about multigenerational incest. There are no explicit sex scenes, certainly no child rape scenes. The reader, already having encountered such elements in numerous other horror novels, takes them as much for granted as the literal presence of the supernatural. The novel, and very possibly the horror field, has moved beyond the need for, or even the possibility of using, such material for shock value.

One might be tempted to criticize Hill, who was brought up in Maine, for succumbing to stereotypes about southern rural degeneracy, as opposed to perhaps writing about the sort of Yankee degenerates familiar from the works of H. P. Lovecraft, but Hill writes authentically and well about the American South, and in any case he never puts across the implication that the sins of Craddock McDermott and his brood in Florida, or Jude Coyne's family in Louisiana, are more than the deviations of individuals. They are not region specific.

The ending turns on Coyne and Marybeth's growing understanding of what is really going on, that, venal and callous as he might have been, Coyne was never the "villain" in the tragedy of Anna's death.

What has all this got to do with the traditional Gothic? If we run down a checklist of standard elements, we find quite a few of them here: vengeful ghosts, dire family secrets, secret sins revealed, inversion (or Jude's fear that he is becoming his opposite, his father Martin), jealousy and revenge, pacts with the supernatural world, animals that detect the occult around them, debasement (falling into the muck and sleeping in hog- and dog-filled barns), bad parenting (or family curses), despair, excess, sexual tension, and so on. Some of the standard tropes are admittedly missing. There are no haunted castles, though there are boyhood or girlhood homes that brim with past and current violence and violation. Craddock has perhaps some of the elements of a traditional Gothic villain, but he lacks the socially upscale elegance of a wicked Italian nobleman from an Ann Radcliffe novel. Jude is a destructive Byronic hero, certainly by reputation: mad, bad, and dangerous to know, if his music (say, the CD *Happy Little Lynch Mob*), the marketing, the rumors, and the drug-use admissions are true ("Fuckin' acid. I had a good memory once" [8]). By action—namely his making both dark art and perverse violence (sometimes with a gun at the head of a girlfriend who fellates him, another time with a tire iron to the throat of the cursed-suit seller Jessica)—he echoes Byron. When Lesley McDowell writes that Hill's novel should actually be called "*Abused Women and Girls*, as they are who this unpleasantly creepy little novel is about," it's a point well taken.[2] What causes the greatest conflict, though, and fuels the entire plot and the vowed "ride together on the night

road" (72) is Jude's current and past Byronic power to seduce effortlessly. To this, Craddock gives this grudged compliment that "there's all sorts of pretty girls happy to lift their skirts for a rock star" (285), and his current girlfriend moans, "Is nine months the limit? Then it's time for some fresh pussy?" (102) and "[Your last wife] catch you in bed with the state of Alaska or something?" (169). The very nature of the book and its position in the genre's development pretty much precludes ambiguity.

Heart-Shaped Box might be fairly described as a post-cliché supernatural horror novel. Its lineage can be traced back even beyond Horace Walpole, to the vengeful ghosts of the Elizabethans or even of Seneca, but it is also a book of a sort which inevitably had to come into existence after the great generic horror boom of the late twentieth century (fuelled very heavily by the books written by Hill's famous dad), the flood of imitations, and the subsequent bust had all run their course. Even as fantastic events are completely taken for granted and regarded as everyday background in Latin American magic realism, for the modern horror reader, all the standard ghostly and Gothic tropes are also taken for granted. Yes, there are ghosts, phantom trucks, spirit messages through Ouija boards, shining doorways into the beyond, and so on. More than that, there is perhaps the most haunting horror theme of all: the loss of identity. This surrender of volition to another is constantly threatened in *Heart-Shaped Box*, most blatantly when Craddock promises that he will control Jude, making Jude see whatever visions Craddock casts, ultimately causing Jude to cut the throats of all around him, just as Craddock was able to make a high-value Viet Cong POW cut off his own fingers. These things cease to be clichés when authors stop trying to *surprise* us with them. As Janet Maslin insightfully observes, "He balances *Heart-Shaped Box* between reality and fantasy in ways that threaten to run the book into an uncharted dreamscape, and away from the palpable suspense on which it thrives. But he holds the italics to a minimum, pulls back from the brink of hallucinatory overkill and mostly keeps this story tightly on track. . . . Though it has the potential to fall back on tricks and pyrotechnics, *Heart-Shaped Box* is firmly rooted in real-world concerns."[3]

This is what Hill has achieved. He does indeed evidence wit (describing a "surprisingly athletic move for a man who was not only elderly but dead" [313], along with an all-too-shabby pale-blue ghost Chevy pickup driven by said ghost), managing to pull a few surprises and turn a few twists in his plot, but not exclusively with the supernatural elements. Circular in structure, the novel takes characters back to where they came from, returning them to the source of their oppression, to their first and as yet unhealed psychic wounds. For all of *Heart-Shaped Box*'s Gothic brooding on death and on the fear of becoming your nemesis, however, it is life itself that in the end scares us and the characters the most. Jude makes this discovery, adding much brooding depth to the novel,

when he comes back home, rests injured on a cot, and hears across from him on an identical cot his aged father:

> Breath yet whined in his throat. . . . Somehow it was more horrible that Martin was breathing. It would've been easier to look upon him, as he was now, if he were dead. Jude had hated him for so long that he was unprepared for any other emotion. For pity. For horror. Horror was rooted in sympathy, after all, in understanding what it would be like to suffer the worst. Jude had not imagined he could feel either sympathy or understanding for the man in the bed across the room. (306–307)

Commingling his memory of the sins of the father with the man's present pathetic decrepitude leaves Jude lost, as confused and vulnerable again as the boy he once was in Moore's Corner. Perhaps this vulnerability finally reopens him to the other's pain, making him more appreciative and protective, too, of those he does love, as he never again calls Marybeth "Georgia," and within seventy pages he will marry her.

Like Stoker writing *Dracula*, who managed to lay out his long book's entire premise by the end of chapter 4, Hill begins where many other writers might have ended, and gets on with his transformation tale. Again, as with *Dracula*, it is women (minimized at first—as "Georgia," "Florida," "Tennessee," and Jessica "the Bitch") who move the plot along, appearing more often—and complicating everything—than the old man's ghost itself.

Whether this approach will be fruitful in the long term has yet to be seen. It could be argued that what Hill has done in *Heart-Shaped Box* is reanimate the corpse of the post-Gothic horror novel for one last shamble—or maybe not.

That is the long sought-after ambiguity implied by this book.

Notes

1. Joe Hill, *Heart-Shaped Box* (New York: William Morrow, 2007), 102. Page numbers appear hereafter in parentheses in the text.

2. Lesley McDowell, review of *Heart-Shaped Box*, by Joe Hill, *Independent*, November 9, 2008, www.independent.co.uk/arts-entertainment/books/reviews/heartshaped-box-by-joe-hill-997441.html (accessed February 9, 2010).

3. Janet Maslin, "Clothes Make the Man . . . Scared," *New York Times*, February 8, 2007, www.nytimes.com/2007/02/08/books/08masl.html (accessed February 9, 2010).

CHAPTER 27

Vlad Lives!

THE ULTIMATE GOTHIC REVENGE IN ELIZABETH KOSTOVA'S *THE HISTORIAN*

Danel Olson

> The historian is a prophet facing backward. . . . The novel-
> ist [is] a historian facing inward. . . . This historian watches
> how his or her fallible characters interpret reality, how they
> inhabit it, how they distort it and force it to accommodate
> to their mental cosmos. . . . The novel itself, ideally, then
> becomes another kind of public record, a rival kind, as *War
> and Peace* is now considered by most readers to "narrate" a
> version of Napoleon's invasion of Russia.
>
> —James Wood, "On a Darkling Plain"[1]

> I'd like to interview Stalin. I'd like to explore with him the
> process of how you go from being an ordinary person to
> becoming a mass-murdering megalomaniac.
>
> —Christiane Amanpour in intervew[2]

> I know the modern world. It is my prize, my favorite
> work."
>
> —Vlad III Dracula speaking
> in Elizabeth Kostova's *The Historian*[3]

Like its main force Vlad III Dracula (as Elizabeth Kostova calls him), *The Historian* is "a strange and curious" creature.[4] Though panned by many critics for its imposing length, similarity in characters' voices, and "anemic" horror, it was nonetheless to date the highest-paid debut novel in American history (with a $2 million advance from Little, Brown following a bidding war, and a $2 million film option secured by

285

Sony[5]). Taking ten years to research and write, it was the best-selling first novel by an American, with four million copies briskly sold in twenty-eight languages. Soaring to the top of the *New York Times* best-sellers list, its publication day broke sales records, outselling Dan Brown's *The Da Vinci Code* on its first day, whose profit-making power Little, Brown hoped to surpass.[6] Yet, for all that, it is not an especially popular-themed or breath-stealing novel; it has not so many scenes of violence, and fewer of sex. It features hundreds of pages of languid descriptions of ports, trains, furniture, curtains, roadways, and communist storefronts from the old, battered Eastern Europe, when the Soviet Empire still stood. Many critics and reviewers have bemoaned its slow pace and uniform voices (probably a valid point, except for the distinct voices of the fascinating Turkish scholar Turgat Bora, the peculiar-tongued Vlad III Dracula, and the wistful unnamed female narrator). *The Historian* tracks the life of a heinous, book-loving monster, his archival minions in a library near you ("inadvertently bolstering the stereotype that most librarians already belong to the undead"[7]), and three generations of historians scarred by Vlad III Dracula, only one of whom, Helen Rossi, is much good with her silver-bulleted gun.

This gun-toting Oxford history scholar Helen Rossi, born from a brief tryst her professor father had in Romania with her Hungarian mother, will be bitten by a vampire-librarian, and she in turn will blast said gun through Vlad III Dracula. Helen acts as time's arrow through history in this novel, and history is its largest theme. She is actually attempting to kill a monster who is an ancestor of hers. He is one who gave life, but damned it. Along with these two, the other major characters are her Oxford history professor father Bartholomew Rossi, her Boston-born Oxford history graduate student husband-to-be Paul, Paul's student at Oxford Stephen Barley, and Paul and Helen's unnamed daughter, who will lose her virginity to her chaperone-cum-lover, Barley. This daughter, whom we meet at age sixteen and who becomes a history scholar as well in America, is the one to open the book (in both senses—as in looking inside a text and as in starting a narrative). She also closes it, and then opens the sad investigation again when she receives a printed dragon, which is Vlad III Dracula's summoning symbol.

Entering the 1400s, the 1930s, the 1950s, and 1972, the novel's characters spirit themselves (or are spirited by another, as in the case of young Vlad III Dracula and also Helen's father, Bartholomew) to Slovenia, Turkey, Romania, and Hungary, as well as studying in the academic bastions of Boston and Oxford. They tell us their three narratives though postcards, over coffee, in letters, through scrawled notes, and in direct address to us via the preface and epilogue (probably composed by the narrator in 2005 or 2006, as she refers to ten years passing since Sarajevo was land mined). What unites all these utterances is a mystery and a slow-motion monster chase leading to Vlad III Dracula's move-

able tomb, which all sense is somewhere in Eastern Europe. In examining *The Historian*, Michael Dirda describes "the basic engine of [such] adventure novel[s as] the quest."[8] Kostova herself has owned that the book is "an adventure story in which the heroes were not Indiana Jones but scholars: librarians, archivists, historians."[9] The quest matters but is actually not the towering factor. Nor is the search by the sixteen-year-old unnamed female narrator what matters most; nor her asking, Where is my Mother? Who is my mother? Where now is my father? And where is Vlad III Dracula, that prince of darkness who is a great grandsire of mine?

This tracking is the plot-driven distraction that carries us along, part of the escapist bait and advertising hype, seducing millions to buy the book, and carrying potentially wayward and word-weary readers to the very end. But once we have found the end, when we have done with chasing, everything fades but two horrible Gothic truths: first, there is nothing that Vlad III Dracula will not do to man, woman, or child, and second, any abuse can be justified as righteous. The darkest Gothic insight we can take away from *The Historian* is the cancerous truth that metastasizes as the hunt goes on: how attractive, alluring, beguiling, and unstoppable a lust is vengeance. To think there is only one way for a vampire to come inside us is a fable. In this novel, we detect many ways to storm and hold our hearts and minds for evil, many ways to enslave us and make us grateful for the bondage. And how easily can Vlad III Dracula arouse and channel the bitterness dormant in human hearts to take, subjugate, torture, and kill.

Before unveiling this vampire's demonic persuasiveness and objectives, it is helpful to observe his provenance. In the first century and a half of its existence, the Gothic novel was propelled in nature, fears, sophistication, and subjects by at least three waves. If the first major wave, at its most basic, gave readers the works of Horace Walpole (including *The Castle of Otranto*, 1764), Ann Radcliffe (*The Mysteries of Udolpho*, 1794, and many others), and Matthew Lewis (*The Monk*, 1796), and the second wave gave us the masterworks of Mary Shelley (*Frankenstein*, 1818) and Charlotte and Emily Brontë (*Jane Eyre* and *Wuthering Heights*, both 1847), it is still the third wave by Anglo-Irish gentlemen that concerns us most here: namely, Joseph Thomas Sheridan Le Fanu's *Carmilla* (1875) and Bram Stoker's *Dracula* (1897). These two works, more than any others at the cusp of the twentieth century, open up *The Historian*. What we see in both *Carmilla* and *Dracula* is a burgeoning interest in the power of political orders. In Le Fanu's novella, which was a huge inspiration for Stoker's famous vampire novel, we see at the end that it is Baron Vordenburg (the descendant of the hero who rid the area of vampires long ago, but also a descendent of the undead Countess Karnstein) who has the directions from his vampire-cleansing ancestor to find Carmilla's hidden tomb. Upon finding the place of the ghoul in southeast Austria, "an Imperial Commission is then summoned who exhume and destroy the

body of the vampire on behalf of the ruling Habsburg Monarchy, within whose domains Styria is situated."[10] What is advanced in Le Fanu is the concept that the beast is in us. Baron Vordenburg's DNA has in it traces of both the hero and the villain; in a sense he must be killing a progenitor, and a little part of himself, which is the dilemma faced in *The Historian* as well. The curious fact that the undead are destroyed by political commissions who wish to control the events in their sovereign territory is another crucial advancement of the Gothic from Le Fanu. This political thinking is inherited in *Dracula*, too, where from the count's point of view, events should strictly move through a chain of command to protect the principality, and at the top of the hierarchy is the dark prince himself. Stoker's Dracula, born in the fifteenth century and now needing real estate help from young English lawyer Jonathan Harker, born in the nineteenth century, has a trace of humiliation in his reaction. As one obsessed with rule and rank, he cannot help but long for the past when he had the answers, when his commands where given and instantly executed in the field, and when no boyish lawyer need ever be consulted. A feudal prince still had all the power in his zone then, and blood was not so expensive. Stoker's Dracula wants not only a return to that kind of power, but an enlargement of it.

The greatest tool yet in spreading war craft is the summoning of our wish to reclaim what was our ancestors, and to punish those who once harmed us, all in the name of relieving us of our shame. This is a rhetoric that both Stoker's and Kostova's vampires understand and apply. Most of all, the cry that spreads war must assure us that we will win, despite all setbacks. How eerily like Bram Stoker's Dracula will be Kostova's Vlad III Dracula's argument, and how persuasive (though without Dracula's signature, vociferous style). Rising alarmingly in Stoker's hands, the "One Who Kills Turks" exclaims in ecstatic Hitleresque flourishes to the disoriented solicitor at his castle that war has the power to wipe away all impurities, wrongs, and degradations. War releases our glorious fate like a battle flag unfurled in the wind:

> He grew excited as he spoke, and walked about the room . . . grasping anything on which he laid his hands as though he would crush it by main strength. . . .
> "We Szekelys have a right to be proud, for in our veins flows the blood of . . . races who fought as the lion fights. . . . What devil or what witch was ever so great as Attila, whose blood is in these veins." He held up his arms. "Is it a wonder that we were a conquering race; that we were proud; that when the Magyar, the Lombard, the Avar, the Bulgar, or the Turk poured his thousands on our frontiers, we drove them back? . . . [Dracula,] who at Voivode crossed the Danube and beat the Turk on his own ground? . . . [Dracula,] who when he was beaten back, came again, and again, and again, though he

had to come alone from the blood field where his troops were being slaughtered, since he knew that he alone could ultimately triumph! They said he thought only of himself. Bah! What good are peasants without a leader?"[11]

What both enthrals and scares in this passage is that killing the enemy is put into glowing terms: it is the only way of fulfilling one's natural ethnic, political, and religious destinies.

Our identity, Stoker's Dracula contends, is that of God's madmen, berserkers for Christianity, defenders of the Holy Empire. On the other hand, the martial talk is pitched as self-defense. The "Turk poured his thousands on our frontiers," and thus there was little choice but to respond. In the historic Vlad Ţepeş case (meaning "Vlad the Impaler" in Romanian, who lived from November 25, 1431, to December 18, 1476), this meant in actual terms outrageous cruelty that Stoker's Dracula glosses over—the staking of tens of thousands of Turks like kabobs, turning an army of captured Ottoman POWs into a writhing and shrieking human forest, leaving speechless German monk witnesses who were passing through Dracula's territory.[12] Why were they staked? Blind hatred? As an example to spread fear into the Ottoman Empire's vast armies? To satisfy certain carnal pleasures on Dracula's part? To show the Turk that Dracula had observed their torture methods but had surpassed them all? That his wolfish warrior Szekely blood was superior in all ways, during the skirmish and afterward as well? It could be yes to all the above. What is certain is that the fictional Dracula's highest bliss was fighting and killing, his joy found in the intoxication of battle. In this, he is an emotional descendent of a revolutionary leader from almost three centuries before his time, Genghis Khan, who lived from 1162 to 1227. Reading Genghis Khan's definition of the good life assists us with what Stoker's Dracula leaves out. Consider how poetically yet brutally the Mongol Empire founder describes his greatest happiness, or what defeating and taking really amount to: "Man's greatest good fortune is to chase and defeat his enemy, seize his total possessions, leave his married women weeping and wailing, ride his gelding, use the bodies of his women as a night shirt . . . gazing upon and kissing their rosy breasts, sucking their lips which are as sweet as the berries of their breasts."[13]

Kostova extracts the lifeblood of Carmilla and Dracula and mingles it with that of historic martial leaders from Genghis Khan to Stalin and Hitler to create a war Gothic of her own. Above all literary genres, it is the Gothic that meditates longest and hardest on what the entire world desires to have—power. While Vlad III Dracula is chased (and chases), we see in the periphery the draconian measures and military extremes to which leaders and states go to control a population, to keep influence in a far-flung part of the world, or to be avenged. We are presented with arguments for using power to shock and awe. Kostova's

Gothic is not outside looking into the castle so much as it looks out from the citadel and reveals the dreamed vision, not just of a supernatural creature's limited marauding, but of massive and horrible violence toward people for questionable reasons, of weaponry that can wreak total destruction, and of the dark mind-set of those who would unleash it. Kostova's Gothic rumination on needless war and genocide is a novelistic unfolding of the seven haunting words said by an American prophet in 1963, not long before his death: "We have guided missiles and misguided men."[14]

Count Dracula's gloating over his past strength is a habit of Vlad III Dracula, too. This enemy of humanity makes a confession to Professor Bartholomew Rossi, who has just been abducted to the fiend's Bulgarian tomb to catalogue a jumbled first-edition death-and-dismemberment library:[15]

> "You cannot imagine what a satisfaction it was for me to see their [Ottoman] civilization die. Their faith is not dead, of course, but their sultans are gone forever, and I have outlived them. . . .
>
> "Yes, my own father left me to the father of [Sultan] Mehmed, as a pledge that we would not wage war against the Empire. Imagine, a Dracula a pawn in the hands of the infidel. . . . That was when I vowed to make history, not to be its victim. . . ."
>
> . . . He brought his great hand to rest on an early edition of Bram Stoker's novel and smiled, but said nothing. Then he moved quietly to another section. . . . "These are works of history about your century, the twentieth. A fine century—I look forward to the rest of it. In my day, a prince was able to eliminate troublesome elements only one person at a time. You do this with an infinitely greater sweep. Think, for example, of the divine fire your adoptive country dropped onto the Japanese cities some years ago." He gave me the trace of a bow, courtly, congratulatory. (583–585)

One of the most memorable scenes in *The Historian* must be that above. Fetishizing torture and execution devices with the creepy glee of the executioner in Kafka's "In the Penal Colony" and idolizing a country that drops atomic bombs, Vlad III Dracula equates mass murder with the work of only the greatest artist.

We may look upon Kostova's steward of evil as a willing member of a sadistic freak show, but this freak of violence looks back at us the whole time. His talk has been the foreword to an indecent offer made to our time; Vlad III Dracula says to Professor Rossi, "History has taught us that the nature of man is evil, sublimely so. Good is not perfectible, but evil is. Why should you not use your great mind in service of what is perfectible? I ask you, my friend, to join me of your own accord in my research. . . . There is no purity like the purity of the sufferings of history. You will have what every historian wants: history will be a reality to you. We will wash our minds clean with blood" (586). As one of the most

barbaric feudal princes of fifteenth-century Europe—when princes knew how to be barbaric—Vlad III Dracula feels most comfortable in the twentieth century. He enjoys it here; he delights at our imagination and ingenuity to kill untold millions, our total warfare more obscene and invidious than such a monster as he could ever have dreamt. Like Stoker's Dracula, this one uses the language that was used on Jonathan Harker and Mina ("my friend," "of your own accord," and "you will come to me when I call for you"), but he goes beyond this to say that he wishes to follow us: "Together we will advance the historian's work beyond anything the world has ever seen" (587). It is implied that Vlad III Dracula knows that the wars and genocides of the twentieth century have made it the cruellest on record, and he applauds us for it. It is a fatal compliment, and the most damning fact is that, as cold and hideously criminal as Vlad III Dracula's acts were, ours are beastlier yet. Beyond nuclear weapons, we have developed neutron bombs that kill people but leave buildings intact, showing how much more they matter than human life. Our violence is unleashed from planes over thirty thousand feet above the kill zone, on people who may never have tried to harm us, loosed by pilots who have no idea of the grotesque carnage resulting below, and who may return to their base afterward for lunch with their commanders. In the case of the historic Vlad Țepeș, he at least had the honesty to face the repression he inflicted. According to a Brother Jacob, who would share what he saw with Michel Beheim, the court poet of the Emperor Frederick III, Vlad Țepeș seated himself among a thicket of Turks he had ordered impaled and dipped his bread in the goblet of their collective blood.[16]

Salting her novel with the tears of the modern horrors of warfare and domination, Kostova engineers one of the more daring exploits of recent Gothic fiction: in a subtle but consistent way, she accuses us of being as blind to our perversity and wickedness as Vlad III Dracula was. We do pay the taxes for the bombs that fall on the people "over there" and then pretend that we just don't see. She is all too aware of that black truth of constant Gothic speculation and sorrow (from Matthew Lewis's *The Monk* to Robert Louis Stevenson's *Dr. Jekyll and Mr. Hyde*): the beast is in us. Though it is an exhaustingly long novel, we recall clearly the self-accusatory line in its first paragraph, from a woman who has witnessed much and in her fifties glances back to when she was sixteen: "It seems peculiar to me now that I should have been so obedient well into my teens, while the rest of my generation was . . . protesting the imperialist war in Vietnam" (3). As she looks back, she might sense another damning war truth, that her nation dropped more bombs on Vietnam, as its war architect Defense Secretary Robert McNamara admitted in his memoir, in just three years of "Operation Rolling Thunder . . . than had been dropped on all of Europe in World War II."[17] She won't know for a while that the Americans had also later shelled a neutral country, Cambodia, as part of Operation Menu, a mission kept secret from the

American public and Congress for four years. But time will eventually show how these bombings not only took innocent lives but helped the Khmer Rouge to give a pretext for saying the Americans were about to bomb Phnom Penh as well, and thus to solidify its bloody, skull-crushing takeover of Cambodia. Indirectly implicated by this faraway crime, a haunting realization comes to Kostova's narrator as she remembers that "terrible things were happening in Cambodia" (234). As an objective point of fact, no other country since World War II has more often threatened, invaded, or bombed foreign soil than the United States of America.[18] The fifth sentence of the first chapter of *The Historian* continues this meditation or wakefulness toward the violence from our own side, showing the anguish it produces in one of its citizens, the narrator's father: "My mother had died when I was a baby, before my father founded the Center for Peace and Democracy" (3). What her father will see, as he understands the hunger for power inside Vlad III Dracula, will make him take up the struggle for peace, no matter how it ends, in his case dying in a Sarajevo minefield in the 1990s (a reminder of the longest siege of a capital city since the end of World War II).

In the decades before this explosion that leaves our unnamed narrator an orphan, her father and mother wander a Europe in the 1950s still devastated by German attacks and genocide, and by the resulting American, British, and Soviet counterattacks and reprisals. The novel does not hesitate to examine the rollover that happens after the young Helen and Paul leave Hungary: the Soviet tanks that will rumble into Hungary only a few years later while the rest of the world stands by, which brings to mind a repeating pattern, that Soviet tanks will also roll into Czechoslovakia a decade later, again while the rest of the world looks on. The great Gothic stories in the end remind us not only of the cost of cruelty to the victim, but how much it disables and dehumanizes the perpetrator, turning the vanquishers (from the politician, to the general, to the tank commander) into monsters that bury the innocent, along with their memories of freedom. Partly a bildungsroman, this book has a narrator who grows and comes to terms with our passive response toward the self-serving politics and vicious history of the twentieth century. She understands the dark truth that the longing for power turns leaders[19] and nations into vampires, draining all the life from those who are weaker.

The epiphany is that the greatest horror story of all is history—and sometimes not ancient or medieval history, but *contemporary* history. This truth must incrementally be discovered by the narrator over the 642 pages of this novel, despite barriers put up by the ones who love her. It is understandable that all parents, like the parents in an overwhelming number of Gothic novels, keep secrets from their children, thinking that it protects. Gothic novels always have mysteries—regarding characters' disappearances, or where and who one's biological mother, father, or long-lost twin might be. This novel has family secrets

that are kept from children (including the secret that the narrator happens to be related to Vlad III Dracula), but also secrets about history's unquenchable blood thirst. This is why Paul can only sigh when his daughter admits that she has brought down the letters of vampire discovery on the sly from his library, those written by her father's mentor (curiously at the same time she lowered a fine copy of the *Kama Sutra* from Dad's shelf, causing an Eden-like simultaneous discovery of thrilling sex and perverse death). Her father is not so much angry as saddened that he must divulge how senselessly violent we are. (In this book, secrets are also kept from spouses, as when Helen, sensing that she is becoming a vampire, jumps off a cliff and simply disappears from Paul and her daughter's life, leaving only blood spoor behind). More vital information is kept quiet by Paul's Oxford mentor, the trusted mentor who would make his student love questioning, investigating, and finding sources to establish the facts of history. Professor Bartholomew Rossi really does not want to reveal what he knows of Vlad III Dracula to his advisee and protégé, Paul, out of fear for his grad student's safety, out of a sense that this is madness anyway, and perhaps out of a dislike for sharing such dispiriting chronicles. The towering, recurring realization for all is that none of the secrets should have been kept. The hiding of these secrets (while thought to be a needed shield) only compromises, disables, and hurts everyone, causing years of disorientation and mourning. If the characters learn nothing else, they learn this: When tracking vampires, let the facts be everyone's friends. However, the characters fail in this. They tell the truth at a slant out of misguided kindness, which hardens into the overarching burden of the novel: the stony resistance that all figures meet to getting straight answers to basic questions on persons, undead or alive. But these secrets about horrors are to be forgiven; they were born from love. And besides, who knows which version of a lie lets someone stumble upon the truth?

The truth is that what the undead want most, besides immortality, is revenge. At first blush—unless one's land has been taken, its cities burned, its religion defiled, and its people killed—*The Historian* and Vlad III Dracula himself may seem abstractions. The Americans in the book have difficulty understanding his hunger for vengeance, having suffered so little destruction on their soil, but Romanian-born Helen Rossi (wife of an American and mother of one) understands well such mordlust. She is the one to whom Vlad III Dracula's charisma should prove most seductive; his promise for reclamation, and his promise that she will never have to fear another person again, should work their black magic.

One curiosity for a Westerner traveling in Helen's home, Romania (as I have done twice, including one arduous journey in the Carpathian Mountains on a rented donkey dubbed Mr. Sugartoes), is the fondness some of the native population have for the historic Dracula. The historical record shows without a doubt that Vlad Ţepeş was not only an enemy of the Turk, but a frequent enemy

of his own people and former neighbors, one who killed, maimed, impaled, and tortured thousands of his fellow citizens, sometimes merely over a suspicion that they had engaged in "unfair trade practices."[20] Astonishingly, his attacks on friendlies were sometimes fiercer than the Turks' pillaging and looting of these same towns and cities from years before. As I once sat on the surrounding hills of the beautiful Transylvanian city of Braşov, I shuddered to think that from this ground once rose "more stakes bearing Dracula's victims rotting in the sun or chewed and mangled by Carpathian vultures than any other place in the principality, . . . [the place where] Dracula is said to have wined and dined among the cadavers."[21] This unhallowed ground was the very location where German sources contemporary to Vlad Ţepeş discovered that "he had mothers separated from the children, . . . [and] the mothers' breasts cut out and their children's heads pushed through the holes in their mothers' bodies and then he impaled them. . . . Such great pain and tortures as all the blood-thirsty persecutors of Christendom, such as Herod, Nero, Diocletian . . . had never thought up."[22] Considering all the real-life horrors and sieges he laid on his own principality's towns, confirmed by German, Russian, and Romanian sources, it is a wonder that Vlad Ţepeş has managed to appear on contemporary Romanian postage stamps and as busts in the middle of village squares. His admirers in Romania may have many enigmatic reasons, but one keeps cropping up. Wherever Dracula ruled for any length of time, extreme order would follow. (The fact that there were fewer people to *make* disorder is brushed away.) A resourceful folklorist named Petru Ştefan Runcan, who is also general director of the Transilvania Târgu Mureş Airport, recalled to me in 2006 a popular tale to explain Vlad Ţepeş's continued surprisingly high approval ratings in this country which has faced drastic change since the death of its dictator couple on Christmas Day 1989. The story goes that a traveler came to a city Vlad Ţepeş ruled and unknowingly dropped his money; when the traveler came back to find the money the next day, no one had touched it—it still sat in the middle of the street. Because of the punishment Vlad Ţepeş would exact on a thief, none dared touch the money. This story occurs in another version in German, Slavonic, and Romanian variants from the fifteenth century: "In a deserted square in Tirgoviste where travelers habitually would rest and refresh themselves, Dracula ordered a golden cup to be permanently stationed here for all to use. Never did that cup disappear throughout his reign. He was, after all, a 'law and order' ruler."[23]

Over five hundred years after his medieval heyday, I took three journeys to Eastern Europe to find the traces of the historic Dracula, seemingly the ultimate in despot depravity. Each time, I was stunned by what I found. Once, I went to his boyhood home in Sighişoara, Romania, where little Vlad reputedly spent his first four years (1431–1435). In the Germanic atmosphere of this beautifully walled town, while his aristocratic father was under house arrest, Dracula

learned the first lessons of his life. Like the characters in *The Historian*, I couldn't escape the uneasy sense of being watched by something as I ate (as the only diner that evening) in the home where the real Dracula took his baby steps, but perhaps I was uneasy from my visit to the clock tower a block from his home. On the first floor of the clock tower stands an exhibit of large and small working medieval torture devices, and the big draw is an inexplicable yearly "torture festival." Once, I also sailed down the Danube from Budapest, Hungary (home of Dracula's sometime allies/sometime enemies to the North), to Constanta, Romania. Again, touring Romania, I was struck that though Dracula's fortress and his castle (and a monastery built for him in Tirgsor, among others) are rubble and ruin, still one senses the dark presence. It is as if the mood of being watched that hovers over all *The Historian* broods over the visitor to Romania, too, despite its peaceful beauty. Perhaps this is a psychic energy leftover of the Ceaușescu regime, when the dictator's Securitate "expanded into one of the world's most dreaded state police forces, . . . and its agents and informers were to be found everywhere, . . . [gathering] to have someone dismissed, blackmailed, evicted from his home, or barred from higher education."[24] Over one green Carpathian mountain after another, though, I found other strange and curious things. Shocked as I was to find some sinister folk customs from Vlad Țepeș's era hanging on, I had to admit how they could enlarge one's perception of life and death and what comes after. For example, I visited a country cemetery near the Tirhuta mountain pass which leads from Transylvania into Moldavia, and there I heard the account (and saw and photographed the evidence) of how one man's remains were actually disinterred and separated (the skull taken to a far corner of the graveyard), under religious ceremony, to disable his vampirism, or to stop his spirit from walking in the night and causing any more harm. Vlad Țepeș seemed to be there, unseen but felt, as I crouched near the man's grave who had been buried twice (once in 1971, and then again, post–skull removal in 2006). Conversely, at an Orthodox painted monastery not so far away, called Stareta Manastirii Sihastria, I found a disinterment about to begin that would prove just the opposite. I happened to arrive the week when the first test for saintliness of a church father was being performed: Would his body when now recovered from the grave be uncorrupted? I could not stay for the whole process, and to this day I wonder if a lack of fleshly decay gave sympathetic evidence of his moral purity. My last tracking of Vlad Țepeș flew me to his old enemy's capital, Istanbul, where Dracula as a boy was held a prisoner from 1442 to 1448 by the Sultan Murad II, father of the notorious conqueror of Constantinople, Mehmed II. Knowing that the capital of the Byzantine Empire had collapsed under Muslim attack just five years after Vlad Țepeș's release, I wandered as if entranced through the Hagia Sofia, which had existed for over nine hundred years as the church that Justinian I had built, but then in 1453 was converted

into a mosque by the son of the very sultan who had held Vlad Ṭepeş. Probably the greatest historical event in his life had already happened by Vlad Ṭepeş's twenty-second year: Constantinople had fallen, and one of the finest basilicas in Christendom and all its treasures were taken, its history stolen. I understood visiting Turkey that the humiliation of the West must have been epic, and the desire for revenge—and for stopping the Ottoman Empire—total. No means would have been taboo, and who could fail to understand why?

We have examined Vlad Ṭepeş's sadism and asked what may have inflamed it. We have investigated how Kostova's version seems much modeled on the Vlad Ṭepeş of record and chronicle, just as much if not more than any fictional model. But besides immortality and beyond the mere "cup of blood" that he quaffs in all of *The Historian*, what does Kostova's Grand Impaler want? How does he live? What is the matrix that holds him in time and where he continues to develop? What is his design? How does he find allies and minions? And how can the good resist him? These are the questions to raise of any worthwhile vampire novel, and they are answered in captivating layers within *The Historian*. For all of these questions, Kostova turns to the past, like a prophet facing backward.

In *The Historian*, Vlad III Dracula apparently did *not* die "pierced by many lances" in battle in 1476 near Bucharest, as did Vlad Ṭepeş. He was *not* buried for all time at the island monastery Snagov,[25] also near Bucharest, as Gothic scholars have learned from the official history of Vlad Ṭepeş. He rose again, in Kostova's imaginings, from "a place in Gaul, . . . where some of the Latin monks have outwitted death by secret means" (640). As red and fresh as a victim's blood, Vlad III Dracula's aristocratic manner, mordlust, and perverse humor are intact. This being who lives in the past as he exists in our present has been like a lost book to history, and now he is found. He has some books to show us. Even when he seems to die again at the end of the novel, we must ask ourselves, is he really dead? We should have reasonable doubts after all the greatly exaggerated accounts of his death. More unsettling is that Kostova's lyrical epilogue presents an action of this profoundly disturbing aesthete of violence, or one like him. When in Philadelphia, of all places, years after Vlad III Dracula was shot by her mother and turned "into dust, into nothing, even his ancient clothes decaying around him" (624), our narrator receives a book with his "ferocious single image at the center" (637). I assume it is of a dragon, as both the historical and the fictional Vlad are members of the Order of the Dragon, as *Dracul* can mean either "dragon" or "devil" in Romanian, and as this is his sign. Our narrator has been summoned.

This dark gifting is one surprise among many that lets Kostova cut a new moonlit path for the Gothic in our time, a way to escort Vlad Ṭepeş into our century. Joseph Ceccio perceptively observes that the narrator receiving this latest book from Vlad III Dracula (or a follower), while she walks in the shadow of

a U.S. federal building that had been bombed the month before, shows that this Dracula "lives on in another evil form, namely, the terrorism and potential for mass destruction in the new millennium. . . . While good may often triumph, evil always returns to challenge people and society. As humans adapt to new forms of evil, so too does evil adapt to the good that opposes it."[26] Indeed, in the way our twenty-first century opens by promptly turning to terrorism and war, Kostova's Vlad III Dracula would be very glad to live to see it. Perhaps not since Stoker's Dracula have we met such a quietly menacing Dracula, often staying offstage (like Stoker's) and thus terrorizing the reader that much more since so much of him is formed by our own worst-fear imaginings. Her Vlad seems akin to and partly modeled on actual vengeful leaders of our own day, and not so far from his old base, which Stoker grandly termed "the Un-Dead home of the King-Vampire."[27] The Balkans (coming from the Turkish word for "Mountain"), as the place where West meets East, has had invaders beyond number, and its cities have been destroyed many times. The capital of the former Yugoslavia, Belgrade (meaning "White City"), has been ruined and rebuilt forty times, and its long memory is necessarily bitter. Indeed, Belgrade gave rise to a politician who is remarkably like Vlad III Dracula, though critics have not dwelled on this. War criminal Slobodan Milošević (1941–2006) had charm, as Kostova's monster has. Milošević was recently remembered by war reporter Christiane Amanpour as the "Most Amiable Dictator: Slobodan Milošević. He would slap you on the back, offer you a drink. He tried to be charming. But many of them do. You have to be on your guard."[28] Having interviewed so many tyrants, Amanpour still sensed this strongman stood out: he was the one who said, "I am just an ordinary man" to *Time* magazine and yet caused four wars in his thirteen years of rule that took 200,000 lives.[29] He embezzled and enriched himself and his cronies along the way, as well as censoring the press and assassinating political foes, as he planned a greater Serbia. Milošević's agenda was to seek total power, igniting revenge, and rebroadcasting past atrocities to manipulate people into war, killing living people to somehow defeat the ghosts of their ancestors and put to rest the ghosts of one's own. All of this destruction was wrought, and then he was found dead in his bed in a Hague jail, apparently of a heart attack. Though the first former head of state to stand trial for genocide before an international tribunal, one that dragged on for four years, he would escape the pronouncement of justice. Like the earliest leaders and purge architects of the French Revolution who became opportunists rather than liberty seekers, and who would become models for many Gothic novels from 1800 on, Milošević was our modern Dracula, adaptable, Machiavellian to the point of madness, and an expert at promoting fear and violence. Influencing state media outlets that would remind Serbs of the atrocities and mass killings they had suffered by the fascist Croatian Ustaše powers during World War II,[30] he would also exploit ancient mistreatments by Muslim

Ottomans against Christian Serbs in Kosovo to defend a massacre of Kosovo Albanians in Racak in 1999. And, like Dracula (the real and the fictional one), Milošević had and continues to have many defenders.

Milošević, again, is our Nosferatu in how he is feared even after death, and how his body is treated, and why. In March of 2007, something shockingly Gothic happened in Milošević's Serbian tomb, an act of such bizarre and macabre intimacy with vampires that even Kostova's brocaded imagination couldn't have invented:

> Days before the first anniversary of Milošević's burial in his home town of Pozarevac, a young self-confessed "vampire hunter" [named Miroslav Milošević, no relation to the dictator] . . . drove a metre-long hawthorn stake through the heart of the dead dictator. In dealing with the "vlkoslak," the local vampire variant, hawthorn is said to be the appropriate weapon. . . . Miroslav is a former member of the Serbian student movement OTPOR, which hastened the political demise of the late dictator with protests and street demonstrations. Miroslav freely informed police of his intended action. "I called the police on my mobile and let them know that I was in the Milošević vault in the cemetery. They said be careful or Milošević's hand might get you from the grave." . . . The late dictator's daughter-in-law, Milica Galici, has lodged a complaint over the "violation of Milošević's grave." The complaint would be sent to the state prosecutor's office.[31]

Valuable things, as Vlad III Dracula would tell Professor Rossi, have this way of being misunderstood.

If the violations of *The Historian* manage to make readers feel more than the average supernatural thriller, it is not only because of their many real-life equivalents. Our stirrings come because of her exquisitely slow burn of disturbance. Though her novel merges with the Dan Brown tradition of treasure hunt/secret heresy/damning revelation/conspiracy trail/entrapment parable, it has few of the mechanically structured Brownian cliff-hangers at each chapter's end; nor does it suffer the limited characterization and simple thriller dialogue of the James Patterson kind. Awe in her novel comes from how Vlad III Dracula and his minions can dispatch people who become problems, and what their greater plans may be. (We seldom see a battle, only the strange evidence, like, say, a splash of blood on a ceiling and an empty desk where once sat a comfy academic, and this is more than enough to scare.) What makes *The Historian* memorable is that the old terrors are not going away. For instance, the eternal distrust between Christians and Muslims, or Jews and Muslims, seems not to be remediable here; the wounds have neither been dressed nor healed, and the butchery goes on. And Vlad III Dracula broods over a final solution, tempting anyone he can. Kostova has drawn him so cunningly that his eyes tell the wary reader what he is longing for, making this

one of the more menacing Gothic novels of the last decade. The ultimate Gothic revenge that this ultimate Islamophobe Vlad III Dracula intimates is obscene: he believes in and welcomes a clash of civilizations. He would like to kill every Muslim man, woman, and child with our nuclear dust. And we are to help him. For him to fawn over the American bombings of Hiroshima and Nagasaki at the same time he speaks of his seething hatred for a long defunct Muslim power is an attempt to bleed his revenge desire with ours. Vlad III Dracula aims to seduce us not by the cheesy trances from the vampire films of old, but by an alliance of hatreds, by arousing our own blindness, frustration, and anger over recent radical Islamist violence and our desire for a solution that restores our hyperpower and security. Nations, history keeps telling us, will do anything to keep their power. The novel asks us how difficult it is to live in a world that is still, five hundred years after the historic Dracula's death, barbaric and desensitized and genocide-prone. The narrator's lament that "I felt a new desolation" comes to us too, when she learns more and more of Vlad III Dracula's atrocities (including when she reads, as we now know, how Vlad Ṭepeş impaled mothers and their infants together). As the narrator and her parents fall into the darkness that is history, as they wander on this Trail of the Dragon, they must wonder what can be a bulwark against sadism, a way to stave off their own soul death. The only solace this novel implies is that forgiveness and sacrifice for those we love, and a surrender to love, are the bulwarks against brutality and smouldering hate. The mystic healing powers of love and sex are stronger than death, and the making of life is greater than the taking of it. The words that make our souls come back from the dead are those of her lover Barley, "Come, . . . come up to bed" (634).

Notes

1. James Wood, "On a Darkling Plain," *New Republic*, April 18, 2005, 28.

2. Christiane Amanpour, interview by Edward Lewine, "Domains: War Rooms— Christiane Amanpour," *New York Times Magazine*, February 11, 2010, www.nytimes .com/2010/02/14/magazine/14fob-domains-t.html (accessed March 20, 2010).

3. Elizabeth Kostova, *The Historian* (New York: Little, Brown, 2005), 572. Page numbers appear hereafter in parentheses in the text.

4. Elizabeth Kostova, interview by Gary Younge, "The Monday Interview: Bigger than Dan Brown," July 18, 2005, *Guardian*, www.guardian.co.uk/books/2005/jul/18/ fiction.news/print (accessed April 15, 2010).

5. Kostova, "Monday Interview."

6. Kostova, "Monday Interview."

7. Michael Dirda, review of *The Historian*, by Elizabeth Kostova, *Washington Post*, June 12, 2005, www.washingtonpost.com/wp-dyn/content/article/2005/06/10/ AR2005061000550.html (accessed April 15, 2010).

8. Dirda, review of *The Historian.*

9. Kostova, "Monday Interview."

10. *Monstropedia: The Largest Encyclopedia about Monsters,* "Carmilla," April 8, 2009, www.monstropedia.org/index.php?title=Carmilla (accessed March 15, 2010).

11. Bram Stoker, *Dracula,* ed. Glennis Byron (Peterborough, ON: Broadview Press, 1998), 59–60.

12. Raymond T. McNally and Radu Florescu, "Dracula Horror Stories of the Fifteenth Century," in *In Search of Dracula: The History of Dracula and Vampires,* rev. ed. (Boston: Houghton Mifflin, 1992), 85.

13. Paul Ratchnevsky, *Genghis Khan: His Life and Legacy,* trans. and ed. Thomas Nivison Haining (Oxford, UK: Blackwell, 1993), 153.

14. Martin Luther King Jr., "The Man Who Was a Fool," in *Strength to Love* (Philadelphia: Augsburg Fortress Publishers, 1981), 76.

15. So what does Vlad III Dracula, dressed in his "red-and-violet finery" (583), sit around reading in this underground, nocturnal existence of his? The kidnapped visiting professor Rossi lifts and peruses with nausea this vampire's rare books that presumably Kostova finds the most coldly calculating, dehumanizing, ghastly, and threatening on the planet, all with good reason: "[There was] an early edition of Machiavelli: *The Prince,* accompanied by a series of discourses on morality I'd never before seen" (578), and "there was a dog-eared first edition of *Mein Kampf* and . . . accounts to chronicle the Reign of Terror from the point of view of a government official . . . [and] an internal memo from Stalin to someone in the Russian military. . . . It contained a long list of Russian and Polish names" (582). Besides the works by amoral advisors, purgers, and genocide architects, Rossi finds a whole cabinet of torture manuals, "some of them dating to the ancient world. They ranged through the prisons of mediaeval England, to the torture chambers of the Inquisition, to the experiments of the Third Reich" (584). Ironically, at the time of publication of *The Historian* in 2006—as readers were watching with dread the vampire's dead eyes kindle alive with the fire of hatred and anticipated tortures—his special books could have been put to use by American intelligence circles. In real life, psychologists and others were being hired by the CIA to develop harsher, or "enhanced" and "alternative," interrogation techniques to use on their persons of interest. See Jane Meyer, *The Dark Side: The Inside Story of How the War on Terror Turned Into a War on American Ideals* (New York: Doubleday, 2008).

16. McNally and Florescu, *In Search of Dracula,* 85.

17. Robert S. McNamara, *In Retrospect: The Tragedy and Lessons of Vietnam* (New York: Vintage, 1996), 174.

18. Richard F. Grimmett, "Instances of Use of United States Armed Forces Abroad, 1798–2004," Congressional Research Service report RL30172, Naval Historical Center, March 14, 2005, www.au.af.mil/au/awc/awcgate/crs/rl30172.htm (accessed April 2, 2010).

19. In a long conversation at an Irish pub with Trinity College, Dublin lecturer Sorcha Ní Fhlainn in summer 2009, I learned her thought-provoking theory of American presidents as bloodsuckers (especially presidents Johnson, Nixon, Reagan, and Bush the Second), expanding Nina Auerbach's arresting thesis of presidents-as-versatile vampires from *Our Vampires, Ourselves* (Chicago: University of Chicago Press, 1995). Ní Fhlainn

reasoned that these leaders, like the Count, can read our desires and fears, charm and persuade when need be, appear cipherlike and furtive in their habits, and hide deadly acts from us, sacrificing the blood of the young and innocent through attacks and wars. As Stoker's Dr. Van Helsing says of the monsters, they are "age after age adding new victims and multiplying the evils of the world." Years into the presidential term or after it, when the public finds what has been hidden from them during the time they were mesmerized, there is outrage, and an investigation, or "vampire hunt," of the president ensues.

20. McNally and Florescu, *In Search of Dracula*, 25.

21. McNally and Florescu, *In Search of Dracula*, 26.

22. McNally and Florescu, *In Search of Dracula*, 195.

23. McNally and Florescu, *In Search of Dracula*, 90.

24. Nicolae Klepper, *Romania: An Illustrated History* (New York: Hippocrene, 2002), 229.

25. McNally and Florescu, *In Search of Dracula*, 27.

26. Joseph Ceccio, "Evil in the Worlds of Bram Stoker's *Dracula* (1897) and Elizabeth Kostova's *The Historian* (2005)," *Popular Culture Review* 19, no. 2 (2008): 59–60.

27. Bram Stoker, *Dracula*, 412.

28. Amanpour, "Domains: War Rooms."

29. Madeleine Albright, "Address by Secretary of State Madeleine K. Albright to the UN Human Rights Commission," United States Mission to the United Nations, March 23, 2000.

30. With any mention of the Ustaše, Milošević must have known the specter raised before Serbian eyes and could count on a frightened response. According to W. G. Sebold's *The Rings of Saturn*, trans. Michael Hulse (New York: New Directions, 1998), 97, which includes photographs, the concentration camps run by the Croatian fascist Ustaše "made even the hair of the [visiting] Reich's experts stand on end. . . . The preferred instruments of execution were saws and sabres, axes and hammers and leather cuff-bands with fixed blades that were fastened on the lower arm and made . . . for the purpose of cutting throats, as well as a kind of rudimentary cross-bar gallows on which the Serbs, Jews and Bosnians, once rounded up, were hanged in rows like crows and magpies." With this historical context of the roundup and mass murder of Serbs and others in the camps near the Sava River during World War II, and the Gothic instruments used to deal the deaths, one begins to understand the fear, suspicion, and ferocious memories fuelling the Yugoslav Wars of the 1990s.

31. Gabriel Ronay, "Vampire Slayer Impales Milošević to Stop Return," *Herald Scotland*, March 10, 2007, www.heraldscotland.com/vampire-slayer-impales-milosevic-to-stop-return-1.829326 (accessed April 2, 2010).

CHAPTER 28

Gothic New York in James Lasdun's *The Horned Man*

Nicholas Royle

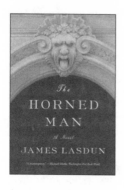

In London-born James Lasdun's first novel, *The Horned Man*, Lawrence Miller is an Englishman teaching at a college just outside of New York City, just as Lasdun himself has taught at three New York City colleges and universities.[1] He discovers that his office was formerly used by a woman, Barbara Hellerman. "You know about her, right?" says Amber, an intern.[2] Lawrence admits that he doesn't, and Amber tells him that Barbara is dead. About to ask for more details, Lawrence feels a blush coming on. He has started blushing at apparently random moments. Later, he finds a Bulgarian coin—in his office. He tells his therapist—in *her* office, or consulting room, in Manhattan—that he just saw her outside on the street. She denies having been outside on the street.

But he's sure he *had* just seen her, just past the Dakota Building, under a "bruise-colored" sky where trees caught "puffy snowflakes on the tips of their purple twigs—[like] a ghostly blossom, almost luminous in the darkening air": she *had* smiled at him, and even said hello.[3] An erotic pulse in him only confirms this memory—in the leather skirt, her "legs were slim and shapely; her hips moved in their gleaming sheath with a sinuous, swaying motion."[4] In the first chapter, then, this is what happens—a lot of contradictions and apparently unconnected stuff. And there are the bits of bland and seemingly benign dead time, waiting for appointments and such, where the scholar admits, "I had half an hour to kill."[5] All of this is, of course, connected, and the link is Lawrence. None of it means anything without Professor of Gender Studies Lawrence Miller. But we don't know that at this stage. It's only the first chapter. We go along with it. His behavior, as he self-describes it, is a bit of absentmindedness, and we have

learned to accept that in an academic. (Even the one element that seems as if it might be a red herring—the blushing—is in fact crucial.)

In chapter 2, Lawrence attends a meeting of the Sexual Harassment Committee, where he is advised to keep an eye on a colleague, Bruno Jackson, who is rumored to be sleeping with students. Somebody mentions Bogomil Trumilcik, a former visiting professor. Trumilcik—our ears, and Lawrence's, prick up—what is that? Bulgarian? The first connection is made. Lawrence goes back to look for the Bulgarian coin. He can't find it. The Bulgarian coin has disappeared.

Thus New York starts to close its mysterious net of confusion and coincidence around Lawrence. My thesis here is that New York, or at least fictional New York, the New York of literature, is essentially a strange place, a place where the Gothic has taken hold. It's in the air; it's in the clouds of subway steam; it's in the grid of streets. It's Gotham City, a city of otherness, a Native American settlement colonized by the Dutch—Chinatown, Little Italy, Spanish Harlem, Koreatown, and Jamaica in Queens—wave upon wave of immigrants: Germans, Irish, Puerto Ricans, Poles, Cubans, Egyptians, Greeks, Russians, and Englishmen like Lawrence—even a Bulgarian.

"How could I have invented such a vivid and detailed memory?"[6] Lawrence asks when he can't find the Bulgarian coin. I asked myself the same question when I read another New York novel. I read Brooklyn resident Siri Hustvedt's first novel, *The Blindfold* (1992), for the first time. Or so I thought. Almost from the very beginning it seemed familiar to me, and this feeling increased as I made my way, slowly, with growing pleasure, through the novel, yet if you had seen me reading it and asked if I had ever read it before, I would have said no. I went from being absolutely convinced I had neither picked up a copy in a bookshop nor chanced upon a review of the book somewhere to feeling distinctly that I had read the novel. *The Blindfold* takes the form of four loosely connected stories, each narrated by graduate student Iris Vegan (the name comes from Hustvedt's Norwegian mother, Esther Vegan). For me, it's a novel of déjà vu. A novel of déjà vu called *The Blindfold*. Perhaps the same unsettling force of familiarity comes for others from reading her husband Paul Auster's obsessive novels and strange stories of New York, full of the coincidence, ambiguity, and dread that we somehow already know. How do we know it, this uncertainty, then? Is it a live feed from those American godfathers of the sinister and the macabre who still speak from the shadows, Poe and Hawthorne?

Wherever the Gothic presence comes from, it comes fast. In chapter 2 of *The Horned Man*, we encounter the first specific reference to the Gothic. Describing the college environment, Lawrence talks about "thick-walled gothic buildings."[7] Waiting for a train to Manhattan, he notices a billboard ad for a podiatrist: "*1-800 why hurt? 1-800 end pain.*"[8] It is so close to the ad in the subway carriage in

Adrian Lyne's *Jacob's Ladder* that it is probably intended as a quotation. *Jacob's Ladder* is one of the great New York movies. It is atremble with the old American unease about what is real, stretching perception for a Vietnam War soldier in the way that Ambrose Bierce's unsparing and still astonishing "An Occurrence at Owl Creek Bridge" did for a Southern planter in the American Civil War. Tim Robbins plays Jacob Singer, a postal worker and Vietnam vet who lives a double life, waking up at one point in the film as a middle-class college professor with a different wife and a son. Back in what we had thought of as his "real" life, he fights with his live-in girlfriend over issues connected to the loss of his son Gabe.

The opening shots of the film show Jacob's unit under attack in 1971 in Vietnam. As Jacob is bayoneted in the stomach, he wakes up on a late-night subway train, a copy of Camus' *The Outsider* open in his hands. He looks around and sees two wall-mounted ads. The first reads, "New York may be a crazy town, but you'll never die of boredom. Enjoy!"[9] Straightforward exposition, an establishing shot. The second shouts, "HELL," in big fat red type on a black background. It goes on: "That's what life can be, doing drugs. But it doesn't have to be that way. Help is available, day or night. Call the drug hotline: 246-9300." The ad provides the key to understanding the film, but you don't realize it upon a first viewing. The podiatrist's ad in *The Horned Man* plays a similar role. We will even see it again.

Lawrence tries to catch an off-Broadway production of a play adapted from a Kafka story, *Blumfeld, an Elderly Bachelor*. The adaptation is by Trumilcik. He fails to get in, but he encounters the actor playing Blumfeld, who relieves Lawrence's migraine by pressing on his forehead. Soon, Lawrence is imagining Trumilcik coming into his office at night. He thinks that the iron bar he finds there must be Trumilcik's. In his fantasy, he and Trumilcik share a kind of double life like Jacob Singer's in *Jacob's Ladder*. He reads an autobiographical story on his computer of Trumilcik's experience at the INS building. Trumilcik, he finds out, used to live in the meat-packing district, like Lawrence.

He goes to print off Trumilcik's story, only to find that it's gone. Had Trumilcik been in the office watching him the night before? He writes a check to his therapist but gets her name wrong, writing *Schroeder* instead of *Schrever*. Of all the names he could have confounded hers with, this is a most interesting accident: *Schroeder* is the German occupational name for a cloth cutter (coming from the German verb *schroten*, meaning "to cut")—more to the menacing point, it is the name of one who also slices hides and trims leathers.[10] Dr. Schrever's leather skirt gleaming black floats up to his mind, but then just as quickly sinks away. The idea of a double life, of actions taking place involving him of which he has no memory, takes on a more worrying turn when a colleague, Elaine, starts to flirt with him. It is a flirtation that seems more like a response to some previous advance than an advance itself. In his office, Lawrence finds a hiding place between the desks. Is this Trumilcik's? While Lawrence is crouch-

ing in the hiding place pondering the actions of the Bulgarian, Elaine enters the office and writes him a note in which she refers to their involvement. What has Lawrence done and failed to remember?

A flashback tells the story of an episode in his adolescence in which he is attracted to Emily—his stepfather's daughter—but she humiliates him in front of her friends. This event prompts Lawrence to think for the first time of a "parallel version of myself."[11] It would seem, in the contemporary story, as if a parallel version of Lawrence is conducting an affair with Elaine. And he seems at least partly willing to go along with it. In chapter 6, he goes to Elaine's address and gives her a sweater that he had bought for his wife. She tries it on. Fingering a little painted box, she says, "Guess what I keep in here."[12] When he says he can't imagine, she says, "Oh Lawrence! Your *letter*, of course."[13] But Lawrence can't remember writing her a letter. When he tries to kiss her, she says no. A little time later, she tells him that Barbara was killed by a crazy man in the subway with a steel bar. Could it be the one in his office? He goes to take another look at it and finds that Trumilcik has left him a deeply offensive message of unparalleled unpleasantness in a coiled pile on his blotter.

Trumilcik's message raises the stakes. Things get weirder. Lawrence receives a note in Latin about unicorns. Amber, the intern, says, "So you did know Barbara,"[14] pointing to a three-year-old flyer on the noticeboard for a conference that Lawrence and Barbara had both attended as guest lecturers.

In a flashback to his first meeting with his future wife, Lawrence remembers her coming to his studio on Horatio Street. A Harvard scholar, Carol had written to Lawrence's father, who had been working on a history of pharmacology, and the letter had found its way to Lawrence, who had written back to explain that his father had died before finishing his book, but that Carol was welcome to come and look through his papers. Carol comes to Horatio Street, and while she reads the material, Lawrence looks out at the Hudson River (which Lasdun, deliberately, calls the West River). "At that hour the river looks taut and self-contained, as if a scooped handful wouldn't run, but wobble on your palm like mercury, burning coldly."[15] This is a world in which normal rules do not apply.

"I seemed to be up against something impenetrably mysterious," says Lawrence a few pages later.[16] His search for Trumilcik, in the context of his wider quest for explanations, his desire for the oddness of the world to make sense, recalls other fictional New York investigations of a similarly Gothic flavor—Jefferson's pursuit of Maya in David Knowles's *The Third Eye* (2000); Patrick McGrath's Empire State tales and novels of abysses and damaged lives, *Ghost Town: Tales of Manhattan Then and Now* (2005) and *Trauma* (2008); Paul Auster's various metaphysical investigations in *The New York Trilogy* (1987); and Iris Vegan's search for her identity—and her sanity—in Siri Hustvedt's previously mentioned *The Blindfold*.

In chapter 8, Lawrence goes back to the theater where he had previously gone to try to see the *Blumfeld* play. It is dark, and he is assaulted (by a unicorn? by Trumilcik?). He discovers the name of the *Blumfeld* actor (an actress, in fact, previously thought to be a man) who had earlier applied pressure to Lawrence's forehead in an attempt to treat his migraine (Lawrence suffers badly from migraines, as does Iris Vegan in *The Blindfold*). The name is Schroeder—the same name Lawrence had written on the check for Dr. Schrever. Plot lines loop around like the West Side Highway and FDR Drive, their linking up being the closest thing Manhattan has to a ring road, while characters' lives intersect like avenues and cross streets, and, cutting across the action diagonally, unexpectedly, like Broadway on a map, is Lawrence.

The novel's second explicit use of the *G*-word comes in chapter 9 as Lawrence looks through the Yellow Pages for a private investigator: "Just glancing down the list of names; the Sentinels and Warriors, the Bureaus, Corporations, Networks and Associates, with their bulleted services—*Digital Lie Detection, Male and Female Armed Agents, Matrimonial Evidence, Nanny Surveillance*—had made me feel as though I'd been waylaid into some realm of existence as absurdly, shabbily gothic as the buildings I worked in."[17] Just a couple of pages later, a confrontation with Bruno leaves Lawrence with "a vivid impression of his physical presence in the room."[18] Bruno was wearing a tailed coat, which he chose to keep on. "His long legs—hind legs, I find myself tempted to call them—were sheathed in skin-tight black drainpipes, tight as an Elizabethan's doublet and hose."[19] He has a handsome face, but "its very handsomeness was of a kind that made you want to avert your eye."[20] As Bruno walks out the door, Lawrence "can almost see a furry tail waving between the split skirts of Bruno's coat."[21] Here we are back in the New York of *Jacob's Ladder*, where tails and horns peep terrifyingly from out of coats and under hats.

On campus, Lawrence comes across a student antiharassment demonstration. When he discovers that they are protesting in defense of Bruno rather than against him, Lawrence is overcome by a terrible weariness.

> I felt I could barely walk. The campus seemed to have extended its dreary footpaths an interminable length. Another image of eternity, I thought: walking forever between the Mulberry Street gates of Arthur Clay, and Room 106; the parking lots, the sooty buildings, the iron-green hemlock borders, the gray clapboard dorms distending themselves one step further into the cold fog with every step you took.[22]

Lawrence, it seems, like Jacob Singer, is blundering around in his own personal hell. There may be a way out. It's even signposted: the podiatrist's ad. While the subway ad in *Jacob's Ladder* is merely a sign intended for the viewer, the podiatrist's ad in *The Horned Man* is an exhortation to the narrator: Why

hurt? End pain. All Lawrence has to do is acknowledge the clear message of his telltale blushes and own up to his dark side, which, in chapter 14, manifests itself externally and unambiguously for the first time. The closing lines of the novel are a quotation from a translation of the Gnostic Gospels—"*If you bring forth what is within you, what you bring forth will save you. If you do not bring forth what is within you, what you do not bring forth will destroy you.*"[23] They are remarkably similar to a line of dialogue spoken by Louis, Jacob's chiropractor, toward the end of *Jacob's Ladder*: "If you're frightened of dying, and you're holding on, you'll see devils tearing your life away. If you've made your peace, then the devils are really angels, freeing you from the Earth."[24]

Notes

1. James Lasdun, "Author of *Seven Lies* Chats with Robert Birnbaum," in *Identity Theory*, February 14, 2006, www.identitytheory.com/interviews/birnbaum168.php (accessed December 19, 2009).

2. James Lasdun, *The Horned Man* (New York: W.W. Norton, 2002), 4.

3. Lasdun, *The Horned Man*, 4.

4. Lasdun, *The Horned Man*, 5.

5. Lasdun, *The Horned Man*, 5.

6. Lasdun, *The Horned Man*, 18.

7. Lasdun, *The Horned Man*, 18.

8. Lasdun, *The Horned Man*, 19.

9. *Jacob's Ladder*, directed by Adrian Lyne, screenplay by Bruce Joel Rubin, performed by Tim Robbins, Elizabeth Peña, Danny Aiello, and Jason Alexander (Carolco Pictures, 1990).

10. Ancestry.com, "Schroeder," www.ancestry.com/facts/Schroeder-family-history .ashx (accessed December 19, 2009).

11. Lasdun, *The Horned Man*, 93.

12. Lasdun, *The Horned Man*, 148.

13. Lasdun, *The Horned Man*, 148.

14. Lasdun, *The Horned Man*, 139.

15. Lasdun, *The Horned Man*, 133.

16. Lasdun, *The Horned Man*, 127.

17. Lasdun, *The Horned Man*, 121.

18. Lasdun, *The Horned Man*, 119.

19. Lasdun, *The Horned Man*, 119.

20. Lasdun, *The Horned Man*, 118.

21. Lasdun, *The Horned Man*, 118.

22. Lasdun, *The Horned Man*, 165.

23. Lasdun, *The Horned Man*, 191.

24. *Jacob's Ladder*.

CHAPTER 29

Economies of Leave-Taking in Mark Z. Danielewski's *House of Leaves*

Laurence A. Rickels

Because it is the documentary record of all the information-gathering efforts of its characters, who must recognize in the "mass of typewriting" at the end only an abyssal absence of proof, Bram Stoker's *Dracula* seems the Gothic novel that "introduces" Mark Z. Danielewski's *House of Leaves*[1] as its "continuity shot" in the tradition or genre. Was *Dracula* at its first reception a recognizable instance of the Gothic novel? In time it became a classic example, even or especially because of its unique "Dracula style."[2] Stoker's novel makes it possible to state that a distinctive trait of the Gothic novel is the attention it gives to its scene of writing, which can extend to and through the brand new media networks reshaping it. *Dracula* becomes the record of media changes in its social context via the alle*gory* of an in-group's struggle against vampirism. Because the documentation of the struggle is without authentication, the existence of vampirism cannot be proved but also cannot be disproved.

House of Leaves allegorizes its new media setting (from an analog to a digital frame of reference) via the reception of a documentary film that doesn't exist about a series of extreme events that didn't happen, but which nevertheless asserts itself as felt absence. What is "new" about digitalization in media is, first, that it opens wide our access to information across all boundaries, and second, that we relate to the excess of information (which is stored as much as it is transmitted) via the supplemental synthesis that digital access also provides. In other words, the abyss of information that digitalization opens up is at the same time a synthetic abyss that fits the screen or page of legibility or that crosses the mind as idea. It's like the divide between the imaginary and the symbolic according

to Jacques Lacan, which through digitalization we fully cross. However, when it comes to psychic reality, not every deposit has the redemption value that could beam it up into the digital symbolic. In E. T. A. Hoffmann's "The Sandman" (the story in which Freud found "the uncanny" allegorized), the protagonist Nathanael's girlfriend Klara points out to her beau, who is beginning to show signs of psychotic disturbance, that his wild imaginings are merely phantoms of the ego that in the light of reason, language, or the symbolic can be effortlessly banished since nonexistent. But her appeal only brings out the psychopathic hostility in the mix and mess of his collapsing psyche.

In the case of the Winchester Mystery House, Sarah Winchester sought to accept or admit haunting while at the same time guiding the vengeful ghosts away from her cosy corner via false leads for thirty-eight years. In what was less a house than an ongoing construction site, the mistress builder seemed always only days away—the time it took to build yet another hallway leading nowhere—from ghostly seizure. On the Internet, this sort of endlessly ongoing construction and misdirection is just a keystroke or link away. But how frightening is it? That is why *House of Leaves* turns to film, the medium that has for the time being absorbed the current media changes rather than be mutated or streamlined by them, as our immediate interface with the abyss of digitalization. It isn't just any film that will do here, but film that transmits the horror of losing it, the horror of derangement and uncontained violence, which keeps coming home where its origin lies. Suggesting one inspiration for the vast hallway suddenly appearing at the Navidson home, Danielewski remembers his own home in a recent interview: the "strange education" his filmmaker father gave him by relentlessly projecting movies, "flung up on the wall [at home] like some magical hallway stretching into far away places. My father in the back, in his chair, still in his shadows."[3]

Dracula was at the hub of media crossovers that also reflected the push and pull between English-language and German-language cultures over the provenance of the Gothic. German cinema made the first move across media to reclaim Stoker's projections. But director F. W. Murnau's *Nosferatu* ultimately led to the relocation of the Gothic genre between Hollywood and "Germany," California's other coast. While the alternate medium of the novel is film, the second language of *House of Leaves* is German, and the metadiscourse surrounding the supernatural house (or housing projection) that the film explores is untranslatably dedicated to "das Unheimliche." That the document inside the novel cites Heidegger on "das Unheimliche" (25, note 33) instead of Freud underscores a tension between its conceptual trajectory (to which so much of the documentary language of the novel contributes as montage element) and the Gothic track, the underworld that the intermediary editor opens up, in which the novel's psychic reality is subtly and implicitly organized around psychoanalytic ready-mades like "The Sandman" or John Carpenter's *Halloween*.

House of Leaves contains a study by a certain Zampanò (a blind man in his eighties who, as a traditional trait of the American intellectual, never got past high school) that documents a legendary film, *The Navidson Record*, and its reception. Discovering the deceased Zampanò's unfinished project, in the apartment he takes from him, is twenty-five-year-old Johnny Truant.[4] Johnny is a "tatts" artist denizen of Hollywood, whose stripper girlfriend, because her name is Thumper, is the reason watching *Bambi* gives him a hard-on. An unlikely academic researcher at first glance, Johnny is nonetheless drawn to conclude the interrupted work. Through his efforts, we soon discover that *The Navidson Record* doesn't exist outside the fictional record of its reception.[5] Truant's notes also record as diary entries the psychopathology of his everyday life that this editorial work either illuminates or triggers. Because he unravels (along the dotted lines of a maternal legacy of psychosis), there is another editor who must give Johnny Truant's wrap the stamp of completion. Just the same, it is not Johnny's doom but rather his trace of survival that *House of Leaves* incorporates as a vital signature of its narrative of loss and mourning. Though Johnny is lost to the novel's completion, he leaves behind the deposit of his mother's letters to him, written from the mental institute where she ultimately killed herself, the collected work of their *dead*ication to each other, which the concluding editor includes as appendix. The mother's letters bear a family resemblance to the goodness of the writing in the Johnny Truant tract. It is in the footnote underworld occupied by Johnny Truant's "good" language (in the Nietzschean sense, and thus in contrast to the bulk rate of the internal faux documents compiled and composed by Zampanò, which must be considered, as language, "bad" or *schlecht*) that a relation to hope and mourning is vouchsafed.

What appears to be press information about the publication's prehistory is also internal to the novel's construct. The cover blurb material refers to the prehistory of Danielewski's novel when, years ago, it was first being passed around as a "heap of paper, parts of which would occasionally surface on the Internet." The only support for this claim is internal to the book.[6] According to Johnny Truant's entry dated August 28, 1999, he encountered a band called Liberty Bell ("cracked," as their guitar player confessed) who cited *The Navidson Record* or its documentation in their song lyrics. "The drummer . . . explained that the lyrics were inspired by a book he'd found on the Internet quite some time ago" (513). On the title page of the band's tattered printout, Truant finds his name credited with composition of the introduction and the notes.

The cover material spreads this internal fiction of a "small but devoted following" that started out "with an odd assortment of marginalized youth" (which when sorted out or listed includes the druggies, clubbers, exotic dancers, and other characters who comprise Truant's milieu) and then spread through "older generations, who not only found themselves in those strangely arranged pages

but also discovered a way back into the lives of their estranged children." Now we hold in our hands in book form these very pages, excerpts, and their first reception. As advertised, then, the book comes to us across a gap in generations. It also comes across to us from three deeply burdened and guilty men who are at a loss that has not been put to rest. As I have argued elsewhere, in relation to Freud's theory of ghosts and his theory of pathological mourning, "those who are incapable of mourning must build inside for the unmourned and, hence, undead."[7]

The jacket material identifies as the content of the novel not Zampanò's study, which is overlooked, though it remains legible, but instead that which is never really available, namely, Will Navidson's document "of creature darkness, of an ever-growing abyss behind a closet door, and of that unholy growl which soon enough would tear through their walls and consume all of their dreams." Navidson, a haunted war photographer who won a Pulitzer for his picture of a starving Sudanese girl collapsing before a vulture (an actual photograph taken by his real-life model, Kevin Carter, who killed himself three months after winning the prize for it), decides to film the happy event of his move with partner and children into a country house in Virginia, "supposedly built back in 1720" (21), where he plans to renew his vows with family life. Staying true to its reputation of having "traumatized in some way" most of its residents for over two centuries (21), one day there is an extra room in the house where before there was none. This room proves to be the opening of a labyrinth in which one can get lost (or find that one is at a loss), not according to a fixed design, but because, in the Gothic mode, it is a space without borders that can undergo instant abyssal changes. *The Navidson Record* is the video- and audio-recorded document of the traumatically close encounter between nine individuals (Will Navidson and his immediate family, plus his twin brother and four friends and colleagues) and this supernatural house, which claims three lives. Though the film cannot be shown to us, the book (or its internal relay of documents) renders itself as visible as it is legible at crucial points of crisis. Thus, as the passageways of the labyrinth close in on Navidson, as the video record allegedly shows, the margins start shrink-wrapping the text in bits that must squeeze through these straitened circumstances on pages left largely blank, like the gray zones that presumably sustain insubstantial traces in the documentary film record of the unknown.

It is not the supernatural house but rather the missing film and the films it summons through which we enter the haunted enclosure that is the site specific to the Gothic genre (and the open invitational for psychoanalytic reading). And yet the players inside *The Navidson Record*, like the scholars who bear testimony to them, are suspended in the faux language of academic journalism. Zampanò's study of *The Navidson Record* completes its range of references within a (largely simulated) scholarly apparatus. In the labyrinth, there is always bull, but there is

one track in the footnotes that is free of the recycling language of simulation. It belongs to the troubled Johnny Truant, who adds to his edition of Zampanò's work.

House of Leaves does have a prepublication history that lies "outside" the book itself (even if, on the other side, the book's frame at times seems coterminous with the Internet). Mark Danielewski's sister Ann, a rock musician who goes by the name Poe, released an album that included recordings of her author brother reading from his book. What was in the foreground, also as the occasion for Poe's composition, was the death of their father, who was an experimental filmmaker from Poland. He left audiotaped communications to his children, which Poe transferred to the record of her work (titled *Haunted*).

The Truant tract is ultimately framed, in the style of *Frankenstein*, by the relationship to a missing mother. But in a more immediate zone within the relay of his diary entries, there is also a story in the mode of "The Sandman" organized around the so-called Gdansk Man, who, like the paternal Sandman figure in Hoffmann's story, cruelly enforces the high-fidelity values of Oedipus at the expense of the libidinal vitality of his wayward sons. Because they messed to varying degrees with his girlfriend Kyrie, Gdansk Man, who "is now officially on some kind of Halloween rampage" (348, note 310), has targeted Johnny and his friend Lude for retribution. That Johnny doesn't die in consequence (as Lude does) is owed to Johnny's own potential for psychopathic violence that he has kept in reserve since childhood and which Gdansk Man's punching releases as a kind of doubling on contact:

> Nothing close to pity moved inside me. I was sliding over some edge within myself. I was going to rip open his skin with my bare hands, claw past his ribs and tear out his liver and then I was going to eat it, gorge myself on his blood, puke it all up and still come back for more, consuming all of it, all of him, all of it all over again.
>
> Then suddenly, drawn in black on black, deep in the shadowy sail of my eye, I understood Kyrie was running towards me, arms outstretched, nails angled down to tear my face, puncture sight. But even as I slammed my fist into Gdansk Man's temple again, something had already made me turn to meet her, and even though I did not command it, I was already hearing my horrendous shout, ripped from my center, blasting into her with enough force to stop her dead in her tracks, robbed instantly of any will to finish what she must have seen then was only suicide. She didn't even have enough strength left to turn away. . . . I should have shifted my gaze. Instead I let her read in my eyes everything I was about to do to her. . . .
>
> Surprised? Really? Has nothing prepared you for this? This place where no eye will find her, no ear will hear her, among pillars of rust, where hawks haunt the sky, where I will weave my hands around her

throat, closing off her life, even as I rape her, dismember her, piece by piece, and in the continuing turn, for these turns never really stop turning, void out all I am, ever was, once meant or didn't mean. (496–497)

While this contact with the psychopath within is contained and Johnny remains at worst a prolonged adolescent, it provides a scene and the language for summoning the films that *The Navidson Record* cites only by implication and exclusion.[8]

The model for the installation of *The Navidson Record* as docu-fiction inside *House of Leaves* (and its World Wide Web) is *The Blair Witch Project* (released the year before Danielewski's novel), which took as its outer and preliminary form and forum an Internet rumor of a real encounter with the supernatural raised to life-or-death stakes. The outside chance that *The Blair Witch Project* was a real posthumous document of a group's violent contact with an unholy abyss, which was rehearsed or repeated on the Internet prior to the film's release, allowed the film to score success and succession as horror.[9]

The Internet occupies the outer limit of that expansion of the press into global media first carried out by telegraphy in the immediate context of *Dracula*. Modern spiritualism syndicated the live connection of telegraphy as the undead tapping that mediums received from spirits and decoded in séances. In turn, the telegraphically expanding news press regularly covered the séances of spiritualism. Often investigative reporting debunked mediums in the course of testing the evidence. That even negative press was thus spreading the good news of (the possibility of) undead networks opening was confirmed when mediums began inviting witnesses, the more skeptical the better, to test their séance activities. The media record of *Dracula* fails to support the reality of vampirism but also doesn't disprove the possibility.

The Blair Witch Project seems, then, a late arrival, within the new media setting, of the *Dracula* effect. But more immediately and more pressingly, this film served in the big picture to bring back "psycho horror." Even the era that *Dracula* documents was home to the primal psycho killer Jack the Ripper. What can be termed the *Psycho* effect was the metabolization in horror films of the traumatic impact of the famous shower scene in Hitchcock's film. *Schauer*, the German etymon of shower, means "horror," as in the German equivalent of the Gothic novel, *der Schauerroman*. While the German word can also designate rainstorm showers—its history tracks back to storms blowing in from the North with disastrous consequences—the German language borrowed from French to name the other shower in a tub or stall. Hitchcock, who came to cinema via German film, reinstalled the *Schauer* in his signature shower scene. After a post-traumatic delay, this *Schauer* scene was symptomatized and syndicated in countless films beginning in 1968 until, around 1990, it had been worked through

and put to rest. This end of treatment came to be another bind we were in. Thus *The Blair Witch Project* marked a return not only of the *Psycho* effect but also of its alternating therapeutic containment. That is why the faux documentary of supernatural events was accompanied by the release of its container, the therapeutic ghost movie *The Sixth Sense*.

When we watched *The Sixth Sense* the second time, we might have had a second thought that, like *The Blair Witch Project*, it was engaged in a reformatting of the end of horror post-*Psycho* as renewal of contact with the medium as sight unseen. *The Sixth Sense* packs a surprise ending that sends the viewer through a flashback loop in part given or modeled at the end of the film. Both *The Blair Witch Project* and *The Sixth Sense*, though certainly in different ways, exceeded the frame of the single screening (as contained in, as containing, a body of work) by networking with outer-corpus experiences of media manipulation and the two-timing of surprise. This larger frame, which comes out of the new interactive media, contains in advance side effects or symptoms that once developed all down the receiving line of films like *Psycho*, *Night of the Living Dead*, and *The Texas Chainsaw Massacre*, which were in themselves, left to themselves, uncontainable. What makes *The Sixth Sense*—like *Scream*—post-*Psycho* rather than pre-*Psycho* is the self-conscious therapeutic momentum that builds (on) resolution.

The metabolism of horror film requires surprise dosages now of hiding the violence, now of showing it all, now of serial interminability, now of termination. Following the success of *The Sixth Sense*, therapeutic closure itself came to be rejected as laughable or as horrifying in its nonexistence. This is where we put *The Ring* on it. This film grabbed us just when and where we thought it was safe to see dead people (in other words in the therapy setting of the movie theater). At what surely looks like the reassuring or therapeutic end of *The Ring*, the adults have tended to the unfinished business of the tormented girl, granted her proper burial, and so on. But when the mother, all upbeat about having done the right thing, tells her son (who is the counterpart to the boy in *The Sixth Sense*) all about the good deed and the dead, the boy is horrified. Don't you know that she won't stop, that she doesn't sleep, that her violence cannot be buried or let go?! Now the mother and we, too, know that the anger of the ghost is interminable and the psycho violence contained in the ghost's video and phone call as death sentence in seven days time can be circumvented only by passing it on before the deadline is reached. You must spread the viewing of contained violence—its death threat—to ever more potential victims, or survivors and collaborators, for your own survival.

The *Psycho* effect raised the figure of the "psycho" to another "Norm" as our double at one decisive remove. In the language of object-relations psychoanalysis, we can say, there but for the grace of the good object go I. In the course

of the *Psycho* effect, we became teenagers at heart who could identify with the psycho. English psychoanalyst D. W. Winnicott argued that in the post–World War II era, teen energy could no longer be harnessed to or through future wars, since the atom bomb had eclipsed total war from the horizon of preparedness.[10] Add to this deregulation of violence control the introduction of effective contraception, and we had to face the adolescent as the site/sight of our ongoing struggle to contain sex and violence. Group or mass psychology thus comes to be circuited through adolescent psychology. The teen prefers starting from scratch to inheriting from the couple of parents. Teens form groups that give them sexual license (which they can't receive from the parents who are too off-limits or out of it) and that calibrate violent acting-out tendencies for them. The group promotes its most ill member to the position of ego ideal or scapegoat. When this identified patient breaks the law, for example, the other members of the group can feel real by proxy. In time, the teen becomes able to tolerate compromise, notably in the form of identifying with and inheriting from parental guidance. A more couplified rapport with the other becomes possible, one that admits, with identification, mourning as well.

The apparent delicacy of Johnny Truant's psychic makeup, who as a boy and young man has painfully moved from orphanage to foster home several times, does not contradict the quality of his escape between the lines. Among the entries or fragments comprising Johnny's narrative, there is the other uncanny episode that stages a violent disconnection between Johnny and a sort of android woman over a stray dog. As preamble to his narration of this episode, Johnny follows Lude's example and tallies his libidinal conquests for that month: "People frequently comment on the emptiness in one night stands, but emptiness here has always been just another word for darkness. Blind encounters writing sonnets no one can ever read. Desire and pain communicated in the vague language of sex" (265). Thus he is brought to tell the story he had "been meaning to tell all along, one that still haunts me today, about the wounded and where I still fear they finally end up" (265). The most basic libidinal connection is to the good object. The story of a threat to this lifeline is what follows his rundown of the connections without answer.

In a bar, Lude directs Johnny's attention to the woman who must be a porn star. With "nails as long as kitchen knives and lips stuffed with god knows how many layers of tissue collected from the ass of some cadaver," her breasts nevertheless stand out: "entire seas sacrificed to fill those saline sacks, Red Sea on the left, the Dead Sea on the right. Given the right storm, they could probably take out coastal townships with no guarantees for inland villages either" (266). In contrast to the truth-pulling conversation from hell back in the bar, when Johnny escorts the woman, who goes by the name Johnnie, to her truck, he can immediately find a connection to the stray Pekinese they encounter on the way.

She offers to take care of the pup since she has a yard, what she calls a "happy pet land" and over which she presides as "the momma to all strays" (267).

Everything about her is near miss: "those cold and indifferent spaces in our talk suddenly full of affection and concern, though the notes seemed wrong, not dissonant or flat or played at an improper tempo, just wrong, the melody somehow robbed of itself, meaning not another melody either, just something else" (266–267). When she gives him a lift to his place, he doesn't ask her in. "Something about her frightened me. The knotted fingers. That blank stare, permanently fixed on some strange slate bare continent lost deep beneath ancient seas, her seas, dark, red, dead. Maybe not. Maybe it was that Pekinese pup, hungry and abandoned, suddenly rescued, suddenly with hope; a projection of myself? my own place in the way of straydom?" (267).

As Johnnie drives away in her truck, she throws the puppy out the window. "She must have thrown it with tremendous force too. In truth an almost unimaginable amount of force. I tried to picture those clawlike hands grabbing this poor creature by the neck and hurling it out her window. Had she even looked at what she held?" (267–268). The strange indecision he experiences over the dead Pekinese raises, like a ghost, the question of his hesitation to revisit his mother at the Three Attic Whalestoe Institute, or to grieve her death: "I couldn't even say anything, not a cry, a shout or a word. I couldn't even feel anything either, shock alone possessing me. . . . I was too late" (268).

The identification with the stray Pekinese belongs to those tendencies that qualify Johnny Truant for the editorial work that claims him. He is a "sucker for abandoned stuff, misplaced stuff, forgotten stuff, . . . goings unheralded, passings unmourned" (21, note 25). Alone, his misspelling when referring to the morning newspaper as "the mourning paper" (31, note 31) gives the novel's greater archival apparatus of nihilistic academic journalism the slip. Deep inside this apparatus, we are informed of the arcane and meaningless speculations advanced at "The Conference on the Aesthetics of Mourning" (386–387). Johnny lets slip between the lines of his morning paper the press of ghosts.

While *Dracula* is transmitted as a document of the survival of the group members who composed it via the new mass-media socius they introduce and project, *House of Leaves* has by the end already taken leave of each group member but one. Though *Dracula* folds mourning into its group bond, it can be argued that the group never really mourns. While a group of editors has turned the internal relay and withdrawal of documents into *House of Leaves*, each group member takes over where another leaves off. *House of Leaves* restages this staggered transmission of its document, its internal posthumous relations, as a closing series of appendices. But what issues from this structure as sole survival is inscribed only in the film document (or its documentation) as the "final shots" Navidson takes one Halloween night: "Navidson does not close with the caramel

covered face of a Casper the friendly ghost" (528). He cannot end with a recognizable representative or representation of group survival. "He ends instead on what he knows is true and always will be true" (528).What you see is what you get—to remember—to forget. "Letting the parade pass from sight, he focuses on the empty road beyond, a pale curve vanishing into the woods where nothing moves and a street lamp flickers on and off until at last it flickers out and darkness sweeps in like a hand" (528).

Notes

1. Mark Z. Danielewski, *House of Leaves* (New York: Pantheon Books, 2000).
2. This "style" refers to Stoker's use of citation only, in the absence of authorial voice or opinion, to build his document.
3. Mark Z. Danielewski, interview by Sophie Cottrell, "Bold Type: A Conversation with Mark Danielewski," Random House, www.randomhouse.com/boldtype/0400/danielewski/interview.html (accessed February 8, 2010).
4. D. W. Winnicott, "The Antisocial Tendency," in *Deprivation and Delinquency*, ed. Clare Winnicott, Ray Shepherd, and Madeleine Davis (London: Routledge, 2000, 129). Winnicott draws a clinical contrast between "a 'going out,' without aim, *truancy*, a centrifugal tendency" and the "centripetal gesture . . . implicit in thieving."
5. In his introduction to *House of Leaves*, xix–xx, Johnny Truant writes, "After all, as I fast discovered, Zampanò's entire project is about a film which doesn't even exist. You can look, I have, but no matter how long you search you will never find *The Navidson Record* in theaters or video stores. Furthermore, most of what's said by famous people has been made up."
6. The Internet provides the perfect technical update of rumor as medium, which in the occult setting transmitted telepathically. On the Web, any fictionalized history can be sustained indefinitely. By the second half of the 1990s, everything in the conservative media could be found exceeded and preceded on the Web. Rather than send printout copies, one could post one's manuscript on the Web for friends and family to encircle and read. Apparently that's what Danielewski did with his seven hundred pages. Did a cult following find its way into this circle, or did the circle open itself by word of mouth? Or is the historical claim of a cult following projected onto a medium that, like the haunted house in *House of Leaves*, is a recognizable size on the outside but incalculably vast on the inside. In an interview, the author claims that the posting of the manuscript was performed "three years earlier" (Eric Wittmershaus, "Profile: Mark Z. Danielewski," *Flak* magazine, May 6, 2000). But since we just learned that the publication process took almost three years, the date mark is unclear. Danielewski had the idea for the book in 1993. But we are also informed that it was ten years in the making. Was the first edition already the so-called second edition? Was there a first edition in which Johnny Truant's mother's letters were not included, since they were published separately as the companion piece, *The Whalestoe Letters*? A 2000 edition of *The Whalestoe Letters* claims

the correspondence, which was "originally contained within the monumental *House of Leaves*," now stands alone but also includes "eleven previously unavailable letters."

7. Laurence Rickels, *Aberrations of Mourning: Writing on German Crypts* (Detroit: Wayne State University Press, 1988), 17.

8. I note here the filmography for movies I will be referring to in the course of my reprojection of *The Navidson Record*.

> *The Blair Witch Project*, directors Daniel Myrick and Eduardo Sánchez, 1999.
> *Halloween*, director John Carpenter, 1978.
> *Night of the Living Dead*, director George Romero, 1968.
> *Psycho*, director Alfred Hitchcock, 1960.
> *The Ring*, director Gore Verbinski, 2002.
> *Scream*, director Wes Craven, 1996.
> *The Sixth Sense*, director M. Night Shyamalan, 1999.
> *The Texas Chainsaw Massacre*, director Tobe Hooper, 1974.

9. *The Blair Witch Project* was conceived and launched in 1993. Ads appeared that year looking for actors for the project who were skilled at improvisation. The film "internal" to the film is an unfinished documentary made by three film students in 1994. The document survived, but the filmmakers disappeared. This faux documentary material was filmed in 1997. Soon the rumor powers of the Internet were pressed into the service of the film's reality effect. By 1999, it was the most successful low-budget film of all time. Because *House of Leaves* coincides with *The Blair Witch Project*, while *The Navidson Record* dates back earlier in the decade, the film inside the book became legend before the Internet; before it was released for a limited but influential run, two shorts or teasers circulated unofficially as VHS copies that were passed around.

10. Winnicott makes this genealogical point about adolescence and the psychoanalytic points that follow on the teen group dynamic in his brief article "Struggling through the Doldrums," in *Deprivation and Delinquency*, ed. Clare Winnicott, Ray Shepherd, and Madeleine Davis (London: Routledge, 2000), 145–155. Winnicott's reading importantly shows that we *double* the psycho because the teen group bond is part of our makeup. When treating juvenile delinquents, for example, Winnicott was kept busy trying to rule out normal adolescence in the course of determining a diagnosis. At the border of doubling, it proves next to impossible to draw a clear line of demarcation. He thus also answers a more specific question: Why, beginning with the film *Halloween*, did the psycho command a group following? But *Halloween* also introduced the survivor as another object of identification, not just as our ego probe in the fantasy of survival but as the other with whom or for whom we, too, can live on. Earlier in the course of the psycho effect, a survivor was admitted to offset the burden of killing. In zombie films, for instance, the guilty pleasure results from the equation between surviving and killing. At the end of *Halloween*, Laurie's survival has the quality of therapeutic achievement. Unlike Sally at the end of *The Texas Chainsaw Massacre*, Laurie is not chained to what she saw.

CHAPTER 30

Dread and Decorum in Susanna Clarke's *Jonathan Strange & Mr. Norrell*

Douglass H. Thomson

Midway through Clarke's 782-page novel, as the magician Jonathan Strange assists Lord Wellington in his Peninsular Campaign against Napoleon, there occurs a scene that epitomizes the crosscurrents of her peculiar shaping of the Gothic spirit. Wellington has asked Strange's help in locating the secret hiding place of some enemy cannons, and the magician decides to use a spell borrowed from the mighty Raven King (more on him later[1]) to reanimate the corpses of seventeen dead Neapolitans to see what they know:

He began muttering to himself in Latin. He next made a long, deep cut in his arm, and when he had got a good strong spurt of blood, he let it splash over the head of the corpses, taking care to anoint the eyes, tongue and nostrils of each. After a moment the first corpse roused itself. There was a horrible rasping sound as its dried-out lungs filled with air and its limbs shook in a way that was very dreadful to behold. Then one by one the corpses revived and began to speak in a guttural language which contained a much higher proportion of screams than any language known to the onlookers.

Even Wellington looked a little pale. Only Strange continued apparently without emotion.

"Dear God!" cried Fitzroy Somerset, "What language is that?"

"I believe it is one of the dialects of hell," said Strange.

"Is it indeed?" said Somerset. "Well, that is remarkable."

"They have learnt it very quickly," said Lord Wellington, "They have only been dead three days." He approved of people doing things promptly and in a businesslike fashion.[2]

319

This droll rejoinder to a gruesome ritual evoking the language of hell typifies what John Hodgman has noted as the play between the "mundane" and the "surreal" in Clarke's novel. Wellington's praise of the dead men's facility in learning a foreign language could pay tribute to English diligence—or satirize it. Either way, the weirdly inappropriate remark abruptly pulls the reader from one of the novel's more viscerally Gothic moments of horror back to a focus on English character and to the business at hand, the war against the French (something covered with meticulous historical accuracy by Clarke, if one looks past the alternate history of Strange's assistance in the British victory). The seventeen animated corpses do give up the secret, and the guns are captured. Two footnotes, a favorite device of Clarke's that similarly straddles the line between seriousness and satire, frame and complicate our reception of the scene. The first, supplying information on the origins of the spell used by Strange, offers a kind of preemptive apology that it should be "so brutal," whereas usually such magic is "mysterious, beautiful, [and] subtle" (329). The second returns us to the cruel exigencies of the battlefield in Wellington's terse letter concerning the fate of the Neapolitans: "They had been so battered about since their deaths. They were not, poor fellows, a sight any one wished to see upon waking. In the end we made a bonfire and threw them on it" (333).

Critical study of the Gothic, especially the "First Gothics" (1765–1825), has stressed its many paradoxes and productive tensions, noting its turbulent energies often framed by conservative morality, its politically subversive plotting meliorated by a middle-class reassurance, and its apparent heresies haunted by traditional Christian doctrines of sin and damnation. Clarke's *Jonathan Strange & Mr. Norrell* references all of these divisions familiar to the Gothic and includes the requisite citations of Radcliffe, Beckford, Lewis, and Byron (who figures as a begrudging friend and double of Strange) to invite our identification of her novel with its Gothic predecessors.[3] What sets her novel apart from the old, hoary tradition is how rarely its crosscurrents appear as tensions or paradoxes or even troublesome matters. As in the episode concerning the belatedly cooperative Neapolitans, the grotesque runs right alongside the comic, with neither too vexed by its opposing term. *Jonathan Strange & Mr. Norrell* has been variously praised as "unquestionably the finest English novel of the fantastic written in the last seventy years,"[4] "a tale of magic such as might have been written by the young Jane Austen,"[5] a successful pastiche "perfectly balanced between outlandish fantasy and richly detailed historical reality,"[6] and a probing meditation on "what it means to be English."[7] The novel has also received its fair share of criticism: Michael Dirda laments the novel's lack of "lyricism and poetry," noting that "Clarke treats magic as simply an arcane branch of learning, like medicine or physics, and its practitioners as essentially applied scientists."[8] Michel Faber relatedly argues that "Clarke is ultimately an arch-rationalist," for whom

"Magic is . . . A Bad Thing." In his view, a "desolate spirit" pervades the novel that reveals a "fear of the very forces it purports to celebrate"[9] (both critics also point out the book's "low emotional temperature" and omission of any matters sexual). So, which is it, a novel of enchantment, "mysterious, beautiful, [and] subtle" (329), or one that hedges upon its own more darkly imaginative energies? A bit of both seems the final answer, and that may well be what makes Clarke's novel such a *strange* read.

Take the novel's presentation of magic for example, a key point of contention among the reviewers. Dirda's complaint about the matter-of-factness shaping the summoning of magic certainly holds true for the bibliophile Mr. Norrell, who distrusts the more anarchic strains of the old enchantments and its folk practitioners, represented by the elaborately tattooed street conjurer Vinculus. As a "practical magician," Norrell seems content to serve as a kind of government bureaucrat in the war against the French. Yet he calls the "gentleman with thistle-down hair"[10] from the world of Faerie he so distrusts to revive the dead Lady Pole and to gain her husband's support, and this self-serving act unleashes the dark enchantment that propels the plot, consigning Lady Pole, the Poles' dignified African servant Stephen Black, and finally, Strange's wife, Arabella, to a zombielike existence in the alternate faerie dimension of Lost-hope. One sees a promising premise on this score with great resonance in the Gothic tradition, a premise that Clarke chooses not to explore: the too narrow rationalist, seeking to deny or repress the imaginative life, inevitably calls forth a malignant, uncontrollable form of the forces he sought to banish (a Freudian logic, well expressed in William Blake's proverb from hell: "The man who never alters his opinion is like standing water, & breeds reptiles of the mind").[11]

The novel's eponymous counterpoint to the pedantic Norrell, the impetuous, intuitively gifted Jonathan Strange, champions the more daring strains of magic but does not really fare all that much better. He, too, serves as a bit of a government lackey, moving rivers and towns to frustrate Napoleon's plans and, for the most part, using his magic to spy on the French. In a scene reminiscent of Victor Frankenstein's wedding night, Strange, monomaniacally devoted to his magic studies, ignores several warnings and loses his wife to the world of Faerie (although he thinks mistakenly that she has died). In order to penetrate the world of Faerie, he must descend to madness by drinking a draught comprised of the chemical remains of a dead mouse he has taken from a mad woman obsessed with cats!—although there also appears to be a de Quinceyesque take on laudanum at work as well. What Strange experiences as he slips into madness comprises some of the eeriest parts of the novel, as Clarke subtly melts reality, shifts scenes, and hints at a yawning abyss from which Strange might not return. These are darkly magical moments, yet counterbalanced, in Clarke's characteristic fashion, with bizarrely light touches, such as Strange's hallucination of pineapples

descending upon Venice, where he admits spending "too much time in Lord Byron's society" (781). The novel's strategic contrasting of Norrell and Strange, almost allegorically signifying Enlightenment reason versus Romantic intuition (or *Sense and Sensibility*[12]), seems to promise a final confrontation between the two, but instead both end up in a Pillar of Darkness or Eternal Night, where the time is always midnight. Despite Norrell's deceptions and nasty pamphlet war against Strange, both are content to work together on their darkling magic now that they are no longer distracted by intrusions from the domestic or political sphere; indeed, the two seem more riveted by "some new conjectures concerning naiads" than in dispelling the dark enchantment that covers them (781).

The most powerful manifestation of magic in the novel concerns a shadowy figure who only appears in three pages of the book (754–756): John Uskglass, aka the Raven King (his actual faerie name is unrecorded, unpronounceable). Hinted at in a poetic prophecy by Vinculus, frequently glossed in the elaborate footnotes, distrusted by Mr. Norrell and ardently pursued by Jonathan Strange, the Raven King embodies the true spirit of English magic. A foundling abducted by the faeries, he held sway in northern England for some three hundred years during the Middle Ages, the last great age of English magic. His very ethereality lends him an aura of mystery, and his spirit, always on the borders, haunts not only the sorcerers but readers of the novel as well. When he finally makes his one brief appearance, his Romantic alliances with nature ("Tree speaks to Stone; Stone speaks to Water" [667]) allow Stephen Black to destroy the malevolent faerie, free himself from bondage, and become the next king of the Faerie realm. The novel ends with the spirit of magic dispersed throughout the land, with commoners and gentlefolk alike able to conjure spells, and with seventeen roads to Faerie land suddenly open to the public in Yorkshire. Clarke has noted with some chagrin that this widespread accessibility of magical forces will present a challenge to her in the follow-up novel: "I have a bit of a problem now that the fairy roads are all open. . . . What do I do with them?"[13] This problem stems from her success in familiarizing the marvelous: making magic so believable and accessible risks losing its, well, magic.

This democratization of magic ushered in by the reappearance of the Raven King points to another of the novel's more perplexing crosscurrents: its treatment of class. The main narrative focuses with Austenesque wit on the genteel world of the Regency upper class, its London dinner parties, gossip, political intrigues, and social maneuvering. Three characters from the lower class, however, assume key roles in the resolution of affairs, although Strange and Norrell never learn of the parts they play in the restoration of English magic. The first is Vinculus, detested and feared by the elitist Norrell as a cheap street magician: his prophecies—"*the nameless slave shall be a king in a strange country*" (124)— simultaneously herald the return of Uskglass and the elevation of Stephen Black

to king of Lost-hope. The tattoos covering his body turn out to be the urtext of English magic, more prescient and organic than any of the books hoarded by Norrell. The second character is the enigmatic John Childermass,[14] the rather independent and secretive serving man for Norrell. First appearing as an ironic foil to Norrell's fussiness, he emerges as a powerful magician in his own right, helping to rescue Lady Pole from Lost-hope and serving as the protector and interpreter of Vinculus and his oracular text. The final economically marginal figure who comes to play a key role in the novel is a child of African slaves, Stephen Black, head servant for the Poles. Forced to wander in the desolate realm of Lost-hope—along with Lady Pole and, eventually, Arabella—because of Norrell's self-serving spell, Stephen finally triumphs over the malevolent faerie by channeling the spirit of the Raven King. He ends up succeeding him as king of Faerie land, with the promise of bringing a more enlightened monarchy to the world of Lost-hope. Elizabeth Hoiem has convincingly argued that the novel explores the "'silencing' of certain voices underrepresented in most historical narratives—those of women, people of color, and disenfranchised poor whites" (both Stephen and Lady Pole endure "muffling spells" [728] inflicted upon them by the "gentleman"). Hoiem concludes that, "in the end, it is Strange and Norrell who are trapped in everlasting darkness while the silenced women, people of color, and poor whites defeat the antagonist."[15] Yet this plausible and reassuringly progressive reading of the novel seems at odds with Clarke's own comments about the "sort of Englishness" she wanted to portray ("something strong and idealized and romantic"). In the interview with *Locus*, Clarke says that she aimed to explore "what it was to be an English gentleman at the time when England was a very confident place. . . . [I]t's the sort of Englishness which is stuffy but fundamentally benevolent, and fundamentally very responsible about the rest of the world."[16] So we are apparently not to be disconcerted that Strange entertains an offer to work for the East India Company or that both Norrell's and Strange's gentlemanly fascinations with magic end up wreaking havoc on those that serve them. In a manner characteristic of its crosscurrents, the novel wants it both ways, offering a celebration of an idealized, romantic England (mainly, it seems, North England) set right alongside a critical questioning of its hegemony. In her next novel, Clarke seems to want to address this issue by focusing on "people basically a bit lower down the social scale" and cutting back the "sort of Jane Austen stratum."[17]

Hoiem's contention that the novel's depiction of women criticizes a patriarchal order that silences their voices and, at the end, affirms their agency points to another of Clarke's suggestive but half-realized re-creations from the Gothic tradition: the Gothic heroine. Many critical studies have focused on the Female Gothic, some arguing how the heroine's victimization reflects critically upon a patriarchal social order, others suggesting that the Gothic genre enabled its many

women writers to challenge culturally constructed notions of gender and bodies.[18] Certainly the imprisonment of Emma Pole and Arabella Strange as endless dancers in the gentleman's fantasy world provides a vivid picture of female exploitation. They have been sent there through the agency of Norrell's and Strange's magic. Lady Pole, newly freed from the gentleman's tyranny, sounds a distinctly feminist note in her expression of rage against Strange: "By negligence and cold, masculine magic he has betrayed the best of women, the most excellent of wives" (729). Railing against "how these men protect one another," she embarks on a letter-writing campaign to the *Times* to expose "the true hideousness of Mr. Norrell's crimes" (761). Yet an important and almost easy to forget factor complicates a feminist reading of the novel: among many other things, *Jonathan Strange & Mr. Norrell* is a love story. Arabella perfectly accepts the fact that "books and magic" are all that her husband really cares about (780), and she waits patiently and lovingly for his return from the world of darkness, "though sleep [does] not come easily to her" (780). For his part, Strange declares, "I have changed England to save my wife" (743). The novel concludes with a quietly powerful scene between Arabella and Jonathan, with his promise that he will do all that he can to emerge from the darkness and rejoin her. Perhaps Dirda goes too far in calling the novel "a very masculine book, with no particular interest in the female characters, who all seem typecast."[19] Yet the power of Lady Pole's attack on "cold, masculine" magic seems somewhat muted by the novel's belatedly romantic (small *r*) interests.

Any consideration of Clarke's novel as belonging to the Gothic tradition must finally address its depiction of terror, and, not surprisingly, the reviewers voice sharply different estimates on this score, reflecting the divisions within *Jonathan Strange & Mr. Norrell* itself. Amanda Craig complains that, "As fantasy, it is deplorable, given that it fails to embrace the essentially anarchic nature of such tales,"[20] and instead treats magic as the "preserve of posh people" (a complaint which does not quite seem fair, given the significant roles of Black, Vinculus, and Childermass). Dirda, while admiring "Susanna Clarke's imaginative dexterity," longs for good, old sources of Gothic terror in such things as "the corruption of the innocent, the Walpurgisnacht orgy, the vampiric Lamia and the Belle Dame sans Merci."[21] While Clarke does not draw upon traditional Gothic sources for the novel's moments of horror, one does come across, in her wintery world,[22] occasionally sublime moments of dread: the endless Black Pillar of Night rising "up into the grey Yorkshire sky" (724), the ghostly ballroom dances in the desolate world of Faerie, the Goyaesque hanging of human bodies on a thorn tree, and the enigmatic King's Roads that may lead to the Faerie world or cast one into oblivion. Clarke's usual method, however, retreats from evocation of the sublime, framing and defusing its power with a return to ordinariness, often via ironic commentary on the very horrors she conjures. In this

world, one finds characters sitting quite comfortably on chairs made of human bones. Her signature treatment of the Gothic actually reverses the direction of a less sublime yet still fertile source of terror, Freud's notion of the *unheimlich* (the nearest English translation is "uncanny"). Freud suggests that terror can derive its power "not from something external, alien, or unknown but—on the contrary—from something strangely familiar which defeats our efforts to separate ourselves from it."[23] Clarke proceeds in just about the opposite way, curiously making "something external, alien, or unknown" seem "strangely familiar." As the author herself notes in her characteristically deadpan fashion, "One way of grounding the magic is by putting in lots of stuff about street lamps, carriages and how difficult it is to get good servants."[24] This domestication of the marvelous may disappoint readers searching for wilder Gothic moments of sexual excess, terror, grotesquery, and unmerciful disaster, but there remains in her vision something undeniably eerie, a suggestion that alternate worlds, dreamlike apparitions, and unimagined forces lie just below the surface of our waking reality. These elsewheres beckon us with their mysterious allure and wondrous otherness, but, the novel suggests, we follow them at our own risk.

Notes

1. One is tempted here to mimic one of the more notorious aspects of Clarke's novel: its copious use of footnotes that range from the mock pedantic to miniessays evoking a bygone period of English magic. My promise to supply information later on the Raven King also mirrors Clarke's "curious narrative strategy of continual deferral and delay" (Gregory Feeley, "The Magic of England: Susanna Clarke's Novel of the Fairy Isle," *Weekly Standard*, October 18, 2004). For example, Strange is mentioned in an early footnote and occasionally thereafter but not introduced until a quarter of the way through the novel.

2. Susanna Clarke, *Jonathan Strange & Mr. Norrell* (New York: Bloomsbury, 2004), 332. Page numbers appear hereafter in parentheses in the text.

3. See the following playful take on the Gothic tradition: "For a while [Mr. Canning] had tried to persuade the other Ministers that they should commission Mr. Beckford or Mr. Lewis and Mrs. Radcliffe to create dreams of vivid horror that Mr. Norrell could then pop into Buonaparte's [*sic*] head. But the other Ministers considered that to employ a magician was one thing, novelists were quite another and they would not stoop to it" (245).

4. Neil Gaiman, cover blurb for *Jonathan Strange & Mr. Norrell*.

5. Amanda Craig, "With the Fairies," *The New Statesman*, October 2004, www.newstatesman.com/200409270052 (accessed January 5, 2010).

6. Anonymous, "Review of *Jonathan Strange & Mr. Norrell*," *New York Post*, October 2004, www.complete-review.com/reviews/popgb/clarkes.htm (accessed January 5, 2010).

7. Susanna Clarke, interview, "The Three Susanna Clarkes," *Locus*, April 2005, www.locusmag.com/2005/Issues/04Clarke.html (accessed January 5, 2010).

8. Michael Dirda, review of *Jonathan Strange & Mr. Norrell*, by Susanna Clarke, *Washington Post*, September 5, 2004, www.washingtonpost.com/wp-dyn/articles/A57806-2004Sep2.html (accessed January 5, 2010).

9. Michel Faber, "It's a Kind of Magick," *Guardian*, October 2, 2004, www.guardian.co.uk/books/2004/oct/02/featuresreviews.guardianreview20 (accessed January 5, 2010).

10. Perhaps nothing better reflects the crosscurrents of the novel and its reception than the following opposing estimates of its chief villain: "Her greatest creation is certainly the fairy king—vindictive, frivolous, self-deluding, charming, utterly full of himself. And very, very dangerous to cross" (Dirda, review). "[T]he arch-villain is a cartoonish fop whose petulant misdeeds lack menace" according to Kate Julian, in "Briefly Noted," *New Yorker*, September 13, 2004, www.newyorker.com/archive/2004/09/13/040913crbn_brieflynoted (accessed January 5, 2010).

11. William Blake, "A Memorable Fancy," in *The Marriage of Heaven and Hell*, introduction and commentary by Geoffrey Keynes (Oxford, UK: Oxford University Press, 1975), xxiv.

12. Lev Grossman, "Books: Of Magic and Men," *Time*, August 16, 2004, suggests that "Clarke could have called the book *Sense and Sensibility* if the title weren't already taken."

13. John Hodgman, "Susanna Clarke's Magic Book," *New York Times* magazine, August 1, 2004, www.nytimes.com/2004/08/01/magazine/01CLARKE.html (accessed January 5, 2010).

14. Clarke notes in an interview given for her Bloomsbury publishers that Childermass grew to become her "favorite character": "He was meant to be a villain at the beginning, but I realized that he's more complex than that. I love that he's so subversive and independent—but he's also (I hope) a man of his period. He begins as a servant and, although he's very bright, he knows he can't expect much more from life, so he sort of makes do with his position."

15. Elizabeth Hoiem, "The Fantasy of Talking Back: Susanna Clarke's Historical Present in *Jonathan Strange & Mr. Norrell*," *Strange Horizons*, October 27, 2008, www.strangehorizons.com/2008/20081027/hoiem-a.shtml (accessed January 5, 2010).

16. Clarke, "The Three Susanna Clarkes."

17. Steven H Silver, "A Conversation with Susanna Clarke," *SF Site*, October 2004, www.sfsite.com/02a/su193.htm (accessed January 5, 2010).

18. See, to cite only two from many sources, Kate Ferguson Ellis's *The Contested Castle: Gothic Novels and the Subversion of Domestic Ideology* (Urbana: University of Illinois Press, 1989) and Adriana Craciun's *Fatal Women of Romanticism* (Cambridge, UK: Cambridge University Press, 2003).

19. Dirda, review of *Jonathan Strange & Mr. Norrell*.

20. Craig, "With the Fairies."

21. Dirda, review of *Jonathan Strange & Mr. Norrell*.

22. From the Bloomsbury interview: "I realized after I'd finished that I'd written a book that spans ten years but which takes place almost entirely in winter."

23. David B. Morris, "Gothic Sublimity," *New Literary History* 16 (1985): 299–319.

24. Hodgman, "Susanna Clarke's Magic Book."

CHAPTER 31

Renovation is Hell, and Other Gothic Truths Deep Inside Jennifer Egan's *The Keep*

Danel Olson

> We have always been surrounded by terror and by the beauty that is an inseparable part of it.
>
> —Josef Škvorecký, *The Engineer of Human Souls*[1]

As one who owns a house that's just turned thirty-one, and who has been victim to more dust-in-the-mouth DIY misadventures than I thought could afflict any man or woman, I cannot imagine fixing a castle built in the fourteenth century,[2] and whose securest tower or keep was first built two centuries before. It is a trembling invitation, a true horror of the imagination. Who but the bravest among us would take it, if we had to renovate the structure by ourselves? But this endless hammering act—on a voluntary basis—is what engages most of the characters' scraped fingers in Jennifer Egan's nested, enigmatic *The Keep*. In the scrubbing, peeling back, and tearing out of the medieval is released much, so much that couldn't be predicted. It is as if every contact from each century leaves a Gothic trace at this castle, and the renovators are discovering them, though they are not always able to interpret the messages of those earlier denizens. This chapter presents interpretation of the phantom messages in the novel, and uncovers how Egan both unearths and reinterprets the old Gothic truths for twenty-first-century readers, as her crew works over a mystery castle which is either "in Austria, Germany, or the Czech Republic"[3] (we never do find out). *The Keep* shows the strange ways the Gothic survives and evolves, stretching its bone-white knuckles into our time (through humor, through post-postmodern information load, through listlessness and paranoia and ghost lovers, and through a longing for the heights and depths of a fully-alive medieval

imagination). Throughout the framed-tale structure of this ambiguous novel, Egan movingly works the theme of "renovation" on several planes simultaneously, from the physical restoration of a castle, to the word's etymology of *renovacyoun* from 1432: "spiritual rebirth."[4] Within the very people who have abused themselves, betrayed and abandoned others, killed out of pain and jealousy, and uneasily lugged the guilt like, as we shall see, a satellite dish over hundreds of pages, comes true neo-Gothic terror, but also *renovacyoun*. The remarkable sedimented structure and emotional depth earn the novel a distinctive place among contemporary spooky books.

Upon its publication in 2006, *The Keep* received deservedly rave reviews for its bold imagination, fully realized characters, enchanting pace, genuine surprises, perfectly pitched and memorable dialogue, and uncommonly successful blend of humor and horror. Even when there were complaints, they were often neutralized in the same review, as in this one, where the book works its weird charm on the commentator: "The beautiful prose doesn't entirely disguise how wildly improbable the novel's events are, . . . [but] the characters' emotions are so real, the author's insights so moving, that readers will be happy to be swept away."[5] Many reviewers, though, seem unable to name the book's secret or deeper appeal, or why they could call it a genre book that's nongenre. The novel's furtive pull is this: it has uncommon fullness for a scary page-turner. It is true that her other novels—including *The Invisible Circus* (1994), *Look at Me* (2001), and *A Visit from the Goon Squad* (2010)—have included flashbacks, scenes of peril, people gone missing, quests to find them, disintegration brought on by time, occasional kleptomania, drug addiction, and other self-destructive behaviors. Still, despite some grim elements, these novels float in the wide category of kitchen-sink realism. Not one of them could be called wholly Gothic until *The Keep*. Like most Gothic novels, *The Keep* positions its tattered characters in an antiquated and decaying place, dwelling on those secrets and violations from the past that curse or limit characters now, physically or psychologically.[6] Chicago-born Egan plays the Gothic game in her own fresh and peculiar way, with a caress and a smile, rather than a death grip and the obligatory "rictus grin of terror!!!" There isn't the clichéd overwrought mood that so many Gothic novels have grave robbed from earlier ones. An unusual softness and pain, identification, and human comedy amidst the bizarre and preternatural may explain why Jennifer Egan's cool, silky touch is unforgettable, disarming, and uncannily inviting. Even Egan herself admits this novel perplexes her in its originality. During the course of its completion, she wrestled with its nature, or "whether a book could be funny and scary at the same time. I couldn't think of models for that."[7] And though *The Keep* literally has a castle full of Gothic paraphernalia, it deals with the standard and nonparanormal woes of imprisonment, professional doubts (especially over teaching), worry for one's children, drug use and its contribution to the death of

a prematurely born child, separation woes, and the dread from relatives for the choices we make and for the supposedly no-account people we love. It is both a laughing and a crying book.

There is much mystery never solved in *The Keep*, including, Where does Ray go at the end? And where does the Baroness vanish to?[8] Some critics, even highly regarded ones, find this lack of closure vexing. Janet Maslin writes, "The potential for writerly tricks is boundless, and Ms. Egan's arresting, twisted cleverness finds many ways to surface. But despite such thoughtful provocations *The Keep* winds up frustratingly unresolved and falls into a moat of its own making. *The Keep* grows more and more hallucinatory, and under these complex circumstances, that vagueness amounts to an easy way out."[9] But the author, if frustratingly so, then also wisely, gives us not what we want, but what we need. The whole book—the whole design of Howie's "new" castle and Egan's neo-Gothic romance—is an invitation for our imaginations to create, rather than for her to neatly finish the job. The modern mind, which has outsourced its entertainment generating to Hollywood, now needs to invent, to see what is not there, and to not see what is: we need to be whole. Like Howie, Egan intimates that we need a hallucination now and again, though preferably not the controlled-substance kind. What she allows is for us to make our own ending, and that is the highest respect an artist can pay her reader. In person, Egan is witty, humble, graceful, and heart-stoppingly lovely. But in her art, she wears spikes. She constantly challenges, seeds ambiguity everywhere, and gives us riddles of life to wake up in the middle of night and ponder. We keep asking, What are we seeing? What is real? Why do these people keep hurting themselves (often by saying nothing, when they should say something)? And why do these people keep getting beaten up (and in spanking new ways)? An unwary or lazy reader *will* be lost beyond reckoning in this fiction. It is not beach-reading Gothic, but is that a flaw? Life is not simple, and lasting fiction should not be so. Human existence in all its terror and love and beauty and violence is principally mysterious. Egan is not afraid of the dark, and she doesn't mind lightly taking our hand into the darkness. And if you want, you can get lost together with her.

Enter into this fictive cult of mystery one Danny King of New York, who has the self-awareness of horseradish. He's a bumbler, a clubber, a believer in "can't-go-wrong" moneymaking schemes, and a guy who wears expensive, slick, and heavy boots, and who will one day slide out of them to the ground from the keep several stories above. The antihero Danny has had girlfriends, models, and model wannabes, probably accessed through his jobs as a front man for restaurants and bars. He has undoubtedly provided them with multiple sarcasms. He has also been played on by the Big Apple mafia a couple of times, right on the head over murky restaurant dealings—hence the flight to Europe. Danny King—with his guilt and his mind-forged manacles—is the perfect protagonist

because he has so far to go, so high to grow. As he seems to have little potential or direction, it will take a consummate deployment of struggle and psychological suggestion from Egan for us to see and believe that he does change. The ultimate challenge will be to convince us that he finds some redemption.

Danny is no Byronic hero in this Gothic romance. He is invited to the castle by his cousin Howard, a once chubby boy who probably liked cake, who grew up into a young man who liked stocks and bonds, and who now is retired and pursuing something greater. Howard is renovating this castle to a state that people from around the world will come to make a pilgrimage of the soul, or rather a pilgrimage into the soul. In a deliberate and ironic twist on the old Gothic meme, Egan has the arrival of Danny take after the Gothic heroine, haunted and harried, guilt drenched, emotionally endungeoned and endarkened, and largely acted upon rather than acting out. And though he is no virgin to be deflowered, he is certainly made love to as if for the first time; an aristocratic ghost has her way with him,[10] an experience he will never want to repeat.

Egan's novel is slippery, sliding between the world of an incarcerated but steadily improving creative writer (who hopes through words to gain sensual access to his teacher) and the world of Danny King (who is introduced to us first before we even know his convict-creator Raymond Michael Dobbs is writing all this). An outline of what happens is needed to savor the novel's Gothic roots. Danny, said victim of mob beatings in New York City, is a happy escapee from more beatings when he arrives at Howie's European castle. But, at the same time, in chapter 1, Danny has two flashbacks that color the rest of the novel and introduce us to his horrifying guilt. The second vision is shattering: it relives the time back in America when, as a boy, he and a friend deserted little cousin Howie in a cave for three days during a family picnic. Young Danny, in a blind moment, and perhaps to escape trouble from his bully friend and possibly for reasons he does not even understand now as an adult, pushed Howie into the cave's small but possibly deep pool before leaving him to drown. Three days later, a ragged Howie has wandered out of the cave and is found by his traumatized parents. Flash to the present: Outside the castle at night now, and with no one sighted, Danny climbs over the castle walls, feeling that he "liked extremes. They were disturbing" (9). Perhaps the whole adventure is to let Howie have a chance to do his sinister will on Danny, to pay him back after all these years; or perhaps it is so Danny can finally lay the dead albatross of guilt and despair and self-hatred down; or perhaps Danny simply has a death wish to fall off a castle wall. The man has a record of putting himself in peril, and self-annihilation is the one sure way of curing chronic guilt spasms. Whatever his psychological reasons for coming, whatever unfinished business beckons, Danny, not having seen Howie in years, now meets the successful, self-assured, seemingly happy adult version called Howard, and is intimidated.

We discover in the last three pages of chapter 1 that all of this is a story within a story. The murder convict Ray is writing this castle story for a class led by teacher Holly T. Farrell, who puts on a brave front and truly tries to help the inmates, despite the fact that she has no writing degree, but mostly dark and application-unmentionable experiences, including a meth addiction, a contribution to the death of her tiny baby Corey, and the threat that child services will take her other children away.

When in chapter 2 Danny meets Howard and his wife Ann, he also encounters Howie's "second man," Mick, who is gruff, suspicious, curt, and monotone. A watchful distrust ensues. Danny looks around at the massive restoration job around him, feeling quite out of place and unable to help, and observes, in his inarticulate but honestly dubious way, "So you're, like, physically renovating the place" (29). With this pointing out of the obvious, Danny is well positioned already as a hapless protagonist, a kind of shaken Shaggy from the *Scooby-Doo* cartoon on whom repeated misfortune will fall. By the third chapter, we understand the castle's new function as a place for haggard Westerners, overcome by media saturation and a lack of true "recreation," to come and allow their heads to rest, and to let their imagination play in the fields of the Gothic. Howard then eloquently and convincingly describes what separated the medieval people from us, their belief in miracles:

> They thought Christ was sitting with them at the dinner table, they thought angels and devils were flying around. We don't see those things anymore. . . . Their imaginations were more active. Their inner lives were rich and weird. . . . They saw one shitty little town their whole lives, their kids caught a cold and dropped dead, they had three teeth left in their heads by the time they hit thirty. People had to do something . . . or they would've keeled over from misery and boredom. So Christ came to dinner. Witches and goblins were hiding in corners. People looked at the sky and saw angels. . . . We've lost the ability to make things up. We've farmed out that job to the entertainment industry, and we sit around and drool on ourselves while they do it for us. (44–45)

Humor and conflict flash together at us, as it does throughout this novel, when Danny ponders Howie's grand dream and finds the whole thing "a little nuts" (47).

Everyone knows that some writing programs are harder than others. In the prison writing class we land in by chapter 4, some of the convicts respond well to Ray's first reading of part 1 of "Danny in the Castle." Others, like Mel, take the writer's desk (with Ray still sitting in it), turn it upside down, and smack said writer's head to the floor. In a scene that will be relived like a precious prison

dream, teacher Holly (Ray's self-declared "princess") touches Ray's beaten head with her cool fingertips. Amazingly, this sudden attack will be worth it to Ray simply for that indescribably healing touch. Again meditating on the entrancing power of women and the three little words they may utter to change a mere man into a prince, in chapter 5 Danny calls his New York love interest from the castle. The forty-five-year-old Martha Mueller back in New York answers, a slightly indolent redheaded cougar who mixes sage with her underpants, but who has a tidelike erotic pull on Danny. She may just be the love of his small life, though actually he finds the au pair at the castle, Nora, rather nice, too. Our Gothic hero is undecided, fickle, and sexually feckless, it's true; yet with Martha, we glimpse more of his romantic being than anywhere else in the book. A secretary who constantly discourages the love (or lust) between them, she nonetheless has feelings for him, too, and neither can quite let each other go, though Martha does try. As she says on the phone, what he has, "it's not love, it's some kind of erotic delusion." Danny gives an amusing, surprisingly wise response: "That's what love *is*" (67). Danny, who has romanced mostly a "clutter of identical girls," certainly enjoys her experience, "that she was wild and dirty in bed. From Martha, *Get away, you fucker* was a come on" (66). Such are her rough charms. But perhaps the real reason he stays with Martha is for her protective softness, though granted, she can tell off the roughs looking for Danny who drive by in black Lincolns: "He's gone. Now leave me the fuck alone" (66). But then there is that adorable, ultrasoft, peachy "fuzz of invisible hair over every part of her" (67). He seems to find maternal comfort in her years above his, some stability in this book of high Gothic instability, someone to watch over him. When a couple of bravos beat him up over some loss from his moneymaking schemes, she actually cares. Fierce older women, as we shall see later, deep inside the keep, have an easy hold on him.

By chapter 6, Danny, who seemed to have little better to do than ramble and search for ways to call people with his phone (complete with a satellite dish he schlepped all the way from the Empire State, until it fell into the pool of evil murk where dead twins appear to bob up alive), encounters the Baroness up close and personal in her keep. With the eerie glide of a renovation ghost—an entity who stirs enough emotional and physical energy to shut down construction on the home she holds dear—she fascinates, repels, and hypnotizes. A stunning character (who, according to Howie, "doesn't look a day over ninety" [42] and who was "inherited" along with the property, as she refused to move from its oldest, safest part) is the Baroness Liesl von Ausblinker. In her elitism, furtiveness, cunning, and viperlike threat, she handily becomes the most captivating character of the book. Danny assumes he has the upper hand and must humor her, as she seems a weak, imperious crone, gabbing about gallantry, her late golf-pro husband, and the reason why men shouldn't wear shorts. She lives entirely

in the past (and I mean *ancient* past—that of battering rams, Tartar sieges, and Greek fire) and seems a harmless nutter. But Danny is no match for her stealth and strength, or her lack of conscience. What's more, she can change from nearly one hundred to twenty years old in moments, twanging his libido. It would have been better if Danny had not quaffed the 1898 burgundy she proffers, with a "reek of decay mixed with some sweet, fresh thing the decay hadn't touched" (88–89). Intoxicated, he is bedded by the old gal in a drolly repugnant scene as old as crones holding poisoned apples in fairy tales. Her perfectly drawn seduction of Danny fits in contemporary Gothic history with Consuelo Llorente's repeated wine drugging of young Felipe Montero in Carlos Fuentes's "Aura," or like Granny Grimes's bootleg Viagra mickey given to decades-younger Hollis Railsback in Nancy A. Collins's tragic shocker "The Pumpkin Child," a gulped fat, shiny-black pill sure "to put starch in yore flag" and get granny pregnant.[11]

In chapter 7, Ray, the creator of Dannyworld, has a dream that he is inside a burning tower. Awakening, he is in his top bunk in a cell with the six-foot-two-inch, 350-pound, glowering cell mate Davis, a no-nonsense hood who routinely puts Ray in headlocks. But Davis is more agreeable today; he has found Ray's opus, and he finds it to be the stuff of life, to which Ray confesses it *is* his life. We won't understand that comment until much later, and it remains as one more generous reward for rereading the novel. With some hard-earned respect toward Ray, Davis now shows his cell mate a machine that lets us hear the dead. It may simply appear as an orange Adidas shoebox with hair (including arm and pubic), accompanied by dust balls of every color and a few broken dials on its long side—because it is. But apparently the thing works: the dead can be reached.

Ray gives a grudging belief in the impossible, just as Danny is accepting the impossible at the castle. Ray's move from "pretending straight into believing" (100) seems recast in Danny's strange wanderings and supernatural discovery on the night he meets that black-magic woman Baroness von Ausblinker, who at one moment calls Americans "mongrels" and Danny a "*homosex-sual*" (84, 82), but then suddenly changes her age, sans L'Oréal, and finds him not a gay dog, after all. We understand the allegorical connection between Ray's and Danny's existences suddenly: Danny's castle is a prison, and Ray's prison transforms into a castle—with a maiden (Holly), spirits (from Davis's ghost communicator), and the everyday supernatural (the smeared prison glass toward the outside world suddenly becoming fully transparent to Ray). Completing the prison-into-castle metamorphosis are the modern cells appearing more like a dungeon's oubliette where the condemned are forgotten. Though dragons and knights are never mentioned in the book, it seems that a dragon, Tom-Tom (this inmate does raise and identify with geckos, and they are merely a sort of tiny, wingless dragon), literally stands in front of a burdened princess (Holly) and emotionally

holds her, while the knight (Ray) is frozen after the symbolic dragon breathes fire (Tom-Tom reads his moving and harrowing story that makes even hardened convicts tear up). The dragon will bite said knight, as Tom-Tom will seriously stab Ray, just as the knight moves closer to the princess's heart.

Making tomfoolery of my careful allegory above, our knight Danny wakes in a bed with some ashes in the keep, following the apparently intense but highly regrettable lovemaking with the Baroness. She is this fairy tale's wicked queen, who seems to emanate from castle wars, and return to them, her wet laughter trickling not "from inside her but below her, from the actual keep" (85). Like a comic plot out of Giovanni Boccaccio's *The Decameron*, Danny has to relieve himself in the morning and stumbles around in this unfamiliar place for release. He finds some, but he also hears voices from below, voices that awaken his gossipy curiosity. As he comes close to an open pointy Gothic window and leans over, he hears Howie's menacing, Heathcliffesque, second-in-command Mick murmuring with Howie's wife Ann of their love affair from six years ago. She wants it admitted to her husband Howard, but Mick (who we find later is the parole ward of Howie) does not. Mick still hungers for love from her. To get a little more of this juicy revelation, Danny leans further, and gravity betrays him—or he gets pushed out to the ground below by the light but dangerous touch of the Baroness. In chapter 9, after a fall that could have killed him, Danny is watched by Howie and others for signs of a concussion. Howard registers honest amazement that the bumbling and dreaming, and now sometimes incoherent, Danny is "telling me stuff I didn't know" (124). As benighted as Danny is, he has a wonderful talent for running into hard truths, for discovering what Howie and Mick and Ann and a gaggle of grad students have been searching for in the castle. Though seeming of rock, the castle is made of dreams, and only fools like Danny know what it means.

Meanwhile, convict Ray, with other inmates, digs a plumbing line twenty feet inside the perimeter of his prison, which looks increasingly like a symbolic moat which he must and will later cross to freedom with his cell mate Davis. Mysteriously, Holly pulls up on Thursday—a nonteaching day—in her Subaru, wearing, for the first time, a skirt and shoes with "a little heel on them" (134), which must be a signal, the first proof-positive one, that she feels something for Ray, that he has made her feel beautiful and that the princess is enchanted by the knight. The repressed inmates are understandably excited. Foot fetishism aside, Ray feels woozy by seeing her, too, and appears so ill that he is offered by the normally harsh commanding officer a rare break from work. This plumbing line, like an underground passageway in Gothic works of old, will naturally be his escape later when he and Davis dig a hole under a guard tower (a representation of the castle tower, with some artistic license), open up a pipe with a blowtorch

(this novel has had an obsession with sewers since page eleven), and crawl under both perimeter fences to freedom.

Inmate Tom-Tom pours out his heart in a meth-case short story in class the next day (about a poor, down-South family, where the mom drops a pot of boiling water on her three-year-old son's arm—the arm stops growing, the boy later does crystal meth, and after his first robbery, breaks an old man's arm in three places). The impressed Ray says nothing, despite Tom-Tom's pleading for some recognition and praise, and despite the fact that others have commented somewhat positively on Ray's own work earlier. This Poesque, "Imp of the Perverse" reticence of Ray's will inspire Tom-Tom to shank him later, respect being almighty in the prison society and no slight going unpunished.

Conveying this outer prison paranoia of revenge and imminent attack to the inner story, the injured Danny leaves the castle, again climbing a wall, fearing that Howie is still building toward a torturous punishment for what he did to him as a boy. Danny feels and surrenders to the much-mentioned "worm" in this novel, which is raised as early as page ten: a sublimely Gothic fear, dread, and terror that disables confidence and invites panic. Danny has ominous visions, yet without enough courage to leave for good, he returns to the castle hopeless, moping with the enervation of other characters from great Gothic novels, especially that drained will evidenced in young British solicitor Jonathan Harker from staying one night too many in Castle Dracula. Just as in Bram Stoker's novel, where Dracula pretends to be Harker's loyal friend and protector, Danny senses that Howie's protectiveness and benevolence are part of a cat-and-mouse game.

In chapter 12, Danny cobbles enough energy to again ascend from his recovery room in the castle, but again he is invaded by "the worm." He roams the town pathetically, worriedly remembering the Baroness's troubling claim that "*The town and the castle have served each other for hundreds of years*" (161). He tries in vain to take a train or bus to the town (which he can only call "Scree-chow-hump" [160]), wonders whether "he ever was really outside, or was it all just a dream" (155), and then rather absurdly ambles into an antique shop where he both nicks a hunting knife *and* buys a wide-framed map of the town and its castle. The map has what looks like paths, but they will turn out to be tunnels, those that would allow allied knights to creep into the ancient keep. He then meets Mick on a bench, and the tension eases. Mick confesses that he is a junkie under conditional parole in Howie's trusteeship. A détente with "his enemy's number two" (164), as Danny calls Mick, ensues, though wary Danny still wonders about Howie's designs and when and how and where the vengeance will fall. He only knows that as long as he "was still in this town, he was under Howard's thumb. And wouldn't you know, he couldn't seem to get out" (161).

Slashing back to the convict world, Ray can't seem to get out either. But in chapter 13, while Ray is in the hospital, Holly visits him and cries. The teacher's love for her student con is now obvious. The knight, by his wounds, is saved.

Stuck in a tunnel in chapter 14, by the Baroness's device, Danny will, with his antique-shop map, find a way out for himself and the flashback-addled Howie (transported in horrible time to his ordeal as a little boy in the cave) and his wife and child, along with Mick, Nora, and a troop of petrified grad students. This party unwisely thought they should immediately clomp underground as soon as they were shown Danny's map (and none of them thought to bring a phone—Danny's was thrown, and Mick, for whatever reason, decides not to bring his). They seek underground entrances to the tower where the Baroness resides. They get in only to quickly discover, in classic Gothic fashion, the remains of others who long ago were trapped in the same fate:

> skeletons . . . on the floor, piled against the walls. . . . Yellow skulls angled up toward the bars as if they were still hoping someone would show up and let them out. Their eye sockets were huge, like flies' eyes, and their grimacing jaws were jammed with teeth. Danny knew what a skeleton looked like, but that was no preparation. His mind went numb. (189)

After this grotesquerie, a conversation ensues with the Baroness, with her on the outside of the locked gate she has just closed on the tunnel entrance. Her comments are what Gothic fans will relish. They embody the chilled evil inside the aristocracy, that they own us, that it is their right to give us life, and theirs to take it: "You think I care what happens to you? To any of you? . . . You can't believe I won't do what you want me to do. You're children, you Americans, every one of you. And the world is very, very old" (192). Indulgent, cocksure, comfortable, and impossibly sensual for her hoary age, the Baroness shows how little the aristocracy has changed from eighteenth-century portrayals to this vivid twenty-first-century image. The classic sexual charge of absolute control of victim is sparking in her, yet underneath is an utterly cool lack of anxiety, guilt, emotion, or fear of punishment. The aristocrat strikes back in *The Keep*, and her love of the godlike power to take life, and the belief that her family did it as an art and a right, has never been more narcissistically and arrogantly displayed.

Despite the moaning cries and collapse of those around him, our lost boy Danny King can in his single-mindedness do one thing for two pages: "[He] started to kick. He kicked and pushed like a madman, like it was the one thing he was made to do on earth. . . . And even after being so long upside down, veins popping, eyes running, lips hanging, sweat making his hand slip on the ring, Danny felt a jolt of strength rock through him from his head to his boots . . . the door lifted away like the top coming off a grave" (199–200). That Danny

saves himself, not to mention all these trapped people, and gets the cheers of all is one of the greatest surprises in a book studded with the unexpected.

No one is king long in Gothic romances, and though witty Nora, the sexy au pair, will kiss Danny after a small hug, before this can register, Danny is shot. He falls and drowns and slowly descends in the black pool that he has so long gazed on, into the stinking water where he envisioned the dead twins (those elder siblings of Liesl von Ausblinker). In one of the most remarkable death scenes since the nearly endless one at the close of Matthew Lewis's no-holds-barred Gothic classic, *The Monk*, Danny sinks into the death pool only to see the killer Ray (who is *Danny's* killer, actually, with the masque of "Mick" at long last dropped). Superbly blending humor and horror, Egan has her flummoxed Ray speak only seven words, "Where the fuck did you come from?" (209). And it is our once-burdened Danny, who first greeted us in velvet coat and inarticulate tongue, who now shares the most haunting line of this haunted book, shadowy because it is true for all of us at all times: "Haven't you learned that the thing you want to forget most is the one that'll never leave you?" (209).

In the Gothic world, nothing disappears, nothing but murderers. And so it goes in *The Keep*. Ray and Davis make their penitentiary getaway and are not heard from again. The only remembrances to come Holly's way—"that pretty princess . . . buried down there like treasure" (214)—are two, and they are both magical. First there is a manuscript from Ray of castle marvels, received "in a big brown envelope with a local postmark and no return address." Holly, who has separated from her addicted man Steve, stays up all night to read it, and confesses, "If I were a crier I'd cry, reading all that, but I'm not. There was a time when all I did was cry, but since then almost nothing. I'm dry" (214). Burying the book out back, she lies to law enforcement when they come by to investigate Ray's disappearance and any contacts he's made. And then she does the most adventurous thing of all. At book's end, Holly cashes part of her 401(k) to travel to a castle in Europe (fittingly, again, this one is not quite in the Czech Republic, but not in Germany or Austria either), one which advertises just the experience Howie once dreamt his could. When she gets there, she discovers the only further traces of Ray she will find:

> I hear a sound and turn. The room is empty but the air quivers against my arms. . .
> "Ray," I whisper. . . . (236)

Egan has called the Gothic genre "a celebration of ghostly traces,"[12] and in the end that's the quietly supernatural reality that Holly leaves us with. This compelling narrative of Extreme Castle Makeover records how every contact leaves a trace. Here we have all the defining features and moments of the great old Gothic—the proud lineages and absent heirs, property battles and haunted

keeps, lost visitors and dead hidden twins, murders and abandonment, facades and dissimulation, endless ironies and shudders, illicit affairs, tests and trials, triumphant superstition and blurred realities, incarceration and the labyrinthine paths characters take for freedom, and the sexual arousal that feels much the same as fright. But this novel has more.

The Keep keeps using the old Gothic tropes to new purpose: to effect a transformation tale. Most of the characters in this narrative have some trauma, and they recast it, relive it, and refashion their response, hoping to get it "right" the second time, either in their actions or in their writing. But they fail; the fantasy is a sham. Poe once identified the mind as a Gothic castle, and Egan understands the simile well, as she has noted that,

> At the center of most gothic stories is an old building—a castle or even just a house—that some believe is a symbol for the . . . mind. I'm thinking of Poe's "The Fall of the House of Usher" or Daphne du Maurier's *Rebecca*. . . . Sometimes the house is haunted—there are actual ghosts—but often it's not clear whether the ghosts are really there or are just internal states of worry or obsession projected onto the landscape. . . . We hear someone whispering into our ear—what does it mean? That a ghost is talking to us? Or that our imaginations have been sparked by the ghostly marks history has left on our surroundings? . . . At which point our selves get confused with our castles, and we've entered the gothic.[13]

But neo-Gothicists like Egan also identify with another organ. One of her characters' most common and serious flaws is going against their own hearts—quickly hurting another to avoid some anticipated hurt themselves. And the whole repair of a nine-hundred-year-old castle, all of its failures and successes, quickly becomes a controlling metaphor for the restoration of the human heart to dignity and compassion. It is hard to tell at times who is more damaged from the traumas of time, the castle or the characters. But what pulls us most tightly in this neo-Gothic work is a longing, a highly contemporary one, for something more, for an exotic place where a keep no longer towers mutely above, but becomes an active presence in shaping behavior.

In the final chapter, Holly screams and uncontrollably sobs in a kind of revelatory ecstasy in the hotel castle.[14] She must be moved by both what is perceived to be the spirit of Ray and also the keep's medieval spirit, making modern people like herself feel more, making them have wonder. Holly's state of awe corresponds with the power of the tower, a Gothic overture to a modern, an attempt to resurrect something of what people of the medieval age felt. It cannot be an accident that after this release she is drawn to the very room where, in her unconsummated lover's fiction, other lovers met for a night, "where Danny met

the baroness: gold, shiny, heavy draperies next to tiny windows, a purple-orange sunset pouring in from outside. The lack of a word to describe the matching up of this place with my expectations is starting to hurt" (235–236). This hurt means *feeling*, a letting go, the longed-for arrival of tears, the kind of sublime sensation with which the new Gothic is obsessed. Alain de Botton, who has studied carefully the world's first Gothic villa (Horace Walpole's fantastic Strawberry Hill in southwest London, finished in 1776), explains the overwhelming feeling when the right spirit, hurt enough from life, meets the right architecture: "We may need to have made an indelible mark in our lives, to have married the wrong person, pursued an unfulfilling career into middle age or lost a loved one before architecture can begin to have a perceptible impact on us."[15] An amazing correspondence is here, as all three of these have afflicted Holly, and in this castle hotel that she spent so much of her limited money to visit, she has a spiritual awakening, "Like a ghost has come in" (236). This castle, now attended by people whose moods do not violate the sublime spirit with which its architect infused it, is spiritually renovated. The broken Holly begins to be renewed. Some buildings can talk back. This castle's old magic touches new skin, and *The Keep* now possesses us all.[16]

Notes

1. Josef Škvorecký, *The Engineer of Human Souls*, trans. Paul Wilson (Normal, IL: Dalkey Archive Press/Illinois State University Press, 1999), 11. This novel, coincidentally, deals with terror, has a Czech connection, and features a protagonist named Danny who chases women, but does not always catch them. And, like *The Keep*, it draws characters we will start to miss and may revisit years later when life's experiences may make us see them differently.

2. In an enlightening e-mail from October 29, 2009, Jennifer Egan shared with me what shaped the castle her readers would wander into: "As to buildings that inspired *The Keep*, the impetus for the book was the ruined castle of Godfrey de Bouillon (who led the 1st Crusade), which overlooks Bouillon, Belgium, and is quite evocative and beautiful. Other inspirations were the sight of all the castles on little promontories along the Rhine viewed from a train; the old house in *Dark Shadows*, the cheesy TV series that I sneakily watched after school when my mom wasn't home; an estate in England that my husband and I visited, which had an overgrown garden and a round, fetid swimming pool; and lots of books on castle architecture that I read, back when I thought 'my' castle needed a real identity and floorplan (before I realized that, actually, it needed to be somewhat illegible and unknowable). And the cumulative impact of occasional creepy old black and white movies involving mouldering castles, scummy pools, eerie music and disappearing children—all of which terrified me back when I used to watch them."

3. Jennifer Egan, *The Keep* (New York: Knopf, 2006), 4. Page numbers appear hereafter in parentheses in the text.

4. *Online Etymology Dictionary*, "Renovation," www.etymonline.com/index.php?sea rch=renovation&searchmode=none (accessed March 14, 2010).

5. Review of *The Keep*, *Kirkus Reviews*, April 15, 2006, 367.

6. This elegant summary of the Gothic comes from editor Jerrold E. Hogle in his introduction to *The Cambridge Companion to Gothic Fiction* (Cambridge, UK: Cambridge University Press), 2.

7. Jennifer Egan, author interview, Random House, www.randomhouse.com/catalog/display.pperl?isbn=9781400079742&view=auqa (accessed March 15, 2010).

8. On the Baroness's disappearance, in an e-mail to me from Jennifer Egan, September 14, 2009: "I don't have a definitive answer to your question; my sense is that the Baroness fades away in the face of the hotel juggernaut, having already done her worst. Maybe she leaves behind an ashy trail like she did in the bed she and Danny shared . . . or perhaps she's handing out towels by the swimming pool! In fact, I rather like that idea. But to my mind, I guess, she sort of seeps into the atmosphere and becomes part of the air, the soil, the walls and floors, just as her hundreds of relatives did before her."

9. Janet Maslin, "Lost Voices, Lost Memories, Inside the Prison of Life," *New York Times*, July 20, 2006, www.nytimes.com/2006/07/20/books/20masl.html?ex=11588112 00&en=d96a05f92a4d9cb8&ei=5070 (accessed March 16, 2010).

10. In another e-mail from Jennifer Egan to me, from September 14, 2009, she generously takes on a question of the Baroness's origin that suggests a source for the whole novel: "It's funny that you keep calling the Baroness the 'Countess,' because she's actually based on a real person who actually *was* a Countess—believe it or not—whom I worked for when I first came to New York, as her private secretary. The Countess so utterly permeated my psyche and dreams that a friend of mine gave me a short story by a Latin American writer Alejandra Pizarnik called 'The Bloody Countess.' My destiny to write at least one gothic novel may have been sealed at that point, though it took me many years to realize it."

11. Nancy A. Collins, "The Pumpkin Child," in *Exotic Gothic: Forbidden Tales from Our Gothic World*, ed. Danel Olson (Ashton, BC: Ash-Tree Press, 2007), 195.

12. Jennifer Egan, "The Ghost in the Renovation," *This Old House*, September 2007, www.thisoldhouse.com/toh/article/0,,1550097,00.html (accessed March 16, 2010).

13. Jennifer Egan, "The Ghost in the Renovation."

14. Novelist Madison Smartt Bell was correct in pointing out *The Keep*'s magic reach: "Egan sustains an awareness that the text is being manipulated by its author, while . . . delivering character and story with perfect and passionate conviction. . . . The emotional authenticity she achieves . . . no other metafictionist has ever delivered." From "Into the Labyrinth," *New York Times Book Review*, July 30, 2006, www.nytimes .com/2006/07/30/books/review/30bell.html (accessed March 15, 2010).

15. Alain de Botton, *The Architecture of Happiness* (London: Hamish Hamilton/ Penguin, 2006), 22. It is noteworthy that Walpole was so delighted with his Medievally-modeled Twickenham home that, "temperamentally disinclined to keep any of his achievements quiet" (de Botton, *Architecture of Happiness*, 36), he issued tickets and invited people inside. De Botton notes that, "within a few decades, a revolution in taste was under way. . . . Gothic buildings began to appear in Britain, then across Europe and North America. . . . [J]ust fifty or so years after Walpole broke ground at Strawberry Hill,

defenders of Gothic could claim—much in the way that the Classicists had done before them—that theirs was the most noble and appropriate architecture of all" (de Botton, *Architecture of Happiness*, 38–39). Baroness Liesl von Ausblinker would no doubt agree.

16. So, is this inspired novel the last Gothic from Jennifer Egan? From Random House's atmospheric Stay at the Keep site (www.randomhouse.com/kvpa/egan), it would sadly appear so. Complete with moody music, splendid pictures of the gleaming Imagination Pool, and the somewhat suspect news of the Baroness's dying "peacefully" in a nursing home at age 108 (what did that woman ever do "peacefully"?), the site offers testimonials from guests. One of them is from Jennifer Egan: "I checked into The Keep anticipating a brief visit, but it was a full three years before I was able to check out again. It's fair to say that my creative powers were stimulated and challenged on a daily basis during that period. I'll remember The Keep fondly, though I sincerely doubt I'll be back." On the other hand, readers could just get lucky. In an e-mail from Jennifer Egan, September 15, 2009, she says, "I've left the Gothic—for the moment, at least. But I do that every time, so it's nothing personal to that genre. When I begin something new, rule number one seems to be that it differ in every possible way from what I've just—and ideally, ever—done. That is certainly true in the case of my new one, called *A Visit from the Goon Squad*. . . . The one I'll begin next may have a noirish feel, so I think I'm inching back toward genre. Another Gothic is not out of the question."

CHAPTER 32

Nancy Drew Goes Gothic?

THE LITTLE FRIEND BY DONNA TARTT

Lucy Taylor

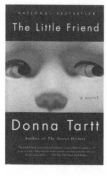

Can a spirited and precocious twelve-year-old girl, her imagination running wild with rumor and speculation about the unsolved murder of her brother Robin, constitute a traditional Gothic hero? Can the now lost family home, aptly named Tribulation, equate to the forbidding hallways of a haunted manor or the crumbling, mysterious ruins of a once grand abbey? And can a tribe of wildly colorful, drug-addled holy-roller hillbillies substitute for lurking ghosts, seductive vampires, and other familiar tropes of the supernatural Gothic?

Although the world of Donna Tartt's *The Little Friend* may lack some elements of the traditional Gothic novel, it is also a brilliant and inventive example of that intriguing subgenre known as Southern Gothic, made popular by writers such as Erskine Caldwell, Tennessee Williams, William Faulkner, and Eudora Welty. And if prepubescent Harriet Cleve doesn't fit the standard mold of a damsel in distress, her wildly improbable, yet thoroughly riveting adventures—stalking snakes in an ill-conceived subdivision development, fleeing a pair of vengeful meth dealers, taking on her nemesis in a thrilling showdown inside a water tower—seethe with melodrama and over-the-top villains.

Written with succulently drawn characters, lush descriptions, and evocative settings, all overhung with a sense of impending doom every bit as irrevocable as that faced by Harriet's hero Captain Scott when he marches off to certain death in the Antarctic, Tartt creates a boiling pot of brooding unease as unsettling as that of any macabre mansion or gloomy heath. Tension crawls across the pages like kudzu over the turrets of the now destroyed family mansion Tribulation as

we become privy to the family secrets and societal taboos of people isolated from one another by hierarchies of class, race, and wealth.

The novel focuses on two eccentric, disparate, and memorably dysfunctional families: the upper-class, aristocratic, and virtually all-female Cleve clan and the drug-crazed, gun-toting, career criminal brood of the paranoid and testosterone-fueled Ratliffs. Set in an unspecified period of the 1970s, the two groups inhabit the same backwoods southern town of Alexandria, Mississippi, but, kept separate by rigid class distinctions, they rarely intermingle. This changes dramatically when Harriet becomes obsessed with the idea that one of the Ratliff boys murdered her brother Robin, who was found hanging from a tupelo tree in their family's backyard when he was nine years old and Harriet was still a baby.

She has good reason to seek vengeance. Had Robin not died, it seems clear that Harriet's world would be far different from the bleak one she now inhabits, with a sedated and bedridden mother, an absent father, and a house weighed low with hoarded newspapers, unwashed dishes, and grief. A mission beckons: "This was Harriet's greatest obsession, and the one from which all the others sprang. For what she wanted—more than Tribulation, more than anything—was to have her brother back. Next to that, she wanted to find out who killed him."[1]

To that end, Harriet embarks upon a quest that is at once ambitious, daring, and perilously lonely. The only person willing to help is her friend and classmate Hely, and even he disappears midway through the book, when he abandons Harriet to join the school marching band. As far as her family is concerned, Robin may be reverently remembered and mythologized, but his death is an inviolate taboo, not to be discussed, let alone investigated. Harriet confronts the herculean task that she has set herself in a vacuum as vast, empty, and daunting as Scott's ice floes, but like the quintessential Gothic hero, she sets forth undeterred.

In *The Gothic Tradition*, David Stevens writes, "The link between the Gothic and the experience of childhood is, perhaps, a strong one," and quotes Robert Bloch, musing that, "On the basis of personal belief and observation, I'd say that those of us who direct our storytelling into darker channels do so because we were perhaps a bit more mindful than most regarding our childhood confusions of identity, our conflicts with unpleasant realities and our traumatic encounters with imaginative terrors."[2]

Indeed, like many Gothic works, *The Little Friend* resonates with the special poignancy of unhappy childhoods, the one Harriet herself experiences, the wretched one recalled by Danny Ratliff and the pathetic childhoods of the neglected Odum children, who wander the more prosperous neighborhoods in squalor, like refugees from some near-by, but seldom visited Third World country.

Harriet's loneliness is depicted with especially wrenching clarity; as a child (and a female one, at that), she is, for all intents and purposes, invisible, extraneous, and unheard. So rare are the times when adults actually see her for who she is that these passages stand out like limpid oases in the otherwise barren wasteland of her youth. When her beloved Aunt Libby, the sensitive and compassionate spinster aunt whom Harriet loves more than her own mother and grandmother, consoles her over the departure of Ida Rhew, the black maid, she states the dreadful truth, not just for Harriet but for many others: "It's awful being a child . . . at the mercy of other people."[3]

The world of Harriet's childhood is, in fact, both enchanted and horrific—enchanted in the sense that she creates a rich fantasy life to counteract the suffocating dreariness of her real-world existence; horrific in that the same fantasy life leads her down paths fraught with peril to undertake a quest that ultimately proves to be based largely on delusion.

Delusional or not, in the tradition of the stoic explorer Scott whom she so admires, Harriet ventures unguided into the vast and dangerous terrain of her imagination, and like some mythical hero, she prepares for the trials she expects to undergo in ways that are at once bold, inventive, and heartbreakingly naive. Sneaking into her absent father's study in the night, she practices loading a firearm for the day she may need to use it against her brother's killer. In the local swimming pool, she exhibits grit and fortitude worthy of a Navy Seal, as she half drowns herself attempting to hold her breath underwater, a discipline that will have ramifications for her in her final showdown with the dreaded Danny Ratliff.

Harriet's determination to find her brother's killer may be a folly that is hers alone, but her fixation on the past puts her in sync, not just with the rest of her family, but with Gothic traditions that go back to the genre's inception in the eighteenth century. A hallmark of Gothic literature is a profound longing for the past, for in it lies both salvation (if it can be recreated in the idealized form of memory) and damnation (when the allure of a fantasy past eclipses any interest in the present).

Without doubt, the past forms the bedrock of life in Harriett's family. Indeed, with the exception of Harriet's sister Allison, the present barely exists except to offer opportunities for reminiscence. From the viewpoint of her relatives, perhaps the strangest thing about dreamy, emotional Alison is that she shuns the past like a bad neighborhood. Of passive, spaced-out Allison, Tartt writes, "She scarcely thought about the past at all, and in this she differed significantly from her family, who thought of little else."[4]

According to some unspoken law of Cleve life, to disrespect the past is to court disaster. Even Robin's murder is linked, in his mother's mind, to her renegade decision "to have the Mother's Day dinner at six in the evening instead

of noon, after church, which is when the Cleves usually had it."[5] This deviation from time-honored tradition was thought to have set forth a chain reaction of events that somehow culminated in death; had she only not tempted fate with dangerous innovation, had she only clung to tradition, Robin might still be flying joyously down the banister at a resurrected Tribulation.

In Tribulation, the Cleves even have their own version of that standard Gothic set piece, the family mansion. The grand old home remains for them a focal point for reminiscence, even though it burned to the ground years earlier and, before that, had been reduced to little more than a ruin after the Cleve fortune was squandered by the family patriarch. Writes Tartt, "The floors were rotten, the foundations were soft with termites, the entire structure was on the verge of collapse, but still the sisters spoke lovingly of the hand-painted wallpaper . . . the marble mantelpieces . . . the handstrung chandelier."[6]

It is in the rewriting and amplification of history that Harriet's mother, grandmother, and aunts seem to find life most real and passionate, the present but a pale tableau upon which to conjure up a grander and more romantic past. Tartt describes the aunts' minds as "besieged constantly by recollections, for whom present and future existed solely as schemes of recurrence. . . . Memory . . . was to them the spark of life itself and nearly every sentence of theirs began with some appeal to it: 'You remember . . . ?'"[7] Tartt's women fully share the Southern Gothic romance for early times with Faulkner's women who, as in his "A Rose for Emily," sense the past as "not a diminishing road but, instead, a huge meadow which no winter ever quite touches."[8]

A measure of the power of Tribulation is that even the rageful, drug-snorting Danny Ratliff retains fond memories of it—one of the rare good memories from his squalid childhood turns out to have been a birthday party for a classmate celebrated at the grand old home, which even then was falling into disrepair. Danny Ratliff recalls the elegant lady (Harriet's Aunt Edie) who saw him cowering in the back and presented him with an extra large piece of cake topped with a pink rose. In an otherwise unfailingly bleak life, the memory assumes an unbearable grace.

Ratliff and his clan may struggle though a sorry existence, but when it comes to suffering, Tartt is nothing if not egalitarian in doling it out. The Gothic, after all, is the realm of despair, hopelessness, and longing, and the harsh fate of the upstanding and socially respectable Cleves is in no way tempered by their decency. Tartt's exquisitely evocative prose conjures up the essence of Gothic literary style: rich, foreboding, redolent of gloom and impending tragedy—and there are tragedies galore. Beginning with the death of Weenie, Allison's adored pet cat, the summer of Harriet's great adventure is one in which loss plays a recurrent, unremitting theme. Even the death of a blackbird mired in tar serves as a taste of what looms ahead. Trying gallantly to save the bird while Allison

whimpers in the background, Harriet rips it free from the hot asphalt with ter-rible results: "There was a hellish screech and Harriet, opening her eyes, saw that she'd ripped the stuck wing off the bird's shoulder. There it lay in the tar, grotesquely elongated, a bone glistening blue out of the torn end."[9]

The doomed bird is but a dark omen. Before the summer's end, Harriet's losses will mount, one upon the other, until the fetid water in which she almost drowns will only mirror the inundation of her sorrows.

But to anyone assuming that *The Little Friend* must be a depressing litany of calamity heaped upon disaster, fear not: despite the ominous and brooding at-mosphere Tartt captures, she simultaneously manages to populate her novel with such outrageous characters and weirdly comedic events that at times it is hard not to laugh aloud. Southern Gothic is known for its predilection for the gro-tesque, the mentally defective, and the outrageously eccentric, and Tartt makes full use of it. She is at her best—keen witted and diabolically funny—when she focuses on the various warped personalities and oddball goings-on around her many damaged, bizarre, and delusional characters—foremost among them the hapless Ratliffs and Odums.

At times her depiction of these backward clans veers between the hilari-ously funny—as when grandma Gum and her grandsons engage in a ritualistic suppertime squabble over who gets a proffered chicken leg that everyone except the mentally retarded Curtis understands must be refused at all cost—and the chillingly sad, as when she portrays the teeth-grittingly unwholesome father-daughter relationship between the barefoot, baby-coddling Lasharon Odum and her drunken father, who has just gambled away the car payment.

The Ratliffs, in particular, are so broadly drawn as to be terrifying in the way of images in a funhouse mirror—their escapades inspire both revulsion and laughter. Certain scenes are impossible to erase from the imagination: a drug-addled brother Farish busily dismantling every mechanical device in his house-hold, looking for "bugs"; the snake-handling, tongues-speaking preachers Eu-gene and Loyal trying to round up an apartment full of poisonous serpents; or the image of Gum careening down the highway in her grandson's convertible as Harriet and Hely toss a live cobra into her car, then staggering along the roadside with seven feet of exotic, deadly reptile clinging to her wattled neck.

And lest we fear for the fate of the cobra, Tartt's omniscient narrator even kindly provides us with a glimpse into the snake's future: "For years to come, farmers and hunters and drunks would sight the cobra; . . . and many, many tales of mysterious death would hover about its silent, lonely path."[10]

The Ratliffs and their cohorts may steal the show for dysfunctionality, but characters with much less stage time are nearly as memorable—Roy Dial, the unctuous car salesman/summer camp director; busybody Mrs. Fountain "in her white cardigan and harlequin glasses"; and Catfish de Bienville, the drug-

dealing, Gran Torino–driving man-about-town who aids and abets the Ratliffs in their nefarious undertakings. Tartt is endlessly inventive with her characters but never strays into the supernatural, that favorite province of the traditional Gothic novel.

Although as David Stevens in *The Gothic Tradition* writes, "Some element of the supernatural may seem to be almost an obligatory component of the gothic,"[11] like many other Southern Gothic writers, Tartt's skillful use of the grotesque and the bizarre substitutes for more traditional supernatural elements. In a few scenes, written from the point of view of the Ratliff brothers, Tartt upends our expectations by letting Harriet herself assume the role of an uncanny being in their eyes. Already driven to paranoia by the methamphetamine they manufacture in the taxidermy shed behind Gum's trailer, Danny and Farish commence viewing Harriet as a kind of private poltergeist, a malevolent imp who pops up seemingly from nowhere to wreak havoc on their lives. They have no way of knowing, of course, that Harriet's ubiquitous presence isn't a coincidence but her intent—that two adult career criminals are, in effect, being stalked by a twelve-year-old girl never crosses their minds.

At other times, however, the very bizarreness and isolation of Harriet's oddly unwitnessed trials take on the tang of the surreal. In one memorable sequence, while being pursued by Danny and Farish, Harriet races desperately in broad daylight from backyard to backyard, scaling fences and agitating pet dogs, but for all the witnesses to this event, the chase might as well be taking place in the middle of the Gobi desert. The one old man she encounters ignores her panic. Finally, it is Chester, the black handyman, who gives her a place to hide, even though Harriet acknowledges to herself the harsh reality that "Chester's word probably wouldn't go very far against two white men."[12]

Even given a generous helping of suspended disbelief, it is hard to imagine a neighborhood so utterly deserted, a town so apparently bereft of a police presence or even Good Samaritans, where two adult men chasing a terrified child can go unobserved and unreported. On the one hand, such scenes strain credibility; on the other, they weave a claustrophobia-inducing sense of isolation so profound that the terrain Harriet traverses is more one of nightmare than reality.

The chase through the suburban neighborhood is just the beginning of Harriet's trials at the hands of the Ratliffs, and in this Tartt brings to mind that standard Gothic trope of the female imperiled or terrorized at the hands of a powerful male. The Ratliffs are, of course, a far cry from more standard Gothic patriarchs such as Harriet's loopy great-grandfather Judge Cleve or even her erratic father Dixon; Danny and Farish are hooligans who wield power only in the crudest, brute-force sense, a fact that magnifies rather than mitigates their capacity to terrify.

In contrast with the macho Ratliff clan, in her depiction of the Cleve family, Tartt has created a world made up almost entirely of women: Harriet and Allison; their mother, grandmother, and aunts; and Ida Rhew, the housekeeper and surrogate mother. The single male presence in the Cleve household is that of the distant and infrequently seen Dixon, Harriet's father, who relocated to Nashville when Robin's murder made the enjoyment of life too difficult in his hometown. Dix's absence seems mourned by no one. His rare holiday appearances are tolerated with the tacit understanding that he will stir up a few arguments, perhaps whip Harriet for insubordination unbecoming her female status, and then—like a spell of bad weather—be gone for a few more months.

While Harriet may be the only female character overtly menaced by dangerous men, on another level, it can be said that the familiar Gothic theme of female subjugation runs throughout the book, with society at large (in the form of restrictive social mores and social conditioning) acting as the oppressor. Even Harriet's own father makes no bones about his "low opinion of girl children," boasting that "no daughter of his . . . would inherit a dime."[13]

In the case of Harriet's mother Charlotte, although the torpor of her life is unrelieved by dangers from outside, she imposes upon herself a degree of isolation and oppression more commonly seen meted out by threatening males in the standard Gothic tale. Following Robin's death, she has retreated into a drugged half life, only vaguely aware of the day-to-day goings-on of her household. In one memorable scene, she berates Harriet for supposedly staying out all night, until Harriet points out that it's seven in the evening, not in the morning. She turns over the running of the household and the raising of her daughters almost entirely to Ida Rhew and, to a lesser extent, her brusquely competent mother Edie, all the while remaining as oblivious to the needs of her daughters as she is to the piles of newspapers and hoarded rubble that fill the upper rooms of the house. In that sense, Charlotte embraces fully the Gothic identity of woman as victim—sequestered, isolated, and incapable of protecting herself or anyone else.

In contrast, Harriet's grandmother Edie is a decidedly different kind of woman from her daughter and sisters, who regard her with something akin to awe. Edie drives a car, takes charge, soldiers on, and can deal with life in a manner that, to her sisters, appears almost masculine when compared with their timidity and propensity for hand-fluttering ineptitude. This contrast between old-style, helpless southern belles and the assertive, independent womanhood evinced by Edie and Harriet reflects a distinctly feminist bent, a trend pointed out by Susan V. Donaldson in an essay for *The Mississippi Quarterly*, in which she observes, "If we take heed to the wealth of scholarship emerging on the gothic and gender in the last twenty years, we might learn in particular that the peculiar propensity of modern Southern writers to evoke the gothic, the macabre, and the grotesque

might very well have a good deal to do with regional anxiety about rapidly changing gender roles in the first half of the twentieth century."[14]

Although Harriet's final showdown against Danny Ratliff atop a crumbling water tower certainly places her in the classical situation of damsel in distress, she also stands out from all the other women in the novel (with the exception of Edie) as someone who not only refuses to be a victim waiting to be rescued by a man, but who takes charge of her own destiny. She scorns the passivity and vagueness of her older sister and refuses the gladiator novels proffered by her Aunt Tat because "they were only love stories in Roman dress, and she disliked anything which had to do with love or romance."[15] She feels only contempt for the boy-crazy, body-obsessed camp mates she encounters while hiding out from the Ratliff brothers at the dreaded Camp Lake de Selby.

Conflict between outdated cultural mores and societal change goes far beyond gender roles, of course, and Tartt skillfully weaves throughout the novel the themes of the white upper classes in lofty ascendance over blacks and lower-class whites. Much as some early Gothic writers used the disparity between the nobility and peasant classes to good effect, Tartt delves into the rigidly partitioned class structure of the Deep South of the 1970s, where upper-class whites inhabit a safe and sanitized cocoon, almost entirely apart from both the black population that serves them and the lower-class, undereducated white population that fears, resents, and ultimately blames them for their debased position.

Seen largely through Harriet's eyes, this hierarchy of social classes creates a toxic blend of pseudointimacy and utter alienation where groups of people interact on superficial levels while rarely connecting in any meaningful or heartfelt way. Rather, they slide silently as ghosts through the slim partitions of each other's lives that social mores permit.

Tartt draws a vivid parallel between the invisibility and marginalization of both blacks and children in the fact that no one bothers to tell Libby's maid Odean—on vacation while her employer presumably goes on a trip—that in reality Libby, her companion of fifty-five years, has died that week and has already been buried. To the horror of the ever-proper Cleves, Odean appears unexpectedly at the wake, rigid with grief and wounded pride, to demand why no one came to tell her of Libby's death. The idea that a deep emotional bond existed between Odean and Libby, an affection more like that of sisters than employer and employee, is so far outside the Cleve's social expectations that they are flummoxed, almost struck dumb (with the exception of Edie) at the sight of Odean's pain.

Only Allison is capable of an emotional response; as Harriet and Hely watch, she throws herself sobbing into Odean's arms while "Harriett's face constricted, not with disgust, or even embarrassment, but with some foreign,

frightening emotion which made Hely step away from her as if she had an infectious disease."[16]

Just as no one thinks to summon Odean to Libby's deathbed, neither does it occur to Edie to pull Harriet out of summer camp so she can say good-bye. Harriet only learns of the tragedy when Libby is already dead. "Why, thought Harriet, blind and sore and dazed from weeping, why did they leave me at that stinking camp while Libby was in the bed dying?"[17]

Likewise, when Ida Rhew leaves the Cleve household for the last time, no one—not even Harriet or Allison—thinks to get her address. Even though she has worked in the Cleve household for decades, no one is completely sure whether or not she even has a phone or how she could be reached, but for the rest of her life, Harriet suffers the knowledge that she let her beloved Ida leave without saying good-bye.

If black servants and their white employees at least coexist in overlapping worlds of poverty and privilege, an even greater isolation afflicts the poor, uneducated white class of Harriet's town. Even Ida Rhew scorns the ragged Odum children, chasing them from the yard when, in years past, they drifted by to play with Robin, who in his carefree way seemed oblivious to their status as undesirables. "Trashy" was how Ida Rhew described the Ratliff and Odum broods, leaving unsaid what everyone else already knew, that "when Ida said trashy, she meant white."[18]

And lest anyone be tempted to overlook the Ratliff's rock-bottom social standing, Tartt courts overkill by adding a few physical defects as well: the terrible burn scar that disfigures Eugene Ratliff's face, Farish's one eye, Gum's revoltingly emaciated body, and Curtis's mental retardation.

Yet if Tartt piles on the defects in true Southern Gothic style, to her credit, she also provides vivid glimpses into the inner worlds of the failed Ratliff men that temper their outcast status with a smidgen of humanity. At first glance (and also second and third), for instance, Danny Ratliff appears to be almost a caricature of the redneck loser male. Later, however, we learn of his aspirations to be a truck driver, of the brief happiness he knew on the road, and of the vicious, soul-destroying put-downs of his grandmother Gum, who makes sure to quash any signs of hope or high spirits in her family. The fact that Gum was married at fourteen to an abusive, much-older man and that, as a female, she derives all her power from subverting and manipulating her grandsons explains a great deal about her bitterness and canker-encrusted soul.

If Tartt's penchant for fleshing out her characters with a wealth of details makes for a more interesting read, it also certainly makes for a longer one. At six hundred plus pages, with long sections of rambling descriptions, *The Little Friend* can seem somewhat daunting upon initial investigation. In the hands of a writer less gifted than Tartt, such a book might soon founder under the weight

of its own verbiage. But Tartt's intricately woven, often meandering narrative is rich with nuance, subtlety, and humor. We could undoubtedly enjoy the novel (and some might argue could enjoy it more) without needing to know every detail of the aunts' home furnishings, Libby's phobias, and Tat's idiosyncrasies, but learning these apparently inconsequential tidbits of Cleve-family trivia becomes in its own way a delight; though riven with secrets and bound by habit and custom, the claustrophobic life of the Cleves is also compelling, fascinating even, given that it provides the backdrop for Harriet's audacious, yet ultimately ill-conceived quest.

Not surprisingly, a good deal of critical comment on *The Little Friend* has focused on the ending, or, in the minds of at least some readers, the lack of a satisfactory one. In this, the novel mimics real life—something that not all who sit down to read a work of fiction are prepared to accept—and deviates from the conventions not only of the Gothic, but of other genres like the detective novel and the romance. Dastardly deeds and appalling predicaments are not neatly resolved in the final paragraphs to return the reader to a satisfying conclusion where loose ends are tied up.

With Harriet's ultimate failure, *The Little Friend* runs true to the tradition of Gothic literature as a genre fraught with despair, for despite all her efforts, including a willingness to risk her life to bring about justice for her brother, at the end of that outlandish summer, her quest comes to naught, and both she and the reader are no closer to knowing who murdered Robin Cleve than when the book first opened with the account of his death. Harriet is left with the blistering knowledge that the man she has pursued and tormented, Danny Ratliff, was in fact not her brother's killer at all, and in fact might even have been his friend.

For some readers, after persevering through such a hefty tome, the realization that Harriet's suspicions about the Ratliffs were ill founded and that Robin's bizarre murder remains unsolved comes as a bitter disappointment, a game of gotcha, with the reader as the loser. Does even Tartt herself know who might have murdered Robin, or did she simply paint herself into a corner? Surely, had she wanted a more neatly wrapped-up ending, it would have been simple enough for Danny Ratliff to make a desperate confession just before (conveniently) drowning in the water tower.

But the convenient path is no more Tartt's choice than it is Harriet's. Never predictable or formulaic, Tartt doesn't tack together a contrived and conventional ending where all questions are neatly resolved. Here, as in Scott's Antarctic adventure, courage and heroism are not automatically rewarded with triumph or even a modicum of serenity.

Given the time and place in which Harriet is growing up, however, it might be suggested that, had her brother's murder not sent her off on a daring quest for justice, even such a spirited little girl might ultimately have been

crushed under the weight of society's misogyny. If Harriet fails in her quest, it is perhaps a deeply redeeming grace that even in failure, she has the possibility of accomplishing something grander than what she set out to achieve: she may not have brought a murderer to justice, but in using the wit, intelligence, and courage necessary to make such a bold and staggering attempt, she may have saved herself.

Notes

1. Donna Tartt, *The Little Friend* (New York: Random House, 2002), 51.

2. David Stevens, *The Gothic Tradition* (Cambridge, UK: Cambridge University Press, 2000), 32.

3. Tartt, *The Little Friend*, 363.

4. Tartt, *The Little Friend*, 24.

5. Tartt, *The Little Friend*, 3.

6. Tartt, *The Little Friend*, 41.

7. Tartt, *The Little Friend*, 24.

8. William Faulkner, "A Rose for Emily," in *Collected Stories of William Faulkner* (New York: Vintage, 1995), 195.

9. Tartt, *The Little Friend*, 132.

10. Tartt, *The Little Friend*, 372.

11. Stevens, *The Gothic Tradition*, 42.

12. Tartt, *The Little Friend*, 509.

13. Tartt, *The Little Friend*, 22.

14. Susan V. Donaldson, "Making a Spectacle: Welty, Faulkner, and Southern Gothic," *Mississippi Quarterly* 50, no. 4 (1997): 568.

15. Tartt, *The Little Friend*, 568.

16. Tartt, *The Little Friend*, 456.

17. Tartt, *The Little Friend*, 433.

18. Tartt, *The Little Friend*, 13.

CHAPTER 33

The Tyranny of Time and Identity

OVERCOMING THE PAST IN GREGORY MAGUIRE'S *LOST*

Jason Colavito

Every few years a scientist, scholar, or skeptic comes along to tell us that ghosts aren't real or that specters are old-fashioned survivals of a more primitive time. While belief in the (meta)physical reality of ghosts waxes and wanes with the current reputation of science, the emotional reality of ghostliness has kept spirits haunting the pages of Gothic fiction for two and a half centuries. When Horace Walpole wrote the first Gothic novel, *The Castle of Otranto* (1764), he made the ghost of a dead medieval prince haunt his former castle, revealing hidden truths, false identities, and romantic entanglements amidst a plethora of otherworldly phenomena. This set the template for future Gothic works, and it was in fact the antique architecture of the novel's gloomy castle that gave the genre its name.

Artifacts of our shared cultural past haunt the works of Gregory Maguire, much as ancient revenants haunt Gothic fiction. Maguire is best known for his retellings of classic stories such as *Wicked* (*The Wizard of Oz*) or *Mirror Mirror* ("Snow White"), but his lesser-known work *Lost* (2001) provides an intriguing example of the way Gothic ideas and themes can be transported into the present—and transmuted. In *Lost*, we see traditional Gothic themes, including ghosts, buried secrets, violent weather, and madness, but we also see contemporary references and elements added to shade the Gothic into a commentary on the fragility and transience of the present and the continuing existence of a half-suppressed past. Throughout *Lost*, two complementary Gothic themes predominate—the imposition of the past onto the present, and the tenuousness of an individual's identity—and it is the interplay of these themes that drives the narrative forward and brings its main character to her moment of catharsis.

For the British writers of the Gothic period (conventionally defined as 1764 to 1818), the "past" was generally imagined as the medieval era, as distinct from "modern times." The Middle Ages were then seen as the great dark space between the light of the pagan past and the flame of knowledge reborn in the Renaissance. Everything about the medieval era, from its gloomy architecture to its embrace of the supernatural, spoke of unreason and fear. The Enlightenment thinkers were particularly appalled by the medieval embrace of religion, which they saw as antithetical to reason and progress. However, materially speaking, for most people the world of 1800 was not far removed from the world of 1400, and many lived in the same hovels doing the same agrarian work as their ancestors had always done. The Middle Ages were not uniformly dead in the Britain of 1800, but in modern America, most now find the medieval European world remote and inconceivable. Contemporary Americans must look for a dark past in a different place. We see this at play in *Lost* from the very beginning.

The novel opens in modern-day Boston where Winifred Rudge is making plans to travel across the Atlantic to England, symbolically going from the present into the heart of the past, the place where her (and America's) ancestors lay. That she does so in the shadow of a great coastal storm, the remnants of a hurricane, that follows her to London is no coincidence, as this gloomy weather predominates in Gothic novels. (It is for good reason that Bulwer-Lytton's "a dark and stormy night" became a latter-day Gothic cliché.) The storm, though, is described not on its own terms but as mediated through "the Weather Channel's computer-graphic impression of the storm."[1] In fact, the early sections of the book are dominated by pop-culture references: Subarus, WGBH (a Boston TV station), the Red Sox, L. L. Bean, Happy Meals, and so on. The modern world is a shimmering mirage of cultural touchstones—consumer goods and products that take the place of landmarks, philosophies, and personalities.

In the first pages, Maguire's overwhelming reliance on such cultural shorthand appears distracting, marooning us in a metaworld bounded by the characters' discussions of *A Christmas Carol*, *Peter Pan*, *The Wind in the Willows*, *Lord of the Flies*, and *Alice in Wonderland*. But this is an illusion; the contemporary world is gradually revealed to be nothing more than a thin tissue of pop culture and a smattering of literature papering over a more solid past defined by architecture and artifacts that in their permanence and presence appear at first more real than the ephemera of a changing modernity. Maguire accomplishes this subtly, by reducing page by page the number of references to popular culture and replacing them instead with increasing references to historical events, places, and objects.

Winnie, as the narration calls her, is a writer of children's books whose income derives mostly from the success of a nonfiction book on astrology, something that embarrasses her to no end. Winnie is a "stone-hearted rational-

ist,"[2] that special species of skeptic who exists in Gothic fiction to have his or her materialist worldview challenged by the appearance of the supernatural. In this, she shares a Gothic heritage with such unbelievers as John Seward, the doubting doctor in Bram Stoker's *Dracula*, and General Browne, who doubted the ghost residing in Sir Walter Scott's "Tapestried Chamber." Needless to say, Seward and Browne eventually came to understand the reality of the supernatural, and Winnie gradually follows in their Gothic footsteps, straight down into the crypt, in both literal and metaphorical senses.

Winnie is on her way to Britain to do research for an adult novel she plans to write—something perhaps about Jack the Ripper, or, better yet, her alter ego Wendy Pritzke's search for the ghost of Jack the Ripper. While in Britain, Winnie intends to stay with her stepcousin John in the ancestral family home, Rudge House, an old pile in Hampstead built by Ozias, the family patriarch. According to family legend, Ozias was the inspiration for Ebenezer Scrooge in Charles Dickens's *A Christmas Carol*. The story goes that the young Dickens spent part of his youth in Hampstead and listened to the wealthy merchant Ozias's tales of being haunted by an indescribable presence around Christmastide. Laundered through sentimental romance, Ozias's haunting became Dickens's morality tale.

When Rudge House was subdivided and sold off seventy years ago, the family held on to a few rooms which might have gone to Winnie, who was heir by blood, had her father's death and his sister's marriage to a widowed father not intervened and placed the remaining flat in the hands of her stepcousin. This development, too, is a legacy of the Gothic, the direct descendent of *The Castle of Otranto*, in which the rightful owner of the title to the castle has been turned out in favor of a usurper, and Ann Radcliffe's *Mysteries of Udolpho*, in which a young heiress is threatened with dispossession at the hands of her aunt's husband. The Gothic frequently concerns itself with ties of blood and dispossession—"that quintessentially Gothic issue"[3]—because these themes are closely tied to legitimacy and, more importantly, to justice flowing from the past into the present.

As the stage for the impending drama, Rudge House becomes a character in itself, a locus of Gothic intrigue that derives in large measure from the picturesque piles of Otranto and Udolpho and the other spooky residences of Gothic romance. However, unlike those original castles, Rudge House is both something less and something more. Unlike the ancient castles of early Gothic novels, "The Rudge family home was recent by English standards, its original rooms dating to the early nineteenth century. Yesterday, really."[4] This was no medieval survival but instead a Georgian edifice full of picturesque detail. Nevertheless, this house is, to Winnie's mind, old because it harks back across the centuries and was the seat of her family, thus symbolically the place of her line's birth. However, in gradually revealing information about Rudge House throughout *Lost*, Maguire translates the Gothic fixation with medieval architecture into a different time

frame, locating the source of horror not in a place but in time. For, of course, Rudge House is not a purely Georgian edifice but contains another part.

Sometime in the nineteenth century, at the height of the Victorian period, Rudge House was expanded, with new rooms added onto the back and abutting another Victorian edifice erected on the adjoining property. These rooms are described as smaller, uneven, and, in the case of the topmost flat (John's), physically crossing the property line to steal space from the adjacent residence—and symbolically crossing other boundaries as well. *Lost* follows the path blazed in the middle of the twentieth century when the Victorian period became associated with a "dismal cloud" of repression and horror.[5] This was for several reasons, which all tie together to inform *Lost* and provide it with its resonance. First, of course, was architecture.

The Victorians drew on historical styles, including the Romanesque, Gothic, and Renaissance, in much of their architecture, and in doing so their buildings appropriated some of the mystery—and even horror—of the great medieval cathedrals and palaces they aped. During the twentieth century, cultural leaders revolted against the Victorians, seeing in them everything that the new century would not be. Their lives, their art, and especially their buildings were reviled. Queen Anne and neo-Gothic mansions were symbols of a nightmare that modernity strived to wake from. Too expensive for Depression-era and postwar populations to maintain, these structures were subdivided into apartments (like Rudge House) or left to rot. Steven J. Mariconda notes that, "as a style favored by the upper class of their era, houses that were once places of privilege became symbols of a decayed aristocracy and places of mystery" for the solidly middle-class middle America of the middle twentieth century.[6] These spooky old homes entered the public imagination by midcentury when Charles Addams's "The Addams Family" cartoons and Alfred Hitchcock's *Psycho* located their transgressive characters in Second Empire–style wrecks, establishing a cliché for houses of horror. In the United States, which has no ancient castles, these homes were the closest thing to hilltop ruins where Britain's ghosts traditionally lived—defiantly opposed to clean, sleek, unadorned modernism.

In *Lost*, the (upper-class) Victorians, like their neo-Gothic architecture, are seen as a corrupting and polluting influence, "corseted, even strait-jacketed by Victorian certainties."[7] They are upper-class patricians whose propriety enforces unwelcome codes on their descendants. Ozias Rudge, of course, is one of these patricians, a wealthy merchant who builds a mansion to house his dynasty. Winnie, by contrast, barely makes ends meet with her declining fortunes. With each generation, her family slips lower down the socioeconomic ladder, something Americans aren't supposed to do. In *Lost*, the Victorian elite are alien people who have usurped the position of the medieval period in older Gothic fiction, the half-forgotten past that reaches out to smite. There is, of course, a paradox here.

In some places, *Lost* views the Victorians as stolidly praiseworthy in contrast with the mad modern world of uncertainty, but also foreign, different, other—the unseen and unloved builders of mock castles in which modern people now squat as unwelcome tenants. (Never mind, of course, that the Victorians were not the gloomy flagellants of popular legend; neither were medieval people the violent, picturesque irrationals that the Gothic writers imagined them to be. Both are literary fictions.) It is from the Victorian section of Rudge House that the first signs of the uncanny begin to emanate.

Winnie discovers that her stepcousin's flat contains not John but workmen whom John hired to break up the Victorian walls and insert an illegal staircase to the rooftop. John is nowhere to be found, and the greater part of the novel involves Winnie's increasingly frantic search for him. Within the apartment, though, strange Gothic doings begin to occur. The workmen find their renovations stalled by unseen forces and strange sounds. Nails, half pulled from the wall, are sucked back in, and damp spots form the shape of a Christian cross with a violent slash through it. The workmen come to believe an angry ghost is out to get them. On a lower floor, the senile old tenant goes slowly mad, with unfortunate results for her poor cats.

The turning point comes when a break in the false wall covering a back chimney reveals a piece of dirty old cloth that a professorial friend of Winnie's learns is a genuine medieval artifact. It had apparently been sealed up when the Victorians built the addition to Rudge House. Though never explicitly stated, old Ozias's death in 1879 placed him just late enough to have perhaps been responsible for the deposition. If not him, then it must have been the son who decamped for America. Winnie consults a psychic, in whose powers she as a skeptic does not at first believe, to learn more about the cloth; but the psychic maintains that the burial shroud—which is what he claims the cloth is—is in possession of a past too traumatic for him to contemplate. Through a series of unfortunate events, Winnie becomes convinced that the old shroud is possessed by a ghost. Only when Winnie opens herself to the ghost does she begin to find answers, answers that leave her half mad herself.

The denouement takes the possessed Winnie to France, where she visits Mont-Saint-Michel, the medieval island abbey. She has deduced from family legend, history, and other evidence that old Ozias had stolen a small statue of the Virgin and Child from the monastery when he helped shore up a failing crypt there in the nineteenth century, a time when builders and architects from all over Britain turned to France's Normandy region as inspiration for their neo-Gothic designs.[8] He smuggled the artifact back to England in the old burial shroud, bringing with it the sad and vengeful ghost of a medieval Norman peasant girl who had been burned alive for crimes she committed to feed herself and her unborn child. Here Maguire skillfully links the prudish and gloomy

Victorians to the barbarous Middle Ages by making Ozias the hand through which the Gothic past travels across space and time to infect the present with its unfinished business.

Once again, it is the architecture that speaks to the continuing existence of the past: "And how much of Mont-Saint-Michel was as it had been in 1350? At least some of it, no doubt."[9] Winnie wends her way to the abbey through a town with houses "dating from the late Middle Ages."[10] With each step, Winnie displaces herself further in both space and time from the ephemeral world of contemporary America. If Victorian England was the antechamber connecting the modern world to its forgotten past, then here, in France, Winnie has completed her journey backward, hurtling from modernity to the neo-Gothic to the very origins of the Gothic in the superstitious, unsettled, and unsettling Middle Ages.

This symbolic voyage across space is paralleled by Winnie's linguistic voyage toward ancestral English. In Boston, she and her companions speak in a contemporary American slang, full of sitcom sparkle and pop culture. Her trip to England introduces British variants and terms into her speech, which she self-consciously adopts and contemplates as she attempts to fit in with the Britons surrounding her. As British English is millennia older than its American cousin, her words have (symbolically, if not literally) begun the regression into the past. This is brought to full force when Winnie becomes possessed by the medieval Norman ghost who speaks a type of Old (Norman) French unremembered today. Norman French, brought to England by William the Conqueror in 1066, was the language of the royal court and government in the Middle Ages and remained the aristocracy's first language into the fifteenth century.[11] Mont-Saint-Michel, it should be remembered, is in Normandy, from which came the Conqueror. In fact, the abbey had been a fort under the protection of the Norman dukes, and the abbey's monks fought with William to conquer England in 1066.[12] In the period when the ghost lived (c. 1350), Normandy (though not the abbey itself) was an English possession.[13] Therefore, in parallel to Winnie's journey backward from America to England to France, her speech revisits its ancestral form, moving her further into the past.

As Winnie comes to lose (and find) herself by surrendering to the atavistic past, Winnie's possession serves as a final exploration of the fragility of modern identity in the face of a tragic history, another of *Lost*'s themes, and one with Gothic literary precedents. As early as the first Gothic novel, issues of identity have bedeviled Gothic heroes and villains alike. In *The Castle of Otranto*, a peasant named Theodore is revealed as the true heir to the duchy of Otranto, and Frankenstein's monster spends most of *Frankenstein* desperately trying to understand himself. But it was the Victorians who, in expanding and developing Gothic themes, brought identity issues to the fore in their Gothic-style novels. From Robert Louis Stevenson's Dr. Jekyll to Oscar Wilde's Dorian Gray, the

Victorians tended to symbolize problematic identity through the existence of doubles—Mr. Hyde, the picture, and so on. As Linda Dryden points out, "The double is a threat to the integrity of the self, and frequently evidence of a Gothic, supernatural force at large that brings with it death and destruction."[14] In *Lost*, Winnie experiences a series of doubles and dualities that culminate in her attempt to fold them all into herself.

When we first meet Winnie, she is already a bifurcated character. She is both Winifred W. Rudge, children's book author, and Dotty O'Malley, her "favorite alter ego,"[15] whom she pretends to be in order to conduct research at an adoption center for the adult novel she intends to write. Winnie reveals to a friend at the adoption center that she is also Ophelia Marley, the nom de plume under which she wrote *The Dark Side of the Zodiac*, her embarrassingly profitable nonfiction book. She uses the same name later to introduce herself to Irv Hausserman, a professor who helps her untangle the mystery of the ghost. Winnie has created a number of identities for herself, the better to isolate aspects of her personality, avoid the demands of reality, and hide from a past she would rather not remember.

Winnie has also created another persona, "Wendy Pritzke," the heroine of the novel she is attempting to write about a woman searching for the ghost of Jack the Ripper. Winnie recognizes the character as an aspect of herself, one that is haunting her and demanding that her story be told, a story of "Gothic excess, born of the grimier side of Winnie's sensibility."[16] Throughout her trip to England, Winnie imagines herself as Wendy, and at intervals throughout *Lost*, we are presented with excerpts from Winnie's evolving manuscript, detailing the reactions and adventures of Winnie's most important alter ego. At first these excerpts seem like standard Gothic-novel melodrama, transmogrifying the events Winnie experiences in her missing stepcousin's flat into a tale of a brave woman investigating the murder of Jack the Ripper, walled up in a Victorian chimney.

But as her book continues, the veil of fiction wears ever thinner, and characters from Winnie's life, like stepcousin John, make their appearance in the story. The tale becomes less the story of Jack the Ripper and more the memoir of a woman who traveled to Romania with her stepcousin, made love to him despite her marriage vows to another man, and lost to hypothermia the baby she and her husband were about to adopt when the orphanage lost its heat in winter. This not-quite-fictional self collapses into Winnie when, at story's end, we learn the author's full name: Winifred Wendy Rudge, ex-wife of Emil Pritzke. Winnie/Wendy feels terrible guilt that her illicit lovemaking occurred in the hours when her baby was freezing to death, and it poisons the rest of her life.

The story of a distraught woman who loses the baby she never knew is paralleled in the ghost, who serves as a double for Winnie/Wendy. Just as Winnie's story is gradually revealed through her writings about Wendy, the ghost's story

is gradually revealed through Irv Hausserman's efforts to have the ghost's Old French translated. The resulting effort reveals that the ghost is named Gervasa, and in her own words, both spoken aloud through her host and mentally via a psychic connection, she tells of her heartbreak and horror at being burned alive while pregnant, and her anger at not knowing whether her child suffered for her sins. Winnie carries the ghost within her—as she never did the baby she could not save—and brings her to Mont-Saint-Michel, where Gervasa was buried beneath a slashed cross. Gervasa mistakenly believes this to be a sign of disfavor, but the priest of the abbey reveals that the slash symbol refers to a sprig of holly, a symbol of life representing the survival of her baby.

However, Wendy, Winnie, and Gervasa cannot all inhabit the same flesh, a body too "stuffed with identity."[17] So, having solved the mystery and provided Gervasa with whatever peace knowledge can bring, Winnie begins her slow journey back to the present, casting aside bit by bit the corruptions and disappointments of the past. She brings Gervasa back to Britain—and out of the medieval (French) past—to bequeath the ghost to a dying woman who can shepherd Gervasa to the next life. The past shed, "what returns is a sense of the present tense as being not only available, but valid."[18] The past's hold is now broken; slowly the present returns to the fore. Winnie then ends her work on "the book that she would not write"[19] and puts aside Wendy, leaving only one person resident in her body—Winnie. The ambiguous last pages leave it unclear whether this one person, Winnie, survives the ordeal bodily or has become a ghost, too, though unlike Gervasa, a ghost of kindness and assistance rather than anger and vengeance. In context, the literal reading of Winnie as physically present in the present seems more appropriate, but either can be supported from the textual evidence.

In the final pages, Winnie is seen traveling to Cambodia with a friend from the opening scene's adoption agency, streaking westward (and thus, in the book's symbolism, toward the future, away from France and England and America) to retrieve the woman's newly adopted baby, a trial run for Winnie's own journey toward a baby and the future "next year." When last we see Winnie, she is on a plane from Phnom Penh arriving back in Boston, the city of the present, whose skyline, "like a film snip from the opening credits of a network news program,"[20] returns her to today and to the ephemeral popular culture that defines the hustle and bustle of modern life. Winnie learns that the essence of life is change, and the past, which is frozen and changeless, brings only death and sorrow to medieval peasants, stuffy Victorians, former lovers, and mourning mothers. Only by putting aside the illusory stability and safety of an unchanging past can Winnie, and the reader, embrace the recklessness and randomness of change and thus truly live again.

Notes

1. Gregory Maguire, *Lost* (New York: Regan Books, 2001), 5.

2. Maguire, *Lost*, 20.

3. Anne Williams, *Art of Darkness: A Poetics of Gothic* (Chicago: University of Chicago Press, 1995), 68, 239.

4. Maguire, *Lost*, 28.

5. John Gardiner, *The Victorians: An Age in Retrospect* (London: Continuum International, 2002), 5.

6. Steven J. Mariconda, "The Haunted House," in *Icons of Horror and the Supernatural: An Encyclopedia of Our Worst Nightmares*, ed. S. T. Joshi, vol. 1 (Westport, CT: Greenwood, 2007), 273.

7. Maguire, *Lost*, 78.

8. Gavin Stamp, "High Victorian Gothic and the Architecture of Normandy," *The Journal of the Society of Architectural Historians* 62, no. 2 (June 2003): 194.

9. Maguire, *Lost*, 316.

10. Maguire, *Lost*, 316.

11. T. F. Tout, *France and England: Their Relations in the Middle Ages and Now* (Manchester: University Press, 1922), 152.

12. Walter Cranston Larned, *Churches and Castles of Medieval France* (New York: Charles Scribner's Sons, 1895), 49.

13. Anne Curry, *The Hundred Years' War*, 2nd ed. (Houndmills, UK: Palgrave Macmillan, 2003), 53.

14. Linda Dryden, *The Modern Gothic and Literary Doubles* (Houndmills, UK: Palgrave Macmillan, 2003), 38.

15. Maguire, *Lost*, 7.

16. Maguire, *Lost*, 23.

17. Maguire, *Lost*, 281.

18. Maguire, *Lost*, 332.

19. Maguire, *Lost*, 334.

20. Maguire, *Lost*, 335.

CHAPTER 34

"And That Was the Reason I Perished"

TRAUMA'S TRANSFORMATIVE POTENTIAL IN ALICE SEBOLD'S *THE LOVELY BONES*

August Tarrier

In the first eleven pages of Alice Sebold's *The Lovely Bones*, the reader is presented with the rape and murder of its fourteen-year-old narrator, Susie Salmon. For the next 317 pages, we witness the aftermath of Susie's violation—her father dissolves into rage and grief, her mother spirals out and away from the family, and her sister Lindsey struggles to survive in Susie's shadow.

Given that *The Lovely Bones* was number one on the *New York Times* best-seller list, it was clearly a widely accepted and accessible novel. Its success could certainly be attributed to the fact that it contains elements of classic horror, a thriller/murder mystery, and a YA coming-of-age novel—it gives us a soupçon of all these, and a huge serving of good old-fashioned family romance. Although *The Lovely Bones* has elements of a murder mystery, it doesn't really focus on the police investigation or the search for and arrest of the perpetrator. One could argue that *The Lovely Bones* could be classified as a horror novel, in that it was awarded a Bram Stoker award for best first novel, indicating that it had enough recognizable conventions of horror to be placed in that genre. And it contains elements of the supernatural (it is, after all, narrated by a dead girl) that we might find in such classic Gothic novels as *The Mysteries of Udolpho* or *Wuthering Heights*, or in the work of Poe or Hawthorne.

A reader might initially conclude that the horror lies in Sebold's depiction of the crime against Susie Salmon—the violated child, her body dispersed in fragments in a sinkhole—as a commentary on what cannot be made whole or explicable to her surviving family or to us. We might imagine that the novel, like many murder mysteries, will resolve with justice served and Susie's perpetrator, Mr. Harvey, caught and punished for his crimes against girls and women.

In fact, a viewing of the film *The Lovely Bones* (directed by Peter Jackson, February 2010) certainly suggests that the novel from which the film was made is a thriller, given the focus on the crime, the role of the detectives, and the unfolding of the case against the perpetrator. The cover of the reissued novel depicts Susie walking in the cornfield where she was murdered, with Mr. Harvey looming; we can imagine the bones of the murdered child crying out from the grave for vengeance. The trailer depicts two scenes that are focused on confrontation with Susie's killer. In one, her father, Jack, broken by his failure to protect her, goes charging into the very cornfield where Susie was murdered, ostensibly to face down her attacker, in order to enact his vengeance. The second is a scene in which Susie's sister, Lindsey, enters the murderer's house and investigates his belongings, making a narrow escape when he arrives home.

But the horror at the heart of the novel has very little to do with Susie's violation; it is the horror of being privy to the deepest pain of a normal, loving family torn apart by the death of one of its members. *The Lovely Bones* conveys its main message in the contemporary parlance of love and healing: we are obligated to heal from our trauma, and its "use" is to bring us closer to our loved ones. The rewards of an earthly life lie in our human frailties, in our vulnerabilities, our reliance on others, the promise of sustaining love. *The Lovely Bones* presents the grief and pain of Susie Salmon's parents, Jack and Abigail, and the temporary dissolution of their marriage, in order to cement those bonds, to make us believers in the power of grief's transformative potential.

A number of critics have taken issue with Sebold's handling of Susie's violation and its aftermath. Sebold presents us with a victim who is posttrauma, the kind of girl who is all bravado; she doesn't want vengeance or confrontation but instead is wholly focused on brokering, as best she can, her family's emotional survival in light of the event. A reanimated Susie, now whole and intact, narrates a tale of intense family bonds sustained across the chasm between heaven and earth. The novel provides an entirely reassuring take on trauma: our loved ones live on in our hearts, and if we grieve them and hold them dear, we will find closure, a way to heal and move on. In this way, *The Lovely Bones* is wholesome and, ultimately, palliative.

Once she is "postmortal," as it were, and residing in heaven, Susie encounters a girl who was also a victim of Mr. Harvey. And as soon as his other victims—girls and women—arrive, "our heartache poured into one another, like water from cup to cup."[1] The narrator continues to explain her own violation, making sense of it via what Daniel Mendelsohn, writing in the *New York Review of Books*, terms "the pseudo-therapeutic lingo of healing."[2] She remembers, "Each time I told my story, I lost a bit, the smallest drop of pain. It was that day that I knew I wanted to tell the story of my family. Because horror on Earth is real and it is every day. It is like a flower or like the sun; it cannot be contained"

(186). What makes this statement disconcerting is that it is delivered to us in a contained fashion, with a flat affect; the message here is not one of unendurable, unending horror, but something more akin to a cataloging of benign quotidian occurrences.

Ali Smith, writing in the *Guardian*, speaks directly to the way in which Sebold, via her nonchalant narrator, appears to undermine the exigencies of traumatic experience. "*The Lovely Bones* is so keen, in the end, to comfort us and make safe its world that, however well-meaning, it avoids its own ramifications."[3] When Smith asserts that the novel "avoids its own ramifications," it is perhaps to take issue with the fact that Sebold appears to bracket the rape and murder: the act itself is contained within the first chapter of the novel. Because Susie does not grapple with her own trauma and is not possessed of any need for vengeance, readers are left to fend for themselves: if Mr. Harvey's victim is happy in heaven, who are we to demand justice?

Phillip Hensher, writing in the *Observer*, looks askance at the novel's nonchalant tone, claiming that the novel is a "slick, overpoweringly saccharine and unfeeling exercise in sentiment and whimsy."[4] What Hensher may be referring to, especially in his use of the word *unfeeling*, is the narrator's tone—a detached and distant voice, pedestrian in its delivery. Susie appears unfazed by the horror of her own violation, and in that sense the novel doesn't signal to us that we are meant to dwell on its disturbing content.

Instead, Sebold is focused on solidifying the bonds of family; she trades in love and forgiveness, not payback. The perpetrator, Mr. Harvey, is bracketed, in that he is the sole inhabitant of what might be termed the sick heart of suburbia, the lone "monster" among all the other good and loving families. What is perverse is contained in the character of Mr. Harvey, the focal point of the horror in *The Lovely Bones*. He inhabits a literal underworld, a subterranean bunker he has built on his property, which is next door to the Salmon's. He makes a couple of dramatic and threatening appearances, but he basically skirts the edges of the novel, quietly building dollhouses and collecting memorabilia, the site of his repressed desire. And even he is given ample motivation for his crimes—we see the nine-year-old boy, abandoned by his grave-robbing mother (reason enough, we suppose, to grow up to be a serial killer). In another scene, the child sleeps in the cab of a pickup with his mother as three men appear outside, menacing her. About to be violated, she enlists her son's aid in escaping the would-be perpetrators. In other words, Mr. Harvey's crimes are motivated and are thus, at least ostensibly, understandable. At the end of the novel, Mr. Harvey is dispatched by an act of providence, thus reassuring the reader that all threats are containable. Vigilantism is quite unnecessary when the powers that be can perform a kind of white magic, invalidating all that is menacing and threatening.

Except for one brief appearance, Susie is offstage for the entire novel, situated in the afterlife, unable to "break through" to earth. But it is earthly matters that consume her: her unfinished business is not vengeance but *completion*. Susie strives to forge a connection across vast worlds. This striving, and the deepening bonds that result, make the novel anything but macabre: the stuff of the Gothic—the dark and foreboding corridors, the icy chill, the creaking door, and evil spirits afoot—is largely absent here. The individual members of Susie's family—her father Jack, her mother Abigail, her sister Lindsey, and her brother Buckley—all can conjure her up, can feel her presence in palpable, tangible ways. She is in touch with them through a kind of spiritual midwifery—she ushers her siblings into adulthood, she shepherds her father through his guilt and rage, she ensures safe passage for her sister when she goes to investigate Mr. Harvey's house. And Susie is there, too, when Lindsey has her first sexual experience and receives a proposal of marriage, functioning as cheerleader ("My sister! . . . My dream!" [241]). The novel creates and embraces normalcy, real-life hugs, and real-time heroic acts. *The Lovely Bones* contains elements of the Gothic in that it views familial connection through the prism of mourning and grief. It provides an atmosphere of menace and foreboding, but it is presented via what might be classified as a kind of Gothic lite, or what Stephen King, writing in *Danse Macabre*, terms "sunlit horror."[5] It makes sense, then, to imagine that Sebold's version of the Gothic might be thought of as a "sunlit Gothic," one that conjures its terror via elegiac moments of loss or regret in order to instruct us about the ways in which we might deepen and solidify our connection to others.

We can look to the tropes of the Gothic to provide us with a version of how trauma is manifested and also how it is contained. One way to think of trauma is as a kind of haunting; the most disturbing aspects of our experience persist, and can easily become repressed, manifesting as oblique or circumspect phenomena that are unapprehendable. We can certainly imagine that this is the case for Eleanor, the central character in Shirley Jackson's *The Haunting of Hill House*, who is haunted by repressed memories of her mother, and by sexual longings for her friend and coinhabitant of Hill House, Theodora.

Another trope of the Gothic is an encounter with the unknown. So much of *The Haunting of Hill House* is confounding and elusive, filled with inexplicable twists and turns, like the long drive one makes in the approach to Hill House itself. The ambiguous and disturbing ending of this novel signals that what is unknowable—Eleanor's fears, her profound sense of being *separate*, the uncontainable depths of Hill House itself—will remain unresolved. "Hill House itself, not sane . . . holding darkness within . . . had stood so for eighty years. . . . [S]ilence lay steadily against the wood and stone of Hill House, and whatever walked there, walked alone."[6]

In this sense, *Hill House* differs strikingly from *The Lovely Bones*, which encodes disturbing experience as ultimately knowable: our desires, our most intimate pain, are available to us and are catalysts to healing. The contrast points up how demonstrably the latter novel refutes the kind of ominous and foreboding content that we find in novels like *Hill House*, which includes the suicide of its protagonist in one of the final scenes. We can only imagine what *The Lovely Bones* might offer if it were to provide such a disturbing conclusion—perhaps a vision of the lost girls, wandering in the purgatory of the cornfield, lingering at the edges of the sinkhole.

The Lovely Bones can be read as providing a counterpoint to the Gothic in that it dispenses with the treacherous corridors, creaky floorboards, and shaky banisters, but also in its bracketing of transgressive content, its omniscient voiceover—Susie knows and sees everything—and in the way it dispels the threat of amorphous identity, the mingling of two women characters, Eleanor and Theodora, in *The Haunting of Hill House*.

The uncanny, shifting ground of the Gothic is rendered as terra firma in *The Lovely Bones*. Susie's presence is ultimately salutary and efficacious: she watches over and enables her family and friends to become stronger and better human beings. She is even a matchmaker, after a fashion, to her separated parents (the novel makes more than a passing nod, via Susie's point of view, to the wish-fulfillment fantasy of every child of divorced parents—if only mommy and daddy would get back together). At every turn, despair is countered by the strong bonds of love. Connection is solidified; even in heaven, our feet are on the ground. It is love that exerts an uncanny force in *The Lovely Bones*—the various family members coming to terms with their love for Susie and eventually finding ways to let her go. In this novel, what is horrifying is unreconciled yearning, the persistence of grief and longing. As Susie says, "In some way I could not account for . . . I was done yearning for them, needing them to yearn for me" (318). *The Lovely Bones* presents trauma as therapeutic, as something that is useful and potentially transformative. It is the letting go, the novel tells us, that we must all strive for, a way to move out of what Susie terms "the Inbetween."

What Ali Smith and Philip Hensher may be decrying in their critique of the novel is Sebold's refusal to allow the exigencies of traumatic experience to reverberate, and instead to tie up too neatly the loose ends of a disturbing or harrowing experience that has enormous destructive potential for the human psyche. Cathy Caruth underscores the role of forgetting in the creation of memories of traumatic experience: "The historical power of the trauma is not just that the experience is repeated after its forgetting, but that it is only in and through its inherent forgetting that it is first experienced at all."[7] If we think about the way trauma works, or rather the way the experience of trauma is recorded in memory, we know that the brain checks out during intense, traumatic

experience. What this means is that we discover trauma as we relive it. So one way to think about the way we process trauma is that we have only wisps and shards of the most horrific experiences of our lives, and as we try to make sense of them, gradually, cumulatively, we end up the authors of our most terrifying moments. An awareness of this reality might result in a focus on uncovering the "truth" of trauma, the way it is remembered, in fragmentary half-light, the way a victim, despite attempts to move forward, often remains frozen in the pain of burgeoning awareness. Instead, Sebold depicts the stitching together, the reassembly, of Susie's heart and soul. In *The Lovely Bones*, the trauma does not so much resonate in disturbing ways so much as it provides an impetus for all of the characters of the novel to deepen their bonds with Susie and with one another. Susie's narrating of traumatic memory is useful, and her death itself is transformative to the other characters. This vantage on traumatic experience is evident in a scene in which Abigail and Lynn, Susie's grandmother, are taking a walk in the neighborhood, discussing the ways in which their working through of grief and pain has changed them:

> "Susie's death brought your father's back to me," my grandmother said. "I never let myself mourn him properly." She goes on to explain to Abigail that there is "something that's coming out of all this. You and me. A nugget of truth between us." (169)

The character of Abigail, Susie's mother, could be read as the one who takes a decided detour in her own attempts to heal from her grief and loss: she has an affair with Len Feterman, the detective who is investigating Susie's murder, and temporarily leaves her family. (He, too, is in mourning—his wife has committed suicide—and their grief provides them the connection they need.) Sebold makes Abigail into a good and loving mother who had to take time out to find herself: all of what she does is permissible and justified in that she was seeking "to find a doorway out of her ruined heart, in merciful adultery" (197). Contrast this portrayal with the wretchedness of grief and loss we find depicted in *The Odyssey*; the devastating effects on those left behind are presented as a kind of horror—unending, irresolvable. When Odysseus visits the Land of the Dead and speaks to his dead mother, Anticlea, she tells him of his wife's incessant weeping and his father's grieving—"and the sorrow grows big within him." She adds, "And so it was with me also and that was the reason I perished. . . . Shining Odysseus, it was my longing for you, your cleverness and your gentle ways, that took the sweet spirit of life from me."[8] Homer conveys that one can die of grief, one can waste away in sorrow. Sebold instructs us very differently about the vagaries of grief: there is a limit to grief, to despair, to the horror of loss.

The veil between Susie and her loved ones is thin indeed, and yet when she makes a return engagement back here on earth, it is not her devastated and

grieving father whom she visits. It is not the sister who has been left to live in her shadow, or the mother who appears haunted by visions of her daughter ("I see her everywhere . . ." [281]). Susie comes back expressly to do the deed for which she must be embodied: to have sex in the back of Hal's Bike Shop with Ray Singh, her first love. In this scene, reparations are made—the violated and defiled body is discarded in favor of an intact one, one that is "pure." Alice Sebold ensures that Susie's first sexual experience will be a virginal one by allowing her main character to return in the body of another girl, Ruth, who hasn't had sexual intercourse (and who is attracted to girls, not boys—perhaps another assurance that her body is safe from male purview).

True love waits. The power of first love enables Susie to "break through" the barrier, what she terms "the Inbetween" (79), and return to earth. When Susie pays a return visit in the body of Ruth, it is a chance for Sebold to undo her main character's violation by addressing it at the corporeal level. The defiled body, once dismembered, is remanifested as whole, purified by "loving" sex. It is as if Sebold tells us here that being murdered permits Susie to move toward acceptance and love. This consummation of first love—in a tender scene of conventional romance—is recompense for the events of the first, harrowing chapter. Once she is able to experience sexual union, the postmortal Susie is fully resolved, and she returns to her place in heaven, unconflicted.

Susie retreats almost immediately back up to a "wide, wide Heaven" (325), presumably more distant than what she originally terms "my heaven," and a place from which she assuredly will not return to earth. She easily breaches that distance, which for the angel Damiel (Bruno Ganz) in Wim Wenders's *Wings of Desire* (1987) has become unbearable. Like Damiel, Susie is an angel who is able to fall to earth and take on a human form. She tells us that

> outside, the world I had watched for so long was living and breathing on the same earth I now was. But I knew I would not go out. I had taken this time to fall in love instead—in love with the sort of helplessness I had not felt in death—the helplessness of being alive, the dark, bright pity of being human—feeling as you went, groping in corners and opening your arms to the light—all of it part of navigating the unknown. (309)

But Susie is content with a fleeting glimpse of the contingent joy of embodiment, the complex vulnerability of being related to others without the scrim of heavenly distance.

Wim Wenders's Damiel is bedeviled by what Milan Kundera termed "the unbearable lightness of being"; he is consigned to be insubstantial, transparent. He, like Susie, is omniscient; along with his fellow angel Cassiel (Otto Saunder), he knows every detail of every occurrence—who folded an umbrella, who read to

whom—and the two provide an inventory of those mundanities at the opening of the film. It is their vantage, the view from above, that is presented to us in the early scenes. But Damiel chafes against the privilege of his secure and omniscient existence, longing to feel the weight of being on earth. Wenders conveys to us the burden of omniscience: his angel longs for the privilege of being human, of living in flawed relation with other humans.

When Susie speaks to Ray about what it's like to be dead, she tells him, "It doesn't have to be sad or scary" (309), and we wonder if she might be suggesting that to be raped and dismembered is neither sad nor scary—it is simply one more opportunity for healing. She asserts that this time she is leaving earth "accompanied" and that it is as if she is taking "a long trip to a place very far away" (311). The attempt at closure here is both magical and literal, childlike in its finality and simplicity:

> These were the lovely bones that had grown around my absence: the connections—sometimes tenuous, sometimes made at great cost, but often magnificent—that happened after I was gone. And I began to see things in a way that let me hold the world without me in it. The events that my death wrought were merely the bones of a body that would become whole at some unpredictable time in the future. (320)

In this way, *The Lovely Bones* is akin to Frank Capra's *It's a Wonderful Life* (1946), another text that depicts both angelic intervention and the transformative power of family connection. The angel Clarence (Henry Travers) tells George Bailey (Jimmy Stewart), "Each man's life touches so many other lives. When he isn't around he leaves an awful hole, doesn't he?" He goes on to point out, "You've been given a great gift, George: A chance to see what the world would be like without you."

Susie tells us of her family, "I became manifest in whatever way they wanted me to be" (321). Unlike Damiel, she does not want to be burdened with the limits of humanness when she can be all things at once, protean, a teenage fairy godmother morphing into whoever she needs to be for those who love her. This is an utterly reassuring message: our relationships to those who have passed on are created by us—they fill a need, they are the connections we seek and maintain. The dead hover above us and can be snatched out of the air at any moment; they are always available when we need them. We are never alone, never without recourse. As Susie hovers near her father's hospital bed, she evokes this connection, which is enshrined in the novel:

> I had left him for hours every day for eight and a half years as I had left my mother or Ruth or Ray, my brother and sister, and certainly Mr. Harvey, but he, I now saw, had never left me. His devotion to

me had made me know again and again that I had been beloved. In
the warm light of my father's love I had remained Susie Salmon—a
girl with my whole life in front of me. (279)

It is those who love us who make us who we are, who create us every day in the
"light" of their love. The message of the novel is that we are lovers and beloveds
both; we are never far from that gentle touch or that kind word.

When she is reunited with Jack near the end of the novel, Abigail, Susie's
mother, says of her daughter, "I see her everywhere. . . . Even in California, she
was everywhere. Boarding buses or on the streets outside of schools when I drove
by" (281). In a novel that depicts the way in which those who love us become
more deeply and fully known to us, it is as if all girls, all daughters, are visible,
known, as if we all exist in a vast nexus of kinship. When Abigail speaks these
lines, she appears to conjure up Susie's presence. Jack asks her, "So if I told you
that Susie was in the room ten minutes ago, what would you say?" (282). This
is the moment at which Susie witnesses Jack and Abigail's kiss. "They kept their
eyes open as they did, and my mother was the one to cry first, the tears dropping
down onto my father's cheeks until he wept too" (282).

The lovely bones—the literal fragments of Susie's dismembered body—are
made whole and comprehensible via her parents' authentic love, and via another
celebration of monogamous, procreative love: a marriage between Lindsey and
Samuel, her first love, which produces an heir, Abigail Susan, a namesake for
Susie. These scenes, and others like them, inscribe normalcy and a reassuring
domesticity. The novel ends with an assertion of domestic bliss (Lindsey and
Samuel's marriage), in very much the way that *Dracula* ends. In both novels,
the monster is dispatched (Dracula requires a stake through the heart, but Mr.
Harvey is taken out by an icicle), thus making way for the ideal of family, which
is constant, unfailing, utterly reliable, and worthy of all faith.

Dracula also ends with the birth of a new baby, the son of Jonathan and
Mina Harker. Van Helsing's words conclude the novel: "We want no proofs, we
ask none to believe us! This boy will some day know what a brave and gallant
woman his mother is. Already he knows her sweetness and loving care; later on
he will understand how some men so loved her, that they did dare much for her
sake."[9] In *Dracula*, the battle between good and evil is undertaken in order to
save and protect the goodness and purity of Mina Harker, the icon of the Victorian New Woman. Similarly, *The Lovely Bones* is about repurifying the violated
girl, providing her with a route to love that is innocent and pure. Susie tells us
"that the dead truly talk to us, that in the air between the living, spirits bob and
weave and laugh with us. They are the oxygen we breathe" (325). Susie's spectral
presence comforts, it knits deeper bonds, it banishes the dark, mysterious depths
of the human psyche, the forces that drive Eleanor to suicide in *Hill House*, the
shards of traumatic memory. As Van Helsing says in Dracula, "We ask none to

believe us." *The Lovely Bones* doesn't see Susie's story as straining credulity, and in that way it prepares no defense.

The novel's final lines provide a halcyon glow, a cheery wave, almost a salute. Susie's last words to us are, "I wish you all a long and happy life" (328). It's not that far off from "Have a nice day," and she is entirely sincere.

Notes

1. Alice Sebold, *The Lovely Bones* (New York: Little, Brown, 2002). Page numbers from the novel appear hereafter in parentheses in the text.

2. Daniel Mendelsohn, "Novel of the Year," *New York Review of Books* 50, no. 1 (January 2003).

3. Ali Smith, "A Perfect Afterlife," *Guardian*, August 17, 2002.

4. Philip Hensher, "An Eternity of Sweet Nothings," *Observer*, August 11, 2002.

5. Stephen King, *Danse Macabre* (New York: Everest House, 1981), 181.

6. Shirley Jackson, *The Haunting of Hill House* (New York: Penguin Books, 1959), 246.

7. Cathy Caruth, quoted in Ann V. Bliss, "'Share Moments, Share Life': The Domestic Photograph as a Symbol of Disruption and Trauma in *The Lovely Bones*," *Women's Studies* 37, no. 7 (2008): 871.

8. Homer, *The Odyssey*, trans. Richard Lattimore (New York: Harper Perennial, 2007), 173.

9. Bram Stoker, *Dracula*, ed. Nina Auerbach and David J. Skal (New York: W.W. Norton, 1997), 327.

CHAPTER 35

Deadly Words
THE GOTHIC SLUMBER SONG OF CHUCK
PALAHNIUK'S *LULLABY*

Sue Zlosnik

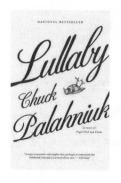

Chuck Palahniuk's 2002 novel *Lullaby* has all the hectic activity of early Gothic novels: the pace and complexity of its plot echo the frenzied activity of Horace Walpole's *The Castle of Otranto* or Matthew Lewis's *The Monk*.[1] Transgression of the most fundamental kind is there in excess too, from the violation of taboo in the form of necrophilia and murder to the supernatural disruption of the laws of physics.[2] And like these early novels, its hybridity is much in evidence: horror and humor sit side by side, precariously balanced as Gothic's comic turn embraces the apocalyptic in the wide-open spaces of the American road trip. Like his eighteenth-century precursor, Matthew Lewis, Chuck Palahniuk is known for his capacity to shock. Lewis became so notorious for his lurid novel that he was nicknamed "Monk" Lewis. Ann Radcliffe had Lewis in mind when she wrote her influential essay "On the Supernatural in Poetry," in which she explored the distinction between "terror" and "horror" that has shaped our understanding of the Gothic ever since: "Terror and horror are so far opposite, that the first expands the soul, and awakens the faculties to a high degree of life; the other contracts, freezes, and nearly annihilates them."[3] At the time of writing (November 2009), Palahniuk's official website, The Cult, is reporting the suspension of a teacher in the Bronx for giving his students the short story "Guts" to read.[4] Palahniuk's first published novel, *Fight Club* (1996), remains his best known, possibly because of the outstandingly successful film adaptation directed by David Fincher (1999). The critical reception of *Fight Club* has focused on its violence and its representation of contemporary masculinity in crisis, placing Palahniuk in a mode of writing associated with figures such as Brett Easton Ellis and Jay McInerny. Ellis and McInerny had become prominent in the literary es-

tablishment by the time *Fight Club* was published, iconic figures in a generation of writers whose work, as James Annesley comments, is characterized by "blank, atonal perspectives and fragile glassy visions" and preoccupied with "the kinds of subjects that obsessed William Burroughs, Georges Bataille and the Marquis de Sade." In invoking the last of these three, Annesley not only emphasizes the predominant themes of "sex, death and subversion" but also identifies implicitly the eighteenth-century inheritance of these writers.[5]

A later arrival on the Generation X literary scene than many of his contemporaries (Douglas Coupland, for example, who tagged the term to fiction with his debut novel of the same name),[6] Palahniuk is more easily placed in relation to Gothic traditions than some of the others. His *Fight Club*, for example, takes the figure of the double, or doppelgänger (familiar to readers of Gothic fiction from works like James Hogg's *Confessions and Memoirs of a Justified Sinner* [1824] and Robert Louis Stevenson's *The Strange Case of Dr. Jekyll and Mr. Hyde* [1886]), as its central plot dynamic. *Survivor* (1999) makes the death wish thematic in a paranoid novel in which organized religion is represented as fundamentally corrupt and life denying in the same way that Catholicism was in the novels of early Gothic writers such as Radcliffe and Lewis; *Invisible Monsters* (actually Palahniuk's first novel but not published until 1999) takes as its themes gender instability, female monstrosity, and abjection, all persistent Gothic concerns; and *Choke* (2001) literalizes physical abjection in a tale of a con man who travels America pretending to choke in expensive restaurants and then preying on the Good Samaritans who save him.

Thus, the earlier novels of Palahniuk's career seem to conform to the idea of "the New Gothic," a term coined by Bradford Morrow and Patrick McGrath in their preface to their 1991 anthology of short stories by the same name. These contemporary short stories, the editors claim, demonstrate that Gothic should no longer be seen merely as a historical phenomenon but as a mode of writing that has survived and is flourishing in mutated forms in the late twentieth century. For Morrow and McGrath, the "fascinating" Gothic tradition evident in these stories is "no longer shackled by the conventional props of the genre" but nonetheless may be seen as "strongly manifest[ing] the gothic sensibility."[7] In a later essay, McGrath identifies "transgression and decay" as the features that define the Gothic in its representation of what Freud identified as "the death wish" and claims that "Gothic allows us to manage the nightmares of a world in which control seems increasingly tenuous."[8]

In order to place *Lullaby* in the context of the New Gothic, however, it is also necessary to recognize another dimension of the Gothic, what Avril Horner and I have termed "the comic turn."[9] Palahniuk himself describes his novel as "an attempt to reinvent the horror novel" and as one in which "humor plays a particularly strong role," adding, "I want there to be the humor, because I think

that people rely on the humor. . . . You need humor to counterbalance the horror."[10] A *Guardian* reviewer concurs:

> *Lullaby* is a very funny novel. Palahniuk, author of the cultish *Fight
> Club*, has a clever and precise way with repetitive prose riffs and
> shorthand wisecracks. He is a macho stylist. Thumbnail sketches of
> numerous secondary characters include the information "His com-
> puter password is 'password'—which is an economical way of saying,
> to a youngish audience, that they are squares."[11]

Humor, however, is not new to the Gothic; it has been there since the founding work of the genre in the eighteenth century. In Walpole's *The Castle of
Otranto*—a tale of death, incest, malevolent machinations, and the supernatural, and the first novel to describe itself as "a Gothic story"—there are several
moments of farcical humor, which comically combine the uncanny and the
melodramatic in a comic turn. Some contemporary critics, notably Victor Sage,
argue that the "surface" quality of Gothic fiction (a quality shared with "blank
fiction") allows for an easy dialectic between the rational and the irrational,
emotion and intellect, artificiality and authenticity, and, above all, between horror and laughter.[12] In his preface to the second edition of *The Castle of Otranto*
(1765), Walpole boasts of the hybrid nature of his work, invoking Shakespeare
as his model for the mingling of the tragic and the comic within the same text.[13]
Taking his cue from Walpole's preface, Fred Botting reminds us that, "A hybrid
form in its inception, the Gothic blend of medieval and historical romance
with the novel of life and manners was framed in supernatural, sentimental or
sensational terms."[14] As Avril Horner and I have argued, the Gothic's emphasis
on fakery[15] in the representation of extremes of feeling and experience inevitably
invites the ludicrous excess of further layers of fakery in the form of parody.[16]
Gothic fiction's tendency to self-parody is well expressed by Chris Baldick when
he says, "Many Gothic tales are already half way to sending themselves up."[17]
What Emma McEvoy calls "a dangerous sense of parody" in *The Monk* we might
simply see as Lewis, Palahniuk's "bad-boy" precursor, daring to push the hybridity so evident in Walpole's work to new extremes to create a heady and salacious
mixture of effects.[18]

Although *Lullaby* may provoke horror and laughter (often at the same time),
it is not sympathetic to the lazy reader. Its narrative is complex and nonlinear
and, like many narratives in Gothic fiction, a framed tale—and like many contemporary narratives, it flaunts its metafictive character. As its narrator tells us in
chapter 1, "*The problem with every story is that you tell it after the fact. . . . Another
problem is the teller. The who, what, where, when of the reporter.*"[19] A journalist
known as Carl Streator, this narrator is a reporter in both senses of the word.
In the outer frame of the story (its chapters interspersed at intervals in the in-

ner narrative and signaled by italicized print), Carl is writing to the moment in *"one café after another"* (7) as he travels America in the company of *"the Sarge,"* *"a baked potato of an old Irish cop"* (8). The Sarge's true identity is not revealed, in one of the novel's many twists, until near the end of the book. This road trip is punctuated by a series of surreal events—*"The Holy Virgin of Welburn,"* *"The Road Kill Jesus Christ," "The Ivy Inferno,"* and *"The Judas Cow"*—which are construed as miracles or portents by those who experience them, and the significance of which only becomes apparent as the inner narrative progresses. As Carl explains in chapter 1, *"this isn't a story about here and now. Me, the Sarge, the Flying Virgin. Helen Hoover Boyle. What I'm writing is the story of how we met. How we got here"* (9).

Prior to Carl's introduction to his story in chapter 1, however, *Lullaby*'s prologue suggests a recognizable haunted house narrative, a tale of terror, which wrong-foots the reader. In an echo of Shirley Jackson's *The Haunting of Hill House*, writing appears mysteriously in the white-oak floor of a newly acquired house; even in these opening lines, there is a hint of the comic, however. This, it would seem, is habitual, and some new owners "are sure it's because they didn't tip the movers" (1). "Our hero" (as the yet unidentified narrator calls her, adding cryptically—and Gothically—"now dead but not dead" [6]), real estate agent Helen Hoover Boyle, has a good line in selling and reselling haunted houses. She exploits people's fears, but there is every indication at this stage of the novel that the supernatural events are to be taken as given, even though much later she asserts:

> I hate people who claim they can see ghosts. . . . There are no ghosts. When you die you're dead. There's no afterlife. People who claim they can see ghosts are just looking for attention. People who believe in reincarnation are just postponing their lives. . . . Fortunately for me . . . I've found a way to punish those people and make a lot of money. (128–129)

Such cynical rationality, however, is another false clue in a novel the very premise of which is profoundly uncanny. In the words of one reviewer:

> *Lullaby* uses all the tools of the supernatural horror novel, but it dissects a different corpse. In addition to the usual victims of the fluffy, friendly horror brick—families—you'll find culture, advertising, New Age bullshit and the oppressive presence of government control (without government, or actually control).[20]

The supernatural driver of *Lullaby*'s plot is the premise that people in contemporary America are doubly vulnerable: to the irruption of the primitive (an enduring preoccupation of the Gothic) and a betrayal by their own senses in a

world of sensory and information overload. The death-dealing culling song is what brings Helen together with Carl Streator. Both, we learn in the course of the novel, have inadvertently killed their close families with the culling song. This is a poem to be found in a book called *Poems and Rhymes from Around the World*, a poem so deadly that just to hear it will kill you. Joined by Helen's assistant, the new age Wiccan Mona, and her amoral but ecologically committed boyfriend Oyster, Helen and Carl join in a quest to hunt down all copies of the book in order to prevent wholesale death. This becomes a quest to find the urtext, the book of spells known as a "grimoire," from which the poem had originally been taken. The recognition that Helen has had this all along, in the guise of her daily planner—and that moreover she has been using the culling song for her own nefarious ends, amassing a fortune in jewels in the process—unleashes mayhem. Most significantly, the book contains an "occupation spell" which "*lets you project your consciousness into the physical body of another being*" (193); this ultimately leads to Helen occupying the body of the Sarge, her own having been destroyed under the occupation of Oyster. In the insistent comic turn of the novel, Carl remarks in the last chapter, "*So I am really in love with Helen. A woman in a man's body. We don't have hot sex any more,*" and adds, "*but as Nash would say, how is that different than most love relationships after long enough?*" (259).

Nash is a peripheral but significant figure in Carl's narrative. His predilection for necrophilia represents the violation of taboo, a Gothic transgression that destabilizes the boundary between life and death. The *San Francisco Chronicle*'s reviewer rightly noted "how difficult it's become to be shocking in 2002. Sex, violence and profanity have been so thoroughly exploited, alone and in combination, that it's almost impossible to scandalize readers. Desecrating corpses is one of the few taboos that's left."[21]

In his role as reporter, Carl has been following a story about sudden infant death syndrome; "it was my editor's idea to tag along with the paramedics" (13). "A big guy" with "his greasy hair . . . pulled into a black palm tree on top of his head" (46), Nash is not averse to violating the dead bodies of attractive women, and, as Carl reflects, "If Nash knew the culling song, there wouldn't be a woman left alive. Alive or a virgin" (48). In the figure of Nash, Gothic's preoccupation with abject acts is given shape, but Carl's past history also makes him complicit in such transgression. The morning after he had unknowingly killed his wife, he made love to her before leaving for work ("it was the best it had been since before Katrin was born") (178). On the run from the police who, in possession of the evidence of postmortem coition, suspect him of murder (as the reader discovers late in the novel), Carl is cursed with a sense of guilt. His pent up emotions mean that he has become a powerful vehicle for the culling song, able to kill people merely by reciting it in his head. As Mona says to him, "My guess

. . . is you're a powder keg of something. Rage. Sorrow. Something. . . . A well-balanced person . . . a functioning person, would have to read the song out loud to make someone fall asleep" (78).

As Carl becomes aware of his power, the dawning horror of what it implies is represented through a comic-book splat fest that would have made Lewis proud. A man pushes him in the street and,

> Hitting me as sudden as a yawn, me glaring at the guy's black leather back, the culling song loops through my head.
> Still crossing the street, the guy in the trench coat lifts his foot to step over the far curb, but doesn't clear it. His toe kicks into the curb halfway up, and he pitches forward onto the sidewalk, flat on his forehead. It's the sound of an egg dropping on the kitchen floor, only a really big, big egg full of blood and brains. (68)

The abject body appears in the novel in other significant images. When the grimoire is found, it is discovered to be bound in human skin. Again, the specificity of detail makes this a gruesome image as Mona observes when she recognizes a pentagram:

> "And before it was a book, this was someone's tattoo. This little bump," she says, touching a spot on the book's spine, "this is a nipple." (202)

Yet, as so often happens in this novel, the comic turn makes its appearance. As Helen and Mona try to guess how to reveal the grimoire's invisible writing, they speculate on the substance used:

> "Try tasting it," Helen says, "to see if it's sour."
> And Mona slams the book shut. "It's a thousand-year-old witch book bound in mummified skin and probably written in ancient cum." She says to Helen, "*You lick it.*" (203)

Much of the body horror in the novel verges on the comic, sometimes through incongruity. Another manifestation of Carl's rage is his stamping barefoot on his intricately made model town. The ensuing infection of his feet is treated by Mona; in the midst of the "yellow ooze" of infection, the miniature detritus of a destroyed civilization—items such as a church steeple, fragments of smoke stack, "the pediment from a Georgian bank building"—emerge from Carl's feet in a bizarre enactment of a toy apocalypse: "All these broken homes and trashed institutions," he reflects (153–154). The dismemberment of Helen's cryogenically preserved baby at her own Oyster-inhabited hands is gruesome but also blackly comic in its devices of defamiliarization. This destruction of a body that

is almost but not quite human is reminiscent of the destruction of Dr. Coppola's lifelike doll, Olympia, in E. T. A. Hoffmann's "The Sandman," the story upon which Freud based his theory of the uncanny.

In Carl's narrative, the baby becomes a doll broken by a petulant child:

> And she tosses the dead child across the room where it clatters against the steel cabinet and falls to the floor, spinning on the linoleum. Patrick. A frozen arm breaks off. Patrick. The spinning body hits a cabinet corner and the legs snap off. Patrick. The armless, legless body, a broken doll, it spins against the wall and the head breaks off. (252)

In this culminating violence, it seems that Helen herself has also been destroyed; her body wrecked at the will of Oyster, her child destroyed forever, she is dispatched by Carl with the culling song as an act of mercy, its original purpose thus revived:

> It's called a culling song. In some ancient cultures, they sang it to children during famine and droughts, anytime the tribe had outgrown its land. It was sung to warriors injured in accidents or the very old or anyone dying. It was used to end misery and pain. It's a lullaby. (255)

With the tricksiness that characterizes the whole novel, however, Helen does not die but is metamorphosed into the Sarge, making sense of the italicized frame and heralding the era of spell-induced signs and wonders of the present time of the narration.

The instability of corporeal identity, a persistent concern of the Gothic, is a major theme of *Lullaby*. The fear of infection and dissolution that is present in so many Gothic texts and so vividly embodied in such abject figures as Dracula takes a new form in this novel. In the midst of modernity, the abhorrent and the supranormal are given full range: it is hearing that will betray humankind in an age full of what Don DeLillo called "white noise":

> The culling song would be a plague unique to the Information Age.
> . . . People have to wear earplugs the way they wear condoms and rubber gloves. In the past, nobody worried too much about sex with strangers. Or before that, bites from fleas. Or untreated drinking water. Mosquitoes. Asbestos.
> Imagine a plague you can catch through your ears. . . .
> The new death, this plague, can come from anywhere. (41)

In a culture saturated by sound, much of it produced electronically, the culling song is a new take on the Gothic's modes of representing modern fears of primitive forces:

> Imagine a world of silence where any sound loud enough or long
> enough to harbor a deadly poem would be banned. No more mo-
> torcycles, lawn mowers, jet planes, electric blenders, hair dryers. (43)

Deriving from an oral culture, the culling song's origins are lost in time. The novel's focus on Carl means that the terrifying potency of the song, linked as it is to his rage and sorrow, is clearly apparent. While his own history is tragic and singular, it is not difficult to identify with his resentment and frustration at the ubiquity of intrusive noise in the modern world. "This is what passes for civilization," he rants:

> People who would never throw litter from their car will drive past
> you with their radio blaring. People who'd never blow cigar smoke at
> you in a crowded restaurant will bellow into their cell phone. They'll
> shout at each other across the space of a dinner plate. (16)

He has to learn to control the temptation to silence them and others who annoy him, and after a series of more or less inadvertent murders, including that of his editor, he adopts the device of counting in his head to prevent the song from running through it and dispatching someone else. "In a world where the culling song was common knowledge," he thinks, "there would be sound blackouts":

> It would be a dangerous frightened world but at least you could sleep
> with your windows open. (60)

In a characteristic comic turn, Carl recites the song loudly in his bathroom and only then notices the air shaft that connects all the apartments: "It could be I've just killed the whole building" (61). The alienation of the man of the crowd is replaced by intermittent news about Carl's hitherto anonymous victims, all of whom are reported by the newspapers to have led exemplary lives.

Comic Gothic is the vehicle for *Lullaby*'s satirical social agenda. The secondary figures of Mona and Oyster counterpoint Helen and Carl and embody an "alternative" counterculture. Mona's claims to be a witch, however, pale beside Helen's occult potency. Mona is a comically grotesque figure who, possessed of the flying spell from the grimoire, appears at the opening of the novel—although chronologically at the end of the story—as "The Flying Virgin." With "long red and black dreadlocks," no knickers, and a gust of wind lifting her skirt, the flying Madonna writes an illiterate message across the New Mexico sky above Main Street with Bug-Off insect repellent: "*stop having babys*" (8). Carl's introduction to Mona's coven is written in ironic vein, the ritual nudity undermined by the suburban details of "bring a dish" catering. The nudity itself is more ludicrous than threatening, and comic disgust is the tone of the account of the adamantly clothed Carl's visit to the coven: "His curly black pubic hair matches the couple

of hairs stuck to my palm after we shake hands" is his comment on one of his new acquaintances (97). Oyster himself is characterized by his "dick," which tapers to "a dribbling pink stalactite of wrinkled foreskin," pierced by a silver ring (96). He is the source of a series of cryptic advertisements appearing in the press inviting class actions; these have appeared sporadically in the novel without explanation, and the current one invites users of Dorsett Fine China to ring a number if nausea or loss of bowel control is experienced after eating (100). Provoked by Oyster, Carl loses his counting battle, leading to an unexpected dramatic climax; he kills someone's parrot, and the scene ends bathetically with its owner prodding poor dead "Plucky" with his sandal. This farcical introduction, however, does not prevent Oyster from being the mouthpiece for graphic denunciations of contemporary farming methods and for apocalyptic warnings of "a biological pandemic" in the wake of rapacious globalization: "The only biodiversity we're going to have," he says, "is Coke versus Pepsi" (115).

Mona and Oyster, Helen and Carl make up "just another dysfunctional family" as they hit the road together in their "quest for an unholy grail" (102). Introduced early on as "our hero," Helen is less Gothic heroine and more Gothic shape-shifter in the tradition of *The Monk*'s Matilda (who turns out to be a demon). Helen's status is more ambiguous. Real estate agent she may be, witch she may be, murderer she may be ("I find that no matter how many people I kill, it's never enough" [195]), but she is also a bereaved mother who is driven by the desire to bring her son back to life. She is, through Carl's descriptions, foregrounded as exemplifying an overdetermined femininity, a construct with her "cloud of pink hair, her fitted pink suit, her legs in white stockings, her feet in pink, medium heels. Her lips are gummy with pink lipstick. Her arms rattle with gold and pink bracelets, gold chains, charms and coins" (29). In this culture of simulation, "the culture that cried wolf" (94), Helen in her original incarnation is an embodiment of the artificiality of her culture. Transformed into the Sarge (a nostalgic stereotype, it might be argued), she becomes transformed into a witch hunter once the spells of the grimoire fall into the hands of Mona and Oyster and are let loose on America. Carl is also an ambiguous figure. His career as a serial killer is at first inadvertent but subsequently tests his self-control and tolerance of his fellow human beings. He is tested and sometimes found wanting. His sense of a compromised masculinity (following the episode of accidental necrophilia, he has not had sex for eighteen years) places him in flight for the whole of the novel: from his own guilt, from the police, and from his own terrifying powers. In an essay on postfeminist Gothic, which takes Palahniuk's *Fight Club* as its key text, Benjamin Brabon argues:

> an inversion has taken place, as the female Gothic heroine cedes her position and role to the postfeminist man. In other words, men's

masculine identity has been transformed from sadism directed at women to masochism aimed at men. Instead of the female Gothic heroine performing her role of victim, it is the postfeminist man "miming" masculinity.[22]

In this way, the status of *Lullaby*'s two dubious heroes remains ambiguous in the outer narration, where Gothic gives way to fantasy. With the spells of the grimoire at large, both miracles and menace populate the American landscape as Carl and the Sarge travel through it. There is a resurrection spell, but this seems to work only on animals. "The Roadkill Christ," who bears a striking resemblance to Oyster, has been seen on the highways bringing dead animals back to life; snapshots on the Internet and video footage validate this modern-day miracle. In Nebraska, a town called Stone River has been renamed Shivapurum and transformed into a Hindu community. Oyster's stories of the atrocities committed in slaughterhouses are evoked in the miracle of the Judas Cow, who one day ceases to lead her fellows to their deaths and, finding a voice, exhorts the townspeople to "*reject your meat-eating ways*" (192). The Sarge identifies this as the occupation spell at work, although at this point in the narrative sequence the significance of this spell has not become fully apparent, so that the Sarge's question to Carl as they leave Shivapurum ("*Do you still love me?*") is unexpected and incongruous. The persistent comic turn of the novel is fully exploited in the description of the Judas Cow as absurdity is pushed to excess: "*It taught them a Hindi song. The cow made the whole crew sing along while it swung its hoof back and forward to the beat of the song*" (193). Seattle fares less well than Stone River. In the case of the ivy, "Hedera helixseattle" as the botanists have named it, miracle gives way to apocalypse. Spreading out from Seattle up and down the Pacific Northwest, "The Green Menace" is inexorably destroying the infrastructure of urban America. This is eco-terrorism, ecological revenge enacted through a literalized green movement: "*The end of civilization in slow motion*" (167). No comic turn here.

For all its social satire, however, this is most of all a novel about the power of words. The potent spells of the grimoire are words endowed with ancient power, yet the novel also shows everyday words, the dynamics of human relations, as inherently dangerous. Even the apparently benign nature of the innocent lullaby is called into question by Helen:

> This isn't about love and hate. . . . It's about control. People don't sit down and read a poem to kill their child. They just want the child to sleep. They just want to dominate. No matter how much you love someone, you still want to have your own way. (148)

Repeatedly, the novelist's own power with words is subjected to a parodic excess. A recurrent motif is Carl's overwrought descriptions of the color of Helen's outfits, for example:

> The suit she's wearing, the skirt is fitted to her hips. It's green, but not the green of a lime, more the green of a key lime pie. It's not the green of an avocado, but more the green of avocado bisque topped with a paper-thin sliver of lemon, served ice cold in a yellow Sèvres soup plate. (82)

In spite of the amusing effect of this striving for exactitude, there is also relish of the self-indulgence that the pleasure of words can offer. Carl recognizes his own tendency to overwrite and is beset by anxiety about himself as a writer. This is an anxiety shared by other Gothic writers, most notably in contemporary Gothic by Stephen King, who returns again and again in his fiction to the figure of the writer.[23] In *Lullaby*, words have transformative powers for both good and evil. They are also often a substitute for direct experience, and in a moment of despair, Carl reflects:

> The best way to waste your life is by taking notes. The easiest way to avoid living is to just watch. Look for the details. Report. Don't participate. Let Big Brother do the singing and dancing for you. Be a reporter. Be a good witness. A grateful member of the audience. (216)

This leaves a final disquieting thought. If writing about life is to waste it, what does that suggest about the writer who writes about other people's writing: the literary critic? Perhaps the best way to end this essay, therefore, is to look to a play that was Gothic before there was Gothic and to quote Hamlet's dying words: "The rest is silence."

Notes

1. Walpole's novel was first published in 1764, with a second edition in 1765. Lewis's *The Monk* was first published in 1796.

2. Fred Botting begins his highly influential 1996 introduction to Gothic with the statement, "Gothic signifies a writing of excess." He goes on to state, "Transgression, like excess, is not simply or lightly undertaken in Gothic fiction, but ambivalent in its aims and effects." Fred Botting, *Gothic* (London: Routledge, 1996), 1, 7.

3. Ann Radcliffe, "On the Supernatural in Poetry" (1826), in *Gothic Documents: A Sourcebook 1700–1820*, eds. E. J. Clery and Robert Miles (Manchester, UK: Manchester University Press, 2000), 168.

4. The Cult, http://chuckpalahniuk.net (accessed November 7, 2009). "Guts" was first published in the March 2004 issue of *Playboy* and is included as a chapter in the 2005 novel *Haunted*.

5. James Annesley, *Blank Fictions: Consumerism, Culture and the Contemporary American Novel* (London: Pluto Press, 1998), 2.

6. Douglas Coupland, *Generation X: Tales for an Accelerated Culture* (New York: St. Martin's Press, 1991).

7. Bradford Morrow and Patrick McGrath, eds., *The New Gothic: A Collection of Contemporary Gothic Fiction* (New York: Random House, 1991), xiv.

8. Patrick McGrath, "Transgression and Decay," in *Gothic: Transmutations of Horror in Late Twentieth-Century Art*, ed. Cristoph Grunenberg (Cambridge, MA: MIT Press, 1997), 158–153; the pagination runs backward in this volume.

9. Avril Horner and Sue Zlosnik, *Gothic and the Comic Turn* (Basingstoke, UK: Palgrave Macmillan, 2005).

10. Chuck Palahniuk, interview by Adam Dunn, *Publishers Weekly*, September 2, 2002, 49.

11. Steven Poole, review of *Lullaby*, by Chuck Palahniuk, *Guardian*, September 28, 2002, www.guardian.co.uk/books/2002/sep/28/fiction.chuckpalahniuk (accessed November 26, 2009).

12. See Victor Sage, "Gothic Laughter: Farce and Horror in Five Texts," in *Gothick Origins and Innovations*, ed. Allan Lloyd-Smith and Victor Sage (Amsterdam: Editions Rodopoi, 1994), 190, 197.

13. Walpole's comments about Shakespeare need to be read in their historical context as endorsing an English identity against the rigidities of European enlightenment taxonomies as exemplified by Voltaire's assertion that to mix buffoonery and solemnity was "intolerable." See Horace Walpole, *The Castle of Otranto*, in *Three Gothic Novels*, ed. Peter Fairclough (1765; Harmondsworth, UK: Penguin, 1986), 45.

14. Botting, *Gothic*, 45.

15. For a detailed analysis of fakery and the Gothic, see Jerrold E. Hogle, "The Gothic Ghost of the Counterfeit and the Progress of Abjection," in *A Companion to the Gothic*, ed. David Punter (Oxford, UK: Blackwell, 2000), 293–304. Also see Jerrold E. Hogle, "Introduction: The Gothic in Western Culture," in *Gothic Fiction*, ed. Jerrold E. Hogle (Cambridge, UK: Cambridge University Press, 2002), 1–20.

16. Horner and Zlosnik, *Gothic and the Comic Turn*, 11.

17. Chris Baldick, introduction to *The Oxford Book of Gothic Tales* (Oxford, UK: Oxford University Press, 1992), xxiii.

18. Matthew Lewis, *The Monk*, with introduction and notes by Emma McEvoy (Oxford, UK: Oxford University Press, 1995), xxviii.

19. Chuck Palahniuk, *Lullaby* (2002; New York: Anchor Books, 2003), 7. Page numbers appear hereafter in parentheses in the text.

20. Rick Kleffel, review of *Lullaby*, http://trashotron.com/agony/reviews/palahniuk-lullaby.htm (accessed November 26, 2009).

21. Charles Solomon, review of *Lullaby*, by Chuck Palahniuk, *San Francisco Chronicle*, September 29, 2002, www.sfgate.com/cgi-bin/article.cgi?f=/chronicle/archive/2002/09/29/RV230937.DTL (accessed November 26, 2009).

22. Benjamin A. Brabon, "The Spectral Phallus," in *Postfeminist Gothic*, ed. Benjamin A. Brabon and Stéphanie Genz (Basingstoke, UK: Palgrave Macmillan, 2007), 60.

23. Ben Mears, for example, in *Salem's Lot*, is one of King's writer heroes who displays anxiety about his compromised masculinity because of his identity as a writer. See Avril Horner and Sue Zlosnik, "Comic Gothic," in *A Companion to the Gothic*, ed. David Punter (Oxford, UK: Blackwell, 2000), 242–254.

CHAPTER 36

His Dark Materials

GOTHIC RESURRECTIONS AND INSURRECTIONS IN PATRICK MCGRATH'S *MARTHA PEAKE*

Carol Margaret Davison

But Britain is the parent country, say some. Then the more shame upon her conduct. Even brutes do not devour their young, nor savages make war upon their families. . . . Europe, and not England, is the parent country of America. This new world hath been the asylum for the persecuted lovers of civil and religious liberty from *every part* of Europe. Hither have they fled, not from the tender embraces of the mother, but from the cruelty of the monster; and it is so far true of England, that the same tyranny which drove the first emigrants from home, pursues their descendants still.

—Thomas Paine, *Common Sense*[1]

Patrick McGrath's *Martha Peake: A Novel of the American Revolution* is a Frankenstein monster of a book. It is not only a brilliant reconfiguration of Mary Shelley's nineteenth-century monsterpiece that places more self-consciously postmodern flesh on the skeleton of that spectacular, philosophical story; it is a work of Gothic recuperation of the highest order whose shrewdly arranged narrative patchwork serves as a uniquely innovative tribute to the Gothic's "greatest hits." In terms of its engagement with ideas, *Martha Peake* cuts a broad swath: it is a brilliantly structured cautionary tale about greed; a trenchant exposé of the dark side of national history, family, romance, and human nature; a self-reflexive meditation on the process of storytelling and history telling; and a beautifully sedimented reflection on the ontology of monstrosity. In an interview with

385

Gilles Menegaldo in 1998 when he was in the midst of composing *Martha Peake*, McGrath openly acknowledged Shelley's influence on his novel[2] and commented on the applicability of the Frankenstein myth to the process of composing historical narratives. According to McGrath, such hybrid creations essentially and necessarily involve a cobbling together from diverse historical and biographical sources. The various technical and thematic ways in which McGrath adapts *Frankenstein*, however, and the ramifications of those reconfigurations, alongside his other Gothic borrowings—which range from minor, passing references to more deeply entrenched motifs and themes—have yet to be identified and dissected. Perhaps McGrath's crowning strategy in *Martha Peake* is to set his doubled Gothic/Female Gothic narrative in eighteenth-century Britain and against the backdrop of the American Revolution. The marriage of form and historical setting is decidedly apropos as this era witnessed the development of the Gothic in its classic phase on two continents—first in Britain and then in America—a literature born of and registering the collision between Enlightenment and pre-Enlightenment belief systems and ideas. That period also saw the broad-scale use of the contentious concept of monstrosity—McGrath's most preeminent motif—in key works of political, philosophical, religious, and scientific discourse.

McGrath's knowledge of cultural history, combined with his skills as a Gothic aficionado, are in evidence on every page of this tantalizing literary romp as he painstakingly rearranges what he has described as the Gothic's traditional "furniture"[3] while incorporating relevant and resonant Gothic allusions that enrich his postmodern narrative tapestry. McGrath has commented on his propensity for Gothic pastiche,[4] and one author has labeled *Martha Peake* a type of "simulacrum of the Gothic . . . that . . . rounds up all the clichés and allows them to converse."[5] McGrath has himself endorsed this critical assessment,[6] but the idea of an intellectually hollowed-out Gothic that such descriptions imply does a disservice to his abilities as one of the foremost developers of the form writing today. The Gothic may be, as McGrath has stated, a stimulating and pleasurable yet mature and mannered form in which it is difficult "to work . . . with any real freshness or originality,"[7] but he manages nonetheless to resurrect and revitalize it successfully toward some grave and resonant ends in *Martha Peake*. Key to this enterprise is his choice of an unreliable, heavy-handed, self-styled historian-"resurrectionist" narrator[8] who fosters, in McGrath's view, a "much more active reader"[9] yet fails, in keeping with that novel's Gothic-related insights, to recognize his own destructive impulses and blind spots. As in the case of *Frankenstein* where Victor Frankenstein effectively misses the point of his own narrative in denying his paternal responsibility toward his creature,[10] and *Wuthering Heights*, another key informing work that features the manipulative yet emotionally infused narration of Nelly Dean, Ambrose Tree proves to be a

biased listener and myopic storyteller. What emerges from between the lines of his agenda-driven tale is a provocatively postmodern and feminist commentary about the politics of historiography, the stark and dark realities underpinning ideals and intergenerational relationships, and the complex desires of the human heart. Thus does McGrath's most accomplished literary work cleverly combine what he has characterized as "Old" and "New" Gothic forms: *Martha Peake* is crowded with "Old Gothic" furniture ranging from an incomplete series of letters, the ambivalent and organic architectural site of Drogo Hall (310) with its disconcerting theater of anatomy,[11] and two key portraits, to a tormented Gothic hero-villain, a fleeing "maiden," and a violent act of sexual transgression. It also fulfills the requirements of the "New Gothic" as described by McGrath in his coedited literary collection devoted to that subject: given that, post-Poe, hell has now been internalized, as he claims in that anthology's introduction, the *New Gothic* explores mental hells and exposes bleak facets of the human soul.[12]

Nowhere does McGrath better uphold what he describes as the New Gothic's "concern with interior entropy—spiritual and emotional breakdown"[13] than in *Martha Peake*'s emotionally, physically, and spiritually traumatized and haunted father-daughter duo. The first section of this novel, entitled "Crooked Timber," recounts the story of Harry Peake who, after being injured in a fire he drunkenly sets and that kills his wife, turns his sufferings to monetary ends and the public eye in his self-styled reinvention as the Cripplegate Monster. This Old World British Gothic story, recounted orally at Drogo Hall by the dying physician William Tree and then committed to paper by his nephew Ambrose, constitutes the first half of McGrath's narrative and doubles its second half—the New World Gothic story ("Cape Morrock") that transpires in America during the Revolution and takes, in true Female Gothic fashion, Harry's daughter Martha as its focus. McGrath smoothly stitches both halves of this intergenerational tale together by way of an overarching narrative framework inspired by Charles Robert Maturin's *Melmoth the Wanderer* (1820). The increasingly emotionally engaged Ambrose insists on producing the novel's second half—the reconstruction of Martha Peake's story after she departs for America. The novel's minor third section, "Drogo Hall," returns the reader to Ambrose's situation in Britain where he, unwittingly and symbolically, becomes a major player in the drama.

In his overarching agenda in *Martha Peake* to examine the anatomy of human psychology in extremis, Patrick McGrath becomes the artistic equivalent of his initially suspect fictionalized collector of curiosities and anatomist, Lord Drogo, who articulates and embraces the monstrously reductive agenda of empirical science with its "relentless application of reason to observed fact" (129) in order to see "what . . . [men] are made of" (119)—of acquiring, examining, and reducing them to their physiological composition on the slab. In adherence to one of Mary Shelley's primary interests in *Frankenstein*—namely, the

identity of monsters—McGrath may perhaps best be classified as a fictional teratologist (one who studies monsters). From the corpses of such iconic figures as Mr. Hyde, the Hunchback of Notre Dame, Heathcliff, Doctor Faustus, and the Elephant Man, McGrath reconstitutes his monster. Armed like his literary foremother with the question "Is the monster made or born?," a question that considers whether the creature's evil actions are attributable to his socialization and abuse in childhood or to his inherently evil nature, McGrath expends a great deal of energy fleshing out his novel's primary abnormality, Harry Peake. In keeping with his conventional "job description," this Gothic hero-villain is a quintessential moral monster capable of great acts of creation and destruction whose personal and political consequences are painstakingly and provocatively delineated by McGrath in this ambitious transatlantic Gothic allegory.

Although Harry Peake is ultimately held up as a monstrous "Everyman" figure who mirrors humanity given the range of his sufferings, he is, in his character makeup, also a monster of his specific historical moment whose creator delights in confounding popular eighteenth-century teratological theories and stereotypes in regard to him. This bastard child, impoverished yet educated, who suffers in his youth from bipolar disorder, which leads to excessive alcohol consumption, seems a natural-born monster given his society's entrenched biases about illegitimacy, literacy, and mental illness. The central trauma of his life that precipitates his entry into greater depravity occurs seven years into his marriage, after the births of several children. It is at this stage that Harry, like Nathaniel Hawthorne's hardheaded Young Goodman Brown, encounters tragedy after denying a minor but significant request from his wife. McGrath's greedy, alcoholic rum smuggler accidentally starts a house fire that results in his wife's death, his family's dissolution, and his deforming spinal injury. Harry's painful and ultimately defective rehabilitation over the course of months in a hellish, coffinlike box splint, a torturous, pseudoscientific machine (21–22), renders him permanently physically deformed.

Harry's subsequent engagement with what might be called his "monster project" involves his re-creation as a freak, a popular phenomenon during this era, exhibiting his spine to paying customers at the Angel Inn. This enterprise is undertaken as a form of penance for his obsession with "greed for profit which he . . . come[s] to see as the root of the evil whose fruit was the death of his wife" (40). It is Harry's hope, during the seven alcohol-free years during which he embraces this monster project, that he will "cauterize his soul, burn[ing] off all that was in him that stank of indulgence and pride, having, as he saw it, a great debt to discharge before he was fit once more to call himself a man" (37). In this reaction to severe personal trauma, Harry is not unlike Victor Frankenstein whose own workshop of filthy creation is engendered by a profound experience of trauma and loss—namely, the sudden death of his mother, which occurs

immediately prior to that seventeen-year-old's departure for the University of Ingolstadt. Frankenstein's experimental attempt to reverse corporeal corruption and effectively rebirth his creature, is inextricably bound up with this loss, as is his horrifying necrophiliac and incestuous dream about a healthy Elizabeth transforming into the corpse of his mother (39). Indeed, the subsequent murders of Justine and Elizabeth, and Victor's dismemberment of the nearly animated female creature, are all, either literally or symbolically, directly or indirectly, related to the death of Victor's mother. As Ann Radcliffe's *The Mysteries of Udolpho* especially makes clear, confronting and accepting the trauma of death, particularly that of one's "double," the parent, is often a key process in the protagonist's development in Gothic fiction.

Repressing the true history of his physical deformity, Harry Peake undertakes a monstrous self-reinvention that affirms such theories as those of Ambrose Paré, a sixteenth-century barber-surgeon, that position the monster at the crossroads of Christian and scientific interpretation. The monstrously well-read Harry draws on the pseudoscientific theory relating to the "forming faculty" to explain the origins of his spine to such curious yet skeptical medical men as Lord Drogo, to whom he feels he sells his soul, Faust-like, by exhibiting himself: he claims that his pregnant mother's encounter with a nefarious, unnatural shadow resulted in her son's horrible spinal malformation. Harry's true self-assessment, however, is far more serious and eminently Christian as he considers himself a moral monster, "a flawed and fallen creature with his sin carried incorporate on his spine, that spine the outward manifestation of a spiritual deformity within" (34). Thus does McGrath proffer a clever sleight-of-hand suggestion that our greatest disfigurement often lies imperceptibly concealed within.

Harry Peake's moral rankness is notably compounded by his alcoholism, an undeniable craving that plays a central role in his various transgressions and that he describes in Jekyll-and-Hyde terms as "a demon within" (78), a "tyrant" (84) that "strips him of reason" (87). Indeed, McGrath lays the Gothic-infused descriptions on thick as he fleshes out Harry Peake's split self in this Gothic pharmography, a subgenre that I have defined and discussed elsewhere as chronicling the process of drug/alcohol seduction and addiction. An indelible, yet physically modified image of Henry Fuseli's *The Nightmare* is evoked by Harry, for example, when he describes the "ghastly black creature that sat on top of him, that hunkered slavering on his spine, urging him to fresh excess" (78–79). Tragically, yet in keeping with the findings of contemporary clinical studies, Harry fails to assume full responsibility for his addiction. His directive to his daughter to keep him from drinking serves, sadly and problematically, to enslave her too by implication (79). Mirroring *Frankenstein*, its mother text, which rendered possible a new way of exploring what Frederick Frank called "the horror of the fragmented self," the "sphere of the Gothic in which all identities are unsure and in which

all selves are perpetually shifting,"[14] *Martha Peake* considers the complex components of personality, often refracting them through the thematic lens of liberty and slavery. This is not only a prominent dialectic in *Frankenstein*, where it is repeatedly employed in relation to the power politics that underpin Victor Frankenstein's sadomasochistic relationship with his creature, it is key to the Enlightenment project that, in its engagement with issues of individual rights and the nature of government, fuelled both the American and French revolutions.

Bringing his complex Chinese-box-style storytelling structure to bear on Harry Peake's ontology, McGrath suggests that environmental factors are also principal ingredients in his protagonist's monstrous makeup. Just as Shelley's *Frankenstein* lends support to the joint critical claims that cultural monsters tend to be "most evident in periods of social, political, and economic crisis"[15] and serve as signposts of the terror of a society split between property owners and propertyless workers,[16] *Martha Peake* portrays late-eighteenth-century Britain as a nation plagued by ghastly social conditions and political despotisms that breed desperate—in part because overtaxed and disenfranchised—monstrous progeny. Thus does the first half of McGrath's narrative set the stage for its second half, lending it a context and a justification. Although Harry's anti-authoritarianism and desire for liberty would qualify him as a "monster" to some thinkers in the late eighteenth century (e.g., Edmund Burke), despotic, Mammonistic British society was likewise indicted as a monster-maker by thinkers from the other side of the political divide (e.g., notably Mary Shelley's parents, William Godwin and Mary Wollstonecraft, along with Thomas Paine). On this front, for example, McGrath's novel suggests that Britain's penal code is wicked, as it values property over humanity and quite grotesquely feeds another Enlightenment-driven institution with the bodies of its victims—namely, medical science. Thus is Enlightenment science exposed, as it is in Shelley's *Frankenstein*, as possessing a dark side in its reductive approach to human beings.

No better symbol for this social disorder exists than Harry Peake's monstrous yet sublime spine that deeply upsets his audience's sense of order, disturbing "the people's confidence in the proper shape and form of things, a confidence they had not known they possessed, it is stitched so deep in their sense of the order of the world" (50). Harry's penitent act of self-exhibition notably aligns him with Christian conceptions of monsters, as referenced by Paré, in their role as signposts both of God's wrath and of forthcoming sociopolitical misfortune.[17] McGrath, however, models his morally conflicted and complex Harry after such Romantic poets as Lord Byron and Percy Bysshe Shelley (Mary Shelley's famous poet-husband) in granting him a powerful voice of protest. Like Victor Frankenstein's self-taught creature of sensibility, the autodidactic Harry becomes increasingly politically and poetically radical subsequent to his move

to London where he and his daughter consort with freethinkers, and produces such compelling and topical works as his "Ballad of Joseph Tresilian," an allegory about monarchic tyranny (51). As this prorevolutionary work makes clear, in combination with the portrait of Harry housed in Drogo Hall entitled *An American Within*, the Cripplegate Monster houses an inner American. Although the idealized, portrait-bound American Harry possesses a straight spine, the real-life, flawed Harry Peake best matches the description of America as a "crippled giant" advanced by McGrath in an interview about *Martha Peake*.[18] As McGrath extrapolates in relation to this paradoxical emblem,

> I wanted him [Harry] to symbolize America. . . . Everything you say about America, you can say the opposite. Then I thought: "I want to create a character of whom it can be true to say 'he's brutal,' but of whom you can also say, 'no, he's tender. He's violent, he's peaceful, he's a tyrant, he's a revolutionary'"—everything that you can say about Harry, you can also say the opposite, he's a completely contradictory character.[19]

The point should not be lost on the reader, however, that this quintessential Gothic hero-villain serves as the double to his British father whose "sins" he transfers to the next generation and, in McGrath's cleverly structured story, the "new" world/nation.

Harry's symbolically sublime spine also tragically serves as an intergenerational bridge—figuratively and biologically—between the two narrative components of *Martha Peake*. Not only, according to the often hyperbolic Ambrose, is "its ridge of peaks down the spine . . . the very image in miniature, of the land itself [and] he . . . himself a *living map* of America" (234), but Harry Peake grotesquely and preternaturally "endows" this singular spine—by way of his appropriately monstrous "great horse-penis" (86) that blurs the animal/human divide—to his son/grandson whose birth occurs in tandem with that of the new and idealized American nation. Significantly, the convergence of these two "great event[s]" (225) occurs only as a result of Harry's most morally monstrous act of incestuous rape. After an earlier attempt to rape and beat his daughter (88), he succeeds in an episode troublingly reminiscent of the early amorous meetings between Mary Shelley and Percy Bysshe Shelley at the grave of Mary Shelley's mother, Mary Wollstonecraft. In the graveyard where Harry and Martha meet secretly after she takes refuge from him at Drogo Hall, a beast rises in her father, savagely violating her while she consoles him over the death of Grace (144–145). This act mirrors Victor Frankenstein's transgression in the original 1818 edition of *Frankenstein* of marrying his half sister Elizabeth, the consummation of which evokes the Gothic's most popular, extreme, and family-endangering transgression.

Harry's sexual attack on his daughter, however, carries other, powerful implications as it irrevocably sullies the popular idealized image of the Adamic American, "a new order of man" (261), directly referenced by McGrath—Martha's American husband, who believes her child to be his, is, significantly, named Adam—and promoted in Thomas Paine's radical work, *Common Sense* (1776), which advocated and justified the American Revolution. (This work is, notably, alluded to in *Martha Peake* as inspirational for that revolution, and Paine is himself featured, as he actually meets little Harry.) McGrath offers a sublimely Gothic corrective to Paine in his depiction of Harry as a brute who, as this essay's opening epigraph describes him, figuratively "devour[s his] . . . young" (149). Paine ascribes such behavior, myopically and exclusively, to Britain. As McGrath makes clear in an interview, the fact that Little Harry possesses "the same deformed back as his father . . . [illustrates how] the deformity of England, its cruelty and its commercialism, are carried over into the New World."[20] This ambivalent, Gothic "sins of the fathers" legacy—"the mark both of his shame and of his glory" (361)—is invested with a profound and typically Gothic supernaturalism in that little Harry's spine cannot possibly be a genetic malformation; his father's/grandfather's spinal defect was the result of physical trauma and a botched medical treatment. This motif of America as Britain's dark double/mirror is especially advanced in the novel by Ambrose's Uncle William who, in response to his nephew's unconcealed allegiance to America (his mother was American, his father British), underscores that nation's hypocrisies: those self-described "Sons of Liberty" are also greedy slavers (200). (Such a complex view of humanity is also proffered in *Frankenstein*, especially in the creature's reading of Volney's *Ruins of Empire* [1791], a powerful polemic on the morally ambivalent nature of empire building.) Thus does McGrath provide a courageous, provocative, and realistic portrait of the dark side of America, revealing that nation to be, as various literary critics have pointed out, fertile territory for the Gothic. Indeed, this popular novel type thrived in the American postrevolutionary period and beyond. In the words of Leslie Fiedler, for example, in his groundbreaking work *Love and Death in the American Novel* (1960), "Of all the fiction of the West, our own [American fiction] is most deeply influenced by the gothic, is almost essentially a gothic one."[21] Fiedler's extrapolations as to the reasons behind this phenomenon reflect McGrath's fictional suggestions in *Martha Peake*:

> In the United States, certain special guilts awaited projection in the gothic form. A dream of innocence had sent Europeans across the ocean to build a new society immune to the compounded evil of the past from which no one in Europe could ever feel himself free. But the slaughter of the Indians, who would not yield their lands to the carriers of utopia, and *the abominations of the slave trade*, in which the

black man, rum, and money were inextricably entwined in a knot of guilt, provided new evidence that evil did not remain with the world that had been left behind.[22]

These various Gothic American threats loom large during Martha's transition into the new world: William Tree regales her with what are essentially captivity narratives, "anecdotes about white women seized by savages, and extraordinary feats of survival in the Wilderness" (141); she encounters "the depths of a wild and chartless forest" (177) reminiscent of the treacherous physical and psychological landscapes popular in the works of Nathaniel Hawthorne; and she is apprised of a tale of terror involving mass family slaughter undertaken by a farmer, which served as the inspirational premise for Charles Brockden Brown's *Wieland, or the Transformation* (1798), the very first work of American Gothic fiction. Perhaps the greatest tragic irony, however, is that Martha—this traditional Female Gothic heroine, this "wild" (183), "lost creature in flight" (188)—has already experienced greater terror and trauma at the hands of her own father prior to her arrival. Such Gothic-infused signs and stories do not bode well for her future, or America's. They also aptly set the stage for Martha's own "witch-like" act of birthing a prodigy.

Martha's dramatic experiences in America, however, prove to be as morally paradoxical as her father's history in Britain, and Ambrose Tree, the self-styled chivalrous chronicler of her life story, is key to this resurrection. Outraged by Harry's brutal act of raping his own daughter and what he perceives to be his uncle's malicious anti-American standpoint, Ambrose hijacks Harry's story in order to reconstruct Martha's with the assistance of some fragments of her letters that remain in his uncle's possession. While Ambrose insists that Martha's tale is not about him, nothing could be further from the truth as McGrath cunningly brings the monster motif to bear on this would-be gallant and his deformed history. A strikingly postmodern, feminist reflection on the fictionality of history ultimately emerges in this neo-Gothic novel, a genre that McGrath deems "perfect . . . for talking about the writing of history as they seem to be about the same thing, which is digging up the past, uncovering the secrets of the past."[23] More often than not, however, the Gothic is a veiled cautionary tale. In this capacity, *Martha Peake* provocatively brings the Gothic to bear on historiography. Over the course of this fictional production, McGrath suggests that historians are, of necessity, unreliable Victor Frankenstein-style producers in their painstaking process, as Ambrose Gothically describes it, of placing flesh on the bones of history. Prejudices, in part due to personal experiences, invariably take root, thus affecting the ostensible objectivity of their enterprise or "black art" (3). What is especially brought to the fore is that, in their required act of deciphering human character and motive, historians assume the role of psychoanalyst, a profession with which McGrath is very well acquainted given his father's lifelong

occupation and position as the medical director of Britain's famous psychiatric facility, Broadmoor Hospital.

The perspective of Ambrose Tree, a "sometime poet" (195) possessed of a romantic sensibility but what he claims is a disciplined imagination, is eventually exposed as monstrously distorted. The reader is blindsided early on by Ambrose's suspicion that Lord Drogo and his assistants (Clyte and William Tree) covet Harry Peake's skeleton for Drogo's cabinet of curiosities. Perhaps in part as a result of Ambrose's unusual nocturnal existence (his drug-addicted uncle, Dracula-like, insists on reciting his story at night) in combination with the unsettling nature of the tale and Ambrose's own increasing drug/alcohol consumption, his narrative reaches a hysterical crescendo whereby he assumes the traditional status of a confined Female Gothic heroine under siege, convinced that his uncle has criminal designs on him just as he had on Harry. The novel's penultimate revelations, that Lord Drogo and his faithful assistants actually served as Harry's charitable protectors after Martha's emigration to America and that Harry Peake still occupies Drogo Hall, echo the mental revolution that concludes William Godwin's *Caleb Williams*, a famous Gothic-infused work—labeled as the first psychological novel—penned by Mary Shelley's father. "Large structures," Ambrose notes, "were collapsing in my mind" (351). The fact that his reading of Harry's situation is exposed as involving heinous projection likewise calls into question his interpretation of Martha Peake's role in the Revolutionary War. Despite her declared commitment to the American cause, Martha betrays it and her newfound family to Giles Hawkins, a treacherous British officer whom she later shoots, in exchange for information about her father in Britain. In order to explain this betrayal, Ambrose posits, in true Freudian fashion, that Martha's compulsion to love her father required her resurrection of an idealized pre-rape image of him. This personal, microcosmic reconstruction process speaks volumes about the sometimes liberating power of denial and repression alongside the power of ideals for an individual's survival post-trauma, a message that McGrath nicely parlays into his reflections on political history. While, in actuality, Martha serves as a traitor to the American cause, her tale is significantly reconfigured by her spin-doctor father-in-law, the novel's foremost American patriot, in order to produce an inspirational tale to promote the American cause. Thus does McGrath advance some compelling insights into the Gothic realities that sometimes underpin ideals and the propagandistic, socially galvanizing power of a falsified history.

Martha Peake's ultimate shocking epiphany recounts Ambrose's unintentional murder of Harry Peake, who is secretly resident in Drogo Hall, ardently stalking Ambrose in his desire to tell his side of the story. This episode beautifully mirrors the creature's similar desire when he arrives on board Robert Walton's ship at *Frankenstein*'s conclusion, after Victor's death and his invocation to

Walton to kill the creature. Harry's dramatic act of homicide cleverly blurs the boundary between fiction and reality. (To this point, Ambrose has conceived of Harry as part of a fiction removed from reality.) Harry's murder is also symbolically apt on at least two fronts: It signals revenge for Martha's rape undertaken by a man who envisions himself as her devotee. It also forcefully suggests the power, offenses, and sacrifices committed by the historian as s/he reconstructs history.

Tragically and ironically, and in keeping with *Frankenstein*, its mother text, where women and the female sensibility are systematically destroyed or suppressed in brutal environments, the greatest offense in *Martha Peake* seems to be against its putative protagonist, a woman of tremendous love and sympathy, manipulated and abused to various ends by numerous men: Martha essentially flees victimization in Britain only to experience another form of abuse in America where she is advised to breed sons for the new world and is ultimately heralded—in a bastardized reconfiguration of her own actions—as a revolutionary feminine ideal. On this front, it is crucial to note that although "many of the early and most prominent figures of the [American] women's rights movement found inspiration in Paine, including Lucretia Mott, Elizabeth Cady Stanton, Ernestine Rose, and Susan B. Anthony . . . Paine never called for enfranchising women."[24] Even Ambrose, Martha's self-styled beneficent biographer, violates his subject. Perhaps out of posthomicidal guilt, this legatee of Drogo Hall, haunted and almost ghostlike at narrative's end, commits a stunningly grotesque offense in his closing words when he envisions a romanticized, supernatural, and posthumous reunion between Martha and her rapist father, a strikingly similar scene to that staged at the end of Emily Brontë's *Wuthering Heights* between the abusive Heathcliff and Catherine.[25] As Martha's life story furnishes a devastating indictment of so-called enlightened attitudes toward women, a more suitable, crowning image at the novel's end suggests itself—namely, of McGrath's titular character hovering ghostlike above this profound postmodernist meditation on trauma, history, and intergenerational relations, hauntingly elusive yet symbolic, a tragic reminder of the often absent, violated, and distorted female subject in history.

Notes

1. Thomas Paine, *Common Sense*, in *Collected Writings*, ed. Eric Foner (1776; New York: Library of America, 1984), 22–23.
2. Gilles Menegaldo, "An Interview with Patrick McGrath," *Sources* (Autumn 1998), 127.
3. Bradford Morrow and Patrick McGrath, eds., introduction to *The New Gothic: A Collection of Contemporary Fiction* (New York: Random House, 1991), xi.
4. Menegaldo, "Interview with Patrick McGrath," 111.

5. Catherine Spooner, "Gothic in the Twentieth Century," in *The Routledge Companion to Gothic*, ed. Catherine Spooner and Emma McEvoy (London: Routledge, 2007), 44.

6. McGrath remembers that "*Martha Peake* was very much an exercise in pastiche. It was a parody of the Gothic form. In some ways it was a large joke. It was a pleasure to write. There are serious ideas in it but the characters, particularly the narrators, Ambrose and Uncle William, and the situation—the old house—and the gin, and the late nights, and the creaky old themes . . . it was all rather ridiculous in a way. I was enjoying myself," in Magali Falco, *A Collection of Interviews with Patrick McGrath* (Paris: Publibooks, 2007), 32.

7. Menegaldo, "Interview with Patrick McGrath," 111.

8. Patrick McGrath, *Martha Peake* (New York: Vintage, 2000), 3. Page numbers appear hereafter in parentheses in the text.

9. Menegaldo, "Interview with Patrick McGrath," 118.

10. William Veeder, *Mary Shelley and "Frankenstein": The Fate of Androgyny* (Chicago: University of Chicago Press, 1986), 203.

11. Not only does Drogo Hall house bodies, but it may be said to be an embodied house in that it is "an asylum for myriad species of bird, mammal, and insect life" (309) and may even, according to Ambrose, possess a soul (312). This trope is in keeping with the Gothic tradition wherein the architectural site of the castle or manor house is frequently represented as an organic site responsive to and expressive of the psyche of its possessor.

12. Bradford and McGrath, *The New Gothic*, xiv.

13. Bradford and McGrath, *The New Gothic*, xii.

14. Frederick Frank, introduction to *"Zastrozzi: A Romance" and "St. Irvyne; or, The Rosicrucian,"* by Percy Bysshe Shelley (New York: Arno Press, 1977), xii.

15. Fred Botting, *Making Monstrous: Frankenstein, Criticism, Theory* (Manchester, UK: Manchester University Press, 1991), 140.

16. Franco Moretti, *Signs Taken for Wonders: Essays in the Sociology of Literary Forms* (London: Verso Editions and NLB, 1983), 83.

17. Ambroise Paré, *Monsters and Marvels*, trans. Janis L. Pallister (1573; Chicago: University of Chicago Press, 1982), 3–4.

18. Falco, *Collection of Interviews*, 39.

19. Falco, *Collection of Interviews*, 47.

20. Falco, *Collection of Interviews*, 43.

21. Leslie A. Fiedler, *Love and Death in the American Novel* (1960; New York: Dell, 1966), 129.

22. Fiedler, *Love and Death in the American Novel*, 130; emphasis added.

23. Falco, *Collection of Interviews*, 53.

24. Harvey J. Kaye, *Thomas Paine and the Promise of America* (New York: Hill and Wang, 2005), 151.

25. Emily Brontë, *Wuthering Heights* (1847; Boston: Bedford/St. Martin's, 2003), 286–287.

CHAPTER 37

The Vigilante in Michael Cox's *The Meaning of Night: A Confession*

Heather L. Duda

What is night? Is it just that time of the day between dusk and dawn when the seedier side of life holds sway? Or is night something even more sinister, a psychological level where darkness rules and goodness seems to be in short supply? In Michael Cox's 2006 novel, *The Meaning of Night: A Confession*, the protagonist Edward Glyver journeys through both possible definitions. His profession as a jack-of-all-trades for a nineteenth-century law firm has him combing the dark streets of London for information while his own personal history and his failed attempt to reclaim his destiny lead him into his own personal night or nightmare. The reader follows Edward's story through a myriad of dark events, glimpsing the best attributes a Gothic novel has to offer. Yet although Cox utilizes several classic nineteenth-century Gothic conventions, his vigilante antihero, Edward, is a distinctly twenty-first-century character. This combination of classic and contemporary creates a fragmented, unreliable, and intriguing narrator who captures the reader's attention from his very first sentence.

Edward's confession is prefaced by a crucial editor's note. According to J. J. Antrobus, professor of post-authentic Victorian fiction at the University of Cambridge, the book which follows is the confession of a man named Edward Charles Glyver. The book itself was discovered among the Duport family papers at Cambridge, is bound with the Duport coat of arms on the front, and is labeled "(Fiction?)." Antrobus has managed to validate the authenticity of many of the people in the narrative. In addition, the professor has included footnotes throughout the novel to further elaborate on locations, translate passages, and explain the famous people mentioned by Edward. Antrobus's editing and preface give the novel some historical accuracy, much like Bram Stoker gives

Dracula with his constant referral to modern nineteenth-century technologies. The text could be true, and, like the original Duport paper cataloger, the reader understands that the following confession may not be fiction. However, Edward Glyver is nowhere to be found in any records. Despite claiming to have been at Eton and to have held mailboxes under the pseudonym Edward Glapthorn, the confessor does not seem to have existed. As Antrobus claims, "Perhaps after we have read these confessions, [Edward's anonymity] should not surprise us; yet it is strange that someone who wished to lay his soul bare in this way chose not to reveal his real name. I simply do not know how to account for this, but note the anomaly in the hope that further research, perhaps by other scholars, may unravel the mystery."[1] This anomaly should come as no surprise to the Gothic reader. Thanks to the editor's preface, the reader is somewhat wary of Edward and his story. Do we trust this strange confession, or has Edward's destructive lifestyle corrupted his brain? The reader is now thrown into turmoil over the authenticity of this document, the typical quandary of a classic nineteenth-century Gothic reader.

Spanning only from October to December 1854, the confession begins with a much-quoted, yet still startling line (the only sentence of fiction included in the *New York Times* 2009 obituary for Cox[2]): "After killing the red-haired man, I took myself off to Quinn's for an oyster supper" (21). And so the reader gets his or her first view of Edward, presumably a cold-blooded killer who cares more about a good meal than his fellow man. Edward has just slain a completely innocent stranger, Lucas Trendle, to prepare for the murder of his true enemy, Phoebus Daunt. Unfortunately, someone else knows what Edward has done and warns his paramour, prostitute, and brothel-owner-to-be, Bella, that Edward is not who he pretends to be. Although Edward does his best to allay Bella's fears and tells her something of his childhood, his entire life story only comes out when his friend, Le Grice, presses him.

Upon his twelfth birthday, Edward received a box from his mother, Simona Glyver, containing two hundred sovereigns and learned that her friend, Miss Lamb, intended him to go to Eton. At Eton, Edward befriends a fellow student, Phoebus Daunt, who ends up framing Edward for stealing a book, thus causing Edward's expulsion. After Simona dies, Edward begins to piece together his true identity, which, it turns out, is entwined with Daunt's. Over time, Edward learns that he is the legitimate heir to Julius Duport, Twenty-fifth Baron Tansor of Evenwood, a very rich and powerful man. As Edward painstakingly unravels the mystery of his birth, he learns that his mother's best friend, Laura Fairmile, Lady Tansor, known as Miss Lamb to him, gave him up out of anger toward her husband and made Simona promise to raise him, never telling Lord Tansor of Edward's conception and birth. However, as Edward is piecing this information together, so is Daunt, who has been named the baron's heir since Lord Tansor's

only known son died as a child, and Daunt's stepmother—a distant relative of Lord Tansor's—has spent much time and energy conniving Lord Tansor into thinking of Daunt as the son he never had.

Edward traces the proof of his lineage as far as possible but can never find absolute legal documentation of his claim. A break comes when Paul Carteret (the baron's cousin and personal secretary) tells Christopher Tredgold (Edward's employer and good friend, as well as Lord Tansor's lawyer) that he has found the possibility of a legitimate heir. Edward goes to meet Carteret—as a representative of Mr. Tredgold—but Carteret is killed and his papers stolen before he can tell Edward the truth. Luckily, Carteret had the forethought to create a deposition, sent to Edward before his death. However, this deposition alone is not enough to convince Lord Tansor and a court of law. Still working under his pseudonym—although it turns out that Mr. Tredgold always knew Edward's true identity—Edward finally discovers the whole truth, including letters from Lady Tansor, buried with her by a close friend, that prove beyond a shadow of a doubt that he is the lawful Duport heir. Unfortunately, Edward has fallen in love with Carteret's daughter, Emily, and gives all the proof to her, not knowing until it is too late that Emily is engaged to and in love with Daunt and the two of them have been plotting Edward's demise. All of Edward's proof and hard work are lost.

After telling his story to Le Grice and bringing the reader back to the opening line of the confession, Edward embarks upon the final part of his plan. Phoebus Daunt has taken everything from Edward, from his education at Eton to the vast Duport inheritance and title. For this, Edward decides to murder him. However, when Edward first gets the opportunity, he freezes, which is why he practices on Lucas Trendle, the red-haired man. In the end, Edward does kill Daunt and avenges the wrongs wrought upon himself. Although he is discovered to be the murderer of both men—Emily sees him after he kills Daunt, and the police link him to Trendle—Edward escapes London. In a letter added to the end of the confession, he writes to Mr. Tredgold from somewhere in Africa and requests that his past employer bind his confession and "then, if it can be so contrived, for the volume to be placed privily in the Library at Evenwood, where it may be found, or not, at some future date" (695). Thus the ending brings the reader right back to the beginning and Professor Antrobus's preface. Full of mystery, betrayal, and darkness, Cox's novel fits well with the classic Gothic novels of the Victorian era.

Cox draws on several nineteenth-century Gothic conventions that enhance Edward's problematic status with the reader, most notably the use of the unreliable narrator. To begin, readers do not even know who Edward is. As mentioned previously, Edward is not a "historical" person since Antrobus has found no record of either Edward Glyver or Edward Glapthorn, the name that Edward

uses as an adult in London. According to David Punter and Glennis Byron in *The Gothic*, "From its beginnings, the literary Gothic has been concerned with uncertainties in character positioning and instabilities of knowledge. Far from knowing everything, like an omniscient narrator, characters—and even narrators—frequently know little or nothing about the world through which they move or about the structures of power that envelop them."[3] Even though Edward claims to be in control of his surroundings and believes himself to be utterly secretive in his mission, he consistently drops clues as to his own instability and unreliability. The main element of Edward's unreliability is his opium/laudanum addiction. Many times Edward goes in search of the drug that will dull his senses; he also thinks nothing of drinking Dalby's laudanum several times a night to help him sleep. It is not unusual for Edward to spend several days or even a week completely high. In addition to his drug addiction, mood swings and severe depression are hinted at throughout Edward's confession. He is utterly unpredictable and either isolates himself or goes on a self-destructive binge when he gets in one of his "glooms." It is also possible that Edward suffers from the sexually transmitted, insanity-inducing neurosyphilis, thanks to the many London prostitutes he visits, as he suffers from lethargy, headaches, irritability, and poor concentration. No matter how much the reader wants to believe Edward, his unreliability is too obvious to ignore. One moment he is extraordinarily happy with Emily, while the next moment he mopes around unsavory parts of London looking for sex and opium, and still later he is complaining of insomnia and taking laudanum. As a narrator, he cannot be trusted, and the reader must recognize how problematic this "confession" really is.

Another classic Gothic convention found in Cox's novel is the desire to retain the status quo. Victorian Gothic texts constantly created images of the Other—such as Mr. Hyde, Dracula, or even Dorian Gray—but the Other always needed to be destroyed or contained by the end of the narrative. In the article "Gothic in the 1890s," Glennis Byron asserts, "There is the desire to identify what is unfixed, transgressive, other and threatening, in the hope that it can be contained, its threat defused; and there is the desire to redefine and fix a 'norm,' to reestablish the boundaries that the threatening other seems to disrupt and destabilize."[4] The boundary Edward desperately wants to reestablish is his father's lineage and his own birthright. Like much of England in the 1850s, Edward is ensconced within a rigid social system. Family lineage, especially within the aristocracy, was of utmost importance to the upper class. Both Edward and Lord Tansor shudder at the lack of a Duport biological heir, and both are attempting to ensure that the line continues. "The absence of . . . a lineal heir, whether male or female," in Lord Tansor's mind, "and the consequences that may flow from it . . . may signal a decline in the family's fortunes" (275). Nothing worries Lord Tansor more than believing his family's title and estate will go to a relative who

is not "appropriate" by early Victorian standards, and he is disconcerted by the mental instability he perceives in Paul Carteret's family, although not in Paul himself. (The irony that his own son demonstrates extreme depression and possible insanity should not be lost on the reader.) Because Edward is also a victim of his society's obsession with lineage, titles, and heritage, he sees the naming of Phoebus Daunt as Lord Tansor's heir as an affront, not just to himself but also to the entire institution of England's class structure. Edward's obsession to set his family's line to rights is a selfish one—he wants the money, power, and title that his birthright promises—but also a social one since Daunt has not been born into the aristocracy. Both Edward and Lord Tansor are attempting to preserve the status quo and reestablish the Duport family boundaries.

Yet Edward himself would be considered an Other by his biological father's social norms, for he demonstrates definite moral decay. In many ways, Edward is a fictional cousin to Stevenson's Dr. Jekyll and Mr. Hyde. On the one hand, Edward, like Jekyll, is a highly intelligent man, a bibliophile conversing with the most learned gentlemen about books. He is also a brilliant photographer, which makes him, in some ways, a scientist. Finally, he can play the part of a good friend and honestly enjoys the company of both Le Grice and Mr. Tredgold. But beneath the proper Victorian gentleman is a drug addict who frequently picks up prostitutes. He is a man who thrives on the darkness of London. His job for Mr. Tredgold involves shady dealings, to say the least, gathering

> information, establishing a network of connexions amongst both high and low in the capital; I uncovered little indiscretions, secured fugitive evidence, watched, followed, warned, cajoled, sometimes threatened. Extortion, embezzlement, crim. con. [criminal conversation], even murder—the nature of the case mattered not. I became adept in seeking out its weak points, and then supplying the means by which the foundations of an action against a client could be fatally undermined. (239)

As a hired thug for Mr. Tredgold and his law firm, Edward relishes London's "many intertwining natures, its myriad distinctions" and dirty little secrets (240). In this way, Edward moves from a Jekyll into a Hyde; their identical first names cannot be coincidence. By spending time with the "dark" city, he embraces the night side of himself. As will be discussed in more depth later, London actually comes to represent Edward's shadowy side, his moral decay. As Alexandra Warwick comments in her article on London and the Gothic, "The crumbling city is the representation of the decadence of empire and the morbid condition of its inhabitants."[5]

Like a shape-shifter in the Gothic novels of the 1890s, Edward literally embodies three different people. To Le Grice and Phoebus Daunt, Edward

is Edward Glyver, the young man who attends Eton on scholarship and has an authoress for a mother. To Bella, Mr. Tredgold, and all those he meets in adulthood, he is Edward Glapthorn, the intelligent bibliophile who is trying to make his own way in the world. But to those who know the truth, he is Edward Duport, heir and rightful Twenty-sixth Baron Tansor. This duplicity would be difficult for anyone to deal with. Somehow, despite his emotional issues, Edward manages to pull off this duplicity in a way Jekyll cannot. However, after losing it all, Edward comes to another, separate identity. After learning the truth about his beloved Emily, her engagement to Phoebus and their possession of the proof of his identity, Edward asks himself the following questions:

> *What do you know?* Nothing.
> *What have you achieved?* Nothing.
> *Who are you?* Nobody. (619)

Edward now gives in to the ultimate Gothic phobia about identity: he has none. This fear has been hinted at throughout the novel in Edward's various dreams. In one, he follows a woman into a deserted ballroom. After the candles are blown out, she says, "But I have forgotten your name. . . . A liar needs a good memory" (410). In another dream, Edward is in court and Mr. Tredgold's sister, Rowena, asks for his name. When he cannot speak to tell her, she states, "Very well. . . . Since you will not tell the court who you are, the verdict of the court is that you shall be taken hence to a place of execution, there to be hanged by the neck until you are dead" (436). The third and final dream he has about his identity has him inside the Tansor family mausoleum where Lord Tansor asks him the three questions mentioned above. Upon answering "nobody," Edward kills the baron. He can never state his name in dreams because even he no longer knows who he is. In the end, Edward is no one because his two names are merely pseudonyms, and his true identity will never be known. In a society where name and lineage mean so much, Edward cannot exist. His life's goal is to prove his own identity, and when that goal is cruelly taken from him, he has no recourse but to leave. Even if he had not committed murder, Edward's loss of selfhood would make it impossible for him to be content in England.

The reader may want desperately to believe and sympathize with Edward, but he cannot be trusted. Constantly the reader asks, "Who is telling the truth? What is the truth? Does our narrator even know the truth anymore, or have his vices removed his sanity?" Le Grice, as he hears his friend's story, perfectly summarizes the reader's quandary: "But what a story, G! I won't say I can't believe it, because I must believe it, if you tell me it's true" (221). Critics like Michael Dirda have had more ominous doubt:

Though the major characters either get what they want or what they deserve, you really don't like any of them very much. Perhaps this shouldn't matter. Yet Dostoevsky's Raskolnikov ax-murders an old woman and Camus's Meursault shoots an innocent Arab, and we still care deeply for both as souls in torment, as human beings. But Cox makes Glyver in particular decidedly, distinctly unsympathetic. *The Meaning of Night* is certainly a more complex novel as a result, but also one without a clear ethical center. . . . One is left drifting in that universe of moral relativity best evoked in the observation of Dickens's villainous Fagin: "Some conjurors say that number three is the magic number, and some say number seven. It's neither, my friend, neither. It's number one."[6]

If Edward is such a problematic narrator, why would readers want to believe him and keep reading about "number one"? The answer lies with the twenty-first-century reader and his or her interest in the vigilante character. As a Victorian narrator, Edward would have been severely punished for his indiscretions. In fact, he most likely would have died by novel's end. After all, characters like Dr. Jekyll and Dorian Gray must die to reestablish the ever-important moral status quo. Edward, however, represents a new Gothic sensibility for a new millennium. No longer do we punish those who dabble in darkness and villainy if they do so for seemingly valid reasons.

While not a new literary phenomenon, the vigilante is not a character one often finds in Victorian Gothic novels, which is what makes Edward, and Cox's novel in general, such an interesting interpretation of the classic Gothic narrative. Edward knows that the legal system can only help him if he has absolute legal proof of his lineage. Once his proof is taken from him through treachery, he knows his only recourse is to take the law into his own hands, especially after the disastrous encounter he has with Lord Tansor when he presents himself as the lord's son, only to be threatened with financial and social ruin. But does Phoebus Daunt really deserve to die? This is not a question Edward even seems to consider. In his mind, Phoebus deserves harsh retribution for Edward's expulsion from Eton. His determination to exact "justice" is greatly enhanced when Phoebus takes away Edward's inheritance. A proportional response to Phoebus's wrongs is never entertained, though. Edward has a good life without his title and money, and he has a good partner in Bella, hardworking prostitute that she is. There is no sense that Edward's punishment fits Phoebus's crimes.

Still, the twenty-first-century reader is not necessarily appalled by Edward's actions. The nineteenth-century reader, in contrast, would certainly have had problems with Edward's murders. Abraham Van Helsing and his band of vampire hunters take great care to make sure Dracula is a vampire before going after

him. Dorian Gray enjoys his spectacularly decadent lifestyle for years, and even though he may soil the reputations of many young men and women, it is not until he crosses the line and kills Basil Hallward that he must be killed himself. Oscar Wilde goes to great pains to ensure that Dorian's punishment fits his crime. Even Dr. Jekyll understands that he must kill himself in order to prevent Mr. Hyde from wreaking unwarranted havoc on London. However, the twenty-first-century social climate is a different one than that of Victorian England. Today's society, at least Western society, seems to love a vigilante. This character appears in everything from Clint Eastwood's spaghetti westerns, to the slasher subgenre of the rape-revenge film, to the popular graphic novels of Frank Miller and Alan Moore. Even our greatest contemporary superhero—Batman—is nothing more than a vigilante who refuses to adhere to the law and accept due process.

There are many possible reasons why contemporary readers respond positively to the vigilante. The most obvious, at least in America, is a distrust for the legal and political systems. Gary Hoppenstand sees this distrust as ironic: "Americans love democracy and equal protection under the law, yet why should we fantasize in our entertainment about a hero who violently breaks all the important social rules?"[7] The answer is that the outlaw becomes a hero because he or she can change things the common person cannot, and American history is full of such people. Laws are made by men and women who, more and more, seem to care little about their constituents. Criminals who get off on a technicality appear in the newspapers on a regular basis. On a global scale, the wars in Iraq and Afghanistan are causing more problems and more violence than they are fixing. It is not surprising that audiences sympathize with Edward for just trying to gain what is rightfully his, and this sympathy is greatly enhanced when the reader learns that his beloved Emily betrays him. This contemporary obsession with and sympathy toward the vigilante may be disturbing because they are no better, and are sometimes worse, than their intended victims; on the other hand, these outlaws are managing to do something that few twenty-first-century citizens can: they take back the night and some control over their lives. In a society where citizens are feeling more and more powerless, these characters, for good or bad, represent a level of control and provide an outlet for readers' frustration and dissatisfaction.

As with Edward, vigilantes elsewhere often struggle with identity and too often see things through a single-minded focus on good versus evil or friend versus enemy. A contemporary figure who best illustrates this tunnel vision is Rorschach from Alan Moore's 1986 graphic novel *Watchmen*. To Rorschach, people are either good or evil. Those who break the law—no matter how major or minor their offense may be—must be punished. Rorschach cannot accept the fact that in some cases the law must be broken to preserve society or to obey a higher law. He cannot even recognize the irony of his own persona: he breaks the

law to dole out punishment. Because he cannot accept the gray area in life, he is murdered by a fellow Watchman to preserve a tenuous world peace. Rorschach's vigilante tunnel vision is his own downfall. The vigilante's identity is so much based on meting out extrajudicial punishment that the character loses a clear identity, as with Edward when he asserts that he is "nobody." And when the vengeance has been completed, the character has no identity whatsoever. A uniting element of the 1890s Gothic narratives is how they "all draw their power from the fears and anxieties attendant upon degeneration, and the horror they explore is the horror prompted by the repeated spectacle of dissolution—the dissolution of the nation, of society, of the human subject itself."[8] Over the last century, fear of degeneration and dissolution have flourished in the vigilante narrative. Only here, in the vigilante text, instead of as in the Gothic novel where the corruption is limited to a single character like Dracula, Hyde, or Dorian Gray, the "hero" must battle back and possibly defeat the degeneration of an entire society. Perversely, the vigilante represents the very baseness of the society that he or she is there to protect. Cox's novel builds on the Victorian fears of dissolution but amplifies them in such a way that everyone and everything seems to degenerate in varying degrees.

In my discussion in *The Monster Hunter in Modern Popular Culture,*[9] I talk about how important a sense of community is to the contemporary monster hunter. Although I am not claiming that Edward is a monster killer, my discussion is relevant to Edward as a vigilante. One of the main elements that moves the contemporary monster from monstrosity to monster hunting is community. For example, in the *Blade* movie trilogy, Blade (Wesley Snipes) is only able to both fight vampires and his own demons with the help of Whistler (Kris Kristofferson) and, eventually, a group of vampire hunters led by Whistler's daughter, Abigail (Jessica Biel). When these characters turn from their communities, they become vigilantes who care nothing about the society they claim to be protecting. These characters trust that their friends will help them be more humane. Edward, however, is lacking a strong community. While he certainly has trustworthy, good friends—Le Grice, Bella, and Mr. Tredgold—he refuses to put his trust in them until too late, if at all. These characters want to help Edward and repeatedly ask him to let them in, but he cannot see past his own pain and anger to the bigger picture. Love makes him ignore the little warning signs such as Miss Buisson's note that says, "But do not fall in love with her. I am serious now" (565), and Emily herself saying, "I would do anything—*anything*—for the man I love" (592). Once again, Edward's tunnel vision causes him harm. In keeping his truth from everyone who truly loves and cares for him, he isolates himself. This isolation forces him to make decisions without consulting others, decisions that turn against him in the end. A man alone—especially a man with a terrible secret—cannot stand alone for long. The result of Edward's lack of

community is a further fragmentation of his self. He is a man apart who does not have a place where he belongs. As the secret gets more and more complex and the betrayal is revealed, Edward becomes even more antisocial and spends more time high on opium and laudanum. He forsakes even the company of those he holds most dear; those who could help him reclaim his inheritance and identity. Unlike contemporary monster hunters, Edward cannot rejoin the community of his peers.

Edward's physical location helps illustrate his fragmentation and isolation and further illustrates his problematic relationship to community. Edward is constantly at odds with "civilized" society. As a child, he loves his ocean-side home with Simona. However, as childhood fades, this unwitting pawn in his true parents' bad marriage finds no location where he feels utterly comfortable. After he is expelled from Eton, he wanders to both Germany and Russia, as well as elsewhere on the continent, looking for his identity. Like many contemporary twenty-somethings, Edward is trying to find himself and, unknowingly, a community, but his communities continue to break apart either through death or Edward's constant movement. After Simona dies, Edward sells his childhood home, a place he can no longer return to with satisfaction, and after his old childhood tutor Tom dies, he loses the connection to his childhood home entirely, the only place he had a sense of community and peace. As an adult, Edward does settle in London, but London is not necessarily the best place for him. While in London, Edward is a detached and shadowy figure. He moves at night; he is two different people. He does not even go to his office every day, for his various tasks take him to a variety of places, so he cannot meet and mingle with his coworkers. As a loner, Edward's disconnect simply fuels the vigilante fire. Even his places of relative safety are dubious: Bella lives and works in a brothel while Mr. Tredgold likes to examine his extensive pornography collection with Edward.

Evenwood, called Edward's "palace-castle," is no better for him. Every time he views the estate, it is through the best of lenses (quite literally, because his first visit, with Mr. Tredgold, is to photograph both the estate and Lord Tansor). Edward refuses to see any negative in his father's home, and these rose-colored glasses cause Edward to lose both his edge and, subsequently, his legal right to the Duport inheritance. Early in the novel, he tells the reader that, given his line of work, he has excellent instincts. But consistently he ignores or discredits them when near or at Evenwood. For example, while staying at a nearby hotel the night Paul Carteret is killed, Edward sees a man smoking outside his window. Edward dismisses the man, saying, "I thought nothing of this at the time. A late dinner guest on his way home, perhaps, or one of the hotel staff. I shuffled back to bed, and fell fast asleep once more" (300–301). Given a later revelation that Edward is being followed, it is clear that this smoker is at the hotel to watch

him. The next evening while staying at Carteret's home, Edward witnesses from his window a clandestine meeting between Emily and an anonymous man (who turns out to be Phoebus Daunt) and still is without suspicion: "So she had a lover. It could not of course be Daunt, for Mr. Tredgold had told me before I left that he was in the West Country, on Lord Tansor's business. . . . Doubtless I had witnessed an assignation with some local buck. But the more I considered the dumb-show that had been played out before me, the more puzzling it seemed" (310). These instances, as well as several others involving Emily's untoward behavior, prove that Edward is out of place at Evenwood. Shockingly, he is far better off in the teeming, morally reprehensible London where fragmentation and isolation is somewhat the norm than at the pristine, agrarian Evenwood where the people of Lord Tansor's estate have a strong sense of community.

Unfortunately, no matter where he is, Edward cannot be happy. As a character bent on vengeance, he cannot accept his surroundings. After Emily betrays him at Evenwood, his instincts are even weaker when he returns to London. He does not realize he is being followed by Phoebus's dangerous associate, Pluckrose. Even though Edward can blend into the night life of London, Pluckrose—a murderer himself—can do so even better. Edward does not even realize until too late that his downstairs neighbor and coworker, Fordyce Jukes, is part of a blackmail scheme created to scare Edward. Edward can no longer find a safe space in London. As Warwick argues, "For the Gothic male protagonist, the will to know, to dominate his environment, deepens his enthrallment, and all objects of desire become objects of fear. He engages in frantic activity seeking pleasure and power, but his actions in attempting to establish control lead to their opposite, complete loss of power."[10] Edward honestly believes that he knows, understands, and controls his environment, whether in London or at Evenwood. However, he is subsumed and controlled by both environments precisely because he cannot create a meaningful, honest, and long-lasting community in either. When Edward flees England, he takes with him two pictures: a watercolor of Simona's home and an out-of-focus photo he took of Evenwood. Neither represents the reality of his situation, and neither is, nor has been, his home. They are only ideals he can never have because he is a man fragmented by his desire to enact a gruesome vengeance.

There is one thing that can redeem Edward: remorse. Nineteenth-century Gothic characters often admit to making bad choices prior to their end. Both Dr. Jekyll and Dr. Frankenstein are sorry for creating monsters, and even Dorian Gray has a slight tweak of conscience before destroying his painting. Though these characters must be punished for their transgressions, they demonstrate a brief return to Victorian sensibilities to ensure a return to the status quo for the reader. This sense of atonement even appears in the contemporary monster-hunting narratives. In those cases where a monster hunter becomes a vigilante for

a short period of time, he or she almost always has some type of epiphany that reminds the monster hunter that he or she is fighting for the greater good, even if it is a constantly losing battle. It is possible that Edward could have redeemed himself by expressing remorse and responsibility. Even a twenty-first-century vigilante often has a redeeming characteristic or two; after all, Rorschach and Batman are just protecting their city's well-being. In the end, Edward does have an epiphany. As he tells Mr. Tredgold in his final communication, "I deserve no sympathy for what I have done" (693). Like all good Victorian Gothic sinners, Edward realizes his mistakes. He accepts responsibility for his actions and even acknowledges that he and his birth mother, Lady Tansor, are cut from the same cloth: "We were both destroyed by believing it was in our own hands to punish those who had done wrong to us" (694). But is this enough? His fragmented psyche has not been magically healed with the death of Phoebus Daunt or even his realization that his vigilante ways were not the best option. His life, his tenuous community, and his dark environment can never again offer him any measure of peace, if any of those things ever really did. As he tells Mr. Tredgold, "I am now a man apart, and can never again put on the life I once knew" (695). Like Frankenstein's monster, who has been physically pieced together and can only find solace in the barren regions of the Arctic, Edward, whose psyche is a fragmented place of night, can only hope to find peace in Africa, never to be heard from again. For all time, to those who read his confession and Professor Antrobus's preface, Edward is nobody.

Notes

1. Michael Cox, *The Meaning of Night: A Confession* (New York: W.W. Norton, 2006), 11–12. Page numbers appear hereafter in parentheses in the text.

2. Margalit Fox, "Michael Cox, Editor and Author of *The Meaning of Night*, Dies at 60," *New York Times*, April 18, 2009, www.nytimes.com/2009/04/19/books/19cox .html (accessed January 13, 2010).

3. David Punter and Glennis Byron, *The Gothic* (Malden, MA: Blackwell, 2004), 273.

4. Glennis Byron, "Gothic in the 1890s," in *A Companion to the Gothic*, ed. David Punter (Malden, MA: Blackwell, 2000), 133.

5. Alexandra Warwick, "Lost Cities: London's Apocalypse," in *Spectral Readings: Towards a Gothic Geography*, ed. Glennis Byron and David Punter (New York: St. Martin's, 1999), 80.

6. Michael Dirda, "Trust No One in This Accomplished Victorian Suspense Novel: *The Meaning of Night*," *Washington Post*, October 1, 2006, www.washingtonpost.com/ wp-dyn/content/article/2006/09/28/AR2006092801373.html (accessed January 13, 2010).

7. Gary Hoppenstand, "Justified Bloodshed: Robert Montgomery Bird's *Nick of the Woods* and the Origins of the Vigilante Hero in American Literature and Culture," *Journal of American Culture* 15, no. 2 (Summer 1992): 60.

8. Byron, "Gothic in the 1890s," 133.

9. Heather L. Duda, *The Monster Hunter in Modern Popular Culture* (Jefferson, NC: McFarland, 2008).

10. Warwick, "Lost Cities," 84.

CHAPTER 38

London Demons

CURSED, TRAPPED, AND HAUNTED IN
WILLIAM HEANEY'S (GRAHAM JOYCE'S)
MEMOIRS OF A MASTER FORGER

K. A. Laity

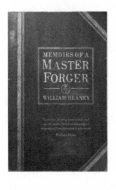

Memoirs of a Master Forger (U.S. title, the infinitely inferior *How to Make Friends with Demons*), although set in modern London, resonates with the echoes of the past. Narrator William Heaney constantly digs behind the superficial modernity of the world—and the people—around him to uncover the lurking Gothic past. His focus is obsessive, as befits his appropriation of the language of addiction narratives. While the neglectful bureaucrat, wine connoisseur, and part-time forger may seem as far away as can be imagined from a Gothic heroine, his narrative (quickly flagged as unreliable) reveals that he is as cursed, trapped, and haunted as any Radcliffe girl. The uncanny surrounds Londoners, who are mostly unaware of what Heaney can see: the demons that hover at their shoulders influencing everything they do. This vision makes Heaney a liminal figure: uncomfortable in every situation, at home nowhere, the perpetual outsider.

As with most of Joyce's books, there are layers of meaning that unpeel like husks. Despite the title, Heaney reveals immediately that he is not the "master forger" but part of a coincidental consortium that produces fake books, although this eventually leads to his forging poetry as well. While the literal acts of forgery concerning old books (primarily a Jane Austen) take center stage, there are other levels of forgery, including Heaney's early successful forgery of a necromantic handbook, which leads to his damnation (though in the end this grimoire, too, is a phony).

The packaging of the original book carried out this theme beautifully with its faux old cover, predistressed to show its age and crediting Heaney as the author even in the indicia. The American edition, which features the Oprah-ready

title and credits Joyce as the author directly, loses this humorous dimension and the additional weight of continuity. It is difficult to say if the publishers assumed merely that Americans wouldn't get the joke or that they would feel cheated (cf. James Frey's *A Million Little Pieces*) or whether it was simply a part of the corporate practice. As Joyce said with regard to another bland American title,

> When you sell a book in America, they feel they must work on it in some way or they haven't earned their money. If they can't change the narrative, because it was already published as a successful novel in the UK, they will look at the title and cover, thinking they could do a better job, but that's not always the case.[1]

Unfortunately, the stripping away of those "forged" elements removes the first layer of rhetoric for the narrative, which relies upon Heaney's fashioning a despairing mood of hopelessness, horror, and decay around his picture of himself as the ultimate forger. He remains unaware of that final layer of deception for most of the narrative.

Demons lie at the heart of Heaney's story. "There are one thousand five hundred and sixty-seven known demons. Precisely."[2] In this opening line, the narrative thrusts the reader into a world not unlike that of Lewis's monk, where dark conjurations are the norm. It also attempts, with suspicious urgency, to establish Heaney's trustworthiness as a narrator. His precision of the number of demons, his disagreement with Fraser's total (1,571), his mistaking psychological disorders for demonic afflictions—all of these appear to establish expertise just as surely as his inclusion of a footnote, despite its "messy intellectuality" and his statement that, "as you will know, it was Goodridge himself who brilliantly identified that the footnoting affliction is itself demonic" (1).

While Heaney teases us with his statement, "I'd been clean for twenty years or so before I picked up my latest demon" (2), it is some time before we get down to the actual practicality of demon keeping. Heaney's narrative circles around in time, first approaching and then shying away from that telling moment of damnation, where the necromantic book he forged as a university student was used in the attic of Friarsfield Lodge to conjure a very real demon and endanger five women he dated, including the one he was dating at the time that his rival Charles Fraser carried out the ritual.

After contemplating ways in which he might get away with murdering Fraser for this attempted sex magic (which involved, among other things, women's hair and a bloody goat's head), Heaney at last comes to the notion of self-sacrifice. There is an underlying message of Christian atonement throughout the book, hardly surprising given the focus on demons, though it is balanced by Joyce's recognition of the absurdity of Heaney's egocentric obsessions. Like the pseudomedievalism of many Gothic narratives, *Memoirs* makes much of the

medieval belief that demons dog our every step, hanging at our shoulders gibbering temptations, and that good people must be ever vigilant to resist their proddings. Even his bibliophilia makes Heaney more susceptible, as he notes, "Demons do tend to cluster around the yellowing pages and racked spines of second-hand books. I've no idea why" (11). Joyce's wink reveals his expectation that the reader, too, has been infected and knows it.

Heaney performs an act of abnegation and self-sacrifice, even though he admits, "I was winging it. I didn't really know what I was trying to do, or undo, or re-do. All I had was the fake manuscript of rituals that I'd concocted only for Fraser to get his diseased hands on it" (167). He abstains from sex, takes up a hermetic existence and studies his forged manuscript. Heaney has become convinced by the veracity of his own creation, even though he declares, "I'd lost all faith in the improvisations of my fake manuscript. I was committed to summoning whatever entity I was about to encounter by mental force alone" (170). This is a subtle clue for the eventual revelation of the ultimate forgery: the reality of the demons Heaney sees throughout the novel. It comes just prior to the scene of his damnation, which invites belief through the lengthy and elaborate form of the ritual, the urgency of the physical descriptions, and his further claim that "I had in my knowledge a *key*, which was not something of my own invention, but which I'd stumbled across in at least two different sources" (170). Everything about this section conspires to make us believe—just as it did for Heaney himself.

Heaney begins the section with an exhortation to the possibilities beyond rationality, just after a scene in which he finally stands up to his ex-wife and her famous chef husband, which itself comes immediately upon the heels of his revealing to Yasmin, his potential love interest, just how disturbed his mind is—and why he's been reluctant to sleep with her. These emotional touchpoints knit the reader's sympathies to Heaney, creating trust for the forger's account of this crucial scene. Heaney removes the last vestiges of doubt with his impassioned paean to the unseen:

> How many coincidences are we prepared to tolerate, how much synchronicity, how many flukes, chances, twists of fate, what degree of happenstance, how much weird correlation will we be prepared to ignore before we finally throw up our hands and say that cause and effect is not the only ballgame in the universe? When do we admit that rationality is just something useful we made up to help us along? (167)

The ritual at last leads to making a deal with a demon who appears in the guise of one of the college chaplains, Dick Fellowes. The scene is handled masterfully to make us read a very straightforward scene, not with logic (the chaplain speaking

to a troubled student who has lied to him about attempting to summon hellish forces), but through Heaney's fevered eyes: "He moved his jaw, as if trying to search for command of his words before speaking. I've seen that gesture since. It is a kind of signature of momentary demonic occupation: . . . he said finally[,] 'You can never walk away from this'" (174). Heaney must suddenly leave the college, freezing all relationships, and damning himself—and the reader along with him—to a life of self-created suffering. A haphazard invocation of demons, he believes, is leading to the bizarre injuries and deaths of the women he loved, or at least heartily lusted for (including the sudden collapse of an inflatable "bouncy castle" upon one of the young lovelies). Like the ultimate revelation of the haunting specter as a fake in so many Gothic novels, especially in the works of Ann Radcliffe, the eventual disclosure of the misreading of this scene releases the reader from the hold of this skillfully woven supernatural spell.

Falsity fills Heaney's life from then on: a forgery of a marriage, a forgery of a career, and of course the forged books and poetry with which he deals. Just as the ritual of his damnation came about for good purpose—saving the life of his girlfriend Mandy, whom he then abandons—Heaney counterfeits for the good of GoPoint, the guerilla homeless shelter run by "the saintly Antonia Bowen" (10)—the necessary healing angel to all these demons—and not for his own gain. He continues to pay the price of his penance for the rest of his life, as if the chaplain-as-demon had commanded that his contrition have physical form. Heaney obsesses over the physical nature of these fabrications, as his raptures over the Austen books demonstrate, including the importance of the wrapper. He reminds us that "it's part of the persuasion" and that, "even though the forgery will fool or at least confound the most trained eye, the cover, the special wraparound, is somehow the clincher" (304). If Heaney's damnation is the forgery, the wraparound for the reader is the rest of the novel. His poetic deception—introduced late, suspicious in itself—seems less important, less obsessive. One quickly suspects that despite all his protesting, Heaney puts far more of himself into the poems he claims not to remember after scribbling them in a drunken state. Yet when tabloids eventually reveal that he is the poet and not his model-handsome fellow forger Jaz, Heaney goes to great lengths to prove that the work was collaboration (in keeping with poetic tag teams like Pound and Eliot), which adds to the suspicion that he reveals more in the poetry "shams" than he would like to admit.

Heaney's obsession with pubs and wine provides another layer of the wraparound hiding his true forgery. While the pubs provide another avenue of Gothic coloring—Heaney never enters one without relating its buried or lost history, those who drank there or those who died and were buried there, whether it's William Blake or Ealing comedians—they also offer the constant distraction of wine. Heaney could be mistaken for an alcoholic, but his real addiction is the

endless cataloging in his head. Wine is a fetish. The compulsive naming of wines seems to calm the eternally restless fear of the demons that hover everywhere in his sight. Whether he's longing for a Mouton Rothschild after a fight with his ex (166) or following an attack on a pretentious poet with a large glass of 1997 Chateau Pichon-Baron, second-growth Paulliac (224), Heaney sublimates every emotional reaction to the naming and consuming of wine.

It's this hunger that leads to his most important relationships, the ones that finally allow him to escape from his darkened confinement and once more embrace the light. Initially, they seem to be an inescapable part of his damnation. When Heaney first gives in to the demon who has claimed him at the ritual of self-sacrifice, he wallows in the worst London offers. When at last his demon relinquishes him, Heaney

> devised a kind of mental yoga to keep [the demon] away . . . the side effect of this yoga was to roll back the surface of the world, and to make plain to me the astonishing array of demonic activity exacting a pull, like the moon and the tides, on every single human life in the capital and beyond. (182)

His family he holds at arm's length, confessing that, "When I met Fay [his ex-wife] I liked her a great deal, and I knew that I wouldn't fall in love with her" (182). He speaks with fondness of his children yet holds them remote until they force themselves upon him. He is close only to the Candlelight Club, his accidental association of brokenhearted men (Stinx and Jaz) who become the band of forgers, their name inspired by Yeats, perhaps his "Phases of the Moon":

> He has found, after the manner of his kind,
> Mere images; chosen this place to live in
> Because, it may be, of the candle-light
> From the far tower where Milton's Platonist
> Sat late, or Shelley's visionary prince:
> The lonely light that Samuel Palmer engraved,
> An image of mysterious wisdom won by toil;
> And now he seeks in book or manuscript
> What he shall never find. (lines 12–20)[3]

The Candlelight Club provides another place to hide, as does Heaney's attraction to GoPoint's Antonia, whom he's able to keep at arm's length because she has no demons and is thus too good for him. Heaney is comfortable only among the damned, yet even there he finds himself in danger because, as Yeats might say, "All dreams of the soul / End in a beautiful man's or woman's body."[4]

When the truth of love is handed to him in an attractive wrapper, he must pretend it is a lie in order to consume it. The beautiful Yasmin is too good to

be true, though not pure like Antonia. Her nigh-on-demonic lure proves an insurmountable temptation for Heaney. The forger transforms most convincingly into a Gothic heroine when faced by Yasmin, for he appears almost helpless as he struggles against sexual allure, like a wan girl struggling against the dark potency of a Byronic hero-villain.

Unlike the careful rituals, harsh denial, and obsessive concentration that Heaney's spells require, Yasmin's magic seems effortless and natural. Every movement enhances her charms, every breath weakens his resolve, until at last he finds himself ready for surrender:

> Then she kissed me, and the kiss drew all the tension out of me and at that moment it was like something else came into the room, riding on smoke. Some dark enfolding power, black like sleep, red like embers, white with snowy wings. She held my face between her hands and gently pressed her tongue into my mouth. I felt myself going under; I wanted to swoon away, like a girl. (286)

Heaney paints himself as helpless, girlish. He can no longer fight the demon within her, the one that desires to be within him: the demon called love. From the time he first experienced its spark with Mandy, Heaney has sought to shut that demon out of his life.

The inescapable lure of Yasmin sets this narrative into action. Heaney lets the careful mental discipline he had maintained for so long slip, though he fights love every step of the way, as if it were a villain trying to spirit him away from a protective convent. The ghosts of the past demand to be heard, and the slow unraveling of the lost time begins, though with the circling and doubling back of the practiced Scheherazade, haunted always by a specter—"Yasmin, who hosted demons but who didn't know it. They flew in and out of her, like dark birds in and out of a tree" (183).

Slowly the walls of Heaney's cobwebbed enclosure begin to tumble, both literally and figuratively as his children invade his home, the safety of the Candlelight Club dissolves, and even the reliable Antonia, who has given him reason to live and a well for his endless outpouring of self-flagellating penance, informs him abruptly that she is dying and that GoPoint will close. When he tells Yasmin that "love is a fraudster. A demon with sweet breath," she counters with the argument "that love is Nature's way of showing you the very best of yourself" (283), which is the one thing Heaney can't bring himself to believe. The reason Yasmin's "magic" appears so natural is because it is; Heaney's artificial world without love requires so much effort to keep in place, it's no wonder that he finds himself depleted.

The key that finally unlocks Heaney's past comes paradoxically from the shell-shocked soldier Seamus's "confession" slipped to Heaney after he blows up

himself and Heaney's friend Otto next to Buckingham Palace; the confession feels jarring because of its ultramodernity. The sudden shift of narrative voice reminds the reader of its peculiar transmission, like the found medieval manuscript within the Gothic novel. It is an insertion and feels like it, at first as unexpected as the *shemagh* that is thrust into Heaney's hands just before the explosion. Yet, as he says later, "in my confused and drunk condition I even believed for a moment that he had written it for me" (227). The narrative—broken up as all the stories within this novel are—seems initially to lead the reader far from Heaney's life and circumstances, though he eventually takes the tale of a soldier who finds himself frozen in place and time upon a landmine as an equivalent metaphor for his life. The demon who rescues Seamus gets passed to him with the testament, but it's a demon of liberation. He seeks out Mandy, for whom he'd damned himself, asking her "permission to fall in love with someone else" (256).

Then, in a scene reminiscent of M. R. James's "Casting the Runes," Heaney decides that the liberation will help his former enemy Fraser, and he slips the testament to him surreptitiously, though Fraser realizes what has happened and angrily berates him. Heaney believes it is the wisdom of Seamus's demon that has freed him, the words of the prophet, "Keep your heart light at every moment, because when the heart is downcast the soul becomes blind" (269). Heaney decides to take his metaphorical foot off the mine—and give in to the desire to love Yasmin—at a pub associated with William Blake, "because he saw angels and demons everywhere, too" (282).

In the end, even his damnation is a forgery. His freedom comes not from Seamus's demon but from Fraser's revelation that the girls he thought to have died from the ritual had not died. He had not saved Mandy with his sacrifice. This is revealed midway through the book but does not sink in until Heaney chooses to embrace the wisdom of Seamus's demon. This lag avoids the blinking disbelief that the revelation of fake ghosts provides in many a Gothic novel; rather than simply a sense of relief that all was right with the world, a euphoria of freedom infuses the narrative at the end. As befits the theme of a kind of purgation and salvation, Heaney stands watching all the demons depart at the stroke of midnight on Christmas Eve, something he calls "the Ascent of Demons" (306): "hundreds of demons, slowly ascending into the night sky over London . . . like floating statues . . . resplendent, golden-brown" (306).

He has accepted love and his children and has even worked out the usually complicated family time-sharing split for Christmas Day itself. While the Candlelight Club has broken up, the members seem to have knit themselves into new and more productive relationships. Yasmin will take over the late Antonia's passionate mission. Heaney finally admits to what he had been told repeatedly as he stands with his chosen ones:

What an odd group. I loved them all. I fancied that I could see my-self in the shining brilliance of their eyes. They reflected back at me, which was appropriate because the biggest demon I faced was the one I saw in the mirror. Because he was the master of all the others. What should I say? I had lived in the shadow of a wrong I didn't commit and in doing so made a counterfeit of my own life. Faked my own death in a way. . . . You let go. No one needs to hang on to a first edition. (307)

Unshackled finally, and scorched by love, Heaney returns to the metaphors that had ruled his life for so long: forgery, demons, and mirrors turned outward. He had made a world of demons to atone for sins he had never committed, had devoted his time to good works in a desperate bid to make reparations for his evil.

In the end, Heaney finds he has unwittingly perpetrated the greatest hoax upon himself. Now blending the wisdom of a saint (Antonia's surrender to death) and Seamus's demon ("levity is the only thing we have in the face of death"), Heaney symbolically takes his foot off the mine, realizing he can't keep it there forever, and experiences the joy of acceptance. "To love me or leave me, to destroy me on the wheel of sex, to crush my heart to dust: I no longer felt I could control it. . . . You cry. You come. You sing. You laugh" (307). And Yeats might agree:

> He'd crack his wits
> Day after day, yet never find the meaning.
> And then he laughed to think that what seemed hard
> Should be so simple—a bat rose from the hazels
> And circled round him with its squeaky cry,
> The light in the tower window was put out. (lines 142–147)[5]

Notes

1. Noga Applebaum, "Graham Joyce," *Write Away*, November 23, 2009, www .writeaway.org.uk/component/option,com_mtree/task,viewlink/link_id,5172/Itemid, 99999999 (accessed January 5, 2010).

2. William Heaney (Graham Joyce), *Memoirs of a Master Forger* (London: Gollancz, 2008), 1. Page numbers appear hereafter in parentheses in the text.

3. William B. Yeats, "The Phases of the Moon," in *Collected Poems of W. B. Yeats*, 2nd rev. ed. (New York: Scribner, 1996), 163.

4. Yeats, "Phases of the Moon," 165.

5. Yeats, "Phases of the Moon," 167.

CHAPTER 39

Haunting Voices, Haunted Text

TONI MORRISON'S *A MERCY*

Ruth Bienstock Anolik

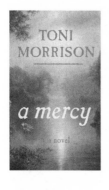

Toni Morrison's novel *A Mercy* (2009) begins with a mysterious voice addressing an unspecified audience: "Don't be afraid. My telling can't hurt you in spite of what I have done and I promise to lie quietly in the dark—weeping perhaps or occasionally seeing the blood once more."[1] The reader does not yet know the identity of the "I" or of the "you"; the situation of the telling will not become clear until the conclusion of the narrative. However, by the first lines of the novel, the reader can be certain that Morrison's narrative is set in the paradoxically familiar and mysterious world of the Gothic: the world in which mystery is as expected as darkness, blood, confusion, and ambiguous identity (3). Indeed Morrison's novel features all of the mandated tropes: a fragmented narrative, destabilized identities, the image of the double, a haunted house, dangerous villains, endangered women, and anxious encounters with the Other and the self.

As the mists of the text clear, we discover that the "I," the writer of the central narrative that overarches the novel, is Florens, a young African American slave living in late-seventeenth-century America. She has been sent by her mistress to fetch an unnamed blacksmith to cure her mistress of smallpox. Florens willingly takes this assignment, even though it means encountering the dangers of the early American woods, because she is eager to join the free African blacksmith whom she passionately loves. The central action of the novel thus suggests an exciting twenty-first-century feminized revision of the epic journey of discovery, adventure, and romance, or a bildungsroman, tracing Florens's development from abandoned girl to self-possessed woman—undergoing the blossoming suggested by her name. However, *A Mercy* ultimately collapses back into the dark,

418

antique Gothic, as Florens's journey leads back to her own dark and despairing past and to the inherited curse of slavery.

"Mine": American Gothic Space

Each space on Florens's journey, the various stations of her failed pilgrim's progress, is an imprisoning Gothic space. Her childhood home, Jublio plantation, is a Gothic home in the tradition of Simon Legree's plantation in Harriet Beecher Stowe's *Uncle Tom's Cabin* (1852). Jublio is located in Catholic Maryland, a dangerous place from the perspective of Jacob Vaark, a trader from the North: "The palatinate was Romish to the core. Priests strode openly in its towns; their temples menaced its squares; their sinister missions cropped up at the edge of native villages" (13). Morrison thus aligns her Gothic site with earlier Gothic locales in which Horace Walpole, Ann Radcliffe, and others express their English Protestant fear of Catholics by creating Catholic villains lurking in monasteries and convents. Fittingly, the master of Jublio is Catholic, and Jacob is appalled by "the graven images" that fill his house. Far more shocking is D'Ortega's ownership of slaves: he complains about his capital loss as a consequence of "cargo" dead of "ship fever" (17), and his house slaves eye him with fear. We later learn from Florens's mother, whom Florens calls *a minha mãe* (Portuguese for "my mother"), that this is a place where Gothic rape takes the place of romantic love. Although Florens never learns this, her mother sends her from this house of horrors to protect her. As Florens's mother kneels before him, begging, Jacob sees "the terror in her eyes" (26). The mother chooses well: Jacob opposes slavery and takes the child from her mother out of kindness and mercy.

The place to which Jacob takes Florens is, on first appearance, a more benevolent place than Jublio Plantation. In fact, at the Vaark farm, Florens finds the kind of community of outcasts that Morrison presents as a sanctuary in many of her books, including *Beloved* and *Paradise*. The community comprises Jacob's wife, Rebekka, as well as a number of servants or slaves whom Jacob has taken in out of compassion. Lina, a Native American woman, had been taken in by "the Presbyterians" after smallpox destroyed her village. But when her sexual activity proved too much for her benefactors, they "abandoned her without so much as a murmur of fare well," and "Sir [Jacob] bought her" (48, 51). Lina, the first and only slave whom Jacob buys outright, is thus rescued as much as bought. Sorrow, the "daft girl" who is "accepted not bought by Sir" (51), had been rejected by a family that had found her as a castaway. In fact, the master and mistress, Jacob and Rebekka, are themselves exiled outcasts. Before inheriting his land and the aristocratic title of patroon from a distant Dutch uncle, Jacob was an orphan from London—his English mother dead, his Dutch father

gone. Rebekka was exiled from the brutal London of her childhood by her father and sold to Jacob, a stranger who could afford to feed her.

Yet Morrison plants early clues, including his name, to suggest that Jacob does not partake of the communal ethos. Jacob is the sly biblical patriarch who tricks his elder brother out of his birthright; *vaark* is the Dutch word for pig. Jacob's self-assessment is that he "continues to feel a disturbing pulse of pity for orphans and strays" (33). That Jacob finds the impulse "disturbing" indicates his character. Although he truly loves his wife and is a good husband to her, Jacob's prime motivation for marrying was that "taking over the patroonship required a wife" (20). As Lina observes, Jacob, an impatient and "poor farmer" (49), is better suited to the quick profits of the capitalist trader. Jacob's affinity for capitalism allows him to be corrupted by his brief visit to Jublio. Although at Jublio, "Jacob sneered at wealth dependent on a captured workforce" (28), a brief conversation with a man significantly named Downes convinces Jacob that "there was a profound difference between the intimacy of slave bodies at Jublio and a remote labor force in Barbados" (35). This is Jacob's moral turning point, as he ceases being a part-time farmer and "a small-scale trader for the Company with a side line in fur and lumber" (33) and embarks on a lucrative career in the rum trade, supported by the suffering of those unknown slaves in the West Indies, whose expendable bodies are "like firewood, what burns to ash is refueled" (30).

Jacob's capitalistic greed drags him and his community from the world of the pastoral to the Gothic, the world of the dark patriarch who destroys everything so that he can acquire property and a dynastic line. This line begins in the English Gothic with Manfred, the villainous patriarch of Horace Walpole's *The Castle of Otranto* (1764), continues through the American Gothic in Colonel Pyncheon of Nathaniel Hawthorne's *The House of the Seven Gables* (1851), and reappears in the character of Jacob Vaark. Like his Gothic precursors, Jacob builds a house for power and pride, because, he says, "What a man leaves behind is what a man is" (89). As Lina recalls, the building of his second house was reasonable: "The first house . . . dirt floor, green wood—was weaker than the bark-covered one she herself was born in." The second house, a simple farmhouse, did not involve a wasteful use of natural resources: "He tore down the first to lay wooden floors in the second." However, "There was no need for a third. Yet . . . he meant to build another, bigger, double-storied, fenced and gated like the one he saw on his travels . . . a profane monument to himself" (44), a monument that "required the death of fifty trees" (43). Rebekka also recognizes the aristocratic pride and greed that the house represents: from her point of view, the house is "something befitting not a farmer, not even a trader, but a squire" (88).

Like all Gothic houses built on pride and on the backs of others, Jacob's house is doomed to haunting and decay. It remains uninhabited; by the time it is built, Jacob's children are all dead, leaving him with no heirs. Jacob dies in

the house, the women dragging him there in the rain to fulfill his last wishes. He orders them to "lift him from the bed and lower him onto a blanket. All the while he croaked, hurry, hurry" (89). Morrison obliquely connects the earlier death of Jacob's beloved last-surviving child, the daughter aptly named Patrician, to the construction of this monument. Rebekka thinks of the building of the house: "Men, barrows, a blacksmith, lumber, twine, pots of pitch, hammers and pull horses, one of which once kicked her daughter in the head." Rebekka also connects the building of the house to Jacob's death: "The fever of building was so intense she missed the real fever, the one that put him in the grave" (89). Some of the characters believe that Jacob's ghost will continue to inhabit the building. Lina thinks, "Now having died in it he will haunt its rooms forever" (44). Willard and Scully, the two bondsmen who work on the farm, believe that "Jacob Vaark climbed out of his grave to visit his beautiful house" (143). They see a shadow and convince themselves it is Jacob: "His glow began near midnight floated for a while . . . moved ever so slowly from window to window" (145).

Indeed, the house is haunted, but not by Jacob. The living ghost of the house is Florens, returned to the farm after being rejected by her blacksmith. The glow that Willard and Scully see is Florens's lamp, as she inscribes the narrative that we read. Writing with a nail, she uses the primitive literacy she secretly acquired in her childhood from the "Reverend Father" (159). She writes first on the floor and then the walls, until "there is no more room in this room. These words cover the floor. From now you will stand to hear me. . . . I am holding light in one hand and carving letters with the other. . . . I am near the door and I am closing now. What will I do with my nights when the telling stops?" (160). Florens writes her life to keep herself alive. She knows that she is to be sold out of the farm community, likely into a more brutal form of slavery. Florens refuses Sorrow's offered plan of escape; she writes, "She wants me to go with her but I have a thing to finish here" (159). Since Florens has already told us that she is finished with the writing, is the thing she needs to finish here her life? Does she recognize that in her future slave life she will be a "thing," and has she decided to end an existence that has been marked by rejection and exile? The historian Jon Butler provides evidence to support this speculation: "Unlike inanimate property, Africans could and did destroy themselves, a prospect owners feared and resented."[2] Certainly Florens knows that her narrative will not endure.[3] She writes, "Lina will help. She finds horror in this house and . . . I know she loves fire" (161). Thus the grand house of the patroon Jacob Vaark is destined to suffer the conventional fate of the Gothic property; it will be burned to the ground to reflect the destruction of the structures of oppression that it represents.[4]

In addition to Ortega's Jublio plantation, and Jacob's unnamed grand house, there is one additional Gothic space in which Florens finds herself enslaved: the home of the unnamed blacksmith. For Florens does eventually achieve her goal,

although "my journey to you is hard and long" (137). She comes to the black-smith's homestead and sees "the yard, the forge, the little cabin." The blacksmith initially greets her with "glee," and Florens believes that finally she has discovered a home: "Here I am not the one to throw out" (136–137).

But the blacksmith's behavior ultimately validates the reader's suspicions about an ardent lover who goes off without farewell and stays away for almost a year, and the skepticism of Lena who realizes in retrospect that "his arrogance was clear" (45). In fact, the blacksmith ultimately literalizes Florens's romantic metaphor: "Before you know I am in the world I am already kill by you" (38), revealing himself to be the traditional murderous Gothic villain, interested in property and dynasty rather than in romance. For immediately after seeing the blacksmith, Florens sees his little foster son. The sight of this little boy sends Florens back to the central moment of her first rejection, that moment when her mother kept her brother and sent her away: "This happens . . . before. The first time it is me around my mother's dress hoping for her hand that is only for her little boy. . . . I am expel" (134). Throughout her life, Florens has been mistaken in her belief that her mother's decision was based on her preference for Florens's younger brother, a preference that would have reflected the values of the patriarchy. However, Florens is quite correct in guessing that she is to be expelled again. When the blacksmith explains that the boy is "a foundling. . . . My mouth goes dry as I wonder if you want him to be yours" (136). As Florens senses, the blacksmith's cabin, despite its humble appearance, is the home of the Gothic dynast whose need for a woman lasts only until his need for an heir is fulfilled. In this, too, Walpole's Manfred sets the tone, eager to divorce his loyal wife and to rape the fiancée of his dead son in order to engender a dynastic heir. We see this model alive and well in the twentieth-century African American novel, in the character of Luther Nedeed in Gloria Naylor's *Linden Hills* (1985). Nedeed is the dark, dynastic patriarch who descends from a line of African American men who dispense with their wives once they have furnished an heir. We know that the blacksmith, a "free man from New Amsterdam," is such a dynast. Florence notes that his craft is a patriarchal inheritance: "The glory of shaping metal. Your father doing it and his father before him back and back for a thousand years" (69).

Florens immediately understands that the foundling has replaced her in the life of the blacksmith. She notes how "you offer and he owns your forefinger. As if he is your future. Not me" (136). Florens accurately senses that she is no longer to have access to the blacksmith's phallus or to his future. Once ensured of his heir, the blacksmith no longer requires Florens's sexuality. All fears are fulfilled when the blacksmith returns just as the young and inexperienced Florens injures the child who is the midst of a tantrum. The blacksmith makes his choice clear: "I am lost because your shout is not my name. . . . No question.

You choose the boy. I am lost" (141). Cheryl Miller argues that the blacksmith helps Florens in rejecting her: "Florens's insane jealousy costs her the love of the blacksmith."[5] The blacksmith does seem to tell Florens some truths. She cannot stay with him, he says, "because you are a slave. . . . Own yourself woman." Yet he also calls her "a slave by choice" and blames her for making herself a slave to her masters and to himself. Ultimately he is blaming the victim of slavery and demonizing the woman; he tells her, "Your head is empty and your body is wild" (141). Perhaps the cruelty of the blacksmith's rejection can be best understood when compared to the compassionate acceptance by Paul D of Sethe, the protagonist of Morrison's *Beloved* (1987), who has done far more harm than Florens in actually killing her own daughter. Instead of abandoning Sethe to the slavery of her memories, Paul D accepts her and realizes that he must slowly teach her to believe that she is her own "best thing."[6]

The comparison of Paul D to the blacksmith points to a radical reversal in *A Mercy*, which disentangles the traditional Gothic association between morality and race. From Walpole's Manfred on, the typical malevolent Gothic patriarch is a swarthy Catholic Italian or Spaniard. All of Ann Radcliffe's dangerous men are dark Italians. Even Charlotte Brontë's English hero-villain, the swarthy Mr. Rochester, fits this mold, as does Emily Brontë's dusky Heathcliff[7] (described as a "gipsy" by six different characters in the novel, and by his adoptive father as "dark almost as if it came from the devil"[8]). In her twentieth-century American Gothic, *Linden Hills*,[9] Gloria Naylor suggests an interrogation of this pattern of creating a Gothic system in which all the characters—evil patriarch, imprisoned wife, and suffering populace—are black. While Naylor's text sets up a fascinating interrogation of the racialization of evil, she ultimately perpetuates the traditional paradigm without altering it. Delores Keller notes that in *Paradise* Morrison also warns of "the atrocities that can occur when black patriarchs imitate the racist, oppressive, and exclusionary ideologies of white society."[10]

Morrison's twenty-first-century Gothic carefully detaches the categories of morality from the categories of race, presenting a spectrum of morality through a racially and gender diverse group of characters. In disconnecting race from moral identity, Morrison not only revises a long-standing Gothic trope but also contests the ideological underpinnings of slavery: the notion that racial identity should dictate freedom or slavery. Morrison suggests that freedom, like moral character, should and cannot be determined by race. In fact, Morrison's stated project for the novel is to "separate race from slavery to see what it was like . . . where your status was being enslaved but there was no application of racial inferiority."[11] The book thus "challenges us to historicize the racialized political momentum that ushered in perpetual servitude based on non-whiteness and to meditate on the analogous forms of early colonial servitude, formal and informal, that might have united rather than divided persons."[12] Natalie Sandison

adds, "Morrison wants her readers to think more generically about slavery here, about freedom and the misuse of power . . . a reflection on the mercy shown when the one who has power over another refrains from using it."[13]

In *A Mercy*, then, morality is determined by deployments of power, rather than by racial identity. Morrison puts the moral of her book in the mouth of Florens's mother: "To be given dominion over another is a hard thing; to wrest dominion over another is a wrong thing" (167). Jennings calls these words "the benediction of the novel,"[14] but they might as well be the novel's curse. For those who abuse power in *A Mercy* destroy their world as well as themselves. Lina, foster mother to Florens, also contributes a central statement to the novel. She tells Florens the mythic story of a traveler who discovers a beautiful countryside. "The traveler laughs at the beauty, saying, 'This is perfect. This is mine.'" The word *mine* booms and "swells" over the countryside. The traveler then strikes a mother eagle, displacing her from her nest and orphaning her babies. Of course this myth is the story of Lina's America and of the versions of America that follow. As Mason notes, this story is "a creation myth. The eagle, our emblematic bird symbol of liberty and freedom sits far above . . . a world . . . jammed with beauty. . . . Alas, the traveler is . . . a consumer, a childish one . . . his 'evil thoughts' betray a drive to possess."[15] Thus, Morrison's American Gothic suggests that greed is the original sin, the underlying evil, of America and of the Gothic tradition. His notion of "mine" is what marks the blacksmith as the evil villain of *A Mercy*, not his vocational and racial blackness. Abusing the power that Florens's love allows him, he casts her away to the living death of slavery, or possibly suicide.

Morrison ultimately aligns the blacksmith with the iconic figure of supernatural evil, Satan, who frequently appears in Gothic texts, from Matthew Lewis's *The Monk* (1796), to Charles Maturin's *Melmoth the Wanderer* (1820), to Charlotte Dacre's *Zofloya* (1806), which features a Moorish slave whose body is possessed by Satan. Morrison deploys a variety of strategies to identify the blacksmith as the iconic font of evil.[16] The trade he inherits from generations of ancestors, providing this nameless character with his only identity, links him to the Roman god Vulcan the blacksmith, a mythological precursor of the devil. Like Satan, Vulcan is flung from heaven by a deity (in Vulcan's case, his mother Juno); both land in the depths of the earth (Vulcan underneath Mount Etna in Sicily), inhabiting realms of fire. Florens says, "The first time I see it [his naked back] you are shaping fire with bellows" (37), one of Satan's lesser-known tools.[17] When Florens arrives at the blacksmith's home, one of the first things she sees is the "forge," the oven that melts metal at a hellish temperature (135). The blacksmith's handiwork also suggests diabolic associations. He enters the narrative when he is brought by Jacob to the farm to create a "sinister gate" for the doomed mansion. The gate is decorated by "two copper snakes [that] met at the top," recalling Satan's appearance in paradise. When Lina goes through

this gate to bring Jacob into the house to die, "she felt as though she were entering the world of the damned" (51). Morrison thus identifies the blacksmith as the Satanic antihuman, the completely unknowable Other, a source of mystery and danger in Gothic texts. Unlike the other major characters in the book, he is nameless[18] and voiceless. Morrison denies him the narrative that would render him human, and he remains the opaque and inscrutable fiend.

Thus, as Morrison's iconography suggests, the blacksmith is the satanic serpent who enters and destroys the fragile paradise of the community of women who inhabit Jacob's farm. For despite Jacob's dynastic ambitions, his farm exemplifies Morrison's female communal paradises, like the ephemeral paradise in *Beloved* before the slave owners track down Sethe and her children, or the community of *Paradise*, also destroyed by men who cannot tolerate female independence. Morrison quite pointedly establishes Vaark's farm as such an isolated paradise. Lina remarks that Jacob and Rebekka's pride made them believe that "they needed only themselves, could shape life that way, like Adam and Eve" (58). Installed as the destructive force of her Gothic text, the blacksmith (the traveler, so like the quintessential Gothic patriarch) looks at those around him—Florens, the boy—and says "mine." The perceptive Lina defines his legal power: "He had rights, then, and privileges, like Sir. He could marry, own things, travel, sell his own labor" (45). Florens grants him emotional power: "You are my shaper and my world as well" (71). A truly inhuman monster, he uses his power to destroy Florens and to destroy her paradise because he cannot partake of a relationship based on a mutual sharing of power.

The Haunted Text

Morrison's central assertion that the will to possess leads directly to the downfall of the American aristocrat, the patroon Vaark, is a recurring Gothic locution and the dictum of Nathaniel Hawthorne's American Gothic *The House of the Seven Gables*,[19] which casts a long shadow over Morrison's text.[20] For Morrison's contention that the corruption of America and Americans begins with the word "mine" is reiterated in Hawthorne's novel. The naïf Clifford Pyncheon pointedly anticipates Morrison's delineation of Jacob when he says, "A man will commit almost any wrong—he will heap up an immense pile of wickedness as hard as granite . . . only to build a great, gloomy, dark chambered mansion for himself to die in."[21] Indeed there are a number of echoes between *A Mercy* and *The House of the Seven Gables*.[22] Mason suggests a connection when he summarizes Morrison's vision of America, the image of Jacob's abandoned house:

> Here we have a great big house, built by a white man and now empty, nobody living there. What happened? Greed drove the white man to

exploit the land and its peoples, to erect a monument to his own presumption . . . by which he—and all those he touched—were undone.
. . . The writing, as it were, is on the walls.[23]

Although Mason does not make the connection, this is an exact description of
the situation within Hawthorne's House of the Seven Gables at the end of the
novel. Yet, while indicting possession of property, and while hinting at the kind
of "immense pile of wickedness" that a nineteenth-century American might ac-
crue in the pursuit of property, Hawthorne represses any overt indictment of
the possession of human flesh from his text; the subject of slavery surfaces only
fleetingly and obscurely in the novel.[24] Morrison thus adds another gable to
Hawthorne's sinful house: the sin of possessing human beings.[25]

The indictment of the evil inclination to possess human beings drives the
text that most visibly haunts A Mercy, Morrison's Beloved.[26] Morrison's two
novels present startling similarities, most notably the event coiled at the center of
each narrative: the dreadful decision by a mother to sacrifice a daughter in order
to save her from a life of slavery. In Beloved, Sethe kills her third child, her older
daughter; ironically this action results in the liberation of the rest of the family.[27]
In A Mercy, the mother of Florens, faced with the possibility of being traded
away from her daughter and young son, begs Jacob to take her daughter from the
harsh plantation and from a future of sexual slavery. The consequences of these
well-intentioned acts are brutal: Sethe is haunted by guilt and ostracized by her
community; the forfeited Florens spends her life believing that her mother has
rejected her in favor of her baby brother.

Yet despite the similarities in these central stories—a similarity that may
be attributed to the Gothic tendency to revisit key themes both within and
between texts—neither A Mercy nor Beloved is an unnecessary duplicate.
Indeed, they are most productively read as a set of doubled texts that reflect
each other, each bringing into focus what is hidden in the other. In Beloved,
the focus is on the mother Sethe, her motivations, and the painful regret that
her decision causes her. A Mercy focuses on the daughter who believes that
she has been cast off because she is not sufficiently loved by her mother; she
never understands her mother's act to be the mercy that it is.[28] Together the
two novels give us the whole story of mother and daughter, just as the separate narratives within A Mercy merge to relate a single story. The two novels
together also give us the entire picture of the experience of American slavery;
as a doubled text they present a diptych, or rather the triptych of slavery: the
"before" of A Mercy; the "after" of Beloved, which focuses on the experiences
of a former slave in 1873; and the tortured memories of "during" that also
surface in Beloved.

The Haunting Voices of History

The care with which Morrison aligns her story to the facts of history indicates that *A Mercy*, a Gothic text that takes on the power of myth or fable,[29] is also a historical novel, taking its power from the reader's understanding that the events it describes happened, although the details might be imagined. Ira Berlin underscores the historical accuracy of Morrison's novel.[30] His observation that slavery developed differently in different times and different places aligns with Morrison's. The distinction Berlin makes between the "Northern nonplantation systems" and the "plantation system . . . around the Chesapeake" is illustrated by the Vaark farm and Jublio plantation.[31]

As Morrison indicates, during the time of *A Mercy*, slavery was a relatively fluid and humane system of servitude. The status of "slave" was not linked to racial identity. Jennings remarks that "economic expediency led the shift to non-white slavery. . . . Race slavery was not an inherent ideology."[32] As we see in *A Mercy*, until the late seventeenth century, there were free blacks, and Native Americans and Europeans were likely to serve side by side in bondage with Africans, functioning more like a household than like the factories of the large plantations. Only starting in the 1680s (the time in which Morrison sets her story) did a loose set of laws develop that over time would concretize into a harsh, brutal, and racialized system of slavery. Morrison's refusal to provide *A Mercy* with a happy restorative ending also reflects her commitment to historical accuracy. For Africans of the late seventeenth century, there were no happy endings. As the historian Jon Butler notes, "by 1700 the free Africans had disappeared—fled or been reenslaved, no one knows . . ."[33]

These humble words of the historian, "no one knows," provide the invitation for the writer of literature to imaginatively access that which remains unavailable to research, to turn toward myth for answers to the questions raised by history. Jean Wilson explains that this strategy aligns Morrison with Northrop Frye, the influential theoretician of literary criticism of the mid-twentieth century. Wilson argues that *Beloved*, a "history book" (238), is also "what Frye would describe as 'a vision of reality that is something other than history or logic.'"[34] *A Mercy*, too, offers "a vision" of reality that is "something other than history." Morrison fills the lacunae of history by drawing on the Gothic trope of the fragmented narrative—the trope that disputes the possibility of a single correct version of any event—imagining voices not recorded in the documents of history. The voices we hear in *A Mercy* belong to the voiceless: the poor, the female, the dark, the enslaved.[35] None of these voices speaks directly to the reader; they are ghost voices—whispering to themselves, whispering to others—and we must strain to understand the confusing utterances. Most of the characters—Jacob, Rebekka, Lina, Sorrow, Willard, and Scully—do not actually voice their stories. Their

perspective is presented by a third-person narrative that positions them, one by one, as the point-of view character. Only two of the characters, Florens and her mother, speak in the hope that they will be heard.

Florens addresses the written narrative of her journey—from Jublio plantation to the Vaark farm, to the blacksmith's home, and back to the farm—to the blacksmith. This is the narrative that is inscribed on the walls of the grand house that Florens knows is doomed to burn. She writes to the blacksmith, "If you never read this, no one will" (161). Nor does Florens have much hope of the blacksmith actually reading her words and thereby correcting his mistaken notion of who she is. At the beginning of her narrative, Florens directs a question to the blacksmith—"One question is . . . can you read?" (3)—conveying an underlying sense that the answer is no. And by the end of her writing, Florens acknowledges that "You won't read my telling. You read the world but not the letters of talk" (160). In fact, since the last we know of the blacksmith is that he was beaten by a frenzied Florens—"the hammer is in my hand" (142)—we cannot even be certain that he is alive to read it.

Nor does the second speaker in the novel, Florens's mother, have any hope of conveying her meanings to the daughter she longs to reach. When Florens describes the fateful moment of her mother's mercy, she shares an incoherent memory of *a minha mãe* "saying something important to me, but holding the little boy's hand" (8). Throughout her time at Vaark farm, Florens envisions her mother silently speaking: "As always she is trying to tell me something" (137). Even when Florens has given up on all happiness, and possibly on life itself, she returns to this loss: "I will keep one sadness. That all this time I cannot know what my mother is telling me. Nor can she know what I am wanting to tell her." And then, in the last lines of her narrative, Florens turns away from the unloving blacksmith, speaking directly to the mother who loves her, sharing a little family joke: "*Mãe*, you can have pleasure now because the soles of my feet are hard as cypress" (161). Unlike Florens, the reader has only to turn the page to read the words that the mother longs for Florens to hear: her explanation that what Florens saw as a rejection was "a mercy," the mother's only way of removing Florens from a place in which "there was no protection" (162); that the stolen lessons in reading and writing were the mother's attempt to help Florens find her own way in the world; that in giving Florens to Jacob she was counting on his humanity to recognize the humanity in Florens, counting on his ability to also offer "a mercy" (167) to a small unprotected child. The final tragic words of the book: "Oh Florens. My love. Hear *a tua mãe*" (167).

Had Florens been able to hear these words and know that she was her mother's love, she might not have made herself vulnerable to a demon. But Florens never will hear them, just as neither the blacksmith nor her *mãe* will hear the last words of Florens's. In this tragic way, Morrison invites us to consider

how many slave children, like Florens, lived their lives believing that somehow lack of maternal love accounted for their expulsion from the paradise of their mother's arms.

As Morrison leaves us with the poignancy of silenced voices, she draws upon yet another timely Gothic trope: the failure of language. Frequently some Gothic narrator will pause on the brink of describing some unimagined horror to the reader to announce that words cannot describe the immensity of the spectacle. Ultimately, the concluding words of *A Mercy* and of *Beloved*—"This is not a story to pass on"—suggest that words fail when confronted with the horrors of slavery. The spectral voices the reader hears are mere words on the page. Morrison obligates us to take the fragmented pieces of the narratives that haunt us and to reassemble them into a whole. As we gaze at the entire picture, we can recognize familiar patterns: a mirrored double of our own historical moment. Like the inhabitants of the ephemeral community on Vaark's farm, we live in dangerous times, poised on the brink of a century that looms, like a dark, uncharted land filled with unimaginable dangers. In fact, the first decade of the American twenty-first century feels no less dark and dangerous, no less Gothic, than the late seventeenth century in America when the horrors of slavery were about to commence.

Notes

1. Toni Morrison, *A Mercy* (New York: Knopf, 2009), 3. Page numbers appear hereafter in parentheses in the text.
2. Jon Butler, *Becoming America: The Revolution before 1776* (Cambridge, MA: Harvard University Press, 2000), 41. My thanks to David M. Carel of Yale University for directing me to this rich resource.
3. In "Mine, Mine, Mine," *Commentary* 127, no. 3 (March 2009): 64, Cheryl Miller argues that Florens is saved by her writing, purging her past "through the act of writing, through art, and thereby find[ing] herself." Yet this elevating moral does not fully conform to what we know of Florens's situation.
4. Wyatt Masons also sees the significance of the burning of the house, while eliding the Gothic context: "For the daughters of the eagle to truly be free, the white man's house must be burned to the ground"; "The Color Money," *New York Review of Books* 56, no. 4 (March 12, 2009): 37.
5. Miller, "Mine, Mine, Mine," 64.
6. Toni Morrison, *Beloved* (New York: New American Library, 1987), 273.
7. For an excellent and comprehensive discussion of this trope, see H. L. Malchow, *Gothic Images of Race in Nineteenth-Century Britain* (Stanford, CA: Stanford University Press, 1996).
8. Emily Brontë, *Wuthering Heights* (1847; New York: Classic Books America, 2009), 3, 35, 37, 48, 87, 95.

9. Gloria Naylor, *Linden Hills* (New York: Penguin, 1985).

10. Dolores Keller, "Toni Morrison's Sermon on Manhood: God in the Hands of Nine Angry Sinners," *Midwest Quarterly* 51, no. 1 (Autumn 2009): 46.

11. Lynn Neary, "Toni Morrison Discusses *A Mercy*," National Public Radio book tour, October 27, 2008; quoted in La Vinia Delois Jennings, "*A Mercy*: Toni Morrison Plots the Formation of Racial Slavery in Seventeenth-Century America," *Callaloo* 32, no. 2 (2009): 645.

12. Jennings, "Toni Morrison Plots," 645.

13. Natalie Sandison, review of *A Mercy*, by Toni Morrison, *Times of London*, June 6, 2009, 10.

14. Jennings, "Toni Morrison Plots," 649.

15. Mason, "The Color Money," 35.

16. In "Remodeling the Model Home in *Uncle Tom's Cabin* and *Beloved*," *American Literature* 64, no. 4 (December 1992): 785–805, Lori Askeland argues that *Beloved* is influenced by Harriet Beecher Stowe's *Uncle Tom's Cabin* (1852). *A Mercy* also reveals traces of this influence. Morrison's satanic blacksmith echoes Stowe's satanic Simon Legree.

17. In *The History of Art in the Middle Ages*, Didron recalls "a picture of a devil blowing a bellows into the face of a terrified angel" in a medieval text. Adolphe Napoléon Didron, *The History of Art in the Middle Ages*, trans. Margaret Stokes, 2 vols. (London: George Bell, 1886), 2:144.

18. On the other end of this spectrum is Sorrow, whose name is imposed upon her by others. Upon the birth of her daughter, she seems to free herself from madness and renames herself "Complete."

19. Nathaniel Hawthorne, *The House of the Seven Gables* (1851; New York: Penguin Books, 1981).

20. Both houses are built upon the suffering of others to satisfy greedy ambition. Like Hawthorne's Colonel Pyncheon, Jacob dies in his house, in the midst of festivity. Both houses are eventually abandoned and haunted by the ghosts of their owners.

21. Hawthorne, *House of the Seven Gables*, 263.

22. Morrison slyly points to this important allusion when Lina sees some runaway slaves "camped in wintergreen beneath two hawthorns" (Morrison, *A Mercy*, 64). The clue becomes even more transparent when we remember that Hawthorne's chapter "The Flight of Two Owls" focuses on Clifford and Hepzibah's escape from the house, the Gothic structure that imprisons them.

23. Mason. "The Color Money," 37.

24. Slavery is suggested in the marginal figure of "Black Scipio" (192) and in the image of the little white boy devouring the Jim Crow cookie.

25. Morrison is certainly not the only African American woman writer to be attracted by the wild freedom of the Gothic text. In addition to revisiting the Gothic in *Linden Hills*, Gloria Naylor creates a magnificent African American revision of the Gothic in her novel *Mama Day* (1988). Nor did female slave narrators fail to see the Gothic lineaments of their situation. Harriet Jacobs's memoir *Incidents in the Life of a Slave Girl* (1861) and Hannah Crafts's novel *The Bondswoman's Narrative* (2002) both draw upon Gothic tropology to amplify and familiarize the horrors of their situation for white readers.

26. A sly textual clue to this connection may be the moment when the slave owner D'Ortega says to Jacob of his slaves, "Do you know the prices they garner?" (23), recalling perhaps Margaret Garner, the historical slave who inspired the story of *Beloved*.

27. Askeland notes that the murder of the child is another moment in which *Beloved* is influenced by *Uncle Tom's Cabin*, which presents a number of wrenching scenes of infanticide by slave mothers.

28. Even though the reader does have the opportunity to hear the voice of the mother in the last section of *A Mercy*, we do not get the same detailed narrative of the effect of the mother's decision on her life that *Beloved* provides.

29. In "Bonds That Seem Cruel Can Be Kind," *New York Times*, www.nytimes.com/2008/11/04/books/04kaku.html (accessed November 4, 2008), Michiko Kakutani praises *A Mercy* as "One of Ms. Morrison's most haunting works yet," rediscovering the poetic voice of *Beloved*, allowing Morrison to move "between the worlds of history and myth, between ordinary daily life and the realm of fable."

30. Ira Berlin, "Time, Space, and the Evolution of Afro-American Society on British Mainland North America," *American Historical Review* 85, no. 1 (February 1980): 44–78. My thanks to David M. Carel for suggesting this fine article to me.

31. Berlin, "Time, Space, and the Evolution," 46.

32. Jennings, "Toni Morrison Plots," 648. Jennings's study examines moments in which Morrison draws on relevant historical events. She explains that Morrison validates her vision of an inclusive community by mentioning "'a peoples' war' of 1676. . . . Nathaniel Bacon, who incited the 'war' alluded to, amassed 'an army' not defined by race, status, or class" (647).

33. Jon Butler, *Becoming America*, 37.

34. Jean Wilson, "Toni Morrison: Re-Visionary Words with Power," in *Frye and the Word: Religious Contexts in the Writings of Northrop Frye*, ed. Jeffery Donaldson and Alan Mendelson (Toronto: University of Toronto Press, 2004), 238.

35. Miller points out harshly, but not inaccurately, that in providing voices for a Native American, a mentally ill slave, two gay men, an African American woman, a white woman, and a penniless orphan, "Morrison thus completes a dramatis personae of contemporary American identity politics," in "Mine, Mine, Mine," 62.

CHAPTER 40

Borderline Gothic

PHIL RICKMAN AND THE MERRILY WATKINS SERIES

John Whitbourn

> I have got a first-rate Gothic woman at last!
>
> —Augustus Pugin (b. London, 1812–1852),
> leading architect of the Gothic Revival.[1]

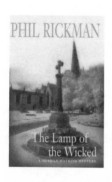

Pugin's words, albeit applied to a very different end (his impending marriage to his third wife), are relevant to the subject of this chapter. For not only does Phil Rickman's character Merrily Watkins provide us with a proper Gothic heroine, but Pugin parallels extend further still. Via indomitable will and skill, Pugin is held to have revived Gothic (architectural) style in the course of his short and driven life. By its close, courtesy of putting myriad concrete (actually, stone) facts on the ground, he changed his chosen world—designing the Palace of Westminster and dozens of Victorian mansions, colleges, and churches—and left a legacy for others to enhance. Willingly overworked to an early grave, he closed his eyes for the last time upon a landscape lastingly enriched by their ever having opened. I shall be arguing that Rickman's ten-book (to date) Merrily Watkins series has similar significance for the Gothic literary genre, but thereafter the Pugin correspondences cease. I am far from wishing Mr. Rickman such an early end. On the contrary, may he have a full crop of years, and Merrily likewise.

The task is to persuade others to be of similar opinion and also to secure Rickman/Merrily a room in the haunted mansion of Gothic literature. Where then to start? Especially with a series already sailing in stately armada past the multi-million-word mark?

Born in Lancashire, Phil Rickman (aka Will Kingdom, aka Thom Madley) lives on the Anglo-Welsh border, just as his series does. Over the course of his

career, he has been successively bracketed in the horror (to his horror) or super-natural or thriller or, mostly recently (and most happily), crime genre—there being, as yet, no bookshop shelves labelled "Gothic." Apparently, Rickman's own preferred best-fit description for the Merrily Watkins books is "spiritual procedurals," in imitation of the police procedural subgenre. Beyond that, such slim Rickman curricula vitae as exist reveal a journalistic past and the existence of an indispensable spouse/muse/editrix, which suffices. Rickman's achievement is in the art of "subcreation," in the Tolkienesque sense. Therefore, the world of Rickman's devising stands alone, and so details of its flesh-and-blood creator are irrelevant. We will see that Rickman's act of subcreation is truly as Tolkien described it:

> What really happens is that the story-maker proves a successful "sub-creator." He makes a Secondary World which your mind can enter. Inside it, what he relates is "true": it accords with the laws of that world. You therefore believe it, while you are, as it were, inside. The moment disbelief arises . . . you are then out in the Primary World again, looking at the little abortive Secondary World from outside.[2]

The supernatural things which Mrs. Merrily Watkins sees and experiences and learns are also our encounters—phenomena possibly awaiting us in our everyday life, and outside our front door, or worse still, given the nature of Merrily's supranormal trade, already within our front door, uninvited! This is not just clever writing or "old tales around the campfire" craftsmanship, but the embedding of a creation into present reality so seamlessly that you feel that the division between the reader's world and Merrily's is merely geographic. The only difference is that, just perhaps, our world is now imbued with fresh signifi-cance, fresh potentialities—in short, enriched. At the risk of repetition, this is subcreation indeed, bearing comparison with such celebrated world making as Tolkien's Middle Earth and C. S. Lewis's Narnia, as well as lesser-known but no less lifelong labors of love like Austin Tappan Wright's *Islandia* or M. A. R. Barker's *Tekumel*.[3]

Watkins first appears in *The Wine of Angels* (1998). Rickman has reportedly confessed that Merrily was not even the intended subject of the book, let alone the vehicle for a series. She walked in and came to life and took over—as only true subcreation can.

The salient points as we meet Merrily are that she is a thirtyish English lady, a widow, and ordained priest in the Church of England. Merrily is described as small and dark haired, and is, it becomes clear from the reviews of others, not unattractive. She smokes, which is fairly unusual nowadays and might be taken as a foretoken of individuality . . . or something. Her widowhood and priest-hood are of recent occurrence (as is the entire concept of female priesthood in

the Anglican communion). Having just lost a husband (faithless, in every sense), she remains both blessed and burdened by an intelligent but stroppy teenage daughter of the marriage. Said daughter, Jane, is unenthused by her mother's faith or role and more inclines to the modern mishmash called "neo-paganism." Both decant into a huge old vicarage (though Merrily has the less secure role of "priest-in-charge" rather than vicar or rector) in the Herefordshire village of Ledwardine, her first parish posting.

"Merrily's world" is the county of Herefordshire, which sits on the English side of the border with Wales. English counties have depth of meaning and are arguably the oldest (Dark Age vintage) surviving units of government in Europe. Their history is thus deep and, human history being what it is, often dark. Over that span of time, they have developed personalities, they pass on atmospheres, and they foster loyalties informed by that past. Prod that background, even lightly, and history exudes. And so our story begins.

And what a story, divided into ten weighty volumes to date! Though thoroughly stand-alone in reading terms, the tales within each installment are not lost from book to book but interweave, overlap, and inform each other, even if only as memory. In movie-town parlance, there are story arcs: time moves on, Merrily acquires experience, and Jane maturity. The claimed truths of Christianity and paganism are tried against unsympathetic reality. Meanwhile, subplots abound, just as they do in reality, and mundane duties (like shopping and remembering to feed Ethel the cat) call, heedless of other important, even life-and-death, things going on. Some matters are resolved, but by no means all. Some lessons are clear to be drawn, but others are merely hints. In short, all is as messy and maddening—but also involving and vital—as life itself. And, as with life and the accumulation of years, throughout the series snatches of secret harmonies are occasionally heard, haunting music on the edge of hearing. Inklings arise from contemplating the books' experiences but are never hammered home as a "message." In some instances, these implications explode later, like delicious delayed detonations. For instance, after *Midwinter of the Spirit*, the second volume, this reader pondered: "If X did indeed do Y, then X's vocation must have been a sham all along, a decades-long deception. And if the support network that X claims is true, then there must be a parallel structure: a whole inverted hierarchy! Which means . . ." And likewise: "That Lolita serial seducer, cutting a scandalous swathe through sexually repressed churchmen—is she powered by her own urges or operating on behalf of a bigger, badder, agenda?" And so on—although such a prosaic phrase doesn't really cover it.

This "trick" is an achievement indeed, but also a fragile flower if handled without care. Though a purpose of this chapter, as stated, is locating and ranking Merrily within the living Gothic tradition, describing her adventures necessarily treads the tightrope between divulging necessary information and draining

the stories of any suspense or joy. However, a sense of the menu and courses in store from the Merrily Watkins decalogy can be conveyed in such a way as to minimize any risk of spoiling the appetite.

Summaries

Book 1 introduces us to Merrily and daughter Jane, and almost as importantly to the village of Ledwardine, the cathedral town Hereford, and the county of Herefordshire, all of whom are set in "the border country" between England and Wales, two similar but profoundly different entities corralled within the same nation-state, the United Kingdom. Wales is tenuously linked by history to the Roman province of Britannia, and England to the Angles, Saxons, and Jutes (*Englaland*) which (mostly) conquered and supplanted it. The extrapolating consequences of that past endure even to the present day, fifteen hundred years later.

Merrily is unusual not only in her Christian name but in that she is a Christian priest(ess), which, as noted, remains a recent and still controversial innovation in the Anglican Church (Henry VIII's creation; equivalent to Episcopalian in America). She has a rural parish to look after (from which comes the archaic term and fourth book title *The Cure of Souls*, an older way of saying "Care of Souls," or the modern "Pastoral Care") and all the daily duties and the seasonal, liturgical round that go with it. By book 2, Merrily has, with much modesty and even more trepidation, accepted the role of diocesan exorcist—or *deliverance consultant*, as it apparently needs to be rebranded in modern mealymouthed church discourse. This is in the teeth of stereo opposition from traditionalist or sometimes reactionary tendencies opposed to priestesses per se, as well as progressive or liberal opponents of literalist theology, especially medieval throwbacks such as the rite of exorcism. On either count, by virtue of merely existing, Merrily is inadvertently either an ambassador of, or affront to, modernity. Meanwhile, whilst Merrily lives in the exact same world that her readers do, she also tries to walk faithfully according to a far bigger truth and oppose the forces that oppose it. We are invited to tag along and consider, at her side, what our response and reactions might be. Merrily has allies within the cathedral administration (some of whom are perceptively revealed as servants of the time-hallowed cathedral itself rather than the here-one-century, gone-the-next, Church which currently runs it); she has the Reverend Huw Owen, a battle-hardened Welsh exorcist, as tutor and continuing mentor, and then a continuum of support ranging from well-wishers through fair-weather friends to covert opponents and underminers.

Investigations ensue. Things are—intermittently, unreliably, least of all when expected—seen or experienced. Merrily, martyred by her overdeveloped sense of responsibility, applies all the diligence at her command, which proves

to be a surprising amount for a diminutive lady swimming against the current of her Church and age. Some case resolutions are made—maybe. Aforementioned inklings unfold in the reader's mind, some merely interesting, others absolutely huge.

And that's about it, really, except that Rickman is also a wizard of characterization, a better-than-Baron-Frankenstein creator of flesh and blood. Merrily is made (and I use the term advisedly, in subcreation terms again) rather than portrayed, a living, breathing person, with all the unpredictable individuality that appends to living breathing persons. Conviction develops, via mere marks upon paper, that a possible encounter with the actual Merrily, or her daughter Jane, or Lol the damaged ex–rock star, or Gomer the village wiseacre, is just a matter of a journey to the actual city of Hereford. More subcreation, this time intersecting like a Venn diagram with the reader's own lived reality.

Simultaneously, the Reverend Watkins is also on that clichéd but no less real thing, a spiritual journey, as she wades through the mundane whilst glimpsing the sublime, and the reader travels irresistibly along with her on that road. In the course of her days, over the never-faltering narrative of such a lengthy series, she encounters good and evil, and quite often an admixture of the two, as one might expect from a faithful depiction of existence. Good and ill often emanate from unlikely sources, and Rickman shows the good as believably human and the evil likewise—except when it's from a superbly hinted-at *beyond* human. As I've fairly warned the reader, the much-mentioned implications do not only leap from the page but also insert themselves, seedlike, in the mind to germinate in slower time and quieter reflection: those stimulating and life-justifying moments of mental growth.

In short, there is philosophical depth in the Merrily series to explore long after each book has been set down, not to mention untelegraphed lines that crackle like electricity and raise the neck hairs—genuine I-think-I'll-just-check-I've-locked-the-doors writing. Rickman can convey malignity like no other writer I've encountered. Ditto unease. Ditto supernatural events forming around you, sudden and clammy as a sea mist.

Now, even simply as a literary experience, this is champagne stuff. In the course of a century, perhaps two, of literary accumulation of the Gothic and supernatural literary field, depending on how you date its nativity, there has been, quite naturally, ample opportunity for familiarity to the point of jadedness with every technique for depicting the uncanny, from high literature to splatter-fests. Yet, time and again, in book after succeeding book, I contend that Rickman astounds with pages that quicken the pulse and chill the room. This is modern and developed Gothic (as we shall see) fiction come of age with meaning beyond its pages and tale-telling.

Therefore, Rickman's Merrily Watkins series is more than the sum of its parts—which, speaking of a decalogy, is a bold statement and praise indeed. It is also, I cannot forbear from advertising, the closest thing you will get to experiencing the supernatural, on demand, in the safety and comfort of your own home.

Having thus, I hope, whetted your appetite for better particulars, I can move on to details of the individual books. In scant (and sometimes facetious) summary, so as to avoid any possibility of spoilers, they comprise:

- *The Wine of Angels* (1998). Cast introductions, apple and orchard lore, ancient injustice, seventeenth-century metaphysical poetry, and sex murders.
- *Midwinter of the Spirit* (1999). Merrily inherits the role of exorcist, her learning curve, apparitions, and Hereford Cathedral.
- *A Crown of Lights* (2001). The interplay of Christianity (committed but uncharitable variant) and paganism (the tree-hugging, not cat-strangling, variety), the inadvisability of buying a decommissioned church.
- *The Cure of Souls* (2002). Hop farming (the bitter flavoring for English ale) and hops lore ("the Lady of the Bines"), gypsies, guitars, and sexual possession.
- *The Lamp of the Wicked* (2002). A horrific (real-world, alas) serial killer and his remains, corporeal and otherwise; a subplot concerning grounds for concern about electricity pylons; and, by the by, page 415 contains an evocation of despair that stands comparison to Macbeth's "Tomorrow and tomorrow" speech, crushingly concluding with, "Nothing. Nothing but going through life . . ."
- *The Prayer of the Night Shepherd* (2004). Sir Arthur Conan Doyle, creator of Sherlock Holmes and the hound of the Baskervilles, among other things.
- *The Smile of a Ghost* (2005). Strange and sinister (can there be any other kind?) suicides in a fashionable provincial town.
- *Remains of an Altar* (2006). Inexplicable road accidents; the composer Elgar and mystical music; prehistoric "old straight tracks" as rediscovered by Merrily's namesake and undercelebrated Herefordshire luminary, Sir Alfred Watkins; an ex–special forces (UK Special Air Service) priest; postmortem bottom pinching of lady cyclists.
- *The Fabric of Sin* (2007). The Knights Templar and one of their churches; something *rum* happening there to famous ghost-story writer M. R. James (1862–1936); dealings with Prince Charles, England's future (?) king; archaeology.
- *Dream of the Dead* (2008). A best-selling professional atheist, biblical-style floods and murder, more archaeology.

The Gothic Mrs. Watkins; or,
How Is the Series Gothic?

It is probably wise to take a stab (an appropriately Gothic action) at a working definition of the New Gothic, which is the depiction of life with both its brighter and darker hues enhanced, for dramatic and stylistic effect. Therefore, Gothic equals the baroque grandeur of the—often grim but always grand—underlying reality of life. And, by that definition, I can confidently report that the Merrily Watkins series cries out with Gothic power. But trust must be put in the beholders; they will know Gothic when they see it, even in the unlikeliest forms. Therefore Gothic is as Gothic does.

Anyone can list a litany of "things Gothic," a tick list of classic, even clichéd elements, from bone-white faces and red lips on introduction, to whitened bones and red gore at the denouement. The supernatural, however defined, also usually shows its generally disobliging face. Along the way, there will probably be castles, heaving alabaster bosoms, and romantically sickly (albeit hygienically so) Byronic youths. Quite possibly on the bill of fare will be some Heathcliff or other on the heath.

However, to delineate Gothic thus, to set a boundary about it, is to court disaster. A modicum of historical knowledge confirms that any entity which is avowedly self-limiting, content to crouch behind confining walls, is destined to first enervate, then ossify, and finally crumble. Ask the Roman Empire—that great wall builder and province downsizer, the emperor Hadrian, doubtless saw the error of his ways in the afterlife, but by then it was too late. That's why it's called the *after*life. As with empires, so with literary genres: the rule of life is to expand or die.

So, in common with all living things, Gothic evolves to survive, and I take survival for the Gothic tradition to constitute continuing stylishness. However, also by definition, the clichéd cannot be stylish, or leastways not for long. Therefore, Gothic must tread lightly and with poise, not plod, for all its serious subject matter. Otherwise it is not Gothic but some lesser breed beyond the pale, like, say, "horror."

Rickman's work contains *none* of the clichés discussed above. Yet the Merrily Watkins series is modern and stylish and, yes, Gothic down to its component atoms. And this is because it conveys a clearer reflection of reality as it is presently lived—and thus Gothically *endarkening*.[4]

In Merrily Watkins's world, the eternal verities and values of nature and tradition—some good or for our own good, but often containing little for our comfort—have the habit, right, and necessity to rudely protrude their unchanging truths into the constructed fiction of bright and shiny modernity. These shock-

ing moments of protrusion constitute a revolutionary subversion of the humanist fable that existence can be comfortably corralled within the fence of reason, science, secularly inspired goodwill to all men, and the like. And this is the precise source of much of the hostility and obstruction that Merrily meets from her surrounding society, namely that she constitutes a challenge to that worldview. Moreover, the phenomena which accompany her work, though usually subtle and subject to interpretation, are occasionally in your face and sweep all disbelief before them. Therefore she makes for unsettling and subversive company. Many people, especially powerful people, do not like their philosophies questioned at all, let alone by things they must countermand their senses to deny.

And of course the rite of exorcism is the very pinnacle of such offensiveness. If accepted, it implies the existence of richer realities, not least that of invisible powers that can possess, or likewise invisible but reliable remedies which should be impotent. Worse still (not only if accepted but even if merely entertained), it presents the notion that the religion Merrily teaches might have, however imperfectly, something in it, some basis in fact. In the words of the 1995 Eric Bazilian song, "What If God Was One of Us?" (covered by Alanis Morissette, Prince, etc.), would you really be so keen on meeting him on the bus, particularly if

> Seeing meant that you would have to believe
> In things like heaven and Jesus and the saints
> And all the prophets?

It is this, surely, that accounts for the curious perennial curiosity about, and fascination for, exorcism, from famous films and novels to surprise best sellers like a recent modest booklet on exorcism in the UK[5] and two volumes of memoirs by the former exorcist of the Catholic diocese of Rome.[6] The latter especially were practical, pragmatic, even prosaic, and were intended as reference works, but nevertheless they proved to be "shelf jumpers," in bookshop parlance.

Therefore, in Rickman's work, Merrily is a both a figure of opposition and the ambassador of the Gothic—that is, a deeper, maybe darker, underlying reality—to the world in which she moves. Being Merrily, she might not see or describe that as so, but it is. One recurrent motif is Merrily's collisions with communication across "great divides." These divides are invariably left for the reader to assess and evaluate postreading, but they seem to be between comparatively wholesome human life and a hinted-at vast hinterland of further realms, further experiences, and further powers, or indeed the great divide of life and death itself. Likewise, we are apparently shown possession, temporary or otherwise, as one should only expect from someone of Merrily's profession and confession. But by what exactly? And to whose end?

Weirdness is also embodied in the nonmaterial residue left by evil and (a Rickmanian trademark, this) the resurrection of memories in the landscape

better left buried. I also cannot forbear to mention the most memorably reported encounter with something that the narrator can only inadequately describe as "blue and gold," something utterly ineffable which sweeps all, including time, away before it.[7] To attempt to identify or label that would be to dishonor the writing, but the incident unavoidably brings in those implications again in the most profound way possible. Albeit brief, the incident may be the crux of the series, or a still higher peak of significance soaring above the rest.

Compounding the uncertainty, creeping anxiety, distrust, and dread are glimpses of secret, inverted structures matching those of the church. The shadow church has friends in very high places, and "dark sanctuaries" where they find shelter and regroup. Almost as troubling, there are the stand-alone anecdotes of wonder arising from the uncanny experiences people confide to Merrily. For example, in *Midwinter of the Spirit*, the phenomena surrounding the hospital deathbed of an elderly farm laborer are introduced by a normally hard-boiled and skeptical nurse. We can, if we so wish, interpret this as his meeting the consequences of, or perhaps even reaping the reward for, a lifetime of active wickedness. The appalling scenes are so well but subtly described that they have clung to this particular reader's memory like an affliction.

Why "Borderline" Gothic?

At this point, it can be revealed that the title of this chapter is as multilayered as the works it describes and seeks to popularize and expound. That subtitle stems not from the plain-sense meaning of *almost* Gothic or *occasionally* Gothic, but instead a play on words. The Merrily Watkins series is Gothic *of* the borderline, namely those borderlines which exist

1. Between prosaic reality and actual (Gothic) reality as—sometimes—sensed.
2. Between Christendom/faith and post-Christendom/secularism.
3. Between traditional/ancient England and modern England.
4. Between England and Wales (two different—and diverging—cultures).

To expound, point one has already been dealt with above in identifying the series as Gothic. Borderline number two follows organically from it. That is to say, Merrily and her profession (profession of faith and profession as exorcist) bestride the borderline between tradition and modernity, where modernity can be taken as a belief in ever-upward progress (where progress equals bright, shiny secularism shedding light into all the dark places of existence, and the triumph of the rule of reason). There is in contemporary Britain, and Europe as a whole, a fervid secularizing drive, driven by law and activists, and, as noted above, Mer-

rily's involvement with exorcism is of itself an intrusion of the Gothic premodern into modernity, to the extent that even within the Anglican Church it must be disguised and sweetened by rebranding it as "deliverance." As Merrily herself sadly reflects, "I might have to operate on the basis that the Unseen permeates everything, but society functions well enough—if a little colourlessly—without it."[8]

This secularizing schism is part, though far from all, of the borderline between two Englands, new and old, the former increasingly dissociating itself from all that went before, except as "tourism heritage." To those not in sympathy with this minority-driven project-cum-process, English modernity seems a frivolous drape over something more substantial and more vital, the shape of which is still visible under the concealing folds. There are moments in the series when some characters express a sort of bewildered lament for this decrease of depth, as when Gomer Parry (traditional "deep England" personified) says of some possibly supernatural event,

> I don't know what to say about this kind of thing. . . . When I was a boy, people laughed. When my granny was a girl, nobody laughed. What's that? Barely a century. For hundreds of years, folk never questions there's more in an orchard, more in a cornfield. Few decades of computers and air-conditioned tractors, even the farmers thinks it's all balls. Sad, en't it? Computers and air-conditioned tractors.[9]

As Merrily herself remarks regarding the likelihood of a third party explaining away (as opposed to explaining) something uncanny, "Everything has a rational explanation, she'd say. Just that most people's idea of what's rational is severely limited."[10]

These two different Englands grind against each other like continental plates, with all the associated friction and generation of subterranean heat. Sometimes volcanoes erupt through. It is over that eruptive border that Mr. Rickman and Merrily Watkins work.

Finally, even if prosaically, there is the boundary between England and Wales, near where Merrily resides. This border is not often evident on the ground: the Dark Age delineating earthwork of Offa's Dyke survives only as a fragmented ancient monument. Certainly, outside of the fevered dreams of some Welsh nationalists (and even a few English ones), no border guards maintain it, and no passport is required to cross. Despite a partly autonomous Welsh Assembly sitting since 1998, it remains a border mostly of the mind and memory. Nevertheless, it is a border still, even in today's globalizing and homogenizing world, and Rickman's characters are actively aware of it. For instance, Ledwardine stalwart and Merrily's prime ally in the village, Gomer Parry, remarks of an undesirable that he appears from time to time from some unknown Welsh

fastness just like one of the Cymric bandits of old (five-centuries-ago old), venturing out to raid and wreak havoc before retreating back over the border. Clearly, though such memories may be ancient, they remain fresh and close to hand, to be applied to current experience. Englishness and Welshness are forces in Merrily's world, and, interestingly, one of Rickman's earlier novels dealt with unpleasant fates befalling English settlers moving into one of the remaining Welsh strongholds.[11]

From this inexorably follows the question, "Is the Merrily series 'Modern English Gothic'?" I affirm that the answer is yes, and furthermore that it is one of the finest—and still unfolding—examples of it.

The source for such confidence lies in the fact that Merrily's England and, as discussed, its more ancient (and Gothic and interesting) doppelgänger-cum-underlay, is simultaneously older and newer than what might be termed the classic Gothic genre. It is older because England is intrinsically very old, the oldest unified nation state in Europe, with roots reaching back before and into the dying Roman Empire, back even to a before-England of Druids, Stonehenge, and folk memory from the Ice Age. Therefore, any literary project intimately connecting with this version of England, which the Merrily series emphatically does, draws its literary energy from deep—and deeply Gothic—wells.

Simultaneously, Merrily's England is also brand new in the sense that England has recently changed from being merely mistaken shorthand for Great Britain into a self-aware cultural entity stirring from centuries-old sleep, buried under the political creation of the United Kingdom and the associated ruling-class-enforced amnesia. England—rightly termed the largest stateless nation in Europe—has, as a deliberate act of government policy, no political structures particular to itself, unlike Scotland and Wales. Officially, it is represented only by its football team and a gaggle of artificial divide-and-conquer regional as-semblies. That is now altering in ways both radical and rapid. I propose that Rickman's Merrily works are identifiably "English Gothic" rooted in both of these disparate Englands, and that, moreover, they are being written in *interest-ing times*. They are a timely surfing upon a wave of history when England and Englishness are reviving from the four-century coma of Britain and Britishness. In other words, twenty-first-century England contains fertile Gothic fields which Mr. Rickman knows well how to plow. The fine harvest that has come forth is Merrily Watkins.

The Significance of the Merrily Watkins Series

I once drew up a personal wish list for a hypothetical work of supernatural fic-tion and arrived at the following unreasonably tall order:

- An English setting, preferably countryside, preferably very English.
- A contemporary setting, but with deep links to a still vital past.
- Profound characterization. Cardboard cutouts, walking placards, and thinly disguised authorial wish fulfillment need not apply.
- The full continuum from unease to terror, expressed with economy in words that thrill even on rereading, but never through the cheap trick of gore, or even worse, gratuitous gore.
- The "glamour of evil" and "all its empty promises"—to borrow phrases from the church's baptismal vows.
- Deep issues like religion and ethics, via the medium of the story itself rather than as a bolt-on or pause in the action—in other words, a realization that all of these ghosties and supernatural shenanigans surely imply something beyond mere thrills.

I've now discovered that such writing and such a writer exists in my day, and herein I've sought, however imperfectly, to convey that the Merrily Watkins series covers all of these and many other bases. I further say that something profound is under creation (that subcreation spoken of above) therein. It may be that the best is yet to come.

Rickman has enriched the Gothic tradition as part of a living and evolving literary genre and culture, and not as a reenactment or pastiche which, like ivy around a tree, can only ultimately harm the host. He has, I suggest, invigorated and adorned the Gothic for our times, creating a corpus of work which crosses great divides. He does so to such effect that I hazard it will find recognition not only now but also beyond our time, when the harsh winnowing of multigenerational quality control has done its necessary worst. In my humble opinion, Merrily Watkins will become part of the canon. Or else there is no justice (which I concede is possible—and very Gothic).

For those of you yet to meet Merrily but now minded to do so, I can only say that the catchphrase of the renowned English comedian, Mr. Tommy Trinder, surges irresistibly to mind: "You lucky people!"[12]

Books in the Series

Volumes 1 through 7 have hardbacks from Macmillan UK and paperbacks from Macmillan UK/Pan Books. The paperback date follows the semicolon. Volumes 8 through 10 have hardbacks from Quercus Publishing, plus a special Quercus mass-media issue for the last volumes that came after the Quercus trade paperback. The paperback date follows the semicolon.

1. *The Wine of Angels* (1998; 1999)
2. *Midwinter of the Spirit* (1999; 1999/2000)
3. *A Crown of Lights* (2001; 2001)
4. *The Cure of Souls* (2001; 2002)
5. *The Lamp of the Wicked* (2003; 2003)
6. *The Prayer of the Night Shepherd* (2004; 2004)
7. *The Smile of a Ghost* (2005; 2006)
8. *The Remains of an Altar* (2006; 2006)
9. *The Fabric of Sin* (2007; TP 2008, MM 2009)
10. *To Dream of the Dead* (2008; TP 2008, MM 2009)

Notes

1. August Pugin, letter to a friend, written on the eve of his third wedding, 1848.

2. J. R. R. Tolkien, "On Fairy-Stories," in *Tree and Leaf* (London: Allen & Unwin, 1964), 60.

3. All readily Googleable. For the last named, also search under "Empire of the Petal Throne." Deep joy awaits.

4. A useful neologism and partner for "enlightening," for which I am indebted to Professor Geoffrey Hunt of the University of Surrey and New Buddha Way community.

5. Fr. Jeremy Davies, *Exorcism* (London: Catholic Truth Society, 2008).

6. Fr. Gabriele Amorth, *An Exorcist Tells His Story* (San Francisco: Ignatius Press, 1999) and *An Exorcist: More Stories* (San Francisco: Ignatius Press 2002).

7. Phil Rickman, *Midwinter of the Spirit* (London: Macmillan, 1999), 66 passim.

8. Phil Rickman, *The Cure of Souls* (London: Macmillan, 2001), 481.

9. Phil Rickman, *The Wine of Angels* (London: Macmillan, 1998), 488.

10. Rickman, *The Wine of Angels*, 354.

11. Phil Rickman, *Candlenight* (London: Duckworth, 1995).

12. Thomas Edward Trinder, CBE (1909–1989), one of the best-loved comedians in England from the late 1930s to the 1960s, also inventor of "Trinder's Impossibility," a paper currency trick.

CHAPTER 41

Narrative and Regeneration

THE MONSTERS OF TEMPLETON
BY LAUREN GROFF

Graham Joyce

The Gothic genre has always occupied that most interesting plot in the garden between literary fiction and popular narrative. Growing particularly well in shade and shadow, it is a genre that always enjoys a melodrama, and yet simultaneously flows toward the poetic. It is also a category of literature with a rich, promiscuous lineage, one that is highly fertile in its modern manifestations. If we can call this category Modern Gothic, it does suggest a reconfiguration of the genre in its attitude to narrative, and this reconfiguration is exemplified in Lauren Groff's haunting work *The Monsters of Templeton.*

The conceit—if that's what it is—of using a real place (Cooperstown, New York) so thinly veiled in its presentation as Templeton, with its antecedent writer James Fenimore Cooper and its Baseball Hall Of Fame so embedded in American folk and literary culture, is a smart one. Even before we are off, we have a ghost, a shadow. Cooper's *The Last of the Mohicans* in particular is a resonating and irresistible story of the violence and tragedy at the birth pangs of American history. That magnificent but deeply flawed novel (Mark Twain was no fan of Cooper's writing style) is still taught widely in American literature courses, and the evocation of its characters and its author instantly wires us into both American history and American literary history. *The Monsters of Templeton* is also a historical novel, and its title does that thing my English high school teacher told me that titles should do, which is to allude to more than one sense of its meaning.

The initial "monster" suggested by the title is introduced in the opening line of the novel, and a very fine crowd-pleaser that line is, too: "The day I returned to Templeton steeped in disgrace, the fifty-foot corpse of a monster surfaced in

Lake Glimmerglass."[1] The supernatural, or at least fantastical tenor of the novel is stated boldly. So is the most ancient sense of what a monster is—a giver of omens (from the word's Latin roots of *monstrum*, "a portent or omen," and *monere*, "to warn"). There is much more trouble and unease coming, and the worldwide coverage of this creature's death (dubbed "Glimmey") is only the first sign. Though the novel locks down into a primarily naturalistic mode of storytelling, the intention is thrilling in its declaration. Take it or leave it (and some readers prefer to leave it), here is a novel in which the magical or the transcendent will not be dismissed.

Monsters in lakes have their own antecedents (most notably on this British side of the Atlantic in the Loch Ness Monster). I have no idea if the Cooperstown lake has similar traditions, but if it doesn't, many neighboring lakes of great profundity will. It is the obscurity and the mystery of the depths that so excites the imagination that the lake itself becomes a symbol of many things: of the unconscious mind, of the unknown historical past, of the power of the irrational over the rational and the classical, and of the source of the imagination itself. In this case, Groff uses Cooper's word for the lake, "Glimmerglass," with its suggestion of *glimmer* (congruent with *glamour*, in the old sense of a spell or an enchantment), and *glass* in the antique sense of a mirror, and a magical one at that. The lake exhales its dark, fairy-tale presence throughout the novel.

Because this is after all a story about the land and the history of the people on the land, I expect that there may have been local people who, misunderstanding the intentions of a novelist, may not have relished what they read as exposing the dark secrets of a real (Cooper) family as if it were all established fact. But then again, there are many people who will reject the dirty, violent, and savage history of our British or American nations in a refusal to recognize where we have all come from. And secrets—secret shame, secret guilt, secret births, secret family dishonor—are of course the sine qua non of the Gothic novel.

The reason why *The Monsters of Templeton* is an important book is that it revivifies the Gothic novel. At a time when the genre has been strip-mined and asset plundered and subjected to the copying of the copying of weak copies, recycled, parodied, and repeated in film and print almost beyond credulity, here is a book that offers something new to the genre, a book that is unafraid to borrow from other genres in the forging of something fresh and yet committed to its root note.

And its root note is the fear that ancestral sins and vices might have the power to blight future generations. This staple of the classic Gothic novel is here offered in a much less literal sense than the traditional "curse" that brings harm to the descendents of a particular family. *The Monsters of Templeton* is a novel in which an investigation into hidden family history is really an inquiry into the soul of a nation. There is indeed vice, murder, poisoning, political skullduggery,

scandals brought on by a viciously antimiscegenation culture, and the massacre of indigenous peoples—lots to generate the sublime Gothic malaise, in other words. But the point is not that a literal curse has been triggered; the point is that modernity is perhaps cursed by its denial of a shared past. Willie's dilemma over whether or not to keep the fetus that is growing inside her is generated by an uneasiness about the past—recent and distant.

It doesn't help Willie that the putative father of the child she is carrying is a feckless professor (of archeology, of course!) offering little in the way of support. He would be an Englishman, too, a degenerated echo of the brooding masculine force, the Byronic hero gone to seed. (Hollywood directors and American authors have a fascinating tendency to repeatedly cast Brits as the convenient stage villain—psychopath, bully, cad, betrayer, feckless philanderer, alcoholic, flim-flam man, ruthless careerist, predator, and so on. This is a psychological habit of Hollywood surely worth exploring.)

The novel, along with the announcement of the presence of monsters—dead or otherwise—in the lake is matched by the announcement of an unplanned pregnancy. Willie Upton (born Wilhelmina Sunshine Upton), our protagonist, returns home from an interrupted affair with her professor, and perhaps it is this state of pregnancy that launches the inquiry into family history, a family history so foggy that even Willie's own father is an unknown. It could have been, both we and Willie are initially informed, any one of three men who took part in a hippy orgy at a commune in the wilder youth of Willie's mother, Vivienne. But this turns out to be a reckless fantasy, a lie devised to protect the identity of the unwitting father, who is really an unassuming local man. So begins the uncovering of a family history reaching right back to the establishment of fictional Templeton, a relentless search for illegitimate ancestors, an inquiry into a lineage that will ultimately reveal the identity of Willie's father. Look into the past to find the present, the author seems to be saying, connecting this new Gothic romance to those of Ann Radcliffe from two centuries ago.

The search for a family history is the engine that drives the story, allowing the author to sample the voices of characters from different eras and genders, both on the legitimate and illegitimate lines of descent. Sometimes these voices are offered up in the form of diary entries or in epistolary sections, but always in the context of the first-person narrator's search for history, and always against the glimmering backdrop of the lake and its now-decomposing fleshy monster.

The backdrop presence of the lake monster's corpse is what gives the book its truly original stamp. Not because it is a monster or a magical figure in the standard trope of fantastical fiction. Another novelist might have deployed its surfacing as a climactic or cumulative moment in the narrative near the end of the novel. Not so here, when the presence of the creature is introduced only to leave it to decay, almost but not quite allowing it to fade from sight. Unlike

many novels, Gothic or otherwise, in which the presence of the monster would have been deployed as a structural device, here it is a *signature* of the presence of the numinous or supernatural but, wonderfully, it never interferes with the progress or resolution of the narrative. Instead of acting as the point of magical possibility in the novel, it admits to the possibility of magic without ever defining or circumscribing it. The casual treatment of this creature—in terms of its place in the complex plot dance—is audacious and effective.

False (for *false*, read *fictional*) documentation is another fascinating motif of Gothic literature, and Lauren Groff anchors her genealogy with numerous letters, diaries, reports, and, most intriguingly in a work of fiction, old photographs and etchings, the status of which I am unsure about. *The Monsters of Templeton* is given a great graphic boost by ingenious illustrations that seem to authenticate the characters: old photographs from Ms. Groff's collection, as well as a computer-generated monster she created using Photoshop. This book's handsome, vaguely sinister family-tree visual design also heightens the impact of Templeton-style hospitality. The fictional documentation allows the novel to be simultaneously leavened *and* complicated, in that we are treated to a diversity of literary styles, a mimicking of antique voices and presentation. This process begins with Old Man Marmaduke in an extract from a putative 1797 document, *Tales from the American Wilderness*: "And as I walked, I believed myself to be an Adam setting foot in a new Eden, sinless and wild-eyed, my sinews still stiff with creation."[2] The fact that Marmaduke had blue eyes and red hair turns out to be diabolically helpful to Willie's investigation. Blue-eyed, redheaded babies had a way of turning up unexpectedly in Templeton, which makes Marmaduke a contender not only for multiple paternity but also for a place in this novel's title. Templeton turns out to have had more than its share of two-legged monsters once Willie begins putting together her evidence. In a family tree that branches out to include slaves, American Indians (James Fenimore Cooper's Chingachgook, the Mohican chief, and his son Uncas), and maybe even the pack of guys who go on shared morning runs and wave fondly at Willie, there are more than a few miscreants along the way. The Gothic must have its grotesques, and in this novel, they do counsel (the lawyer Chauncey Todd who addresses women's breasts), piss in place and sometimes touch themselves in front of girls (the town crazy, Piddle Smalley), or threaten to castrate (Dean Jan, the wife of Willie's lover). And grotesqueries are accentuated when the town feels stress. As the Running Buds observe sadly, "Secretly, in our deepest of our deep hearts, we think it is the monster's fault. As soon as it died, our lives spiraled down."[3] The secret sins naturally follow, but meanwhile these devices lend verisimilitude to the act of exploring the family tree as at the same time they fatten the ancestral history. The technique, as far as the Gothic romance is concerned, goes back to Horace Walpole's *The Castle of Otranto* (1764).[4]

Perhaps the most successful of these fictional documents that figure in Willie's research is a packet of letters exchanged between two seemingly genteel ladies. The impeccable manners, the stilted, formal language, and the circumlocution of the age give way to seething darkness. The letters are marked "Contents disturbing and painful," and the formality of the diction stands in neat counterpoint to depravities both implicit and explicit. There are in the exchanges references to sexual abuse, blackmail, brothel creeping, ghost hauntings, husband poisoning, and, thrillingly, remote fire-raising. But through it all one feels that the mid-nineteenth-century crinolines were maintained in good order throughout.

In a further clever stroke of unreliable documentation is the presentation of the changing family tree—changing, that is, as further discoveries are made in the investigation. Yes, the mystery is ultimately solved, or at least the formal mystery of paternity, but not before a sense of provisional heritage is established. It is a wise child, so the saying goes, who knows its father, and the provisional nature of the information available from pursuing the family tree shows us that the history of all families and of all nations can only ever be at least partly fictional, partly mythologized, partly convenient. The roots of the tree are dark and twisted, and its branches wave and threaten in the storm of the present.

Plot twists like these ancestral revelations are certainly intriguing enough to captivate readers. Some readers might reasonably complain, though, that the trouble with *The Monsters of Templeton* is that its complications seem nonstop. Does the town really need a monster *and* ghosts *and* eerie Temple family portraits? ("You rapscallion," Willie says endearingly to one of them, a painting of fleshy Marmaduke Temple circa 1800, "I think we know your little secret, my old friend.")[5] How many illegitimate pregnancies can one book follow? Even the monster turns out to have been ready to procreate—though at least no red hair or blue eyes are genetic factors. How many old Templeton boyfriends can Willie reactivate once she gets to town? How many subplots, like an out-of-town best friend suffering from lupus, can accumulate to no finality, out of thin air? The answer seems to grow out of the genre itself. The Gothic is the grand garden of despair, that semishade zone always hospitable to another distress, doubt, cry, or woe. It is the literature of excess. Its soil feeds on lies, and they are ever abundant. The author introduces yet another storytelling device, not Gothic at all, but drawn from the genre of detective fiction. A set of candidates for the role of Willie's father is introduced early in the form of the Running Buds. This cluster of six middle-aged joggers all offer themselves as potential fathers. We learn early in the novel that Willie's true father was not, after all, a West Coast hippy, nor was she conceived in a steamy commune. He was instead a local man who knows nothing about the fact that Willie is his daughter, and Vivienne seems to want to keep it that way—for as long as the duration of the novel, at any rate.

So the hares—the Running Buds—are set in motion in a delightfully literal sense. They have been running together for years, and Willie knows all of them. The reader is led to sense that any one of these men could be her father (though this possibility does seem to elude the otherwise highly intelligent Willie.) In classic detective fiction style, each of the Running Buds carries with him an aura of, or at least a hint of, circumstantial identification. It's a charming method of presenting a rather tired narrative device. All six suspects are kept jogging in the suburban loop ("Nobody leaves this room"), and within more or less equal prospect of being the father.

At large throughout the book is the creeping shadow of deviant sexuality, a shadow cast from the origins of the Gothic genre itself. Matthew Lewis in *The Monk* perhaps initiated this focus with a work that portrayed a corrupt monk having sex with an initiate, who happens to be a woman in disguise, who later appears to be his sister, and who of course may have been an incarnation of the devil all along. This convoluted trail of abnormal sexual relations then became a staple of Gothic fascination.

The Brontë sisters in particular cemented this fascination even if the social mores of the time demanded a more implicit depiction of abnormal sexual relations. Charlotte Brontë's *Jane Eyre* offered the Byronic form of Rochester who is punished for the libertine excesses of his youth by being chained (in marriage) to the violently insane Bertha. The not-so-veiled suggestion is that Bertha's madness occasionally expresses itself in outbursts of nymphomania. Her semi-incarceration becomes a notorious motif of repression, sexual and otherwise, in the influential feminist study of Victorian Gothic literature *The Madwoman in the Attic*.

Meanwhile, in Emily Brontë's *Wuthering Heights*, the establishment of sexual guilt as a pre-echo to the tumultuous drama is only slightly more hidden. Heathcliff, so the family tale told by a servant goes, was a "foundling" plucked from the streets of Liverpool by Mr. Earnshaw and brought home. Heathcliff grows up alongside Catherine in a passionate intensity of love in which they are almost like brother and sister and therefore are denied consummation by the incest taboo as well as by an inherent class difference. But the decision by Earnshaw to bring home the street urchin Heathcliff has to be questioned. It is a decision that first haunts and then governs the entire narrative. Are we to seriously believe that this was a random act of kindness? One that led only to tragedy and heartbreak? The streets of the industrial cities of that time were teeming with street urchins, and the hideous class system of the British had arrived at its most impervious and solidified condition. The induction into a middle-class family of a street orphan would have been an extraordinary act at that time. This extraordinary act—while not completely unthinkable—becomes explicable if Earnshaw's compassion is underscored by culpability. The spectral

suggestion that Heathcliff was Earnshaw's illegitimate child won't go away. What *is* unthinkable is that this never occurred to Emily Brontë. The implication is a structural ghost that twists and shapes the subsequent narrative. We are not dealing with pseudoincest at all, but incest in all its colors. A decision *not* to confirm the biological status of Heathcliff is the mark of true narrative genius and a stroke which would be implicitly understood by any novelist. Great novelists also operate on the principle of the happy negative, an understanding of the power of what is not told but is seeded in the clouds.

So a giant theme of Gothic fiction—that of deviant sexuality and dangerous progeny—is spun into modern form in *The Monsters of Templeton*. The family tree has a shadow line, and the report of miscegenation goes off like distant gunfire. It is interesting that this sexual deviancy—or rather its progeny (hideous or otherwise)—is demarked by the motif of red hair. This is the forensic clue offered in the lineage detective game, of course. The fact that old Marmaduke Temple at the apex of the family tree had blue eyes and red hair is helpful both to the reader and to Willie in her investigations. Red-haired babies have a habit of turning up in Templeton, by way of slaves, Native Americans, and even through the Running Buds. Willie is actually conceived after her mother, perched on a stepladder, drops a pigeon-poo splash of white paint on her biological father's red head.

The red-hair motif does of course have sinister antecedents and sexual associations beyond the Gothic. Traditionally the color accorded to those of the faerie realm and viewed with suspicion, red hair has often been associated with sexual intemperance (a belief satirized by Swift in *Gulliver's Travels* in the "Voyage to the Country of the Houyhnhnms," where "it is observed that the red-haired of both sexes are more libidinous and mischievous than the rest, whom yet they much exceed in strength and activity.")[6] In some traditions, red hair denotes unreliability, and often it is the mark of a witch. (More than one author writing about witchcraft has instinctively given his protagonist a head of flowing copper-colored hair.[7]) Mary Magdalene was formally depicted as a redhead by medieval and Renaissance painters. Whichever way you look at these prejudices and assumptions, red hair, because of its minority status, has always carried with it the suggested threat of a genetic outsider, and red hair in this book is a banner for original sin in the genealogical line. The presence of the red-haired gene reminds us of the venerean impulse, playfully suggesting how easy it is for human beings to step out of orthodox (or socially approved) behavior. In case we've forgotten, even Willie's lover, the feckless British professor with whom she has had an affair and by whom she appears to be pregnant, is also a redhead. By making him married *and* Willie's professor, the author violates a modern sexual taboo as well as an old one.

And thus it is the pregnancy (though it may turn out to be phantom) that triggers the narrative and the hunt for paternity, but which also gives birth to

the strangest and most original dynamic element of the novel: the supernatural presence of the sea monster in this otherwise naturalist drama. The sea monster itself is a bloated symbol of sexuality and reproduction. It lives a semisecret life in the great amniotic sac of the lake, occasionally signaling its presence, but mostly hiding, living, and breathing underwater—a great heartrending miracle of a beast, a universal pregnancy and an unknowable mystery, a Gothic secret, itself pregnant and never properly revealed until it is ready to move over for the next generation.

The fact that the monster in the lake is pregnant at the same time as Willie is not a coincidence. The monster's fetus when it emerges is almost human, with limbs and features like those of a human baby. The gestation period was twenty years, which roughly equates to a modern generation. Willie frequently addresses the "lump" in her belly, and the same word is used to describe the sightings of the monster. With Willie's pregnancy ultimately declared phantom, this other swelling in the amniotic lake is a poetic projection of the protagonist's search and the author's concerns; a restless subconscious is at large in the distorting mirror of the lake.

But to call the monster a mere symbol of sexuality would be to reduce its power in the novel. It is the author's courage and audacity to make this poetic projection a fleshy concern that makes it a new, and very modern, Gothic construct. The gestation of the fetus links the cycle of narrative to the cycle of procreation—transgressive or otherwise—and the book celebrates both, narrative and regeneration. The monster functions as a representation of both of these entrained forces. Almost like a thought bubble rising from the unconscious lake, the monster delivers itself and makes way for the next story.

Notes

1. Lauren Groff, *The Monsters of Templeton* (New York: Voice/Hyperion, 2008), 1.
2. Groff, *Monsters of Templeton*, 13.
3. Groff, *Monsters of Templeton*, 147.
4. *The Castle Of Otranto* is generally considered to be the first Gothic Romance. The first edition was published as a "recovered" medieval romance and brought from Italy by a fictitious translator, though a similar game had been played in 1508 by Montalvo in his chivalric romance *Amadis of Gaul*.
5. Groff, *Monsters of Templeton*, 304.
6. Jonathan Swift, *Gulliver's Travels*, part 5, "A Voyage to the Country of the Houyhnhnms" (1726; New York: Penguin English Library, 1967), chap. 8, 314.
7. Graham Joyce, *Dark Sister* (London: Headline, 1992). This wasn't an afterthought. The protagonist, Maggie, appeared in my imagination with a full head of chestnut curls before the writing was begun.

CHAPTER 42

Educating Kathy

CLONES AND OTHER CREATURES IN KAZUO ISHIGURO'S *NEVER LET ME GO*

Glennis Byron and Linda Ogston

> Give me the child, and I will mould you the man.
>
> —Jesuit maxim

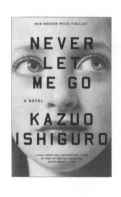

While early Gothic is absorbed by the past as a site of terror, and by the impingement of that past upon the present, contemporary Gothic frequently turns an uneasy eye toward the future. In *Never Let Me Go* (2005), Kazuo Ishiguro imagines a world in which disease is being conquered with the help of healthy new organs harvested from the bodies of human clones. The clones are fully exploited, their role being to become, in the society's euphemistic terms, "carers" for those who are "donating," and then "donors" themselves until, after up to four donations, they "complete." Kathy, herself a clone, narrates the story, which is set back in the late 1990s, soon after the actual cloning of Dolly the sheep in 1997. Cloning resurrects old anxieties about the mad scientist violating the natural order and unleashing potentially uncontrollable forces, and the Gothic prototype for this scientist is, of course, Mary Shelley's Victor Frankenstein. *Never Let Me Go* may look toward the future, but like much contemporary Gothic, it remains haunted by its own past, by the Gothic tradition from which it has emerged. This is most clearly demonstrated by the way the text appropriates and rewrites *Frankenstein* (1818).

In creating his being, Victor Frankenstein disturbs accepted notions of the human. This fundamental challenge to conceptualizations of the human is also levied by cloning. The clone disrupts the humanist idea of the self as a fixed, stable, and unique individual and raises questions about some vital life

principle linked to the concept of the immortal soul. With this in mind, critics have devoted endless pages to the question of whether the clones in *Never Let Me Go* are indeed human, an issue which is, however, something of a moot point. The question is directly raised only when the clones Kathy and Tommy visit their former guardians, believing that if they can prove themselves to be in love they will be granted a "deferral," a few years together before continuing on their set path as donors. As Miss Emily and Madame explain the idea behind Hailsham, the school in which the clones were raised, their nostalgic revival of liberal humanist ideas appears quaint, even risible, in the overall context of *Never Let Me Go*. Even if one accepts what they claim—and it is something we challenge—that their main concern was to prove the clones human and show that they had souls, it does not necessarily follow that this is the primary preoccupation of the text. Looking at this novel through the Gothic lens, *Never Let Me Go* rewrites *Frankenstein* at the same time that it insists on *difference* from its prototype. Ishiguro gradually turns the focus to other questions, concerns over education and indoctrination, and, more generally, our increasing entrapment by the systems in the contemporary world.

Unlike Frankenstein's creature, the clone is visually indistinguishable from the norm. While Kathy says little about interaction between clones and those she refers to as "normal" people, during the one incident described in any detail, the woman in the art gallery shows no sign that she recognizes them as different. They comfortably revert to the role of students, listening as they did at Hailsham when a guardian started to speak. Somewhat ironically, only those who profess to care *about* and *for* them, and more importantly those who know what they are, respond as though the children are different, monstrous. This is first seen when Kathy's friend Ruth puts forward a theory that Madame is afraid of them, a theory which the students test by choosing to "swarm out"[1] around her. Madame freezes, forcing herself to suppress a shudder, fearing their touch, and Kathy concludes, "Madame *was* afraid of us. But she was afraid of us in the same way someone might be afraid of spiders."[2] The first time you see yourself through the eyes of another, Kathy recalls, "it's a cold moment. It's like walking past a mirror you've walked past every day of your life, and suddenly it shows you something else, something troubling and strange."[3] Like Frankenstein's creature discovering his monstrous self in the pool, the clones are defined as Other through the eyes of the "normal." Retreating from this clear definition of their difference, the clones say no more of what happened, and while Kathy's reading of Madame's response is subsequently shown to be flawed, the incident nevertheless imposes the need for later reflection on, and redefinition of, the self.

Mirrors and reflections frequently show the clones what they are in the eyes of the world, although what is revealed is shied away from or misunderstood. The image of the mirror returns when Kathy, now her carer, visits Ruth. The

rooms at this recovery center are furnished with gleaming white tiles; it is like entering a hall of mirrors. Kathy reveals more than she realizes in her description. In this sterile environment, clones are reduced to their functions: "You don't exactly see yourself reflected back loads of times, but you almost think you do. When you lift an arm, or when someone sits up in bed, you can feel this pale, shadowy movement all around you in the tiles."[4] The moment reverberates later when Miss Emily describes how clones were initially "kept in the shadows," seen as "shadowy objects in test tubes," and, after the Morningdale scandal, relegated "back in the shadows where [they'd] been before."[5] The gleaming tiles, reflecting Kathy's self back to her, show only these shadows, only endless copies to be used.

"Who was I? What was I? Whence did I come? What was my destination?"[6] Frankenstein's abandoned creature asks as he begins to educate himself through books taken from the cottage by the hovel in which he finds refuge. The clones come close to vocalizing such questions only upon their movement from the protective world of Hailsham to the ruined farm called the Cottages—and the name may echo tellingly. Awaiting their next role as carers, the clones become fascinated with "possibles," with finding the people from whom they had been copied. The clone, a literal mirror image, reworks the Gothic doppelgänger that is often, as in the case of Frankenstein and his creature or Jekyll and Hyde, markedly different from, and set in opposition to, the original "self." The moment of encounter reveals another way in which the use of the doppelgänger motif differs from that of earlier Gothic fictions. Frankenstein responds with horror and fear at the first sight of his creature, and when they meet again on the summit of Montanvert, he is "troubled": "A mist came over my eyes," he records, "and I felt a faintness seize me."[7] Encountering one's double in *Never Let Me Go*, at least from the perspective of the clone, is not remotely haunting or disturbing, not a threat to the self, but a way of understanding the self. They believe that "when you saw the person you were copied from, you'd get *some* insight into who you were deep down, and maybe too, you'd see something of what your life held in store."[8] The dangers of looking too closely become clear during the search for Ruth's possible. Pushing beyond the safety of a limit imposed by a window, they become "too close, much closer than we'd ever really wanted."[9] They find only disappointment. In her subsequent outburst, Ruth expresses a growing sense of her own worthlessness: "We're not modelled from that sort. . . . We're modelled from *trash*. Junkies, prostitutes, winos. . . . If you want to look for possibles . . . look in rubbish bins."[10] They do indeed see what their lives hold in store: fantasies of the possible—deferrals, being allowed to work in a shop or office—will always be exposed as illusions.

The notion of the copy emerges throughout the text, intricately involved in their attempts at self-definition. The clones at Hailsham learn to value the original above all else, something evidenced most clearly at the Exchanges when

they prize books of poetry written by other students, poetry they could have borrowed to copy out any time they wanted. The veteran students copy their mannerisms from the television, and while this is in some sense a variation on Frankenstein's creature learning from the family in the cottage, there is an important distinction. When Ruth follows suit, Kathy confronts her: "It's not something worth copying. . . . It's not what people really do out there, in normal life, if that's what you were thinking."[11]

Kathy seeks to define herself in other ways. Significantly, it is immediately after Ruth's disappointment in her possible that Tommy and Kathy search the secondhand shops of Norfolk for the much-loved tape that Kathy has lost, the tape containing the song which shares the novel's title, "Never Let Me Go." When Kathy finds a copy, Tommy excitedly marvels, "Do you think it could be the same one? I mean, the *actual* one. The one you lost?" Kathy is skeptical: "There might be thousands of these knocking about."[12] She comes to question the authority of the original, valuing each one of her cassettes, whether original or not. For Kathy, the importance of copies lies elsewhere. As a carer, she collects desk lamps and has four in her bedsit, different colors but all the same design. These lamps, like the "little tribe" of balloons she sees held "securely twisted together and in a tight grip"[13] in a clown's fist, suggest that she defines herself not as an original but through her community. Her only fear is that one string may unravel, and a single balloon will sail off into the cloudy sky.

Kathy's narrative voice adds another layer to this attempt at self-definition through community. The narrative is presented solely through her eyes, and Kathy repeatedly reaches out to her readers as though we have shared her experiences: "I don't know how it was where you were," she wonders, or, "I don't know if you had 'collections.'"[14] In this way, *Never Let Me Go* follows a trend found in many recent Gothic narratives: the monster becomes the site of sympathetic reader identification. While Shelley's *Frankenstein* initiated this shift in sympathies by giving the creature a voice, his narrative nevertheless remained contained within that of his creator. Now the creature's voice is all we have. As the creature becomes the site of identification, it becomes ultimately irrelevant whether the clones are fully human or not, and in contrast to their creators, they are certainly fully humane. In *Never Let Me Go*, as in *Frankenstein*, society is the site of the monstrous. It is society's discomfort with the existence of the clones that for so long keeps them in the shadows. It is society's determination to believe the clones are not human that allows them to be "reared in deplorable conditions."[15] Miss Emily's explanation for how these circumstances come about is revealing:

> Suddenly there were all these possibilities laid before us, all these
> ways to cure so many previous incurable conditions. This was what

the world noticed most, wanted the most. And for a long time, people preferred to believe these organs appeared from nowhere, or at most that they grew in a kind of vacuum. Yes, there *were* arguments. But by the time people became concerned about . . . about *students*, by the time they came to consider just how you were reared, whether you should have been brought into existence at all, well by then it was too late. There was no way to reverse the process. How can you ask a world that has come to regard cancer as curable, how can you ask such a world to put away that cure, to go back to the dark old days?[16]

Utilitarianism, the greatest good for the greatest number, emerges here in horrific form. As Miss Emily explains it, the system takes over: a "process" is put in motion, and for normal society to exploit the possible, all possibility for the clone must be shut down.

The scene in which Tommy and Kathy confront their creators is central, not because of the questions it raises about the human, but because, after focusing so long on the personalities of the controlled, the narrative turns to reveal the nature of the controllers. Miss Emily's campaign was not to save the students, or even to extend their lives, but simply to improve the conditions in which they were reared. The experiment, attempting to prove to "cabinet ministers, bishops, all sorts of famous people"[17] that clones had souls, appears of far more importance than the clones themselves. One of Kathy's enduring memories is of Miss Emily apparently acting "potty," pacing an empty classroom, "pointing and directing remarks to an invisible audience."[18] While Kathy assumes she addresses an imaginary student, in retrospect it seems likely she is practicing with a more elevated audience in mind. She expresses pride in her achievements, saying, "I think what we achieved merits some respect." She even goes so far as to look to the students for gratitude: "It might look as though you were simply pawns in a game. . . . But think of it. You were lucky pawns."[19] Throughout their visit, Miss Emily appears primarily concerned with the fate of her furniture, the beautiful bedside cabinet she has possessed since Hailsham. Beneath the patina of her liberal humanism lies a tough and uncompromising message: "Your life must now run the course that's been set for it."[20] When Miss Emily, now in a wheelchair, explains, "I'm hoping this contraption isn't a permanent fixture,"[21] there is even the suggestion that she hopes to benefit from the system, that she is waiting for a donation.

If Miss Emily appears remorseless, Madame shows some understanding: "All they feel now is disappointment, because we haven't given them everything possible."[22] It is Madame who expresses some responsibility as she exclaims, with tears in her eyes, "Poor creatures. What did we do to you? With all our schemes and plans?"[23] However, her continual reference to them as creatures, with all of the word's Frankensteinian echoes, indicates a need to distance herself from both

them and her remorse, from her sense of responsibility, much as she distanced herself at Hailsham. What Kathy interpreted as revulsion, what made them feel like spiders, is now revealed to be more complex. Madame, shuddering, fearing their touch, physically evinces something much deeper: her perception that what was done to the Hailsham clones was ethically wrong. This is also suggested through Kathy's earlier misinterpretation of Madame's sobbing as the woman watches her dance. It was not the predicament of an individual clone that Madame mourned, but the loss of a way of life, the replacement of an "old kind world" with one "harsh and cruel."[24] Such nostalgia is nevertheless both suspect and ultimately futile. For all their apparent liberal thinking, both Miss Emily and Madame are products of the system.

The real benefits of the Hailsham educational experiment become clear when put in the context of *Frankenstein*; for all the talk of souls, what they do is manipulate personalities. The students are provided with at least some form of the nurturing, education, and companionship that Frankenstein's creature is denied. But while he rages against his fate, they generally remain unnervingly passive and accepting. At Hailsham, one of their favorite films is *The Great Escape*, and they repeatedly replay the scene in which the American sails over the barbed-wire fence on his motorbike. The prisoners of Hailsham, however, show little sign of rebellion themselves. The education they receive ultimately functions only as a systematic and effective way of making them malleable. Even more disturbingly, as Ishiguro himself notes in an interview, "Far from feeling they should rebel or run away, they feel a certain sense of duty to do these things well."[25] Hailsham, the site of the experiment, is little more than another test tube. The text provides merely a glimpse of the horrors that these "lucky pawns" were spared, but when the children play at pretending to touch electrified fences, Miss Lucy's reaction is telling. As she watches, a "ghostly expression" comes over her face, and then, so softly that only Kathy hears, she remarks, "It's just as well the fences at Hailsham aren't electrified. You get terrible accidents sometimes."[26] Elsewhere, clones may throw themselves upon electric fences in desperate attempts at escape, but there is no need for such measures here; it is the educational experiment itself that controls them. The system is a success: no waste at Hailsham.

Hailsham House, as an architectural structure, updates an old Gothic trope. Like the castles of eighteenth-century Gothic romances, this isolated house can, depending on perception, appear as the secure domestic sphere or as the terrifying site of incarceration. What initially appears as a caring boarding school where kindly guardians nurture their charges gradually comes to seem like something quite different: an institution run by guards, a place where clones are closely monitored and lulled into acceptance of the unthinkable. From the students' point of view, however, Hailsham is a place of protection; it is their home and

school and all they know. Their lessons nevertheless seem something of a farce. Geography lessons rely on picture calendars and are limited to learning about the different counties of England that they will someday travel through as carers. They will never have the opportunity to travel further, so there is no need for knowledge about the wider world. While there are practical reasons for limiting their knowledge, there is also the sense that the guardians are carefully controlling information so as not to suggest possibilities beyond the prescribed limits of their lives.

Their real education lies in the way they are "told and not told,"[27] protected from full knowledge, enabling them to distance themselves from the reality of their life to come. Unwilling to test the precarious foundations of their fantasy world, the students erect mental fences to reinforce the literal fences that surround the property. Repeatedly, their discussions falter at the boundary of "territory we weren't ready for yet," "dodgy territory," "territory we didn't want to enter."[28] When Moira challenges Ruth's story about the plot to kidnap Miss Geraldine, Kathy rejects the alliance Moira seeks through this challenge and instead reaffirms Ruth's imaginings. "What it was," she speculates later, "is that Moira was suggesting she and I cross some line together, and I wasn't prepared for that yet. I think I sensed how beyond that line, there was something darker and I didn't want that. Not for me, not for any of us."[29] It is hardly surprising that so little is revealed about the process of making clones and harvesting organs—just which four organs are taken, and which one goes last—or why the clones cannot have children. We have only Kathy's thoughts, and to speak of such things would be to cross the line into that darker, disturbing territory. If the personalities of the clones sometimes appear odd, it is because they are so well indoctrinated that they remain forever in a malleable state of arrested development.

While at Hailsham, the students' unformulated fears are embodied within the woods behind the house. The stories that circulate suggest anxiety about what awaits them in the outside world. Rumors spread about a boy who ran beyond the boundaries and was found tied to a tree with his hands and feet chopped off: their future fates as donors are translated into more acceptable tales of terror. Another story concerns the ghost of a girl who haunts the woods. Having climbed over the fence "just to see what it was like outside," she is not allowed back in and wanders the woods, gazing over Hailsham, "pining to be let back in."[30] Echoes of another Gothic text, *Wuthering Heights*, resonate here, with the ghost of Cathy wandering the moors, crying and pleading to be let back into the Heights.[31] The echoes of *Wuthering Heights* may extend even further. Both female protagonists spend their lives yearning for a past world: as Cathy mourns the Heights, so Kathy mourns Hailsham, and her early years "tend to blur into each other as a kind of golden time,"[32] a world from which she is forever

banished and which will haunt her until the end. Once the students leave Hailsham, they can never return. For all the years she spent there, Kathy has no idea where Hailsham is located and can never find it again. Hailsham is unmapped territory, uncharted space. Kathy's golden world never did exist as an actual place; it is, rather, the locus of her desire, and the desire of those less fortunate clones who wish to replace their grim memories with her own.

Despite the echoes of *Wuthering Heights*, Ishiguro's Kathy is different from Brontë's Cathy in striking ways: certainly, she is no rebel. Tommy, on the other hand, potentially is. As a child, he dreams of fighting Roman soldiers, suggesting resistance to authority, and it is this that draws Miss Lucy to him, the guardian dissatisfied with a system filled with lies and deception. "If you're to have decent lives, you have to know who you are and what lies ahead of you," she tells the students, but she can say no more; nevertheless, she encourages Tommy to question: "There are all kinds of things you don't understand. . . . Perhaps one day, you'll try and find out. They won't make it easy for you, but if you want to, really want to, you might find out."[33] After she is dismissed from Hailsham, her subversive voice silenced, Tommy has no further encouragement.

Tommy's childhood tantrums, however, as Kathy later speculates, indicate that "at some level [he] always *knew*."[34] Seeing him "raving, flinging his limbs about, at the sky, at the wind, at the nearest fence post," one student suggests he is "rehearsing his Shakespeare."[35] The comment may be said in jest, but the analogy with King Lear raging in the storm—"is man no more than this?"[36]—is apt. Knowledge is also implicit in his densely detailed animal drawings. Kathy's initial impression is that it was like when "you took the back off a radio set: tiny canals, weaving tendons, miniature screws and wheels."[37] It is only on closer inspection that she becomes "genuinely drawn to these fantastical creatures" and recognizes something "sweet, even vulnerable about each of them."[38] These complicated drawings reveal some repressed awareness that, in the eyes of the "normal" people, they are nothing more than components.

Furthermore, Tommy's studious *avoidance* of the body, the flesh, its replacement by mechanical parts, suggests some deep-seated rejection of his fate, or at the least a refusal to confront directly what he knows. One of the most striking features of recent Gothic has been a return to the body, to the horrors of the body, but for the most part, *Never Let Me Go* demonstrates a quite extraordinary avoidance of the body. The clones are known only through their personalities; Kathy gives no sense of what they look like. Apart from the sexual intimacies of the older students, they rarely touch each other; little pats on the shoulder are as far as they like to go. There is the sense of an anaesthetized horror here, a Gothic drained of its corporeal horror. The closest the clones come to an open acknowledgement of the fate of their bodies is during their last years at Hailsham, when, marking a stage in their development and acceptance, at mealtimes they play

at unzipping "bits of themselves"[39] and piling them on another student's plate. It is a way of holding off horror through outrageous—or outraged—laughter. In their disengagement from the idea of themselves as no more than sources of organs, they disengage from the bodies that will be harvested.

It is only after Tommy and Kathy face their creators that the futility of their lives is fully realized. They have in a sense already had the only deferral possible. Playing God, like Victor Frankenstein, the guardians brought them out of the shadows and gave them a semblance of normal lives while molding them into malleable beings; Miss Emily admits that "in many ways we *fooled* you," but justifies this: "We gave you your childhoods."[40] For Tommy this is no consolation: "I think Miss Lucy was right," he tells Kathy, "not Miss Emily."[41] His subsequent outburst takes us back once more to *Frankenstein*. Tommy disappears, and Kathy, hearing his screaming, follows him into a muddy field: "The moon wasn't quite full, but it was bright enough, and I could make out . . . Tommy's figure, raging, shouting, flinging his fists and kicking out. . . . I caught a glimpse of his face in the moonlight, caked in mud and distorted with fury."[42] As in *Frankenstein*, where the glimpse of the Other is usually facilitated through moonlight (Victor's dream, the destruction of the female, the death of Elizabeth[43]), here there is a sense of all he has learned to repress emerging in monstrous, violent form. Caked in mud, raging against his fate, against being "fooled," brought out of the shadows, Tommy truly becomes Frankenstein's creature:

> Did I request thee, Maker, from my clay
> To mould Me man? Did I solicit thee
> From darkness to promote me?[44]

Both he and Kathy nevertheless now recognize there is nothing to be done: "I reached for his flailing arms and held on tight."[45]

All that remains after this is fear: fear that is most clearly vocalized as the body resurges and the Gothic trope of premature burial is given chilling new form. Awaiting his fourth donation, Tommy crosses the line into darker territory when he confesses the ultimate fear of all donors, that, after technically completing, "you're still conscious in some sort of way: how then you find there are still more donations . . . how there's nothing to do except watch your remaining donations until they switch you off."[46] For Kathy, this is "horror movie stuff"; she cannot cross that line with him, and once she dismisses these fears as "rubbish," they "both shrank back from the whole territory."[47] Restrained and subdued, Tommy is resigned to both death and their separation. In a romantic image of doomed love, he sees them as two people in a river, "trying to hold onto each other, holding on as hard as they can," but "the current's too strong. . . . They've

got to let go," and Tommy can only repeat with the typical understatement of the clones, "It's a shame, Kath. . . . It's a shame."[48]

The lack of all possibility in their lives is most poignantly shown in a richly suggestive scene when Kathy takes Ruth and Tommy to see a boat stranded in the marshes. Barbed wire once again imposes limitation, and Ruth, frail from her donation, expresses fear. Kathy is reassuring: "We can go under it. We just have to hold it for each other," and "with us there for support," Kathy remembers, "she seemed to lose her fear of the fence."[49] As the group comes together to overcome the obstacle, the possibility of conquering fears, of crossing boundaries, seems within grasp: never let me go. There is a wood, but they move through it together, and in front of them lies open marshland as far as they can see; the pale sky looks vast, a world of endless possibility. Then, before them is the boat: beautiful, but with its cracking paint and crumbling timbers suggesting the impossibility of escape. Limitation immediately imposes itself again as they enter a landscape beyond their control; their feet sinking, the marsh prevents them from advancing further, and only dead tree trunks offer support. In the far distance they see "the vapour trail of a plane . . . climbing slowly into the sky."[50] This is freedom beyond their grasp, and the conversation turns to death, completion, acceptance. "I was pretty much ready," Ruth says of becoming a donor. "It felt right. After all, it's what we're *supposed* to be doing, isn't it?"[51] Even working together in that tightly bonded group for which Kathy yearns, this scene suggests that the current that works to separate them, the system itself, is too powerful, and the clones have been too well indoctrinated to fight it.

The book concludes when, soon after Tommy completes, Kathy allows herself one "indulgent thing"[52] and drives to Norfolk, that lost corner of England where, as children, they had imagined all lost things converged. The barbed-wire fence recurs, preventing her from stepping into the field. Along the fence, "all sorts of rubbish had caught and tangled."[53] Once he has served his purpose, Tommy, like all clones, is dispensable, and "looking at that strange rubbish," "thinking about the rubbish," Kathy mourns the loss of her lover:

> If I waited long enough, a tiny figure would appear on the horizon
> across the field, and gradually get larger until I'd see it was Tommy,
> and he'd wave, maybe even call. The fantasy never got beyond that—
> I didn't let it—and though the tears rolled down my face, I wasn't
> sobbing or out of control. I just waited for a bit, then turned back to
> the car, to drive off to wherever I was supposed to be.[54]

The flood of emotion never comes. Kathy does not allow herself to become "out of control" but instead quietly continues with what, echoing the resignation of Ruth, she is "supposed to be" doing. While Kathy comments early in the text that "carers aren't machines,"[55] ultimately the truth of this is not entirely uncon-

tested. Then again, to act like machines is precisely what they have been taught, and Kathy, stoic, accepting, doing her work well, keeping her donors calm, is a Hailsham success story. In appropriating and rewriting the early Gothic, Ishiguro offers a new Gothic tale for our times: he shows not so much our simple conformity to the system, but our absolute helplessness before it.

Notes

1. Kazuo Ishiguro, *Never Let Me Go* (London: Faber and Faber, 2006), 34.

2. Ishiguro, *Never Let Me Go*, 35.

3. Ishiguro, *Never Let Me Go*, 36.

4. Ishiguro, *Never Let Me Go*, 17.

5. Ishiguro, *Never Let Me Go*, 258, 256, 259. In the novel, James Morningdale, like Victor Frankenstein retreating to the Hebrides to create the female, goes to a remote part of Scotland and begins to experiment with clones superior to humans; the consequent public outcry leads to the shutting down of "privileged" institutions like Hailsham.

6. Mary Shelley, *Frankenstein*, ed. M. K. Joseph (Oxford, UK: Oxford University Press, 1980), 138.

7. Shelley, *Frankenstein*, 98.

8. Ishiguro, *Never Let Me Go*, 138.

9. Ishiguro, *Never Let Me Go*, 161.

10. Ishiguro, *Never Let Me Go*, 164.

11. Ishiguro, *Never Let Me Go*, 121.

12. Ishiguro, *Never Let Me Go*, 170.

13. Ishiguro, *Never Let Me Go*, 208–209.

14. Ishiguro, *Never Let Me Go*, 13, 38.

15. Ishiguro, *Never Let Me Go*, 255.

16. Ishiguro, *Never Let Me Go*, 257.

17. Ishiguro, *Never Let Me Go*, 256.

18. Ishiguro, *Never Let Me Go*, 43, 45.

19. Ishiguro, *Never Let Me Go*, 251, 261.

20. Ishiguro, *Never Let Me Go*, 261.

21. Ishiguro, *Never Let Me Go*, 251.

22. Ishiguro, *Never Let Me Go*, 260.

23. Ishiguro, *Never Let Me Go*, 249.

24. Ishiguro, *Never Let Me Go*, 267.

25. Kazuo Ishiguro, interview by Karen Grigsby Bates, National Public Radio, May 4, 2005, www.npr.org/templates/story/story.php?storyId=4629918 (accessed April 20, 2010).

26. Ishiguro, *Never Let Me Go*, 77.

27. Ishiguro, *Never Let Me Go*, 79.

28. Ishiguro, *Never Let Me Go*, 37, 40, 137.

29. Ishiguro, *Never Let Me Go*, 55.
30. Ishiguro, *Never Let Me Go*, 50.
31. Emily Brontë, *Wuthering Heights* (London: Penguin Popular Classic, 1994), 36.
32. Ishiguro, *Never Let Me Go*, 76.
33. Ishiguro, *Never Let Me Go*, 80, 106.
34. Ishiguro, *Never Let Me Go*, 270.
35. Ishiguro, *Never Let Me Go*, 10.
36. William Shakespeare, *The Arden Shakespeare: King Lear*, ed. K. Muir (London: Routledge, 1991) 3.4: 99.
37. Ishiguro, *Never Let Me Go*, 184–185.
38. Ishiguro, *Never Let Me Go*, 185.
39. Ishiguro, *Never Let Me Go*, 86.
40. Ishiguro, *Never Let Me Go*, 263.
41. Ishiguro, *Never Let Me Go*, 268.
42. Ishiguro, *Never Let Me Go*, 269.
43. Ishiguro, *Never Let Me Go*, 58, 166, 196.
44. Shelley, epigraph to *Frankenstein*, from *Paradise Lost*, 10: 743–745.
45. Ishiguro, *Never Let Me Go*, 269.
46. Ishiguro, *Never Let Me Go*, 274.
47. Ishiguro, *Never Let Me Go*, 274.
48. Ishiguro, *Never Let Me Go*, 277.
49. Ishiguro, *Never Let Me Go*, 218, 219.
50. Ishiguro, *Never Let Me Go*, 221.
51. Ishiguro, *Never Let Me Go*, 223.
52. Ishiguro, *Never Let Me Go*, 281.
53. Ishiguro, *Never Let Me Go*, 282.
54. Ishiguro, *Never Let Me Go*, 282.
55. Ishiguro, *Never Let Me Go*, 4.

CHAPTER 43

Cormac McCarthy's *No Country for Old Men*

WESTERN GOTHIC

Deborah Biancotti

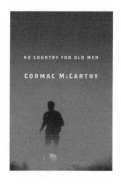

Welcome to *No Country for Old Men*. Welcome to a new style of Gothic, a modern tale of manners and morality, a battle between good and evil for the soul of one man. Welcome to mortal fear and immortal dread, the isolating effects of the western frontier, the harbingers and supernatural horror of a place populated by good old boys and the shadowy, anonymous face of drugs. Welcome to a world where Satan is more real than God.

In this 2005 publication, Cormac McCarthy becomes a kind of genre thief, taking tropes from the thriller, the road movie, the western, and—most notably—Gothic literature to build a tale that feels both modern and timeless. He uses Gothic structure in particular to examine modern anxieties: loss of faith, anonymous violence, angst, madness, and moral decline.

For *No Country for Old Men* is a Gothic story, a struggle for and with God, an examination of a humanity haunted by its past and condemned to the horrors of its future. It's an examination of class and inheritance, with the good ol' boys of Texas up against anonymous drug barons in high (and high-security) glass towers. It's a story about the mess and unholiness of modern human existence.

And it's a tale of unrepentant evil, the frightening but compelling bad guy who lives by a moral code that is unrecognizable and alien. The wanderer, the psychopath, Anton Chigurh, is a man who's supernaturally invincible. He's a man with no particular class loyalties, no particular background, no particular—and this is important—community.

Unlike previous Gothic wanderers in, say, *Frankenstein* or Maturin's *Melmoth the Wanderer*, however, Anton Chigurh is not wrestling internal demons. He's not a man condemned through self-pity or rage or remorse to keenly feel

and regret his isolation. He has none of these traits, and hardly anything human by which to recognize him. He is truly in a class all by himself. He is "the other."

In opposition to Chigurh's evil is Sheriff Ed Tom Bell, a local law enforcer and community-minded man who tends to his flock and comments that he has "*pretty much the same authority as God.*"[1] Bell will battle Chigurh for the body and soul of a third character, Llewellyn Moss, who is good and bad in about equal measures. But by the end of the book, Bell will admit he doesn't have the same belief he used to. He will find it easier to believe in Satan than God. And he will confess his terror of Chigurh, part ghost, part prophet, part man.

What McCarthy does with the story of Chigurh and Sheriff Bell is create something stylistically different from its parent genre. This isn't *exactly* the Gothic of damp castles and windswept isolation. And this isn't *exactly* Southern Gothic, either, with its grotesquerie and domestic horror. Yet it has elements of each, and it includes something new, something unique to its own subgenre. Contemporary Western Gothic is a new kind of story, a new kind of madness, a new kind of isolation and dread.

It's a story that begins in the sunlit desert of a western-style frontier, where drugs and crime are sweeping in from Mexico and from the southern cities of America. It moves to the crowded, populated cities where it doesn't pay to be working the hotel desk and it doesn't protect you to have an office high above ground. It's a thriller. It's a hunt. It's a road movie and a gangster tale, but it's also, at its core, undeniably Gothic.

And, crucially, it's a modern story. Set in the 1980s, it uses modern fears and ideas and a kind of timeless accent, a style of speech that belongs specifically to a place if not a time. In this novel, evil doesn't hide in coffins or dark corners. Evil carries a cattle gun and steals police cars and is, in modern parlance, a psychopath. Though the novel's antagonist, Anton Chigurh, lacks the brooding, sexually threatening "appeal" of earlier Gothic novels, he is, in part—at least by implication—supernatural. He is cold enough to be a machine (the new nightmare for a population now steeped in the mythology of *The Terminator*), he is the world's most unkillable man (according to one opponent), and he is wholly terrifying.

This new evil, McCarthy argues, is a product of its time, a waking nightmare that couldn't exist without narcotics and "Mammon." Moss wouldn't be pursued and Bell wouldn't be haunted like this at any other point in history. You can't go to war without God, Bell is told by a fellow "old man." But Bell does, or tries to. And by the closing chapter, he fails.

With the tension between the settled and nomadic, young and old, Anglo and Mexican, law abiders and lawbreakers, old ways and new ones, fear and hope, good and evil, and love and something colder than hate, this is a novel of unbearable horror and dread.

The Voice of Dread: Sheriff Ed Tom Bell

> I sent one boy to the gaschamber at Huntsville. One and
> only one. My arrest and my testimony.[2]
>
> —Sheriff Tom Bell

Bell is the mouthpiece of the novel. It's his testimony that starts and finishes the novel, and it's through his eyes that we come to see the world of McCarthy's terror. Bell's is the Gothic voice of despair: a narrator in mortal fear, compulsive and anxious. Bell is ashamed of his past and his present, and he's frightened as hell of his future. But just like in all good Gothic novels, the past cannot be left behind. Ghosts will exact their revenge. In Bell's case, the "coward" he was as a young man is the coward he'll find out he still is, and all his failed attempts at faith will not improve that.

Bell's is a voice that is slightly old fashioned but no less contemporary for that. His values are slightly old fashioned, too, and that's crucial to McCarthy's argument that the modern era is one of descent into evil. Bell's theory is that in modern times we've turned away from God toward Mammon. Money. It starts "when you begin to overlook bad manners."[3] Like so many Gothic novels before it, this social decline is the beginning of the descent into evil (witness Radcliffe's mannerless antagonists and the terror they wreak over their more graceful charges). Where God doesn't exist, the beast rises, and Bell himself seems to be having an easier time believing in Satan than God: "*He [Satan] explains a lot of things that otherwise don't have no explanation.*"[4]

Central to the book is this: the challenges of believing in God. Gothic novels will often examine our relationship to the divine (see the agonies of the protagonist in *The Monk*), and in this book we find not so much that God doesn't exist, but that he can't help. Fellow old man Uncle Ellis waited for God to enter his life. He didn't. "I dont blame him," says Uncle Ellis.[5]

As academic Fred Botting's critiques suggest, internal angst and anxiety are crucial to "the Gothic,"[6] making Bell the archetypal hero. Bell's terror reflects the wider concerns of society at large: senseless violence, a world that's become incomprehensible, a world without the comfort of God. It is Bell's mortal anxiety that makes him so recognizable. It's his failure that makes him human. And perhaps ironically, it's all this that makes him inadequate to save the world. Humanity hasn't made him stronger.

In Bell we have a man who talks to his dead daughter and pays homage to the corpse of a dead eagle. He attends to the needs of the missing (Moss) and the dead (community cemetery cleanings), and those unable to help themselves (the prisoners in his care). And he tracks Moss not out of vengeance but protectiveness. Moss is a member of Bell's flock.

He's a decent man, a common man, the everyman, with a strong respect for the living and the dead. He is the greatest example of humanity the book has. He is as close to God as we'll get in McCarthy's grim world. And yet, by his own admission, he's a man who's lost belief and suffers for it in the way of the Gothic hero. He is the best hope we have. And he fails us.

For the reader, this loss throws us from the real world back into the chaos of the world McCarthy has so artfully described. We at once relate to Bell regardless of our own religious beliefs because he's trying to do good. Bell cannot understand this world and this bad guy, and neither can we. He is not just the mouthpiece of the novel, but our mouthpiece. He is us: "I'm not the man of an older time they say I am. I wish I was. I'm a man of this time."[7]

That's the existentialist angst at the heart of this Gothic tale: what defines us as human ultimately makes it impossible for us to succeed in the modern world. In the end, concerns of the flesh undermine us. Bell's sensitivities in effect unman him. Ultimately, perhaps it is his own fears, his own superstitions, that make him run from a fight with Chigurh. It isn't death Bell fears. It's the loss of his immortal soul.

It's this greater-than-mortal fear that immobilizes him in the last instance. Bell resigns from the hunt and his job because he doesn't want to walk in front of "*those eyes*" again.[8] He's afraid of the world and what it has produced. More than anything, Bell wants to *understand*. And he can't.

Bell's uncle accuses him of doing what old men do: they try to set things right. And since this is "no country for old men," the implication is that he can't possibly set things right. This is not a place that will allow that. Old people, Bell observes, don't look so much confused as "crazy . . . like they just woke up,"[9] and you have to wonder how much of that comes from their failed attempts at rightness in a world gone wrong.

Of Chigurh, Bell says, "He's pretty much a ghost."[10] He's the prophet of doom, a harbinger of even worse tidings. But Chigurh is also all too real.

Living is harder than dying, Bell implies, and some things are worse than death. Anton Chigurh is one of those things.

The Wanderer: Anton Chigurh

> I thought I'd never seen a person like that and it got me to
> wonderin if maybe he was some new kind.[11]
>
> —Sheriff Tom Bell

A psychopathic killer with a dangerous, twisted philosophy, an assassin who imbues his actions with a kind of divine retribution, a monster incapable of pity, a man who sees himself as the hand of fate—meet Anton Chigurh.

Chigurh colors the entire book, even when he's "offscreen." It's his presence, his power, his very existence that determines the lives of every other key character. Moss and Carla Jean die because of him. Bell retires into a life of doubt and fear.

Just as Bell typifies the everyman, Chigurh is the everymonster. Part ghost: rising from nowhere, untrackable, mysterious. Part amoral beast: killing for reasons wholly his own and unrelated to any worldly code. He is evil not because he wants to cause pain. He is evil because he's indifferent to pain, even, it seems, his own, patching up his own gun wounds in a hotel bathroom. Chigurh is, by any rules we have access to, insane. Transgressive and particular, he is—according to most other characters—psychologically disturbed and disturbing.

Chigurh is a return to the horrific enemy of early-eighteenth century Gothic novels, rather than the sexually charismatic bad boy of more recent Gothic fantasy. This is an evil we don't want, or want to be near. This is not a reflection of our own inner demons. Chigurh is not even the id, the "otherness" inside ourselves (psychoanalysis is fond of the Gothic), because he is too alien. He does things we don't dream of. He is truly other than human.

Ultimately, we cannot come to understand "the other" in this book. It's important for McCarthy's depiction of evil that we don't understand or relate to Chigurh. The world is changing. This new era is no place for old men. Chigurh is an omen with a cattle gun. He embodies the oldest sense of what a monster is—a figure who dramatizes that the old order is falling to chaos, and that there are more of his ominous kind coming.

His lack of humanity is what makes him uncharismatic. He is asexual and isolated. He is sinful (greed and pride are two of his traits), and he exemplifies the Gothic liberation from transgression. He is not of the world, so he does not suffer the world's rules, not even the rules of the society from which he apparently comes (even his fellow drug runner doesn't understand him). And he perpetrates a kind of sublime violence that even mercenary Carson Wells can't accept. Gothic horror often obsesses over social and moral boundaries, and through Chigurh we examine where our boundaries lie on violence. His particular brand of tortuous, anonymous, cobalt-steel assault is frightening in its alienating matter-of-factness.

Whereas the famous Melmoth the Wanderer roamed the world looking for some way to be released from the Faustian bargain he'd made, Chigurh's wanderings allow him to make those bargains. By the toss of a coin, Chigurh can determine whether to release people of their lives.

Chigurh is silent for much of the book, and when he does speak, he talks an odd, individual, self-justifying philosophy that makes no particular rational sense. In this way, despite his veneer of intellectualism, he is the voice of the beast—the loner who pursues nothing but death, and is somehow immortal, immune to humanity's best efforts to capture or stop him. There is often no

reason for Chigurh's killings apart from the toss of a coin, which Chigurh chooses disingenuously to interpret not as chance but as fate, a nod from the divine for him to continue his work. In this killer's mind, doesn't he, too, have the same authority as God? But instead of grace, there is only vengeance.

He is power and impulse, a Nietzschean nightmare made flesh. He allows himself to be arrested because he wants to see if he can extricate himself "by an act of will."[12] "God is dead," you can hear Nietzsche cry. "We have killed him."

"If the rule you followed led you to this, of what use was the rule?" Chigurh asks one victim.[13] The same could be asked of Chigurh, of course—not that the answer would make any sense.

McCarthy gives us something new: his evil isn't hoary, trapped in the moldering cellar of a church or castle dungeon. His evil is modern, the cold self-serving rationality of the psychopath, not the unleashed, raging, manic beast. His evil is entirely at home in the hotel rooms and skyscrapers of the modern world. His evil is a product not of ancient times but of modern moral chaos.

His evil couldn't exist without the modern world. What McCarthy is really saying through Chigurh is this: God is irrelevant. Fate is everything.

Chigurh, whose name at one point is ironically heard as "Sugar," makes just as surprising a description of himself: "I live a simple life."[14] Is there anything simple, really, about his world of drugs and death? Basing his murders on the toss of a coin or a cold requirement to get someone out of his way, can he really claim that a simple life? And if this is a simple life, did any of us ever realize how awful it would be?

Even his motivation—as simple as his revenge appears to be at first—isn't simple. Anton Chigurh lives in a world of self-referential make-believe. Too bad it's our world.

Supernatural 1: The Machine in the Monster

We never see him eat, or drink. We watch him watch television, but even that he does like a machine, never changing the channel. It's not so much as though he's relaxing as like he's powering down, a machine with few needs. A monster for the post-*Terminator* era. A killing machine. A horror that was made, like Frankenstein's monster was made, by ill motives. A product of drugs and Mammon.

Reactive, not proactive, he moves forward as a machine in want of a program. He operates on his own bullet wounds. He decides on murder by the toss of a coin. He kills and blames his victims for choosing the wrong "rules." He excuses himself by pretending he is the hand of fate, the divine will to power. In a way, he reasons, the victims summoned him, and so it's their fault what happens next.

The common misperception about Chigurh is that because he reacts without passion, he is not a beast, that because he uses a self-justifying (and bizarre) rationalization for his actions, he is an intellectual. I don't think Chigurh would agree with this principle, and I don't think McCarthy would. Chigurh is monstrous not because of his emotions, his bestiality, his base humanity. He is a "goddamned psychopath," as bounty hunter Carson Wells aptly describes him, because of his *lack* of humanity.[15] He is a triggerman who seems driven more by curiosity than reward, as cold and random as a lethal disease. Even the Houston drug-cartel manager who hires Wells, as he stands behind his stainless steel and walnut desk without one picture or piece of paper, wonders aloud if they aren't up against an "invincible Mr. Chigurh."[16]

Lost in his own rationalizations, he demonstrates a kind of anti-intellectualism that aligns him less with humans and more with the hunters of the animal world. His reasons for the hunt, though, have nothing to do with food or need, and even less with honor. Chigurh himself might disagree, of course. When he returns the drug money to its "owner," Chigurh tells the unnamed man that he wants to be seen "as someone who is completely reliable and completely honest. Something like that."[17] The monster has been programmed with principles after all. It's only their application that is inexplicable.

The closest-to-human trait he has is narcissism. He is in love with his own mind. He lacks remorse or rage, he doesn't come from any identifiable community. Even his colleagues in the drug trade are against him. Carson Wells calls him an "outlaw," invoking western tropes.[18] Other labels—psychological and religious—are also used.

Chigurh is peerless, a one-of-a-kind monster. But unlike Frankenstein's monster, he feels no loneliness. Death, he says, "doesn't mean to me what it does to you."[19]

What, after all, *can* death mean to the hand of God? "Getting hurt changed me," he tells mercenary Wells, but it's hard to see how.[20] Perhaps by finally facing his human weakness, he realized he lacked godhead, but this is never spelled out.

Chigurh possesses a different morality, but it's not a morality that is ancient or old fashioned like Bell's. It is entirely new. He is repulsive but not unattractive. He is, according to Bell, "a true and living prophet of destruction."[21] Coming apparently from nowhere, Chigurh's last act in the novel is to disappear, to walk away from a car crash that should have killed him. He is invincible, supernatural. He has not only the presence but the luck, it must be argued, of the devil.

He's out there, says Bell. He is real. And the world is more frightening for that.

Supernatural 2: Portents, Harbingers, and the Claims of the Dead

As any student of the Gothic will tell you, harbingers should be avoided. They spell bad news. Take the limping, earless dog at the beginning of the book. Surely the only right response to that sight is to leave, to go home and lock the door. Portent number one, and we haven't even moved off the first page. But what Llewellyn Moss does instead is follow the dog's path backward into the mess of a drug deal gone wrong. Moss—perhaps intrigued, perhaps a man too at ease in his world, a man not used to failing—apparently takes no heed of this unsettling sight. If he'd had more of Bell's superstitious dread, he might still be alive by the end of the book.

Later that night, after waking into a light like a "winter moon" (a vapor lamp Moss uses because he's afraid, notably, of the dark), Moss returns to the desert. As the hunt begins and Moss flees for his life, he unsettles a hawk who takes flight ahead of him. The hawk—chief carnivore among birds with its cousin the eagle—will appear again and again in *No Country for Old Men* as a symbol of the hunter. Thematically this ties the greater world to the human story, as is often found in Gothic works. The hawk as hunter reflects the human predators in the book: Bell, chasing Chigurh, chasing Moss, chasing money.

Its next appearance will be when Sheriff Bell finds "a hawk dead in the road" and, acting out of respect for the hunter, moves its body out of the way of traffic.[22] Even later, as Chigurh pursues Moss south toward the Mexican border, he uses "some kind of large bird" for target practice.[23] We assume it's a hawk, and we read that moment for what it is: a demonstration of Chigurh's attitude, so at odds with the respect and moral integrity of Bell. But it's also a portent of Chigurh's impending failure, because he fails to hit the bird, and later he fails to kill Moss.

That bird will make another appearance as the namesake at Eagle Pass. It's here (in the Eagle Hotel, in fact) that Moss and Chigurh confront each other— the first and last time this will happen.

Then there are the ghosts. Or as Sheriff Bell accurately observed earlier, "the dead have more claims on you than what you might want to admit. . . . You get the feelin they just don't want to turn loose."[24] When Moss—bleeding profusely from the gun battle with Chigurh—crosses the border into Mexico, he haggles with a group of four teenagers to buy a coat. It's only as the boys walk away that he realizes there are, in fact, only three boys, not four. "That's all right," he tells himself, barely reacting to the curious tally.[25] This is similar reasoning to Bell's when he admits that he talks to his dead daughter and finds comfort in it. The supernatural exists, and Gothic novels will rely on it.

Death is not the end. And it's not the end for Moss, either. Rolling down the stairs after being fatally shot in the head, Moss raises his gun once more and kills the man who has shot him. It's a typical piece of McCarthy irony and Gothic surprise that it's not Chigurh who kills Moss. Like Bell, he shows up too late. And in a way, that's a kind of victory over Chigurh, the only victory we achieve.

Chigurh himself also transcends death, walking away from a car accident that kills two kids in the other car (ironically, again, the kids are high on drugs—McCarthy again invoking the downfall of the world) and leaves Chigurh himself with a bone jutting from his arm. It's hard to escape the conclusion that Chigurh has survived based on nothing other than his will—his compulsion—to live. This is an encounter with the weird that, as Bell confides, we may "not be equal to. . . . When you've said that it's real and not just in your head I'm not all that sure what it is you have said."[26]

And then we have Carla Jean, the damsel in distress who foresees her meeting with Moss, the love of her life. She must confront Chigurh alone (who tells her that this ending, too, was foreseen, though he's not so much prescient as crazy). Unlike Bell, who has a relationship with the past via the ghost of his daughter, the halfway psychic Carla Jean has a relationship with the tragic future.

Just as Chigurh mirrors Moss's transcendence (momentary though it was) over death, he mirrors Bell when he refutes Carla Jean's assertion that the dead have no claims. Chigurh is the other side of the coin, the other face of God—the other to all of us.

The book does have its believers. Carla Jean, Moss's young wife, shows the last vestiges of a world outside money and religious struggle, outside the life of greed and violence. Just as Bell finds comfort in a life outside the violence and chaos—just as he finds love in his wife Loretta—Carla Jean signifies her husband's best hope of redemption. She even convinces him to give back the dirty money. She's only hours too late. Chigurh has killed Wells and cut off Moss's one chance.

Carla Jean is the book's Gothic maiden stalked by Death. Upon her ultimate meeting with Chigurh, she does something no one else has managed: she invokes Chigurh's pity, and he gives her an out from his crazed intentions. He gives her the toss of a coin—not death by his homegrown principles, then, but death by fate. Death, however, it is, and Carla Jean gives up the struggle to live when Chigurh convinces her—evilly—that her husband wanted her dead. Without faith in her husband's love, Carla Jean's life is meaningless. "You shouldn't be more frightened to die because you think I'm a bad person," Chigurh tells her.[27] Chigurh's "revenge" against Carla Jean, if you can call it that, is simply the alien destroying the outsider. For Carla Jean, like Loretta Bell, has always been outside of masculine violence and the love of power.

Descent into Chaos: The World

> It starts when you begin to overlook bad manners. Anytime
> you quit hearin Sir and Mam the end is pretty much in
> sight.[28]

—Sheriff Tom Bell

In Gothic literature, there is often the clash of "classes," discrepancies in manners that lead to social anxiety and fear. The bestial wealthy man who eats with his hands versus the charming but broke young heroine, for example. In *No Country for Old Men*, classes don't so much reflect money as time—the old man Bell versus the new, unrecognizable creature of Chigurh, tradition versus modernity, benevolence versus vengeance.

From the descent of manners we have the descent into evil. The end of the world as we know it isn't a godly apocalypse but an ungodly moral wasteland. It's a world (a country, to invoke the book's title) that drives old people crazy, but it's clear McCarthy isn't saying the fault lies with the aged. As Bell visits with the "old men" of his community (his uncle, Moss's father), he finds a shared sense of loss: "All the time you spend tryin to get back what's been took from you there's more going out the door. After a while you just try and get a tourniquet on it."[29]

The world has made it easier to believe in Satan than God. Bell's afraid of what Chigurh represents. His theory is that psychopathy (such as Chigurh displays) is a modern malady, brought about by the contemporary turning away from God, from manners, and a turning toward Mammon. To Bell's mind, Chigurh is not a lunatic. He is too much part of a lunatic world: "I think if you were Satan and you were settin around tryin to think up somethin that would just bring the human race to its knees what you would probably come up with is narcotics. Maybe he did."[30]

Evil is sweeping the country on the same tide that's bringing drugs, violence, and dread, the same tide that brings Anton Chigurh the hunter. From murder to drugs to, fundamentally, the worship of money over the worship of God. "You cant go to war without God," says Moss's father. "I dont know what is goin to happen when the next one comes. I surely dont."[31]

Good and evil battle each other through the character of Moss. It's a struggle for Moss's soul by one powerful opponent (Chigurh) and one flailing defender (Bell). In fact, Bell and Chigurh are like two sides to a coin, two faces of God—the one, merciful and caring, tending to his flock, the other appropriating the godlike role of death and vengeance, slaying the guilty and the innocent.

As Moss makes off with the drug-running millions of dollars, sides are drawn. People try to take over the battleground of the American Southwest.

Will the law win? Will it be Chigurh, or the Mexicans, or the other unnamed drug dealers? Will it be the mercenary? Will money, drugs, or justice win? In the tradition of Gothic literature's battle for inheritance (Radcliffe's heroines are occasionally forced out of their homes for the sake of some less deserving but more powerful man, for example), fairness and equity are not always the winners.

But when the novel ends, it ends with a dream of fire, with Bell reunited with his dead father, carrying fire, the symbol of tradition assured. Bell, childless, can still feel part of the ancestry of the human race. The future may be a foreign land, but the past is reassuringly familiar. It's true, then, that as isolating as this modern world is, there is something supernatural going on around you. Something to ensure that you are never alone.

Conclusion

In a book set on the modern western frontier, which features a hunt on foot and by car, which takes us from Texas-Mexico borderland desert to Houston skyscraper, from poverty to ill-gotten (and lost) wealth, we find loss of faith versus crazed faith in oneself, a tale of mortal terror and immortal angst. Part western (outlaws and bounty hunters), part thriller (pursuit by a psychopath), part road movie, part Gothic morality tale, one thing unites the whole narrative: the pursuit across a modern American landscape. The questions the relentless chase raises—questions pertaining to both Moss's actions and the actions of the hit man from hell—are the central moral questions of good versus evil, modern anarchic life versus the anachronistic lifestyle of Sheriff Bell.

What, after all, is Moss's mistake? Is it taking drug money? Or is it returning with a bottle of water for a dying man? Most of us will be surprised by Moss's apparent indifference to the scene of carnage and the dying man he finds begging for *agua*. But most modern people won't struggle with the concept that Moss takes over $2 million in cash from the dead and missing drug dealers.

However, once he does that, almost everyone will agree he shouldn't return with the water. If the dying man is on his conscience, what Moss should probably do is call the local constabulary and stay the hell away. It's his return as much as his theft that marks him as a dead man. It's his morally righteous act, preceded by the morally dubious one, that launches him into the pitiless gaze of Chigurh.

Take the money and die—that's the moral of the book.

But in a world without justice, without comprehensible moral structure, ultimately the last word belongs to our struggling hero, Sheriff Ed Tom Bell, since he's spoken for us all the way through: "You know that gospel song? We'll understand it by and by? That takes a lot of faith."[32]

Notes

1. Cormac McCarthy, *No Country for Old Men* (New York: Knopf, 2005), 64.
2. McCarthy, *No Country for Old Men*, 1.
3. McCarthy, *No Country for Old Men*, 304.
4. McCarthy, *No Country for Old Men*, 218.
5. McCarthy, *No Country for Old Men*, 267.
6. Fred Botting, "Aftergothic: Consumption, Machines, and Black Holes," in *The Cambridge Companion to Gothic Fiction*, ed. Jerrold E. Hogle (Cambridge, UK: Cambridge University Press, 2007), 277–300.
7. McCarthy, *No Country for Old Men*, 279.
8. McCarthy, *No Country for Old Men*, 278.
9. McCarthy, *No Country for Old Men*, 304.
10. McCarthy, *No Country for Old Men*, 299.
11. McCarthy, *No Country for Old Men*, 1.
12. McCarthy, *No Country for Old Men*, 175.
13. McCarthy, *No Country for Old Men*, 13.
14. McCarthy, *No Country for Old Men*, 177.
15. McCarthy, *No Country for Old Men*, 178.
16. McCarthy, *No Country for Old Men*, 140.
17. McCarthy, *No Country for Old Men*, 252.
18. McCarthy, *No Country for Old Men*, 157.
19. McCarthy, *No Country for Old Men*, 177.
20. McCarthy, *No Country for Old Men*, 173.
21. McCarthy, *No Country for Old Men*, 4.
22. McCarthy, *No Country for Old Men*, 44.
23. McCarthy, *No Country for Old Men*, 98.
24. McCarthy, *No Country for Old Men*, 124.
25. McCarthy, *No Country for Old Men*, 117.
26. McCarthy, *No Country for Old Men*, 299.
27. McCarthy, *No Country for Old Men*, 257.
28. McCarthy, *No Country for Old Men*, 304.
29. McCarthy, *No Country for Old Men*, 267.
30. McCarthy, *No Country for Old Men*, 218.
31. McCarthy, *No Country for Old Men*, 295.
32. McCarthy, *No Country for Old Men*, 268.

CHAPTER 44

Jeffrey Ford's *The Portrait of Mrs. Charbuque*

A PICTURESQUE TERROR

Charles Tan

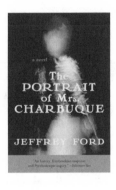

When I first read *The Portrait of Mrs. Charbuque*, Gothic wasn't the word that first came to mind. Jeffrey Ford's language was rich without being too elaborate, and his descriptions were detailed and evoked a sense of wonder. It featured none of the stereotypes of the Gothic genre: there were no haunted houses or castles, the atmosphere was neither dark nor foreboding, and there were no outright monsters, supernatural or otherwise. In fact, I could easily imagine the novel being classified under other genres such as magic realism, the *fantastique*, or even mystery. It wasn't until Danel Olson showed me the proposal for *21st Century Gothic* and mentioned *The Portrait of Mrs. Charbuque* that I considered the novel to be Gothic in nature. And yet, the longer I thought about it, the more that made sense. For example, the narrative was littered with tragic characters, and there were elements of horror and suspense sprinkled here and there. The question for me was whether there was enough material for it to warrant inclusion in this book.

After rereading the novel, this time with a keener eye on the Gothic elements, it shouldn't come as a surprise what my conclusion was. In that sense, *The Portrait of Mrs. Charbuque* shares a quality with some of the other novels included in *21st Century Gothic*: at first blush, they don't seem like classic Gothic novels, but delving deeper into them reveals elements that are neo-Gothic, those dark fascinations of our own period.

Rereading *The Portrait of Mrs. Charbuque* using this paradigm revealed layers I had not seen before. My epiphany is similar to that of the protagonist, Piero Piambo, a painter who survives on commissions. In the second chapter, he comes upon this realization with regard to his most recent work: "If this was

the first time, I doubted it would be the last, but now, with each future assault on her dignity, the charming, ageless beauty in my painting would forever bear witness to the increasing ugliness of her marriage and her life."[1]

There's an inherent contradiction in this statement, the way ageless beauty is combined with ugliness. The fact that it pops up so early in the book is also part of Ford's legerdemain. The entire book could be summed up by that particular passage, as the clash between these two opposites is a recurring theme, preparing readers for what is to come. And yet, when I initially encountered the book, I missed this particular fact. Or rather, I was focused more on the ageless beauty aspect and neglected the ugliness part. I wouldn't claim that the Gothic aspects were concealed, but rather my oversight is part of Ford's sleight of hand. His fusion of elements of the fantastic with romanticism and horror is so elegant that he produces a text that is both picturesque and terrifying. It is all too easy to fall in love with the prose and forget that *The Portrait of Mrs. Charbuque* is a frightening tale. This also mirrors the plight of Piambo, who as an artist is surrounded by so much beauty, and yet lurking behind each painting are tragedies and failures. The constant clash between the two—and the way we believe we are reading one kind of text when in fact the author is presenting us with something more—makes *The Portrait of Mrs. Charbuque* one of the most original and refreshing Gothic narratives of the past few decades.

The Gothic Elements

Before I talk about the characteristics that make *The Portrait of Mrs. Charbuque* unique, it is important to establish that this is indeed Gothic fiction.

One element is the setting. *The Portrait of Mrs. Charbuque* takes place in 1893 New York, and at first glance, Gothic isn't the image that comes to mind. It is a civilized locale that is not only heavily populated but seemingly at the height of modernity: aristocrats congregate for art exhibits, the police patrol the streets, and people have easy access to one another. There are no medieval buildings, baroque atmospheres, or isolated venues.

This is, however, only the surface. There is a certain Victorian quality to New York society presented in the novel, the way one's true emotions are repressed for the sake of appearing prim and proper. Take for example Piambo's painting in the first chapter. It is commissioned by a wealthy patron, supposedly to appease his wife for his adulterous transgressions. Readers never get to see his conflict, although we are led to suspect it. Piambo himself is not too thrilled at his patron's party although he never says this out loud. The turning point in the chapter is when Piambo says his farewell to the wife, Mrs. Reed. She responds, "in a voice no louder than the sound of a wet brush gliding across canvas, 'I hope

you die.'"[2] He seems to hear this in the same breath that she smiles and thanks him for the painting. What this bizarrely cold wish mixed with polite gratitude means is hard for readers to gauge at such an early moment in the novel: perhaps it is that the surface never equals reality here? Despite being surrounded by society, few people in the novel will have genuine communion with each other, as they lack the liberty to be themselves. Our artist seems to take his own meaning from this exchange: that he is one more agent that her resented husband has bought. For Piambo, "trained for so many years to see into the souls of those who sat for me,"[3] now detects a beast in the room. He looks at this model-wife now held by her husband and beholds an anemic, "mortally weak woman in the clutches of a vampire."[4] Then Piambo turns away and flees, stumbling down the stairs.

The New York where our twitchy artist lives has an intense sense of decadence. It isn't so much what is described as what isn't. Piambo, while a struggling painter, is surrounded by the life of the aristocracy, from parties to art exhibits to theater. The only time we see the plight of the common man is when the mysterious murders occur later in the story, or when Piambo begins his investigations of Mrs. Charbuque.

Another aspect of the setting is the flashbacks, which occur repeatedly throughout the book, especially when it comes to the character of Mrs. Charbuque. If Piambo's sense of isolation is metaphorical, Mrs. Charbuque's is literal. For example, as far as her childhood is concerned, she grew up in an isolated mountain, with her doting father and her apathetic mother as her only companions. Later on, even as she travels around the world and becomes part of society, she is still isolated, as all her interactions take place behind a screen. The only people with whom she has any intimate conversations are Watkin, her servant and representative, and Piambo.

It is only fitting that the climactic scene takes place outside of the city. By then, both Piambo and Mrs. Charbuque feel solipsistic, although the former is conscious of it, while the latter is presumably driven mad by it.

The second Gothic element that is prevalent in the book is the noble but tragic characters, reminiscent of classics such as *Frankenstein* and *Dr. Jekyll and Mr. Hyde*. Right from the outset, we have our hero Piambo, who, as an artist, is forced to survive on commissions. In the second chapter, with the revelation of his role in aiding Mr. Reed's psychological torture of his wife, his doubt is made manifest when he asks himself, "Piambo, what have you become?"[5] He compares himself to Albert Pinkham Ryder, another artist that he sensed had a "palpable innocence about him,"[6] and it is implied that Piambo has lost his own when it comes to art. Weighing on Piambo's mind is the legacy of his father, an artisan who created war machines: "I began life wanting to create something as beautiful as this, but all my time and energy, all my talent, has gone to waste. . . . I have

won battles and in the process lost my soul."[7] Compounding this is Piambo's crime of denying association with his mentor, M. Sabott, a fate that Piambo would later share, as well as infidelity to his lover, Samantha.

And then there is the enigma that is Mrs. Charbuque, who perpetually hides behind a screen. Whereas Mrs. Reed in the first chapter conceals her true feeling behind a smile, Mrs. Charbuque employs a more literal barrier. Her anonymity gives her a certain sense of power that other women of her period do not have. As Piambo observed, "She could have been anyone, the woman sitting next to me, the young girl passing outside on the street."[8] And yet, this same anonymity is what heightens Mrs. Charbuque's sense of isolation. Watkin describes her at the end: "She was already more at home behind the screen than in the everyday world. There, she had a sense of power and confidence, and her performances reinforced that feeling."[9] Even her name—Mrs. Charbuque—is false, as *Mrs.* implies companionship with the Mr., yet Mrs. Charbuque does not have even that. Throughout the story, we get a sense of Mrs. Charbuque's cruelty: the way she challenges artists to paint her portrait and in their failure breaks them psychologically, or the way she pries into Piambo's personal life in a way that goes beyond that of a mere patron. Finally, there is also the sense that Mrs. Charbuque is an unreliable voice. Readers are left wondering, is there really such a thing as a crystalogogist? Are Mrs. Charbuque's psychic powers real? What is it about her father and mother that she's not immediately revealing to Piambo? And then there are the contradictory accounts that continue to crop up as Piambo's investigation progresses.

Even the supporting characters are haunted. Piambo's faithful companion, Shenz, is in many ways one of Piambo's possible futures: an artist who has grown cynical, devoid of friends or lovers to anchor him, and has failed in Mrs. Charbuque's commission. On the other end is Mrs. Charbuque's lone servant, Watkin. What would cause such a man to follow Mrs. Charbuque so devoutly? And juxtapose that fact with one of his final statements in the novel: "I don't know, but now I owe it to the world to stop her. I can't let this go on."[10]

Finally, there is the conflict in the novel. As doomed as the characters seem at the outset, they are not wholly irredeemable. Piambo is an artist we'd label today as a "sellout," although he attempts to redeem himself by doing the impossible: painting the portrait of Mrs. Charbuque without ever seeing her. In the end, he is not only doing it for himself, but to represent the artists that have come before him and failed, whether it's Shenz or Sabott.

And then there are the murders, which seem peripheral in the beginning but come to the fore toward the end. The victims die gruesome deaths as they cry tears of blood. It is also worth noting that, save for a few exceptions, the victims are female, proxies for Mr. Charbuque's retribution against his wife, another sign of indulgence given to the male gender during that period. There is also the sup-

pression of the news by the police, a cover-up so as to not stir up the paranoia of the city. Still, one must wonder, is the peace of the city so fragile that such grisly murders would unravel it all? The police and the government seem to think so, yet by the story's end, the city still goes on, apathetic to such macabre crimes.

The Neo-Gothicness of
The Portrait of Mrs. Charbuque

Where *The Portrait of Mrs. Charbuque* truly shines is the way it innovates the Gothic movement, or the elements that make it unique for its time. The most obvious is the way the book stimulates the senses, most notably the reader's sense of sight. Paintings, after all, are a recurring element in the story, and if Ford could not describe or evoke the emotions instilled in the portraits he mentions, the book would have faltered. But this is not the case, as we are lost in the sensuousness of Ford's descriptions.

When Piambo first meets Watkin, the latter is pretending to be blind. Again, when Piambo first meet Mrs. Charbuque, the stipulation with regard to his commission is that he can never look at Mrs. Charbuque without her screen. There is an aversion to blindness, and this is presented in the book in several ways. Aside from the challenge faced by Piambo, there is the fact that the agent used to commit the murders initially targets the eyes, blinding the victim before the organism finally consumes the host. The act of being blindfolded is also Piambo's downfall, as this has become Mrs. Charbuque's signature ensemble and is used by Samantha to test Piambo's fidelity.

The success of our hero lies in the fact that he eventually resorts to his other senses. Nutmeg is a recurring element in the story, and this spice relies on scent. It is ultimately nutmeg that saves Piambo from the Tears of Carthage, the application of which leaves him temporarily blind. It is during this state that Piambo has an epiphany regarding Mrs. Charbuque's character.

Piambo also rises to the challenge of painting Mrs. Charbuque's portrait without ever glimpsing her. He accomplishes this by relying on his mind's eye, incorporating all the stories he's heard and experienced into the painting. In a way, the role of paintings here is the complete opposite of the Gothic novel *The Picture of Dorian Gray*. In Oscar Wilde's book, the painting is a symbol of Dorian Gray's debauchery. It is his true image, and very ugly. In the case of Mrs. Charbuque, however, her real persona is duplicitous—especially with her numerous aliases, from Luciere to the Sybil—and it is in the painting that we see her true beauty, the innocent woman that possibly still resides within her. It is for this reason that Mr. Charbuque hunts Piambo, because he uncovers that which could not be seen—something that all the other artists have failed to do.

Whereas Dorian Gray's demise is the destruction of his portrait, Mrs. Charbuque's salvation is the completion of hers, and while the ending is bittersweet, it is also fitting. Mrs. Charbuque finally finds her Gothic twin in the form of her painting: "But I tell you that the figure in my portrait and the woman in the coffin were one and the same. Yes, they were twins."[11] Mrs. Charbuque's redemption is also emphasized by the fact that the final scene takes place in a church, and Piambo uses her profile as a model for the characters most associated with creation, Adam and Eve.

Then again, not all the paintings in the novel are concerned with Mrs. Charbuque. The aristocracy are prominent early on in the book, and because of their wealth, they are given privileges. This is highlighted by Piambo's comment that portraits are the aristocracy's medium of choice as opposed to cheap cameras which even the commoners were able to use.

There is also Ryder's painting, *The Race Track* or *The Reverse*, which is Piambo's reminder of what he had lost. Whereas Piambo's paintings were beautiful, Ryder's was horrific, especially with its inclusion of Death himself. The appeal of the painting to Piambo is how it reveals humanity's condition: "That picture had truths to tell and was the opposite of the technically perfect, stylistically safe work of Sargent's that was so popular with the moneyed class."[12] On the other hand, John Singer Sargent's paintings tend to have a macabre element despite seeming gorgeous on the surface. Take for example one of his most famous works, the *Portrait of Madame X*, a life-sized portrait that was controversial for its time. While it bespoke sensuality and grace, it also had blackly Gothic, tensely erotic, and taboo elements. The woman-subject looks away from the painter though her torso projects toward him; the background is gloomy, her black gown is deeply recessed and one dress strap is fallen, her neck is strained, and the skin of her chest and long bare arms is an unnatural corpselike white (composed, Sargent confessed, of "lead white, vermillion, bone black, rose madder, and even viridian green"[13]). The subject, the American wife of a French banker who gained high-society interest for her illicit affairs, was one of great allure. She was a woman whom an American art student in Paris, Edward Simmons, "could not stop stalking . . . as one does a deer."[14] Sargent's fate, alone with this large painting, is similar to Piambo's toward the end of the novel, where he has Mrs. Charbuque's naked portrait as his only companion.

Another trend is the juxtaposition between the grotesque and beauty. In the middle of the book, we are led to believe that Mrs. Charbuque is some sort of Monkey Queen. This revelation, of course, confounds Piambo as it clashes with his image of a woman. And yet, for Mrs. Charbuque, he indulges this possibility. We can also go back to Mr. Reed, who is, in a certain way, the personification of Dorian Gray. He is a man Piambo detests, yet Piambo never publicly denounces him. On a remote level, there is the cover-up regarding the murders. The civility and sophistication of the city is preserved, even when horrible crimes are being

committed. It seems that if you dig beyond the surface, what appears to be beautiful is accompanied by horrible complications.

Mystery working in tandem with the fantastical is another element that is effective in *The Portrait of Mrs. Charbuque*. On one hand, you have elements that are too coincidental and appear supernatural. There are Mrs. Charbuque's accounts of her past: "the Twins" snowflake, her ability to foretell the future, and even her relationship with Mr. Charbuque seem ludicrous. Nevertheless, when the reader first encounters them, we take them at face value. On the other end is a tendency to debunk the myths that are presented. Watkin, for example, initially appears to be a skillful blind man, but it turns out he isn't blind at all but merely faking it. Mrs. Charbuque herself downplays her ability to portend the future by giving rational explanations. There is also the bizarre method of how the various victims die—crying tears of blood—which seems fantastical, yet Ford gives us a rational explanation by the end. The methodology of Piambo and Shenz for discovering Mrs. Charbuque's image is also very logical, as they employ the means that a detective would use. Curiously, even the most realistic explanations are accompanied by an element of surrealism. In order to break into Mrs. Charbuque's warehouse, for example, the thief that Shenz contacts is a man whose fingernails are in the shape of keys. While there is nothing that prevents this from occurring in real life, it is also a very unlikely possibility that borders on the mythical. Thus, the way Ford combines these two elements is part of his sleight of hand. As readers, we are not entirely sure which to believe: is this purely a fantastical story or a realistic one? What we end up with, however, is a fusion of the two that constantly leaves even the most astute reader guessing.

Finally, there is the concept of twins. This is a recurring theme that expresses itself in many ways, but always revolving around Mrs. Charbuque. First, there is Mrs. Charbuque's numerous aliases. How could a single woman have so many monikers? This raises the issue of multiple personas, and Mrs. Charbuque is indeed a different person depending on whom she is talking to: she is a seer when she is known as the Sybil, regal when she is Mrs. Charbuque, arguably the most vulnerable when she is Luciere, and mean and powerful when she is Mr. Charbuque.

Twins in literature have also been known to possess what seem to us like mystical qualities, whether it's sharing their own private language or telepathy. It is interesting that Ford uses Mrs. Charbuque's association with the Twins snowflake to explain the beginning of her portentous abilities. Yet the Twins also cause a rippling effect which creates complications in Mrs. Charbuque's life. Her knowledge of the "Wolf," for example, is what eventually causes a rift in her family. And her current prestige is attained through her success as the Sybil. But the Twins are not entirely bad luck. It is significant that at the end of the novel, Piambo picks up Mrs. Charbuque's locket (an old Gothic trope) from her corpse. And while, in the last paragraph, Piambo experiences a momentary

fear of Mrs. Charbuque, he is actually comforted by the implied appearance of Samantha.

Lastly, the concept of twins keys into the idea of paintings. In creating the latter, one arguably makes a clone of the person the artist is copying. Here, the mystical aspects of art come into play, as paintings in the novel are agents of truth: either they are used to lie to people—which is the case with Mrs. Reed's portrait—or they reveal what is hidden, whether this is Piambo's final portrait of Mrs. Charbuque or the work of Ryder. The dilemma for Mrs. Charbuque is that she feels alone and isolated, as if lacking a soulmate. Perhaps the appeal of twins to her is that she would have a partner that would stay true to her. Despite being accompanied by a man devoted to her—Watkin—she never sees this aspect of her life (a metaphorical blindness on her part, going back to one's reliance on the visual sense) and instead resorts to other means for creating the perfect double for herself. On one end of the spectrum is the persona she fabricates: Mr. Charbuque is everything she is not, complementing her existing traits, albeit in a darker direction. On the other end is the painting of herself. The beauty of the painting is that it is possibly eternal: "After all, a photograph yellowed and cracked within a generation or two, but an oil painting would carry its exalted subject intact into the distant future."[15] The trick, of course, is that the painting should capture Mrs. Charbuque's essence, hence her rigorous strictures on the various artists who have attempted to paint her portrait. If Mr. Charbuque is her darker side, then the painting would have been Mrs. Charbuque's positive aspect.

But what's great about *The Portrait of Mrs. Charbuque* is that Ford does not really favor any one of those two aspects. They go hand in hand, the horridness of Mr. Charbuque along with the beauty of Piambo's painting of Mrs. Charbuque. This duality, this yin and yang if you will, is at the heart of the novel. Piambo, for example, is both a failure (in the beginning of the book) and a savior (as he finishes the painting). Mrs. Charbuque is both his patron and his nemesis. His art requires much from him, yet Piambo needs to paint in order to live. Even New York, for all its decadence and debauchery, is still home for Piambo. The fate of Watkin is also most ironic: whereas he always stood by Mrs. Charbuque's side, it is by his hands that she meets her end. The lone character who is untouched by all of these events is Samantha, but at the novel's end, Ford gives us hope by implying her return to Piambo. In the same way that Piambo ultimately saves Mrs. Charbuque, here it is Samantha who saves Piambo, a reversal of the male role as savior.

Conclusion

What readers need to understand when reading *The Portrait of Mrs. Charbuque* is how two opposing elements are constantly at work and how it runs this fic-

tional world. This is stressed by the theme of the twins—not as identical copies of one another, but more like the relationship between Dr. Jekyll and Mr. Hyde, wherein one cannot exist without the other. The terms *picturesque* and *horror* might seem contradictory, but in the context of *The Portrait of Mrs. Charbuque*, it is the reconciliation between the two that makes it worthy of being one of the decade's essential Gothic novels.

Notes

1. Jeffrey Ford, *The Portrait of Mrs. Charbuque* (New York: William Morrow/Harper Collins, 2002), 8.
2. Ford, *The Portrait of Mrs. Charbuque*, 5.
3. Ford, *The Portrait of Mrs. Charbuque*, 5.
4. Ford, *The Portrait of Mrs. Charbuque*, 5.
5. Ford, *The Portrait of Mrs. Charbuque*, 8.
6. Ford, *The Portrait of Mrs. Charbuque*, 11.
7. Ford, *The Portrait of Mrs. Charbuque*, 19.
8. Ford, *The Portrait of Mrs. Charbuque*, 106.
9. Ford, *The Portrait of Mrs. Charbuque*, 299.
10. Ford, *The Portrait of Mrs. Charbuque*, 301.
11. Ford, *The Portrait of Mrs. Charbuque*, 306.
12. Ford, *The Portrait of Mrs. Charbuque*, 10.
13. Deborah Davis, *Strapless: John Singer Sargent and the Fall of Madame X* (New York: Tarcher/Penguin, 2003), 139.
14. Davis, *Strapless*, 59.
15. Ford, *The Portrait of Mrs. Charbuque*, 9.

CHAPTER 45

Gothic Maternity

THE PUMPKIN CHILD BY NANCY A. COLLINS

Karin Beeler

 Flannery O'Connor (1925–1964), an American writer of Southern Gothic fiction, made the observation that "anything that comes out of the South is going to be called 'grotesque' by the northern reader, unless it is grotesque, in which case it is going to be called realistic."[1] While many readers might hesitate to call Southern Gothic writing "realistic," there is still a certain coexistence of the grotesque with traditional social realities below the Mason-Dixon line. Social strata in the regions of the American South tend to be fixed, there is a high level of poverty, and crime is high despite the amount of funding that is channeled into law and order.[2] Some of these socioeconomic realities often serve as a backdrop for the literature of the American South. However, O'Connor's statement about the coexistence of the "realistic" and the "grotesque" also suggests the possibility for shifting perspectives and ironic twists that inform Gothic stories. The narrative of concealment and the partial uncovering of hidden truths characterize contemporary Gothic narratives, including Nancy A. Collins's unusual novella, *The Pumpkin Child*, set in the Mississippi Delta corner of her native Arkansas. Collins uses the concepts of the supernatural and a grotesque maternity to weave a tightly knit plot of irony and fate reminiscent of Greek tragedy while still creating the local ambience of the American South through language, landscape, and the agricultural motif of the pumpkin.

Collins is perhaps best known for her popular vampire novels, but one particular example of Gothic storytelling, *The Pumpkin Child*, proves just as captivating as her bloodsucking fiction. First published in Collins's *Knuckles and Tales* (2002, Cemetery Dance Publications) and then later in the collection *Exotic Gothic* (2007, Ash-Tree Press), *The Pumpkin Child* reads like a Greek tragedy set in Arkansas. The novella focuses on the character Hollis Railsback

who has just returned from active World War II military duty in the Pacific theater only to find out that his business and social rival, Virgil Bayliss, has secured the affections of his girlfriend and nearly put his father out of business. The narrative initially generates feelings of sympathy for Hollis who tries to reverse his fate by enlisting the aid of Granny Grimes, the local "witch" or "folk doctor." The connection of Collins's novella to Greek tragedy is not farfetched; like the ironies and the twisted truths which pervade the genre of a classical tragedy such as *Oedipus Rex*, the Gothic is rife with moments of darkness and light. However while there may be some element of anagnorisis, or recognition, for characters in *The Pumpkin Child*, the Gothic is as a rule a more ambiguous genre than most examples of classical tragedy, perhaps because of its grotesque and macabre elements that highlight a certain incongruity. The experience of full recognition for characters and for the reader of Collins's work remains elusive because of the ambiguous aspects of the narrative which tend to prevent the notion of an easily discernible truth at the very end of the tale.[3] In *The Pumpkin Child*, this incongruity is manifested in the multiple and sometimes eerie representations of maternity. *The Pumpkin Child* is a Gothic work that continues a Southern Gothic tradition of foregrounding desire and tragedy. Other writers of Southern Gothic, like Tennessee Williams and William Faulkner, have funneled the plots of Greek tragedy into their works in order to highlight a sense of doom and the taboo of forbidden love. This love can take the form of incestuous desire or desire for someone who is already bound to another. In Williams's play *Suddenly Last Summer* (1958), for example, the Oedipal sexual tension between mother and son are part of the dark drama, and in Faulkner's *Absalom, Absalom!* (1936) the timeless elements of tragedy enter Sutpen's narrative and heighten the novel's Southern Gothic style.[4] Like Oedipus's absent yet present mother, Jocasta, the feminine principle in *The Pumpkin Child* is both present and absent, manifesting itself in the paradoxical figure of Granny Grimes. She was "as much a local fixture as the river," and the rumor in the community was that many people consulted her about spells, yet Hollis "had never once laid eyes on the woman, as she refused to set foot in town."[5] Granny incorporates the ordinary and the supernatural; she is "a midwife, of sorts,"[6] yet she offers magic pills which facilitate the reversal or restoration of a romantic relationship between Hollis and Joslin ("this spell will swap out yore luck for another's"[7]). Community members, even the Baptist minister, often consult Granny Grimes; she is gifted and clever, but she is also dangerous, manipulative, and vindictive as she controls the fate of individuals in the community, determining whether their lives will have tragic or felicitous outcomes.

The grotesque figures prominently in *The Pumpkin Child* in both supernatural and more ordinary social contexts. The origin of the word *grotesque* may be traced back to the Italian word *grotte* for caves or underground chambers,[8]

and it therefore suggests that which is hidden. At the same time, the term has been linked to extravagance and excess[9]: the grotesque denoted the "freakish and unnatural . . . aberrations from the desirable norms of harmony, balance and proportion,"[10] norms which were valued during the "Age of Reason" by neoclassicists. In grotesque painting, for example, the fantastic appears to dominate through the representation of demons, perverted creatures, and images of death, yet the grotesque may be asserted in tandem with the ordinary and with social realism, as the work of French writer Rabelais so aptly demonstrates. In *Gargantua and Pantagruel*, for example, the realm of the body, including bodily functions and sexuality, contributes to the corporeal subversion of the sacred. Flannery O'Connor's link between the malformed and the realistic in Southern Gothic writing, and the presence of these seemingly incongruous elements in *The Pumpkin Child*, are not entirely incompatible with these earlier literary representations, since Collins's work also highlights the relationship between the outlandish or preternatural elements (spells and miraculous events) and realistic experiences (envy, pregnancy, and desire).

As a pivotal character in Collins's novella, Granny Grimes is identified with both the fantastic and the realistic. She has a role as a local midwife, but she also appears to be able to exceed the normal length of a mortal life: "some things grow old, but they never die."[11] As an archetype of the crone, the hag as witch (in the most negative tradition, the one who could turn humans into pumpkins), Granny embodies a certain Gothic incongruity. She is a fixture in the community, yet she is not bound by the ordinary laws of time and space since she appears to have been around forever. It is also interesting that her mysterious character is linked to a certain ambiguity surrounding her racial origins: it is "impossible to tell if she was Black, White, or Indian, or a mix of all three."[12] As Justin D. Edwards argues, the Gothicization of racial ambiguity is already evident in nineteenth-century Gothic literature.[13] However, the enigma surrounding Granny's origins also suggests an affiliation with another story about unclear origins, the drama of *Oedipus Rex*, connecting classical tragedy to Collins's Southern Gothic narrative.

Yet even as *The Pumpkin Child* resonates with the supernatural elements of myth or the taboos characteristic of ancient tragedies, it does so through the specificity of the agricultural and social landscapes of the American South, as well as the historical moments of the 1940s and 1950s. The tone of the novella develops with reference to the Second World War and to changes in the community of Seven Devils, Arkansas. During the war, Hollis Railsback "got close to dyin'."[14] The Second World War thus serves as a reminder of how tenuous the balance between life and death, fortune and misfortune, can be. Social conditions in Hollis's own community have also changed, dividing the town into winners and losers. Ironically, even though Hollis has been spared death while

fighting "Japs" in the context of combat, and while he supposedly helped win the war for the Americans, when he returns to Seven Devils in 1946, he experiences loss. He hears about his father's reversal of fortune; the latter's business, Railsback Feed and Seed, has suffered, and so has his personal health, while another business, Bright Star Agricultural, owned by Virgil Bayliss, Hollis's rival, has become increasingly successful, and Virgil's romantic interests have followed suit: "Virgil Bayliss wasn't content with simply stealing his girl; he had to steal Daddy's business, too."[15] Virgil, who was able to escape the draft because of a football injury, happens to have secured the affections of Hollis's girl, Joslin Simms, the most "perfect example of womanhood,"[16] thus resulting in Hollis's decision to change his fortune with the "supernatural" assistance of Granny Grimes. (This encounter with Granny is similar to Oedipus's consultation with seers and prophets in Sophocles' play.) Granny's luck-changing spell, secured with Hollis's blood which drips on a "sick pumpkin," enables Hollis's change in fortune. He unwittingly pays for this spell when Granny drugs him and has him engage in a sexual encounter with her, thus illuminating the ghastly aspect of Granny as a wrinkled and naked witch who resorts to mickey trickery to claim a sexual favor. The scene also echoes the social taboo or Oedipal fear of sleeping with a maternal figure; thus Granny functions as an example of incestuous dread.

The narrative depicts the kind of exchange, loss and balance that is so prevalent in classical Greek tragedy. When one character's luck rises, another often experiences misfortune. In *The Pumpkin Child*, a love triangle between Virgil and Joslin and Hollis serves as a means of demonstrating the fine line between fortune and misfortune or abundance and loss in *The Pumpkin Child*. The profit of one individual is offset by the loss of the other. For example, as Hollis regains his love Joslin and turns his father's ailing business around in the 1950s, Virgil, the former football star, becomes disabled with polio. Yet there is a catch in Hollis's change of fortune; since he acquires Virgil's "luck" he also "acquires" Virgil's inability to have "young'uns"; in other words, Joslin continues to have miscarriages until Hollis makes another deal with Granny Grimes to grant his wish to be a father.

The social and physical landscape of Collins's novella includes the blend of financial mobility combined with the backdrop of superstition that has characterized the American South. Hollis may appear to experience upward mobility by renaming and relocating his father's growing business, but his lot ironically appears to be determined by an individual who lives in poverty herself: Granny Grimes. Her name also suggests a symbolic affiliation with that which is "unclean" (grime) and dark (etymologically, Grimes is derived from the Anglo-Saxon term "grim," which also evokes the tale-collecting brothers who have been an inspiration to much of Collins's finest work) while also embodying her

Southern heritage, since the name Grimes is also a recurrent family name in Arkansas.

Other aspects of Collins's far southeastern old home-corner of Arkansas contribute to the Gothic texture of the novella. Gothic landscapes often include dark settings such as subterranean passages and hidden entranceways, and indeed the entrance to Granny's place offers little in the way of landmarks, inadvertently first arrived at when Hollis takes a wrong turn at a fork near the levee. In *The Pumpkin Child*, the Gothic landscape takes the form of settings or features such as the swamp, the river, coonhounds, the pumpkin patch, and the Caddo Indian mounds (ancient burial sites of Native American people who lived in Arkansas). All of these elements contribute to the weird imagery of the narrative while reinforcing the realism. One reference to swamp consists of Hollis's recollection of a swamp on a Pacific island during his war experiences, but it also functions as a key entry point to his future fortunes, and swamps also happen to be a geographical feature of the Arkansas landscape. Hollis remembers slogging through "those damned swamps, up to his armpits in slime and leeches" [17] and the imagery emphasizes a certain darkness or a fear of that which lurks beneath the surface. This doom and gloom characterizes both Gothic and tragic narratives. Another example of water, the Mississippi River, acquires a kind of otherworldly force as well with its power to flood the Arkansas area. A river of "mystery and romance" (190), the muddy waters of the Mississippi have the ability to obscure and destroy, and in this sense the river can be equated with Granny Grimes who also remains within the "consciousness" of the people in the community of Seven Devils. The force of the river thus echoes the inevitability of fate that appears in the context of tragic drama and is linked to the witchcraft of Granny Grimes.

Other examples of local color which are presented in *The Pumpkin Child* with Gothic flair are Pappy Pritchett's coonhounds. The coonhound, like many other tracking breeds, was developed in the Southern United States. When Hollis visits Pappy's place, a pack of hounds emerge from the darkness and appear dangerous. While "Pappy" Pritchett may serve as an illustration of a rather shady character in his own right (he provides "jars of shine" for the community), he and his hounds are also introduced in the narrative as a way of foreshadowing the dog-like familiar that hides under Granny Grimes's porch. After witnessing Pappy Pritchett's hounds emerge from under the stoop, it would be natural for Hollis to assume that the creature under Granny Grimes's porch is a dog as well. However, the creature that she keeps underground and calls Sathan turns out to be much more than "somethin' like a dawg." [18] The end of the novella suggests that this animal is some kind of supernatural beast, but the ordinary language used by Granny to describe this monster demonstrates how smoothly the ordinary and the supranormal co-exist in *The Pumpkin Child*. In other words, depictions of the coonhound and the Southern porch still create the kind of regional

ambience that places Collins's novella within the framework of Southern Gothic writing despite the presence of hidden supernatural elements.

Perhaps the most prominent element of local landscape in *The Pumpkin Child* is the pumpkin patch, and this is not surprising given the novella's title. This setting facilitates the creation of what could be called the agricultural grotesque in *The Pumpkin Child*. The "punkin patch" in Choctaw County is used to illustrate the unstoppable forces of tragedy and the force of Gothic maternity symbolized by Granny Grimes's power as a sexually active witch. The pumpkin functions in an important way as an ordinary object transformed into a grotesque symbol that conceals and eventually reveals the horror of other examples of Gothic motherhood in Collins's world. In the context of contemporary Arkansas, pumpkin patches are a favorite attraction for locals and tourists much like corn mazes and contribute to the colorful autumn landscape. However, they also function in a mythic capacity as a way suggesting the juxtaposition of fertility and blight. For example, when Granny Grimes asks Hollis to find the most beautiful pumpkin and the most dried up "blighted punkin" in her pumpkin patch, she uses the ritual power of a natural object to recreate a mythic narrative of life and death. Cynthia Ott has commented on the element of transmutability that is associated with the pumpkin.[19] Like corn, the pumpkin has been associated with fertility and change. An American Indian (Penobscot) myth of the corn mother or the First Mother, for example, presents the interrelationship between maternity, mutilation, and consumption that symbolically describes a people's relationship to the harvest. In this myth, corn is the image of sustenance but also the image of death since the First Mother sacrifices herself to feed others; she asks her son to kill her and then drag her back and forth by her silky hair until she loses all of her flesh. Her bones are then buried and several months later her flesh is miraculously transformed into corn.[20] In a similar fashion, the pumpkin in Collins's novella is linked to consumption because of its realistic association with harvest time throughout North America. Since the pumpkin patch is a symbolic site of abundance or fertility, the expression "pumpkin child" is used in the narrative to suggest a child born during the fall season, and especially on that night when traditionally the souls of the dead made their way back to their old hearths to warm themselves—Hallowe'en. In Collins's novella the pumpkin is definitely associated with the demonic, and an otherworldly genesis, especially in Hollis's dream about a pumpkin and the birth of his child. The dream foreshadows the grotesque climax of *The Pumpkin Child* when Hollis finds his dead wife Joslin carved up "like a jack o'lantern"[21] (the very image once thought to drive demons away on Hallowe'en) while Granny has transplanted the baby into her satchel, a symbol of the womb.

Feminine fertility along with the atmosphere of Gothic doom in the narrative are further inscribed in *The Pumpkin Child* through the geographical

feature of the Caddo Indian mounds. Like Granny's working one form of nature until it becomes something else, the ancient natives deliberately heaped soil, rock, ash, shell, and the remains of burned buildings onto natural land surfaces making them into their Archaic religious symbols, ritual centers, and territory markings.[22] Some of the mounds are as old as 3500 years in Arkansas, and the Caddo people lived in the area of this story in the 18th century, then but moved farther down the Red River.[23] The mounds are suggestive of maternity in the narrative as well as death, contributing to the novella's mythic hybridity and Gothic incongruities. The shape of the mounds also approximates the roundness of a pumpkin, which in turn resembles the appearance of a woman's pregnant body. This interrelationship is made clear in Hollis's dream which co-mingles the promise of a birth with death/loss through the presence of the mounds, the pumpkin patch, and the supernatural aspect of Granny's luck-changing spell. Hollis's dream echoes the transformation of the dream-into-reality that takes place in Sophocles' tragedy. In *Oedipus Rex*, Oedipus's wife/mother Jocasta mentions that a man often dreams about marrying his mother, but this dream becomes a reality when Oedipus discovers that he has wed his mother. Similarly, in *The Pumpkin Child* Hollis has a horrific dream about a birth that involves a pumpkin. In his dream he stands on the Caddo mounds and then searches for his unborn son in the pumpkin patch: the "pumpkins were unnaturally large and extremely orange."[24] Inside the pumpkin is a mewling infant that seems more like a half-formed fetus with wiggling split feet and a tail, which he regards with horror since he has apparently created this "thing." Hollis suddenly realizes that he cannot find the Indian burial mound again, and his thoughts about these mounds segue into the scene when he wakes up and makes contact with his wife's swollen belly. The examples of the ugly and awry in this dream (the freakishly large pumpkins and the devil-baby) are reminiscent of the kind of "difference" that is so often present in traditional Gothic writing. Joslin's pregnant "mound" along with the Caddo mounds are also presented as images of otherness in the text to highlight the alienating experience of pregnancy (especially for Hollis). It is also ironic that Hollis is so busy asking about the "son" he and Joslin supposedly conceived, that he does not "recognize" his own son, Jasper, the young boy that lives with Granny Grimes. If Jasper is Hollis's son, his birth can be traced back to Hollis's sexual encounter with Granny Grimes, the payment for Granny's change in luck spell, thus providing a revelation that simulates a moment of tragic recognition (anagnorisis). Thus *The Pumpkin Child* captures a feeling similar to the moment of horror experienced by Oedipus during his moment of tragic recognition (he has killed his father, he has bedded his mother, his children are his sisters). However, the landscape of Arkansas, the character of Granny Grimes, the pumpkin patch, and the aboriginal burial mounds provide a regional specificity for this Gothic and tragic narrative.

Several events which form *The Pumpkin Child*'s climactic conclusion combine to create a tale of tragic misfortune while retaining the ambiguity and lack of closure which are such an important part of Gothic fiction.[25] The pumpkin continues to function as the paradoxical source of joy and horror since it becomes a substitute for the maternal womb and for Granny Grimes, who is accused of being a "baby farmer." It would appear that Granny has swapped babies by "giving" Hollis's child to Naddy Creek, a thirteen-year-old girl, who is the victim of incest. Hollis is instead left with the deformed baby of Naddy Creek that her father had given to Granny Grimes to dispose of. When Naddy searches for her missing child, she finds what she believes to be her baby inside a pumpkin in the pumpkin patch. These events highlight the ongoing importance of concealment, fate manipulation, and the tragic theme of incest in Collins's Gothic text. Just as the pumpkin in Hollis's dream contained the seeds of horrific "truths" (he appeared to father a child with Granny Grimes—the wary and quiet Jasper; worse, the child he conceived with Joslin is stolen away), so the baby that Naddy finds in the pumpkin patch (if it is in fact Hollis's child, created with Granny's spell), is still "marked to serve the Dark One" [26] and is also taken away by Social Services. Naddy's joy is short-lived. Thus Granny Grimes is presented as the driving force in Collins's story of secret sin, Gothic motherhood, and usurped destiny. But not even Granny can out-trick fate, as she is dispatched not long after Hollis is: "they found the old hoodoo-woman stretched out on her bed, her head laid open like one of her prize pumpkins."[27] Waddy Creek, her nearest neighbor as well as an incest-committing father (and seemingly passed out drunk at the time of Granny's murder), takes the fall; that seems fair enough for the residents of Seven Devils.

These chilling events—with the haunting question of *Who Killed Granny?*[28]— would appear to signal the end of the narrative proper, but *The Pumpkin Child* actually ends with a kind of epilogue that transports the reader some 40 years into the future. The year is 2001 and the place is Atlanta (like Arkansas, another one-time home of Collins). A couple visits a gynecologist to help them conceive a child, a certain Dr. Grimes. This doctor could be Granny Grimes's son Jasper since Granny had wanted her son to get "his-self a proper education,"[29] and Hollis had paid $10,000 towards Jasper's college fund (as the price tag for Granny's continued magic). Collins thus sustains the Gothic ambiguity of her novella until the very end, beckoning and mystifying like "the old Caddo burial mound that was located on [her] family farm."[30] Hidden elements resurface but they do so in only a partially recognizable form. The phantasmagoric and the commonplace co-exist. With this novella, and the fourteen other astonishing tales of *Knuckles & Tales*, Collins conjures some of the most fraught and affecting Southern Gothic short works of the last ten years. Defying clear cut boundaries between the realistic and the fantastic, Collins blends the fairly ordinary experiences

of life (courtship and competition, infertility and pregnancy, success and misfortune) with mythic, freakish, and supernatural elements, partially unmasking the truths, temptations, and fears that still haunt us into the twenty-first century.

Notes

1. Flannery O'Connor, *Mystery and Manners: Occasional Prose*, ed. Sally Fitzgerald and Robert Fitzgerald (New York: Farrar, Straus and Giroux, 1969), 40.

2. Collins herself in a revealing introduction regarding the complicated feelings of an author to her home (written for the preface in the volume where "The Pumpkin Child" debuted) noted that "Arkansas was perennially hovering in the second-or-third-to-last spots for public education, literacy, and high school graduations. (The standard, half-joking, response of native Arkansans when faced with such depressing statistics has traditionally been: 'Thank God for Mississippi!'" In "Introduction: Gonna Send You Back to Arkansaw," *Knuckles and Tales* (Baltimore, MD: Cemetery Dance Publications, 2002), 9–15.

3. In *Reforming the Past: History, the Fantastic and the Postmodern Slave Narrative* (Columbus: Ohio State University Press, 2005), A. Timothy Spaulding discusses the Gothic in Toni Morrison's work and comments on the ambiguous and supernatural qualities associated with Gothic elements; the real thus becomes an aspect of the Gothic.

4. Glenn Meeter, "Quentin as Redactor: Biblical Analogy in Faulkner's *Absalom, Absalom!*" in *Faulkner and Religion*, ed. Doreen Fowler and Ann J. Abadie (Oxford: University Press of Mississippi, 1991), 103.

5. Nancy A. Collins, "The Pumpkin Child," in *Exotic Gothic: Forbidden Tales from Our Gothic World*, ed. Danel Olson (Ashcroft, BC: Ash-Tree Press, 2007), 191.

6. Collins, "The Pumpkin Child," 191.

7. Collins, "The Pumpkin Child," 193.

8. C. Hugh Holman and William Harmon, *A Handbook to Literature*, 6th ed. (New York: Macmillan), 219.

9. Philip John Thomson, *The Grotesque: The Critical Idiom* (London: Methuen, 1972), 22–23.

10. J. A. Cuddon, *Dictionary of Literary Terms and Literary Theory* (London: Penguin, 1991), 393.

11. Collins, "The Pumpkin Child," 190.

12. Collins, "The Pumpkin Child," 191.

13. Justin D. Edwards, *Gothic Passages: Racial Ambiguity and the American Gothic* (Iowa City: University of Iowa Press, 2003), xii.

14. Collins, "The Pumpkin Child," 182.

15. Collins, "The Pumpkin Child," 183.

16. Collins, "The Pumpkin Child," 183.

17. Collins, "The Pumpkin Child," 184.

18. Collins, "The Pumpkin Child," 191.

19. Cynthia Ott, "Squashed Myths: The Cultural History of the Pumpkin in North America" (Ph.D. diss., University of Pennsylvania, 2002).

20. David Adams Leeming, *Mythology: The Voyage of the Hero*, 3rd ed. (New York: Oxford University Press, 1998), 165.

21. Collins, "The Pumpkin Child," 211.

22. Ann M. Early, "Indian Mounds," *The Encyclopedia of Arkansas History & Culture*, www.encyclopediaofarkansas.net/encyclopedia/entry-detail.aspx?entryID=573 (accessed December 24, 2009).

23. Cecile Elkins Carter, "Caddo Nation," *The Encyclopedia of Arkansas History & Culture*, www.encyclopediaofarkansas.net/encyclopedia/entry-detail.aspx?search=1&entry ID=549 (accessed December 24, 2009).

24. Collins, "The Pumpkin Child," 203.

25. Danel Olson mentions that Gothic writing is "mired in ambiguity—this could be Heaven or this could be Hell—even to the last sentence, even unto the character's last breath." Charles Tan, "Interview with Danel Olson," *The Shirley Jackson Awards Blog*, http://shirleyjacksonawards.blogspot.com/2009/06/danel-olson-interview-by-charles-tan.html.

26. Collins, "The Pumpkin Child," 212.

27. Collins, "The Pumpkin Child," 145.

28. In an e-mail to Danel Olson on Christmas Eve, 2009, Nancy A. Collins shared her conclusions: "Jasper killed Granny Grimes because he was nothing more than a slave to her, born out of Granny's need for a servant instead of love, and was resentful towards both parents. There is also the suggestion towards the end (more clearly stated in the original draft of the novella) that children conceived using this particular method are born without souls. It is also up to the reader to decide if the monstrous baby found dead at the murder-suicide scene is actually that of Naddy Creek, and the baby in the pumpkin shell the Hollis child. This [novella] was originally the preface to a novel, most of which was set 30 years later and the reader had to figure out who is the soul-less 'pumpkin child' responsible for a string of murders."

29. Collins, "The Pumpkin Child," 200.

30. Collins, "Gonna Send You Back to Arkansaw," 14.

CHAPTER 46

Natsuo Kirino's *Real World*
MURDER AND THE GROTESQUE THROUGH TEENAGE EYES

Edward P. Crandall

"Living in Japan itself is a horror story."

—Masato Harada, director of the gothic horror film
Inugami (2001)

If you look at Japan National Police Agency statistics on crimes committed by juveniles, you will find that felonies such as murder, robbery, and arson are all on downward trends.[1] Regardless, several sensational crimes committed in recent years by people under the age of twenty have contributed to the image—fueled by the domestic media—that Japan's children are running amok.

Some of the more gruesome crimes are still fodder for TV "infotainment" programs. In 1997, a fourteen-year-old Kobe boy who went by the nickname Seito Sakakibara murdered, beheaded, and mutilated two other children. In 1998, a thirteen-year-old boy in Tochigi Prefecture knifed his teacher to death. In 2000, a seventeen-year-old boy hijacked a bus at knifepoint in Fukuoka Prefecture. He injured two passengers and killed one other before the bus was stormed by police a day later. Also in 2000, a seventeen-year-old boy in Okayama Prefecture murdered his mother with an aluminum baseball bat. In none of these cases has a specific, concrete motive been identified. When interrogated by police, the children said things like, "I wanted to see how fragile human beings are," "I didn't like the way my teacher talked to me," or "People were cruel to me."[2] None of these statements seems to have satisfied the public, social commentators, or child psychologists.

Author Natsuo Kirino sets the reader up to expect that her novel *Real World* will offer an explanation. Early in the story, a seventeen-year-old boy kills his mother with a baseball bat and then steals the bicycle of his next-door

neighbor, a high school girl. He uses her cell phone, which she had left in the bicycle's basket, to contact her and her friends, and four girls become involved in his flight from the police. The murderer and the girls, who take turns narrating parts of the story, discuss the boy's possible motive and their own feelings toward murder, death, parents, and a lot of other things, but they never manage to answer the question, "Why do children kill?" Even the murderer, whom the girls have nicknamed "Worm," is not able to give a convincing explanation for his actions. Instead, *Real World* portrays a gruesome, menacing modern Tokyo and the ways, including murder, in which the teenage characters try to cope. The novel does this by using and modernizing many elements of the Gothic fiction tradition.

The Grotesque: Tokyo through Teenage Eyes

Gothic fiction, like utopian and dystopian fiction, relies on exaggeration, often to grotesque extremes. But the Tokyo of *Real World* is at best "based on" the real capital city of Japan.

As in the Gothic fiction of Radcliffe, Shelley, Lovecraft, and others, the stage upon which the action is set is filled with weirdness and danger. But in *Real World*, this stage is not a crumbling castle, the windswept wastes of the Arctic, or "teeming labyrinths of ancient streets that twist endlessly from forgotten courts and squares and waterfronts to courts and squares and waterfronts equally forgotten, and . . . the Cyclopean modern towers and pinnacles that rise blackly Babylonian under waning moons."[3] Kirino's Tokyo is not nearly as highly wrought as Lovecraft's New York City. It seems to be the Tokyo of the real world.

Kirino uses the first line of the novel to set up her real/unreal Tokyo: "I'm penciling in my eyebrows when the smog alert siren starts blaring."[4] These sirens can be heard in most large cities in Japan during summer, and in the novel—as in real life—the obvious suggestion is that the environment of Tokyo is poisoned. This line, however, contains a small but significant difference from the original Japanese. The word rendered *smog* is in the original *koukagaku-sumoggu*, which translates to "photochemical smog." The term used in the Japanese version indicates a specific type of smog, one that occurs when chemicals such as the carbon monoxide in car exhaust are struck by sunlight and turn into a low-lying ozone layer (known as the "tropospheric ozone") that causes respiratory and other health problems. The idea contained in the original but absent from the English translation is that "things go out into the atmosphere of Tokyo and are transformed into something deadly." Throughout the book, Kirino will play with this idea of an environment that poisons things that enter it.

Almost immediately, Kirino takes the commonplace smog alert siren and runs it through the perception of one of her characters. Worm's next-door neighbor, a girl called Toshiko Yamanaka but who goes by the nickname "Ninna Hori" and is one of the five high school students who take turns narrating the tale, says that people pay little attention to the sirens because they have become so routine. Then, "What I'd like to know is where they hide those speakers. To me, that's creepier and weirder than anything about smog."[5] With these two sentences, Kirino twists the idea of smog in the environment into the suggestion that there is something sinister going on not overtly but behind the scenes. For the character Ninna Hori, the adult world—the world of the people who, as she sees it, are able to broadcast warnings with no visible means of amplification—fills her with unease.

Kirino deepens the sense of danger by sending the character Ninna Hori through a kind of gauntlet while she's on her way to "cram school." She is approached separately by a fortune-teller and a survey taker. She says the fortune-teller was "creepy looking" and tried to "grab" her, though all the fortune-teller did was offer to peer into her future. Regarding the survey taker, Ninna Hori explains that she is usually careful enough to avoid these people, but she let her guard down momentarily and got cornered. To an adult reader, the encounters seem innocuous enough: if you don't want to talk to these people, just say so. But to Ninna Hori, we are made to understand, simply being approached and spoken to by these people is tantamount to being trapped. She concludes her description of the encounter with the person conducting the questionnaire by saying, "You have to be careful . . . or you'll wind up in some database. Then adults will *control* you."[6] And the point is underscored: the fear of adults who can broadcast smog warnings from invisible speakers is the same fear of adults who will "control" you if they can get your name in a database. These are modern, urban fears, and as such they are the perfect choice for an author writing a modern, urban Gothic novel.

So far it is hardly obvious that the book is set in Japan. The stage where the action is unfolding could easily be any technologically advanced nation. But soon, the unique Japanese nature of the environment becomes clear.

One early example of this comes as Ninna Hori arrives at her "cram school." These after-school schools are notorious in Japan for being harder on students than their normal teachers and studies. By the time a student is in the upper grades of high school, the main focus of the instruction in cram schools is preparation for college entrance exams, which themselves are notorious for being difficult to score well on and for being specifically designed to control the number of passing students to match the limited number of available spots in the best colleges. A teacher, who is actually a college student tutor assigned to the class, gives the students a chilling lecture on the advantages of "doing your best":

It's summer vacation already. Now's the time you've got to do your best and don't let yourself give up. There's still time. It's only the beginning of August. So no more complaining, just do the very best you can. If you don't, believe me—come next spring you won't be smiling. The spring when I became a senior in high school I was told to forget about getting into the university I was hoping for. It'll never happen, they told me. But no exaggeration, that summer I spit up blood. I never worked so hard in my life.[7]

Ninna Hori reflects on the dangers and stresses of her life as a high school student in Tokyo—encountering bullies, hawkers, prognosticators, data collectors, lechers, and extreme tutors. Her conclusion, one the reader is made to sympathize with, is that she would rather not live in this "real world." And her solution is to take on a new identity: "That's why I became Ninna Hori. Otherwise I couldn't keep myself together, couldn't survive."[8]

This strategy of becoming someone—or even something—else is a leitmotif in the novel and a Gothic hallmark. All the girls in Ninna Hori's group of friends have nicknames. What's more, in the original Japanese, their nicknames are written in katakana characters rather than the normal kanji and hiragana, a fact which gives the nicknames the impression that they are not Japanese people's names, and perhaps not even human names (animals, plants, and pet names are written in katakana). This is a typographical trick Kirino uses as reinforcement of a major theme of her novel, but it is unfortunately lost in the English-language version.

Other girls in Ninna Hori's high school belong to groups defined by their fashion, such as the *kogyaru*, called "Barbie girls" in the English translation, and *yamamba* groups. *Kogyaru* is a portmanteau word combining the Japanese *ko*, which is an abbreviation of the word for "high school student," *kokosei*, and *gyaru*, which comes from the English word "gal." These girls dye their hair light brown or blonde and wear outlandish, garish fashions consisting of miniskirts, tight shirts, extremely high heels or platform shoes, and lots of sparkles and sequins. *Yamamba*, a word which originally meant a wild woman who lives in the mountains, dress in fashions similar to *kogyaru*, but in addition tan their skin as dark as they can and often wear stark-white eye shadow and color their eyebrows jet black with magic marker.

The *kogyaru* and *yamamba* have changed their appearance so drastically that to older Japanese people such as their parents and grandparents they are hardly even human anymore. To the older generation they look—and this is especially true in the case of *yamamba*—like the *obake* of folktales. And here it is important to understand exactly what the term *obake* means.

According to the dictionary, *obake* means "something that changes or transforms." The *bake* of that word is the noun of the verb *bakeru*, which means "to

change or transform."⁹ The kanji character this is written with is the first of two kanji in the word for "cosmetics," another item with widely known transformative powers. Ghosts are considered *obake* because they are the form a living person has transformed into after death. Most *yokai* (supernatural creatures) are considered *obake* because they are usually shape-shifters, some with the ability to transform into human shape, but more often simply the animated spirit form of household items such as spoons and bowls or other normally inanimate objects. And Worm, the murderer of the story, is the most significant modern-day monster or "*obake*" in *Real World*.

Worm's real name is never revealed in the story. Ninna Hori and her girlfriends gave him this nickname because they think his tall, lanky frame makes him look like a worm. So the first transformation he undergoes is forced upon him by his neighbor and her friends. Later, after he kills his mother and is on the run, he walks into a convenience store. He describes the sensation of standing at the entrance of the store, where the air conditioning is strongest, after being outside in the August heat all day. He feels the sweat evaporate quickly, leaving a layer of salt on his skin:

> I had the illusion that my whole skin was covered with a thin layer of glittering white salt. With my salt suit on, I was better than any other person around. I am a mother-killer, after all!¹⁰

He identifies so strongly with the image of his "salt suit" that he even begins to think that killing his mother and what has happened to him since has transformed him into something new. The Gothic irrationality is complete: "It felt like I'd . . . crossed over to a completely different world. . . . With this salt suit on, am I no longer going to be human?"¹¹

But, like the maddening lack of any explanation for why children kill, the idea that Worm is transforming himself into something other than human is subverted, and the reader is led to believe it was just a blind alley. Later on, during Worm's flight from the police, one of Ninna Hori's friends who goes by the nickname "Kirarin" joins him in an attempt to affect her own transformation from the "nice girl" to the "dark girl" who hangs around with a murderer, even though she constantly has sex with older men she meets in Internet chat rooms. Since she has money—Worm ran out of his early on in his flight—they are able to spend the night at a hotel. There, Worm takes his first shower since murdering his mother. "As soon as my salt suit was washed away I completed my new personality. The soul of the former Japanese soldier."¹² Worm now tries to become a World War II soldier that he had once seen being tortured in a film. Later, he will suffer a crisis brought about by his inability to come up with a new identity that satisfies him, and he asks Terauchi, another of Ninna Hori's friends, to write a "murderer's manifesto" for him. He specifically asks her to model it after the infamous one actually written by the real-life killer Sakakibara,

suggesting that he means to take on a new identity, that of Sakakibara. But even this falls short of satisfying him with yet another new identity. His instructions to the girl he hopes will ghostwrite the manifesto make him sound as though his heart isn't in it:

> Sprinkle in some Dostoyevsky or Nietzsche or whatever. But do a good job of incorporating those, so nobody can trace the source. Then sort of wrap it up like "Evangelion." Or maybe—it might be better to make it all avant garde-ish, know what I mean?[13]

Worm seems to have resigned himself to letting someone else create his new identity for him.

A weird, fearful environment, the violence and cruelty of a murder, characters trying to transform themselves and others—even into grotesque things (like a worm)—other characters seeking the thrill of the bizarre—like the girl Kirarin who joins Worm—all of these elements combine to give the novel its Gothic flavor. And they all could have been taken out of the table of contents of Eiri Takahara's wonderful study of the Gothic in modern Japanese society, *Goshikku Haato* (Gothic Heart), published in 2004 in Japan but unfortunately not available in English translation. In this sweeping survey, Takahara mentions artists associated with this tradition that range from Edogawa Rampo to Marilyn Manson. But we do not find, say, Kyoka Izumi or the ghost stories of Lafcadio Hearn (often known in Japan by the name he took upon naturalizing as a Japanese citizen, Koizumi Yakumo). Why? To answer this question requires a look at the Japanese tradition of "Gothic."

This tradition has two streams. One stream can be called "refined" and is found in Noh plays and the macabre tales of writers such as Ueda Akinari and Shusaku Endo. These are all linked by their concentration on ghosts, a detailed examination of human relationships, and eerie atmospherics.

The other stream is that of the "vulgar." These works have in common a lurid fascination with murder, death, and the grotesque in realistic settings. The two streams have not always been distinct—many stories and works of art have elements of both—but the two tended to diverge more and more during the late nineteenth and twentieth centuries. The vulgar stream leads directly to *Real World*.

Murder and the Grotesque in Japanese Art

Works that could be considered part of the vulgar Gothic tradition can be found as far back as the *Konjaku Monogatari-shu* (literally, *Anthology of Tales from the Past*, compiled around the year 1120).[14] But if we restrict the discussion to more recent arts, *ukiyo-e* artists who lived and worked into the Meiji period (1867–1912) provide a convenient starting point. *Ukiyo-e* are most well known

by mid-Edo-period (the Edo period was 1603–1867) paintings and prints of traditional sites of scenic beauty, kabuki actors, and beautiful women. Many of these artists, such as Hokusai, depicted *O-iwa* and *O-kiku*, both ghosts with eerie and deformed appearances, but these depictions did not evoke a sense that the ghosts were in any way "real." They were clearly pictures of imaginary beings.

It is the later artists who gained a reputation for their realistically macabre works. Two late-Edo- and Meiji-period artists in particular are known for depicting the graphically grotesque.

Kyosai Kawanabe (1831–1889), known as an excellent draughtsman and caricaturist who was jailed several times for his politically satirical images, produced many disturbing works. One is an undated painting called *Kuso-zu* (undated, collection of Stadtmuseum Hornmoldhaus Beitigheim-Bissingen). This hanging scroll depicts two corpses abandoned on the bank of a river. They lie side by side, face up. One is bloated, the flesh dappled here and there with the gray-green of putrefaction. The surface of the body is covered in ripples that suggest the rotting and liquefaction taking place within. The corpse beside this one is further along in the process of decay. On the bones bleached white by the sun only small fragments of flesh cling. Four crows are busy picking at these last edible bits, and two of them are pulling the remains of the eyes out of their sockets. Three crows circle overhead, one with what looks like a section of intestine in its beak. The scene is utterly repulsive for its almost scientific accuracy. The title of the work, *Kuso-zu*, means "The Nine Stages [of Decomposition]." We are being shown two of these stages.

Tsukioka Yoshitoshi (1839–1892, sometimes known as Taiso Yoshitoshi) is another artist who focused much of his work on the macabre. One of his most famous images is called *Okushu Adachi-ga-hara Hitotsu Ie no Zu* (1885, collection of the National Museum of Japan, Tokyo). It depicts a young woman, clearly in the last stage of pregnancy, naked from the waist up and wearing only a red wrap to cover the lower half of her body. Her arms are bound behind her back and she is gagged. Around her ankles is a knotted rope from which she is suspended upside down, her luxuriant long hair spilling below her nearly to the floor. Her distended belly sags beneath its own weight. A very old and savagely shriveled woman, also naked from the waist up, is drawing the blade of a large knife across a sharpening stone as she looks up at the suspended woman. There is a tub of water standing ready nearby. The old woman's intentions are clear even if one did not know the tale this image was taken from: she means to violently extract the unborn child. The subject matter of the image is horrific enough, but what makes it all the more disturbing is the accuracy and nonjudgmental realism with which it is depicted. More than simply an artist's conception of what such a scene would look like, Tsukioka's painting makes the viewer feel like a witness to an actual crime. You want to alert the authorities before the revolting deed is done.

This almost scientifically (perhaps it would be more correct to say medically) accurate realism made Tsukioka a popular producer of images for the illustrated newspapers—called *nishiki-e shimbun* in Japanese—that were published in the late nineteenth century in Japan.[15] The stories published in these newspapers were similar to modern tabloid news stories, featuring abduction, rape, murder, and other vicious crimes, as well as ghostly and macabre tales. One such illustration (not by Tsukioka) depicts a husband and wife. The man has just murdered his wife by thrusting his sword nearly to the hilt straight down into her open mouth. Both are splattered and smeared with the dead woman's blood. Another shows a certain Ryujiro Hirata as he is hoisting the corpse of a recently deceased seventeen-year-old girl out of her grave (the Japanese were not at the time required by law to be cremated). The written commentary explains that he intends to have sex with the corpse in order to cure his impotency. It goes on to note that, after committing the act, he failed to rebury the corpse and was subsequently arrested.

This focus on the bizarre and the sexually pathological, the ghastly, and the physical rather than the emotional aspects of murder and the grotesque was carried into early-twentieth-century art and literature. Edogawa Rampo's 1929 short story "The Caterpillar," for example, includes a revolting depiction of erotic desire, transformation (the husband of the female protagonist is a soldier who is a quadruple amputee and whose face has been horribly disfigured), and tormenting violence (his wife becomes a sadist, taking guilty pleasure in his helplessness alone with her, finally shaking him and gouging his eyes until they bleed). Even so, the story is a famous example of the tamer end of the spectrum of what is known as "*Ero-guro-nansensu*" (erotic-grotesque-nonsense).

This phenomenon was influenced heavily by the contemporary European avant-garde, including Dada, and was developed over time in particularly Japanese ways. One example of this is *shibari* (also called *kinbaku*), or the art of erotic rope binding. The painter Seiu Ito (1882–1961) was the first to use the Edo-period police technique of binding prisoners with rope as an art form. He began by drawing and painting women in poses he found in Edo-period illustrations and later began actually binding women—often completely or partially nude—in reality and then sketching and painting the results.[16] While his images never really become out-and-out pornography (there is no intercourse or other sexual activity involved), they are disturbing to the extent that the bound models are treated as objects rather than people. They are often forced into poses that contort their bodies into twisted and clearly painful shapes. The models, therefore, are one of the main materials—along with the rope—that the *Shibari* artist uses to express himself. *Shibari* clubs, where women are bound live on stage, exist today in Tokyo,[17] and many models have reached a level of fame usually associated with movie stars. *Butoh*, and especially *Sakai Juku* (a school of *Butoh*),

which also features grotesque contortions of the body, though in the context of dance, has an aesthetic that is close to that of *shibari*.

And then there are the films. The postwar period was a boom time for the Japanese film industry, with a few major production companies—such as Nikkatsu—churning out low-budget thriller, mystery, melodrama, horror, and *yakuza* films. There are too many to allow an exhaustive list, but major contributions to the developing vulgar Gothic tradition were *Daydream* (1964), *The Horror of Malformed Men* (1969), and *In the Realm of the Senses* (1976). These films all feature the macabre, cruelty, and a morbid fascination with pain, murder, and death, more often than not with erotic overtones.

Taking a cue from the sensation caused by crimes like those mentioned in the beginning of this chapter, author Koushun Takami in 1999 published a novel called *Battle Royale* that became a watershed in the vulgar Gothic tradition in Japan. The story, which was made into an infamous film the following year, is about a group of junior high school students who are forced to participate in a murder game that leaves most of them dead. The "murderous teenager" genre was born. Sion Sono's 2001 film *Suicide Club* (in Japanese, *Jisatsu Circle*) carried on this new trend. The opening scene and defining event in the film shows fifty-four high school students simultaneously throwing themselves in front of a train and committing suicide. Many elements of this film evoke *Real World*. Both deal with the pressures that high school students suffer; both focus on fads, fashions, and consumerism; and both explore senseless death.

Death as a "Bummer": Twenty-first Century Japanese Gothic

The vulgar stream of Japanese Gothic has since the end of the twentieth century completely broken from the refined stream. It is senseless death and meaningless, motiveless murder that are its main subjects. All hints of the spiritual and emotional have been stripped away, leaving only violence and a sense of confusion that may, and often does, cross over into chaos.

Most of the high school students depicted in *Real World* seem gravely affected by everything going on in their lives, except the most significant thing that has happened: Worm's murder of his mother. Only one character seems to grasp the horror of this crime, and she commits suicide. Ultimately, the reason that Kirino's novel fails to answer the question, "Why do children kill?" is that there is no answer, and there is no "real" world. And this is the enormous spiritual and emotional vacuum that forms the center of both the novel and much of twenty-first-century Japanese Gothic fiction: death is a bummer and nothing more.

Notes

1. See Japan National Police Agency white paper *"Shounen hikou nado no gaiyou"* (A Summary of Juvenile Delinquency), www.npa.go.jp/safetyflife/syonen38/syonen-hikou_h20.pdf (Japanese language only).

2. See, for example, Kyodo News article *"Shounen A kara 10 nen—Kobe renzoku jidou sasshou jiken"* (Ten Years After "Youth A": The Kobe Serial Murder Case), reprinted in the *Saga Shimbun* newspaper, May 20, 2007.

3. H. P. Lovecraft, "He," in *The Transition of H. P. Lovecraft: The Road to Madness* (New York: Ballantine, 1996), 213.

4. Natsuo Kirino, *Real World*, trans. Philip Gabriel (London: Vintage, 2008), 3.

5. Kirino, *Real World*, 3.

6. Kirino, *Real World*, 11.

7. Kirino, *Real World*, 12–13.

8. Kirino, *Real World*, 16.

9. *Koujien* (dictionary of the Japanese language) (Tokyo: Iwanami shoten, 1978), 1773.

10. Kirino, *Real World*, 69.

11. Kirino, *Real World*, 73.

12. Kirino, *Real World*, 113.

13. Kirino, *Real World*, 123.

14. For example, *Yamashina no kijo* (literally, The Demon Woman of Yamashina). It appears as the fifteenth story of the twenty-seventh scroll, where the demon-woman of the story eats babies.

15. See Katsuhiko Takahashi, *Shimbun Nishiki-e no Sekai* (Tokyo: Kadokawa Shoten, 1992).

16. See Youji Takahashi, ed., *Bessatsu Taiyo no. 88 Winter/1994 Ranpo no Jidai: Showa Ero-Guro-Nansensu* (Tokyo: Heibonsha, 1994).

17. Giovanni Fazio, "It Is Easy to Find Lashings of Rope on Show in Japan," *Japan Times*, May 22, 2008, http://search.japantimes.co.jp/cgi-bin/ff20080522r3.html (accessed January 28, 2010).

CHAPTER 47

The Longest Gothic Goodbye in the World

LEMONY SNICKET'S *A SERIES OF UNFORTUNATE EVENTS*

Danel Olson

I cherished, you perished,
The world's been nightmarished.

—Lemony Snicket, *A Series of Unfortunate Events: The End, Book the Thirteenth*[1]

If there has been a saga that most successfully and profitably appropriated the love and loss of the traditional Gothic and revisioned it for the twenty-first century, it must surely be Lemony Snicket's *A Series of Unfortunate Events*. Among recent series that have collectively sold hundreds of millions of copies, Philip Pullman's *His Dark Materials* omnibus (consisting of *The Golden Compass*, *The Subtle Knife*, and *The Amber Spyglass*, from 1995 to 2000) may have astonishing Gothic flashes, and the much straighter-faced seven books of the *Harry Potter* series (from 1997 to 2007) may have tingling moments of peril and fantasy (with its castles, supernatural visitations, magic, endless conflicts and melodrama, questions of lineage, and assumptions of wizardly power), but it is *A Series of Unfortunate Events* that has all the Gothic rites. As *Son of a Witch* author Gregory Maguire imaginatively and accurately opines, "Had the gloom-haunted Edward Gorey found a way to have a love child with Dorothy Parker, their issue might well have been Lemony Snicket."[2] These dire, inventive, and outlandishly witty books, now translated into forty-one languages and having sold sixty million

copies as of November 2009[3] (and *The Bad Beginning, Book the First* has recently been offered for free download to an audience of untold size), offer all the iconic features of the old Gothic, but with a new-millennium twist. We rattle along for thirteen dangerously addictive volumes that unveil resourceful orphans of unstoppable curiosity, shabbily Byronic heroes, secret societies, abduction, large contested estates, grotesqueries, cruel authorities and heartless institutions, sexual threats, murder most foul (offering 1,001 fiendishly clever ways to die over 170 chapters), frequent conflagrations, imprisoned victims, an ignorant public that ranges from passive to mobbish, myopic guardians and slain rescuers, ghastly and consuming lake-, sea-, and landscapes, and, the most moving motif of all, an irrecoverable past. Running through these fifteen classic features of Gothic misery, betrayal, and forlorn hope are also abundant humor and aggressive wit, acidic word play and metaphors, absurdly morose asides and warnings, outlandishly funny deliverances, some hard-earned wisdom, and, occasionally, a baby biting a blackguard's fingers. With both a Romantic-era melancholy and a fin de siècle decadence all merging with the comic, San Francisco–born Daniel Handler (writing as the narrator/character Lemony Snicket) manages to revitalize and revamp the hoariest Gothic truths, characters, troubles, and sensibilities in every volume—keeping the Gothic true, but making the Gothic anew. Composing these books at the turn of the century, just when such uneasy and ominous books about the past and the future tend to bloom, he has created a series that continues to surprise us, to stay unclassifiable (Is this for adults? Is it for kids?), to evenly split critics on its literary value, to astound all with adrenaline-addled adventures in alliteration, to offer satirical commentary on innumerable follies, and to make us shudder as we laugh.

For readers not yet aware, the novels concern the three Baudelaire children—oldest sister Violet, middle brother Klaus, and baby Sunny—who are orphaned by page eight in the series' starting point, *The Bad Beginning*. Entrusted to the care of a chronically coughing Mr. Poe, of Mulctuary Money Management, they are then placed in the homes of various incompetent or inappropriate guardians who, despite the repeated protests of the Baudelaires, singularly fail to recognize the controlling villain of the series, their distant relative and first guardian, Count Olaf. It is Olaf whose lousy disguises and scheming presence haunt each fresh start the orphans make. His declared motive, consistently held even by the final volume when he is lost at sea, is to swindle the orphans so that "the Baudelaire fortune is mine. Finally, I [will be] a wealthy man, so everyone must do what I say."[4]

Though talentless in countless ways, Olaf has the uncanny ability to divine what people want and then promise to get it for them. Doing what the count wants without him actually acquiring the fortune, some of the guardians become his lady friends (possibly victims of his unctuous charm, money promises, and

empty flattery) before being tossed, sometimes literally, just as lonely heart Aunt Josephine Anwhistle is unceremoniously thrown to Lake Lachrymose's devouring, aerial leeches in *The Wide Window, Book the Third*, creatures that would best be at home in a Hieronymus Bosch painting. Another enamored one and Baudelaire guardian is fashion-conscious girlfriend Esmé Gigi Genevieve Squalor, she of the stiletto heels, from *The Ersatz Elevator, Book the Sixth* and following. She gets her rough Olaf treatment later by being fired Donald Trump style. Like the classic case of the confidence man/pedophile who wishes proximity to the children through their mother, Count Olaf ingratiates his way in with guardians and squeezes menacingly close to the orphans, who can sniff his never-washed theatrical costumes and stale breath of egg sandwiches from thirty feet away. A predictable, but no less gasp-worthy, pattern ensues then in each volume of capture, some form of imprisonment, hard or tedious labor, disclosure, high-energy and inventive close escapes, and a few *unfortunate* deaths.

By *The Hostile Hospital, Book the Eighth*, a turnabout occurs that will shape the rest of the series and haunt the Baudelaire orphans evermore. When Violet escapes a suspicious operation at the hospital, which was to be executed by Olaf and his henchpeople, she and her siblings end up fleeing the burning hospital and hiding in the truck of Olaf's car as he speeds off to the Caligari Carnival. In fact, because the orphans were accused of murdering Jacques Snicket in the previous volume (*The Vile Village, Book the Seventh*) they are technically fugitives until the end of the series. With a bold and impressive logic, absent from many Gothic victims, they decide to limit their open exposure and vulnerability by shadowing Olaf himself (akin to hiding on a dragon's back), so that he cannot find them yet again in the foreground and dash whatever adjustment and small happiness is theirs. From now on, rather than Olaf routinely tracking them and donning disguise (and a poor one at that, as it *is* hard to kid a kid), they appear incognito behind the charlatan until *The Penultimate Peril, Book the Twelfth*. A crucial switch is activated, one that disqualifies criticism that the series is mere "kid noir" and that the three lead characters display no roundness and the narrative no depth. Their proximity to Olaf will lead the Baudelaire orphans to commit a crime that makes them question who they are—they will, in order to effect escape, light afire a hotel and continue the intergenerational curse of fire starting that plagues many of the characters in these books, including our narrator Lemony. The narrator meditates on a serious Gothic fear in the final volume, namely, that

> although each scheme had failed, it appeared as if some of the villain's wickedness had rubbed off on the children, and now Olaf and the Baudelaires were all in the same boat [just as physically they happen to be in the same boat]. Both the children and the count were responsible for a number of treacherous crimes, although at least

the Baudelaire orphans had the decency to feel terrible about this, whereas all Count Olaf had been doing for the past few days was bragging about it.

"I've triumphed!" Count Olaf reiterated.[5]

In this series of parody, mockery, and what critic Do Rozario calls "cheerful nihilism,"[6] one heartrending Gothic truth has been whispered, the most shattering one that creeps through *Dr. Jekyll and Mr. Hyde*, *Frankenstein*, *Dracula*, and all their ilk: We are the beast. Symbolically, we have drunk the elixir; embraced the undead one, been thrice bitten, and returned to him; abandoned our hideous offspring and then tried to kill him; and *worse*. This identification—or this becoming the monster—is what helps form the last volumes into a Gothically involving, potent, guilt-ridden experience. The villain is shown to have something of the hero in him, and the heroes are shown to have something of the villain in them.

Though space limits make it impossible to discuss the ramifications of each delectably dismal plot movement in the series' 170 chapters, it is possible to anatomize this mammoth work's Gothic body parts. Thus we can gain appreciation for how this comic yet bitter series superbly maintains its satisfyingly Gothic mood where tragedy and absurdity pal around for thousands of pages. More crucially, we can trace the imaginative way it reimagines Gothic possibilities for twenty-first-century fiction. The vital organs in the whole work are artifacts, time, sublime nature, and lost symbols; villains, heroes, and those in between; sexual threats; morality, mortality, and fate; and memory, hope, and despair.

Artifacts, Time, Sublime Nature, and Lost Symbols

To quote the perceptive children's literature scholar Bruce Butt, "Each of the [Snicket] novels possesses the same curiously timeless mood, despite the incidental references to cars, telephones, faxes, and even computers."[7] The novel's mansions and decor could arise from the cartoon, TV, and movie versions of *The Addams Family*, as do its deadpan humor and eccentricity, moribund taste, and precocious outsider children (repeatedly called "orphan brats" by Olaf and "cakesniffers" by their little-girl nemesis, Carmelita Spats). As Butt puts it, "There appears a mixture of not-quite-contemporary modernity and a heavily stylized choice of characters and settings that seems curiously familiar and yet unplaceable at the same time: buildings are improbably located and architecturally implausible, as if taken from the pages of a Dr. Seuss story."[8] It is true that the antagonists and their oddly Edwardian wardrobes—often adorned by a forbidding eye image—are right out of Edward Gorey's cartoons.

If the manmade objects in the books are grim, those that nature made are even blacker. Perceptions of the natural world are rarely appreciative in these books, and understandably so. More often than not, nature offers additional obstacles rather than any temporary relief from the trials of the plot. Nature is Gothically sublime and coldly indifferent. Closely following Edmund Burke's design for making readers tremble in his famous *A Philosophical Enquiry into the Origin of our Ideas of the Sublime and Beautiful* (1757), Snicket puts before the orphans towering cliffs, deep waters, great winds, uncontainable fire, and sudden death—sometimes all in the same book. The children often find themselves in open and barren landscapes, symbolic shorthand to show that these orphans on the run have nowhere to hide, and to keep their melodrama burning.

But the thirteen novels actually teem with more dread than brilliant Burke dreamt. Treacheries for the children include being entrapped by a giant pincher machine in *The Miserable Mill, Book the Fourth*; dropped to the bottom of an elevator shaft in *The Ersatz Elevator, Book the Sixth*; hanging from a hot-air balloon/Airstream trailer in *Book the Seventh, The Vile Village*; at the edge of a lion pit in *The Carnivorous Carnival, Book the Ninth*; and never far from a killer fungi called the Medusoid Mycelium for the last three novels.

How do they survive? is one great question of the series. *What got them into this?* is another. Improbably enough, a stolen sugar bowl is the lost symbol of this series. It is of momentous value to members on both sides of a schism that has developed in a secret society, a vortex that pulled in Olaf, the orphans' parents, and apparently all of the orphans' other relatives. While its significance is never fully revealed, its secret code never cracked, and the bowl itself never recovered, the damning fact is that it was purloined. The sugar bowl is known to have belonged to Esmé Squalor, who supposes Beatrice stole it. However, Lemony finally admits to taking it (at least to the readers) and to his sorrow for how one act of grabbing a pretty bowl (and whatever was inside it) has led to a catastrophe of fighting, separation, arson, and murder. This trivial theft and its massive human injury can explain where some of Lemony's regretful, plaintive, and weary tone comes from, as in this meditation that opens *The Penultimate Peril, Book the Twelfth*:

> Certain people have said that the world is like a calm pond, and that anytime a person does even the smallest thing, it is as if a stone has dropped into the pond, spreading circles of ripples further and further out, until the entire world has been changed by one tiny action. If this is true, then the book you are holding is the perfect thing to drop into a pond. The ripples will spread across the surface of the pond and the world will change for the better, with one less dreadful story to read.[9]

These lines shed much sad light on why Lemony has given us this grim story over such a vast canvas. I suggest these volumes are not just a meditation on Beatrice, the woman whom he lost to another man, and the recorded destiny of her children, the Baudelaires. These books are his mea culpa, Lemony's way of facing the endless tragedy, recrimination, and villainy that his small mistake unleashes.

Betrayal, Peril, and Melodrama

The single greatest thing that distinguishes the brutal nature, constant horror, disappearance, and threatened death here from most other shudder novels and series is that the menace is directed constantly at children. While children have traditionally appeared in Gothic novels (suffering exploitation, abandonment, and disinheritance), they will suffer it here repeatedly and with no surcease of sorrow for thirteen vile volumes.

In truth, some book critics have sincerely worried about children's reactions to the images, pessimistic tones, and violence in these books. Cynical themes, as well as the psychological and physical torture, have made for blistering reviews. Beyond complaints about the woeful fates and recurring endangerment of the youngsters, detractors detect a note of nihilism in the series, suggesting to young readers that any meaning and purpose and wider trust in life are all out of reach. Children reading the series are relentlessly reminded, too, that they will die. If they chance to forget, this motto will appear emblazoned as memento mori for the kiddos above an archway at the Austere Academy in *Book the Fifth*. As reviewer-bookseller Christine Heppermann puts it, "A condensed analysis of the distinction between *Angelwings* [by Donno Jo Napoli] and *Unfortunate Events* could be that one series promotes good, old-fashioned 'values,' and the other series . . . doesn't."[10] Heppermann claims that Snicket never allows that "a positive attitude and a little moral backbone could make everything right for his characters. . . . No guardian angels swoop in, . . . and no one believes them, . . . [so, as the narrator says,] 'sometimes not only is it good to lie, it is necessary to lie.'"[11] She ventures, with a dubious quotation from former American drug czar, secretary of education, and moralist William J. Bennett (who was also a Las Vegas high-stakes gambler), that this series is "vapid or even corrosive to the spirit."[12]

Among nonprofessional critics who would normally be the closest allies to fiction—say, librarians who would order, catalog, and champion the books, and the teachers who would assign them—the objections are even fiercer. One teacher blasted the series thus:

> I fail to see any productive purpose in scaring children with the idea
> of both their parents dying in a fire and then having those children

ending up with a distant relative who emotionally and physically abuses them, with strong hints of adults wanting to inflict sexual abuse on the children, and the kids being threatened with murder to top it off. The sickness of the content by far overpowers the author's evident talent.[13]

A Series of Unfortunate Events finds itself in the crosshairs from the very people who would request the books for their collection and direct readers to them, possibly because the moral battle between good and evil is not so clear cut, everyone is compromised, and young victimhood in Gothic texts is a dire thing indeed. Hence a children's collection librarian shrilly complained,

> This series is being pitched to Harry Potter readers, but it lacks the adventure and the aesthetic and moral appeal of J. K. Rowling's books. The creepy freak-show characters and situations were nauseating. The scene where a baby girl tied in ropes is imprisoned in a cage with her mouth taped shut while the cage dangles high above the ground is not the sort of thing I would promote for 10 year olds to read. While the children do manage to overcome their situation, it seems almost by accident. In the Harry Potter books (and Aiken's fine books), the characters have some character. They reach heroic stature because they possess compassion, intelligence, bravery, loyalty, moral principles.[14]

Abandoned by some librarians for their absent "moral principles," baby Sunny, Klaus, and Violet seem orphaned twice.

School boards have weighed in negatively, too. As Daniel Handler puts it in an interview,

> We were banned in one school district in Decatur, Georgia. I'll always have that. . . . I hate to get too catty about Decatur, Georgia, but they were very concerned in *The Bad Beginning* that Count Olaf wants to marry Violet, who is a distant relative. And this strikes me as something that, without being too stereotypical about the South, but perhaps Decatur, Georgia, has heard of before, let's just say. And also, I'm at a loss for how to construct a villain who isn't doing villainous things. If Count Olaf were only doing things that no one would object to, then he really wouldn't be much of a villain.[15]

Handily defending his work from obscenity charges through accusatory wit, Handler flips the Gothic taboo of incest onto the back of the Decatur School District, which understandably had no comment.

The harshest trashing probably comes from parents themselves, calling the series "Horrible," "Awful," and "Sadistic." One quipped at Handler, "You, sir, are no Roald Dahl." Another parent's review showed how far *A Series* detractors

and fans will always be from each other, and ultimately how one person's droll satire or mock Gothic is another person's torture porn:

> If you're a good parent you won't want your kids to read these books. I heard good things about them, so I read the first two books myself. These are sick books. There is little character development and the plot is ridiculously repetitive and redundant. Worse, the books contain graphic, gory details about murder, dead bodies, the color of dead bodies, using a syringe to poke a hole in someone and kill them, breaking glass to slit someone, kidnapping, polygamy (yes the actual word is even defined in this series). . . . Please do not buy these. Our children need good examples of moral behavior in their reading. They don't need gruesome specifics about . . . how to kill people, and all other sorts of evil and darkness.[16]

One wag—perhaps Count Olaf himself?—shot back to the above parent in a sarcastic blaze: "I agree with this reviewer—these are depraved books that NO child should be reading! . . . For some books that praise the word of God, teach universal lessons, inspire the whole family, and give real examples of social and moral behavior that Mr. Snicket should be writing about (and with more fun!), I recommend unreservedly: *120 Days of Sodom, Maldoror, Last Exit to Brooklyn,* . . . [and] *Our Lady of the Flowers.*"[17] One young fan backed the wag, suggesting how reading does not blindly cause acting out: "Parents are just trying to protect their kids from everything under the sun, including the sun itself, (SPF 70 sunscreen? are you kidding?). . . . I personally enjoyed these books when I was a child, and I am 16 now. . . . I have not done anything remotely evil after reading these books. If your kids are evil, blame yourselves!"[18] It is no surprise that many young readers would reject parental fears of *The Complete Wreck* (as the whole series is boxed and sold by HarperCollins) when they realize that any wrong click on the Internet would deliver them depravity worlds beyond the Baudelaires' worst misfortunes. Indeed, the complaint seems quaint. It is an antiquated view to think that little nippers could be much harmed by the Snicket books in an age when anyone can log on to something unspeakable and innocence robbing—from mind-boggling sexual acts to a flood of war porn, like Iraqi inmates forming naked pyramids, images of the headless corpses and body parts of both civilians and enemy combatants, and streaming video of insurgents in the cross hairs and blown apart three seconds later.

Sexual Threats

Though the peril and images may seem old fashioned by comparison to the Web, still the distressing fact is that Violet Baudelaire, who turns fifteen by *The*

Grim Grotto, Book the Eleventh and is most likely sixteen years old by the series' end, is under immanent sexual threat throughout the volumes. The first obvious use of this standard Gothic trope of the chased maiden comes in the first volume, when Count Olaf arranges to marry her, during a shamelessly wooden performance of *The Marvelous Marriage*, with his malignant troupe. The marriage scene in the play is even conducted by an actual judge, the kind but unwitting neighbor, Justice Strauss. Though the orphan trio manages to dig into the law books of their neighbor and take a momentary victory—as Violet is only fourteen, she is not of legal age to marry—one sinister fact is unfurled by Olaf: Violet's guardian may give her hand in marriage before the legal age, and the Count *is* her guardian. Moreover, she will act in this play, or someone will get hurt: in a traditional Gothic trope with a modern twist, Violet's baby sister will fall from an iron cage suspended from a tower at the count's walkie-talkie signal. A crooked, toothy, and unnecessarily yellow smile spreads on Olaf's face, and the old goat we love to hate is in butting against us, and Violet, again.

Thankfully the marriage is foiled—along with the acquisition of their estate, which is the official reason Olaf gives for marrying her. But the sadistic attempts on Violet's virginity continue, and neither adult men nor women seem able to protect her, or even to be aware of the crime. By the next volume, Olaf has slimed himself into the orphan's next new world, one that they will eventually call the happiest they knew, at herpetologist Uncle Montgomery's home. Monty's assistant has disappeared (most probably bumped off by Olaf), and a new one appears, Stephano, a man with Olaf's unibrow and unsettling manner and banter (played with nasally, gloating perfection by Jim Carrey in the 2004 film version). The orphans are on to him, but Monty senses that Stephano's snake ignorance merely suggests that he is a plant, an eavesdropping pawn of the reptile society he has fallen out with. The series will now take a growing interest in phallic substitutes that point and eventually touch Violet's skin, often overtly but sometimes covertly, and in that hidden way make us all the more squeamish. One of the most piercing images happens at the supper table in *The Reptile Room, Book the Third*, when the newcomer is at his jolliest, and Violet despairs:

> Stephano told funny stories and praised Monty's scientific work, and Uncle Monty was so flattered he didn't even think to guess that Stephano was holding a knife under the table, rubbing the blade gently against Violet's knee for the entire meal. And when Uncle Monty announced that he would spend the evening showing his new assistant around. . . . He was too eager to realize that the Baudelaires simply went up to bed without a word.[19]

Rubbing a knife—under the noses of all—on the innocent girl's knee makes the dark Gothic promise of a hundred novels before this one: Stephano/Olaf can

rape and kill her at any time if she violates any wish, so she must obey. Much later in the series (especially in the final two books), Olaf keeps his hand on this spectral phallus as it metamorphoses: the knives that point and touch Violet will be replaced as she grows a little older. A harpoon gun will be pointed at her midsection instead, with Olaf "happier than a pig eating bacon!"[20] and her constantly talking him out of using it.

One of the creepier ways that older, grotesque men get at Violet is by medical means. "She's a pretty one even when she's unconscious," croaks Olaf's hook-handed man as he hovers and leers over Violet while she is anesthetized, her hair tangled and her gown stained, stretched out on the operating table for an involuntary "cranioectomy" procedure by the count's goons (where the head is removed to save the patient!), performed before an uncommonly gullible and bloodthirsty surgical theater. Curiously, in *The Carnivorous Carnival, Book the Ninth*, not long after Violet escapes this operation which would render her mindless, she discovers that the three orphans are troublingly like Olaf. "We fooled them. We're as good at tricking people as Olaf is. . . . And lying to people. . . . Maybe we're becoming villains after all. . . . Olaf has to do tricky things to save his life."[21] These are staggering admissions not heard before in any of the volumes. It is the first identification (perhaps a kind of Stockholm syndrome[22]) with the very man thought to have burned their parents to death. The comment only registers shudders and disbelief from the other Baudelaires, but it is telling, and it wears on them. This indicates character change and recognition in a series lambasted for featuring none. Violet before has seen the lies, frauds, arson, and prison escape as necessary for life (a case of understandable situational ethics), but now she is saying that the count sees lies, thievery, escapes, and bloodshed as necessary for leading the only kind of life he knows. Superbly placed, her confession, which horrifies Klaus, precedes one of the longest sections where Count Olaf speaks privately to his confederates of his motivations and goals, all overheard by the orphans who secret themselves in the rattling car's trunk. This is also one of the rare, almost surreal sections where the pursued and the pursuers decide to use the same getaway car. The children simply have no one to save them this time—Mr. Poe hasn't been spotted in at least two volumes— and they must hide away among those who would murder them to escape the Heimlich Hospital where they are hunted for arson, for the murder of Count Omar (a misspelling of *Olaf* courtesy of the dependably sloppy *Daily Punctilio*), and, worst of all in the Hostile Hospital administration's mind, for a rampant disregard of paperwork.

Regardless of what Violet's identification with the count means, she understands the continued threat to her maidenhead. As the Baudelaires bump down the road stowed in the hatch, they eavesdrop on an awful conversation about which of the orphans will live the longest. Olaf is overheard to say, "We only

need one of them alive to get the fortune. . . . I myself hope it's Violet. She's the prettiest."[23] The series' "pretty girl" may be saved, but for what worse-than-death fate? Snicket's narrative queasily combines a melodramatic escapism with the adult menace of rape by her one-time guardian.

Villains, Heroes, and Those in Between

Traditionally the Gothic features the fantastic and an interest in destruction, a wandering evil force (perhaps the Devil himself) beyond human understanding, and an irresistible terror, *fascinating*, in the Latin origin of the word, meaning to charm or use witchcraft. A sign of this force—like the enchanting Fascinum, the phallic amulet worn in Roman times, often by children—had a talismanic power: it could ward off other evils. In *A Series of Unfortunate Events*, the mysterious ankle tattoo of an eye functions like a twisted Fascinum, inspiring dread and, for a while, depicting evil. Later, the orphan trio realizes this tattoo was worn by their own parents too, not just by Count Olaf and his dark accomplices. The tattoo is a sign of membership in the ultra-ambiguous VFD, first mentioned in *The Austere Academy, Book the Fifth*, which stands for many things, often absurd, throughout the books (Vernacular Fastening Device, Village of Fowl Devotees, Verdant Flammable Device, Volunteers Fighting Disease, Very Fancy Doilies, etc.), but it most commonly stands for Volunteer Fire Department. There is duality again, just as with the tattoo. For some, the VFD is a way of volunteering to start fires, and for others it is volunteering to put them out.

The duality of human nature, a motif especially developed in the Victorian Gothic (say, *Jane Eyre, Wuthering Heights, The Moonstone, Dracula*, and *Dr. Jekyll and Mr. Hyde*), runs through the series as well. Indeed, the latter of the thirteen volumes announce this duality much more strongly, showing how easily the moral compass faults, and how no villain starts out to be evil. Perhaps since the Baudelaire siblings spend so much time imprisoned, they start to see the world as one of the most famous prisoners of the twentieth century did. Their maturing thought is like Aleksandr Solzhenitsyn's in the *Gulag Archipelago*: "If only there were evil people somewhere committing evil deeds, and it were necessary only to separate them from the rest of us and destroy them. But the line dividing good and evil cuts through the heart of every human being. And who is willing to destroy a piece of his own heart?"[24] In the end, the trio discovers that they are more like Count Olaf than they ever imagined—after all, they did turn Hotel Denouement to ash in *The Penultimate Peril, Book the Twelfth* (it was Sunny's bright idea), and not all the lodgers may have gotten out in time.

In constructing the perfect villain to forever disturb the peace of the Baudelaires and cause them no end of harm, Handler adroitly infuses Olaf with every

one of formalist Vladimir Propp's signature descriptions of how the villain enters and disturbs in folktales. Many a folktale informs the Gothic genre ("Bluebeard" is only one notorious example). Through Propp's analysis, we readily see what a traditionally structured evildoer the count is. Indeed Olaf's lurking presence walks all the paths a villain takes to execute his schemes. First, as Propp diagnosed in a multitude of tales, there is "reconnaissance," with "the aim of finding out the location of the children, or sometimes of precious objects."[25] Throughout these novels, we find very late that Olaf has used his neighbor Justice Strauss, along with an accurate psychic named Madame Lulu, to watch the movements of the Baudelaires. Second comes "trickery." According to Propp, "The villain attempts to deceive the victim to take possession of him or his belongings. The villain, first of all, assumes a disguise . . . [and then] employs other means of deception or coercion."[26] Olaf dons innumerable costumes and applies loads of makeup, morphing into an interior designer, a snake man, a pregnant woman, a Sikh gym coach, and an old salty dog, Captain Sham. When the disguise is inevitably revealed, he threatens to kill one or more of the orphans if he doesn't get his wishes.

Following many of Propp's sightings of intimidation and violence in dark tales to an eerie degree, the fiend Olaf "causes bodily injury . . . [and] a sudden disappearance, . . . entices his victim, . . . expels someone, . . . orders someone to be thrown into the sea, . . . effects a substitution, . . . orders a murder to be committed, . . . commits murder, imprisons, . . . threatens forced matrimony, makes a threat of cannibalism, . . . [and] torments at night."[27] Propp has uncannily anticipated by seventy years every wrong the count commits, save for the malefactor's joy in setting fires and dangling babies over heights. Tracing every Proppian nuance of the archetypal wicked one, Handler forms his Olaf into what one eloquent character analyst calls "the Ultimate Villainous Character."[28]

Olaf does so many of these prescribed dastardly deeds—and will seem so much a folktale stereotype or an 1880s black-hatted stage heavy—that it stuns us to find that he is more, that he is a round character of sorts. The count's Snidely Whiplash persona starts eroding in the last four novels. Intriguingly, it comes at the hands of a little vain girl we first met tormenting the Baudelaires at the Austere Academy in *Book the Fifth*, nasty Carmelita Spats. Little Carmelita, in league with Olaf's mistress Esmé, through wheedling and cunning begins to dominate the archfiend by the very end of *The Slippery Slope, Book the Tenth*. By the start of *The End*, Olaf is reduced to sheepishly following the orders of another young girl, asking twice, "'What about me?' . . . His voice was a little squeaky, and it reminded the Baudelaires of . . . people who were [once] frightened of Olaf himself."[29] By the end of *The End*, he is begging for the trio's help to unlock him from the golden cage where Ish, the leader of the island (one who knows much about their parents and Olaf, but tells so precious little) has trapped him, as the waves rise on the coastal shelf.

Olaf's accomplices, and there were once many, grow in character as well. The two "white-faced ladies" in his gang openly question him, complaining that it may be difficult for a baby to light a fire *and* cook meals for the company of rogues, and they absolutely balk at tossing Sunny Baudelaire down the mountain at the end of *The Slippery Slope, Book the Tenth*. This refusal causes their expulsion from the group, and possibly their deaths. Their fate remains unknown. Madame Lulu plans to stop helping Olaf and join the twins but is thrown to hungry lions before she can do much good. Another minion, the man with hooks for hands, is found out to be the brother of an ally of the Baudelaires; he leaves crime for a while, and though he will ultimately deceive the trio (and his long-lost sister Fiona regretfully joins him), the hooked one does for a time provide the Baudelaires reconnaissance. Four other villains show no change at all—the bald man, the one who was neither man nor woman, the man with beard but no hair, and the woman with hair but no beard—but neither are they much remembered. They are essentially stock characters, making their entrances and final exit, dwarfed by bigger and more rounded characters that create greater unpredictability, action, and ambiguity.

One of the great tensions of the series is the desire to be noble, despite all the treachery one does. Something that makes this series remarkable is how Olaf steps out of his bossing mentality and sheds some character armor to show vulnerability, speechlessness, a longing for his lost parents (he is, after all, an orphan too), genuine shock at the orphan's long-held secret (that they think he killed their parents), and, at the orphans' request, a genuinely heroic act. In a jaw-dropping scene reminiscent of Gothic romances, Olaf rescues Lemony Snicket's pregnant sister Kit from the top of a raft on the waves and carries her safely to shore, before delivering a momentous kiss. With no financial gain to be had, this act of our guardian-killer seems impossible, but perhaps we have known all along that buried somewhere in the dark chambers of Olaf's heart was the intimation that what he wanted was not money but the acceptance that money could bring. "A lot of life," horror director and villain specialist Wes Craven observes, "is dealing with your curse, dealing with the cards you were given that aren't so nice. Does it make you into a monster, or can you temper it in some way, or accept it and go in some other direction?"[30] At the very end, Olaf does temper it in some way. Another film expert, screenwriter David Lubar, advances Craven's view, and we can use it to suggest what makes Olaf an enemy that we never stop wanting to understand: "The bad guy isn't doing bad stuff so he can rub his hands together and snarl. He may be driven by greed, neuroses, or the conviction that his cause is just, but he's driven by something not unlike the things that drive a hero."[31] Accepted as he is in this moment, Olaf saves a woman who will successfully deliver her baby girl, Beatrice, named after the mother of the orphans (and like Dante Alighieri's, the narrator's one true but lost love). And then Olaf dies.

Olaf was largely a destroyer, but he was the one figure that, after their parents' death, would pay the orphans the most attention, though admittedly of a mendacious kind. Still, like so many other hunted figures in great Gothic literature (like Frankenstein's creature lingering with his creator's body after Dr. Frankenstein's death), the Baudelaire siblings are haunted by him: they never can let him go. This contradiction of returning to the one whom they tried to escape and who relentlessly tried to ruin them is the eternal Gothic paradox. On the abandoned island where the orphans, now four, live, "Sometimes they would visit . . . the grave of Count Olaf, where they would merely stand silent for a few moments."[32] Why come back to the one who did them ill? Why even properly bury him rather than simply toss him to the surf and the sharks? Is it to prove that their souls were better than his? Or, oppositely, is it a helpless attraction back to what is also in them? Whatever Olaf was and discovered, he was a constant presence, albeit a hellish one, in their lives. He was their immoral guardian, this one-eyebrowed lunatic, and he has helped shape the only perspective of reality they have, a view of good and evil all clouded together.

Morality, Mortality, and Fate

Much is scripted already in a reader's mind after reading the first two novels in the series. We appreciate this dramatic irony: that the Baudelaires will suffer, be taken in, have their guardian duped by wily Olaf, and will soon be on the run for their lives. Benighted Mr. Poe, who knows their past, will always be too slow to detect anything, too late coming in an emergency, unable to apprehend Olaf, and incapable of listening carefully to the children. With so much that is predictable, there is a strong suggestion that these are books where fates are merely played out and free will is a fanciful notion. One of the serious questions of these often cheeky books is whether we are in control of what we are doing, or if we are somnambulists. Nothing comes to a sleeper but dreams. Divining this, "Life is but a dream" is the one lyric Violet could never stand to hear.

Lemony himself likes to brood on the topic of fate as the books play out, never with a conclusive answer, but certainly with a compelling question that connects his musing to literature and opera, to the orphans, and to us:

> Some people think destiny is something you cannot escape, such as death or a cheesecake that has curdled, both of which always turn up sooner or later. Other people think destiny is a time in one's life, such as the moment one becomes an adult. . . . And still other people think that destiny is an invisible force, like gravity, . . . that guides everyone throughout their lives. . . . In the opera *La Forza del Destino*, various characters argue, fall in love, get married in secret, run away to

monasteries, go to war, announce . . . revenge, engage in duels and drop a gun on the floor, where it goes off accidentally and kills someone . . . [just like what] happens in chapter nine of this very book. They wonder and wonder at all the perils in their lives, and when the final curtain is brought down even the audience cannot be sure what all these unfortunate events may mean.[33]

A harder question presents itself to Sunny, Klaus, and Violet: "They wondered . . . if it was the force of destiny that was guiding their story, or something even more mysterious, more dangerous, and even more unfortunate."[34] Many a Gothic figure has wondered the same: Am I under a curse, that thing "more unfortunate"? For instance, the Baudelaire orphans may be under an intergenerational curse, and it is Olaf who suggests why, all in front of witnesses who do not deny the charge—that the orphans' parents may have killed people in a theater with poison darts, perhaps the "wrong" people. Another question may swell in the orphans' minds: if their lives are run by fate, are they liable for what they do? Are their character traits essentially locked in place, not growing in personality, insight, and behavior after each trauma and crime? The most memorable Gothic novels do have round characters—*Jane Eyre* and *Wuthering Heights* both have figures that, despite all their melodrama, quicken with life, depth, and changeability. But does *A Series* have them? Hundreds of Gothic novels do not have such multidimensional personalities and are still entertaining. What can be said for certain is that the three children go from utter innocence to becoming liars, thieves, and arsonists (probably killing some of the Hotel Denouement guests in a horrible way). Will they continue now as if in a somnambulistic trance to kill someone they *do* know well?

Gregory Maguire, an interviewer of Daniel Handler and a fan of his work raises this question: Are the books formulaic? He answered that they are: "Selfconsciously, generously, joyously so. The fun derives from watching the formula at work. . . . He has taken a small handful of storytelling tricks . . . and he has made them convulse in convincing sequence, so that despite the contrivances there is something vivid and even urgent about these tales."[35] Maguire's point is well taken, and yet the orphans do grow—they may have sported "the slimmest of personalities"[36] from the start through the fifth book (which Maguire reviewed), but by the end they move from innocence to experience. They know this world, and most sadly, they recognize how it has changed them.

In *The End*, unknowing Olaf almost reaches his own end a little early, and it would have come at the hands of three juvenile killers. In the first pages, altogether in a boat, the three orphans study Olaf leaning over the side, and all feel a powerful attraction to murder. Littlest Sunny breathes it first: "'Push Olaf overboard,' she whispered."[37] Again we get a pondering about human nature,

how much of it is instinctive and how much is learned. As the three debate on whether to kill, Lemony has a moral-development rumination:

> Some believe that everyone is born with a moral compass already inside them. . . . Others believe that a moral compass develops over time, as a person learns about the decisions of others by observing the world and reading books. In any case, a moral compass appears to be a delicate device. . . . The Baudelaire orphans were not sure what they should do with this villain who was leaning so far over the boat that one small push would have sent him to his watery grave.[38]

Spinning in the Baudelaires' minds is the murderer's dream from time immemorial: "Imagine how simple it would be to push him, just hard enough." This pause before murder helps dismiss critics' views that the series has essentially a cast of static characters in revolving situations. Fated or not, Olaf straightens and grins, and the three did not have to make the decision. For whatever perverse reason, Snicket will not show us what the three would have done. But if Olaf had stared one more minute at sea, I believe—from the short but mighty arguments made by the orphans for drowning him—the count would be undersea now.

Memory, Hope, and Despair

Despair is Gothic DNA. The last few chapters of four of the most famous novels in the genre close repeatedly with the words *despair*, *despaired*, and *despairing* (namely, *The Castle of Otranto, Vathek, The Monk,* and *Frankenstein*). Likewise, *The Bad Beginning* opens early with the worst despair, the death of parents. And *The End* closes with the death of another's parent. Snicket erects a marvellous frame to makes readers feel more. Our introduction to these children is when they are playing on Briny Beach and out comes Mr. Poe (the estate executor) with the sad news, "Your parents have perished in a terrible fire."[39] This scene of brutal desolation echoes the children's loss sublimely. An empty beach and a sea with nothing on it, which now Violet stares at, uses limited yet bold and vast elements—a dramatic perspective—to emphasize the imposing aloneness of their lives. The unrelenting landscape helps dramatize the grisly news more than tears could, though tears still will come. One thing to count on, besides bad luck and Count Olaf's nonstop scheming, is that at least two times in each volume the trio of siblings will sob in each other's arms, crying into their Nazi-like gruel or actually weeping themselves to sleep. In the last volume, the trio is still by the water, actually not so far from Briny Beach where misfortune first befell them, and the memory of happiness (their family's once safe and cool-marbled mansion, and the love and security it gave) must be the most unfortunate event of

all. Though a plethora of literary references are made in the series, largely decadent and Gothic, two world authors stand out—Tolstoy and Proust. Tolstoy's famous first line to *Anna Karenina* is reworked many times in the novels, perhaps as some solace for the parentless trio, and the spirit of Proust's seven-volume *À la recherche du temps perdu* broods over this long chronicle of these desperate children. Memory—or tasting Proust's madeleine and receiving the flood of memory that washes over him—is a constant in the books, because memory is the inheritance of these children. There is no evidence that they ever receive their earthly one.

Now at closing they sail out from an island where they have lived for over a year, with a new orphan under their care—little Beatrice, daughter of another vanquished VFD member. In the midst of so many narrative high jinks and so much lampooning of mordant literature, some wisdom manages to bob up. In the play of shadow and light that fills these thirteen books, each of thirteen unlucky chapters, there is this happy anomaly: the last book includes a fourteenth chapter, and a tantalizing suggestion that the unfortunate cycle may yet be broken. For the Baudelaire orphans, and for us, there is the grounded hope in that final chapter that "the world, no matter how monstrously it may be threatened, has never been known to succumb entirely."[40] We leave the Baudelaires as castaways on a boat in search of all the people they hoped to see again; it might seem unlikely, but "not impossible," for the Baudelaires to find again some of the people who loved them.[41]

The Last Good-bye

In the follow-up treatment to *A Series* entitled *The Beatrice Letters*, little Beatrice (Lemony's niece) has become separated from Klaus, Violet, and Sunny. The letters and notes are a mixed file (some from Beatrice Baudelaire, the mother of the three orphans, some from Lemony, but most from little Beatrice, who is searching for the orphans, but also for Lemony). She movingly mentions what happens after *A Series* cuts off, that "Violet told me once that I saved her life, and Klaus claimed that without me he would have died in despair not long after the destruction of the Hotel Denouement. Even Sunny said that she could not have survived without me."[42] As mentioned, the three orphans understand how the coldness of human nature has changed them, but they are apparently saved from utter despondency by little Beatrice. By their self-sacrifice and caring for a helpless one, their world must have been born anew. Beatrice wanders toward and narrows on Lemony several times, and can even hear him breathing on the other side of his office door. One of the last mysteries is why Lemony doesn't open the door and present himself to little Beatrice after all her pleading. Why

doesn't he let her innocence heal him? How can a narrator with seemingly boundless sympathy of the most profound kind for the orphans—and himself an orphan—not reveal himself? Is the pain of facing someone young who has lost so much too painful? Does he fear that if he gets attached to his darling niece and takes her in he will only get hurt later when she is abducted by an Olaf replacement? After recording all this tragedy and villainy over thirteen books of misery, does he simply not want to be hurt by anyone or anything anymore? An answer would mean closure, a forgetting, and a heart that stops sobbing. I choose to let the mystery be.

Books in the Series

Lemony Snicket's *A Series of Unfortunate Events* includes thirteen novels as follows:

Hardback American publications from HarperCollins:

1. *The Bad Beginning* (1999)
2. *The Reptile Room* (1999)
3. *The Wide Window* (2000)
4. *The Miserable Mill* (2000)
5. *The Austere Academy* (2000)
6. *The Ersatz Elevator* (2001)
7. *The Vile Village* (2001)
8. *The Hostile Hospital* (2001)
9. *The Carnivorous Carnival* (2002)
10. *The Slippery Slope* (2003)
11. *The Grim Grotto* (2004)
12. *The Penultimate Peril* (2005)
13. *The End* (2006)

American paperbacks mostly from Scholastic, except where otherwise noted:

1. *The Bad Beginning* (2000; HarperCollins, 2007)
2. *The Reptile Room* (2000)
3. *The Wide Window* (HarperCollins, 2007)
4. *The Miserable Mill* (2001)
5. *The Austere Academy* (2000)
6. *The Ersatz Elevator* (HarperCollins, 2001)
7. *The Vile Village* (2001)
8. *The Hostile Hospital* (2001)

9. *The Carnivorous Carnival* (2002)
10. *The Slippery Slope* (2003)

UK hardback volumes from Egmont Publications (Egmont published the UK paperback issue of these thirteen volumes in 2010):

1. *The Bad Beginning* (2003)
2. *The Reptile Room* (1999)
3. *The Wide Window* (2003)
4. *The Miserable Mill* (2001)
5. *The Austere Academy* (2003)
6. *The Ersatz Elevator* (2003)
7. *The Vile Village* (2003)
8. *The Hostile Hospital* (2003)
9. *The Carnivorous Carnival* (2003)
10. *The Slippery Slope* (2004)
11. *The Grim Grotto* (2004)
12. *The Penultimate Peril* (2005)
13. *The End* (2006)

Notes

1. Lemony Snicket (Daniel Handler), *A Series of Unfortunate Events: The End, Book the Thirteenth* (New York: HarperCollins, 2006), epigraph page.
2. Motoko Rich, "An Unfortunate Event for HarperCollins," *New York Times* (in "Arts, Briefly"), November 12, 2009, www.nytimes.com/2009/11/13/books/13arts-ANUNFORTUNAT_BRF.html?_r=1 (accessed January 8, 2010).
3. Gregory Maguire, "Review of *The Austere Academy*, by Lemony Snicket," *New York Times* (in "Children's Books"), October 15, 2000, www.nytimes.com/2000/10/15/books/children-s-books-523372.html (accessed January 9, 2010).
4. Snicket, *The End*, 8.
5. Snicket, *The End*, 5.
6. Rebecca-Anne C. Do Rozario, "Pedagogy and Other Unfortunate Events: Cheerful Nihilism in Popular Children's Books," *Papers: Explorations into Children's Literature* 17, no. 1 (May 2007): 36–42.
7. Bruce Butt, "'He's behind you!': Reflections on Repetition and Predictability in Lemony Snicket's *A Series of Unfortunate Events*," *Children's Literature in Education* 32, no. 4 (December 2003): 283.
8. Butt, "'He's behind you!'" 283.
9. Lemony Snicket, *A Series of Unfortunate Events: The Penultimate Peril, Book the Twelfth* (New York: HarperCollins, 2005), 1.

10. Christine Heppermann, "Angel Wings and Hard Knocks," *The Horn Book Magazine*, 77, no. 2 (March 2001): 239. The vices of Mr. Bennett, editor of *The Book of Virtue*, have made for good copy. See David von Drehle, "Bennett Reportedly High-Stakes Gambler: Former Education Secretary Lost $8 Million in Past Decade, Magazines Find," *Washington Post*, May 3, 2005, http://articles.chicagotribune.com/2003-05-03/news/0305030138_1_high-stakes-casino-gambler-washington-monthly-slot (accessed March 23, 2010).

11. Christine Heppermann, "Angel Wings and Hard Knocks," 239.

12. Christine Heppermann, "Angel Wings and Hard Knocks," 239.

13. Winifred (teacher), "Horrible Story," Amazon customer review, February 12, 2004, www.amazon.com/review/R3C0PFJU7A915M/ref=cm_cr_rdp_perm (accessed April 1, 2010).

14. Children's librarian, "Not appropriate fare for its intended audience," Amazon customer review, March 10, 2003, www.amazon.com/review/R191SEXY8SUDX6/ref=cm_cr_rdp_perm (accessed April 1, 2010).

15. Daniel Handler, interview by Terry Gross, *Fresh Air*, National Public Radio, WHYY, December 10, 2004, www.npr.org/templates/story/story.php?storyId=4212818 (March 11, 2010).

16. Calming Tea (parent), "Sick books not for good parents," Amazon customer review, September 22, 2008, www.amazon.com/review/R36ARMCHFECU79/ref=cm_cr_rdp_perm (accessed April 1, 2010).

17. Woland, Amazon comments, September 30, 2008, www.amazon.com/review/R36ARMCHFECU79/ref=cm_cr_pr_cmt?ie=UTF8&ASIN=0061119067&nodeID=#wasThisHelpful (accessed April 1, 2010).

18. Michael J. Montgomery, Amazon comments, February 14, 2009, www.amazon.com/review/R36ARMCHFECU79/ref=cm_cr_pr_cmt?ie=UTF8&ASIN=0061119067&nodeID=#wasThisHelpful (accessed April 1, 2010).

19. Lemony Snicket, *A Series of Unfortunate Events: The Reptile Room, Book the Third* (New York: HarperCollins, 1999), 63.

20. Lemony Snicket, *A Series of Unfortunate Events: The Grim Grotto, Book the Eleventh* (New York: HarperCollins, 2004), 277.

21. Lemony Snicket, *A Series of Unfortunate Events: The Hostile Hospital, Book the Eighth* (New York: HarperCollins, 2001), 241–242.

22. Though Sunny gets the idea for burning down Hotel Denouement, and Olaf fully helps her, she never considers him to be any part of her—there is no Stockholm syndrome. In *The Slippery Slope, Book the Tenth*, where Sunny utters her first whole sentence ("I am not a baby," 306), we see how different the sisters can be. Sunny, who has been alone on a mountaintop and cooking over a frozen waterfall with Olaf, Squalor, and assorted fiends, has the opposite appraisal of Violet's, not seeing any of Olaf in herself. She has become an independent little person, a cunningly resourceful cook, and no longer merely a sharp-toothed baby with one-word retorts. And she loathes Olaf: "There is another expression . . . when a prisoner does not become friends with such people [criminals and abductors], but instead . . . despises them more and more with each passing moment. . . . The expression is 'Mount Fraught Syndrome,' and Sunny Baudelaire was experiencing it" (258).

23. Lemony Snicket, *A Series of Unfortunate Events: The Carnivorous Carnival, Book the Ninth* (New York: HarperCollins, 2002), 10.

24. Aleksandr Solzhenitsyn, *The Gulag Archipelago, 1918–1956: An Experiment in Literary Investigation*, trans. Thomas P. Whitney (Boulder, CO: Westview Press, 1998), 168.

25. Vladimir Propp, *Morphology of the Folktale*, ed. Louis A. Wagner, trans. Laurence Scott, 2nd ed. (Austin: University of Texas Press, 1968), 27.

26. Propp, *Morphology of the Folktale*, 29.

27. Propp, *Morphology of the Folktale*, 33–34.

28. "Villains Don't Always Wear Black," *Fiction Notes*, January 28, 2008, www.darcypattison.com/characters/villains-dont-always-wear-black (accessed April 1, 2010).

29. Snicket, *The End*, 42.

30. Robert Mancini, "Return of the Mack, Horror Kingpin Wes Craven is Back, with Bite," Movies on MTV.com, www.mtv.com/shared/movies/features/c/craven_wes_050225 (accessed April 1, 2010).

31. "Villains Don't Always Wear Black."

32. Snicket, *The End*, 323–324.

33. Snicket, *The Penultimate Peril*, 17–18.

34. Snicket, *The Penultimate Peril*, 18.

35. Maguire, "Review of *The Austere Academy*."

36. Maguire, "Review of *The Austere Academy*."

37. Snicket, *The End*, 16.

38. Snicket, *The End*, 19.

39. Lemony Snicket, *A Series of Unfortunate Events: The Bad Beginning, Book the First* (New York: HarperCollins, 1999), 8.

40. Snicket, *The End*, 6 (in supplemental chapter 14).

41. Snicket, *The End*, 6 (chapter 14).

42. Lemony Snicket, "BB to LS #5," *The Beatrice Letters* (New York: HarperCollins, 2006).

CHAPTER 48

A Labyrinth of Mirrors

CARLOS RUIZ ZAFÓN'S *THE SHADOW OF THE WIND*

Romana Cortese and James Cortese

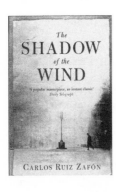

Carlos Ruiz Zafón, the author of *The Shadow of the Wind*, the novel for which he is best known, was born in Barcelona in 1964 and currently lives in Los Angeles, where he settled in 1993. Zafón's first books were novels for young adults. *The Shadow of the Wind* (*La sombra del viento*), his first novel for adult readers, came out in 2001 and was almost immediately successful, selling millions of copies worldwide and winning many awards. His subsequent books have been published in forty-five countries and translated into more than thirty languages. It has been said that Zafón is one of the most successful contemporary Spanish writers. A prequel of *The Shadow of the Wind*, called *The Angel's Game*, was published in 2009. Both books were translated into English from the Spanish by Lucia Graves, the daughter of the English poet Robert Graves.

Critical Reception

The opinions of professional reviewers of *The Shadow of the Wind* have been varied. Some were entirely laudatory, as was Michael Dirda's in the *Washington Post*: "Anyone who enjoys novels that are scary, erotic, touching, tragic and thrilling should rush right out to the nearest bookstore and pick up *The Shadow of the Wind*. Really, you should."[1] Amy Mathieson in *The Scotsman*, was similarly unambiguous in her praise: The combination of thriller and love story "gives his tale a dramatic tension that so many contemporary novels today seem to lack. This is highly sophisticated, fun reading that keeps you gripped and tests

527

the brain cells all at the same time. What more could you ask for?"[2] In some of the more effusive reviews, the book was sometimes compared to the novels of such giants of literature as Jorge Luis Borges, Gabriel García Márquez, Umberto Eco, and even Franz Kafka.

Other reviews were mostly laudatory, but with qualifications. *Entertainment Weekly* called the novel "wondrous," with the qualm that "there are places in which the book might seem a little over-the-top." Nevertheless, the novel is "ultimately a love letter to literature."[3] Richard Eder in the *New York Times Book Review* offered the same sort of ambivalence: "The melodrama and complications of *Shadow* . . . can approach excess, though it's a pleasurable and exceedingly well-managed excess. We are taken on a wild ride [that] . . . we may occasionally feel executes its hairpin bends with breathtaking lurches."[4] Michael Kerrigan of the *Guardian* puts his finger on what he sees as the novel's best attributes:

> Novels constructed like Russian dolls, stories within stories, with terraced layers of surveillance and interpretation embedded in texts which advertise their own artificiality: this is the standard stuff of doctrinaire postmodernism. That this elaborate nest of narratives stacks together so neatly is impressive; that the cogs which drive the action whir quite so swiftly and smoothly is little short of miraculous. Zafón's real virtues are more old-fashioned ones, though: what makes this novel so irresistibly readable is the emotional energy generated by the ups and downs of a big and varied cast of memorable characters.

But elsewhere Kerrigan pointed to some flaws of style: "an overvaluing of words at the expense of things," "a tendency to daub on description without too much thought for either precision or consistency," and a reliance on cliché: "There are too many enigmatic smiles and impenetrable gazes here by half."[5] Similarly, the reviewer of the *Sunday Times*, having noted Zafón's skill at set pieces, complained that "the characters seem hand-me-downs" and concluded, "For those who like their escapism dark and melodramatic, the novel could provide a good week's beach reading. For the more hard-hearted, it remains a piece of hokum."[6] Robert Colvile, writing in the *Observer* liked the fact that "the language purrs along, while the plot twists and unravels with languid grace," but "the medley of genres (mildly supernatural thriller, against-the-odds love story and period coming-of-age saga) never quite fuses into a satisfying whole."[7]

Other reviewers have not been so kind. Jennie Yabroff in the *San Francisco Chronicle* warned that any potential reader "must be forgiven for looking for literary high jinks in this otherwise tiring, meandering tale. . . . Mist, fog, haze, shadows, gloom, dusk, rain, snow, clouds and plain old darkness obscure the landscape and the action, adding to the sense of sameness every time [the hero] sets out to meet yet another shadowy figure. He is constantly pushing open

doors into dank, dusty, foul-smelling mansions and crumbling monasteries, where he stumbles around in the dark, looking for clues—an experience the reader will well relate to." Yabroff labeled the book a "tepid potboiler."[8]

Reader reviews tend to be much more enthusiastic. On Amazon.com, 85 percent of readers gave the book four or five stars. Typical is this comment: "Zafón's storytelling skill is quite remarkable, his prose doesn't just take you into the story, it completely transports you. In only a few sentences, Zafón crafts a world of remarkable visions and events—just a little bit magical (as all the best stories really are) but grounded in characters who live, breathe, and merrily cavort off the page and into your heart."[9] Or this one: "I finished reading this intensely seductive and rewarding masterpiece two days ago. Since then I've been unable to get it out of my mind, and I think you won't either. The characters, the plot and especially the extremely powerful and clever brand of storytelling deployed here seem to have left me under a spell that I can't remember experiencing with any other book I've read in the last 25 years."[10] At the other end of spectrum, one two-star reader wrote, "This bloated Spanish novel boasts the most overwrought prose this side of a Harlequin romance in a mix of thriller, historical fiction, tragic romance, gothic horror, and most of all, soap opera."[11] Other disappointed readers offered similar criticisms.

The critical reviews and readers' responses that concentrate on various aspects of the novel are predicated upon personal and literary tastes. The plots and subplots, told by multiple narrators, have led critics to describe Zafón's novel as "sprawling." Typically, the narrative is advanced by having one character tell the details of a story to another character in dialogue. At some point, Zafón (or an editor) must have realized that he was overusing this approach and that the length of the book was ballooning beyond what was sellable. To solve that problem, instead of expository dialogue, Zafón resorted to some chapters set entirely in italics and written from the third-person point of view.

Patience is a virtue when reading *The Shadow of the Wind*. One of the challenges to the reader's memory is the innumerable characters that appear at nearly every turn of the page. They are often described in minute detail. We learn of their peculiar histories, habits, and possessions, much of which is either irrelevant or tangential to the main narrative. They illustrate the intricacies of the trivial connections of relationships that are curiosities in themselves but dilute the narrative tension and strain the reader's memory. But once the focus is on the central characters and the threads begin to come together, the narrative moves quickly and achieves moments of tension and suspense worthy of the classic Gothic stories.

For those readers who have fallen in love with *The Shadow of the Wind*, a sprawling novel is just what they want. Readers who have praised the book like to mention its narrative complexity, its obvious symbolic scheme, its Gothic

atmospherics, its slow unraveling of the mystery, and the many scenes of dramatic tension and suspense. They don't mind that the sun never shines in Zafón's Barcelona.

The Scheme of the Novel

The Shadow of the Wind is a novel within a novel, a labyrinth of plots and subplots, told from the point of view of multiple narrators. It begins in the summer of 1945 in Barcelona and ends in 1966. Daniel Sempere, a young boy of ten, is taken to the Cemetery of Forgotten Books by his father, a secondhand bookseller. The Cemetery of Forgotten Books is a secret place, where a huge collection of books that have been forgotten or have fallen into oblivion is kept. Here, under the auspices of his father, Daniel ostensibly chooses a book to read, *The Shadow of the Wind*, written by a man called Julián Carax.

However, this event is more destiny than choice. Daniel says, "Perhaps the bewitching atmosphere of the place had got the better of me, but I felt sure that *The Shadow of the Wind* had been waiting for me there for years, probably since before I was born."[12] All that Daniel discovers at the beginning of the action about the author who immediately engages his imagination is that Carax was a young Spaniard who lived in Paris and apparently died in a duel. Daniel's continuing interest in the life of this author leads him to the disturbing knowledge that someone has been systematically destroying all of Julián Carax's work and is seeking to do the same with his own, and presumably last, copy of *The Shadow of the Wind*. Thereupon, Daniel embarks upon an obsessive search to find out more about the book and its mysterious author whose memory someone has been trying to obliterate.

In the process, the events of the book increasingly become mirrored in Daniel's own life. From the moment that Daniel chooses and feels chosen by the book *The Shadow of the Wind*, the Gothic motif of duality pervades the novel. Both character and novelist fall for a love thwarted by societal rules and patriarchal tyranny. Both defy the authority of the father and use subterfuge, secretly rendezvousing with their beloved in attics and abandoned houses; both struggle to assert the purity of their intentions; and both "die" in order to be reborn. For Carax, it is an artistic rebirth; for Daniel a personal one. In structuring the two narratives as foil mirrors of each other, Zafón weaves a tale of innocence and experience, personal and historical violence, life and death, resolution and redemption.

For Daniel, the reconstruction of Carax's life begins with the knowledge of a few biographical facts: a trip to Paris, a job as a piano player in a bar, publication of his work by a second-rate publishing house, an announced marriage to a rich

and older heiress, a duel, and a mysterious death on a Parisian street. In the quest to find out who exactly Carax was, Daniel Sempere meets an ever-increasing number of characters who give him fragments of information, taking him deeper and deeper into the complexity of human relationships as he learns the extent to which the past impinges on the present.

Not until the last narrator, Nuria Monfort, writes a memoir intended for Daniel does he learn that Carax is still alive and is, in fact, the "ghost" that has appeared to him at night with strange warnings. Carax, disillusioned with the outcome of his love relationship and life in general, has been systematically destroying his own books and is after the last copy owned by Daniel. At the very center of things, hidden for most of the novel but exerting a powerful and malign force, looms the threatening figure of a depraved chief inspector of police, Francisco Javier Fumero, a matricidal Fascist thug, whose sporadic appearance and violent encounters with Daniel and his acquaintances drive the dramatic tension of the plot. Holding a childhood grudge against Julián Carax, Inspector Fumero has been after revenge ever since and stalks Nuria Monfort whom he suspects of knowing Carax's whereabouts. Nuria not only knows, but she is the one who has been hiding the writer out of a hopeless love for him. Violence, lies, forbidden love, freaks, superstitions, and shadows—atmospheric and metaphorical—propel the action in a complex series of stories by first-person narrators who help Daniel uncover not only Carax's mystery but Daniel's own sense of purpose.

Daniel Sempere's interest in solving the mystery that is Julián Carax intersects with Daniel's own coming of age. Through the personal transformation of the novel's hero, Zafón implies a national regeneration—the rebirth of Spain from its Fascist past. Daniel is young and impressionable, and he experiences the usual disappointments of adolescent love and the temptations of the flesh before meeting his soul mate, Beatriz. As he matures and his love deepens and develops, his sensitivity and kindness to others are shadowed by acts of cowardice and indecision. He finds himself unable to stand up to the anarchist violence and depravity that characterize his world. He is troubled by what he perceives as a paralyzing concern for his physical safety when he fails to defend his friend, Fermín Romero de Torres, against the savagery of a police beating.

Daniel is eventually able to overcome his cowardice through an act of self-sacrifice as Chief Inspector Fumero is about to shoot Julián Carax. As he comes to understand the tragic end of Carax's own love story, Daniel redeems the mistakes of the past and asserts the primacy of love and loyalty as redemptive principles. His personal "death" is symbolic of an historical transition for Spain as well: from a Gothic worldview, full of shadows, secrets, and violence, to an enlightened present, from a fractured society to social reintegration and harmony. Romance and capitalism triumph—or do they? The social order, fractured by

patriarchal privilege before the Spanish Civil War and by repression and violence during the Fascist regime, heals itself through the constancy and idealism of Daniel Sempere. The conclusion of the two narratives marks the end of Fascism, patriarchy, and social hierarchy. Daniel wakes from his physical wound into a world of light: "The room was white, a shimmer of sheets and curtains made of mist and sunshine" (469).

But this is not the end. In the next-to-last section of the novel, called "Dramatis Personae," the loose ends of the relationships of Zafón's various characters are brought to a happy conclusion. Julián Carax ends his novel, *The Shadow of the Wind*, with "a brief coda" (483), and so does Zafón, who adds a coda to Daniel's own story. It is a recapitulation of the beginning of the novel as the then ten-year-old Daniel now initiates his own ten-year-old son, Julián, into the mystery that is the Cemetery of Forgotten Books.

A Tale of Three Mothers

Like many contemporary novels that find their inspiration in a genre, *The Shadow of the Wind* is not afraid to explore the inner depths and outer reaches of the familiar, using the genre as a way to analyze the dark areas of human experience in the process of maturation, discovery, and the transition to order and stability. One of the most enduring themes in Gothic literature is the theme of the forbidden, especially in the realm of love and sexuality. Because the novel takes place in Spain and is suffused by a particularly potent patriarchal culture and history, Zafón explores the dark side of this theme in great detail. "The sins of the males" is dramatized in Zafón's novel through the sexual exploitation and domination of women. A woman who indulges in a sexual relationship outside of marriage must face rejection, isolation, violence, or any combination of these. The young man who defies the cultural restrictions of social standing and sexual freedom finds an enemy in a father for whom his daughter is a commodity to be disposed of according to his wishes.

At the bottom of the historical and personal rottenness lies the family. Absent, passive, or indifferent mothers; possessive, castrated, and violent husbands; and alienated sons and daughters are all caught in a web of deceptions, betrayals, and lies. The only parent that is capable of nurture is Daniel Sempere's father, who must be both mother and father to the motherless Daniel.

The novel begins where everything begins: with the mother. Many of the families in the novel have either a dead or an ineffectual mother, and the hero's journey of maturation is also a recovery of the mother figure. On page 4, we learn that Daniel's mother has been dead for six years. "As a child," Daniel tells us, "I learned to fall asleep talking to my mother" (4). The morning he is taken

to the Cemetery of Forgotten books, Daniel wakes up from a nightmare that shakes him to the core of his being. When his father rushes into his room to calm him down, he cries, "I can't remember her face. I can't remember Mommy's face" (4). Daniel will not be able to visualize his mother's face again until the end of the novel when he throws himself on Inspector Fumero to prevent him from killing Julián Carax. As Daniel is losing consciousness from the bullet that strikes his chest, he sees Carax jump on Fumero, dragging and impaling him on the uplifted hand of the Angel of Mist, a dilapidated statue in the fountain in front of the Aldaya house. Only then, near death and about to be reborn, is Daniel finally able to see his mother's face.

In a book with so much mirror doubling going on, it is no surprise to find the opposite of the good mother in the form of a grotesque perversion. This is Fumero's mother, Maria Creponcia, aka Yvonne. She is a "dim-witted woman with delusions of grandeur and the looks of a scullion," who "dressed skimpily in front of her son and the other boys" (212). Calling her son a "little shit," she is utterly ignorant of her insidious influence on her son's psychic development. It is a failure that costs her dearly when one day Javier takes a shotgun and blows her head off "like a ripe watermelon" (215). When the civil guards arrive, they find him starring impassively at his mother's body, covered in insects, his face splattered with blood "as if he were being ravaged by smallpox" (215). The murder is classified as a tragic hunting accident, and Javier avoids punishment, allowing him to continue to murder and torture as a policeman.

The third important mother is Julián Carax's. In pre–Spanish Civil War Spain, she works at a music school as a tutor at a time when the social milieu is composed of rigid social hierarchies. She meets a man named Antoni Fortuny, the owner of a hat shop, and tries to balance her ambivalence at his persistent but respectable advances with her need for companionship. At a house of one of her promising female students, she meets Ricardo Aldaya who seduces her and gets her pregnant. Aldaya beats her and demands that she abort the child. She refuses and turns to Fortuny who offers to marry her. She accepts. Once married, she sees his kindness turn to cruelty because he suspects her of adultery. "He spit as he threw her out onto the landing, after flaying her with blows from his belt" to the point of fracturing "her right hand completely" (127). When the baby is born, Fortuny cannot bring himself to love the child, who turns out to be Julián Carax. Tired of the abuse and slavery to one whose mind seemed more and more unhinged, Sophie eventually leaves Fortuny. Sophie is yet another helpless mother who cannot protect her son from the violent vindictiveness of his stepfather and rescues herself only by running away.

The standard Gothic absence of the mother, physically or psychologically, speaks to a fundamental lack of wholeness, of personal and cultural dysfunction. This theme is expanded to address the area of human sexuality and freedom

in men and women's relationships. It underscores the importance of an active and positive female influence to counterbalance a world dominated by the law of the father for whom female sexuality is an extension of male identity——in effect, male property. Patriarchy is the shadow that casts a pall over everything and everyone in the novel; it is the corruption within, the monster that must be confronted, violence with violence, in order to "atone for the sins of the males" (239). Restoring the family unit in which mothers and fathers are co-nurturers and equal partners is one of the central struggles of the novel.

Romantic Love

If Julián Carax and Daniel Sempere are the mirror-image male protagonists of *The Shadow of the Wind*, then Penélope Aldaya and Beatriz Aguilar are their mirror-image female counterparts.

The beautiful Penélope, Ricardo Aldaya's daughter, is Julián's obsessive love. When Ricardo takes the young Julián under his wing and invites him to make use of his library, Julián sees Penélope there, and the two fall in love. What they don't know is that they are brother and sister—incest, the ultimate forbidden love, being another familiar Gothic theme. Nevertheless, their love flourishes, and they plan to escape to Paris. But they are thwarted by Mrs. Aldaya, another damaged mother, who suffers her husband's philandering with resignation. She tells Don Ricardo that she saw Julián and Penélope make love in the governess's room. Don Ricardo leaps from his armchair and slaps his wife so hard she falls to the floor. To the terrified Mrs. Aldaya, he looks as if "possessed by all the devils in hell" (278). He then goes to Penélope's bedroom and drags her by the hair to a room in the attic, locking her inside.

Penélope's subsequent screams and violent poundings on the door fall on deaf ears. Her mother, too afraid of her husband, is unwilling to defy him, and Penélope, soon discovered to be pregnant, eventually delivers a son, but both mother and son die, and the two are entombed in the basement of the home. Two years later, Mrs. Aldaya, the mother who was psychologically absent in Penélope's life and affections and who did not dare to question her husband's murderous violence, dies from what is presumed to be a terrible sense of guilt.

Carax's relationship with Penélope closely resembles Daniel's relationship with the upper-class Beatriz Aguilar. Daniel and Bea's relationship is also shadowed by the tyranny of a father, Mr. Aguilar, whose plans for Bea are for her to marry within her class. In addition, both mothers are pathologically passive, allowing the fathers to exert total control over their daughters and determine their destinies. The relationship between Daniel and Bea must therefore grow in secrecy, under the threat that Aguilar would break the boy's legs if he knew the name of the person with whom Bea is infatuated. Daniel and Beatriz seal

their commitment to one another by revealing a secret to each other. Secrets, the essential life force of the Gothic, are a way in which humans develop their bonds and subvert the established order. Daniel shares with Beatriz the secret of the Cemetery of Forgotten Books, and Beatriz takes Daniel to the abandoned and dilapidated mansion of the Aldaya family where she recounts the story of the cursed mansion and the secrets it hides.

One of the peculiarities of the mirror relationship between Daniel and Julián is the shared relationship they have with Nuria Monfort, the daughter of the caretaker of the Cemetery of Forgotten Books. Upon meeting her, Daniel immediately is attracted and finds himself "filled by an almost painful desire to kiss that woman" (172). Ignorant as to the reason for Nuria's tenderness toward him, Daniel misreads the situation as a sexual invitation. Nuria, as Daniel will eventually find out, knew Carax when she worked for Carax's publisher; she met him in Paris on a business trip, fell in love and had an affair with him, and then protected him from those who wanted to do him harm. Daniel's visit and questions threaten to uncover the secret she is keeping and thus expose Carax to danger. Like Daniel, Nuria is motherless. Like Julián, she has a problematic relationship with her father, who disapproves of her lifestyle and sexual freedom. "According to him, I run after any pair of pants, like a bitch in heat" (165), she tells Daniel.

Unmarried Nuria has the misfortune of loving Carax who cannot reciprocate with anything more meaningful than periodic moments of sexual intimacy. Nuria is particularly vulnerable to male sexual advances. As a self-supporting female, she sees herself as part of a breed of "women adrift," casualties of the Spanish Civil War and World War II. Difficult economic times force her to find work in a publishing house whose owner is another male predator, exploiting his position of power "to court young ladies half his age by presenting himself as the self-made man, an image much in vogue at the time" (434). Ironically a publisher of moral literature, this man finds it unacceptable that Nuria should reject his sexual advances. He ultimately fires her, exploiting the unequal power distribution between men and women. This moral and social violence is paired with another form of brutality along with which it functions: the abusive system of male sexual prerogative. Nuria goes home and tells Julián Carax about the publisher; the publisher is discovered dead the following morning from a broken neck.

Setting as Symbol and the Archeology of Memory

The Aldayas' decayed mansion, erected on fraud and violence, embodies the past of pre–Civil War privilege and the Fascism that replaced it, neither one a

viable social or legal system that nurtures the individual or the creative impulse. The house's unkempt garden, stripped rooms, dark corridors, and subterranean chambers reflect the state of moral decay of Franco's Spain, the putrescence of which can be cleansed only through personal nobility and courage. A symbol for the fractured family and splintered state, the house has a reputation of being haunted, of hiding secrets. Daniel will not only come across the coffins of Penélope and her newborn, but he will also discover the very much alive, albeit disfigured, Julián Carax, the arsonist who attempted to obliterate his memory by burning his own books and nearly succeeded in killing himself. The house symbolizes the patriarchal system of repression and violence, a repression directed primarily against women, homosexuals, and dissidents. The resolution of the action, then, appropriately and symbolically takes place in the mansion where history resides. Here Inspector Fumero meets Carax and Daniel, here Daniel throws himself on Fumero to prevent him from shooting Carax, and here both Daniel and Carax are reborn.

From the moment that the house is introduced, its symbolism is made apparent from its description. In front of the house sits a fountain from which the hand of a broken statue of an angel, the Angel of Mist, is seen pointing toward the sky and "rising from the waters that were tinted scarlet. The accusing index finger seemed sharp as a dagger" (299). The house is the central locus that unites the historical and familial themes, embodying a past of violence and horrors that are uncovered by Daniel's persistence and redeemed in his noble attempt to sacrifice his life for Carax. Daniel's life, maturation, and singleness of purpose revitalize the ghostly Carax who, once Daniel is shot, finds the strength to grab Inspector Fumero, drag him to the fountain, and impale him on the Angel of Mist's hand. Daniel's near-death experience changes Mr. Aguilar's objections to Daniel's and Bea's union, and he becomes "resigned to the fact that his grandson would soon call [Daniel] Dad" (476). The house where Carax's potential family was destroyed and where other families self-destructed becomes the place where the wholeness of the family and the nation are reconstituted and healed. During the confrontation with Fumero, Carax tells Daniel, "Take Beatriz away from here, Daniel. She knows what you must do. Don't let her out of your sight. Don't let anyone take her from you" (463).

In killing Inspector Fumero, Carax thus ends a period of state-sponsored persecution and violence, turning self-hatred into an act of moral justice. From a person who at the beginning of the novel was bent on erasing all memory of himself, he changes into someone who trusts again in the power of the imagination. He finds new life and purpose by watching Daniel Sempere grow and mature. In Daniel's purity of purpose, Carax comes to see in the young hero "the son he had lost, a blank page on which to restart a story that he could not invent but could remember" (444).

The Ultimate Mirror

Of all the mirror doubling in *The Shadow of the Wind*, the one that subsumes all the others is time itself—the present reflected in the past, a past preserved both in books and in the memories of the characters. In a sense, Daniel is an archeologist of memory. In one of his books, Carax wrote, "As long as we are remembered, we remain alive" (446). A book, Bea tells Daniel at the end of the novel, "is a mirror that offers us only what we already carry inside us" (484). So, too, is cultural memory reflected in the story, providing a metafictional element through the many references to writers, philosophers, and musicians.

Thus the classical Penelope, Odysseus's faithful wife, that symbol of the hearth and of constancy, is ironically recalled in the unfortunate Penélope Aldaya. By the age of thirteen, Carax had read Joseph Conrad's *Heart of Darkness* three times, a novel that undermines the certainties of civilization as it takes us on a journey into the darkness of man's heart. When Daniel introduces Beatriz Aguilar to the Cemetery of Forgotten Books, she picks Thomas Hardy's *Tess of the d'Urbervilles*, a tragic story of a young girl who is seduced and abandoned. Like Daniel's statement in the opening pages of the book, Beatriz says of her chosen novel, "It feels as if it's been waiting for me. As if it has been hiding here for me since before I was born" (182).

The nature of human experience is a circular reenactment of old stories, of either foil mirrors or echoes that inform and invest our own stories with meaning and purpose. One cannot overlook the name of Daniel's love, Beatriz. His adulation and adoration for Bea, as he calls her, is evocative of an older story told in Dante's *Divine Comedy*. The love of a good woman, Fermín tells Daniel, makes one want to be a better man: "I want to be someone she can be proud of" (186). Daniel's love for Beatriz turns out to be the kind of love that makes a man go through hell, and at the end of it, like Dante, reemerge a new and better person.

Typical of the classic Gothic novel, all the labyrinthine plot lines are satisfyingly resolved in the end, but Zafón refuses to stop at the finish line and takes the story further in multiple codas, disturbing our newly found security and returning us to the mystery of human experience. The darkness temporarily resolves itself in a new redemptive light, restoring the authority and faith of the imagination, but the tale of mystery continues as the final chapter of the novel reiterates the first, and a new labyrinth of mirrors awaits us.

Notes

1. Michael Dirda, review of *The Shadow of the Wind*, by Carlos Ruiz Zafón, *Washington Post*, April 25, 2004, www.washingtonpost.com/ac2/wp-dyn?pagename=article& contentId=A35314-2004Apr22&notFound=true (accessed March 31, 2010).

2. Amy Mathieson, review of *The Shadow of the Wind*, by Carlos Ruiz Zafón, *The Scotsman*, June 19, 2004, www.scotsman.com (accessed March 31, 2010).

3. Rebecca Ascher-Walsh, review of *The Shadow of the Wind*, by Carlos Ruiz Zafón, *Entertainment Weekly*, April 16, 2004, www.ew.com/ew/article/0,,609551,00.html (accessed March 31, 2010).

4. Richard Eder, "In the Cemetery of Forgotten Books," *New York Times Book Review*, 25 April 2004, www.nytimes.com/2004/04/25/books/in-the-cemetery-of-forgotten-books.html (accessed March 30, 2010).

5. Michael Kerrigan, "Under the Dictator," *Guardian*, June 26, 2004, www.guardian.co.uk/books/2004/jun/26/featuresreviews.guardianreview25 (accessed March 31, 2010).

6. Adam Lively, review of *The Shadow of the Wind*, by Carlos Ruiz Zafón, *Sunday Times*, August 1, 2004, http://entertainment.timsonline.co.uk/tol/arts_and_entertainment/books/article462282.ece (accessed March 31, 2010).

7. Robert Colvile, "Barça Loner," *Observer*, June 6, 2004, www.guardian.co.uk/books/2004/jun/06/fiction.features (accessed March 31, 2010).

8. Jennie Yabroff, "The Paper Trail Begins at the Cemetery of Forgotten Books," *San Francisco Chronicle*, April 18, 2004, www.sfgate.com/cgi-bin/article.cgi?f=/chronicle/reviews/books/THE_SHADOW_OF_THE_WIND.DTL#ixzz0kL2eRSoe (accessed March 31, 2010).

9. A. L. Spieckerman, "As Good as a Caráx Novel," Amazon customer review, July 29, 2004, www.amazon.com/review/RVTZFOXSP0ORU/ref=cm_srch_res_rtr_alt_2 (accessed March 31, 2010).

10. Mike Harrison, "Perhaps the Best Novel I've Read in My Life," Amazon customer review, May 7, 2004, www.amazon.com/review/R2I64AMQ81LAG8/ref=cm_srch_res_rtr_alt_1 (accessed March 31, 2010).

11. A. Ross, "A Bloated and Overwrought Soap-Opera of a Book," Amazon customer review, February 20, 2005, www.amazon.com/review/R2KK7URDAP9YWY/ref=cm_srch_res_rtr_alt_2 (accessed March 31, 2010).

12. Carlos Ruiz Zafón, *The Shadow of the Wind* (New York: Penguin, 2004), 7. Page numbers appear hereafter in parentheses in the text.

CHAPTER 49

An Icy Allegory of Cultural Survival

GOTHIC THEMES IN DAN SIMMONS'S *THE TERROR*

Van Piercy

> And through the drifts the snowy clifts
> Did send a dismal sheen:
> Nor shapes of men nor beasts we ken—
> The ice was all between.
>
> The ice was here, the ice was there,
> The ice was all around:
> It cracked and growled, and roared and howled,
> Like noises in a swound!
>
> —Samuel Taylor Coleridge, "The Rime of the Ancient
> Mariner" (1798)[1]

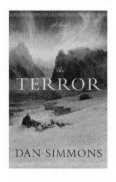

The physical sounds of ice moaning and cracking, sheets of ice flows separating and merging, haunt Dan Simmons's 2007 Gothic horror novel of arctic exploration and depravation, *The Terror*. There is certainly something of an education in this novel, and this speaks to Simmons's own nearly twenty-year teaching background. We learn something of the language of freezing, particularly through the ice masters of the historic Franklin expedition, Mr. Blanky and Mr. Reid. There are different kinds of ice, such as pancake ice; sludge ice; old pack ice or screw pack ice, which are pressure ridges of ice that are constantly forming anew and then dissipating; and seracs, which are massed columns of ice that can topple at any time. The men on the expedition face two principal monsters, the sublime ice and a supernatural terror that stalks them, periodically killing them, usually

only one or two at a time. Compounding the menace and despair, they also face *"everything"* existing in the arctic environment:

> Captain Francis Crozier . . . knew something that the men did not; namely that the Devil trying to kill them up here in the Devil's Kingdom was not just the white-furred thing killing and eating them one by one, but *everything* here—the unrelenting cold, the squeezing ice, the electrical storms, the uncanny lack of seals and whales and birds and walruses and land animals, the endless encroachment of the pack ice, the bergs that plowed their way through the solid white sea not even leaving a single ship's length lee of open water behind them, the sudden white—earthquake up-eruption of pressure ridges, the dancing stars, the shoddily tinned cans of food now turned to poison, the summers that did not come, the leads that did not open—*everything*. The monster on the ice was just another manifestation of a Devil that wanted them dead. And that wanted them to suffer.[2]

The treacheries of the ice will give Simmons occasion, in Gothically interesting ways, to rework historical characters—resurrected out of the merest documentary scraps—from the hubris-driven 1845 Franklin expedition.

The Terror is a long (769 pages) story of the now legendary arctic expedition led by fifty-nine-year-old Captain Sir John Franklin, the Admiralty's sixth unofficial choice for commanding the hoped-for voyage through Canada to China. Captain Francis Crozier, the leader of real ability, was passed over and placed second in command of the expedition because he was Irish and Presbyterian. The expedition consisted of two ice-cutting ships (modern for the time), 134 men including the officers, and "cockeyed optimism."[3] Apparently the overly hopeful and historic mission ended in that most Gothic and taboo of acts. As *National Geographic* editor Anthony Brandt puts it, the macabre finish came on King William Island with "human arms and legs cooking in a kettle while starving men stare[d] with deadened eyes at the ultimate consequences of this spectacular piece of folly."[4]

Simmons's book can reasonably be criticized by the impatient for the sin of tedium, for spending so many pages in an arctic hell, damned faintly as "reasonably creepy entertainment."[5] Still, Simmons's large novel rewards its most stalwart readers with an eventful story, realized characters, plenty of Gothic thrills and horror chills, and a surprising climax involving the survival of its lead character through an astonishing transformation that, in the best way, speaks well of human possibility. The ending is satisfying, despite the amount of reader patience needed to get there. The story and characters are engaging, but one should be forewarned that endless ice and cold and bodily failure and death among the men of the expedition has a certain brutality to it, a certain abuse of

the reader. Simmons himself may be herculean in his capacity to persevere, willing this material into an artistic whole, but numerous readers looking only for a dark winter encounter of the pulpier, popular, or one-hour variety, may not be willing to go with him where his one-and-a-quarter-pound, doorstop hardback asks them to go.

This artistic stressing of the reader is not unlike John Fowles's in some ways similarly punishing novel *The Magus*,[6] in which the main character and narrator is forced to watch a pornographic film of a lovely young white woman with whom he is smitten coupling with another man, a black man in fact. Fowles himself discusses this operation of his, this purgative "heuristic mill" (10), stating—in reference to the protagonist of *The Magus*—that essentially he wanted to destroy "human illusions," that is, take apart the identity of a conventional middle-class suburban white man by breaking his psyche, confronting something basic, unspeakable, and horrifying in this man with something more real and demanding than his prejudice. Forcing him to watch breaks him of his illusions of control and centrality. Simmons ends up participating in this same withholding of reader satisfaction, pressuring his characters and the reader throughout *The Terror*. His aim appears in a mock Holy Communion scene where Francis Crozier kneels naked before the monster in a pose of taking the sacrament, tongue held out in weird supplication. Then his tongue disappears, thanks to the monster's violent devices we assume, and he, transformed, joins the First Nation woman Silna among the God-Walkers, to live out his life with her, have children, and presumably keep the peace with the monster north of where the Inuit are allowed to go.

The novel challenges the reader with many pages following the expedition's crew of doomed, struggling, tortured, and expiring characters. They experience terrible cold, long bouts of darkness, fear, terror, general mayhem, murder, betrayal, physical exhaustion, injury, depression, and starvation. The psychological torment these characters endure, and vicariously so the reader, clearly reaches back in the tradition of Gothic fiction to the long, dark, often subterranean or deep forest journeys of Horace Walpole's Isabella in *The Castle of Otranto* (1764) or Ann Radcliffe's heroines in such famously stout Gothic novels as *The Mysteries of Udolpho* (1794) and *The Romance of the Forest* (1791). In these and in many similar stories from the period, typically female characters experience anxieties about being imprisoned in a castle or trapped in a marriage not of their choosing. In both cases, the then typically female reader—and now with Simmons, as likely a male—experiences injustice, or justice much delayed and executed by an unlikely source. In *The Terror*, the villain crewman Cornelius Hickey murders a promising young lieutenant and mutilates his body. This young man may have gone on to become a lover of the one female protagonist in the novel, the Inuit Lady Silence (Silna). The lieutenant's death is used to cover the murderer's

homosexuality, a crime committed to cover what at the time in the Royal Navy was typically a crime punishable by death (487). The lieutenant had caught the murderer, Cornelius Hickey, and his giant idiot lover, Magnus Manson, in the throes of something that would be a hanging offense (226–227), but decided, ultimately to his own undoing, that reporting the two men would cause him more trouble than it was worth:

> What had he just seen? What could he testify to, his hand on the Holy Bible . . .? He hadn't *seen* any unnatural act. He'd not caught the two sodomites in the act of copulation or . . . any other unnatural posture. Irving had heard the breathing, the gasps, something that must have been whispered alarm at the approach of his lantern, and then seen the two struggling to raise their trousers and tuck in their shirts.
>
> That would be enough to get one or both of them hanged under normal circumstances. But here, stuck in the ice, with months or years ahead of them before any chance of rescue?
>
> For the first time in many years, John Irving felt like sitting down and weeping. His life had just become complex beyond all his imagining. If he did report the two sodomites, none of his crewmates—officers, friends, subordinates—would ever look at him quite the same way again.
>
> If he did not report the two men, he would open himself to endless insolence from Hickey. His cowardice in not reporting the man would expose Irving to a form of blackmail for weeks and months to come. Nor would the lieutenant ever sleep well again or feel comfortable on watch in the darkness outside or in his cubicle—as comfortable as anyone could be with that monstrous white thing killing them all one by one—waiting, as he would be now, for Manson's white hands to close around his throat.
>
> "Oh, bugger me," Irving said aloud into the creaking cold of the hold. Realizing exactly what he had said, he laughed aloud. (226–227)

When later Irving is killed, Simmons ratchets up the dramatic moment well because Irving has just completed successful diplomatic contact with the one group of people that may be able to save the men of the expedition: the Inuit. In rushing back to tell the others of these friendly Inuit who had just shared seal blubber with him, Irving unfortunately meets Hickey, who then proceeds to slaughter him. The rest of Irving's men then begin, we find out later, to kill most of the Inuit party. This has the dramatic effect of the lost or stolen confession or the unknowingly hidden dowry in such old Gothic tales as the anonymously written "The Friar's Tale" (1792) or Isaac Crookenden's highly melodramatic and

entertaining "The Ring, or The Vindictive Monk" (1802). Tragedy and hidden injustice occur together for the reader who helplessly watches the tale unfold.

If one asks how the novel reshuffles the elements of Gothic fiction, there are no physical structures in the arctic setting other than the ships, the impermanent igloos, and an Inuit seasonal village or two somewhere. There are no forbidding towers, no castles, no subterranean passages through which hunted heroines stumble before they are free. Again, characters in *The Terror* are often inside wooden ships, and only three ever go into an igloo. Other than that, we find them braving the ice, extreme cold, and lightning, physically exhausting themselves by pulling "sledges" of equipment. The men themselves, their equipment, and their expedition eventually decay and fall apart. As Chris Baldick has no doubt taught a generation of Gothic fiction scholars through his perennially popular *Oxford Book of Gothic Tales*, along with inherited legacies and constricted space, decay is at the heart of Gothic's effects:

> For the Gothic effect to be attained, a tale should combine a fearful sense of inheritance in time with a claustrophobic sense of enclosure in space, these two dimensions reinforcing one another to produce an impression of sickening descent into disintegration. . . . Typically a Gothic tale will invoke the tyranny of the past (a family curse, the survival of archaic forms of despotism and of superstition) with such weight as to stifle the hopes of the present (the liberty of the heroine or hero) within the dead-end of physical incarceration (the dungeon, the locked room, or simply the confinements of a family house closing in upon itself). Even more concisely, although at the risk of losing an important series of connected meanings, we could just say that Gothic fiction is characteristically obsessed with old buildings as sites of human decay.[7]

Rather than old building in decay or the decline of the family line, we have in *The Terror*, read as Gothic fiction, *the decay of a whole cultural inheritance* and its possible rejuvenation through hybridization or admixture, and the individual cost of the ensuing transformation, made possible by access to *living* (as opposed to museum set pieces) aboriginal or indigenous cultures. The novel invites one to rethink the old Gothic categories through our contemporary context, especially regarding globalization (the sweeping away of cultural otherness) and gender (physically battling ice and fatigue versus the easy—or unmanly—pleasures of melodrama and consumer media culture).

True to melodramatic and conventional form, the hero (Crozier) gets the girl (Silna) in the end, but his substance as a man, his cultural identity, his understanding of his place in the natural order, is dismantled and rearranged. Silna is the new center, or the point of identification that has not changed but rather

been discovered (or rediscovered), fought for, and "won." While one would not want to characterize Crozier's triumph as Pyrrhic, his is perhaps the triumph of survival itself or of a man discovering in himself the capacities to love and endure, and indeed to be, beyond what his culture has taught him. He has essentially changed not just his cultural identity but his species being, joining a whole new cosmological scheme complete with new enhanced biological powers in his tongueless life now as a telepath.

While mostly women wrote and consumed Gothic fiction in its first wave, recognizing in these fictional flights and subterranean journeys the effort to exorcise anxiety about patriarchal domination in their culture, we now have Simmons presenting men on dark journeys, not to escape female power—not in symmetry with women's struggles against a repressive patriarchal order in the eighteenth and nineteenth centuries—but to escape something unleashed by the (ecological) gods of this earth. The Inuit divinities left a demoniacal killing machine where our explorers land, a prehistorically oversized polar bear called the *Tuunbaq* that could only "be *appeased*," not killed (266).

Between the *Tuunbaq*'s feasts, the novel portrays many men living together in cramped conditions and invites the suspicion that the novel harbors a genuine interest in human suffering and degradation. There is an abundance of bodily fluids, smells, flatulence, excrement, shared or observed pain and fear, lack of modesty, and paradoxically, as a result of the bonds of mutual survival and hardship, a deep camaraderie between the over 128 men living on two ships for three years. There is a constant danger of losing one's body parts, of exploding teeth (9) and the freezing that threatens hands, nose, and more, a Canadian promise that "in less than a minute . . . any fleshy appendage" can "freeze solid" (9)—a bogus story we are told "at a mere fifty below," but believable nonetheless, and true enough at lower temperatures. There is physical endurance in the pain of the journey, "the tortures of the Long March" (545) that the men undertake when their coal finally runs out.

Simmons's Dr. Harry Goodsir as well as the monster perform the evisceration, or rather the anatomization, of male bodies, a violence done to them in the name of testing their limits and answering the question, "What makes a man?" or "Of what is man composed?" (499). In one of Simmons's sets of characters, we find that a man can be a man of culture and a tradesman. One of the surprises in the novel is the unbelievably well-read pair of former lovers, Henry Peglar and John Bridgens. Simmons takes literal textual scraps (whatever later archeological studies have left us of the expedition's effects) to create the characters and relationship of Peglar and Bridgens. The reader finds both sympathetic and unsympathetic treatments of homosexuality. The pairing of Bridgens and Peglar contrasts starkly with the murderers Hickey and Manson, the idiot lover Hickey likes to use to murder others. Simmons's treatment of same-sex attraction possesses the virtue of recognizing a normative range of human qualities, from gross

demonic urges, comprising even abuse and rape when one considers Manson's idiocy, to the beautiful and touching tribute to deep friendship and shared intellectual interests. The only criticism one might have of Simmons's handling of his asymmetrical homosexual pairs is that the virtuous homosexuals are desexed; they no longer have sex together, thus making them more acceptable than the demonic Hickey and the ludicrous Manson who can neither control their urges on board ship nor be held safe among the cabin boys.

Simmons's handling of character is further shown in the believable, if possibly foreseeable, development of the character of Dr. Harry Goodsir. At the beginning of the story, Goodsir is devoted to the somewhat ridiculous Sir John Franklin. He comes aboard the *Erebus* just before the expedition departs Greenhithe in Kent, England. Trained in anatomy, he writes in his diary that while he is employed by the expedition "as a mere assistant surgeon, I am, in Truth, no mere surgeon but a Doctor" (47). The reader must decide here whether this is mere pretension or special truth. Does Goodsir bring more to the expedition than is apparent in his pedantic descriptions and "amateurish" interests in "arctic flora and fauna" (55)? Intent on sailing through the arctic, mainly in order to study "the life-forms of the Icy Realms," Goodsir feels certain that his "Expedition with Captain Sir John Franklin already promises to be the Experience of a Lifetime" (48). Simmons also mocks Goodsir's faith in gentlemanly ways, partly through the latter's very name, and in his often elaborate gestures of courtesy and trust in protocol. His naïveté and enthusiasm are obvious when Franklin's beloved daughter, Eleanor, sees a dove from dockside as her father's ships depart, and she points the flying bird out to her father aboard *Erebus*. Goodsir sees the dove as a "good omen," marking him, despite his scientific training, as a surprisingly superstitious man (as were many of his fellow seafaring crewmen). Christian man that Goodsir is, Simmons seems also here to mock a religious mind's addiction to psychological anesthesia for salving the psyche with essentially irrational, accidental events or "omens" by attaching wished-for meaning to them. A belief in folklore (a Gothic hallmark) and wish-fulfillment fantasy seems hardly the stuff of a people who put so much trust in steam engines, hardwoods, metallurgy, various implements of innovative technology, and mathematical navigation to challenge hostile arctic environs. Though Goodsir's name invites one to imagine, and the author confirms, a right, prim, and proper fellow, a pedant even, and shallow fool, inept at pulling a sledge, his true courage is revealed in one of the book's most moving moments, just past the midpoint. As the monster rampages through the ship, killing and maiming, Goodsir accepts his medical responsibility and goes back to the hold to try to retrieve one or two of the giant bear's victims even though he himself is injured (421). He is recognized for his bravery by the bona fide war hero Captain Fitzjames (239) when the latter addresses him as "doctor," a usually withheld element of address protocol that had previously vexed Goodsir.

In the old Gothic tales written in England in the late eighteenth and early nineteenth centuries, the construction of space, its use and imagined status, is a constant feature. Space itself became a way to represent the self's constriction or repression (usually this has been interpreted by later critics as a repression by social forces, mechanisms, or codes) by producing anxiety about enclosed spaces and loss of freedom. In *The Terror*, we have for enclosures the ships themselves, trapped within the ice, not for days or weeks but for years. Here is enclosure enough to induce panic, fear, dread, and an overpowering wish for home. The paranoia and terror are caused not only by the threat of a skull-crushing thwack from *Tuunbaq*, but by −50 °F temperatures, which threaten injury and death merely from contact or a moment's inattentiveness—for instance, grabbing a metal gun without one's gloves. The sense of entrapment, both on the ships and in the unforgiving, unrelenting ice, contributes to a well-known aspect of experience in the Gothic genre: anxiety and the induced paranoia of closed spaces. This spatial ordeal transfers to anxieties about sex and sexuality and the codes and regulations society uses to contain sexual desire.

Captain Franklin's puritan morals and state of repression are apparent when he is shocked by the "Esquimaux" maiden's nudity. Franklin reflects on a previous arctic expedition he was on when he tries to recall the name of "that fifteen-year-old Copper Indian girl that Back was going to fight a duel over at their winter quarters of Fort Enterprise" (17):

> That girl was evil. Beautiful, yes, but evil. She had no shame. Franklin himself, despite all efforts never to look her way, had seen her slip out of her heathen robes and walk naked across half the length of the cabin one moonlit night.
>
> He was thirty-four years old at the time, but she was the first naked human female he had ever seen and even now the most beautiful. The dark skin. The breasts already heavy as globed fruit but also still those of an adolescent, the nipples not yet raised, the areolae strange, smooth dark-brown circles. It was an image Sir John had not been able to eradicate from his memory—try and pray as he might—in the quarter of a century since then. (17–18)

Thinking of her pubic hair, the puritanical Franklin imagines it "as pitch black as sin itself" (18). Later in the novel he sees Lady Silence naked and almost faints (155). Sir John Franklin, deliverer of long sermons to his men on Sundays, is shocked by the strange sexual mores of the "Esquimaux" and haunted by the dusky "globed fruit" (18). Established religion, as troubled here as it was in the older Gothic works, has as its representative an incompetent and sexually repressed leader, a sentimental and rather bumbling man, who is to be pitied. As an historical figure, he has power, but his potency as a religious figure or

religious leader in this neo-Gothic fiction is surprisingly curtailed. His power is clearly recognized as that of the figurehead, the semblance of the real-world competence that saves men's souls; material competence and leadership is actually embodied in the narrative's central character and captain of *The Terror*, the whip-smart commanding drunk, Francis Crozier.

The name of Crozier's ship, the *Terror*, leads elegantly and metaphorically to the idea that we bring terror with us. The whole opening paragraph of the northern lights reaching for the ship Gothicizes nature: "Captain Crozier comes up on deck to find his ship under attack by celestial ghosts. Above him—above *Terror*—shimmering folds of light lunge but then quickly withdraw like the colourful arms of aggressive but ultimately uncertain spectres. Ectoplasmic skeletal fingers extend toward the ship, open, prepare to grasp, and pull back" (3). The ship that carries the men is a Gothic attractor and the principal site and vehicle of terror. Terror, of course, is something that brews from the human imagination, whether it's "our" ship, "our" mental state, or "our" treatment of the world, of nature, and of others.

Meeting terror best are the Inuit, who according to legend chose to stay in communion with the demon monster of the Far North. The conclusion of *The Terror*, with its sense of awe and human promise, confirms the novel as an allegory of cultural survival and personal transformation, of Captain Crozier's conversion from curmudgeonly tippler to shaman. This is "going native," to be sure, but also submission and humility, the changing of one's basic understanding of life and what it is to be human, and the acceptance of the impossible—the supernatural experience of this new world. As humans are cultural beings, they can change their cultures as they change themselves. Change comes in many ways. Sometimes a man has to change, and sometimes a culture has to change. Judged as art, this novel makes us believe in change, for however briefly, in the need for it, in the heroic human possibility of it when confronted with the wholly alien environmental other and in the protection and profound respect for cultures not our own. To confront arctic conditions well, one doesn't easily make up for the specialized knowledge and practices of the Inuit, built up over millennia, with reinforced wooden hulls, extra layers of English wool, and two low-horsepower steam engines.

Silence and Crozier mutually benefit from the tightly fastened nature of their intercultural relationship and then intracultural marriage. She even communicates to him at one point that she had been waiting for him (760). The story pings for us the myth that our one true love awaits, if only we will recognize him or her and pledge devotion. The reader hopes for that romantic conclusion, having endured so much death and despair during the failed expedition, that is, that Crozier will make the right decision and bond completely with Silence. He kneels in his visions and then in his final "surrender" to Silence—with their

mutual blowing of air over each other's vocal chords, a strange communion—
and to the beast, to another way of life, in another sacrament of change, as the
beast takes his tongue and speech (his Western humanity) forever (744–745,
746). Once mated, she goes where he goes, even taking the children into the
forbidding, haunted wreck of the *Terror*. They find the ship after it has been
sailed south by some remaining crew members and once again has been frozen in
place, before the old hulk's final conflagration which is viewed by Crozier, Silna,
their children, and the small Inuit hunting party that had found the wreck. She
follows him because she is his wife now, not in some formally ceremonial sense
but in the sense that matters to two human beings facing a truly cold and hostile
world together:

> None of the Real People wanted to go through that hole.
> *I will see you in a few minutes*, Crozier signed to Silence.
> She actually smiled. *Do not be stupid*, she signed. *Your children and
> I are coming with you*. (758)

This view of partnership, of husband and wife, of being in a deep psychological
and emotional communion where one casts one's lot in life forever with this
other forms part of the Gothic romance of *The Terror*: "*I was always waiting for
you*" (760), Silna signs to Crozier. The hero is rewarded. Here is where the "native" woman shows the adulterous and lustful Western men of the crew the true
meaning of integrity and commitment to another human being. The marriage
customary among a people living in a dangerous place during a changing time
means that they are dependent on one another for survival: there is the fastened
partnership, the union, and nothing else gets in its way or questions it. This no
doubt is the moment to compare Crozier's love with Silna to his fantasized love
and ultimately humiliating and pointless dalliance with the opportunistic Miss
Cracroft, who is so outwardly and conventionally desirable (211)—she'll play
with him sexually for amusement and pleasure, but she won't marry him. He
proposes marriage the day after their intimacy, and she counters coldly with her
frank ambitions and elitism: "'If I were to marry,' continued Sophia, opening
her parasol again and spinning it above her, 'it would be to our dashing Captain
Ross. Although I am not destined to be a mere captain's wife either, Francis. He
would have to be knighted . . . but I am sure he will be soon'" (211). Crozier recognizes years later, after forming his native "marital" bond with Silna, that Miss
Cracroft had been a "spoiled child" who "used him" as he had used women before, those "dockside chippies." He recognizes himself by the end of the novel as
both subject and object, neither in the margin nor in the center of control (734).

Lady Silence, as she is known by the Westerners, contains a double enten-
dre: her name and lost tongue suggest her not saying anything to the white men
of the expedition and fits with what little real interest they have for listening to

the indigenous people anyway. She is not just a Rousseauian child of nature or noble savage, naive and innocent in so many things, as the English men at first see her. She comes and goes mysteriously, a completely independent (female) being, and thus doubly other for the Westerners (culturally other and gendered other), beyond their understanding and control.

Contrary to some of Simmons's horror novels (especially *Song of Kali*, 1985), Crozier's redemption and transformation serve as an allegory for the always-ready possibility that Westerners may need to give themselves over to another way of life. Crozier realizes the futility and absurdity of the European approach to these lands, that too many die, that England throws too many men away for voyages of exploration, as well as for the rescue parties (189–190). When he comes upon the remnants of the expedition, a pile of goods, furniture, tools, and luxury items, he asks, "Did we really haul all this shit hundreds of miles in our boats?" (753). He finally comes to realize that "the only paths left now are surrender or death. Or both" (743). It is then that he aligns himself completely with Silna, taking the sacrament from the monstrous *Tuunbaq*.

Simmons lends his hand to tradition, revitalizing Gothic fiction in his novel, applying the Gothic's peculiar resources to questions about masculinity and to Western concepts of technology and purpose, focusing on how Western man must overcome his techno-fascist view of nature and (the value of) other cultures, relearning the ancient Greek tragic conception of hubris. The taboo of changing cultural premises, of moving beyond one's most basic, lifelong-held terms of reference (e.g., Western science and technology, know-how, and military power as a force for conquering others, as well as nature, all in the quest for wealth, fame, and dominion)—these elements of firm belief get shaken by the long, dark night of arctic cold, as well as, incidentally, by the allegorical Everest that the reader must climb in reading through this long, productive, and cathartic novel.

Reason, exemplified by science, the scientific method, and that coolest language of science, mathematics and quantitative measures, explains objects and physical forces in the world, but imagination courts our senses too: The reliance on reason and science by the *Kabloona* (the pale humans, the men from the West) struggles with the irrationality of what appears to their senses while trudging through the lands of the First Nation:

> Pulling up his collar and tilting his head back, out of forty years' habit of checking the status of masts and rigging, Crozier notices that the stars overhead burn cold and steady but those near the horizon not only flicker but shift when stared at, moving in short spurts to the left, then to the right, then jiggling up and down. Crozier has seen this before—in the far south with Ross as well as in these waters on earlier expeditions. A scientist on that south polar trip, a man who

> spent the first winter in the ice there grinding and polishing lenses
> for his own telescope, had told Crozier that the perturbation of the
> stars was probably due to rapidly shifting refraction in the cold air
> lying heavy but uneasy over the ice-covered seas and unseen frozen
> landmasses. In other words, over new continents never before seen by
> the eyes of man. Or at least, Crozier thinks, in this northern arctic,
> by the eyes of white men. (3–4)

His mind is settled only in part by the sanguine explanations of science and its measurements. Scientific explanation provides a reasonable, known, trustworthy interpretation of natural phenomena. Crozier critically notes that there are other people who have seen these arctic phenomena before, people who aren't from the minor promontory of Asia otherwise known as Europe, the others who properly and rightly dwell here.

Besides the conflict with nature in this forbidding landscape, there is Western man's barely tolerant response to indigenous peoples, a response that led not only to technological or instrumental approaches to nature, and to thinking of nature as a passive object for alien tools and purposes, but to the worst problems of modernity, to colonialism and imperialism, world wars, nuclear arms races, and the destruction of native and traditional cultures. The reason that Crozier meets with success is that he is able to integrate his past self and his new identity as one of the "God-Walking People" (747). Like those who have no tongues, who have made a pact with a monstrous arctic bear, who can "think" thoughts to one another, and who have the gift of "second sight"—which had been denounced in Crozier's England as witchcraft—he is liberated by his new faith, particularly in this Lady of Silence, mother of his children.

Crozier is ushered through a voluntary death and rebirth. In May 1851,[8] he becomes *Taliriktug* ("Strong Arm"), the husband of Silence (747). He now cares for her and their children. He joins her tribe of silent, telepathic "God-Walking people." He has given up what many have considered the one thing that makes human beings human, distinguishing them from animals—speech. Communication, however, if not language as such, persists for these people in the form of hand gestures and mental telepathy, "mind speech."

The novel's triumph—besides teaching us about a historical mission, imagining it from the inside, showing us the limits of human endurance in miles of ice, and questioning unconsidered domination—must be its intense, love-affirming, and revolutionary ending. The "steady blue flame of hope in Crozier's aching chest" (433) remains a strange testament to the will to survive and has indicated all along that this novel is, in part, a Gothic transformation tale that takes an "older life away" (936). In his determination to lead his men and to abandon alcohol, in his acceptance of the grandmother who taught him to use his "second sight" (334), and in his transcendent lovemaking with Silna (which

leads to kneeling at the altar of the supernatural and losing his tongue to a god-like beast), a new man has been created.

Notes

1. Samuel Taylor Coleridge, *The Rime of the Ancient Mariner* (New York: Dover, 1970).

2. Dan Simmons, *The Terror* (New York: Little, Brown, 2007), 189. Page numbers appear hereafter in parentheses in the text.

3. Anthony Brandt, *The Man Who Ate His Boots: The Tragic History of the Search for the Northwest Passage* (New York: Knopf, 2010).

4. Brandt, *The Man Who Ate His Boots*, 396.

5. Terrence Rafferty, "Ice Men," *New York Times*, Sunday book review, www.nytimes.com/2007/03/18/books/review/Rafferty.t.html (accessed March 18, 2007).

6. John Fowles, foreword to *The Magus* (New York: Dell, Bantam, 1965, rev. 1978), 6–11.

7. Chris Baldick, introduction to *The Oxford Book of Gothic Tales*, ed. Chris Baldick (Oxford, UK: Oxford University Press, 1992), xi–xxiii.

8. Lastly, I would like to note what seems a slight problem with the text related to a Gothic-inspired warping and twisting of time in the narrative. Odd things happen with the dates in *The Terror*. Is the first instance a typo or not? Chapter 13, where Franklin sees the returning party with the shot "Esquimaux," is dated June 1846, but all the other chapters related to the event date it as 1847. The second instance occurs when Crozier and Fitzjames go to a mapped cairn to leave a record of their expedition and see that a previous note penned by Sir John Franklin mistakes the year (526–527). Simmons might have been bitten by the *Lost* television series bug, given that show's penchant for delving into alternative timelines. Time fragments, as does the readerly consciousness, in sympathy with the horrors visited on the men; this vertigo of time displacement captures readily the supernatural time entered into by the expedition.

CHAPTER 50

Are They *All* Horrid?

DIANE SETTERFIELD'S *THE THIRTEENTH TALE* AND THE VALIDITY OF GOTHIC FICTION

Reggie Oliver

"But, my dearest Catherine, what have you been doing with yourself all this morning? Have you gone on with *Udolpho*?"

"Yes, I have been reading it ever since I woke; and I am got to the black veil."

"Are you, indeed? How delightful! Oh! I would not tell you what is behind the black veil for the world! Are not you wild to know?"

"Oh! Yes, quite; what can it be? But do not tell me—I would not be told upon any account. I know it must be a skeleton, I am sure it is Laurentina's skeleton. Oh! I am delighted with the book! I should like to spend my whole life in reading it. I assure you, if it had not been to meet you, I would not have come away from it for all the world."

"Dear creature! How much I am obliged to you; and when you have finished *Udolpho*, we will read *The Italian* together; and I have made out a list of ten or twelve more of the same kind for you."

"Have you, indeed! How glad I am! What are they all?"

"I will read you their names directly; here they are, in my pocketbook. *Castle of Wolfenbach, Clermont, Mysterious Warnings, Necromancer of the Black Forest, Midnight Bell, Orphan of the Rhine,* and *Horrid Mysteries.* Those will last us some time."

"Yes, pretty well; but are they all horrid, are you sure they are all horrid?"

—Isabella Thorpe and Catherine Morland in Jane
Austen's *Northanger Abbey*

While looking through the "customer review" section for books on the Amazon website, I am sometimes reminded of this delightful snatch of chatter about Gothic novels from Jane Austen. The "reviews" rarely affect my decision to buy, but they do offer a fascinating glimpse into the tastes and insights of ordinary readers from all over the world. Someone will write an illuminating study based upon them one day.

Diane Setterfield's *The Thirteenth Tale* is an interesting case in point. It had received, when I last looked, well over a hundred customer reviews which range, in a fairly even distribution, all the way from extravagant five-star praise to one-star vituperative dismissal. These extremes of opinion, I discovered, depended very much upon whether its readers accepted the premises on which the Gothic novel is founded. Differing opinions about style, characterization, plot, and structure of course remained, but these seemed to me to be secondary to the fundamental issue: is it possible to write a Gothic novel that is also a substantial work of literature?

This is a question which, as the above quotation suggests, Jane Austen might have answered in the negative. But then she was writing before *Jane Eyre*, *Wuthering Heights*, *The Woman in White*, *Rebecca*, and, for that matter, *The Thirteenth Tale*. Sheridan Le Fanu and Poe were yet unborn. On the other hand, Ann Radcliffe, the author of *Udolpho*, was very much alive and was to outlive Austen by several years even though her best work had already been done by the time *Northanger Abbey* (composed between 1798–1803) was written.

The Gothic novel has, as I see it, three primary characteristics. Those who respond more favorably to qualities which the Gothic novel does not possess will find that *The Thirteenth Tale* is not for them. Though by no means short of originality, Diane Setterfield's work is an exemplary Gothic novel and, in its particular way, features all three of the principal characteristics of the Gothic novel.

1. The Gothic Novel is Primarily a Work of the Imagination

Of course all works of art depend upon the imagination of their creator, but the Gothic novel does so in a special way. The works of Austen, Trollope,

Dickens, Waugh, and for that matter Balzac, Flaubert, Tolstoy, and many of the great European masters, are human dramas which derive their strength from a close and often humorous observation of the manners and morals of their time. Their narratives are washed by the tides of history and fashion; they are as much concerned with society as with the individual. The little dialogue above quoted would adequately demonstrate to the reader that *Northanger Abbey* is *not* a Gothic novel. It is detached, gently mocking, acutely aware of the follies of its time. Social observation has no place in the Gothic novel because it is about the inner world. Humor, if present at all, is traditionally confined to minor characters: rustics, servants, and the like.

The setting of a Gothic novel is both specific and imaginary. To take Ann Radcliffe's *The Mysteries of Udolpho* as a classic example, it begins in the year 1584 "on the pleasant banks of the Garonne,"[1] but the scenery that Mrs. Radcliffe so luxuriantly describes comes straight out of an idyllic landscape by Claude Lorrain.[2] Later, when things get wilder, one is reminded of Salvator Rosa,[3] but always of an imagined landscape. Mrs. Radcliffe, by all accounts, was a retiring lady and as far as I can ascertain never ventured abroad, though her descriptions are no less vivid for that. Moreover, while she dresses her characters in the picturesque costumes of two hundred years before her time, they are all of them, from her heroine Emily to the proto-Byronic villain Montoni, of the eighteenth century. This applies particularly to her important subsidiary characters like Madame Cheron and Cavigni. Emily in particular is a child of the eighteenth century, a young lady of sentiment, whose very characteristic and all too prolific effusions in verse belong to the age of James Thomson, William Collins, Thomas Gray, and Edward Young's *Night Thoughts*, with its picturesque pastoralism and classical melancholy. Setterfield's protagonist, Margaret Lea, is similarly bookish and pensive, though, fortunately for us, her literary inclinations are more prosaic.

Like Radcliffe, Setterfield has a certain disregard for chronological authenticity. She sets some of the action in the past (at a guess, about sixty or more years ago) and some presumably in the present, though it is not a present in which either computers or mobile phones play a part. The past is equally vague: it is one in which servants and governesses exist as a matter of course, but neither of the world wars, nor indeed any other historical event is mentioned. This was something that greatly annoyed some of the Amazon critics, who did not perhaps realize that these omissions were deliberate and not the product of carelessness. Setterfield is aiming to cut the reader off from the moorings of contemporary reference in order to concentrate more fully on the inner drama of the mind.

The story tells of a bookish woman, Margaret, daughter of the proprietor of a secondhand bookshop, who is called to write the biography of famous author Vida Winter, well known for her many and disparate accounts of her life.

Gradually, Margaret is drawn into the world of Vida and sees parallels with her own upbringing. Mysteries are uncovered. Its central theme is that of identity and of the role that storytelling plays in its discovery.

The plot motif of an innocent drawn into a different and more dangerous world than that to which she is accustomed is one that is shared by *The Mysteries of Udolpho* and many another Gothic novel. A comparatively recent modern example is Daphne du Maurier's *Rebecca*. The assault being made is not so much upon the heroine's person as upon her innocent imagination. Had Margaret, or Emily, or the nameless narrator of *Rebecca*, been more worldly and sophisticated, they might have borne their experiences, for which they are magnificently unprepared, with less trauma. Emily's eighteenth-century pastoralism is assaulted by the romantic and the sublime; Margaret's bookish academicism is invaded by psychological ambiguity and moral chaos. Ultimately, however, their lack of sophistication is not necessarily a disadvantage: innocence emerges relatively unscathed and wiser if not stronger from the ordeal.

There is always an archetypal, fairy-tale element to the plot; in the above instances (including *The Thirteenth Tale*), that of the ordeal of innocence. It is not surprising therefore that dreams play a major role in the Gothic novel. After all, at least two of its earliest examples, *Frankenstein* and *The Castle of Otranto*, were inspired by dreams. *Rebecca* begins, "Last night I dreamt I went to Manderley again."[4] There are dreams too in *The Thirteenth Tale*, and they perform the traditional dual function of dreams in the Gothic novel, that of revealing the inner world of the protagonist, and of offering cryptic warnings to the reader of coming events. With characteristic subtlety, Diane Setterfield does not make her dreams into discrete imaginary incidents but rather the continuation into another state of consciousness of the narrator's work and anxieties:

> As I started to sleepwrite my questions, the margin seemed to expand. The paper throbbed with light. Swelling, it engulfed me, until I realised with a mixture of trepidation and wonderment that I was enclosed in the grain of the paper, embedded in the white interior of the story itself. Weightless, I wandered all night long in Miss Winter's story, plotting its landscape, measuring its contours and, on tip-toe at its borders, peering at the mysteries beyond its bounds.[5]

In a few short sentences, Setterfield has delineated the book's inner landscape. Another means whereby Setterfield enriches the imaginary landscape of her novel is that of literary allusion. In this she displays both skill and considerable originality. In the same way that the landscapes conjured up by Mrs. Radcliffe are those of Claude Lorrain, Gaspard Dughet,[6] and Salvator Rosa, so the atmospheric landscape of Setterfield reminds one of *Jane Eyre*, *Wuthering Heights*, and *The Woman in White*. The difference is that Setterfield's use of artistic reference

points is more self-conscious and cunning. These books are all mentioned by name. They are to be found on the bookshelves of the heroine and narrator who later finds them on the shelves in the house of Vida Winter, the writer whose biography she is writing. These books are later joined by *The Turn of the Screw*.

In *The Thirteenth Tale*, one is deliberately invited to draw parallels with these books. Vida's house on the moors suggests *Wuthering Heights*; motifs of a fire and a hidden presence in the house remind one of *Jane Eyre*. Isabelle, mother of the fateful twins, is said to appear like the Woman in White. Enigmatic children, one quite possibly intrinsically evil, and apparitions in the garden seen from a window suggest *The Turn of the Screw*. The presence of a governess who writes a journal to make sense of strange happenings reminds one of both *The Turn of the Screw* and *Jane Eyre*. These echoes are not introduced out of a lack of originality or, as more than one Amazon reviewer irritably suggested, to place *The Thirteenth Tale* self-consciously on par with a great classic like *Jane Eyre*. They provide a web of reference and suggestion for the intelligent reader; they give the narrative depth and background. Similes and metaphors often reflect the bookish theme, such as "a silence as unambiguous as the white space at the end of a chapter." The central figure is a writer and also a fabricator of her life story. We have entered a strange ambiguous world in which apparent facts turn out to be fictions, and apparent fictions reveal the truth.

But would readers unacquainted with the classics to which Setterfield refers miss out? I do not think they would to any great extent, as long as they grasp Setterfield's essential point: that we are all enriched and defined by narrative. Human identity is discovered through storytelling, and its authenticity is dependent not on an accurate correspondence with external events but on the way it resonates in the inner world. Her theme, in other words, is a kind of manifesto for the Gothic novel itself.

2. The Gothic Novel Is Transgressive

It is ironic that Horace Walpole, in so many ways an exemplary product of the Age of Reason, should also be the pioneer of an art form that reacted violently against it. This school friend and companion of Thomas Gray, the neoclassical elegist, was the author of *The Castle of Otranto* (1765). Yet this is perhaps not so surprising: neoclassicism always contained in it the seeds of its ruination. Even in Pope you will find the odd Gothic moment. Some of his poems teem with Gothic imagery, in particular, "Eloisa to Abelard" from 1717:

> See in her cell, sad Eloisa spread
> Propt on some tomb, a neighbour of the dead.[7]

While the Palladian style still held sway in country house building, rich men were beginning to embellish their properties with Gothic accessories. In George Colman and David Garrick's *The Clandestine Marriage* (1766, produced only a year after *Otranto*), the vulgarian arriviste Mr. Sterling is showing Lord Ogleby around his property:

> Ay ruins, my lord! And they are reckoned very fine ones too. You would think them ready to tumble on your head. It has just cost me a hundred and fifty pounds to put my ruins in thorough repair.[8]

(Sterling's sister, Mrs. Heidelberg, has "a little gothic dairy.")

The mention of ruins is significant. The Gothic novel, like the fashionable eighteenth-century landscaped garden, would be incomplete without a ruin. Decay, decline, and corruption is a persistent theme. The house in which "Vida Winter" grows up is a veritable House of Usher, and by the time her putative biographer Margaret Lea visits it, it is a ruin. We tend to think of "decadence" as a late-nineteenth-century phenomenon, but you will find it from the first at the very heart of the Gothic novel.

The fascination of the Gothic novel with ruin is more than mere morbidity, the half-reluctant compulsion to look on corpses and corruption that was observed as far back as Plato. In the Gothic novel, the destructive element is also the most potent source of energy. The transgressions of Montoni (in *The Mysteries of Udolpho*), Schedoni (in Mrs. Radcliffe's *The Italian*), and Ambrosio (in *The Monk*) are what drive these books, not their passive heroines. Incidentally, both Schedoni and Ambrosio are doubly transgressive in that they were once monks and have therefore fallen, like Satan, from the ranks of the blessed: *Corruptio optimi pessima* (the corruption of the best is the worst). According to Montague Summers's pioneering study of the Gothic novel, *The Gothic Quest*, the very first Gothic novel ever written, *Longsword, Earl of Salisbury* (by Thomas Leland, 1762), features a villainous monk with the improbable name of Reginhald who was "the ancestor of a whole progeny of villainous cowlmen and friars."[9]

This cannot be put down to a simple Anglican bias against Catholic monasticism. It has deeper roots in a belief in the dynamics of transgression and corruption which came to dominate the Gothic sensibility. It was William Blake, that philosopher of the Gothic mind, who believed that Milton was secretly "of the Devil's party" when he created *Paradise Lost*. He may have been right about Milton, or he may not, but he was certainly uttering a truth about himself and his contemporaries for whom "energy is eternal delight." Some romantics like Byron even managed to live out this Gothic role in their lives and were in their turn fictionalized into Gothic villains. Polidori in his novel *The Vampyre*, like *Frankenstein* a child of the Villa Diodati, describes his central character Lord Ruthven in terms that make it unmistakably a portrait of his friend Byron. There

is no doubt that the passive heroines of Gothic fiction—Emily, Camilla (*The Monk*), the nameless narrator of *Rebecca*—have little glamour when compared with their diabolical adversaries, Montoni, Ambrosio, and Rebecca herself. Even Dr. Van Helsing is dwarfed by his eponymous opponent, Dracula. These creatures are the destructive creators of the Gothic world.

The Thirteenth Tale has its own brand of dynamic corruption. There is more than a hint of a very Byronic act of incest (Byron had an affair with his sister Augusta). Without revealing too many of the secrets of the plot, the very Gothic theme of the doppelgänger puts in an appearance, in the apparently prosaic form of twins. In fact, the whole structure of the book is binary: there are two narrative streams, Vida's and Margaret's. Vida's narrative originates with the binary of a brother and sister in one generation and then a set of twins in the next. Margaret's narrative will discover another set of twins altogether. Two is traditionally the Devil's number, the number of division and separation.

In the duality of the twins is reflected the traditional Manichean duality of light and dark, good and evil, but the final resolution provides a more complex and subtle meditation on this theme. The fire which destroys the house of secrets destroys one duality and creates another. It also creates a writer. Vida Winter, whose true identity we only discover at the end of the book, rises phoenix-like from its ashes. She also is not one but two: a writer of fiction who tells the truth and an autobiographer who tells a lie. One of the more intelligent of the Amazon.com critics observed, "As a scholar of André Gide, Ms. Setterfield is understandably keen to evoke the phenomenon he termed 'dédoublement,' splitting of the self into two: one who experiences the world and one who only observes."

The Thirteenth Tale, like all Gothic novels, is also transgressive in that it is antirationalistic. This manifests itself blatantly in many Gothic novels through supernatural happenings, but this is not always the case. Both *The Thirteenth Tale* and *The Mysteries of Udolpho* endeavor to explain away what appears to be obviously supernatural, but a residue of mystery remains. In *The Thirteenth Tale*, the specter of the heroine/narrator's missing twin may be only in her head, but it is real for all that, and it plays a key role in her journey of self-discovery.

There is an episode in the middle of the book that is part of the narration of Vida Winter's supposed past as one of twin girls. When the twins' mother, Isabelle, is taken to an asylum, a governess called Hester Barrow, of prosaic name and appearance, is employed to look after Adeline and Emmeline. Sanity takes over from madness, apparently. In collaboration with the local doctor, the governess embarks upon a scientific study of the twins. However, the study fails because the twins' behavior does not conform to any kind of rational psychological pattern, but also because the doctor and the governess fall in love. This leads to a scandal that exiles the governess. The forces of rationalism are therefore twice defeated by the forces of irrationalism, from without and within. (The bi-

nary motif yet again!) The doctor and the governess are all the more vulnerable because their scientific minds fail to comprehend the mysteries at work inside them.

3. The Gothic Novel Is about Secrets and Their Revelation, Imprisonment, and Release

The Thirteenth Tale is a story about biography, the search for identity, and the relationship of the biographer to her subject. It is a fruitful motif for a writer of Gothic fiction, which depends so much upon mystery, concealed identity, and shocking revelation.

Even in real life, biography has its Gothic aspects. I remember how when I was writing a biography of the writer Stella Gibbons,[10] I happened to buy a volume of her poetry from a book dealer. In it I found some scrawled marginalia which I was able to identify as being in the handwriting of the writer's former lover. That, together with the discovery of a death certificate and a letter from a mutual friend, allowed me to uncover a relationship about which the writer had been extremely secretive, even misleading, in her lifetime. The elusiveness of the subject, and the curious feeling that you are discovering as much about yourself as about the object of your researches when writing a biography, is extremely well conveyed by Setterfield. Being herself the author of literary and biographical studies, she can speak from personal experience.

It is a commonplace of the early Gothic novel that the heroine or hero discovers that she or he is the inheritor of a great fortune or the heir to a noble title. The novel generally takes the form of a quest, sometimes deliberate, sometimes unconscious, to discover these hidden treasures of the self. Deep within all of us is the myth that we are something special, that we are gods and goddesses in disguise, and that sometimes we are not ourselves aware of our own imprisoned splendor. By "myth," I do not mean something that is necessarily untrue, but rather something that is true but not necessarily in the form in which it is revealed.

To put it perhaps simplistically, the Jane Austen heroine is in search of a husband, and through that husband self-discovery and self-fulfilment; the Gothic heroine is in search of identity and fulfilment and may emerge at the end with a husband. In *The Thirteenth Tale*, there is a hint of potential romance in the form of Aurelius Love, the man whom Margaret Lea meets in the ruins of Angelfield House. By the end of the novel, however, the potential romance is unresolved, but they have helped each other to discover their true selves. In the case of the orphan Aurelius, Margaret has helped him to find his real family.

The quest necessarily entails a visit to some deep and dark places. In the earliest Gothic novels, these took the form of dungeons, locked rooms, and cloistered convents where nuns were frequently immured for their transgressions.

There are various dungeons in *The Thirteenth Tale*. There is the rotting house of Angelfield with its paralyzed, immured owners, Charles and his sister Isabelle. There is the institution to which the insane Isabelle is taken. There is the strange, trapped existence of "Vida Winter" in her lonely house on the moors where Margaret Lea visits her.

More importantly, there are mental dungeons. Vida the writer creates a kind of labyrinth of truth and lies through which her biographer must thread her way to arrive at the truth. Then Margaret herself is tied to the secret of her dead twin from which only her voyage of discovery can release her. In both the narratives of the past and present, there are hidden presences thought to be ghosts but revealed to be prisoners of circumstance and trauma. The final revelation of mystery and the release of the protagonists from their neuroses prove to be one and the same thing.

At the end of the book, Vida Winter is at last truly released by death (cf., *Dracula*):

> Miss Winter died and the snow kept falling. . . . The snow that had already deadened the telephone now reached the window ledges, and drifted half way up the doors. It separated us from the rest of the world as effectively as a prison key, Miss Winter had escaped.[11]

Finally, her biographer Margaret Lea is released from the dungeons of the past, and even from the necessity of publishing Vida's biography. She is no longer chained to her dead twin: "She had come and she had gone. I would not see her again this side of the grave. My life was my own."[12]

Conclusion

The Gothic novel has had many progeny. In the nineteenth century, it evolved into the "sensation novel," many of whose female exponents like Mary Elizabeth Braddon (*Lady Audley's Secret*), Mrs. Henry Wood (*East Lynne*), and Sheridan Le Fanu's niece Rhoda Broughton (*Cometh Up as a Flower*) enjoyed a remarkable if transitory success. The sensation novel was essentially a Gothic novel in a contemporary setting, shorn of its most wildly romantic and potentially supernatural elements. Through Wilkie Collins and such works of his as *The Moonstone*, the Gothic novel evolved into the thriller and the "whodunit." The whodunit in its archetypal Agatha Christian form is arguably a debased Gothic novel in which mystery is reduced to a mere puzzle. But despite these evolutions,

the Gothic novel itself has persisted and like one of its most famous offspring, *Dracula*, has refused to die.

What gives the Gothic novel its validity is that it can be a particularly potent form of the archetypal quest narrative. It begins in innocence and ignorance. It travels through wild landscapes and languishes in dungeons both physical and mental. It emerges at last into the light with a solution of the mystery, or a partial solution. If this is a reasonable definition of the Gothic novel, then *The Thirteenth Tale* both fulfills and validates that definition.

The Thirteenth Tale has certainly put a spring in the step of the Gothic novel. If I were to call Diane Setterfield the Ann Radcliffe of the twenty-first century, I would mean it as a compliment. Diane Setterfield, like the author of *Udolpho*, is, I understand, happily married, shy, retiring, and not at all enamored of her newly found celebrity. She writes lovingly and structures meticulously. Her book, like *The Mysteries of Udolpho*, offers an intense, cloistered experience. We can be grateful, though, that, unlike Radcliffe, she does not allow her heroine to break into poetry. *The Thirteenth Tale* is itself a poem of the imagination.

Notes

1. Ann Radcliffe, *The Mysteries of Udolpho*, ed. Bonamy Dobrée (Oxford, UK: Oxford University Press, 1998), 1.

2. Claude Gellée (1600–1682), known as Claude Lorrain, was one of the most popular and influential painters of his day. His output consisted entirely of landscapes, serenely classical, with either mythological, pastoral, or (very occasionally) historical and Biblical figures in the middle ground. His inspiration was the picturesque landscape of the Roman Campagna. His taste is pre-Gothic and pre-Romantic in that he has no taste for the wild or sublime. Everything seems tranquil and is usually glowing in a golden evening luminescence. His rendering of light was to influence J. M. W. Turner.

3. Salvator Rosa (1615–1673) was, in life as well as in art, a forerunner of the Gothic and Romantic. Though a contemporary of Lorrain's, his work was in complete contrast to his. His subject matter was usually violent—battle scenes, bandits, storms at sea—his landscapes were rugged and sublime.

4. Daphne du Maurier, *Rebecca* (New York: Avon, 1994).

5. Diane Setterfield, *The Thirteenth Tale* (London: Orion, 2006), 80.

6. Gaspard Dughet (1615–1675) was a painter of landscapes, heavily influenced by Lorrain and Poussin (who married his sister). His works combined Lorrain's and Poussin's classicism with a touch of the wild and sublime, especially in his stormy skies. He was enormously popular in England. Almost every major country house in England has one or more Dughets collected by their young eighteenth-century masters on the Grand Tour. Ann Radcliffe would have been very familiar with his work.

7. Alexander Pope, "Eloisa to Abelard," in *Alexander Pope: The Major Works*, ed. Pat Rogers (Oxford, UK: Oxford University Press, 2008), 137–146.

8. David Garrick and George Colman, *The Clandestine Marriage*, ed. Noel Chevalier (Peterborough, ON: Broadview Press, 1995), 82. This play, inspired by one of Hogarth's *Marriage á la Mode* paintings (the first in the series), was one of the most popular comedies of its time. Contemporary audiences would have particularly enjoyed the elements which satirized current trends, in particular the affectations of the urban commercial middle classes, who were, as in the play, attempting to marry into the landed gentry and ape their manners. These affectations included the newly found taste for the Gothic, or "Gothick."

9. Montague Summers, *The Gothic Quest: A History of the Gothic Novel* (London: Fortune Press, 1968), 160.

10. Stella Gibbons (1902–1989) is the author most famously of *Cold Comfort Farm* (1932), a brilliant comic novel that satirizes, among other things, the rural gothic novels of Mary Webb, Sheila Kaye-Smith, H. A. Manhood, and the like, as well as the rugged neopaganism of D. H. Lawrence and the Powys brothers. She was also a notable poet and a writer of over twenty-five other novels and volumes of short stories. Most of them are satirical and domestic in the manner of a latter-day Jane Austen; others, like *The Shadow of a Sorcerer*, *Starlight*, and *Fort of the Bear*, are more Gothic in feel.

11. Setterfield, *The Thirteenth Tale*, 389.

12. Setterfield, *The Thirteenth Tale*, 408.

CHAPTER 51

Snakes, Bulls, and the Preoccupations of History

ALAN GARNER'S *THURSBITCH*

David Punter

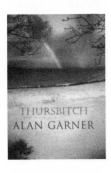

Alan Garner is a writer whose whole oeuvre has been determined by questions of location and topography. His earliest—and probably still best-known—novels, including *The Weirdstone of Brisingamen* (1960), *The Moon of Gomrath* (1963), *Elidor* (1965), and *The Owl Service* (1967), were classified at publication as "children's fiction," but this labeling did scant justice to the continuing depth of their involvement with the landscape and with the uncanny historical links that persist throughout the history of a certain terrain, affecting and potentially determining the lives of those who inhabit specific places.

There are two aspects to this preoccupation of Garner's. One is general: it concerns his conviction that character is in the end formed in response to habitation, that as we live within an environment, we are all the time imbued with the characteristics of that environment. So much of who we are is where we have been. We could refer to his approach as "environmentalist" or "ecological," but these terms probably fall a little short of the complex imbrication between person and nature which Garner posits. The second is far more specific, in that many of Garner's writings are set in a particular part of Cheshire and aspire to reveal some of the richness of myth, legend, and dialect peculiar to that place. This is not to say that Garner's interests are restricted to the rural; elsewhere he is more concerned with the irruptions of the past into urban or suburban life. Still, as he looks back to the past, what he inevitably investigates are forces that preexisted the industrial age, and that continue to persist—even if in only virtual form—within modernity as a kind of underlay to the world we so frequently take for granted.

Thursbitch (2003) exemplifies these preoccupations of Garner's, and indeed the very word *preoccupation*, in its fuller meaning, could be taken as emblematic of the themes which run through the novel. The entirely real valley which purportedly gives the book its name (although it is in fact more commonly known to the Ordnance Survey as "Thursbatch") is, above all, "pre-occupied": it is occupied, as far as the modern protagonists Ian and Sally are concerned, by other figures from the past, specifically from a particular moment in the eighteenth century; and, as far as those historical figures are themselves reflected, it is also "pre-occupied" by timeless, ageless forces which have no obvious origin but whose behavior inevitably colors the life of the valley, both hidden and overt, determining its weather, the state of the harvest, and the condition and health of all living beings within it.

The plot of *Thursbitch* is not easy to summarize. On the face of it, Ian and Sally have come to the valley of Thursbitch for unresolved reasons which include geological investigation and the possibility of some form of spiritual and/ or physical healing. Sally is a scientist who suffers from a fatal motor-neuron disease; Ian, who may or may not have been her lover in the past, is a Catholic priest and now her caretaker. While there, they—and we—receive a series of intimations of the valley's history, and especially of the mystery of the death of Jack Turner, a traveling peddler whose body was found in the valley long ago, with beside it a mysterious woman's footprint.

But this is not a detective story; it would be difficult indeed to say whether the reader feels more or less enlightened by the end of the book than at the start, although in between he or she will have been subjected to a remarkable set of oscillations of time and history, between past and present, and across a landscape sometimes perceived as claustrophobically constraining and at other times as opening onto the wild spaces of the universe.

What it certainly is, though, is a story of the uncanny. We can ascribe this to the most simple of definitions of the uncanny, those of Jentsch, Schelling, and Freud[1]: it is a story about the homely and the unhomely; it is a story about the domestic and the strange; it is a story about the sense of being left forever "outside" in the howling blizzard, which apparently kills Jack Turner, and the sense of being "inside," for example in the intimate albeit unorthodox relationship between Ian and Sally. We can say also that it is weird in terms of its problematic relationship to death. Garner does not go quite so far as to suggest that one of the secrets of Thursbitch is that it is a site of reincarnation (there would actually, in Garner's universe, be nothing unusual in that), but he certainly suggests that there is some way in which the life stories of Jack Turner and his lover "Nan Sarah" come to have a kind of second life two centuries later.

It would, however, be by no means fair to translate this set of collisions and collusions between past and present into that most frequent of Gothic topoi,

namely the simple haunting of the present by a past which is proving unwilling or unable to lie down and respect the passing of time and history. So frequently this becomes the site of horror—or at least of the apprehension of horror—as the undead rise up against the occupants (we might perhaps helpfully call them "post-occupiers") of the place, be it house, mansion, or graveyard, which they consider it their right to call home. But in *Thursbitch*, it is difficult to say whether there is horror; if there is, then it would most obviously be in the wildly hallucinatory scene in which we appear to be uncannily present at a ritual dominated by the Bull God, but here we as readers are in a continuing state of uncertainty.

For where *Thursbitch* most fully meets the Gothic, it might be said, is in the uncertainty of vision. In traditional Gothic—in, for instance, *The Mysteries of Udolpho* (1794)—the text inculcates uncertainties as to what is being seen, for instance, by Emily and by ourselves: are there really ghosts and skeletons within Udolpho, or are we being invited to share in Emily's heightened imagination and thus to enter into the text as a way of sharing in her experiences before being returned, with a more or less violent shock, to the outside world?

If anything, the world of *Thursbitch* is even more unstable. It appears that in the "bull scene" Jack Turner blinds and slaughters a bull, but the bull itself—if there really is a bull—seems unnaturally passive and accepting of his place in the ceremony. Is what we are watching a simulation of a scene rather than the scene itself, a ritual in the full sense of the word as a *recapitulation* of a set of acts which, if ever they were done at all, were done at some remote and only half-remembered stage of history? There is a darkening sense that, if some kind of sacrifice is performed during this ritual, then the sacrifice is of Jack himself.

And yet, it is history which is the real subject of *Thursbitch*—the question of who, on the cusp of a moment when Christianity may take over and erase pagan customs, will get to tell the history. This erasure is suggested early on by the all-encompassing snow that covers the early pages of the novel, where Jack muses on the conflict between the Christian creation myth and the harsher but perhaps more probable story that has the world born of the primal encounter between "Night and Mither" (modern Cheshire dialect word for *confusion*, from Middle English mīþen).[2] But this, of course, is the eighteenth-century world; in the parallel—or dependent—world of the modern, it does not take long for the Gothic to make an explicit appearance. Sally is amazed by a geological feature:

> It was a cube of rock sticking out of the peat a little below them. Its back was buried, its top flat and tilted to give a launch out across the valley. The sides were layered bands, disturbed by running cracks. The front was an arch, and all was hollow within; a cave, a hive, an oven, curved round, with more layers lying on each other, and at

the back an upright crevice in the crag, going into the ridge but not
through the slab of roof nor through the slab of floor.
    "It's classic."
    "More Gothic. It's not on the map." (10–11)

So something "Gothic" is here "from the beginning"—from, perhaps, even before the beginning. But is it on the map? More to the point, what map might be
truly appropriate to a landscape that is intelligible more as a series of historical
and geological layers than as a site of surface geography?

    One thing is certain in this uncertain world, and that is that Jack Turner
knows, through and through, what his actions must be. There is no real question
here of free will: the life of a wandering peddler, or "jagger" as he is called, is
occupied with reading signs and following them, knowing what has to be done
at what season and how the land will lie come snow, come rain, come storm.
The figure of "Bully Thrumble" (which seems a stone, although by whose provenance it has become set in its present position nobody knows, but which may
also be the supposed bull in the scene mentioned above) is as active a participant
in this world of ritual and ceremony as any of the human—or indeed animal—
characters. Jack

> went down the slope to Bully Thrumble, walking quietly. He sat
> with his back against the pillar, on the other side from the water,
> and listened. The sound of the brook entered him, and he grew to
> the stone. He waited. The sun was singing, but not loudly, and the
> small white clouds rang against each other, soft as Jinney's bells. (45)

This is a world where the boundaries between human, animal (Jinney is Jack's
leading packhorse), and all the other elements in nature do not exist: they have
not yet come into being, they have not been mapped, and the possibility remains
of being entered by the brook, of growing into the stone. In this world, the sun
sings and the clouds ring, yet there is not a trace of sentimentality in *Thursbitch*.
Rather—and indeed we should sense this from the title—there is a harshness, a
sense of being bowed before necessity, which inflects even the most rapturous
of scenes.

    From the comparatively new term "eco-Gothic" is often implied a Christian
notion of human stewardship of nature. Such a notion of stewardship would,
however, seem deeply disrespectful in the world of *Thursbitch*; it would seem as
though man had arrogated to himself a kind of guardianship of the valley and
was now generously dispensing care. This is the opposite of the kind of sensibility Garner develops, which is one where nature itself (whatever that might be)
has the power. The task of humans is to try to fit into nature's ways, and it is

only by doing this that we might be able to share something of nature's munificence.

Again, *munificence* may seem a strange word to use up here amid the bleakness of the bare high valleys and hill slopes—a strange word indeed until we hear the unending resonance throughout the text of honey, a kind of honey that appears to have been made by no natural bees but that nevertheless occurs and remains as a trace of the moment of rapture, as a kind of sign of memory, even as the promise of salvation, at all events as an essential element in the rituals that keep Thursbitch alive. But the main thing that keeps the valley alive, over and above the ever-elusive trace and memory of honey, is the endless circlings of Jack himself: in his ridings, in his fetchings and carryings from one place to another, and above all in his walkings, he maintains a kind of equilibrium that serves to keep the countryside around him in being. In the end, in the dispute between the incoming Christians and the threatened pagans as to who created the world, the most probable answer is that it is in fact Jack himself who created—or better still, continually creates—the world by his journeyings, which also mimic the "natural" order of the rising of the sun and the setting of the stars.

In *Thursbitch*, though, nothing is as it seems; or rather, everything is a sign that points toward another sign, like the stone posts—inexplicable to their modern viewers—which point up and down the hillside, but which also appear and disappear in the mist, or point to each other, or on occasion may turn and move themselves to prevent the trail from being followed and the secret from being unveiled. And there are many "secret places" in the text: one of the most important is known as Pearly Meg's, a well that clearly serves a sacred function but which perhaps is also full of snakes:

> At the bottom, he listened to what the water told him, and then tapped the stones lightly; and from the cracks between, the snakes came and curled themselves round the twists of his stick, and when they were all counted and quiet he laid the stick below the roof and reached into the hill. With both hands he felt in the dark for the shelf over which water ran, and took the weight that sat there, holding its wetness to him until he was free to turn and put it into the sack. (47)

But then perhaps it isn't; perhaps there are no snakes (or at least not until the coming of Christianity). What Garner is trying to do, here and more generally, is to depict a world in which our actions are not chosen but run in accordance to an ancient script, even a script of which we have no conscious recollection. One could think of this in Freudian terms and hypothesize that what Jack Turner is obeying—and even more so his modern counterparts Ian and Sally—is the promptings of something repressed into the dark, something which may indeed

flash with unseen and fleshless snakes; but this might not be the best way to conceive of the universe Garner is creating. Better might be to follow the clue of the "sign": everything in the valley of Thursbitch is a sign; the only difference between one human and another—or perhaps again we might extend this also to include the animals, some of whom also have what we are now inclined to call an "uncanny" ability to read the signs—is whether they can make sense of these signs, whether they can metaphorically, literally, and geophysically align themselves with them in such a way as to make sense of their lives even in the very moment of abandoning the hubris of any pretense of sense-making ability.

"Signs taken for wonders" is perhaps a familiar phrase,[3] but in *Thursbitch* the signs are absolutely not taken for wonders; instead they are taken as evidence of an everyday order in the universe, but not one which is revelatory or even benevolent. Instead, these signs are the supposedly eternal indicators of a world that may visit good or ill upon its inhabitants, that may be the harbinger of a good summer or a terrible winter, or that may herald new birth or lingering death. The world of *Thursbitch* is stony in every way: the most significant forms in the valley are stones, the apparent participants in the rituals are very probably themselves stones, and stony is the face of whatever god it is that looks down on the valley or is continually incarnated within it.

Hubris—as in all Gothic fiction—is also a factor in *Thursbitch*. It is located in the modern retelling, or "recapitulation." Sally, whose illness—which remains to an extent mysterious in the novel—involves, at the very least, physical deterioration and memory loss, and is therefore perhaps not as indescribable as the text claims, has to use sticks to walk (even, or perhaps especially, within this most difficult of terrains) but does not want to. Indeed, she gets very angry with Ian when he recommends that she use them, but then, along with her other mood swings, there are also uncustomary fits of anger, violent outbursts—indeed all the phenomena that go along with a gradual and feared draining of human individuality, the incarnation of a terror at the end of life which has now in the early twenty-first century become almost commonplace, as though the unseating of reason is now expected before the end of physical life.

This, then, is one of the true terrors of the book: a sense of imminent paralysis, of the body but also perhaps of the mind, within which it is impossible to react to half-glimpsed events which are unfolding around us. And so one might say that in a peculiar way Sally, sensitive as she is to the complexities, the peculiarities, and the embedded stories of Thursbitch, is in some way actually returning to that world of the primitive past herself. The question would be whether what she loses as a result of her slipping away from the assumptions and conventions of "civilization" is compensated by her understanding of the barbaric, for we need make no mistake: the world of eighteenth-century Thursbitch is barbaric, full of sudden death and awful accident. And indeed this might be the place to

remind ourselves that the world of this older Thursbitch is in fact far older again; the reason why the eighteenth century is the setting is in order to contrast most starkly the last survival, the last throes of the "ancient" with the coming of what the novel regards, with some justification, as the earliest avatar of modernity, a certain version of Christian orthodoxy. And so here we can see *Thursbitch* as definitively linked in to the Gothic tradition, in the sense that it tells a story, or a series of stories, whose origins remain forever unknown but which effect their force through their haunting and domination of the present.

Thus, in several ways, *Thursbitch* replays older Gothic conflicts: between the civilized and the barbaric, between the urban and the rural, and between what might be seen as the possibility of a physical cure (which is what Ian, alongside and despite his more significant role as a priest, appears to represent, unlikely though such a cure may be) and an acknowledgment of a malaise of the soul for which no cure may be available given the distance between modernity and the problematic yet undeniable healing powers of, say, Pearly Meg's snake-polluted water. But the role of Jack Turner in the "bull ceremony" confuses and complicates all this, for within the confines of the valley itself, and in accordance with the cocktail of hallucinatory drugs which he has taken, Jack figures both as the killer of the bull and as the bull itself.

Perhaps a further link to the Gothic would then be this: who achieves mastery and who is the victim? Within the modern story, Sally becomes very angry when Ian, in his role as supporter and carer, attempts to assert control over her, or even to make what may appear to be sensible recommendations; in the "old story"—and that is probably the best description of it—Jack Turner, the life and soul of the community but also dead almost as soon as the story begins, is both instigator and victim. However, much of what we as readers think about these matters will hinge on Garner's description of what we might call either the Christian "conversion" or "invasion," which only fully becomes apparent to the reader as a major topos quite late in the novel, although that very thought reinvites one to speculate as to whether the more visible scenarios of the novel are always already, in some sense, too late—too late, certainly, to save Sally from death, but perhaps also too late to save Thursbitch from having to sacrifice its autonomy, its topographical uniqueness, and become subject to the indifferent, imperialist geographizing imposed by a proselytizing religion.

It is this religion which Jack Turner hears whispers of as he travels his routes, a religion which has nothing to do with the "old ways." As he says on one of his periodic returns from his traveling, he has heard "some queer chaps this last jag":

> They were promising as we were all going to burn in big ovens when
> we die, because we were all born nowty, and there was some gover-
> nor as had it in for us, choose how much we said we were sorry. But
> sorry for what? No matter o' that, his gang were going to shovel us in

> ovens and roast us on forks, day and night for evermore. Leastways,
> that's what I made on it. . . . Where are they from? And is it catch-
> ing? (102–103)

It *is* "catching" (so, as we shall see, is the cause of Nan Sarah's death): as the novel proceeds, we are left in no doubt of that. As with so many postcolonial texts, from Chinua Achebe to Brian Friel to Thomas Keneally,[4] the invading force arrives with a Bible, or a version of the Bible, in its hands, but also with a pair of compasses, a set of devices to divide the land and to sever the old, mobile links which have held the land together, to disrupt the "song lines" and separate communities. The trade of the "jagger," of course, is—as it is in Wordsworth, although he uses a different term—one of the principal ways in which those communities have been held together: the arrival of the form of the protostate renders his job impossible, or at least perceived as unnecessary.

But the trajectory of Christianity has to encompass both the "original" story and the modern one, and in the latter we as readers are continually disturbed by our awareness of Ian's genuine care for Sally and her periodic furious rejections of this care as sanctimonious, self-serving, and in the end designed for his own ends, whatever they may be. "I do not feel sorry for you," Ian says at one point, although he means, we presume, that the emotion he feels is higher and more complex than pity. "Show some emotion, damn you," she explodes:

> You, you do it all in your head! The rest of us have to do it out in a
> real world! Christ Alcrappingmighty! And those notes! What are you
> going to make of them? Write a bestseller? Become an authority?
> Have your own website? And why not? Help yourself! Mate! You've
> put enough hours in! I hate you! I hate your self-righteous bloody
> face! (105)

Back, however, in the eighteenth century, it is the land that is threatened; it is threatened most obviously by the arrival of a "new master" who wants to settle the desolate but sacred valley of Thursbitch, build a farmhouse, and disrupt the ceaseless silent singing of the stones. It falls to Jack to try to prevent this, but at the same moment Nan Sarah contracts and dies of the plague (which is obviously "catching"), and Jack disappears. When he returns, he is a changed man; or perhaps, indeed, he is not the same man. At any rate, his talk is no longer of the stones and the old ways. Now it is the voice of the Christian apocalypse:

> God passed me by when I was polluted with innard filth, and let me
> live; He passed me by, and let me live so as I could fetch you news
> of His great anger against you, and to bruise the heads of snakes as
> they will bruise your heels. For you shall all, every one, be surely cast
> into yon flames, where the worm does not die, and the fire is not

quenched. For you wicked shall go away into everlasting torment. (128)

The men of the community are initially not impressed: "Give over," says one of them. "We piss out bonfires, so what's the odds?" (128). But the forces of change at work are, of course, greater than they are: a chapel is built in the valley, and the transformed Jack becomes the converted fire-and-brimstone preacher.

Yet by the end of the novel, all is again uncertain. Jack appears to awaken from a great madness and to be returned to the old faith; but what he is also returned to is his memory of the terrible death of Nan Sarah, and because of this he returns to his old walkings and dies himself—and this returns us to the beginning of the novel, when his body is found with a woman's footprint marked in snow next to it, the print we now suppose of the dead Nan. Meanwhile, in the modern story, Sally settles down to die on the high passes, and Ian is dismissed, with unanswered questions raised about the meaning and impact of his faith.

Thursbitch is an intensely moving book: a large part of its emotional force rests on language and events all pared down to their barest essentials. It is a book of stone and rock, a book which seeks to release—and yet also, necessarily, to conceal—some of the secrets from which the landscape is formed. It is in one sense a book of ghosts, but the ghosts have a flesh-and-blood reality that constantly seduces the reader into belief.

In the end, perhaps it is a book that tells us more about the Gothic than Gothic tells us about *Thursbitch*. What it tells us is, first, that all moments of history can be seen as moments of passing and becoming, that even when and where the world appears most stable, most unchanging, there are forces massing that will uproot the strongest and sturdiest of stones. Old beliefs will quail and melt before the onrush of modernity; and this is surely also one of the lessons of the Gothic, in which older beliefs, superstitions, call them what you will, have become mere shadows of their former selves, either a stock of past legend to be drawn on to frighten us in the present—as in, say, Matthew Lewis—or a partly laughable background to an overexcitable imagination, as with Ann Radcliffe's heroines.

It has often been remarked, perhaps most forcefully and eloquently by Victor Sage,[5] that Gothic is essentially about religion, or perhaps more accurately about conflicts between different forms of religion. Certainly that was true of the "original," late-eighteenth-century Gothic; arguably the relevant conflicts were played out over the succeeding century more in terms of religion itself in conflict with Darwinian and Freudian insights. But in any of these incarnations, the issues had to do with how we manage the relics, the "things which survive": past beliefs, conventions, habits, and indeed bodies and souls from the past which cannot stay still. *Thursbitch* dramatizes a moment of change, but it does

so without coming to a final conclusion as to what succeeds what, as to whether the sheer force of modernity can ever entirely eradicate older systems and signs.

The Gothic also, of course, often explores issues of madness, dislocation of perception, or an athwartness toward or a transgression of society's norms. *Thursbitch* challenges us as readers to recognize differences of perception and perspective, to reflect not merely on how we may be influenced by a particular landscape, but also on how the construction of the landscape and the construction of our inner world(s) may be mutually geared, and on how if we come adrift from that gearing, from that sense of innate connectedness, then we may find that we have lost everything—even though, by a type of saving grace which is also a tragedy, in the end it will not matter because we shall anyway have forgotten what it is that we have lost, as Sally gradually through the book loses not only her memories but also her sense of what it might even mean to forget or to have forgotten, and thus experiences even her own existence as a kind of madness.

We are accustomed to thinking of the Gothic as offering us a distorted view of history; *Thursbitch* in a sense reverses this view, offering us instead a version of history that rings true, or would if only it were not the case that this history has been supplanted, rewritten. I have already mentioned Wordsworth; of the other writers around the period of the early Gothic—which is also of course the precise period in which *Thursbitch* is, not by accident, set—the most suitable comparison might be with Scott and his enduring attempts to keep the memory of the past alive. But of course in *Thursbitch* there is one huge difference: it is not a singular account of a historical moment, but rather an attempt, hugely ambitious in its aim and successful in its execution, to bring two moments of history together, moving beyond the simplicities of allegory to suggest a far more complex sense of how, in true Gothic mode, the past and the present are inseparable in the uncanniness of their mutual hauntings.

Notes

1. See Sigmund Freud, "The 'Uncanny'" (1919), in *The Standard Edition of the Complete Psychological Works of Sigmund Freud*, eds. James Strachey et al., 24 vols. (London: General Books, 1953–1974), 17: 217–252.

2. Alan Garner, *Thursbitch* (London: Harvill Press, 2003), 3. Page numbers from this edition appear hereafter in parentheses in the text.

3. In the Gothic context, see Franco Moretti, *Signs Taken for Wonders*, trans. D. Miller, David Forgacs, and S. Fischer (London: Verso Books, 1983).

4. See, e.g., Chinua Achebe, *Things Fall Apart* (London: William Heinemann, 1958); Brian Friel, *Translations* (London: Faber & Faber, 1981); Thomas Keneally, *The Chant of Jimmie Blacksmith* (Sydney: Angus & Robinson, 1972).

5. Victor Sage, *Horror Fiction in the Protestant Tradition* (London: Macmillan, 1988).

CHAPTER 52

Gothic, Romantic, or Just Sadomasochistic?

GENDER AND MANIPULATION IN STEPHENIE MEYER'S TWILIGHT SAGA

June Pulliam

Many reviewers are at a loss to explain the enormous popularity of Stephenie Meyer's Twilight saga, as well as that of the films *Twilight* (2008) and *The Twilight Saga: New Moon* (2009), both based on the first two books in Meyer's series. The phrase "Harry Potter for girls" is bandied about, but this characterization refers more to the books' marketing success than it does to their content, since after *Twilight*'s enormous commercial success, subsequent installments in the series were premiered by booksellers at midnight release parties that were similar to those that accompanied the release of Rowling's later Harry Potter books. *Bitch* magazine's Christine Seifert approaches the reason the series is so popular with teens when she dubs the Twilight saga "abstinence porn," a descriptor which highlights the series' erotic elements.[1] The Twilight saga's success is due in part to its following the predictable patterns found in contemporary Gothic romance fiction, a well-established genre that explores women's erotic desires.

Both contemporary horror fiction and contemporary romance fiction have their origins in the Gothic. Meyer herself says that her novels were inspired in part by many classic works of Gothic and/or romance fiction, including *Wuthering Heights* (echoed in *Eclipse*, 2007), *Jane Eyre* and *Romeo and Juliet* (in *New Moon*, 2006), and *Pride and Prejudice* (within *Twilight*, 2005).[2] The Twilight saga is a work of paranormal romance, a type of romance fiction that includes "any element beyond the range of scientific explanation, like ghosts or time travel."[3] It also often includes vampires and werewolves. The supernatural elements of the paranormal romance give authors license to metaphorically

examine erotic feelings that might be considered politically incorrect in more realistic romance fiction.

In *Loving with a Vengeance*, Tania Modleski divides romance fiction into three distinct subgenres, two of which are the Harlequin romance and the contemporary Gothic romance. One distinction between the Harlequin and the Gothic is in how each corresponds to different phases in a typical woman's life, namely courtship and marriage.[4] Because romance fiction as a whole focuses on the formative events in the average woman's life, works in the genre (the Twilight saga included) can be considered feminine bildungsromans.[5] Furthermore, the length of the Twilight saga permits it to straddle both events, as well as both genres: *Twilight*, *New Moon*, and *Eclipse* chronicle Bella and Edward's courtship, while *Breaking Dawn* focuses on the couple's marriage. All four books have elements found in both the Harlequin and the contemporary Gothic romance.

The Twilight Saga as Harlequin Romance

Edward and Bella's relationship mirrors the power imbalance between the principals found in the typical Harlequin romance, novels in which "a young, inexperienced, poor to moderately well-to-do woman . . . becomes involved with a handsome, strong, experienced, wealthy man" who is considerably older.[6] Edward, who has been seventeen for several decades, is technically old enough to be Bella's great-grandfather, and he is fabulously wealthy. The virginal Bella, on the other hand, has no experience with dating boys even her *own* age, and her divorced parents will more than likely have difficulty sending her to college on their salaries as a preschool teacher and a small-town sheriff.

Much of the Twilight saga's plot also follows the trajectory of the typical Harlequin, in that "the heroine is confused by the hero's behavior since, though he is obviously interested in her, he is mocking, cynical, contemptuous, often hostile, and even somewhat brutal."[7] Edward's behavior can certainly be described as mocking, cynical, hostile, and even brutal when the two first meet, reactions that confuse Bella. When Bella first sees Edward, she senses that he is "hostile, furious," a reaction that she cannot fathom, as she is a stranger to him.[8] Edward's confusing and inconsistent behavior toward her continues into *New Moon*, in which Edward professes his love for Bella one moment, while in the next instance, he and the whole Cullen clan depart without saying good-bye or telling anyone where they are going. While we later learn that Edward has taken these drastic actions to protect Bella from his kind, to Bella his behavior is incomprehensible. As a result, she goes into a deep depression after he leaves. In this impossible period for Bella, the text suggests with surprising grace how she

drags lost in time with an empty heart, showing in all-caps only one word page after page—the passing month.[9]

Furthermore, Edward is controlling and manipulative in the relationship. Some of the decisions that Edward makes against Bella's will—but "for her own good"—are merely laughable, such as insisting that she attend her prom even though she hates dancing and has a broken leg at the time. But other instances of Edward's manipulative behavior would be read in other genres (or in real life, for that matter, as Rebecca Housel observes) as harbingers of a potentially abusive partner, rather than evidence of caring. Edward becomes particularly controlling in *Eclipse* while he is trying to protect Bella both from Victoria, the vampire who wants to kill her to settle a grudge against the Cullens, and from Jacob and the other Quileute werewolves, which he believes are too dangerous. For this reason, Edward becomes furious when he learns that while he was away on a hunting trip Bella visited Jacob. When Edward must leave on his next hunting trip, he arranges for his sister Alice to kidnap Bella for an evening of "girl fun," a ruse to prevent her from seeing Jacob, despite the fact that Bella does not enjoy typically feminine activities involved in an evening of "girl fun," such as shopping and hair play. As a consequence, Edward's planned diversion becomes a punishment. On other occasions, Edward has resorted to disconnecting the battery cables in Bella's car to prevent her from visiting Jacob. In this way, Edward is similar to Bella's father, who has also disabled her car in the past in order to limit her mobility. Edward further controls Bella by keeping information from her. For example, in *Eclipse*, Edward does not tell Bella that Victoria is nearby, as he reasons that this information would needlessly worry her rather than help her take precautions to ensure her own safety. Abusive partners similarly attempt to control their mates through limiting their mobility and their access to information.

Worse yet, Edward stalks his beloved. In *Twilight*, we learn that Edward has been in Bella's bedroom every night, even before the two have become a couple, watching her as she sleeps. In any other genre, this behavior would be classified as the sort of stalking that an abusive partner would resort to in order to try to achieve control over the other. However, because the Twilight saga is paranormal romance, Edward's stalking is couched as evidence of the depth of his love for Bella rather than a worrisome obsession.

While Edward's controlling behavior vexes Bella, she fails to see it as a warning that he is dangerous, as it falls within the realm of normal masculine behavior as perpetuated by contemporary discourses of gender. Lynn Phillips defines discourses as sets of "prevailing ideas or cultural messages [that] tell us what is natural, inevitable, desirable, and appropriate in human behavior and social phenomenon."[10] Discourses of gender, which define what it is to be a "good" woman or a "normal" man, are perpetuated in popular media, such

as romance novels. Bella is a voracious reader of classic romance fiction; she is particularly fond of the works of Jane Austen and the Brontë sisters. So it is not surprising, then, that Bella is predisposed to see Edward's controlling behavior as evidence of his ardor rather than a sign that he has the potential to become abusive. Prevailing cultural ideas about "normal" heterosexual relationships, such as what Phillips terms the danger/dichotomy discourse, lead Bella to believe that women can avoid becoming involved in abusive relationships because "clearly perceptible, static, and enforceable lines" separating the good guys from the bad make it easy to differentiate between dangerous and safe men.[11] Because many of Edward's actions are compatible with prevailing ideas about how an ideal male suitor should behave, Bella (and the reader) view Edward as a good guy rather than as a dangerous, perhaps deadly bad guy, and his controlling behavior is not indicative of his potential for abuse.

Jacob, Bella's other love interest, also fits the mold of the typical Harlequin hero. After Jacob becomes a werewolf in *New Moon* and declares his love for Bella, he begins behaving more like Edward. Lycanthropy has made Jacob conventionally masculine: he shaves his long hair and becomes larger and more muscular. But Jacob's facial expression is the most masculine feature he now sports, for Bella observes that Jacob's "open, friendly smile was gone like the hair [and] the warmth in his dark eyes altered to a brooding resentment that was instantly disturbing."[12] The new, more masculine Jacob is also inexplicably hostile to Bella. He refuses to see her for weeks, or even to return her phone calls. We later learn that the reason behind his baffling behavior is similar to Edward's—Jacob, too, fears that as a supernatural creature, he could unintentionally harm Bella. However, unlike Edward, Jacob never demonstrates his love for Bella through any controlling behavior. While he frequently tries to warn Bella off Edward and exhibits jealousy even when she goes to the theater with a relatively innocuous male classmate, he does not disable her car battery or arrange to have her "kidnapped" in order to prevent her from seeing his rival.

Bella, with her girl-next-door beauty, is a typical Harlequin heroine. She is unmistakably feminine in appearance, describing herself as having ivory skin that could be pretty.[13] Nevertheless, Bella never thinks of herself as beautiful, and readers are to see her preference for wearing old sweatpants and her refusal to wear makeup as evidence of her modesty rather than as a rejection of a sexist beauty culture. Similarly, Bella's hatred for dancing is due to the combination of her clumsiness and her reluctance to be on display. Bella has no desire to manage her appearance for those two most important feminine rites of passage, her senior prom and her wedding. Alice has to dress Bella for her prom, as well as select her wedding gown and trousseau, while Bella is so unconcerned about her looks that she does not even bother to glimpse at herself in a mirror on her wedding day.

But most importantly, Bella is virginal. She is, as Edward puts it, someone for whom "lust and love keep the same company," and so she has not had *any* sort of sexual encounter.[14] While Bella's lack of sexual experience makes her a fairly typical Harlequin heroine, this quality is not part of the vast imbalance of power between the couple; Edward is equally sexually inexperienced, and his morality causes him to wait until after he is married to consummate their relationship.

The Twilight Saga as Contemporary Gothic Romance

While much of Edward and Bella's relationship follows the trajectory of the Harlequin romance, Meyer's saga has more in common with the contemporary Gothic novel, itself a descendant of classic Gothic fiction such as *Wuthering Heights*. Modleski describes both the Gothic and the Harlequin romance as genres dealing "with women's fears of and confusion about masculine behavior in a world in which men learn to devalue women."[15]

Women's fear and confusion about masculine behavior in the Gothic novel is underscored by the typical heroine's anxiety that her beloved is actually trying to kill her. Some of this apprehension is dealt with through the device of the double—in this case, another vampire. *Twilight* opens with Bella's relating her experience with this double, though the reader is not in a position to know that at the time. In *Twilight*'s preface, Bella sets up the whole novel as a flashback; She is about to be killed when she begins her narration. After the first few chapters, readers suspect that "the hunter" who "sauntered forward to kill" Bella in the preface is Edward, since at the end of chapter 4, he tells her that she "really should stay away from [him]."[16] However, we later find out that the hunter Bella refers to in the preface is James, a vampire who tries to kill Bella as a way of settling a grievance he has with Edward.

Nevertheless, Edward is a danger to Bella. When Edward reveals to Bella that he is a vampire, he confesses his fear that he could be so overcome by her scent that he might not be able to stop himself from killing her. Meyer's vampires and werewolves can harm humans without meaning to, so sexual intimacy between a supernatural creature and a human is particularly perilous. As a consequence, Edward's old-fashioned sense of morality is not the only reason he is reluctant to be intimate with Bella.

Meyer's werewolves are similarly dangerous to humans. We learn in *New Moon* that Sam Uley accidentally mauled his fiancée Emily while in his wolf form. When Bella and Edward finally marry in *Breaking Dawn*, we have the

ultimate proof of Bella's feminine fragility. Bella's wedding night leaves her covered in bruises in spite of Edward's attempts to restrain himself.

Bella's frailty makes her a typical Gothic heroine. Bella is "slender, but soft somehow, obviously not an athlete," as she lacks "the necessary hand-eye coordination to keep from humiliating [herself]."[17] In addition, she is afraid of blood—to the point of swooning when she pricks her finger. Bella's frailty means that she constantly requires saving. In *Twilight*, Edward describes Bella as "a magnet for trouble" after rescuing her from a gang of thugs in Port Angeles.[18] Bella even requires saving when she comes to Edward's rescue, as happens in *New Moon*.

But Bella's frailty is not the only quality that makes her a typical Gothic heroine. She also actively participates in her own victimization. Michelle A. Massé describes the Gothic heroine as someone who helps shape the system that oppresses her by internalizing its values.[19] Bella's attitude toward Edward's controlling behavior demonstrates this internalization. We have already explored how Bella is predisposed to see Edward's rudeness and hostility as evidence of his caring nature. Granted, in the beginning of their relationship, some of what Bella ignores is excusable since Edward is a supernatural creature whose existence is difficult for her to grasp. But later, when Bella can accept that vampires are real and fully comprehends how dangerous they can be to humans, she continues the relationship. She decides that she is absolutely positive about three things: "First, Edward was a vampire. Second, there was part of him . . . that thirsted for [her] blood. And third, [she] was unconditionally and irrevocably in love with him."[20] In short, Bella completes her own damsel-in-distress role. Indeed, even when Edward is absent, she remains the menaced waif. As Edward's wise vamp sister Alice Cullen puts it, "He was a fool to think you could survive alone. I've never seen anyone so prone to life-threatening idiocy. . . . Leave it to you, Bella. Anyone else would be better off when the vampires left town. But you have to start hanging out with the first monsters you can find."[21]

Bella's ambivalence about Edward's expression of anger and her desire to be powerful further underscore her participation in her own victimization. At the end of *Twilight*, Bella wants to be a vampire so that she can be Edward's equal—but he denies her this until the last novel. In the face of this denial, Bella is ambivalent about her desire to be powerful; she is even tentative about her feelings of anger. When Jacob and his fellow Quileutes, in their new, frightening lupine bodies, scare Bella, she wishes she were a vampire because she wants to be "fierce and deadly, someone they wouldn't dare mess with."[22] Yet afterward, Bella waffles, despite her anger being a logical response to stimuli, now believing that "the violent desire caught me off guard and knocked the wind out of me."[23]

Finally, Bella's relative frailty is emphasized by how her relationship with Edward is more similar to a parent-child bond than to a romantic one. Edward is an ideal parent of sorts to Bella, providing her with the discipline and protection

that she has never received from her mother or father. While Bella describes her mother Renée as her best friend, readers realize that she is too giddy brained and childlike to adequately parent her daughter. Though Renée is not much of an actual presence in the Twilight saga, Bella's occasional references to her mother reveal how the mother-daughter roles have been reversed. Renée calls her daughter when she gets lost driving, and e-mails her regarding the whereabouts of a missing article of clothing that she left at the cleaners. And while Charlie is by no means a bad father, he is also not wholly prepared to parent Bella. Bella functions as Charlie's wife, taking over all of the housekeeping and cooking duties upon her arrival in Forks, since her bachelor father is not capable of performing these tasks. And although Charlie is a police officer, he cannot protect Bella from vampires or werewolves.

Edward, then, becomes both mother and father to Bella. He has an omnipotence that young children often imagine their parents to possess, and while he can't hear Bella's thoughts, he can hear everyone else's thoughts to the degree that for all intents and purposes he is omniscient. Furthermore, Edward is strong enough to balance Bella's clumsiness and human fragility. On many occasions, Edward carries Bella the way a parent would carry a child whose small legs make it difficult for her to keep up on her own. Finally, Edward's often condescending and preemptory behavior toward Bella is characteristic of a parent-child relationship, for Edward controls her, and he refuses to explain his actions, a posture that makes Bella feel safe rather than indignant.

In *New Moon*, Edward comes off as a bad parent, something that further emphasizes the parent-child nature of his relationship with Bella. He abandons Bella, ostensibly for her own good, as he is convinced that he and his kind are a danger to her after she is nearly killed by his brother Jasper, who went into a feeding frenzy after she cut her finger. However, Edward's attempt to protect Bella backfires, and he puts her life in even more danger. After Edward leaves, Bella becomes dangerously depressed. As a result, she gets lost in the woods for days and then goes into a stupor for months afterward. When Bella emerges from her lethargy, she engages in near suicidal behavior, taking up dirt-bike riding and cliff diving, since putting her life in danger is the only way she can hear Edward's voice. Bella's inability to care for herself while away from Edward emphasizes her almost childlike dependence and poor judgment. Alice Cullen speaks truth to Bella: "You are so bizarre, even for a human."[24] Meyer eroticizes this imbalance of power rather than problematizing it, as she reproduces the imbalance of power characteristic of too many actual intimate partner relationships in junior and senior high school. In the time that Meyer was writing her saga, the Centers for Disease Control reported that 72 percent of actual eighth and ninth graders were dating. By the time they were in high school, one in four adolescents reported verbal, physical, emotional, or sexual violence each year from their partner, and

one in five high school women had been physically or sexually abused by a dating partner.[25] The CDC warns that this obvious lack of respect and abusive dating experience during adolescence "may disrupt normal development of self-esteem and body image, . . . and adolescents in abusive relationships often carry these unhealthy patterns of violence into future relationships."[26]

The Twilight Saga as Paranormal Romance

Finally, we must also consider the Twilight saga as a quintessential example of paranormal romance. Lee Tobin-McClain argues that the paranormal romance "tells us more about women's needs, feelings, and fantasies than any other genre of the fantastic."[27] As Tobin-McClain explains, the genre's unique perspective on women's feelings and fantasies derives in part from how it allows for the "exploration of unspeakable elements of contemporary gender identity and relationships."[28] Some of these "unspeakable" elements are progressive, such as plots exploring gender role reversals, while others, such as female masochism, are more regressive. The saga permits its mostly female readership to explore exaggerations of traditional gender roles in a way that is not obviously threatening, since they are mediated metaphorically, through the narrative's paranormal elements. In other words, what is unacceptable behavior in humans is perfectly acceptable in vampires, even those pursuing a relationship between themselves and a human, despite the imbalance in power between the two.

In small ways, the Twilight saga does explore role reversal. In chapter 20 of *Eclipse*, Bella pressures Edward to take her virginity, but Edward refuses to have sex with his beloved before marriage. Part of his argument hinges on the old "why buy the cow when you can get the milk for free?" canard: he declines Bella's premarital sexual advances, as he wants to get married more than she does, and he has promised to make Bella a vampire only on the condition that she become his wife. If he sleeps with Bella before they marry, Edward reasons, then there is nothing to stop her from getting a member of his vampire family to turn her. Then she can refuse to marry him.

While the Twilight saga contains a few feminist elements, it primarily valorizes female masochism. Each novel of the saga begins with Bella's sober consideration of her impending death at the hands of an unknown assailant and ends with her miraculous survival. Perhaps this is because Bella continuously puts the needs of others before her own—to the degree that her life is imperiled. In *Twilight*, for example, she willingly goes to James so that she can save her mother, never stopping to think about other methods at her disposal, and never suspecting that James might not honor his promise to leave her family unharmed if she surrenders to him. With the fawn eyes and baby cheeks of Mary Pickford, Bella

is the perpetually persecuted and inarticulate ingenue to the end; in another age she would have been tied to locomotive rails or placed on a giant band saw as the black-hatted, mustachioed villain laughed. And then there is Edward's condescending, manipulative behavior. Meyer attempts to normalize it by creating Edward as a vampire whose adult identity was formed in an era when women were subordinate to men and could not even vote, but to the modern feminist, these attempts come across as weak. And Bella's love for the vampire Edward, a man who could easily kill her without even meaning to, is the ultimate demonstration of female masochism. Jacob posits that the supernatural elements of Bella's relationship with Edward have permitted her to explore what he calls the unspeakable, masochistic side of herself. He tells Bella that "if the world was the way it was supposed to be, if there were no monsters and magic," then her life would have taken a different path, one where she ended up with him in a quiet, comfortable existence.[29]

Breaking Dawn, in particular, contains a good deal of sadomasochism. The novel's prologue prepares us for this with Bella's reasoning that "when you loved the one who was killing you, it left you no options" but to give your life to your beloved.[30] After Bella's one act of marital coitus with her spouse (while she is still mortal), she is covered in welts, and the bed has been smashed. Nevertheless, Bella feels no pain; instead she is blissful.

But the strongest evidence of Bella's masochism is in how she deals with her unplanned pregnancy. Since vampire-human couplings are rare in Meyer's mythology, Edward and Bella did not use birth control during their lovemaking (since no one thought that vampires could produce sperm). As a result, Bella becomes pregnant on her wedding night, and within a matter of weeks, it is obvious that her fetus is no normal creature. In short, Bella's pregnancy jeopardizes her life. Her half-vampire fetus robs her of nearly all the nutrients she takes in and leaves her covered in bruises that are reminiscent of her wedding-night encounter with Edward. After Edward consults with Carlisle, his physician father, the two attempt to coerce Bella into an abortion for her own good. Bella, true to character, refuses and even goes so far as to enlist her sister-in-law Rosalie as the fetus's own personal protector.

As Carlisle predicted, the birth nearly kills Bella. Her vampire daughter, Renesemee, bites and claws her way out of the womb and leaves Bella dying. Of course, it is Bella's right to determine how she will deal with her pregnancy. What is most disturbing about this plot thread is how Meyer emphasizes Bella's masochism. The violence done to Bella's body as a result of her pregnancy is described in far more graphic detail than the results of any kill made by any vampire in the saga. In fact, the scenes of Bella's suffering in book 2 of *Breaking Dawn* are told in more loving detail than Meyer's description of Bella's ordeal at the hands of James in *Twilight*. Also, while most of the Twilight saga is related

through Bella's perspective, her crisis pregnancy in book 2 of *Breaking Dawn* is related by Jacob.

Most unsettling of all is how masochism as a strategy pays off for women, a common theme in romance and Gothic fiction. Bella's choice ends her mortal life; Edward *must* finally turn her into a vampire immediately after Renesemee is born, lest Bella bleed to death. Disturbingly, Bella is richly compensated for her helplessness and naïveté with immortality and eternal youth, as well as the companionship of a loving and extended family. And at last the vampire Bella is a true equal in her relationship with Edward. In fact, as a newborn, Bella is physically stronger than all of the Cullens, and Bella the vampire has a powerful sense of self-control that some vampires can never achieve.

Like the heroine of most Gothic romances, Bella must endure great pain to achieve her heart's desire. In this way, the Twilight saga's message is no different than that of most romance fiction, which offers readers discourses of normative femininity and normative masculinity. A good woman, and apparently a good female fledgling vampire, demonstrates her femininity through her capacity for enduring abuse, and if this suffering occurs at the hands of her beloved, that is to be expected.

Books in the Series

1. *Twilight* (Little, Brown, 2005)
2. *New Moon* (Little, Brown, 2006)
3. *Eclipse* (Little, Brown, 2007)
4. *Breaking Dawn* (Little, Brown, 2008)

Notes

1. Christine Seifert, "Bite Me! (Or Don't): Stephenie Meyer's Vampire-Infested Twilight Series Has Created a New YA Genre: Abstinence Porn," *Bitch*, 2008, http://bitchmagazine.org/article/bite-me-or-dont (accessed August 16, 2009).

2. "Stephenie Meyer Talks about Breaking Dawn," June 11, 2008, online video clip, YouTube, www.youtube.com/watch?v=UVEvEtF08S8 (accessed April 18, 2009).

3. Lee Tobin-McClain, "Paranormal Romance: Secrets of the Female Fantastic," *Journal of the Fantastic in the Arts* 11, no. 3 (2000): 294.

4. Tania Modleski, *Loving with a Vengeance: Mass-produced Fantasies for Women* (New York: Methuen, 1982), 61.

5. Harriet Margolis, "A Childe in Love, or Is It Just Fantasy? The Values of Women's Genres," *Paradoxa: Studies in World Literary Genres* 3, nos. 1–2 (1997): 127.

6. Modleski, *Loving with a Vengeance*, 36.

7. Modleski, *Loving with a Vengeance*, 36.

8. Stephenie Meyer, *Twilight* (New York: Little, Brown, 2005), 23.

9. Stephenie Meyer, *New Moon* (New York: Little, Brown, 2006), 85–92.

10. Lynn M. Phillips, *Flirting with Danger: Young Women's Reflections on Sexuality and Domination* (New York: New York University Press, 2000), 16.

11. Phillips, *Flirting with Danger*, 52.

12. Meyer, *New Moon*, 262.

13. Meyer, *Twilight*, 10.

14. Meyer, *Twilight*, 311.

15. Modleski, *Loving with a Vengeance*, 60.

16. Meyer, *Twilight*, 1, 4.

17. Meyer, *Twilight*, 10.

18. Meyer, *Twilight*, 174.

19. Michelle A. Massé, *In the Name of Love: Women, Narcissism and the Gothic* (Ithaca, NY: Cornell University Press, 1992) 195.

20. Meyer, *Twilight*, 195.

21. Meyer, *New Moon*, 386–387.

22. Meyer, *New Moon*, 263.

23. Meyer, *New Moon*, 263.

24. Meyer, *New Moon*, 437.

25. Centers for Disease Control and Prevention, "Intimate Partner Violence: Dating Violence Fact Sheet," www.cdc.gov/ViolencePrevention/intimatepartnerviolence/datingviolence.html (accessed December 15, 2009).

26. Centers for Disease Control and Prevention, "Intimate Partner Violence."

27. Tobin-McClain, "Paranormal Romance," 294.

28. Tobin-McClain, "Paranormal Romance," 300.

29. Stephenie Meyer, *Eclipse* (New York: Little, Brown, 2007), 599.

30. Stephenie Meyer, *Breaking Dawn* (New York: Little, Brown, 2008), 1.

CHAPTER 53

Shaggy Dog Stories

JONATHAN CARROLL'S *WHITE APPLES* AS UNCONVENTIONAL AFTERLIFE FANTASY

Bernice M. Murphy

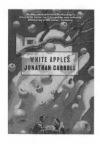 Around thirty pages into Jonathan Carroll's twelfth novel *White Apples*, womanizing ad man Vincent Ettrich is asked the following question by his latest lover, a young woman named Coco Hallis: "Do you remember your life before we met?"[1] As is the case so often in Carroll's fiction, the question is an apparently straightforward one, but the answer is anything but, and the consequences for the protagonist are terrifying and genuinely profound:

> The question was so peculiar and out of place that he wasn't sure he'd heard her correctly. "Do I remember my *life*? Of course I remember it." Anger like a blowtorch flared in his chest. What was this bullshit? "Why wouldn't I remember my life?"
>
> "Then do you remember the hospital? Do you remember all the time you spent in the hospital when you became sick?"
>
> "*What?*" Ettrich had the constitution of a dray horse. He was never sick. Once a year he caught a mild winter cold that usually lasted three days and gave him the sniffles. Sometimes he took an aspirin for a mild headache. Nothing else—even his teeth were healthy. The only reason he ever went to a dentist was to get them cleaned.
>
> "What hospital? I was never in the hospital!" (29)

Despite his frantic initial denials, at Coco's insistent prompting, memories of his previously unremembered time as a patient *do* start to quickly flood Ettrich's mind, and the events of the past few months begin to emerge. Most terrible of all, he suddenly remembers the point at which his cancer-ravaged life ended. "His whole being felt like a tent, a big circus tent, and someone jerked away the poles that held it up. . . . Watching two nice people laugh, Vincent

Ettrich died" (30–31). Like Vincent himself, at this juncture the reader of the novel must suddenly reevaluate everything that has happened up until that point. It is a sensation of Gothic doubt that those already familiar with Carroll's work will be well used to, for more than any other current writer of the fantastic, he excels at pulling the narrative rug from under us, wrong-footing the reader as much as his characters. Again and again in Carroll's novels and short stories, "normal" life is suddenly derailed by the intrusion of supernatural or fantastical forces which can be alternatively life affirming, terrifying, and deeply unsettling. He is the literary equivalent of David Lynch, whose finest films also tend to blur the lines between fantasy and reality in a manner that is as disorientating as it is exhilarating. Like so many of his characters, the reader who has just immersed himself or herself in a Carroll story or novel really never quite knows just what is coming round the corner.

White Apples—a tale of the fantastic, a horror story featuring some genuinely brutal interludes, a touching romance and an afterlife fantasy as indebted to Frank Capra as it is to the Orpheus myth—is in many respects a typical Carroll novel, its resistance to conventional categorization emblematic of that of the author himself. His first novel, *The Land of Laughs* (1980), begins in a conventional enough manner, as Thomas Abbey, a young school teacher and obsessive bibliophile, travels to the small town of Galen, Missouri, in order to write a biography of its most famous citizen, children's author Marshall France. However, as Abbey and his equally obsessive companion Saxony Gardner begin their work on the text, they begin to realize that the relationship between France and the town itself is of a far stranger nature than it initially appears, and that the author's creative powers are much greater than anyone could have ever imagined.

Like many of Carroll's novels to follow, *The Land of Laughs* frustrates conventional generic classification and is by turns playful and genuinely sinister. As in *White Apples*, whimsy frequently intrudes in the form of talking animals and the like (here, it's a dog which takes the leading role, only the first of many significant animals in Carroll's work), but the comedic, often downright goofy edge often present in his work is always evened out by the deeply serious philosophical and theological thrust of the narrative arc. Nothing is what it seems in the initially bucolic town of Galen, and as often recurs in Carroll's work, the relationship between an artist and his work, as well as being a richly rewarding one, also has its dangers. The book remains one of Carroll's most famous, a cult classic in the truest sense of the word, and was even recently referenced in the popular science fiction/thriller television series *Fringe*.

Carroll's follow-up to *The Land of Laughs* was *Voice of Our Shadow* (1983), which, like its predecessor, was recently chosen to be reprinted as one of the Gollancz Fantasy Masterworks series. It is a narrative which again explores the relationship between the world created by a writer and the reality that surrounds

him, about a successful author named Joe Lennox who uses his traumatic childhood relationship with his bullying older brother (whose death may have been Joe's fault) as the basis for a highly successful literary work. As so often in the Gothic, the past, of course, refuses to stay buried, and as the novel progresses, it becomes clear that Joe's youthful experiences have left even more of a mark than he himself truly recognizes. *Voice of Our Shadow* is also the first of Carroll's novels to feature his adopted home city Vienna, whose characters' "inner lives are enriched and animated by the sights of Jewish cemeteries, opera houses, and cafes, [as well as] Grimm's fairy tales or the European tradition of the fantastic."[2]

Given his recurrent focus upon American expats, then, it seemed fitting that his 1987 novel *Bones of the Moon* would focus upon the unusual travails of a young American woman recently returned to New York after spending several years living in Europe with her husband, a genial professional athlete. *Bones*, the first volume in Carroll's so-called Rondua trilogy, is his first novel focusing upon a female protagonist, a warm, witty, and ultimately violent exploration of the porous boundaries between the real and the imagined.

His narrator, the laconic Cullen James, who in almost every other respect seems to be living a charmed life, complete with a kind, thoughtful husband, beautiful baby, and supportive best friend, finds that motherhood inspires in her strange and compelling dreams of a fantasy land named Rondua, the presence of which becomes stronger and stronger as the novel develops. As she journeys through her rich and unusually vivid dreamscape, Cullen is accompanied by a young boy named Pepsi (who we later find out is an incarnation of the little boy she would have given birth to several years previously if she had not had an abortion). Pepsi is on a quest to find the five magical bones that will allow him to control the moon. This being Carroll, a dog again has a prominent role (although this canine is rather larger than most). As she grows increasingly engrossed in the world of her dreams (which unfold sequentially, like a story), Cullen fails to notice the real-world peril that is coming ever closer to her cozy life: the bogeyman next door. Her former next-door neighbor, an incarcerated ax-murderer named Alvin Williams, has becomes dangerously fixated upon her, and in the novel's genuinely disturbing climax, Rondua and the real world collide with devastating and bloody consequences. As this chilling sequence suggests, Carroll is as adept at depicting scenes of graphic violence and their aftermath as are his contemporaries Peter Straub and Stephen King, and for this reason *Bones of the Moon* owes as much to horror and the Gothic as it does to the fantastic.

Many of the characters—both major and minor—from *Bones of the Moon* recur in the follow-ups *Sleeping in Flame* (1988) and *A Child Across the Sky* (1989), in which the fantastic yet again intrudes into the lives of jet-setting, imaginative young Americans whose complacent worldviews are suddenly up-

ended by the intrusion of magical (and often sinister) outside forces. *Sleeping in Flame*, set in Vienna, is about an actor and writer named Walker Easterling who discovers that his mysterious father is a murderous immortal who comes from the world of fairy tales—and definitely not the Disneyfied world of fairy tales, but the sinister, bloodthirsty realm of the Brothers Grimm. Weber Gregston, the arrogant young filmmaker whose initial encounter with Cullen James in *Bones* was a bruising but ultimately eye-opening one, is the narrator of *A Child Across the Sky*, in which he investigates the suicide of one of his closest friends, a successful horror film director tormented by his own creation.

The protagonist of *Outside the Dog Museum* (1991), Harry Radcliffe, is, like Vincent Ettrich, a highly successful and creative professional (in this instance, an architect) with a complicated personal life for whom conventional reality soon takes a sharp left turn into the surreal. It is also, along with the award-winning short story "Friend's Best Man," surely the apotheosis of Carroll's canine admiration, featuring as it does an eccentric sheikh who commissions Radcliffe to build a billion-dollar dog mausoleum in, of course, Austria.

After Silence (1992) is about yet another creative male, an LA cartoonist who falls in love with a free-spirited waitress who is mother to a captivating little boy named Lincoln. In a narrative that starts off in a relatively cozy fashion, yet another Carroll male has his life upended (seemingly for good) by the love of a captivating and mysterious woman. The narrative quickly descends into nightmare when the hero discovers that his new lover is actually a kidnapper, and Lincoln is not her own child. Rather than disrupt their lives, Max decides to keep Lily's terrible secret, a decision that will ultimately have devastating consequences. *From the Teeth of Angels* (1993) is a philosophically inclined meditation on mortality in which characters approaching the ends of their lives are granted the opportunity to question Death himself in their dreams—a theme which has much in common with both *Bones of the Moon* and *White Apples*.

The Panic Hand (1995), originally published in German, collects together twenty of Carroll's high-concept, thought-provoking, and often uncanny short stories, including the grimly hilarious afterlife story "The Jane Fonda Room" and the genuinely bizarre "My Zoondel," about a special breed of dog bred to detect werewolves. As with his previous novel-length pieces, many of the stories collected here feature European settings, but with his next major piece of writing, the so-called Crane's View trilogy (comprising *Kissing the Beehive*, 2000; *The Marriage of Sticks*, 2001; and *The Wooden Sea*, 2002), Carroll returns to the upstate New York of his youth, as well as the small-town setting of *The Land of Laughs*. As Hantke observes, "This change of setting constitutes, in one sense, a move away from the originality of Carroll's earlier work, as he abandons the expatriate theme in favour of one of the central tropes of American horror fiction throughout the 1970s and 80s—the American small town and its dark

underside. In another sense, it has opened Carroll's work towards an examination of his own past as a source of inspiration."[3]

As this overview suggests, metaphysical doubt and cultural displacement (alongside a very Gothic preoccupation with the inherently deceptive nature of human perception) form the remarkably consistent principal strands of Carroll's oeuvre.

White Apples (2002) is no exception, for the novel is in many respects a fairly familiar recombining of many of the thematic and narrative characteristics present in his earlier work, and indeed, the novel's protagonist is Carroll's most avid skirt-chaser to date. In *White Apples*, America and Europe once more combine, this time in the form of urbane Manhattan ad man Vincent Ettrich and his on-again, off-again Austrian lover Isabelle Nuekor, who has taken offense, is away for three months, and is pregnant with their uniquely gifted child. The novel begins as the successful, suave, and good-looking cad Vincent, ever confident in his ability to charm the opposite sex, picks up a young woman named Coco during an encounter in the lingerie store in which she works. But just as Vincent's charming exterior disguises the fact that he is in actuality quite an empty man whose endless pursuit of attractive women can never quite dull the pain caused by the failure of his relationship with Isabelle, it is also the case that Coco isn't quite what she seems on the outside. In fact, the first hint as to her real nature comes during the couple's first date at an up-market restaurant, during which she is unaccountably offended by a misprint on the menu: the dessert "Chocolate-covered Gob" is accidentally rendered as "Chocolate-covered God" (22). Though Vincent finds the mistake mildly amusing, his companion does not and insists upon bringing the mistake to their waiter's attention, much to his discomfort, and the incident, in which Vincent feels the first vague stirrings of disquiet about his new companion, is typically Carrollesque.

The awkwardness of the moment is broken only when an old business acquaintance of Vincent's, the significantly monikered "Bruno Mann," approaches their table (27). The two men shake hands, but while Mann seems curiously shaken by the couple's presence, nothing significant is said. It is just then, however, that reality, as both the reader and Vincent have understood it up to this point, is suddenly and devastatingly undermined. Vincent receives a phone call from his ex-wife Kitty, who informs him that none other than Bruno Mann himself has just died—a fact that Vincent obviously finds difficult to believe, given that Mann is sitting right next to him at that exact moment, chatting pleasantly with Coco. From this moment on, the scene has the narrative texture and fluid logic of a dream. Just as his brain tries to process this new and very disturbing piece of information, Vincent finds himself transported, without any warning, to a bed where he lies alongside Coco. He quickly dismisses what has

just happened as a dream—that is, until he notices something written on her nape:

> He didn't remember her having anything back there like a mole or a birthmark of any sort. Holding her hair up, he leaned over and looked more closely. It was a tattoo. Looking black in the room's dim light, it was definitely a tattoo. Simple block letters that spelled "BRUNO MANN." The dead man's name was written in the back of Coco Hallis's neck. (27)

Moments later, Vincent is forced by Coco's insistent questioning to face the fact that he is no longer in the land of the living. This Gothic message, which never comes at a convenient time, arrives at Vincent's unconscious by all the referents to the color brown, which is the shade of the grave's open maw, the very color to which we all return. *Bruno* is German for "brown," and *Coco* is Spanish for the brown "coconut," as well as an English homonym for steaming chocolate, reminding us of the brown "kakao" that Isabelle loved to drink every afternoon in her grandmother's kitchen. The ghost of Grandma confides to Isabelle that she never liked drinking the stuff herself during this after-school ritual—the cocoa made her "throat feel mossy"—but that she did it to please Isabelle (248). One of the truths of the book is that there are some things we should do even though they go against our immediate instinct and nature, like maintaining fidelity to a partner. Isabelle's grandmother is a protective spirit who considers sharing even more wisdom along with facts of the afterlife, but explaining them to the living is like lecturing someone while they are "having an orgasm" (249). (This insight prompts Isabelle's crooked smile and musing: "I thought life was supposed to be a cabaret. Now you're telling me it's an orgasm?" [249])

Indeed, as Vincent soon discovers, Coco herself is actually a kind of guardian angel, a benign emissary from the other side (purgatory, to be exact). Vincent is not quite dead yet either. As it turns out, he has literally been willed back to life by his own unborn child, currently being carried by the ever-enticing but always elusive Isabelle.

The novel is therefore a typically unusual combination of afterlife fantasy, off-beat detective story (in which the newly resurrected Vincent must try and piece together his fragmented memories of life before his death in order to figure out just what is going on), horror story, Gothic romance, and urban fantasy. The story of Vincent and Isabelle's powerful but complex romantic relationship is interwoven with a complex battle of wits between the forces of good and evil. However, the narrative's more fantastical elements (and there are plenty) are anchored by the fact that, as ever, Carroll's protagonists are deeply flawed individuals all too aware of their own shortcomings. Vincent is a rather shallow,

glib man whose insatiable love of women has destroyed his marriage; Isabelle is a high-strung neurotic who uses her inherited wealth to run away the moment it looks like she will be asked to make a lasting commitment to someone—even Vincent, the love of her life. One of the novel's many strengths, therefore, is the way the reader gradually comes to understand these characters as they slowly begin to truly comprehend the geography of their own souls, and of each other's.

The novel's surreal combination of fantastic and mundane elements aligns it neatly with Carroll's earlier works, but in particular the likes of *Bones of the Moon*, in which an unborn child again plays a key role. While Pepsi in that novel was fated never to be born, however, Vincent's son Anjo is a kind of future messiah in waiting who will one day be of immense importance to the universe, and who is able to help his parents even while still in utero. Carroll has certainly never shied away from exploring the big issues before, but in *White Apples*, and in its sequel *Glass Soup*, he delves into the very meaning of existence in a manner even more dogged than in his earlier works. The confusion and disorientation experienced by Vincent Ettrich as he comes to terms with a completely new way of thinking about life, death, and the very meaning of existence parallels that of the reader, who similarly never quite knows what Carroll will pull out of his bag of tricks next. As the story progresses, Vincent soon discovers that he is not the only person who has recently been resurrected; it seems that Bruno Mann has risen again as well, but although the two men talk about their mutual situation, they are of little real help to one another. Resurrection has other side effects as well: on the way to his meeting with Mann, Vincent brings a taxi driver stricken with a fatal heart attack back to life, although even he isn't quite sure how this was done.

The lovers are reunited when Isabelle flies to New York, but she stops him in his tracks with a single question that reveals she knows even more about his new state than he does himself: "Vincent, what's it like to be dead?" (66). It turns out that in a reversal of the gender dynamic of the Orpheus legend, it was *she* who descended into the underworld in order to bring him back, because "he [Anjo] needs both of us to be alive until he's born" (103). During a long conversation over coffee and pie in a nondescript diner, Isabelle reveals to Vincent what she knows about their unborn child, and about the forces that are gathering against them. It seems that Anjo first made his power felt when she was on a dinner date with a suitor who threatened to become violent. As Isabelle tells her story, Vincent suddenly finds himself transported to the exact time and place at which the incident occurred, in yet another example of the way in which conventional reality so often changes in the blink of an eye in Carroll's work. When it looks as if her date might hit her, Isabelle is rescued by the restaurant owner's dog, a shaggy beast five feet tall on its hind legs and 150 pounds. Isabelle describes it in what could almost serve as a description of the novel itself: "It was

like a beast out of Greek mythology or a German Folktale" (103). However, as she explains to Vincent, "Anjo isn't a dog. He's whatever he wants to be, whatever is convenient for him. He goes in and out of things—minds, people. He has that power" (90).

Despite their unborn child's considerable abilities, however, Vincent remains in terrible danger: "Death wants you back . . . because you belong to it" (107). And indeed, an indication of the fact that the forces of chaos are determined to prevent Anjo from being born comes the next day, when Vincent wakes up next to Isabelle with no memory whatsoever of their relationship or of recent events. This section of the novel resembles the film *Memento* (2000), in which the lead character, an amnesiac, must attempt to reconstruct his life from clues he himself has left written on his own body, as though he were a giant Post-it note. However, while the protagonist of *Memento* tattooed *himself*, it turns out here that Vincent left a message inked on someone else—Coco. The name "Bruno Mann" inked on her neck is, as it soon turns out, a warning, for Mann is actually an agent of chaos itself, the recently appointed "King of the Park"—which is a roundabout way of saying that he rules the forces of chaos, which have recently started to become self-aware, and therefore more dangerous than ever. In one of the many lengthy philosophically inclined passages in the novel, Coco explains to Isabelle, using Scrabble tiles, the fact that "God" (at least as we understand the concept) is like an ever-shifting mosaic—and we are the individual tiles:

> The black tile lay in the middle of Coco's open palm. "Imagine this is your whole mosaic shrunk down to this size." She pointed to the large one hanging in the air. "Your tile completes that. Alone it looks small and unimportant. Until you see what the finished one looks like *without* it. Are you with me?"
>
> Isabelle nodded.
>
> "That big mosaic is not death—It's *God*. The tiles that create Him are all the completed lives that have ever existed. Every single one of them has its place in Him. And without them all, He is incomplete." Coco handed her the black one. "Put it back in." Isabelle reached in and stuck the tile in place with her thumb. "So God is a mosaic and we're the tiles. How we choose to live our lives gives our tile its specific shape?"
>
> "Right." (173–174)

What's more, Coco further explains that purgatory exists for the purpose of teaching every individual about the mosaic and their place in it. As each tile joins the mosaic and is thrown back out again into the universe, the very mosaic itself—God himself—changes as the tiles themselves change. "They travel a certain distance, stop and return. But while they're returning they change into

completely different things. So that when they are joined again, the mosaic is of course different—God is different" (176). This, in turn, means that there is not just one God, but many different Gods, all ever changing; and all "are necessary, and always will be" (177).

Chaos, too, is always part of the ever-changing pattern of existence, but whereas before it was an unthinking force, "like nature," as Coco puts it, it has, in this incarnation of the mosaic, somehow become conscious, aware of its own existence—and what's more, chaos likes this feeling and is willing to do anything to hang on to it. For that reason, chaos doesn't want a new mosaic to be formed and for a long time has been doing all it can to prevent this from happening—which is why Anjo, along with others like him, has been sent into the world, by the mosaic itself, in order to prevent Bruno Mann and his fellow agents of chaos from completing their nefarious mission.

One of the most dramatic confrontations between our protagonists and the forces of darkness takes place in the unlikely setting of a zoo, in a scene that showcases Carroll's ability to create scenes of genuine horror. Because animals are protectors of mankind (a conceit found elsewhere in Carroll's fiction, in particular his award-winning short story "Friend's Best Man," in which they can sense a coming global catastrophe), Coco, Isabelle, and Vincent believe themselves to be, for the moment, safe. But then they hear a terrible shriek from the elephant enclosure and are confronted by a scene of absolute horror as a gang of monstrous children—actually agents of chaos in disguise—mercilessly attack April, the baby elephant within:

> The children had already pulled April's giant head halfway through the bars of the cage, killing her. The skull had burst and there was blood everywhere. The last synapses, messages, and commands from the crushed brain were still travelling down to the distant corners of her great body, making it appear as if she were still living. Some of her did not yet know that it was over. Parts still moved, twitched, reacted, and tried to escape the death that had already come. Her legs crumpled and the body sank to the floor except for her head, still high and wedged between the now glistening bars. (198)

There follows a gruesome, violent, and bizarre battle between the terrified zoo animals and the "children" who have brought death to their home. When it looks as if the animals will win (for, as Carroll points out, "children, no matter how strong and vicious, were no match for a zoo full of enraged animals" [200]), chaos breaks another rule that has existed since the beginning of time, and the children are suddenly transformed into animals themselves, which turns the battle decisively in the other direction. "All of the animals that had come to defend these human beings were now being slaughtered by their own. It was

beyond sacrilege" (200). Even Coco is torn apart by a chaos "lion," although Vincent and Isabelle do manage to escape harm when he is able to access the memories that had been lost to him and find a way to hide their presence from the forces of darkness.

The remainder of this complex, constantly shifting narrative is taken up with Vincent's efforts to protect Isabelle and Anjo, and to figure out just how the forces of chaos, epitomized by Mann, can be defeated. Along the way, Isabelle gets to have a poignant meeting with her dead grandmother, and Vincent spends time with his young parents on the very day of his conception. There is also a particularly inventive scene in which Bruno Mann visits the barber and gets rather more than a haircut: his entire physical appearance is completely altered. Mann's plan to end Anjo's life before it even properly begins is a particularly devious one, which hinges upon Vincent and Isabelle's unconditional love for one another: "There I was, thinking up all kinds of cunning ways to ruin them. Then it dawned on me—all I had to do was stand back and let their love do it for me" (294). In a plot twist that may admittedly strike some readers as a little glib, Mann's scheme is this: He engineers a terrible car crash that leaves Vincent in a coma and in need of a blood transfusion. The catch is that he has a rare blood type, and the only other person nearby with the same blood type is, of course, Isabelle. Mann knows that Isabelle will not be able to let Vincent die, even if the transfusion does irreparable harm to their unborn son and thus renders Anjo incapable of fighting the good fight in later life.

In the hands of a lesser writer, the many lengthy passages in which the meaning of existence is thrashed out between various characters and the slightly saccharine ending would all combine to make *White Apples* a rather tedious "meaning of life" novel in the tradition of the likes of Paulo Coelho. But what ultimately saves Carroll's novel from this fate, apart from the sheer quality of his prose and his breathtaking inventiveness, is his subtle wit and his ability to conjure up moments of genuine unease. In any Carroll novel, there is generally at least as much horror as there is fantasy, and *White Apples* is no exception. The Gothic is a constant presence throughout the book, embodying itself in dark discoveries, a threatening lineage, characters who are the walking dead, displacement and emotional captivity, excess and sexual transgression, melodrama, humorous juxtaposition of menace and the absurd, the all too active supernatural, and the intensely malign power of the agents of Chaos whom our frail and initially uncomprehending humans must resist. For both Isabelle and Vincent, the extraordinary sequence of events they experience forces them to truly embrace adulthood and come to terms with both their own and each other's many flaws. No "matter what kind of life [they've] lived," they realize they are still an indispensable part of the God-mosaic (177). Typically, however, their journey toward self-realization is interspersed with as much terror as wonder. The fact

that Carroll felt the need to continue their journey in a sequel—*Glass Soup*, in which God turns up in the form of a talking polar bear named Bob—suggests that like the characters he evidently has so much fondness for, the author himself felt the need to continue his speculations upon the nature of existence.

Despite his considerable success in Europe, Carroll still remains more of a cult figure than a mainstream "name" in the United States, a "writer's writer," lauded by the likes of Neil Gaiman (whose fiction bears a strong resemblance to Carroll's own work) and Stephen King, who has yet to receive the critical attention that he so richly deserves. Yet, as *White Apples* and the rest of his oeuvre demonstrate, Carroll remains a remarkably inventive, ambitious writer who always manages to be both witty and humane. Few contemporary writers can reverse expectation and astonish as adeptly as he can. In Carroll's fiction, reality as we know it is a thin veneer, beneath which teem forces more fantastic, and more terrifying, than anyone but he can imagine. There is magic in the lives of his characters, but, as if to compensate for some sort of cosmic imbalance, there are frequent infusions of terror, too. It is for these reasons that he deserves to be considered one of the very finest writers of twenty-first-century Gothic.

Notes

1. Jonathan Carroll, *White Apples* (New York: Tor, 2002), 29. Page references to the primary text hereafter appear in parentheses.

2. Steffen Hantke, "Jonathan Carroll," *The Literary Encyclopedia*, www.litencyc.com/php/speople.php?rec=true&UID=5206 (accessed December 5, 2009).

3. Hantke, "Jonathan Carroll."

Consultants and Contributors

The Gothic narratives this guide lists or discusses were suggested by the more than 180 authorities listed below for their art, freshness or originality (including inventive structure, curious characters, and memorable language), experimental nature, genre-bending and blending, influence on other writers and the market, emotive power, continued conversation with the Old Gothic, metaphysical/cultural/historic resonance, or unstoppable drive to scare, disturb, transgress, or shock us. The books had to have that strange alchemy of literary elements that make their words come back to us in dreams. Through their interviews, online sites, award giving, World Fantasy Convention panels and World Horror Convention panels, Gothic courses, symposia, anthologies, reference guides, book-length studies, reviews, articles, and more, the following experts nominated these post-2000 Gothic fictions, and many through e-mail, phone, or in-person conversation voted for them. Novels or novellas receiving the most votes have essay treatments in *21st Century Gothic*.

If "myth is truth" and literature is simply "words that provoke response," as the Cheshire novelist Alan Garner suggests, then which books seemed truest, most provocative? Which were the ones in the world with more mystery and secrets, melodrama and murder, than we could reasonably hope for? Which best redefined the Gothic?

A gracious thank-you to all the people who helped to answer these Gothic questions, and then raised more.

Dean Francis Alfar, author of *Salamanca* and *The Kite of Stars and Other Stories*
Douglas A. Anderson, independent scholar and editor of *Tales Before Tolkien: The Roots of Modern Fantasy*
Ruth Bienstock Anolik, professor of English at Villanova University

Nina Auerbach, professor of English and comparative literature at the University of Pennsylvania

Chris Baldick, professor of English at Goldsmiths College, University of London

Karin Beeler, professor and chair of English at the University of Northern British Columbia

Peter Bell, senior lecturer in history and American studies at York St. John University, England

Deborah Biancotti, author of *A Book of Endings*

Leigh Blackmore, graduate student/lecturer at the University of Wollongong, Australia

Richard Bleiler, humanities librarian at the University of Connecticut

Bernadette Lynn Bosky, reviewer for *Strange Horizons* and author of "None of the Above"

T. C. Boyle, creative writer and professor of creative writing at the University of Southern California

Marshall Brown, professor of English and comparative literature at the University of Washington

Karen Budra, professor of literature and cinema studies at Langara College, Canada

John Bushore, author of *Friends in Dark Places* and *The Prisoner of Gender*

Bruce Butt, instructor at the City Academy, Bristol, England

Glennis Byron, professor of English and Gothic studies at the University of Stirling, Scotland

J. R. Campbell, coeditor (with Charles Prepolec) of *Gaslight Grimoire* and *Gaslight Grotesque*

Ramsey Campbell, author of *The Darkest Part of the Woods* and *Creatures of the Pool*

Isobelle Carmody, author of *The Obernewtyn Chronicles* and *Green Monkey Dreams*

Lynette Carpenter, professor and chair of English at Ohio Wesleyan University

Margaret L. Carter, author of *Embracing Darkness*

J. Kathleen Cheney, author of "Early Winter, Near Jenli Village" and "Iron Shoes"

Alan Cheuse, NPR book commentator and professor of creative writing at George Mason University

George Makana Clark, creative writing professor at the University of Wisconsin, Milwaukee

Simon Clark, author of *The Midnight Man* and *Ghost Monster*

Peter Coady, independent scholar

Venita Coelho, creative writer and filmmaker

Jason Colavito, author of *A Hideous Bit of Morbidity* and *Knowing Fear*

Nancy A. Collins, author of *Knuckles & Tales* and *Sunglasses After Dark*

Bill Congreve, creative writer and founder of MirrorDanse Books

Scott Connors, editor and independent scholar

James Cortese, creative writer and adjunct professor of English at Lone Star College, Montgomery

Romana Cortese, professor of Italian and English at Lone Star College, Montgomery

David E. Cowen, poet of *Sixth and Adams*

The late Michael Cox, editor and author of *The Meaning of Night* and *The Glass of Time*

Edward Crandall, creative writer and journalist for *Saga Shimbun*

Gary William Crawford, creative writer and founder of Gothic Press

Peter Crowther, creative writer and founder of PS Publishing

Shane Jiraiya Cummings, creative writer and editor

Don D'Ammassa, independent scholar and author of *Wings Over Manhattan*

Ellen Datlow, anthologist extraordinaire

Andrew Davidson, author of *Gargoyle*

Carol Margaret Davison, associate professor of English at the University of Windsor, Canada

Stephen Dedman, author of *Foreign Bodies* and *Never Seen by Waking Eyes*

Guillermo del Toro, screenwriter and filmmaker

Dejana Dimitrijević, creative writer

Michael Dirda, Pulitzer Prize–winning *Washington Post* book critic

Chitra Banerjee Divakaruni, professor of creative writing at the University of Houston

James Doig, editor of *Australian Nightmares* and *Australian Gothic*

Hiromi T. Dollase, professor of modern languages and literatures at Beloit College

Doug Dorst, author of *Alive in Necropolis*

Terry Dowling, author of *Blackwater Days* and *Clowns at Midnight*

Heather Duda, professor of English at the University of Rio Grande

Steve Duffy, author of *The Moment of Panic* and *Tragic Life Stories*

Stefan Dziemianowicz, anthologist, editor, and coeditor of *Supernatural Literature of the World* (3 vols.)

Jennifer Egan, author of *The Keep* and *A Visit from the Goon Squad*

Brian Evenson, author of *Last Days* and *The Wavering Knife*

Paul Finch, author of *After Shocks* and *Walkers in the Dark*

Rob Fisher, retired professor of philosophy, Westminster College, Oxford University, and founder of Inter-Disciplinary.Net

Christopher Fowler, author of *Old Devil Moon* and the Bryant & May Mystery series

Sir Christopher Frayling, author of *Nightmare: The Birth of Horror* and *Vampyres: Lord Byron to Count Dracula*

Neil Gaiman, author of *Neverwhere* and *American Gods*

Alan Garner, OBE, author of *The Weirdstone of Brisingamen* and *Thursbitch*

Nick Gevers, horror/fantasy reviewer and PS Publishing editor

Laura Anne Gilman, author of *Hard Magic* and *Staying Dead*

Adam Golaski, author of *Worse Than Myself* and publisher of the journal *New Genre*

Helen Grant, author of *The Vanishing of Katharina Linden*

Lauren Groff, author of *The Monsters of Templeton* and *Delicate Edible Birds and Other Stories*

Genni Gunn, author of *Tracing Iris* and *Faceless*

Paula Guran, editor of *Embraces: Dark Erotica* and *Best New Paranormal Romance*

Cheryl Hague, university lecturer in English at Governors State University, Illinois

Peter Halasz, administrator of Canada's Sunburst award

Joe Haldeman, adjunct professor in the School of Humanities at MIT

Tunku Halim, author of *The Woman Who Grew Horns* and *Gravedigger's Kiss*

Melissa Mia Hall, creative writer and *Publishers Weekly* reviewer

Elizabeth Hand, *Washington Post* reviewer and author of *Illyria* and *Mortal Love*

David Hartwell, anthologist, editor, and publisher of the *New York Review of Science Fiction*

Mavis Haut, author of *The Hidden Library of Tanith Lee*

Rick Hautala, author of *Untcigahunk: The Complete Little Brothers* and *The Mountain King*

Jerrold E. Hogle, university distinguished professor of English and director of undergraduate studies and English honors at the University of Arizona

Robert Hood, author of *Robot War Espresso* and the Shades series

Douglas L. Howard, editor of *Dexter: Investigating Cutting Edge Television* and coeditor of *The Gothic Other*

William Hughes, professor of Gothic studies at Bath Spa University, England

Stephen Jones, editor of *The Mammoth Book of Best New Horror* series for over twenty years

S. T. Joshi, coeditor of *Supernatural Literature of the World* (3 vols.) and editor of *Icons of Horror and the Supernatural* (2 vols.)

Graham Joyce, author of *The Facts of Life* and *Memoirs of a Master Forger*

T. E. D. Klein, author of *The Ceremonies* and "Children of the Kingdom"

Robert Knowlton (Bob Hadji), World Fantasy Award judge and founding editor of *Borderland*

Charles Kroll, professor of English at Stephen F. Austin University

K. A. Laity, author of *Unikirja: Dreambook* and *Pelzmantel: A Medieval Tale*

Margo Lanagan, author of *Tender Morsels* and *Red Spikes*

John Langan, professor of English at SUNY, New Paltz

Rob Latham, professor of English and cultural studies at the University of California, Riverside

Thomas Ligotti, author of *The Agonizing Resurrection of Victor Frankenstein & Other Gothic Tales* and *The Conspiracy Against the Human Race*

Stephen Lockley, coauthor of *The Ragchild* and coeditor of the Cold Cuts series (both with Paul Lewis)

Bruce Machart, professor of creative writing at Lone Star College, Houston

Anthony Magistrale, professor and chair of English at the University of Vermont

Violette Malan, author of *The Sleeping God* and editor of *Dead in the Water*

James Marriott, coauthor of *Horror: The Definitive Guide to the Cinema of Fear* (with Kim Newman) and contributing editor of *My Bloody Valentine*

Valerie Martin, author of *Mary Reilly* and *The Confessions of Edward Day*

Elizabeth Massie, author of *Sin Eater* and *Shadow Dreams*

Patrick McAleer, author of *Inside the Dark Tower Series: Art, Evil and Intertextuality in the Stephen King Novels*

Elizabeth McCarthy, coeditor of *Fear: Essays on the Meaning and Experience of Fear* and cofounder of the *Irish Journal of Gothic and Horror Studies*

Kenneth McKenney, author of *The Changeling* and *The Moonchild*

Gabriel Mesa, reviewer and interviewer for *All-Hallows* and *Fantastic Metropolis*

Randy B. Money, reviewer for *Conspire*

Amy L. Montz, professor of English at Texas A & M University

Rev. Stephen Morris, Eastern Orthodox chaplain of Columbia University and hub leader for Inter-Disciplinary.net

Farnoosh Moshiri, author of *The Bathhouse* and *Against Gravity*

Marie Mulvey-Roberts, reader in literary studies at the University of the West of England

Bernice Murphy, lecturer in popular literature at Trinity College, Dublin, and cofounder of the *Irish Journal of Gothic and Horror Studies*

Adam L. G. Nevill, author of *Apartment 16* (an Amazon.uk number-one best seller on its 2010 release) and *Banquet for the Damned*

Kim Newman, coeditor of *Horror: 100 Best Books* and *Horror: Another 100 Best Books* (both with Stephen Jones)

Sorcha Ní Fhlainn, lecturer in American literature and cinema at Trinity College, Dublin

William F. Nolan, author of *Dark Universe* and *Nightshadows*

Joyce Carol Oates, editor, author, and professor of creative writing at Yale University

Linda Ogston, Ph.D. student in English at University of Stirling, Scotland

Reggie Oliver, playwright, actor, director, and author of *Madder Mysteries* and *Dramas from the Depths*

Catherine Olson, professor of English at Lone Star College, Tomball

Danel Olson, editor and professor of English at Lone Star College, Houston

Norman Partridge, author of *Dark Harvest* and *Lesser Demons*

The late Milorad Pavić, author of *Dictionary of the Khazars* and *Landscape Painted with Tea*

Van Piercy, professor of English at Lone Star College, Tomball

Sarah Pinborough, author of *The Language of Dying* and *A Matter of Blood*

Rosemary Poole-Carter, author of *Women of Magdalene* and *What Remains*

Charles Prepolec, coeditor (with J. R. Campbell) of *Gaslight Grimoire* and *Gaslight Grotesque*

Robert M. Price, founder of *Crypt of Cthulhu* and the *Journal of Higher Criticism*

Cherie Priest, author of the Eden Moore trilogy and *Fathom*

Melissa Pritchard, author of *Spirit Seizures* and *Selene of the Spirits*

June Pulliam, professor of English and gender studies at Louisiana State University, Baton Rouge

David Punter, professor of English at the University of Bristol

Katherine Ramsland, professor of forensic psychology and criminal justice at DeSales University

Walter Rankin, author of *Grimm Pictures: Fairy Tale Archetypes in Eight Horror and Suspense Films*

Tina Rath, author of "A Trick of the Dark" and "Extended Family"

James Reese, author of *The Dracula Dossier* and *The Witchery*

Laurence Rickels, professor of German and comparative literature at the University of California, Santa Barbara

Thomas S. Roche, coeditor of *Noirotica* and coeditor of *His: 30 Erotic Tales* (both with Alison Tyler)

Jim Rockhill, reviewer and editor of three Sheridan Le Fanu story collections (for Ash-Tree Press)

Barbara Roden, cofounder of Ash-Tree Press and the *All Hallows* journal, and author of *Northwest Passages*

Christopher Roden, cofounder of Ash-Tree Press and the *All Hallows* journal

Cameron Rogers, author of *The Music of Razors*

Nicholas Royle, author of *Antwerp* and *Mortality*

R. B. Russell, author and founder of Tartarus Press

David J. Schow, author of *Pamela's Get* and the screenplay *The Crow*

Darrell Schweitzer, former editor of *Weird Tales* and author of *Living with the Dead* and *The White Isle*

Ekaterina Sedia, author of *The Secret History of Moscow* and *The Alchemy of Stone*

Bill Sheehan, reviewer for the *Washington Post* and author of *At the Foot of the Story Tree*

Lucius Shepard, author of *Viator* and *Beast of the Heartland*

Brian J. Showers, reviewer, interviewer, and author of *The Bleeding Horse* and *Literary Walking Tours of Gothic Dublin*

Michele Slung, editor of *Slow Hand, Shudder,* and *Shudder Again*

Mary Ellen Snodgrass, professor of English and Latin at Lenoir Rhyne University

Catherine Spooner, lecturer in the Department of English and Creative Writing at Lancaster University

Brian Stableford, author of *The Cassandra Complex* and the *Historical Dictionary of Science Fiction Literature*

Mark Steensland, lecturer in media at Penn State University

Karen F. Stein, professor of English and women's studies at the University of Rhode Island

Jonathan Strahan, editor of the yearly *Best Short Novels, Fantasy: The Very Best of,* and *Science Fiction: The Very Best of* series

Peter Straub, author of *A Dark Matter* and *Ghost Story*

Anna Taborska, creative writer, and director and screenwriter of *My Uprising* and *The Rain Has Stopped*

Charles Tan, creative writer, interviewer, and founder of *Bibliophile Stalker*

August Tarrier, editor, and author of "I Hold You Harmless" and "Field Notes"

Lucy Taylor, author of *Dancing with Demons* and *The Safety of Unknown Cities*

Steve Rasnic Tem, author of *In Concert* and *The Man on the Ceiling* (with Melanie Tem)

Thomas Tessier, author of *Phantom* and *Fog Heart*

Douglass H. Thomson, professor of English at Georgia Southern University

Dale Townshend, professor of English and Gothic studies at Stirling University, Scotland

Tia V. Travis, author of "Down Here in the Garden" and "One Thousand Dragon Sheets"

Lee Tulloch, author of *Wraith* and *The Cutting*

Lisa Tuttle, author of *Stranger in the House: The Collected Short Supernatural Fiction* and *The Silver Bough*

Douglas Unger, author of *Voices from Silence* and *Looking for War*

Simon Kurt Unsworth, author of *Lost Places* and contributor to *Creature Feature*

Jeff VanderMeer, editor of *The New Weird* and author of *City of Saints and Madmen*

Stephen Volk, author of *Vardøger* and screenwriter for Ken Russell's film *Gothic*

Sean Wallace, founder of Cosmos Books and Prime Books editor and anthologist

Jerad Walters, founder of Centipede Press

Marina Warner, distinguished visiting professor of humanities at Queen Mary, University of London, and visiting professor of animation at the Royal College of Art, London

Kaaron Warren, author of *Walking the Tree* and *Slights*

David Wellington, author of the Monster trilogy, the Laura Caxton/Vampire series, and the Frostbite series

John Whitbourn, author of *A Dangerous Energy* and *Binscombe Tales: Sinister Saxon Stories*

F. Paul Wilson, author of the Repairman Jack series

Judith Wilt, professor of English and Newton College alumnae chair at Boston College

Antoinette F. Winstead, professor of communication arts at Our Lady of the Lake University

Gary K. Wolfe, professor of humanities and English at Roosevelt University and reviewer for *Locus* magazine

Chelsea Quinn Yarbro, author of the Saint-Germain cycle and the Madelaine de Montalia novels

Jason Zerrillo, artist for *Ghost Realm, Rope Trick*, and *Exotic Gothic 3* (all for Ash-Tree Press)

Zoran Živković, professor of creative writing at the University of Belgrade

Sue Zlosnik, department head of English at Manchester Metropolitan University

APPENDIX B

Honorable Mentions

These Gothic-oriented novels and novellas also received votes for being most stylistically artistic, experimentally successful, influential on other writers and the market, innovative at genre bending and blending, original, emotive, metaphysically/culturally/historically significant, or authentically scary/disturbing/transgressive/shocking.

Margaret Atwood, *Oryx and Crake* (2003)
Clive Barker, *Mister B. Gone* (2007)
Max Brooks, *World War Z* (2006)
A. S. Byatt, *The Biographer's Tale* (2001)
Mary Caponegro, *All Fall Down* (2009, includes two novellas)
Gail Carriger, *Soulless* (2009)
Jonathan Carroll, *The Ghost in Love* (2001), *The Wooden Sea* (2001), *Glass Soup* (2005)
Simon Clark, *The Midnight Man* (2008)
Michael Cox, *The Glass of Time* (2008)
Bret Easton Ellis, *Lunar Park* (2005)
Virginia Renfro Ellis, *The Wedding Dress* (2002)
Leif Enger, *Peace Like a River* (2001)
Justin Evans, *A Good and Happy Child* (2007)
Brian Evenson, *The Open Curtain* (2008), *Last Days* (2009)
Michel Faber, *Under the Skin* (2000)
Jana French, *In the Woods* (2007), *The Likeness* (2008)
Neil Gaiman, *American Gods* (2001)
Carol Goodman, *The Lake of Dead Languages* (2002)
Elizabeth Hand, *Mortal Love* (2004), *Illyria* (2006), *Generation Loss* (2007)

APPENDIX B

Charlaine Harris, the Southern Vampire series/Sookie Stackhouse series (starting 2001)
Joanne Harris, *Sleep, Pale Sister* (2004), *Holy Fools* (2004)
Glen Hirshberg, *Snowman's Children* (2002)
Stephen Graham Jones, *Demon Theory* (2006)
Graham Joyce, *Dreamside* (2000), *Indigo* (2000), *The Facts of Life* (2003)
Sue Monk Kidd, *The Mermaid Chair* (2005)
Caitlín R. Kiernan, *Threshold* (2001), *Low Red Moon* (2003), *The Five of Cups* (2003)
Stephen King, *Lisey's Story* (2006)
Natsuo Kirino, *Grotesque* (released in Japanese, 2003, as *Gurotesuku*; English trans. and pub. 2007)
Rachel Klein, *The Moth Diaries* (2002)
Margo Lanagan, *Tender Morsels* (2008)
Tanith Lee, *Death of the Day* (2004), *L'amber* (2006)
John Ajvide Lindqvist, *Let Me In* (released in Swedish, 2004, as *Låt den rätte komma in*; English trans. and pub. 2007, and re-released in 2008 as *Let the Right One In*)
Jeff Lindsay, the Dexter series (starting 2004)
Margot Livesey, *Homework* (2001), *The Missing World* (2005), *Criminals* (2005), *The House on Fortune Street* (2008)
Nick Mamatas, *Northern Gothic* (2001), *Move Under Ground* (2004)
Hilary Mantel, *Beyond Black* (2005)
Graham Masterson, *A Terrible Beauty* (2003)
Patrick McGrath, *Ghost Town: Tales of Manhattan Then and Now* (2005)
James Meek, *The People's Act of Love* (2005)
Stephenie Meyer, the Twilight saga (2005–2008)
China Miéville, *The City & The City* (2010)
Kate Morton, *The House at Riverton* (released in Australia as *The Shifting Fog*, 2007; elsewhere in 2008)
Joyce Carol Oates, *The Tattooed Girl* (2003), *The Gravedigger's Daughter* (2007), *My Sister, My Love: The Intimate Story of Skyler Rampike* (2008)
Stewart O'Nan, *Songs for the Missing* (2008)
Anthony O'Neill, *The Lamplighter* (2003)
David Oppegaard, *The Suicide Collectors* (2008)
Chuck Palahniuk, *Haunted* (2005)
Norman Partridge, *Dark Harvest* (2006)
David Peace, *Tokyo Year Zero* (2007)
Rosemary Poole-Carter, *Women of Magdalene* (2007)
Anne Rice, *Merrick* (2000)
Cameron Rogers, *Music of Razors* (2001)

Nicholas Royle, *Antwerp* (2004)

Will Self, *Dorian: An Imitation* (2003)

Lucius Shepard, *Louisiana Breakdown* (2003), *Viator* (2005), *Trujillo* (2005)

John Shirley, *Demons* (2002)

Koji Suzuki, *Promenade of the Gods* (released in Japanese, 2003, as *Kamigami no Promenade*; English trans. and pub. 2008)

Thomas Tessier, *Father Panic's Comic Opera* (2000)

William Trevor, *The Story of Lucy Gault* (2002)

John Updike, *Eastwick* (2008)

Luis Alberto Urrea, *The Hummingbird's Daughter* (2005)

Jeff VanderMeer, *City of Saints and Madmen* (2004)

Carlos Ruiz Zafón, *The Angel's Game* (released in Spanish, 2008, as *El Juego del Angel*; English trans. and pub. 2009)

APPENDIX C
Novel Publication Details

Key:

H	hardback
HLP	hardback large print
HDE	hardback deckle edged
P	paperback
PLP	paperback large print
TP	trade paperback
MM	mass market paperback

The Angel Maker (2005) by Stefan Brijs

H	The Netherlands (Atlas, 2005, titled *De Engelenmaker*)
H	UK (Weidenfeld and Nicholson, 2008, trans. from Dutch by Hester Velmans)
P	US (Penguin, 2008, trans. from Dutch by Hester Velmans)

Banquet for the Damned (2004) by Adam L. G. Nevill

H	UK (PS Publishing, 2004)
P	UK & US (Virgin, 2008, 2010)

Beasts (2002) by Joyce Carol Oates

H	US (Otto Penzler Books/Da Capo Press, 2002)
HLP	US (Thorndike, 2004)
P	UK (Orion, 2004)
TP	US (Carroll & Graf, 2008)

The Blind Assassin (2000) by Margaret Atwood

H	UK & US (Bloomsbury, 2000)
HLP	UK & US (Bloomsbury, 2000)
P	UK (Virago, 2001)
MM	Canada (Seal, 2001)
HDE	US (Nan A. Talese, 2000)
P	US (Anchor, 2001)

The Book Thief (2006) by Markus Zusak

H	UK (Bodley Head, 2006)
H	US (Knopf, 2006)
H	US (Doubleday, 2007)
P	UK (Black Swan, 2008)
P	US (Knopf, 2007)

The Bride of Frankenstein: Pandora's Bride (2007) by Elizabeth Hand

P	US (Dark Horse, 2007)

Candles Burning (2006) by Tabitha King and Michael McDowell

H	US (Berkley, 2006)
P	US (Berkley, 2007)

The Casebook of Victor Frankenstein (2008) by Peter Ackroyd

H	UK (Chatto & Windus, 2008)
MM	UK (Chatto, 2009)
P	US (Vintage, 2009)
HDP	US (Nan A. Talese, 2009)
P	US (Anchor, 2010)

Clowns at Midnight: A Tale of Appropriate Fear (2010) by Terry Dowling

H	UK (PS Publishing, 2010, signed and tray cased)
H	UK (PS Publishing, 2010)

Cold Skin (2002) by Albert Sánchez Piñol

H	Spain (La Campana, 2002, titled *La Pell Freda*)
P	UK (Canongate, 2006, 2007, trans. from Spanish by Cheryl Leah Morgan)

H	US (Farrar, Straus and Giroux, 2005, trans. from Spanish by Cheryl Leah Morgan)
P	US (Canongate, 2007, trans. from Spanish by Cheryl Leah Morgan)

The Crimson Petal and the White (2002) by Michel Faber

H	UK (Canongate, 2002)
P	UK (Canongate, 2003, 2010)
H	US (Harcourt, 2002)
P	US (Mariner, 2003)

A Dark Matter (2010) by Peter Straub

H	US (Doubleday, 2010)
PLP	US (Random House, 2010)
MM	US (Anchor, 2011)

The Dark Tower series (seven novels, 1982–2004) by Stephen King

H	US (Fantasy Books, 1998, The Dark Tower gift collection, books 1–3)
P	US (Pocket, 2003, The Dark Tower boxed set, vols. 1–3)
P	US (Plume Books, 2003, The Dark Tower boxed set, vols. 1–4)
MM	US (New American Library, 2003, The Dark Tower boxed set, vols. 1–4)
P	UK (New English Library, 2003, The Dark Tower boxed set, vols. 1–4)
H	UK (Hodder & Stoughton, 2004, *The Dark Tower*, book 7)
P	UK (Hodder, 2005, *The Dark Tower*, book 7)
P	UK (Hodder, 2009, The Dark Tower set, vols. 5 and 6)
H	US (Donald M. Grant/Scribner, 2004, *The Dark Tower*, book 7)
MM	US (Pocket, 2006, *The Dark Tower*, book 7)

The Darkest Part of the Woods (2002) by Ramsey Campbell

H	UK (PS Publishing, 2002)
H	US (Tor, 2003)
MM	US (Tor, 2004)

The Dracula Dossier (2008) by James Reese

H	US (William Morrow, 2008)
P	US (William Morrow, 2008)

The Eden Moore trilogy (2003–2007) by Cherie Priest

P   US (Marietta Publishing, 2003, *Four and Twenty Blackbirds*, vol. 1)
P   US (Tor, 2005, *Four and Twenty Blackbirds*, vol. 1, longer, revised edition)
P   US (Tor, 2006, *Wings to the Kingdom*, vol. 2)
P   US (Tor, 2007, *Not Flesh Nor Feathers*, vol. 3)

Eva Moves the Furniture (2001) by Margot Livesey

H   US (Henry Holt, 2001)
P   UK & US (Picador, 2002)
P   UK (Methuen, 2005)

Fatal Women (including novellas *Rherlotte; Virgile, the Widow;* and *Green Iris*, 2004) by Tanith Lee

P   UK (Egerton House, 2004)

Fingersmith (2002) by Sarah Waters

H   UK (Virago, 2002)
P   US (Riverhead, 2002)

The Forgotten Garden (2008) by Kate Morton

H   Australia (Allen & Unwin, 2008)
H   US (Atria/Simon & Schuster, 2008)
P   US (Washington Square Press, 2010)

Four Souls (2004) by Louise Erdrich

H   US (HarperCollins, 2004)
P   US (HarperCollins, 2005)

The Gargoyle (2008) by Andrew Davidson

H   UK (Canongate, 2008)
H   US (Knopf/Doubleday, 2008)
P   UK (Canongate, 2009)
P   US (Knopf/Doubleday, 2009)
P   Australia & New Zealand (Text Publishing, 2009)

The Ghost Writer (2004) by John Harwood

H	UK (Jonathan Cape, 2004)
P	UK & US (Vintage, 2005)
H	US (Houghton Mifflin Harcourt, 2004)
P	US (Houghton Mifflin Harcourt, 2005)

Gould's Book of Fish: A Novel in 12 Fish (2001) by Richard Flanagan

H	Australia (Pan Macmillan Australia, 2001)
H	US (Grove Press/Atlantic, 2002)
P	US (Grove Press, 2002)

The Graveyard Book (2008) by Neil Gaiman

H	UK (Bloomsbury, 2008)
P	UK (Bloomsbury, 2009)
H	US (HarperCollins, 2008)
P	US (Trophy Press, 2008)
P	US (HarperCollins, 2010)

Heart-Shaped Box (2007) by Joe Hill

H	US (Subterranean Press, 2007, advance edition)
H	US (William Morrow, 2007)
MM	US (Harper, 2008)
TP	US (Harper, 2010)
H	UK (Gollancz, 2007)
P	UK (Gollancz, 2008)

The Historian (2005) by Elizabeth Kostova

H	US (Little, Brown, 2005)
HLP	US (Little, Brown, 2005)
P	US (Sphere/Little, Brown, 2006)
MM	US (Little, Brown, 2008)
P	US (Back Bay, 2009)

The Horned Man (2002) by James Lasdun

H	US (Norton, 2002)
P	US (Norton, 2003)
P	UK (Vintage, 2003)

House of Leaves (2000) by Mark Z. Danielewski

H   US (Random House, 2000)
P   US (Pantheon/Random, 2000)

Jonathan Strange and Mr. Norrell (2004) by Susanna Clarke

H   UK & US (Bloomsbury, 2004)
P   UK & US (Bloomsbury, 2005)
MM   US (Tor, 2006)

The Keep (2006) by Jennifer Egan

H   US (Knopf, 2006)
HLP   US (Thorndike, 2007)
P   US (Anchor, 2007)
P   UK (Abacus, 2008)

The Little Friend (2002) by Donna Tartt

H   UK (Bloomsbury, 2002)
H   UK (Bloomsbury, 2009, *The Secret History* and *The Little Friend* special edition box set)
P   UK (Bloomsbury, 2002)
H   US (Knopf, 2002)
P   US (Vintage, 2003)

Lost (2001) by Gregory Maguire

H   US (William Morrow, 2001)
H   UK (Headline Review, 2010)
P   US (Harper, 2002)

The Lovely Bones (2002) by Alice Sebold

H   US (Little, Brown, 2002)
H   UK (Picador, 2009)
H   US (Little, Brown, 2009, as *Looking Glass: A Special Letter Edition of The Lovely Bones*)
PLP   US (Large Print Press, 2006)
P   UK (Picador, 2003)
P   US (Back Bay, 2004)
MM   US (Little, Brown, 2006, 2009)
MM   UK (Picador, 2009)

Lullaby (2002) by Chuck Palahniuk

H	US (Doubleday/Random, 2002)
H	UK (Jonathan Cape, 2002)
HLP	US (Thorndike Press, 2003)
P	US (Anchor, 2002)
P	US (Random/Vintage, 2003)

Martha Peake (2000) by Patrick McGrath

H	US (Random, 2000)
H	UK (Penguin/Viking, 2000)
P	US & UK (Vintage, 2002)

The Meaning of Night: A Confession (2006) by Michael Cox

H	UK (John Murray, 2006)
H	US (Norton, 2006)
P	US (Norton, 2007)

Memoirs of a Master Forger (2008) by William Heaney (Graham Joyce)

H	UK (Gollancz, 2008)
H	US (Night Shade Books, 2009, as *How to Make Friends with Demons*)
P	UK (Gollancz, 2009)
TP	US (Night Shade Books, 2010, as *How to Make Friends with Demons*)

A Mercy (2008) by Toni Morrison

H	US (Knopf, 2008)
H	UK (Chatto & Windus, 2008)
PLP	US (Random, 2008)
P	US (Vintage, 2009)

The Merrily Watkins series (ten novels, 1998–2008) by Phil Rickman

H	UK (Macmillan)
P	UK (Macmillan)
H	UK (Quercus Publishing)
MM	UK (Quercus Publishing)

The Monsters of Templeton (2008) by Lauren Groff

H	UK (William Heinemann, 2008)
H	US (Voice/Hyperion, 2008)
P	US (Voice, Hyperion, 2008)
HLP	US (Thorndike, 2008)
P	UK (Windmill Books, 2009)

Never Let Me Go (2005) by Kazuo Ishiguro

H	UK (Faber & Faber, 2005)
H	US (Knopf, 2005)
HLP	US (Thorndike, 2005)
P	UK (Faber & Faber, 2006)
P	US (Vintage, 2006)

No Country for Old Men (2005) by Cormac McCarthy

H	UK & US (Picador, 2005)
HLP	US (Random House, 2005)
HDE	US (Knopf, 2005)
H	US (B. E. Trice Pub., 2005, leather bound and signed)
P	US (Vintage, 2007)
P	UK (Picador, 2008)
MM	US (Random, 2006)

The Portrait of Mrs. Charbuque (2002) by Jeffrey Ford

H	US (William Morrow, 2002)
TP	US (HarperCollins, 2003)
P	US (Tor, 2004)

The Pumpkin Child (2002, a novella in the collection *Knuckles & Tales*) by Nancy A. Collins

H	US (Cemetery Dance Pub., 2002, leather bound and signed)
H	US (Cemetery Dance Pub., 2002)
TP	US (Biting Dog Pub., 2003)
H	Canada (Ash-Tree Press, *Exotic Gothic*, 2007, a multiauthor collection)
TP	Canada (Ash-Tree Press, *Exotic Gothic*, 2007, a multiauthor collection)

Real World (2006) by Natsuo Kirino

H   Japan (Shueisha, 2006, originally titled *Riaru Warudo*)
HDE   US (Knopf, 2008, trans. from Japanese by Philip Gabriel)
P   US (Vintage, 2008, trans. from Japanese by Philip Gabriel)

A Series of Unfortunate Events (thirteen novels, 1999–2006) by Daniel Handler/Lemony Snicket

H   US (HarperCollins, 2006, thirteen-volume box set titled *The Complete Wreck)*

The Shadow of the Wind (2001) by Carlos Ruiz Zafón

H   Spain (Editorial Planeta, 2001, originally titled *La Sombra del Viento*)
H   US (Penguin, 2004, trans. from Spanish by Lucia Graves)
H   US (Subterranean Press, 2008, trans. from Spanish by Lucia Graves)
H   UK (Weidenfeld & Nicolson, 2004, trans. from Spanish by Lucia Graves, illustrated edition)
P   UK (Phoenix, 2004, trans. from Spanish by Lucia Graves)
P   US (Penguin, 2005, trans. from Spanish by Lucia Graves)

The Terror (2007) by Dan Simmons

H   US (Little, Brown, 2007)
H   US (Subterranean Press, 2009, signed and lettered)
P   US (Back Bay, 2007)
P   US (Bantam/Random, 2008)
MM   US (Little, Brown, 2009)

The Thirteenth Tale (2006) by Dianne Setterfield

H   UK (Orion, 2006)
P   UK (Orion, 2007)
H   US (Atria, 2006)
H   US (Turtleback Books/Sanval, 2007)
PLP   US (Center Point, 2007)
P   US (Washington Square Press, 2007)

Thursbitch (2003) by Alan Garner

H   UK (Harvill Press/Random, 2003)
P   US & UK (Vintage/Random, 2004)

Twilight (2005) by Stephenie Meyer

H	US (Little, Brown, 2005)
H	UK (ATOM, 2006)
P	US (Little, Brown, 2006)
P	UK (ATOM, 2007)
MM	US (Little, Brown, 2008)
MM	UK (ATOM, 2009)

White Apples (2002) by Jonathan Carroll

H	US (Tor, 2002)
TP	US (Tor, 2003)
P	US (Tor, 2004)

Index

Eagle. See Arend
Earnshaw, Catherine, xxviii, 395, 450
East Lynne, 206, 560
Eastern Europe, 160, 286, 287, 294
Eastwood, Clint, 137, 139, 404
Eckhart, Meister, 242
Eclipse, 573, 574–75, 580, 582
Eco, Umberto, 528
eco-Gothic, 226–41, 232, 381, 566–68
ecstasy, state of (not the drug), 114, 130, 165, 338
Eddison, E. R., xv
Eden Moore trilogy, 171–81
Edible Woman, 35
Edogawa Rampo, 501, 503
Edwardian era, 22, 253, 255, 509
Egan, Jennifer, vi, xvi, xx, xxi, xxiii, xxvii, 327–41, 597, 611
eggs, human, 7
ego, 162
Egoyan, Atom, 242
Egypt, 117, 195, 303
Egyptian, ancient beliefs or practices, 74, 162, 164
Egyptian Books of the Dead, 164
ejaculation, 74, 114
electricity, 58, 73–74, 78–79, 155, 436–37
elementals, 150, 246, 347
The Elementals, 66
elements, 161
elephants, 592
Elidor, 563
Eliot, George, 118, 621
Eliot, T. S., 413
Ellis, Bret Easton, 269, 372, 603
"Eloisa to Abelard," 556
embryo, 2, 7, 77
Emerson, Ralph Waldo, xxvi
empire: British, 113; Byzantine, 295–96; *Encyclopedia of the Literature of Empire* (Snodgrass); Holy, 289; Mongol, 289; Ottoman, 289–90, 296; penetrating it, 162; Roman, 438, 442; remains of, 72, 401; *Ruins of Empire* (Volney),

392; Second, 356; Soviet, 286; State (NY), 305, 332
enchantments. *See* spells
endings: ambiguous or unresolved, 10, 351–52; *A Book of Endings* (Biancotti); Grimm Brothers, 224; happy, 224; unhappy, 47
England, xiii, xv, xvi, xxv, 78, 115, 161, 189, 218, 242–43, 252, 256, 300, 322, 323–24, 339n2, 354, 357–60, 385, 392, 400–402, 404, 407, 435, 437, 440–42, 459, 462, 545, 546, 549, 550
enigma, xxiv, 28, 67, 73, 81, 91, 177, 191, 195, 294, 323, 324, 327, 480, 488, 528, 556
the Enlightenment, 72, 354, 390
entrapment and confinement, xxvi, 28, 33, 96, 150, 156, 162
epic, 21, 141
epilepsy, 165
epistolary novel, 99, 111, 161, 250, 447
Erdrich, Louise, vii, 226–41, 609
Erebus (ship), 545
erections, 332
eros, xxiv, 25, 199
erotica, xxv, xxx; *Embraces: Dark Erotica*, 598; *Man with a Maid*, 210; *My Lustful Adventures: A Nocturnal Meeting*, 210; *My Secret Life*, 210; *A Night in a Moorish Harem*, 210; *Randiana: The Adventures of Grace & Anna*, 210; *Venus in India*, 210; Victorian, 111, 210
estates, xxvi, 507
Etchison, Dennis, xvii
eternity, 45, 155, 306
Eton, 406
Etrustrans, 89, 91, 94
Eva Moves the Furniture, vi, 182–94, 609
Eve (biblical), 51, 57, 425, 482
Evenson, Brian, vi, 124–34, 597, 603, 622
evil, xxiv, xxvi, 17, 25, 28–29, 30, 38, 52, 54, 58, 66, 130, 140, 144–46, 149,

Morrison, Toni, viii, xvii, xxiii, xxvii, 121, 418–31, 495n3, 612; Karen Stein title, 627
Morrow, Bradford, 269, 273
mortality, 38, 45, 73, 258, 263, 509, 519, 587
Morton, Kate, 87, 215–25
mosques, 296
mothers, 532–34; absence of, 533–34; fairy-tale, 220; mourning of, 360; murder of (matricide), 493, 496; Norman Bate's and Freddy Kruger's, 243; slave mothers, 418–31; surrogate, 4; torture of, 294, 299; working, 212. *See also* stepmothers
motives, xxvii, 6, 12, 177, 187, 197, 202, 243, 280, 470
Mott, Lucretia, 395
mounds, earthen, 154
mountains, 149, 189, 293, 499
mourning, 74, 117, 200, 220, 234, 293, 310, 311, 315–16, 360, 365, 367, 458, 459, 462
mouse or mice, 321
mouths, 17, 34, 252
Mr. X, 124
multiple personality disorder (dissociative identity disorder), 168
Mulvey-Roberts, Marie, v, x, 50–59, 96n1, 189, 193n8, 194n14, 599, 624–25
Murad II, Sultan, 295
murder, ix, xxv, xxvi, xxx, 8, 22, 34, 38, 50, 54, 55–56, 61–62, 65–70, 76, 80, 81, 85, 96, 117, 124, 128, 141, 145, 154, 159–60, 162, 166, 176, 179, 184, 186–88, 197–98, 204, 206, 208, 215–16, 221, 230–32, 233, 254, 265, 273–74, 277, 285, 290, 331, 337–38, 342–44, 348, 351–52, 359, 372, 376, 379–80, 389, 394–95, 398–99, 401–3, 405, 411, 442, 437, 446, 470, 474, 479, 480–82, 490, 503–4, 507–8, 510, 515, 517, 533–34, 541–42, 544, 586, 587, 595; ax,

586; contemplation of, 520–21; of a girl, 362–64, 367–68; Seito Sakakibara manifesto on, 502; serial and Katherine Ramsland studies, 626; underage killers, 496, 500–501. *See also* killing
Murnau, F. W., 309
Murphy, Bernice M., ix, xx, 584–94, 599, 625
museums, 37, 164, 226–27, 502, 543, 587
Muslims, 295, 297–99
mutability, 263–65
muteness, 76, 547, 550. *See also* silence
mutilation and dismemberment, 62, 126, 156, 158, 166, 236, 496
The Mysteries of Udolpho, xi, xii, xxvii, xxxi, 3, 21, 32, 92, 93, 98, 110, 134, 143, 171, 182, 189, 231, 233, 271–72, 283, 287, 339, 340–41n15, 353, 372, 374, 383n13, 419–20, 422–23, 448, 541, 556
Mysteries of Winterthurn, 23
mysticism and mystics, vi, 21, 77, 82, 95, 111, 118, 126, 143, 149–157, 161, 242, 244, 247, 260, 263–64, 437, 440, 483–84; mystical tattoos, 246
mythology, xxv, 33, 53, 93–94, 264, 466, 581, 591; Finnish myths and K. A. Laity, 624
"My Zoondel," 587

Nagoya, 244,
nakedness, 9, 28, 107, 131, 202, 246, 248, 424, 482, 489, 502, 513, 541, 546
Naples, 182
Napoleon, 119, 285, 319, 321
Napoli, Donno Jo, 511
narcissism, 61–62, 67, 113, 336, 471
Narnia, 433
narration, unreliable or compulsive, xxvi, 44, 173, 195, 302–8, 339
The Narrative of Arthur Gordon Pym, 99, 102

National Library of Australia, 261

Native Americans, vi, 177, 226–41, 303, 419, 427, 451, 490; slaughter of, 393; negative portrayals of, 236–37

naturalism, 37, 111

nature: laws of, xi, 150, 215; power of, 145, 510

nausea, 165, 300n15, 380, 512

Navy, Royal, 542

Naylor, Gloria, 32, 422, 423, 430n25

Nazis, xxiii, 42–48, 58, 230–31, 292, 521, 626; and Ingrid Pitt, xxxiin1

necronomicons, 259

necrophilia, 85, 216, 221, 372, 376, 380, 386

Nelson, Victoria, 19

neo-pagan, 434, 437, 562

Nesbit, E., xv, 161

neuropsychology, 159, 166

Never Let Me Go, viii, 453–64, 613

Neverwhere, 274, 598

Nevill, Adam L. G., v, vi, 14–20, 149–57, 599, 606, 625

The Netherlands, 1, 167

The New Gothic, 21, 269–70, 373, 387; *Conjunctions* magazine, 124

new or neo-gothic, xxvii, xxx–xi, 11, 22, 339, 387, 403, 438, 447, 463, 617; *Exotic Gothic: Forbidden Tales from Our Gothic World*, 340n11, 486, 494n5, 613, 617; *Exotic Gothic 2: New Tales of Taboo*, 86, 617, 619, 621, 623, 626, 629; *Exotic Gothic 3: Strange Visitations*, 602, 617, 621, 622, 623; *Exotic Gothic* series, 617

New England, 23, 27

new literary forms, creation of. *See* innovations in fiction

New Mexico, 379

New Moon, 573–74, 576–79

New Orleans, xxii, 62, 64–65

New Prometheus, 53, 196

New South Wales, Australia, 86

New Woman, 78, 120, 370

New World, 50, 52, 57, 230, 235, 264, 385, 387, 391–93, 395, 514, 547

New York City, 142, 302–6, 330, 497

The New York Trilogy, 305

New York Times best-sellers list, xvi, xxii, 72, 265, 286, 362

newspapers, 35, 180, 316, 343, 348, 379, 404, 503; Edward Crandall, reporter, 621

Nick of the Woods, 236–37

Nietzsche, Friedrich, 310, 470, 501

Nigeria, 15, 184

night, 43, 565; night-gaunts, 273; night terrors, 15; nightmares, xxx

Night of the Living Dead, 281, 314, 318

the Night Sun, 91

Night Thoughts, 554

The Nightmare (painting), 14, 389

The Nightmare Before Christmas, 60

The Nightmare Factory, 86

A Nightmare on Elm Street, 15

nihilism, 24, 27–28, 138, 316, 509, 511

Nile River, 164

"Nights at Totem Rule," 87

nipples and aureoles, 210, 248, 377, 546

Nirvana (band), 280

No Country for Old Men, viii, 465–76, 613

"no man is an island," 99

Nobel Prize for Literature, xxii–xxiii

Noh, 501

noir, 341n16; kid noir, 508; noirotica, xxv, 600

Normandy, 357

North Dakota, 228–29, 232, 239n3, 239n15, 239–40n16

Northanger Abbey, 553–54

Nosferatu (Murnau film), 309

nosferatu, 161, 298

nostalgia, xxix, 118, 181, 244, 380, 454, 458

Not Flesh Nor Feathers, vi, 171–81 609

novel: of manners, 111; mash up, 158, 265; sensation, 206–7, 560

radicalism, Romantic, 75
rage or anger, 62, 312–13, 314, 398
Railsback, Hollis, 333, 486–95
Rain Main, 233
The Rainy Moon, 197
Ramsland, Katherine, vi, 158–70, 600, 626
Rankin, Walter, vi, 215–25, 600, 626
ransom, 62, 64, 70
rape and ravishing, 34, 36, 70, 74, 113, 166, 184, 187–88, 193, 229, 232, 282, 313, 362, 364, 369, 391, 394, 395, 404, 419, 422, 503, 515–16, 546; rape-murders, 166; *The Rape of Martha Teoh*, 622
"Rappaccini's Daughter," 87
rapture, 116, 413, 567
"Rapunzel," 216, 221–22
Raskolnikov, 199, 403
rats, 161
Real World, ix, 496–505, 614
realism, xii, xv, xvii, 30, 37, 179, 208, 257, 283, 328, 488, 490, 502, 503
reality, alternate, 261–62
reanimation, xxvi, xxviii, 80–81, 284, 319, 363
reason and rationality, v, xxvi, 14, 250, 375, 412, 470
Reason, Age of, 488, 556
Rebecca (novel), 212, 338, 553, 555, 558
rebirth, 62, 126, 328, 389, 530–31, 550–51
records and documentation, 262, 448–49
red-headed, 1, 198, 332, 448; babies, 451; fathers, 451; lover professors, 451; Maggie (character in Joyce's *Dark Sister*), 452n7; minority status, 451; Peter Quint, 25; victims of murder, 398–99
Reese, James, vi, 158–70, 600, 608
Reformation, 19
Regency era, 265, 322
regeneration, viii, 246, 445–52, 531
Reginhald, 557

reincarnation, 64, 173, 177, 185, 375, 564
reinvention, 74, 260, 387, 389
rejection, 5–8, 18, 37, 80, 181, 196, 243, 421, 422–23, 428, 460, 532, 570, 576
religion, xi, xxvi, xxxi, 8–10, 43, 48, 91, 101, 245, 293, 354, 373, 439, 443, 494, 546, 569, 571, 629
remains, human, 156, 220
remorse, 113, 145, 407–8, 458, 465
Renaissance, 19, 242, 248, 354, 356, 451
Renault, Mary, 88
Rendell, Ruth, 269
renovation, vii, 264, 327–41, 357
reproduction, monosexual, v, 1
reptiles and reptilian, 106, 321, 346, 514; *The Reptile Room*, 523, 524
reservations, Native American, 226–39
resistance, 40
resurrection, viii, xiii, xxiii, 51, 59, 79, 155, 176, 182, 176, 338, 345, 381, 385–86, 393, 394, 439, 453, 540, 589–90; Christ, 247; resurrection men, 78
retellings and intertextuality, 32–40, 50–59, 72–82, 389
retribution, 230, 330, 332, 335
reunions, 65, 395
Revelation, Book of, 272
revenants, xxix, 121, 180, 181, 353
Revolution, American, 385–95; *Martha Peake*, 385–95
Revolution, French, 78, 297, 390
Rherlotte, 197–99, 609
Rice, Anne, xvi, 121, 243, 604; biography by Katherine Ramsland, 626
Richards, Keith, 280
Rickels, Laurence, A., vii, xx, 308–18, 600, 626
Rickman, Phil, viii, xvii, 432–44, 612
Riddell, Charlotte, 22, 119
Rilke, Rainer Maria, 107
"The Rime of the Ancient Mariner," 539
The Ring (film), 314

About the Editor

DANEL OLSON at a young age fell for the insane passions, accursed lands, frothy plots, and violent femmes of the Gothic. Having taught "Horror, Ghost and Gothic Fiction" at Lone Star College in Texas since 2000, he has taken sabbaticals and international exploration grants to roam and rest in the deserted graveyards, ruined abbeys, and collapsed castles of Ireland, the UK, the Czech Republic, Slovakia, Hungary, Croatia, Bulgaria, Serbia, and Romania. Meetings with writers in these lands have enriched the trademark fiction series he compiled and named *Exotic Gothic*. A literary venue for new Gothic fiction set outside of its traditional homelands, the sequence which he teaches includes *Exotic Gothic: Forbidden Tales from Our Gothic World* (2007), and the Shirley Jackson Award finalists *Exotic Gothic 2: New Tales of Taboo* (2008) and *Exotic Gothic 3: Strange Visitations* (2009), which was short-listed for the World Fantasy Award. They are all published by the World Fantasy Award–winning Ash-Tree Press. A new guide to Gothdom, *Exotic Gothic 4*, appears in 2011. A recent Faculty Excellence Award winner, Danel's articles and interviews have been featured in *Commonwealth*, the *New York Review of Science Fiction*, and *Cemetery Dance*.

About the Contributors

RUTH BIENSTOCK ANOLIK teaches at Villanova University. Most of her work focuses on the Gothic with a special interest in the interplay between Gothic literature and social and cultural structures. She has published essays in *Modern Language Studies, Legal Studies Forum, Partial Answers,* and *Studies in American Jewish Literature.* She has also edited three collections of essays on the Gothic—*The Gothic Other: Racial and Social Constructions in the Literary Imagination* (2004), *Horrifying Sex: Essays on Sexual Difference in the Gothic Imagination* (2007), and *Demons of the Body and Mind: Essays on Disability in Gothic Literature* (2010). Recently, she authored the entry "Sex" for *The Blackwell Encyclopedia of the Gothic* (eds. William Hughes, David Punter, and Andrew Smith, 2011).

KARIN BEELER is professor and chair of the English Department at the University of Northern British Columbia in Prince George, Canada. She has published on Canadian culture and on film and television studies as well, including *Tattoos, Desire and Violence: Marks of Resistance in Literature, Film and Television* (2006) and the coedited anthology with Stan Beeler, *Investigating "Charmed": The Magic Power of TV* (2007). Her fascination with Fantastika is evident in her most recent book, *Seers, Witches and Psychics on Screen: An Analysis of Women Visionary Characters in Recent Television and Film* (2008).

PETER BELL is an historian, living in York, England. As well as academic works on the international history of the 1930s, he has written articles for *Ghosts & Scholars, Faunus,* and *Wormwood,* including the article "Joyce Carol Oates: Artiste of the Grotesque." His strange tales have appeared in several magazines and anthologies including *Exotic Gothic 2* and *Running with the Pack* (2010), edited by Ekaterina Sedia. A collection of his stories is forthcoming in 2010.

DEBORAH BIANCOTTI is a Ditmar Award-winning writer based in inner-city Sydney, Australia. Her first published story, "The First and Final Game," won the 2001 Aurealis Award for Best Horror Short Story, and her first collection, *A Book of Endings*, was shortlisted for the 2010 William L. Crawford Award. Her fiction has appeared in *Australian Dark Fantasy and Horror* several times, and more recently in the Prime international *Year's Best Dark Fantasy and Horror*. Lately she's been working on a contemporary urban fantasy novella about the return of the goddess Ishtar. She is also wrapping up her first novel and planning a short story suite called *Bad Power*. She studied Gothic literature all too briefly at Sydney University and still remembers the heart-stopping glory of her lecturer's psychoanalytic dissection of Jane Austen's *Emma*. Deborah most likes to read and write fiction that is "unsettling."

LEIGH BLACKMORE is a widely published critic, editor, poet, writer, and occultist who lives in Wollongong, Australia. Recent critical work has appeared in *Studies in the Fantastic* and *Lovecraft Annual* and in the book *Robert Bloch: The Man Who Collected Psychos* (2009). Leigh is president of the Australian Horror Writers Association and the editor of issue 5 of their journal *Midnight Echo*. He is also the official editor of the Sword & Sorcery and Weird Fiction Terminus amateur press association and runs its blog at http://sswftapa.blogspot.com.

RICHARD BLEILER is the humanities librarian at the University of Connecticut. He is the editor of *Supernatural Fiction Writers: Contemporary Fantasy and Horror* (2000, 2 vols.) and, with his father Everett F. Bleiler, assisted on *Science Fiction: The Early Years* (1990) and *Science Fiction: The Gernsback Years* (1998). He has contributed over twenty essays, including one on Neil Gaiman, for S. T. Joshi and Stefan Dziemianowicz's prize-winning *Supernatural Literature of the World: An Encyclopedia* (2005, 3 vols.).

KAREN BUDRA, winner of the 2010 Langara College Teaching Excellence award, teaches literature and cinema studies at Langara College in Vancouver, where she specializes in exploring the Gothic as well as the power of popular culture. She believes firmly in the transcendent and transformative power of narrative, visual, and performing arts. A current member of the Transylvania Society of Dracula and, yes, a former Goth, she continues to dress the part and write poetry as well as academic papers.

GLENNIS BYRON is professor of English at the University of Stirling, Scotland. She is interested in both Victorian and contemporary Gothic and has edited a casebook on *Dracula* (1999) and a critical edition of it (1998). With David Punter, she coedited the essay anthologies *Spectral Readings: Towards a*

Gothic Geography (1999) and *The Gothic* (2003). Glennis is presently planning a book to be called *Gothic Relocations*, focusing on twenty-first-century texts.

JASON COLAVITO is an author and editor based in upstate New York. His books include *Knowing Fear* (2008), a study of science and knowledge in the horror genre, and *A Hideous Bit of Morbidity* (2009), a collection of early horror criticism. His website is www.jasoncolavito.com.

NANCY A. COLLINS is the author of numerous short stories and novels, including the Bram Stoker Award–winning *Sunglasses After Dark* (1989). A recent new story of hers, "The Ice Wedding," appears in *Exotic Gothic 2*. She is currently working on the Golgotham series, the first novel of which, *Right Hand Magic*, is scheduled for December 2010. A native of Arkansas, she currently lives in the Cape Fear area. Visit www.golgothamonline.com.

JAMES CORTESE, husband of Romana Cortese, is an adjunct professor and writer of satiric fiction in which Gothic elements are some of its key ingredients, but not serendipitous encounters or affective relationships. His published work includes short stories for such magazines as *Epoch* and *Carolina Quarterly* and the anthologies *Exotic Gothic* and *Exotic Gothic 3*. He also has written two short-story collections—the award-winning *What the Owl Said* (1979), for which he was awarded a grant from the National Endowment for the Arts, and recently *The Very Last Thing*.

ROMANA CORTESE, wife of James Cortese, was born in Rome and is a professor of English and Italian at Lone Star College, Montgomery in Texas. A lover of Dickens and George Eliot, she revels in intricate plots and large casts of characters whose destinies are determined by serendipitous encounters and affective relationships. She also gardens, paints (houses, that is), sews, cooks (when she has to), does crossword puzzles, and loves her dog, Ginger.

EDWARD P. CRANDALL writes in Japanese on the arts for the *Saga Shimbun* newspaper and is a translator. He also lectures on politics and economics at Saga University and elsewhere. His published short fiction includes "The Arrangement" in *Exotic Gothic 2*) and Swan River Press. He has lived in Saga, Japan, since 1998.

DON D'AMMASSA is the author of seven novels and three reference books, as well as more than one hundred short stories. His most recent is the chapbook *Wings over Manhattan* (2010). He has written extensively on horror and science fiction for various encyclopedias and other books.

CAROL MARGARET DAVISON is an associate professor of English at the University of Windsor, Canada, who is currently at work on a monograph devoted to the Scottish Gothic. A former Canada-U.S. Fulbright scholar, she is the author of *History of the Gothic: Gothic Literature 1764–1824* (2009) and *Anti-Semitism and British Gothic Literature* (2004), and the editor of the award-winning collection *Bram Stoker's Dracula: Sucking Through the Century, 1897–1997* (1997).

JAMES DOIG works at the National Archives of Australia in Canberra. He has edited several anthologies of colonial Australian Gothic fiction, most recently *Australian Ghost Stories* (2010). He has a Ph.D. in medieval history from Swansea University in Wales.

HEATHER L. DUDA is an assistant professor of English at the University of Rio Grande/Rio Grande Community College where she teaches composition, literature, and film courses. She is the author of *The Monster Hunter in Modern Popular Culture* (2008) and loves all things Gothic.

BRIAN EVENSON is the author of ten books of fiction, including *Last Days*, which won the American Library Association's award for best horror novel in 2009. His novel *The Open Curtain* (2006) was a finalist for an Edgar Award and an IHG Award, and his story collection *Fugue State* (2009) was recently nominated for a Shirley Jackson Award and World Fantasy Award. He lives and works in Providence, Rhode Island, where he directs Brown University's creative writing program.

TUNKU HALIM lives in Australia but is a frequent visitor to his country of birth, Malaysia. He has worked as a corporate lawyer in Kuala Lumpur and an IT lawyer in Sydney. He has his own publishing company and is interested in design and environmentally friendly urban development. His first novel, *Dark Demon Rising* (1997), was nominated for the 1999 International IMPAC Dublin Literary Award and analyzed by Professor Glennis Byron in her essay "When Meaning Collapses . . ." in *Asian Gothic*. His second novel was the gruesome *Vermillion Eye* (2000), and his five short-story collections are entitled *Bloodhaze* (1999); *The Rape of Martha Teoh* (1997); *44 Cemetery Road* (MPH, 2007); *Gravedigger's Kiss* (2007); and *The Woman Who Grew Horns* (2001). His work (including the tale of a Malaysian shrine in *Exotic Gothic 3* called "Keramat") is praised by Rich Horton in *Locus* for its "evocations of ghost traditions unfamiliar to most Westerners." He is working on a third novel.

MAVIS HAUT is the author of *The Hidden Library of Tanith Lee: Themes and Subtexts from Dionysos to the Immortal Gene* (2001) and is at present working on a book on feminism entitled *Sixteen Takes on a Self-Invented Woman*. She is currently living in southwest France.

JERROLD E. HOGLE (Ph.D., Harvard University) is professor of English, university distinguished professor, and director of undergraduate studies and honors in English at the University of Arizona. The recipient of Guggenheim and Mellon fellowships for research and a national Burlington Foundation prize for excellence in teaching, he is the author or editor of numerous studies of Romantic and Gothic literature, among them *The Cambridge Companion to Gothic Fiction* (2002) and *The Undergrounds of "The Phantom Of The Opera"* (2002). He is also a past president of the International Gothic Association, a frequent guest editor of the journal *Gothic Studies*, and cochair of the senior general editors for the new International Gothic book series from Manchester University Press.

ROBERT HOOD, a much-published author of Gothic and fantastical tales, often takes diversions into genre literature and film commentary and has won awards for the latter. Other recent fiction includes tales of vengeful ghosts (as in "Kulpunya" for *Exotic Gothic 2*), dark alternate Australian history (with "Behind Dark Blue Eyes" *in Exotic Gothic 3*), zombies in *The Mammoth Book of Zombie Apocalypse!* (ed. Stephen Jones), and robots in *Robot War Espresso*, a YA novel.

S. T. JOSHI is the author of *The Weird Tale* (1990) and *The Modern Weird Tale* (2001), as well as coeditor with Stefan Dziemianowicz of the three-volume International Horror Guild winner *Supernatural Literature of the World* (2005). Along with additional critical and biographical studies, he has prepared annotated editions of the work of H. P. Lovecraft, Arthur Machen, Lord Dunsany, Algernon Blackwood, Ambrose Bierce, and other writers. He is at work on a comprehensive history of supernatural fiction.

GRAHAM JOYCE is the author of sixteen novels, most recently *Memoirs of a Master Forger* (2008)/*How to Make Friends with Demons* (2009); a collection of short stories; a nonfiction sporting memoir about goalkeeping; and several YA novels. Prizes earned include the World Fantasy Award for his novel *The Facts of Life* (2002), the British Fantasy Award for Best Novel five times, and the O. Henry Award for his short story, "An Ordinary Soldier of the Queen" (2007). His work has been translated into more than twenty languages. A forthcoming novel is *The Silent Land*, and his website is www.grahamjoyce.net.

K. A. LAITY received a 2006 Finlandia Foundation grant and the 2005 Eureka Short Story Fellowship to work on *Unikirja: Dreambook* (2009), a collection of short stories inspired by the witches, sages, and giants of Finnish mythology and *The Kalevala*. A new expanded edition of her novel *Pelzmantel: A Medieval Tale* appeared in 2010 with an introduction by Elizabeth Hand. The original small press edition (2003) was nominated for the Aesop Prize and the International Reading Association Children's Book Award. Kate is associate professor of English at the College of Saint Rose in Albany, where she teaches medieval literature, film, new media, and popular culture, and serves as director of the Women's and Gender Studies Program. In addition to her fiction, she publishes and presents papers in the areas of comics, humor, drama, film, writing, medieval studies, fantasy, and horror, including a contribution to Ruth Bienstock Anolik's *Horrifying Sex*. She has tried her hand at a silent comic ("Jane Quiet, Occult Investigator," with Elena Steir, 2008) and is a weekly columnist for BitchBuzz.com. Her comic Gothic novel *The Mangrove Legacy* (2010) was published under the nom de plume Kit Marlowe.

TONY MAGISTRALE is professor and chair of the English Department at the University of Vermont. He has published twenty books, most of them specialized studies of Poe, the American horror film, and the films and fictions of Stephen King.

JAMES MARRIOTT is the coauthor (with Kim Newman) of *Horror: the Definitive Guide to the Cinema of Fear* (2008). His other nonfiction includes *Horror Films* (2007); *Horror! 333 Films to Scare You to Death* (2010); and a series of film essays for Creation Books. As Patrick Blackden, he has written true crime including *Danger Down Under* (2002), *Tourist Trap* (2003), and *Holidaymakers from Hell* (2004, a *Sunday Times* travel book of the week), and is a contributing editor for *My Bloody Valentine*. He has had a novel and a collection of short stories published and has contributed to *SFX*, *Headpress*, and *Arthur*.

MARIE MULVEY-ROBERTS is a Reader in Literary Studies in the Department of English at St. Matthias, the University of the West of England, Bristol, in the UK. She is the author of *British Poets and Secret Societies* (1986) and *Gothic Immortals: The Fiction of the Brotherhood of the Rosy Cross* (1990). Marie has edited many books including *Secret Texts: The Literature of Secret Societies* (1995) with Hugh Orsmby-Lennon and *The Handbook to the Gothic* (1998; 2nd ed., 2009), and is the editor of the journal *Woman's Writing*. With Alison Milbank and Peter Otto, she has also coedited selections of *Gothic Fiction: Rare Printed Works from the Sadleir-Black Collection of Gothic Fiction at the Alderman Library,*

UVA (2003). Her current work is on Gothic, gender, and the body, and she presently writes *Dangerous Bodies: Corporeality and the Gothic.*

BERNICE M. MURPHY is a lecturer in popular literature at the School of English, Trinity College, Dublin, Ireland. At the age of fifteen her career path was inadvertently determined when she read Stephen King's *Danse Macabre* and decided to read every novel that he mentioned. She recently published *The Suburban Gothic in American Popular Culture* (2009) and also edited the collection *Shirley Jackson: Essays on the Literary Legacy* (2005). Bernice is cofounder/editor of the online *Irish Journal of Gothic and Horror Studies* (irishgothichorrorjournal .homestead.com), which began in 2006 and publishes bianually.

ADAM L. G. NEVILL was a long-time erotica editor and is a writer of supernatural horror, including the novels *Banquet for the Damned* (2004) and *Apartment 16* (2010). His next novel, *The Ritual,* will be published in May 2011. He lives in London and can be contacted through www.adamlgnevill.com

LINDA OGSTON is a Ph.D. student at the University of Stirling in Scotland working on a thesis entitled "New shades of grey: The clone as a Gothic trope in speculative fiction." She also runs a fundraising consultancy business.

REGGIE OLIVER is a professional playwright, actor, and theater director. His publications, besides plays, include *Out of the Woodshed* (1998), the authorized biography of Stella Gibbons, and four volumes of stories, some of which have appeared in over twenty-five anthologies including the *Exotic Gothic* sequence ("A Donkey at the Mysteries" and "Meeting with Mike"). A collection of his short fiction, essays, and illustrations appeared in 2009 entitled *Madder Mysteries.* An omnibus edition of his stories entitled *Dramas from the Depths* was published in 2010.

VAN PIERCY has his Ph.D. from Indiana University, Bloomington. He has taught English at Lone Star College in Tomball, Texas, including "Horror, Ghost, and Gothic Fiction" since 2004, and now with the Exotic Gothic series. Van writes on educational issues at http://vpiercy.wordpress.com. His research interests include rhetoric and composition pedagogy, Hegelian philosophy, Mormon studies, and Gregory Bateson.

JUNE PULLIAM teaches courses in the horror genre, adolescent literature, and gender studies at Louisiana State University. She has written several articles on zombies and werewolves, and coedited with Anthony J. Fonseca *Necropsy: The*

Review of Horror Fiction, an online journal, until 2008. She has also coauthored with Anthony J. Fonseca three editions of *Hooked on Horror: A Guide to Reading Interests in the Genre* (1999, 2003, 2009), and *Read On . . . Horror Fiction* (2006). June lives in a creaky old house in Baton Rouge with several cats and shakes her fist at the occasional squirrel that wanders across her lawn.

DAVID PUNTER is professor of English at the University of Bristol, UK. His many publications on the Gothic include *The Literature of Terror* (1980; 1996, 2 vols.)—praised by scholars for setting "off a three-decades-long proliferation of studies in the Gothic"—as well as *Gothic Pathologies* (1998) and *A Companion to the Gothic* (2000). He is also a well-known poet.

KATHERINE RAMSLAND has published thirty-eight books (including biographies of Anne Rice and Dean Koontz), sixteen short stories, and over nine hundred articles. She is an internationally recognized expert on serial murder, as well as an associate professor of forensic psychology and criminal justice at DeSales University. Her latest book is *The Forensic Psychology of Criminal Minds* (2010). The Investigation Discovery channel soon airs her most recent TV series, *American Gothic*, about criminals who commit occult-oriented crimes.

WALTER RANKIN is the author of *Grimm Pictures: Fairy Tale Archetypes in Eight Horror and Suspense Films* (2008). He has taught a variety of literature and film courses at Georgetown, George Washington, George Mason, and Hampton universities. He currently serves as the associate dean of academic affairs for Georgetown's School of Continuing Studies. He is also working on a new book examining Nazi imagery in American popular culture.

LAURENCE RICKELS, following graduate study at Princeton University, moved to the West Coast where he taught as professor of German and comparative literature at the University of California, Santa Barbara, and wrote psychoanalytic criticism and trained as a psychotherapist. His *The Vampire Lectures* (1999) represents a sifting through the mythology of vampirism and its movements through film. A short vampire film, *Spout*, which was based on Rickels's feature screenplay, began making the festival rounds in the summer of 2010, while his newest book, *I Think I Am: Philip K. Dick*, appeared at the end of the same season.

NICHOLAS ROYLE is a frequent reviewer and the author of five novels, two novellas, and a short-story collection. His short story from *Exotic Gothic 2*—"Very Low-flying Aircraft"—was republished in Ellen Datlow's *The Best Horror of the Year: Volume One* (2009). Born in Manchester in 1963, he teaches creative writing at Manchester Metropolitan University; he has won three Brit-

ish Fantasy Awards, and the Bad Sex Prize once. Nick also runs Nightjar Press, publishing original short stories as signed, limited-edition chapbooks.

DARRELL SCHWEITZER is a former editor of *Weird Tales*, a World Fantasy Award winner, the author of *The Mask of the Sorcerer*, *The Shattered Goddess*, *The White Isle*, *Living with the Dead*, and hundreds of published short stories. He has written or edited eighteen volumes of nonfiction, including criticism and interviews, along with compiling one of the early scholarly treatments of Stephen King, *Discovering Stephen King* (1985). The best of his nonfiction is collected in *Windows of the Imagination* and *The Fantastic Horizon*.

BRIAN J. SHOWERS is the author of *The Bleeding Horse and Other Ghost Stories* (2008), winner of the 2008 Children of the Night Award, and *Literary Walking Tours of Gothic Dublin* (2006). He currently resides somewhere in the verdant and ghost-haunted wilderness of Dublin, Ireland, where he is busy at work on his next collection of strange tales. His website is www.brianjshowers.com.

MARY ELLEN SNODGRASS is an award-winning author, having written and compiled more than one hundred reference works and textbooks on American literature, mythology, fable, feminism, and history, including the *Encyclopedia of Gothic Literature* (2005). She teaches English and Latin at Lenoir Rhyne University in Hickory, North Carolina, and her latest studies are *Peter Carey: A Literary Companion* (2010) and *Encyclopedia of the Literature of Empire* (2010).

KAREN F. STEIN is professor of English and women's studies at the University of Rhode Island. A recipient of the Woman of the Year Award from the URI Association of Professional and Academic Women in 1993 and from the Rhode Island Commission on Women in 2007, she is the author of *Margaret Atwood Revisited* (1999) and *Reading, Learning, Teaching Toni Morrison* (2009) and is currently writing a book about Rachel Carson. An article, "Problematic Paradice," comparing Margaret Atwood's *Oryx and Crake* to Mary Shelley's *Franken-stein* will appear in a book on Atwood's recent work edited by J. Brooks Bouson.

CHARLES TAN's fiction has appeared in publications such as *The Digest of Philippine Genre Stories* and *Philippine Speculative Fiction*, as well as the anthology *The Dragon and the Stars* (edited by Derwin Mak and Eric Choi). He has contributed nonfiction to websites such as the Nebula Awards (http://nebulaawards.com), the Shirley Jackson Awards (www.shirleyjacksonawards.org), the World SF News Blog (http://worldsf.wordpress.com), and SF Signal (www.sfsignal.com). You can visit his blog, Bibliophile Stalker (http://charles-tan.blogspot.com), or the two online

anthologies he edits, the *Philippine Speculative Fiction Sampler* (http://philippine speculativefiction.com) and *The Best of Philippine Speculative Fiction* (http://best philippinesf.com).

AUGUST TARRIER works as an editor and manuscript consultant, specializing in novels and screenplays, as well as scholarly and academic work. She has won four national awards for her short stories, among them the Zoetrope Prize for "I Hold You Harmless" and the DIAGRAM Prize for "Field Notes." August is currently at work on a novel.

LUCY TAYLOR is acclaimed as the most "highly regarded American woman writer" of "graphic erotic tales of terror," according to the *St. James Guide to Horror, Ghost, & Gothic Writers.* Her sensual prose of spiritually wayward characters, shocking revenge, and epiphanies has turned heads since her debut novel, *The Safety of Unknown Cities* (1995), which received Bram Stoker, Deathrealm, and IHG awards. Novels following include *Dancing with Demons* (1999); *Eternal Hearts* (1999); *Nailed* (2001); *Saving Souls* (2002); and *Left to Die* (2004), under the nom de plume Taylor Kincaid. Five short-story collections have appeared as well, and a sixth collection is in preparation, perhaps with some of the tales she first published in each volume of the Exotic Gothic series. A passionate traveler, she often sets her stories in the places she adventures.

STEVE RASNIC TEM's most recent book is a collection of all of his short collaborations with his wife Melanie Tem, *In Concert* (2010). Steve has written over three hundred short stories and has won the IHG, Stoker, British Fantasy, and World Fantasy awards. The Exotic Gothic series has featured one of his new works in each of its volumes, starting with "The House by the Bulvarnoye Koltso," "Burning Snow," and an excerpt from his novel *Deadfall Hotel.* You can read more of his recent work in *Asimov's, Interzone, Crimewave,* and John Skipp's *Werewolves and Shapeshifters.*

DOUGLASS H. THOMSON is professor of English at Georgia Southern University. His most recent work on the Gothic includes a critical edition of M. G. Lewis's *Tales of Wonder* (2009) and an entry on "The Gothic Ballad: 1790–1805" for the forthcoming *A Companion to the Gothic* (2011).

LISA TUTTLE, a Texan by birth and current resident of Scotland, has been writing fiction professionally since the 1970s. She has created a dozen widely praised speculative novels since her first with George R. R. Martin, *Windhaven* (1981). Her most recent novel is a romantic fantasy set in a Scottish village overwhelmed by creatures and events from ancient legend, *The Silver Bough* (2006).

Her *Stranger in the House*, the first volume of *Stranger in the House: The Collected Short Supernatural Fiction* is scheduled for publication in September 2010.

JOHN WHITBOURN (born 1968) is an English author and reformed archaeologist who has published nine novels to date, commencing with the prize-winning *A Dangerous Energy* (1992). Many of his stories have been anthologized, including his tale "Enlightenment" in *Exotic Gothic 2: New Tales of Taboo*. His works have been described as a sustained meditation on power, politics, and religion. More revealingly, a rare press interview with Whitbourn (2000) was entitled "Confessions of a Counter-Reformation Green Anarcho-Jacobite."

JUDITH WILT is professor of English and Newton College Alumnae Chair at Boston College, where she teaches courses in British fiction, women's studies, popular culture genres, and religion and literature. Among her books are *Ghosts of the Gothic: Austen, Eliot and Lawrence* (1980) and a combined edition of *Frankenstein* and *The Island of Dr. Moreau* titled *Making Humans* (2002). Her current work is on women writers and the heroes they create.

SUE ZLOSNIK is head of the Department of English at Manchester Metropolitan University, UK. She has published extensively on women's writing and coauthored two Gothic studies with Avril Horner—*Daphne Du Maurier: Writing, Identity and the Gothic Imagination* (1998), *Gothic and the Comic Turn* (2005), and coedited a third, *Le Gothic: Influences and Appropriations in Europe and America* (2008). Her most recent book is a study of the fiction of Patrick McGrath (2011). With Avril Horner, she has an edition of Eaton Stannard Barrett's *The Heroine* due to be published in 2011.